Understanding Low Vision

**Edited by
Randall T. Jose**

**American Foundation
for the Blind**

New York

To my parents

Frances and Dean Jose

Library of Congress Cataloging in Publication Data

Understanding Low Vision

  Bibliography: p.
  Includes index.
  1. Visually handicapped—Addresses, essays, lectures.
2. Visually handicapped—Rehabilitation—Addresses,
essays, lectures.   3. Vision disorders—Diagnosis—
Addresses, essays, lectures.   I. Jose, Randall T., 1943–
[DNLM: 1. Vision disorders. WW 140 U55]
HV1593.U45 1983   362.4'1   83–21446
ISBN 0–89128–119–3

2nd printing 1985
3rd printing 1989
4th printing 1991
5th printing 1994

Published by American Foundation for the Blind, 15 West 16th Street, New York,
N.Y. 10011. Printed in the United States of America.

ISBN: 0–89128–119–3

Contents

Section I   Understanding Low Vision
1. The Eye and Functional Vision 3
2. Psychosocial Aspects of Low Vision 43
3. Psychosocial Aspects of Aging and Visual
   Impairment 55
4. The Low Vision Rehabilitation Service 61

Section II   Assessment of Low Vision
5. Minimum Assessment Sequence: The
   Optometrist's Viewpoint 75
6. Comprehensive Preliminary Assessment of
   Low Vision 85
7. Assessment of Children with Low Vision 105

Section III   Clinical Services
8. Clinical Examination of Visually Impaired
   People 141
9. Optics 187
10. Treatment Options 211

Section IV   Training and Instructional Services
11. Establishing a Training and Instructional
    Program 251
12. Distance Training Techniques 277
13. Near Training Techniques 317
14. Training Programs for Individuals with
    Restricted Fields 363

Section V   Special Considerations
15. Assessment of Multiply Handicapped People 379
16. Assessment of Lighting 403
17. Role Model for an Orientation and Mobility
    Instructor and a Teacher of the Visually
    Handicapped 415
18. Delivery Systems 441
19. Resources 497
20. Selected References 515
About the Authors 537
Index 539

SECTION I
Understanding Low Vision

The four chapters in this section provide the reader with sufficient background on low vision to understand the person who will be receiving low vision services. Without an understanding of the impact of vision (or loss of vision) on functioning, learning, and psychosocial areas, the professional will not be able to provide effective services. Thus, the section gives the reader a thorough "philosophical" understanding of low vision care and lays the foundation for future chapters on the actual provision of care.

Chapter 1, "The Eye and Functional Vision," by this editor, reviews the anatomy of the eye from a functional standpoint. The reader is made aware of the problems caused by various structural changes to the eye and what diseases cause these structural changes. Suggestions for simulating various functional sight losses are presented.

Chapter 2, "Psychosocial Aspects of Low Vision," by Dr. Morse presents an important aspect of low vision. Although the impairment discussed in chapter 1 is important, an understanding of the effects of visual loss is vital to the successful rehabilitation of the low vision patient.

In Chapter 3, "Psychosocial Problems of Aging and Visual Impairment," Mr. Negrin describes the specific problems faced by visually impaired elderly people and how services should be structured for them.

Chapter 4, "The Low Vision Rehabilitation Service," this editor offers a model of low vision services which is applicable to any setting and resources. The three-phase series of services discussed in the chapter is then used as the structure of the remainder of this book.

Randall T. Jose

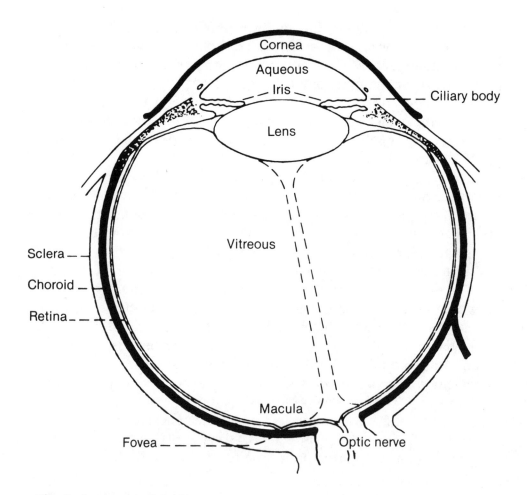

Fig. 1. Anatomy of the Eye.

CHAPTER 1

The Eye and Functional Vision

RANDALL T. JOSE, O.D.

This chapter reviews the anatomy of the eye and discusses the types of loss of functional vision that may occur when the various ocular structures are affected. The purpose of the discussion is to familiarize low vision instructors with the effects of specific diseases on the anatomy of the eye and how these changes, in turn, influence the individual's ability to function visually. The review of pharmacology is included as a reminder to instructors to consider information on drugs in their evaluations. A vision loss or "sight" loss simulation kit is described in the hope that such a kit will be used by each person who works in the low vision field to experience the uncomfortable feeling of losing acuity and visual fields.

ANATOMY OF THE EYE

The *cornea* is the outer, almost circular, clear part of the eye. It protects the inner contents of the eye, allows light to pass through it, and is the strongest converging lens of the eye. Together with the lens, the cornea focuses the optical image on the retina; it provides about 65 percent of the refractive power of the eye. Although it is much thinner than the lens, the cornea has such high refractive power because its front surface is in contact with the air, to give a refractive index ratio of 1.377 to 1.000 (i.e., light bends more when it goes from the air to the cornea than from the aqueous to the lens). The cornea is avascular and in a relatively dehydrated state, both of which factors contribute to its transparency. It is also the most highly sensitive tissue of the body, containing about 70 naked nerve fibers, which accounts for the severe pain that results from seemingly minor irritations. If the cornea becomes damaged, the eye's inner, more delicate, structure may become infected. If, as a result of injury or disease, all or part of the cornea becomes opaque, light transmission is reduced and acuity may be severely affected.

The *aqueous* lies just behind the cornea in the space known as the *anterior chamber*. The aqueous is a watery fluid, continuously produced in the

3

eye and continuously drained away. The aqueous is manufactured by the *ciliary body* and drains out through the filtration canal system at the *limbus.* It brings nutrients to and removes waste products from the back surface of the cornea and the lens. It also helps maintain the shape of the eye.

The *iris* is the colored part of the eye. It controls the amount of light that comes into the eye by regulating the size of the pupil. The iris, together with the ciliary body and the choroid (described below) make up the *uveal tract.*

The *crystalline lens* is a biconvex, avascular, colorless, transparent structure that consists of 65 percent water and 35 percent protein; there are no pain fibers, blood vessels, or nerves in the lens. The lens is suspended behind the iris by fibers that connect it to the ciliary body. The lens becomes larger and less elastic throughout life, which is the reason for presbyopia (a reduction in accommodative ability that occurs with age). The sole function of the lens is to focus light rays on the retina.

The *ciliary body* is a muscular structure which, in addition to secreting the aqueous fluid, serves as the mechanism for focusing the lens. There are three types of *ciliary muscle* which control accommodation and help maintain clear images on the retina.

The *vitreous* is a clear, avascular, gelatinous body that comprises two-thirds of the volume and weight of the eye. It is about 99 percent water. The remaining one percent includes two components—collagen and hyaluronic acid—that give the vitreous its specific physical character. The vitreous plays an important role in maintaining the transparency and form of the eye; if it were removed, the eye would collapse. When the vitreous is replaced by saline, as in certain forms of vitreous surgery, cellular matter and particulate debris are free to migrate into the optical pathway. If it becomes hazy as a result of infection in the surrounding structures or opaque because of hemorrhages, visual acuity may be affected since light transmission to the retina is reduced.

The outermost part of the eye is a white tough coating called the *sclera,* which encloses the eyeball except the cornea. The sclera protects the inner more delicate structures of the eye. If it becomes diseased (which rarely occurs) or damaged, a severe infection of the inner contents may result. The conjunctiva is a thin transparent membrane which covers the sclera and the inside of the lids. Its purpose is to serve as a protective coating and to help keep the cornea moist through the production of mucous cells. The conjunctiva has many blood vessels and few pain fibers. This means a person can have a major inflammation with little pain.

The *choroid* is the layer between the sclera and retina. It contains many blood vessels and carries the blood supply for the eye. In very young children, the outer layer, the sclera, is very thin and allows the choroid to show through, which gives it a bluish tinge.

The *retina* is a multilayered sheet of neural tissue. It is the innermost part of the eye and the most delicate. As a sensory structure, the retina contains cells that respond to visual stimuli by a photochemical reaction. Light must traverse most of the retinal layers to reach and stimulate the layer of rods and cones. Cones function best in bright light and mediate both vision and color. In central areas of the retina, cones are more numerous than rods. In the *macula* (the area of best vision) and the *fovea* (the area of most acute vision) only special cones are present. In contrast, rods are most numerous in the periphery of the retina. Since rods are extremely light sensitive, they function best in reduced illumination. Thus, the purpose of the retina with all its layers and specialized cells is to initiate impulses to the cortex via the optic nerve for visual perception.

The *optic nerve* carries the message to the brain. It is actually the brain that "sees." If the optic nerve is damaged, vision is severely disturbed.

REFRACTIVE AND OCULAR ABNORMALITIES

The sense of sight depends on an external light stimulus that the eye receives in the form of light rays that pass to the retina through the cornea, aqueous, lens, and vitreous and are transmitted along the optic nerve to the visual cortex. The varying optical densities (or refractive indexes) of these structures cause the light rays to change direction (converge) as they pass through. If the image does not focus on the fovea of the retina, the object will appear blurred.

Light travels in the form of rays. When the source is close, the rays are divergent when they reach the viewer's eye (see Chapter 9). When the light source is distant, the rays are parallel. Because of the relatively small aperture (pupil) of the eye, it is customary in optometry to consider rays of light originating farther than 20 feet away to be parallel.

In the emmetropic (normal) eye, parallel rays of light are brought to a focus on the fovea without the use of accommodation or lenses. (Accommodation is the mechanism by which the focusing appartus of the eye adjusts to objects at different distances.) Contraction of the ciliary muscle causes the lens of the eye to become more convex, which increases the power of the eye. Divergent rays of light coming from within 20 feet are focused on the retina through accommodation. The mechanism is largely reflex and so well adjusted that normal individuals are not aware of the process.

A hyperopic (farsighted) eye is either smaller than normal or its component refracting parts are weaker than the normal system (see Chapter 9). In this condition, the rays of light fail to converge enough to focus on the fovea. The act of accommodation or placing convex (plus) lenses in front of the eye helps converge the light rays more so they are focused on the retina. A myopic (nearsighted) eye is either larger than normal or its component refracting parts are stronger than the normal eye. The rays of light tend to focus in front of the fovea. Accommodation, since it makes the lens more convex, cannot be used to correct the optical error of myopia.

Degenerative Myopia. Degenerative myopia is extreme nearsightedness

5

(myopia). Individuals with this condition generally are myopic from a very early age (sometimes from birth) and their myopia increases progressively through adolescence. The diagnosis of degenerative myopia can be made when the myopic progression is accompanied by marked degenerative changes of the posterior portion of the eye. This increase in myopia is due to the lengthening of the eye, which results in the stretching of the posterior portion of the eye and accompanying degenerative changes that may progress to the point where vision is impaired significantly. The degeneration may occur very early or later in life, and its extent cannot always be predicted accurately.

The initial symptom of degenerative myopia may be only blurred distance vision from the myopia, and acuity can be improved with conventional eyeglasses. As the condition progresses, the decreased visual acuity may not be correctable to 20/20 with conventional spectacles or contact lenses because of the stretching of the retina and the accompanying degenerative changes. Near vision will generally be unaffected, although it may be impaired in more advanced conditions. Complaints of flashing lights or sharp pain may indicate retinal detachment and should be investigated immediately owing to the serious implications involved. If the retina is detached, there will be a corresponding field loss, although such detachments generally occur in the peripheral fundus and may not be debilitating at first. The individual may complain of spots before his eyes, which are due to floaters in the vitreous.

In the more advanced stages, the macula may be involved, which results in problems with central vision. Swelling of the macular area (macular edema) may cause distortion when viewing an object (metamorphorsia). Hemorrhages in the macular area, although rare, may cause further degeneration, including central vision defects.

Little can be done to stop the progression of degenerative myopia. Generally, the condition levels off after adolescence, although detachments of the retina may occur later in life. It seems to be genetic and may be transmitted as an autosomal trait. However, it has not been established whether degenerative myopia is a dominant or recessive trait, and the mechanism for its transmission is not completely understood.

Astigmatism. Astigmatism is distorted vision caused by a variation in refractive power along different meridians of the eye. Most cases occur from irregularities in the shape of the cornea. It is probably easiest to think of this refractive error as a condition in which the eye is out of focus for a vertical part of an object and more out of focus for the horizontal parts of an object. This means that a point of light will be imaged as an oblong shape rather than as a point, which distorts the edges of an image and creates a blur. Astigmatism may be simple or may be combined with hyperopia or myopia. With mild degrees of astigmatism, there may be no immediate symptoms, though it may initially cause asthenopia (headaches, tired eyes, a sandy, gritty feeling in the eyes, and so forth) when the eyes are used for a long time. The person with astigmatism tries to achieve a clearer image by rapidly changing focus (which results in fatigue and asthenopia). With greater degrees of astigmatism, clear visual acuity may not be possible. The person will squint the eye to try to get a clear image. Most cases of astigmatism can be corrected to 20/20 with cylindrical lenses.

Many eye reports list a child's problem as being due to congenital astigmatism. This condition is diagnosed when the astigmatic refractive error is associated with nystagmus (the rapid, rhythmic side-to-side movement of the eyeball) and a reduction in central acuity (amblyopia) probably because of poor macular development. Since these three anomalies are usually found together, the terms "congenital astigmatism," "congenital nystagmus," and "congenital amblyopia" often are used interchangeably to refer to the same functional congenital problem. Acuity usually improves with age (or at least the child learns to interpret the blurred imagery better), as does the nystagmus. Conventional spectacles to correct astigmatism usually do not improve acuity because the damage is cortical as well as corneal or refractive. The acuity is typically in the 20/200 to 20/400 area.

Presbyopia. Presbyopia is a reduction in accommodative ability that occurs with age. It causes difficulty in focusing on near objects and reading fine print. The average person requires his first reading glasses between the ages of 42 and 45. Because the power of accommodation is well correlated with age, a fairly accurate estimate of a person's age may be made by measuring the power of accommodation.

With this basic understanding of the general refractive conditions that affect the eye, the discussion will proceed first to functional losses and then to the major pathologies that affect the important components of the eye. An overview of the major pathologies appears in Table 1.

FUNCTIONAL LOSSES

In the low vision field, persons studying ocular pathology are usually required to memorize the names of pathologies and a few descriptive terminologies or to suffer through yet another course in ocular anatomy. Because the Vision Rehabilitation Service emphasizes function, knowledge of the specific pathology is of minimal importance in the rendering of services. Rather, the interests of the service are directed toward the functional losses in visual activity that have occurred as a result of the eye disorder or pathology. However, knowing and understanding the pathology involved sometimes helps the low vision team formulate appropriate treatment programs more quickly.

Before a low vision patient becomes involved in evaluative and instructional services, the team must make sure that all appropriate medical care has been provided. In addition, the ophthalmologist and optometrist on the

Table 1. Overview of Ocular Diseases and Disorders*

Condition	Affected Area	Cause	Visual Effects	Mode of Detection	Treatment	Prognosis
Achromatopsia (total color blindness)	Retina (cone malformation)	Hereditary	Decreased visual acuity to 20/200, extreme photophobia, and nystagmus. Visual fields are normal.	Color vision screening test and electrodiagnostic tests, especially using the electroretinogram (ERG).	Optical aids, sunglasses, and dim illumination.	Nonprogressive; nystagmus and photophobia reduce with age.
Albinism (total or partial lack of pigment)	Macula (underdeveloped)	Hereditary	Decreased visual acuity (20/200 to 20/70), nystagmus, photophobia, high refractive effor, and astigmatism. Visual fields variable and color vision is normal	Family history and ocular examination.	Painted or pinhole contact lenses, absorptive lenses, optical aids, and dim illumination.	Nonprogressive.
Aniridia	Iris (underdeveloped)	Hereditary	Decreased visual acuity, photophobia, possible nystagmus, cataracts, displaced lens, and underdeveloped retina. Visual fields are normal. Secondary complication: glaucoma, with accompanying constriction	Clinical observation of missing iris tissue	Pin-hole contact lenses, sunglasses, optical aids, and dim illumination.	Milder forms develop slow, progressive cataracts; severe forms develop glaucoma and corneal opacification.

| Cataracts (congenital) | Lens (opacity) | Hereditary, congenital anomalies (rubella, Marfan's syndrome, Down's syndrome), infection or drugs during pregnancy, and severe malnutrition during pregnancy. | Decreased visual acuity, blurred vision, nustagmus, squint, photophobia, slight constriction in the peripheral visual fields is possible, but visual fields are generally normal. | Ophthalmoscopy and slit-lamp biomicroscope. | Surgery as early as possible. cases of severe visual impairment. | After surgery, inability to accommodate; problems with glare, which are corrected with spectacles or contact lenses. Complications from surgery: secondary cataracts and detachment of the vitreous or retina. |
| Cataracts (senile) | Lens (opacity) | Age | Progressively blurred vision; near vision is better than distance vision. | Same as for congenital cataracts. | Surgery, with resultant cataract spectacles, contact lenses, lens implant, (IOL, intraocular lens). | Same as for congenital cataracts. Complications from surgery: glaucoma, retinal detachment, hemorrhage of the vitreous, infection. Better candidate for intraocular lens (IOL) implants. |

*Developed by Dr. Dr. Jose and Ms. Nance Baumann, O.T., at the Pennsylvania College of Optometry.

Condition	Affected Area	Cause	Visual Effects	Mode of Detection	Treatment	Prognosis
Cataracts (traumatic)	Lens (opacity)	Head injury or metallic foreign body in the eye.	Blurred vision, redness and inflammation of the eye, and decreased visual acuity. Complications: infection, uveitis, retinal detachment, and glaucoma.	Same as for congenital and senile cataracts.	Surgery after inflammation subsides.	Same as for congenital and senile cataracts.
Coloboma	Various parts of the eye may have been deformed, severity depending on when deformity occurred during development.	Hereditary	Decreased visual acuity, nystagmus, strabismus, photophobia, and loss of visual and superior fields. Secondary complication: cataracts. Associated conditions: microphthalmia, polydactyly, and mental retardation.	Fundus examination	Cosmetic contact lenses, sunglasses, and optical aids.	Usually fairly stable.
Diabetes Mellitus	Retina	Hereditary	Diplopia, inability to accommodate, fluctuating vision, loss of color vision or	Ophthalmoscopy; reports of fluctuating vision	Insulin injections, dietary controls, spectacles, and laser-beam surgery.	Variation in acuity common.

	visual field, refractive error, decreased visual acuity, hemorrhaging of blood vessels in the retina, retinal detachment. Secondary complications: glaucoma and cataracts. Associated conditions: cardiovascular problems, skin problems, and kidney problems.			Various illumination control aids	
Degenerative Myopia (nearsightedness)	Hereditary	Elongation of the eye; stretching of the posterior of the eye.	Decreased visual acuity in the distance, vitreous floaters, metamorphopsia. Normal visual field unless retina is detached. Secondary complications: retinal detachment and swelling or hemorrhaging of the macula.	Fundus examination	Prescription correction, preferably contact lenses; optical aids, and high illumination.

Unpredictable rate of progression.

Condition	Affected Area	Cause	Visual Effects	Mode of Detection	Treatment	Prognosis
Down's Syndrome (mongolism)	Various parts of the eye.	Hereditary; extra No. 21 chromosome.	Decrease of visual acuity, squint, nystagmus, severe myopia, Brushfield spots, congenital cataracts, and keratoconus. Color vision and visual fields are normal. Associated conditions: mental retardation, cardiac abnormalities, hypotonia, saddle-shaped nose, large protruding tongue, and a short, squat stature.	Physical appearance. Complete medical work-up	Depending on patient's intellectual level, optical aids, prescription correction.	Medical problems more severe than usual. Good prognosis.
Glaucoma (congenital)	Tissues of the eye damaged from increased intraocular pressure.	Hereditary	Excessive tearing, photophobia, opacity or haze on lens, buphthalmos, poor visual acuity, and constricted visual fields.	Tonometry, study of the visual fields, and ophthalmoscopy.	Eye drops; surgery as soon as possible to prevent extensive damage.	With treatment, depends on the innate resistance of the structures of the eye. Blindness if not treated.
Glaucoma (adult)	Same as for congenital glaucoma.	Hereditary or the result of changes in the eye after surgery.	Headaches in front portion of the head, especially in the	Same as for congenital glaucoma	Eye drops, optical aids, sunglasses.	Same as for congenital glaucoma.

Glaucoma (acute attack)	Same as for congenital and adult glaucoma.	Inability of the aqueous to drain.	morning; seeing halos around lights; decreased visual acuity, loss of visual fields, photophobia, and constricted peripheral fields in severe cases. Nausea, severe redness of the eye, headache, and severe pain.	Same as for congenital and adult glaucoma.	Emergency surgery.	Without emergency surgery, permanent damage to the ocular tissues and loss of visual acuity and in peripheral vision.
Histoplasmosis	Macula or periphery (scattered lesions)	Fungus transmitted by spores found in dried excrement of animals.	In the macula: decreased visual acuity, central scotoma, and deficient color vision. In the periphery: scotoma corresponding to the area of lesions.	Ophthalmoscopy	Optical aids for visual problems; steroids for physical condition.	Can be life threatening if not treated.

Condition	Affected Area	Cause	Visual Effects	Mode of Detection	Treatment	Prognosis
Keratoconus	Cornea (stretched to a cone shape)	Hereditary. Manifests in second decade	Increased distortion of entire visual field; progressive decrease in visual acuity, especially in the distance. Associated conditions: retinitis pigmentosa, aniridia, Down's syndrome, and Marfan's syndrome.	Ophthalmoscopy, retinoscopy, keratometry, and slit-lamp biomicroscope.	Hard contact lenses in the early stages; keratoplasty (corneal transplant) as needed.	Without keratoplasty, progressive degenerative thinning of cornea until cornea ruptures and blindness ensues.
Marfan's Syndrome (disease of the connective tissues of the body)	Various parts of the eye.	Hereditary	Dislocation of the lens, decreased visual acuity, severe myopia, dislocated or multiple pupil, retinal detachment with accompanying field loss, different-colored eyes, squint, nystagmus, and bluish sclera. Associated conditions: skeletal abnormalities, long, thin fingers and toes, cardiovascular prob-	Medical examination and evaluation.	Optical aids. Surgical or optical management of the disclocated lens.	Vision problems stable; medical problems are more significant.

...lems, and muscular underdevelopment.

Condition	Part Affected	Causes	Symptoms	Diagnosis	Treatment	Prognosis
Retinal Detachment	Retina (portions detach from supporting structure and atrophy)	Numerous, including diabetes, diabetic retinopathy, degenerative myopia, and a blow to the head.	Appearance of flashing lights; sharp, stabbing pain in the eye; visual field loss; micropsia, color defects, and decreased visual acuity if the macula is affected.	Ophthalmoscopy and an internal eye examination.	Laser-beam surgery and cryosurgery, depending on the type and cause of the detachment; optical aids; and usually high illumination.	Guarded.
Retinitis Pigmentosa	Retina (degenerative pigmentary condition)	Hereditary	Decreased visual acuity, photophobia, constriction of the visual fields, (loss in the peripheral field), and night blindness. Usher's syndrome, Laurence-Moon-Biedel's syndrome, and Leber's syndrome are associated with R.P.	Electrodiagnostic testing, especially ERG, and ophthalmoscopy.	Optical aids, prisms. No known medical cure; genetic counseling is essential.	Slow, progressive loss in the visual fields that may lead to blindness.

Condition	Affected Area	Cause	Visual Effects	Mode of Detection	Treatment	Prognosis
Retrolental Fibroplasia	Retina (growth of blood vessels) and vitreous.	High levels of oxygen administered to premature infants; occasionally found in full-term infants.	Decreased visual acuity, severe myopia, scarring, and retinal detachment, with resultant visual field loss and possible blindness. Secondary complications: glaucoma and uveitis.	Ophthalmoscopy.	Optical aids and illumination control devices.	Poor, in severe cases, where further detachments can be expected in third decade.
Rubella	Various parts of the eye.	Virus transmitted to the fetus by the mother during pregnancy.	Congenital glaucoma, congenital cataracts, microphthalmia, decreased visual acuity, and constriction of the visual fields. Associated conditions: heart defects, ear defects, and mental deficiency.	Ophthalmoscopy, slit-lamp biomicroscope, tonometry, and family history.	Surgery for glaucoma and cataracts, optical aids, establishment of appropriate educational goals.	Poor; post-surgical inflammation.

Toxoplasmosis	Retina, especially macula (lesions)	Intraocular infection caused by *Toxoplasma gondii*. In congenital type, fetus exposed to organism; in acquired type, through contact with infected animals or ingestion of raw meat.	Loss in visual fields corresponding to location of lesion, squint, decreased visual acuity if macula is affected, severe brain damage if congenital.	Ophthalmoscopy.	Optical aids—usually good responses to magnification.	Nonprogressive, although new lesions may develop.

17

low vision team should determine if the characteristics of the pathology (such as diabetes and fluctuating vision) are interfering with the success of the program or if they are related to some unusual functional observations. Once medical care has been provided, the low vision team must concentrate on the functional aspects of the visual system.

Some of the visual disturbances caused by ocular pathologies and disorders that the low vision instructor will encounter are as follows:

Lowered Central Acuity or Fluctuating Vision. Persons with this condition may indicate a dimness of vision, haziness, a film over the eye, foggy vision, or a need for glasses. Usually they first report that they cannot read small print.

Metamorphopsia. Persons with metamorphopsia describe a distortion of vision and may complain of a haze all the time. Objects appear to bulge, curve, or "look funny."

Photophobia. Persons with photophobia either complain of an abnormal sensitivity to light or do not report the problem but use very dark glasses or avoid high levels of illumination. Recovery from glare is slow, and adaptation to light is difficult.

Color Distortions. Persons with this condition indicate they cannot detect colors, or functional observations show they have trouble identifying colors.

Field Defects. Persons with field defects report they have no vision in specified sectors of the visual field; objects disappear to the right, left, and so forth; and parts of an object being viewed are always missing. Frequently, field loss is detected through functional observations, rather than from direct reports from the person experiencing it. Common losses include: (1) general contraction or depression (objects in the periphery are not seen), (2) hemianopsia (the right half, left half, upper half, or lower half of the visual field is missing), and (3) scotoma (seen mainly as a central scotoma in which the macula is no longer functioning but all the retinal tissue around the scotoma area is intact. Scotoma usually results in vision of 20/400 or more).

Night Blindness. Persons who have night blindness indicate a decreased ability to see at night and difficulty in performing specific tasks at night or are observed to function worse at night. This condition can be confirmed by clinical tests, especially electrodiagnostic testing.

Entoptic Images. Persons with this condition see floaters or spots before their eyes, including stationary spots that move with the eye; these floaters or spots momentarily interfere with vision. Such symptoms may indicate an active pathology, so appropriate care should be provided by the staff optometrist or ophthalmologist.

Oscillopsia. Persons with oscillopsia report that the world seems to be moving or jumping around. This condition may be a sign of a neurological disorder; therefore, persons suffering from it should be referred to a neurologist or another appropriate physician.

DEFICIENCY OF TEARS

Tears are a mixture of three separate layers—the outermost oily layer, the central aqueous layer, and an inner mucoid layer. Tears form an almost perfect optical surface (a film) on the cornea. The tear film fills in all the irregularities, thus producing a smooth refractive surface. Tears also lubricate the eye as the lids move over its exposed surface and provide bactericidal action to protect the sensitive corneal epithelium. Deficiency in any components of the tear film may lead to the dry-eye syndrome. Patients with dry eyes complain most frequently of a scratchy or sandy sensation, although when the eyes are observed casually, they appear normal. The dry-eye syndrome may be caused by (1) old age, (2) trachoma, (3) drugs, (4) chemical burns, or (5) inflammations. It may lead to reduced acuity, photophobia, and metamorphopsia.

CORNEAL CONDITIONS

Diseases of the cornea are serious because improper management of them may result in permanent visual impairment ranging from slight blurring to total blindness. Most of the disabling complications of corneal diseases can be prevented by prompt and accurate diagnosis and appropriate treatment.

Since the cornea serves as the window of the eye and refracts light rays, corneal lesions cause some degree of blurred vision. The blurring is greater if the lesion is centrally located. Scarring or perforation from corneal ulceration is a major cause of blindness throughout the world. Most forms are corrected by medical therapy, but visual impairment can be avoided only if appropriate treatment is instituted promptly; in some cases, treatment must begin within a few hours of onset. Corneal ulceration is caused by many agents: bacteria, viruses, fungi, hypersensitivity reactions, vitamin A deficiency, as well as by causes that are not yet known.

Keratoconus
Keratoconus (kera = cornea, conus = cone shaped) is exactly what its name indicates: a cone-shaped cornea. It first becomes noticeable during adolescence and occurs primarily in females. The condition, which usually affects both eyes, may initially present itself as a progressive decrease in visual acuity. There is generally no observable loss of visual field, but, rather, an overall distortion of the visual field. The person may find herself needing a new prescription every six months to a year at a time when her refractive error should be fairly stable. Distance vision is generally worse than near vision because as the cornea becomes progressively cone shaped, nearsightedness is being induced. Visual acuity depends on the extent of the condition and may range from mild distortion to severe visual impairment that cannot be adequately corrected with spectacles or contact lenses. If the condition progresses to the point at which the cornea ruptures, blindness will result.

The optometrist or ophthalmologist identifies the condition by noting shadows in the reflex when looking into the eye with the ophthalmoscope or measuring the refractive error with the retinoscope. These shadows are due to folds or ruptures of the various layers of the cornea. Diagnosis is made by measuring the curvature of the cornea (keratometry) and closely examining the cornea under the slit-lamp biomicroscope. As the condition progresses, the lower lid bulges when the patient looks down (Munson's sign). Contact lenses are often used to retard the bulging of the corneal cone; however, they are not always successful. In severe cases, corneal transplants (keratoplasty) may be successful if performed before the condition progresses to a more advanced stage.

Keratoconus generally occurs in both eyes. It is generally believed to be a hereditary condition although the mode of transmission is not completely known. It is thought to be an autosomal recessive trait. Keratoconus may be seen in conjunction with other conditions such as retinitis pigmentosa, Down's Syndrome (mongolism), Marfan's syndrome, aniridia (congenital absence or defect of the iris) and Apert's Syndrome. The mode of transmission when associated with one of these anomalies is probably related to the major anomaly present.

Corneal dystrophies are a rare group of slowly progressive, bilateral, degenerative disorders that usually appear in the second or third decade of life. Some cases are hereditary, others follow an ocular inflammatory disease, and some are of unknown cause. In most cases, the symptoms and signs are slowly progressive until useful vision is lost. Corneal transplants improve vision significantly in most cases.

DISEASES OF THE AQUEOUS HUMOR

Glaucoma is the main pathology that occurs in the aqueous humor. In the United States alone, 50,000 persons are totally blind as a result of this disease, and each year some 95,000 people lose some vision from glaucoma (NSPB,1980). Glaucoma is a disease in which the intraocular pressure is so high that it damages the tissues of the eye, resulting in some loss of vision. This loss may be a decrease in visual acuity, a loss in the visual field, or both. There are many types of glaucoma, each with its own signs and symptoms. Detecting the condition in the earliest possible stage is the most important factor in determining the success of treatment.

Glaucoma may be divided into two broad categories: adult and congenital. Congenital glaucoma is present at birth or soon after and generally requires surgery as soon as possible to prevent extensive damage to the eye. It may be primary (not associated with any other ocular disease) or secondary to some other ocular condition. Patients with congenital glaucoma may have hazy, opaque corneas. In severe cases, the cornea actually is pushed forward in a bubble-like effect. An internal eye examination in such cases usually reveals extensive damage to the optic nerve. Vision is usually poor (sometimes no more than light perception) and visual fields are generally constricted (resulting in tunnel vision).

Adult glaucoma may also be of two types—primary or secondary—although the primary type is by far the most common. Patients with adult glaucoma often have headaches in the front portion of the head, especially in the morning. This condition frequently can be treated with eyedrops to control the pressure. The drops themselves may have annoying side effects, such as a slight blurring of vision and constriction of the pupils.

Some persons are subject to acute attacks of glaucoma that occur when the aqueous cannot drain because of defects in the physical structure of the eye. These attacks may be painful and may require emergency surgery. Such attacks can do permanent damage to the ocular tissues and may cause a loss in the visual field. An episode of nausea, headaches, severe redness of the eye and pain may be indications of an acute attack of glaucoma. Unfortunately, many persons ignore these symptoms. Since the central vision is the last to be affected, individuals often are not aware that the damage being done to the tissue by the high intraocular pressure is robbing them of their peripheral vision. Thus, they first notice that something is wrong when they no longer see the edges of doorways as they pass through them or notice cars or other objects approaching from the sides.

The optometrist or ophthalmologist can detect glaucoma early during a general examination. For example, tonometry—a test that measures the pressure inside the eye—detects any elevation of pressure. Furthermore, a close examination of the internal structures of the eye during ophthalmoscopy will indicate any disturbance to the tissue caused by the elevated pressure. Also, careful testing of the visual field will determine any defects in that area.

There is evidence to support the fact that glaucoma—especially congenital and adult, primary glaucoma—is hereditary. Although the exact mechanism for transmission of glaucoma is not completely known, glaucoma probably is autosomal with more than one type of inheritance pattern.

There is also a condition in which the intraocular pressure is too low. This condition often leads to retinal detachment and uveitis, which will be discussed in the section on the iris. A sustained, abnormally low, intraocular pressure usually causes shrinkage of the entire eye until is is nonfunctional—a condition called "phthisis bulbi."

CONDITIONS OF THE IRIS

Inflammation of the uveal tract is called uveitis and its symptoms are injection or redness of the eye, photophobia, and blurred vision. The blurred vision is caused by a cloudy aqueous or vitreous.

Aniridia is the failure of the iris to develop fully so that the iris is partially

21

or almost completely absent. This condition usually affects both eyes, although in rare cases it may affect only one eye. Aniridia is a congenital defect (present at birth) that is transmitted as an autosomal dominant pattern and may vary from a minor abnormality to an almost total structural lack of iris tissue. There is always some iris developed although it may not be visible to the naked eye.

In aniridia, the general appearance is that of an extremely large pupil. Persons with this condition are extremely senstitive to light (photophobic), have decreased visual acuity, and may demonstrate nystagmus (rapid, involuntary movement of the eyes). Glaucoma is a secondary problem in many cases when the iris remnants interfere with the drainage of the aqueous. The increased pressure may cause pain, constriction of the visual fields (tunnel vision), and cloudiness of the cornea, which further decreases visual acuity. Cataracts, a displaced lens, and underdevelopment of the retina are frequently associated ocular defects.

Persons with aniridia are sometimes helped with sunglasses, optical aids, dim illumination, and pinhole contact lenses to decrease the amount of light reaching the back of the eye. Aside from reducing the patient's photophobic complaints, pin-hole contact lenses will slightly improve visual acuity and may reduce nystagmus. Because of its hereditary nature, genetic counseling is recommended for patients with aniridia who wish to have children.

DISORDERS OF THE CRYSTALLINE LENS

The only disorders of the lens are opacification (cataracts) and dislocation. Because there are no pain fibers, blood vessels or nerves in the lens, the patient with an opacity or dislocation of the lens will complain of blurred vision without pain.

Cataracts

Cataracts are any opacification of the lens; they vary markedly in degree of density and may be due to a variety of causes; however, they usually are associated with aging. Some degree of cataract formation is to be expected in persons over age 70. Most cataracts are bilateral, although the rate of progression in each eye is seldom equal. They often are not visible to the casual observer until they become dense enough (mature or hypermature) to cause blindness. The clinical degree of cataract formation, assuming that no other eye disease is present, is judged primarily by visual acuity. Generally speaking, the decrease in visual acuity is directly proportional to the density of the cataract. However, some persons who have clinically significant cataracts when examined with the ophthalmoscope or slit-lamp biomicroscope see well enough to carry on with their normal activities. The decrease in visual acuity in other persons may be out of proportion to the degree of opacification of the lens because of a distortion of the image by the partially opaque lens.

In cataract operations, the procedure of choice is generally to remove the

22

entire lens. The patient's condition is now called aphakia and he or she must wear a thick plus lens or a contact lens to compensate for the loss of the crystalline lens. An increasing number of people are being successfully fitted with plastic lens implants that "normalize" postsurgical vision.

Two common forms of cataracts that the low vision instructor will encounter are congenital cataracts and posterior subcapsular cataracts.

Congenital Cataracts

Congenital cataracts are opacities present at birth or developed shortly after birth. They are generally bilateral, although they may be unilateral, especially in the case of intraocular disease. As is the case with other forms of cataracts, with congenital cataracts, the optometrist or ophthalmologist observes the opacity grossly with the ophthalmoscope or in greater detail with the slit-lamp biomicroscope to evaluate the involved portion of the lens and the density of the opacity.

Surgery may be necessary in cases of severe visual impairment. It should be performed as early as possible to allow for the development of normal vision. Failure to perform surgery at the right time may result in the development of a squint (turning in or out of the affected eye). Complications that occur from the removal of congenital cataracts are fairly common and take the form of secondary cataracts (opacification of remaining lens material) and possible vitreous or retinal detachment. The latter are due to the strong adherence of the vitreous to the back portion (posterior capsule) of the lens. Even though improved surgical techniques have reduced the incidence of such problems, surgery is advocated only in cases of marked visual impairment. The presence of other ocular disorders would further contraindicate the surgical removal of congenital cataracts.

The effect of congenital cataracts on vision varies greatly, depending on the size, position, and density of the opacity. Generally, persons with cataracts have blurred vision. Visual acuity may be near-normal or greatly reduced. Nystagmus may be manifested in severe cases of congenital cataracts. The person may complain of serious glare problems. Night vision is not generally affected. Visual fields are generally normal, although there may be some reduction in the peripheral fields. One early sign of a congenital cataract may be the development of a squint or strabismus because of the lack of visual stimulation of the affected eye, which results in a type of amblyopia (reduced visual function).

Centrally or posteriorly located congenital opacities (such as posterior congenital subcapsular cataracts) may affect near vision more than distance vision and are more debilitating in bright light. Cortical cataracts (those opacities located in the cortex, or outer portion of the lens) may result in poor color discrimination owing to the abnormal scattering of light rays. In nuclear opacifiction (when the central portion of the lens is affected), visual acuity may be improved significantly by applying dilating agents (in the form

23

of drops or ointments) on a regular basis. Dilation of the pupil allows the patient to see around the cataract; it is an alternative to surgery.

After cataract surgery, a refractive correction is needed, which may be provided in the form of a spectacle correction or a contact lens. If the patient had a cataract removed from one eye only, a spectacle correction would be undesirable because of the magnification effects of the spectacle lens. A contact lens would be preferable because it would minimize the problems the patient would experience. Removal of the lens also takes away the ability of the patient to accommodate; therefore, a bifocal correction or reading correction is necessary for the patient to see objects close up. The use of sunglasses and visors can alleviate the increased glare that many patients experience after cataract surgery.

The causes of congenital cataracts are many. Approximately 25 percent of all cases are hereditary. Therefore, prospective parents with congenital cataracts should seek genetic counseling to determine the probability of future children exhibiting the condition. Congenital cataracts may also be associated with other congenital anomalies, such as the rubella syndrome, Down's syndrome (mongolism), and Marfan's syndrome. They may be caused by intrauterine infection during pregnancy, the administration of drugs during pregnancy (particularly during the first three months), or severe maternal malnutrition or systemic disorders of either the mother or the infant.

Posterior Subcapsular Cataracts

In posterior subcapsular cataracts, the posterior or back portion of the lens becomes hazy or cloudy. Because of the position of the opacity, the effect on vision can be devastating (as is true with posteriorly positioned congenital cataracts). Individuals with this type of cataract will generally notice poor vision in bright sunlight and poor near vision. Such complaints are caused by a loss of acuity when the pupils are constricted, which maximizes the effect of the cataract by preventing the patient from seeing "around" the opacity. Distance vision is generally minimally affected in the early stages.

Posterior subcapsular cataracts are generally bilateral, although they may be unilateral in cases of traumatic injury. Visual fields are generally normal; however, some central distortion may be evident. Patients may notice some distortion of color and may experience glare (particularly at night) owing to the scattering of light by the opacity.

Gross observation of such individuals may indicate no abormality. Only by careful examination of the internal aspects of the eye (using the slit-lamp biomicroscope) will the optometrist or ophthalmologist be able to detect the cataracts and localize the position of the opacity. Since the changes are generally irreversible, the only treatment is surgical extraction of the lens when the cataract has reached the stage of severe visual impairment.

Posterior subcapsular cataracts have numerous causes. They may be the result of the normal aging process, of traumatic injury to the eye, or of the long-term taking of drugs (particularly steroids), or they may accompany other ocular conditions, such as retinitis pigmentosa. Posterior subcapsular cataracts, it is thought, are transmitted genetically in the form of an autosomal dominant trait.

Partial or complete dislocation of the lens may be hereditary or may result from trauma. Hereditary dislocation of the lens usually is bilateral and may be associated with coloboma of the lens, Marfan's syndrome, and Hallerman-Streif syndrome. The vision is blurred particularly if the lens is dislocated out of the line of vision. If dislocation is partial, the patient may complain of monocular diplopia (double vision). When a lens is dislocated, it may be removed to prevent blockage of the aqueous outflow, which can lead to glaucoma.

PROBLEMS WITH THE VITREOUS

Two conditions involve the vitreous. They are the appearance of flashing lights and retrolental fibroplasia.

Flashing Lights

Flashing lights are a common symptom. The person is aware of a localized streak of light or flashing in the field of vision for which there is no reasonable explanation. The light seldom persists for more than a fraction of a second. It frequently recurs at short intervals for a few minutes and then disappears for hours, days, or even weeks. The person notices it most readily when moving the eye, especially when there is little or no illumination. Although this phenomenon is unilateral, a similar episode commonly occurs in the other visual field. The flashing light represents a cerebral awareness of a new abnormal vitreous stimulation of the retina. It is most commonly associated with a recent collapse and detachment of the vitreous. The ophthalmologist or optometrist who takes a careful history of the patient will readily distinguish this symptom from the scintillating scotoma of migraine, which is characterized by a symmetric quivering scotoma in both eyes, predictable configuration and progression, and variable nausea or headache.

Flashing lights visually require no treatment. The patient may be reassured that the symptom will pass. However, they may be caused by a retinal tear, retinal detachment, or vitreous hemorrhage. Therefore, this symptom must be carefully watched and monitored by an optometrist or ophthalmologist.

Retrolental Fibroplasia

Retrolental fibroplasia is commonly seen in premature infants who received oxygen therapy, although it occasionally occurs in full-term infants. Its mechanism is not completely understood, but the condition does not seem to be genetic in origin. The severity of RLF may range from minimal ocular damage with no visual impairment to complete retinal detachment and scarring that causes total blindness. The extent of the condition depends on many factors, including the length of time the infant received oxygen and the amount of oxygen that was administered. The condition may be avoided or minimized by careful monitoring of the oxygen levels in incubators for premature babies.

When an infant receives high levels of oxygen in the incubator, the retinal vascular system fails to develop normally. After the infant is removed from the incubator, the blood vessels of the retina cannot supply the necessary levels of oxygen, which causes the blood vessels to grow rapidly and to develop fibrous tissue. The new vessels and fibrous tissue stretch the retina and may eventually lead to retinal detachment when a person reaches the late twenties. These changes are generally first observable, with an ophthalmoscope, when the infant is about one month old. Once they begin, it is difficult to say how far they will progress; approximately 20 percent of persons with RLF eventually become totally blind.

Externally, the eye of individuals with RLF may appear normal. In severe cases, the ophthalmologist discovers a leukocoria (white pupil) and microphthalmus (a small underdeveloped eye). Persons with retrolental fibroplasia generally have no usable vision or have extremely low levels of visual acuity. Such low vision aids as telescopes and microscopes can usually help those individuals with very low visual acuities.

Severe myopia (nearsightedness) is common among persons with retrolental fibroplasia. It may be significantly improved by the use of a contact lens. Glaucoma and uveitis are common secondary problems that may create further complications.

DISORDERS OF THE RETINA

Most disorders of the retina cause blurred vision. If the macular area is diseased, the person's central visual acuity will be affected and the person will have difficulty reading and discerning objects in the distance (such as street signs). If the peripheral portion of the retina is diseased, side vision is impaired but the person is able to read. Because the retina contains no pain fibers, there is no pain with retinal disease, and the eye does not become red or inflamed.

In central retinal artery occlusion, the central retinal artery that feeds the retina becomes obstructed. The result is a sudden complete loss of vision in the affected eye. If the afflicted person is seen within two hours of the onset of the symptoms, medical treatment may be successful. The ophthalmologist may attempt to restore the flow of blood by massaging the globe or by using vasodilators.

In central retinal vein occlusion, the central retinal vein becomes obstructed. This condition results in retinal hemorrhages and a sudden painless loss of vision. As the hemorrhage clears, vision is usually decreased but not lost. Young persons with central retinal vein occlusion have a better prognosis for maintaining some visual function than do older individuals.

Diabetes Mellitus

Diabetes mellitus is the leading cause of blindness in the United States. It is a systemic condition that is due to the lack of insulin in the bloodstream. Insulin, which is produced by specific cells in the pancreas, is necessary to control the amount of sugar circulating in the bloodstream. Insufficient amounts of insulin result in hyperglycemia (high blood sugar levels) and in problems in metabolizing carbohydrates, fats, and proteins. These high blood sugar levels, in turn, affect many parts of the body, including the eyes, the kidneys, the skin, and the circulatory system (heart, blood vessels, and so forth).

Symptoms experienced by diabetics include excessive hunger (polyphagia), excessive thirst (polydypsia), excessive urination (polyuria), poor wound healing, impotence, and lethargy. The practitioner tests for a high blood sugar level, excessive sugar levels in the urine, and possibly a high sugar content in the tears.

Treatment generally depends on the severity of the condition and the age of the patient. Juvenile diabetics (those afflicted prior to age 20) are usually treated with insulin injections and a controlled diet. They are generally the most severe cases and the most difficult to treat. Mature diabetics (whose onset is around age 40) typically are treated with oral medication (to stimulate insulin production) and dietary controls. Senile diabetics (whose onset is about age 70) are generally the least severe cases and often are treated only by dietary controls.

Systemic complications from diabetes are related to the severity and onset of the condition. They include premature aging of the blood vessels, which results in a high incidence of stroke and heart problems; an elevated blood cholesterol level; and neurological problems, such as diplopia (double vision) in patients aged 40–60, caused by a paralysis of one or more of the muscles that move the eye. Among the earliest signs of diabetes are the general loss of the ability to accommodate (focus the eyes for a near object) and a fluctuating refractive error, which usually remains stable if the condition is under control.

The main ocular problems associated with diabetes stem from changes in the blood vessels of the eye. The blood vessels in the retina may hemorrhage and the hemorrhage may spread into the vitreous. The hemorrhaging of blood vessels results in the growth of new blood vessels and eventual retinal detachment. (A patient's complaint of "flashing lights" often indicates retinal detachment.) Visual impairment may be insignificant or severe (total blindness) and its extent varies from one episode of hemorrhaging to the next. Visual acuity is reduced according to what parts of the retina are affected. In the more advanced stages, a person may show varying losses in the visual field owing to retinal detachments and hemorrhaging and may lose color vision if the macular area is affected. Glaucoma may develop as a result of the growth of new blood vessels extending from the back toward the front of the eye into the vitreous. Laser beam surgery will sometimes retard the progression by sealing off the hemorrhaging blood vessels, but this is not always successful. Diabetics are also predisposed to cataracts. However, surgery to remove the cataracts is difficult because of the poor wound-healing capabilities of diabetics.

Diabetes mellitus is inherited as a simple Mendelian recessive trait with incomplete penetrance. Thus, if both parents are diabetics, the probability of transmitting the trait is 100 percent; if one parent is a diabetic, the chance of transmission is only 20 percent (less than 25 percent because of incomplete penetrance).

Diabetic retinopathy may also be classified into two main types—nonproliferative and proliferative—and the course and prognosis of each type differs. In nonproliferative retinopathy, the changes in the eye are confined to the retina. These retinal changes include dilation of the veins, microaneurysms, and retinal hemorrhages. Edema or exudates in the macular area are responsible for the impairment. In general, the prognosis for persons with nonproliferative retinopathy is better than for those with the proliferative type.

The most outstanding feature of proliferative retinopathy is the formation of new blood vessels, which may be limited to the surface of the retina or may involve the vitreous as well. Persons with this condition have a poor visual prognosis, and there is no effective treatment for most stages of advanced proliferative retinopathy.

Retinitis Pigmentosa

Retinitis pigmentosa is a retinal pigmentary degeneration of unknown etiology—an inherited disease that primarily attacks males. The disease is acquired by all forms of genetic transmission, the recessive variety being the most serious and the sex-linked being the least severe.

In this disease, the rods of the retina are slowly destroyed, and the remainder of the retina atrophies. These changes usually begin in the mid periphery, sparing the macula and extreme peripheral areas until later. The ophthalmologist or optometrist detects the disease through electrodiagnostic testing and ophthalmoscopy.

Night blindness, the first symptom of retinitis pigmentosa, usually occurs in early youth. Thereafter, the visual fields gradually constrict to become disabling between ages 40 and 60, at which time macular vision also may be lost. Photophobia is usually reported. The development of posterior cataracts and glaucoma are often secondary complications. Retinitis pigmentosa may be associated with other ocular problems, such as Usher's syndrome (retinitis pigmentosa plus cataracts and deafness), Laurence-Moon-Biedel's syndrome (retinitis pigmentosa plus mental retardation, obesity, and hypogenitalism), or Leber's syndrome (retinitis pigmentosa plus cataracts plus atrophic changes in the disc).

There is no specific therapy for retinitis pigmentosa although low vision aids and prisms are sometimes helpful. Therefore, genetic counseling should be offered to patients in order to reduce unwanted propagation of the disease and to prepare them for the likelihood that their male childen will have it. Appropriate services can be provided to children with retinitis pigmentosa at an early age to minimize the debilitating effects of the disease.

Retinal Detachment

In retinal detachment, the retina is separated from its supporting structures. Because it receives no nourishment, the detached portion of the retina atrophies, and a blind area develops in the field of vision corresponding to the area of the detachment. Retinal detachment occurs in many forms and is associated with various causes. To a large extent, the type and cause of the detachment determines the treatment procedures used.

Visual symptoms of retinal detachment vary. The appearance of flashing lights accompanied by a sharp, stabbing pain in the eye are significant indications of a recent or impending detachment. (Such complaints always should be followed up by a careful ocular examination.) If the macula is involved, visual acuity may be markedly decreased; the retina may swell, causing micropsia (objects appearing smaller when viewed with the affected eye); and color vision may be impaired.

The examining physician may first notice a retinal detachment when performing ophthalmoscopy. The retina in a normal eye is transparent; however, when the retina becomes detached, it appears milky white. A careful internal eye examination will determine the extent and severity of the detachment.

Most detachments are caused by an accumulation of fluid under the retina that pushes it away from its supporting structures. The excess fluid may be the result of many other ocular or general physical conditions, such as diabetes or a sharp blow to the head.

Surgery is generally necessary, particularly if there is a hole or break in the retina. It may be accomplished by various means, the most common being photocoagulation (application of a laser beam to seal the retina to its supporting structures) and cryosurgery, which involves using a cold probe to freeze the retina to its underlying structures. Although these procedures are usually successful, it is difficult to predict how much vision can be restored. The length of time between the detachment and surgical procedures is crucial. In many cases, postsurgical improvement is slow; it may take months before vision reaches its best level of improvement.

Since retinal detachments are caused by trauma, ocular disease, or a general physical condition, they are not an inherited trait. The causative condition (such as diabetes) may have genetic tendencies; if so, the diabetic person may benefit from genetic counseling.

Toxoplasmosis

Toxoplasmosis is a severe intraocular infection caused by a small organism called the *Toxoplasma gondii*. It may be congenital, in which case the fetus was exposed to the organism prior to birth, or may be acquired. The organism may be transmitted through contact with domestic animals such as cats or chickens or by ingestion of raw meat that contains the organism. Since the organism is destroyed by heat, cooking will generally insure against infection.

Congenital toxoplasmosis is much more severe owing to other complications: the organism seems to have a predilection for nervous tissue and may cause severe brain damage. Ocular involvement is much more common in congenital cases.

Toxoplasmosis is first diagnosed during an ophthalmoscopic examination when a lesion or lesions, seen as punched-out areas of the retina, are detected. These areas demonstrate corresponding blind areas on visual field testing. If a lesion impinges on the macular area, as is frequently the case, the effect may be devastating: a greatly reduced visual acuity as well as accompanying field defects. The decreased acuity in an affected eye often results in a squint, which may be one of the first observable signs of the infection, particularly in young children.

The condition is generally not progressive, although new lesions may develop; thus, periodic examinations are important. There are no indications of genetic involvement.

Histoplasmosis

Histoplasmosis—a fungus infection that can affect various parts of the body—is prevalent in the Midwest. It is caused by inhalation or ingestion of spores of an organism called *Histoplasma capsulatum* that may be found in the dried excrement of animals.

The condition is life-threatening. Its general symptoms may be similar to pneumonia or tuberculosis. The condition affects the eye in the form of scattered areas of inflammation (lesions) in the back of the eye that, in the absence of external symptoms, generally are first detected during an ophthalmoscopic examination.

The effect on vision depends on the location and extent of the lesions. If the infection develops in the macular area, visual impairment is serious and includes greatly reduced visual acuity both at distance and at near (which may result in the development of a squint), a central scotoma, and deficient color vision. Lesions in other portions of the retina are less severe. A scotoma corresponds to the area of the lesion or lesions, and, depending on its size and location, may cause mobility problems or may interfere greatly with reading if it involves all or part of the area of central vision, especially in the right field.

Management of histoplasmosis usually involves steroid therapy to control the body's inflammatory response to the organism. Since the condition is caused by an infectious agent, there are no hereditary implications. Although a pregnant mother can transmit the organism to the fetus, which will, in turn, become infected, future children will not be affected if the mother is not in an infectious state during pregnancy.

Senile Macular Degeneration

Senile macular degeneration is a common disease in people aged 65 and older. It may also occur in young people who inherit it as juvenile macular degeneration. This disease primarily affects both eyes, although only one eye is significantly involved at first. Progression is gradual, but the end result usually is a dense central scotoma. Patients should be reassured that the disease does not lead to total blindness, although central vision may be extremely poor. The extent of photophobia and glare varies, and the major problem is to teach older patients to look around the central blind spot.

Albinism

Albinism is a congenital condition characterized by a fair complexion, platinum-blonde hair, and light-colored irises and eyebrows owing to the lack of pigment or the body's inability to produce pigment. It may involve all pigmented structures (the hair, the skin, and the eyes) or just one. When only the eyes are affected, the condition is termed *ocular albinism.* Carriers of this hereditary condition may exhibit other minor forms of albinism.

Albinism is a hereditary disorder. The mode of transmission of albinism depends on the type of condition present. Ocular albinism is a sex-linked recessive trait characteristically limited to the eyes. Thus, males exhibit the condition while the females are carriers. Although female carriers typically exhibit minor ocular manifestations of the condition, they are not generally impaired. One out of every two female carriers has a chance of exhibiting the trait, while all the daughters of an affected male will be carriers.

Because affected individuals are severely photophobic, lighting conditions are important; appropriate illumination control aids often reduce the photophobia. Nystagmus may occur because the macula is underdeveloped. Albinos usually have high refractive errors and may exhibit severe astigmatism. However, because the macula did not develop fully, they do not show the expected increase in acuity when the refractive error is corrected. Visual fields are generally normal or slightly reduced if no other ocular conditions are present. Mobility skills are minimally affected in relation to the level of visual acuity.

Treatment of affected individuals may involve the fitting of contact lenses to provide the best possible visual acuity. A pin-hole or painted type of contact lens frequently is effective in reducing glare as well as in providing an optical correction for refractive error, and may be of some benefit in reducing nystagmus.

Oculocutaneous albinism is transmitted as an autosomal recessive trait. It affects all the pigmented structures (the hair, the eyes, and the skin) to various extents. Carriers of this condition clinically exhibit no symptoms of albinism. A careful family history and ocular examination will help the ophthalmologist or optometrist to diagnose the type of albinism present. This differentiation is important for determining the prognosis of the condition for the patient as well as the need for genetic counseling.

Achromatopsia

Achromatopsia (total color blindness) is a hereditary condition in which the individual is unable to distinguish colors because of a malformation of the neural portion of the eye that normally distinguishes colors. The retina contains two types of neural receptors: cones, which allow one to see detail and color in illuminated (photopic) conditions, and rods, which allow one to see under dark (scotopic) conditions. Achromats have improperly developed cone systems and thus are sometimes referred to as rod monochromats. Since cones are the major form of receptor in the macular area, they are responsible for normal central visison. They also function in the determination of colors. A deficiency in the cone system (such as that seen in achromatism or any ocular condition that affects the macular area) results in decreased visual acuity (generally to a level of about 20/200), which cannot be corrected with conventional spectacles, and an inability to discriminate colors. Near vision is generally less affected than distance vision.

Achromats cannot function adequately under normal illumination and exhibit photophobia and nystagmus. They may compensate for their color blindness by detecting brightness or differences in the gray intensity of colors and associating appropriate color names with these differences. The nystagmus and photophobia are significantly reduced at low lighting levels. Thus, the application of sunglass aids or shields is usually beneficial. These conditions may reduce in severity with age and many times are minimal by the time these individuals reach the mid-teen years.

Visual fields are generally normal in the absence of any other ocular abnormalities. Mobility skills are basically related to the level of visual acuity.

In addition to noting a history of photophobia and acuity loss, the optometrist or ophthalmologist will generally detect this condition during an examination with any type of color vision screening device. Further evaluation should include electrodiagnostic testing (especially an electroretinogram), which is important in determining the extent and prognosis of the condition.

Achromatopsia or rod monochromatism is a hereditary condition found in about 3 males per 100,000. It has a slightly lower incidence in the female population. The mode of transmission is not completely understood, but it is thought to be inherited as an autosomal recessive trait. Although it sometimes appears as a dominant trait, such cases are rare and may be linked to various other ocular and systemic anomalies that would determine the mode of transmission.

Coloboma

A coloboma is usually seen as a notch or cleft on the pupil. In a colobomatous eye, the pupil has a characteristic tear-drop shape owing to a malformation of the eye during development. The coloboma is a congenital condition. Its location and extent depend on when, during development, it occurred. The coloboma may extend from the back of the eye, where the optic nerve enters the eye to the iris or colored portion of the eye. It is generally bilateral and may be associated with other conditions such as microphthalmia (small, underdeveloped eye), abnormalities of the head and face, multiple fingers or toes (polydactyly) and mental retardation.

If the retina is involved, there is an associated field loss because the coloboma affects the lower portion of the eye. Although the field loss does not significantly impair an individual's mobility skills, he or she may find it difficult to detect low overhanging obstructions such as tree limbs or doorways. An affected eye may develop a strabismus (turning in or out of the eye) and/or nystagmus; these conditions generally are secondary to the decreased visual acuity. Furthermore, a colobomatous eye may also have difficulty with glare because of the tear-drop shaped pupil; however, this problem can be alleviated with sunglasses. If the pupil is cosmetically unattractive, the patient may be fitted with a contact lens to make the pupil appear more normal.

The mode of inheritance is not completely clear. It is believed that the condition is transmitted as an irregular, autosomal dominant trait. However, a coloboma involving the macular area may be transmitted in a different fashion.

ATROPHY OF THE OPTIC NERVE

Atrophy of the optic nerve can be caused by a multitude of diseases or it can be inherited. When it is atrophied, the optic nerve head is pale, and the patient loses visual acuity and undergoes changes in the visual field. It is rarely possible to treat the atrophy unless the underlying cause is found early and treated effectively. A good example is glaucoma, which eventually leads to atrophy of the optic nerve and then total blindness. By treating glaucoma in its early stages and keeping it under control, further atrophy can usually be prevented. Optic atrophy can create a variety of visual field and ocular losses ranging from those that are barely discernible to total blindness.

SYNDROMES

Congenital rubella, Down's syndrome, and Marfan's syndrome are three syndromes or diseases that are commonly associated with or are causes of low vision.

Congenital Rubella
A person with congenital rubella was exposed as a fetus to the rubella virus, which was transmitted by the mother to the fetus through the placenta. The severity of the resultant defects depends, to a great extent, on how early in the pregnancy the virus was introduced. (The first trimester and, particu-

larly, the first four weeks are critical.) The rubella virus, it is believed, is able to interfere with the division and multiplication of cells, thus causing nonspecific chromosomal changes that are responsible for the resultant birth defects. An adequate vaccination is the only treatment to prevent maternal infection during pregnancy. Without immunity, there is no sure way to prevent the viral infection.

Classically, the rubella child exhibits eye, ear, and heart defects, although other organs are commonly involved. Generally, ocular abnormalities are evident. Congenital glaucoma and congenital cataracts give the eyes a hazy, whitish appearance and prevent the examining physician from viewing the back of the eye. The eyes are generally very small (microphthalmia). Viral inflammations of various parts of the eye may be added complications. The back of the eye sometimes is similar to that seen in retinitis pigmentosa. However, in congenital rubella, the condition is nonprogressive and does not, in itself, seem to interfere with vision. However recent research suggests that further deterioration may occur as the child grows.

Visual acuity is generally reduced because of the cataracts and opaque cornea. Congenital glaucoma also results in severely constricted visual fields. Nystagmus may be present as well as an obvious squint. Mobility skills will depend greatly on the extent of the ocular damage as well as other physical problems.

The treatment of such patients is discouraging. Although cataracts and glaucoma can be treated surgically, the prognosis is poor. Viable viruses persist in the lens and may cause a subsequent inflammation as a result of the surgery. Severe complications occur in 35 percent of rubella eyes after cataracts have been extracted.

Down's Syndrome

Down's syndrome (mongolism) is a congenital condition caused by a genetic abnormality—an extra No. 21 chromosome, the most common chromosomal syndrome. The condition is more prevalent in children born to women over age 40. Because the condition is genetic in origin, women over age 40 who wish to have children should receive genetic counseling, and those who become pregnant should undergo amniocentesis.

Persons with Down's syndrome generally are short and squat and have narrow, slanted eyes and a thick, protruding tongue. They usually are mentally retarded, with an I.Q. in the 20–50 range, and have cardiac abnormalities. Furthermore, they frequently have ocular problems, such as nystagmus, and severe myopia. About 50 percent of these persons have congenital cataracts; however, surgery is rarely performed because it can result in various complications.

The level of measurable visual acuity in persons with Down's syndrome depends on their ocular condition as well as their level of intelligence. Visual fields and color vision are generally normal. Although their distance vision is generally reduced, their near vision may be adequate.

Marfan's Syndrome

Marfan's syndrome is a congenital abnormality of the connective tissues of the body. It is believed to be transmitted as an autosomal dominant trait that affects both eyes equally. There is some indication that the condition may be more common in males than in females. Since Marfan's syndrome is an inherited condition, genetic counseling is recommended. Persons with this syndrome are characterized by long thin fingers and toes as well as a generalized elongation of the extremities. Cardiovascular problems are common among such individuals, as is muscular underdevelopment.

Marfan's syndrome has many ocular complications. The most frequent complication is dislocation of the lens of the eye, which can cause a general blurring of vision or, in some instances, double vision in one or both eyes. When the affected person looks through the lens, he or she may be nearsighted or have normal vision; however, when looking around the dislocated lens, the person is much more farsighted. Such a condition will often result in decreased visual acuity even with conventional correction.

Persons with Marfan's syndrome may also have a displaced or multiple pupil. Severe myopia is common and results in retinal detachment, which causes a visual field loss corresponding to the area of detachment. A squint may develop owing to the decreased visual functions. Surgery is not generally recommended except as a last resort. Externally the individual may also demonstrate heterochromia iridis (different-colored eyes), a bluish sclera, and nystagmus.

OCULAR SIDE EFFECTS OF DRUGS

Many individuals seen in a low vision service take various drugs for ocular or systemic problems. These drugs have side effects that may influence diagnosis and training. A brief synopsis of the more commonly seen drugs and their ocular side effects follows. Space does not permit an extensive discussion of ocular pharmacology and the various drugs involved. The reader may obtain such information from Fraunfelder's *Drug-Induced Ocular Side Effects and Drug Interactions* (1976) and *Physicians Desk Reference for Nonprescription Drugs* (1981).

Drugs that are frequently seen include the following:

Antibacterial agents (e.g., Argyrol, mild Protargin, silvol, silver nitrate, and Silveo Protein) are used in the treatment of conjunctivitis and to prevent ophthalmia neonatorum in infants. Some ocular side effects are irritation and photophobia, ocular pain, allergic reactions of the lids and conjunctiva, decreased visual acuity, and a color-vision defect in which objects appear to have a yellowish tinge.

Antiviral agents (e.g., Ara-A, Vidarabine, Dendrid, Herplex, and F_3T) are used in the treatment of herpes simplex. Some ocular side effects include excessive tearing, photophobia, ocular pain, clouding of the cornea with reduced acuity or increased sensitivity to glare, and ptosis (drooping of the eyelid).

Carbonic anhydrase inhibitors (e.g., Diamox, Oratrol, Cardase, Neptazane) are used in the treatment of glaucoma to lower intraocular pressure. Some ocular side effects are reduced visual acuity, increased nearsightedness, decreased accommodation, hemorrhages of the conjunctiva, and a color-vision defect in which objects have a yellowish tinge.

Decongestants (e.g., Afrin, Albalon, Clear Eyes, Murine, Privine, Visine, and Vasocon) are effective in the relief of nasal and ocular congestion from allergies and inflammations. Some mild ocular side effects are slight irritation to the eyes, mild dilation of the pupils, and occasional blurred vision.

Miotics (e.g., Isopto Carpine or Pilocarpine, Ocusert, Michol, Humorsol, Phosphaline, Fluropryl, Prostigmin, and Physiostigmine Pilocarpine) are used to constrict the pupil in the treatment of various ocular diseases and inflammations. Functional visual side effects are few. Reduced acuity from accommodative spasms is possible, as is the development of cataracts.

Mydriatics and cycloplegics (e.g., Cyclogyl and Mydriacyl) are used to dilate the pupil and relax the accommodative muscles in refractions and ocular examinations. Some ocular side effects are reduced acuity, photophobia, ocular irritation and a burning sensation, and possible visual hallucinations.

Topical osmotic agents (e.g., Adsorbonac 2 + 5%) are used to reduce corneal edema. The only side effects are local irritation and discomfort, which are reversible.

The foregoing represents a broad classification of drugs that the low vision instructor may encounter in working with low vision patients. As new drugs appear on the market, they are described in the *Physicians Desk Reference,* which should be in every low vision clinic. It is important that the instructor be alerted to the types of side effects that drugs can cause.

If low vision patients are experiencing any of the side effects that follow and are taking medications, the instructor should seek consultation. The symptoms or signs may be due to medications being prescribed. However, never assume they are due to the drugs or advise the person to stop taking the drugs. If you observe any possible side effects, refer the person for medical consultation. Such referrals are particularly important if more than one physician is presribing medications for the individual.

Side Effects

- Eye turns of recent onset.
- Abnormal visual sensations.
- No pupillary response.
- Blurred distance vision.
- Color-vision disorders.
- Unequal pupil sizes.

- Blindness for any period.
- Cataracts (reports of decreased vision, haziness, cloudy vision, and so forth).
- Field losses.
- Inability to see objects at near (of recent onset).
- Inability of eyes to turn in to see near objects (possible double vision).
- Changes in dark-adaptation time.
- Loss of depth perception.
- Dry-eye syndrome.
- Decreased acuity.
- Double vision.
- Changes in color or swelling of external parts of the eye.
- Onset of nearsightedness.
- Night blindness.
- Nystagmus of recent onset.
- Seeing color tinges to objects.
- Reports that world is "jumping around" (oscillopsia).
- Inability to move eyes in a particular direction.
- Photophobia.
- Ptosis (drooping of eyelid).
- Random eye movements.
- Visual hallucinations.

VISION SIMULATION

To obtain a more practical understanding of the loss of functional vision that a low vision patient experiences, it may be valuable to try to perform some daily activities utilizing simulation. Although simulators do not accurately portray the various disease processes, they give the instructor a realistic experience with the frustrations and anxieties faced daily by the low vision patient.

An inexpensive simulator kit was designed by Kent and Connie Carter [O&M consultants, 105 Strong St., Amherst, Massachusetts] and Gerald Friedman, O.D. The instructions for making the kit are as follows:

Kit Materials

1. Six pairs of Airco Welding Goggles, Model No. 2205 with a screw-off lens cap on each eye. Available at most welding supply companies for a cost of approximately $12.00 a pair.

2. Three opaque plastic funnels: small, medium and large. Available at most kitchen utensil supply stores for a cost of approximately 50¢ per funnel.

3. Twelve rubber "O" rings, 2 inches in diameter. Available at most hardware or plumbing supply stores.

4. Miscellaneous items: epoxy glue, dull black spray paint, a fine-tooth

37

hacksaw, heavy scissors, a butane torch, and a briefcase or other such container.

5. Convex lenses: two +1.25D, three +2.25D, and two +4.50 Diopter Ground 50 mm round with no bevels on edges.

Assembly Procedures

1. Take goggles apart by unscrewing the lens cap and removing the two lenses (tinted and clear) in each cap. Paint all tinted hardened lenses on both sides with two or three coats of dull black spray paint. Retain cardboard "O" rings that separate the two lenses in each cap. The black painted lenses can be used as occluders in the kit.

2. With a hacksaw, cut the base of each funnel slightly larger than necessary to fit into the goggle cap. Make the cut at approximately a 25 degree angle to allow the funnel to rotate in the cap to simulate a particular quadrant loss once in place. Trim, with scissors, to fit cap tightly.

3. Heat the edge of each funnel until it is soft and pliable (the color will change from opaque to clear when it has been heated an appropriate amount) using the torch. While still warm, form a lip on the funnel edge by using a pair of pliers. Place the funnel base on a flat surface while still warm, after making the lip, and press down to ensure an even base. Fit it into the goggle cap. If the funnel lip is now too large, simply trim off the excess edge with the scissors.

4. Drill out the tapered end of the funnel or cut off a small length of the funnel spout to enlarge the viewing hole. Test the actual field loss in degrees by testing at a tangent screen or using a chalkboard. At 15 feet allow 8cm [3.2″] for every degree of field from the fixation point to the point where viewing is still possible. Paint the funnels with three or four coats of dull black spray paint, inside and out.

5. Using the spare +2.25 convex lens, place a glob of epoxy glue in the center and spread the glue around with a toothpick or finger. When dry, the ridges left by the glue will refract light causing an effect similar to that of a cataract. This will be the cataract lens simulation part of your kit.

6. The rubber "O" rings are used to take up space and block any excess light from entering the goggles once the funnel has been placed in the cap and an "O" ring placed in after it.

7. The cardboard "O" rings can be used to separate various convex lenses when used in tandem within one goggle cap.

8. The lenses will simulate certain acuity restrictions, such as 20/60 = +1.25; 20/200 = +2.25; 20/400 = +4.50. These are approximate acuities; the individual who is not 20/20 without glasses will achieve different acuities with each lens. Therefore, it is important to test the individual with a distance chart once he has the goggles and lens in place over the eyes.

9. It is virtually impossible to obtain binocularity with a funnel over each eye. Therefore, simulation of field loss should be restricted to one eye at a

time by using an occluder lens in the opposite goggle cap.

10. The convex lenses may be placed one on top of the other in the cap if greater losses in acuity are desired below 20/400.

Uses

The simulator kit can be used by vision professionals, parents, public school teachers, peers, and friends of the low vision client. Anyone who wishes to try some of the problem solving that a low vision client goes through will find the kit useful. The tasks that are not simulated effectively are near-point reading and the eye scanning techniques available to persons with a severely restricted field. It is important to discuss and react to any statements that may be expressed by the simulator wearers. Since what the low vision individual sees cannot as yet be closely approximated, it is not possible to make specific points based on simulation activities. Therefore, the low vision instructor should be careful in using the simulators with emotionally involved parties. John and Sandy Ferraro, of the University of Houston, developed the following activities for use with the simulators.

Distance Activities

Aid Used _____

Distance: 15–20 feet

Activity 1
While looking through the telescope, copy the material from the blackboard onto the lines below.

_____

_____

_____

_____

Comment on the difficulties encountered in localizing, shifting your gaze from the blackboard to the paper, and note the quality and accuracy of your copy.

_____

_____

_____

_____

Understanding Low Vision

Activity 2

Find the curved-line pattern on the blackboard. Locate the arrow on the left end. Follow the line, writing down the numbers in the sequence you see them on the line below. The end of the line is marked with the letter z.

_____

Comment on your ability to trace the line and accuracy of copying.

Intermediate Distance Activities

Aid Used _____

Focal Distance of the Aid (compute using the formula F(cm) = 100/diopters) _____

Working Distance (distance from the lens to the material when using the aid)

_____

Activity 1

While wearing a low vision optical aid, completely fill out a check. Comment on the comfort of the working distance, your field of view (how much of the check you can see without scanning), your ability to track the movement of your pen, and the quality of the finished product.

_____

_____

_____

_____

Activity 2

While wearing the same aid, deal out and play a partial game of solitaire. Comment on the comfort of the working distance, your field of view, and your ability to manipulate the cards.

_____

_____

_____

_____

If there is extra time, try to sew on a button or take some stitches while wearing the aid.

Near Activities

Aid Used _____

Focal Distance of the Aid (compute using the formula F (cm) = 100/diopters) _____

Working Distance (distance from the lens to the material when using the aid)

_____

Activity 1
While using a low vision optical aid, read the material typed in regular-size print for one minute. Record your reading speed in words per minute and the difficulties encountered while scanning a line as you read, scanning back and locating the next line, and reading long words.

Speed _____ Comments _____

_____

_____

_____

Activity 2
Using the same aid, read the material typed in large print. Again, read for one minute. Record your reading speed and the problems encountered while reading across a line, locating the next line, and reading long words. Indicate which size print was easiest to read using this aid.

Speed _____ Comments

_____

_____

_____

_____

Activity 3
While looking through the aid, measure the field of view in terms of the number of visible letters and the number of usable letters. Do this for regular and large print. Make sure you do not move your head as you count the letters.

Typewriter-size print: visible letters _____ usable letters _____

Large print: visible letters _____ usable letters _____

Bibliography

Adler, F. M. *Textbook of ophthalmology.* 7th ed.; Philadelphia: W. B. Saunders Co., 1966.

Davan-Langston, D. *Manual of ocular diagnosis and therapy.* Boston: Little, Brown & Co., 1980.

Faye, E. E. *Clinical low vision.* Boston: Little, Brown & Co., 1976.

Faye, E. E. The role of eye pathology in the low vision evaluation. *Journal of the American Optometrical Association,* **47**(11), 1976, 1395–1401.

Fraunfelder, F. T. *Drug-induced ocular side effects and drug interactions.* Philadelphia: Lea & Febiger, 1976.

Human eye. Southbridge, Mass.: American Optical Corp., 1976.

National Society to Prevent Blindness. *Vision Problems in the U.S.—Facts & Figures.* New York: NSPB, 1980.

Normal and abnormal vision. Southbridge, Mass.: American Optical Corp., 1976.

Physicians desk reference for nonprescription drugs. Oradell, N.J.: Medical Economics Books, 1981.

CHAPTER 2

Psychosocial Aspects of Low Vision

JOHN L. MORSE, ED.D.

Some potentially successful low vision clients are lost because psycho-social considerations are not evaluated in the determination of a treatment plan. This chapter provides the reader with basic insights into the types of psychosocial problems the low vision client may be facing and how these problems may affect the low vision services being offered.

Any discussion of the psychosocial aspects of low vision must acknowledge the formidable task of defining the partially sighted population, which, it has been estimated, numbers about six million (Goldish, 1973). People with low vision are, without question, heterogeneous with regard to degree, ·type, and amount of remaining vision (a considerable number being considered "legally blind"); age; onset of the condition (congenital versus adventitious); educational status; receipt of various services; and adjustment or maladjustment to the condition. Consider, for example, these statements derived from authors who allude to the aforementioned difficulties:

> A partially sighted person considers himself sighted and functions visually long after he has reached a level that others may consider blindness [Adams, Personal communication].
>
> •••••
>
> The partially sighted seem to have greater difficulty adjusting to their remaining vision than individuals who lose their sight and have no hope of recovering it, or the congenitally blind who have no conception of what it is like to see [Cholden, 1958, p. 15-31].
>
> •••••

The terms "sighted" and "blind" represent groups possessing well-established stereotypes and culturally expected rules of behavior. The position and role of the partial is much less clear owing to the tremendous range of variability in partially sighted types. Generally, society

43

views the partial as sighted and expects him to function as such [Faye, 1970, p. 415].

•••••

Children with partial sight are often misdiagnosed, misunderstood, undereducated, and socially ostracized. They are neither blind nor sighted —society doesn't acknowledge their existence [Jan, Freeman, & Scott, 1977, p. 326].

•••••

The low vision person would like to be included in some grouping, needs and seeks an identity, and learns to behave and respond in accordance with the expectations of others. If they expect him to act blind, he may try. If expected to act sighted, he may try. People then think they know how to treat him and he thinks he knows how to behave ["The Partially Sighted Person," A Marginal Man, Group 5, p. 109].

The purpose of this chapter is not to describe all the parameters of the psychosocial aspects of low vision, but, rather, to discuss the issues of visual deficits, the development of the self-concept, and the adjustment difficulties and to suggest intervention procedures and their implications for service providers.

THE IMPLICATIONS OF VISUAL DEFICITS

The importance of vision and the role it plays in the development of the psyche has been recognized by numerous authors. The early bond between mother and child (known as "attachment") is considered necessary for feelings of security (Adler), the transmission of empathy (Sullivan), and the establishment of trust (Erikson). Since ordinarily an adultlike plasticity of convergence and accommodative responses are present in the visual behavior of 2-month-old infants, vision must inevitably contribute to attachment (White, 1971). Therefore, Jackson (1978) and others have stressed the importance of maximizing the behaviors of visual functioning as early as possible.

The effective utilization of vision by low vision people is dependent on their overall physical and emotional health status in relation to environmental factors, such as the size of print, lighting, contrast, changes in the environment, and figure-ground requirements, to name a few. These variables often result in the inconsistent visualizing of certain sights at certain times. Unfortunately, parents and service providers often assume that low vision persons can see ("If once, why not all the time?"). Performance difficulties are then attributed to inattention, lack of ability, or poor coordination. Moreover, apparent contradictions (not seeing the blackboard or reading signs, yet being able to run or ride a bicycle—behaviors to be expected in those with a central field loss) often are deceiving to the public (Jan, Freeman, & Scott, 1977). It is difficult, as well, to understand that a person with a severe peripheral field loss can "see" an object across the room, yet fall over a foot stool. Low vision persons with fluctuating acuity may miss visual nuances on certain occasions yet have no difficulty at other times. Moreover, they may find it necessary to develop and utilize behavioral changes (e.g., squinting, tilting the head, performing slowly and compulsively, being orderly, subvocalizing, and using their finger to keep their place on a printed page) to compensate for their visual difficulties. For low vision people, such behaviors are "normal," necessary, and must be allowed, but they are often misunderstood and discouraged.

The type of visual deficits that a low vision person has affects the person's level of functioning. Optic nerve and pathway disorders are the result of various causes (atrophy, infectious disease, injury, growths, degeneration, heredity, or prenatal problems). The site of the disorder is the single most important factor in determining the level of functioning (Dennison, 1974). Each visual task needs to be analyzed in relation to the known area of visual loss. If the loss is the lower half of the visual field, mobility will be affected. A loss of the right field of vision will affect reading, since reading print requires a left-to-right progression of eye movements and scanning.

If central vision is lost, academics become a problem. Some physical activities are difficult if peripheral vision is affected. With either loss, the person will have significant problems in social adjustment. Frequently, the appearance of the eyes give no evidence of injury or insult (Dennison, 1974)—a situation that, unfortunately, makes it easy for the "sighted" population to expect a normal performance by the low vision person. Furthermore, it is difficult for the low vision person to explain all the conditions of his or her ·loss. To say nothing invites false perceptions; yet, to offer a detailed account of what he or she cannot be expected to perform may be interpreted by meaningful others as offering excuses. Accordingly, low vision individuals require the assistance of all involved "significant others" (family members, close friends, teachers, and service providers) to recognize their limitations, to make the best use of all clues, to learn coping responses and compensatory techniques, and to acquire the means by which they may assist others to acquire a realistic understanding of their visual problem.

For some unexplained reason, according to Dennison (1974), persons with albinism and glaucoma often exhibit extreme types of behavior. They may appear excited, distracted, and flamboyant in their actions and verbalizations or may have compulsive and perfectionist tendencies. Persons with albinism may be compulsive and perfectionist as a way of compensating for the difficulties associated with their eye condition. That is, albinos are light sensitive, fatigue easily when performing fine-detailed paper-and-pencil tasks, and find it difficult to visually scan and track (smoothly and in a coordinated fashion) and to shift their visual focal points effectively and rapidly. Persons with glaucoma require a constant monitoring of their intraocular pressure and thus are continuously reminded of their condition; they worry and feel depressed about the prognosis, they notice continual changes in their visual efficiency, and they frequently experience pain and discomfort.

THE DEVELOPMENT OF SELF-CONCEPT

To understand the adjustment problems of low vision persons and how to help them resolve these difficulties, it is important for the low vision professional to be knowledgeable about how the self-concept is formed and the factors that hinder its development. Each person, visually handicapped or not, continually and reciprocally interacts with his environment, a process which results in the feeling that, "How I see myself may bear little relationship to how others see me and both of these will differ from how I really am"(Mehr & Freid, 1975, p. 16). Maltz (1960) stated that one's perceptions of the self and the environment are based on imagination, not fact. A person performs according to what he believes is true of himself and his environment. Therefore, his self-image is what he believes to be true of himself. Davis (1959) believed that without an adequate body image, the self-concept will be distorted. Pearson stated that the self-concept should be closely related to both the abilities and the limitations of the body structure so that internal motivation will be realistically related to one's physical and mental abilities. Consider, therefore, the difficulties experienced by sighted adolescents when their body structure changes during puberty, or the problems of all sighted people when an insult to bodily functioning occurs. Again, consider the difficulties encountered by visually handicapped persons, with or without usable vision, in establishing an adequate body image when deprived of accurate visual feedback regarding the functioning of their body or of the feedback of significant others. Obviously, if visual efficiency fluctuates or visual status suddenly deteriorates or improves dramatically these changes have an impact on self-concept.

All individuals have a need to feel adequate and competent; however, for certain individuals, the need is greatly intensified because, as Adler believed, some people compensate for their feelings of inferiority by striving for superiority, and others compensate by denying all inadequacy. Visually handicapped people find it is difficult to master their environment and easier to deceive themselves. They may ignore feedback from the environment by avoiding certain situations or by blocking negative feedback. They may be "aided" in this process by the overprotection of sighted people. Nevertheless, the defense mechanism of avoidance is helpful because, in its absence, there would be a difference between how the visually handicapped perceive themselves and how they think others perceive them. Such a discrepancy creates anxiety and the the need to manage their anxiety. Low vision people frequently use three methods to avoid anxiety. First, they obtain information about their performance (selective perception) and thus shun certain new or unpredictable situations. Second, they rationalize their inadequacies, project them onto others, or displace them onto the "handicap" ("But I can't do that, I'm visually handicapped"). Third, they collapse or expand their perceptual field; that is, they become an expert in and devote their whole lives to a single endeavor or become involved in a multitude of activities and responsibilities.

Low vision individuals may differ in their adjustment to their visual condition as it affects their self-concept (Davis, 1959). They find it difficult to perceive themselves as "sighted" or "blind"—perceptions that are encouraged by attitudes or environmental demands made by significant others. They feel neither "fish nor fowl" because they are able to function differently in various situations and to conform to the various expectations expressed by different adults and peers. The conflict between dependence and independence further complicates the process of acquiring an adequate self-concept. Mehr and Freid (1975) noted that fulfilling the need for dependence may be more rewarding than striving for independence.

Visually handicapped people often use hearing to acquire environmental feedback. As Lowenfeld (1980) noted, through practice, visually handicapped people develop the ability to discern certain moods, emotions, attitudes, and traits in voices and may rely too heavily on the voice as an indicator of a person's character. This process is similar to that experienced by sighted individuals who form impressions and make judgments about people according to their physical appearance. Furthermore, Allport (1980), in his study of the ability of blind and sighted subjects to judge personal characteristics by voice alone noted that, contrary to popular belief, the blind were less accurate in their judgments than were the sighted. Allport also noted that the absence of visual clues prevented the correction of errors by blind people. It may be conjectured as well that the distorted or limited visual feedback received by low vision people is of no greater assistance. That is, facial and postural nuances are missed. However, facial and postural gestures, not verbal responses, are of prime importance; sighted individuals use them, consciously or not, to express their feelings and attitudes and rely on them to determine the environment's response to them. Consider, therefore, the problems experienced by low vision persons who are denied accurate visual images in interpersonal relations and attempt to obtain and rely on auditory feedback. Their inaccurate and undetailed visual system is combined with an unreliable or unavailable auditory source of information relative to their environmental needs and feedback regarding their performance. Obviously, intervention—in the form of instruction, interpretation, role playing, and group sessions—is required to assist low vision persons to develop coping skills.

ADJUSTMENT DIFFICULTIES

Numerous studies of various aspects of adjustment have been made, over the years, by a variety of authors. For the purpose of clarity, the results of these efforts will be grouped according to the following classifications: the difficulties of adjustment to low vision, comparisons between the adjustment of low vision persons and blind persons, sighted people's perceptions of low vision people, and requirements for successful adjustment.

Adjustment to Low Vision

Bateman (1962) stated that partially sighted children pity themselves more and are less able to accept their visual limitations than those whose handicaps are more severe. Moreover, the parents of partially sighted chldren are less understanding than those of totally blind children. Karnes and Wollerstein (1963) found that 75 percent of the partially sighted children they studied had moderate to severe adjustment problems and that the remaining 25 percent had mild problems in specific areas even though these children were considered to be adequately adjusted. Peabody (1967) supported these conclusions and indicated that the outstanding characteristics of partially sighted children are underachievement, fatigue, and emotional problems.

Glass (1970) studied the psychosocial responses to residual vision of persons with adventitious low vision. He found that these individuals adjusted to their condition by modifying their expectations. However, because they did not know how to adapt to low vision, their adaptation was random and trial-and-error in nature and often resulted in increased tension and accumulated frustrations. Glass noted the preponderance of three personality types in low vision people: (1) those who use their condition to gain an advantage, (2) those who identify themselves as sighted, and (3) those who try to maximize their use of residual vision. Glass also discussed the rewards offered by sighted individuals and the penalties offered by knowledgeable individuals when low vision persons engaged in "shamming" (pretending they can see). These rewards are occasional, however, and reinforcement may be withheld in other areas. Therefore, Glass recommended that low vision persons develop skills in communicating experiences to significant others.

Numerous studies and investigations, as reported by Lowenfeld (1980) and others over the years, have confirmed the belief that a visual handicapping condition is not the etiology of emotional difficulties. Although the emotional status of a visually handicapped person is influenced by and affects the reciprocal interactions in a family constellation, the stresses that other family members feel when a family member loses vision represent the reemergence of earlier unresolved emotional reactions.

Extensive investigations have been made of the role of the mother in the development of the visually handicapped person. In addition to the typical "reactions" so aptly described by many writers, parents are faced with the difficult task of dealing with these reactions and making adjustments in their daily routines that affect the whole family. The task is complicated by the parents' lack of knowledge and experience; such knowledge would give the parents the conceptual background to deal realistically with the situation. If, in addition, the prognosis is uncertain, the extent of residual vision undetermined, the degree of useful vision unknown, and if there is a possibility of additional difficulties, it is impossible for the parents to grieve when they are unsure of what they are grieving for or to accept when they are unsure of what they should accept. What a task—to struggle with one's emotions and feelings and simultaneously to give to others!

Comparative Adjustment

Jervis (1959) and the University of Rochester group conducted studies to determine whether the self-concept of blind adolescents differed significantly from that of sighted peers. Both studies found no significant differences between the blind and sighted except that blind adolescents used more extreme statements to describe themselves. Jervis noted that more blind subjects had either high positive or high negative attitudes toward themselves. Yet, the question remained: Are there differences within the visually handicapped population? Will significant differences in adjustment be found when comparing low vision and blind individuals?

Meighan (1971), using the Tennessee Self-Concept Scale, found that the self-concepts of the blind who attended residential schools were in an extreme negative direction. No significant differences were found between the blind and partially sighted. These results differed from those obtained by Bauman (1964). Bauman found, utilizing the Adolescence Emotional Factors Inventory, that partially sighted students showed a significantly higher level of anxiety and insecurity and a greater sense of loneliness and were less well adjusted to their handicap than were blind students. In support of these differences, Cowen and Benham (1961) found that partially sighted adolescents ranked slightly lower in adjustment than did the legally or totally blind. Without question, more research is required to determine the differential self-concepts of the blind and partially sighted and to identify, in general, the variables responsible for poor adjustment and, in particular, the effect of age, educational placement, etiology of the visual condition, onset of the condition, and level of remedial intervention, if any.

Perceptions by Sighted Peers

The image one has of onself is affected by the opinions of and feedback received from others; therefore, it is important to know the perceptions that sighted peers have of visually impaired individuals. Bateman (1962) investigated sighted children's perceptions of the ability of blind children. She found that the more blind people a sighted child knew, the more likely the sighted child was to appraise the abilities of blind people in a positive way. In addition, positive feeling toward blind people increased with successive grade levels, particularly grades three and six, and more favorable responses were made by urban than by rural children. Jones, Lavine, and Shell (1972) investigated the acceptance of blind children by their sighted peers and the sociometric characteristics of those sighted children who showed a high degree of acceptance of their blind classmates. They found that sighted children accepted blind children less than they did other sighted children and that those sighted children who accepted blind children tended to be social isolates. However, few specifically addressed the perceptions of sighted people toward the low vision population.

SUCCESSFUL ADJUSTMENT

Numerous studies and investigations have attempted to define and describe the characteristics of low vision individuals who successfully adjusted to their condition or the aids prescribed for increased visual functioning. Freeman (1954) reported that the attributes of the examiner, the personality and outlook of the patient, and the type of adjustment the patient made to visual impairment, were important factors in determining the successful utilization of low vision aids. Kelleher, Mehr, and Hirsch (1971) found that successful rehabilitation and the voluntary use of low vision aids were due to many factors, the most important being the positive attitude of the subject. In attempting to discover why low vision persons often chose not to use a low vision aid, Mehr, Mehr, & Ault (1970) conducted discussion groups with low vision patients. From these discussions, they discovered that the duration of the condition and its severity; the patient's age, degree of motivation, and level of intelligence; and the nature of the pathology were factors that contributed to use or nonuse. Successful patients were found to be more flexible, had a higher level of self-regard, and developed stronger peer-group relationships. Faye (1970) described similar characteristics as well as a sufficiently strong central acuity, adequate eye motility, and a stable pathology of long duration.

Bishop (1972) cited the importance of the following factors in the successful adjustment of the visually impaired: positive self-attitudes, self-acceptance, and self-expression and frequent positive contacts with people who offer the low vision individual security and acceptance. Allen (1972) thought that the key to adjustment is the development in the low vision individual of an awareness of that person's interrelationship with the rest of the world. Both Bishop's and Allen's studies stressed the necessity for an experimental and interpersonal approach to rehabilitation and the need for low vision individuals to receive accurate and frequent feedback from the environment. McGuiness (1970) compared the advantages and disadvantages of various educational settings and concluded that students in itinerant programs develop a stronger self-image than do students in special schools owing to the number of friendships they develop with sighted peers.

"Normal" development, the achievement of an adequate self-concept, and the ability to act maturely and confidently do not happen automatically and are not solely the result of the type of educational placement or rehabilitation setting attended. Direct interventions that stress accurate feedback from the environment, that offer the means to cope with less-than-reliable visual information, and that assist the individual to function with ease, maturity, and confidence in relationships are necessary and must be provided to insure competence and adequacy.

SUGGESTIONS FOR INTERVENTION

Burlingham (1941) concluded that the lack of sight diminishes the ability to test reality—an important function of the ego. Instead of compensating for the lack of sight, the visually handicapped person turns to fantasy. It is imperative that low vision individuals be helped to obtain, interpret, and express auditory information from the environment. Although it is difficult for anyone to verbalize all thoughts, impressions, and attitudes and to request verbal feedback from significant others regarding one's performance, nevertheless there is no substitute for role modeling by significant others. That is, significant others should offer themselves as "models" to demonstrate to low vision persons how to integrate what is happening nonverbally in the environment or within themselves and to show, through their actions, that it is acceptable to request verbal feedback regarding their performance. However, successful role modeling requires that significant others be well versed in what constitutes successful and unsuccessful communication patterns.

One indication of a successful interaction using effective communication skills is the absence of conflict regarding the expectations of the two parties. It involves, more often than not, speaking in the first person, predominantly using the present tense, and spontaneously expressing feelings and impressions. There is no hidden agenda. When conflict occurs or when expectations conflict, the following subtle changes occur:

1. There is a tendency to speak of what the other person does, feels, or is responsible for.

2. There is a tendency to stress or react to the inaccuracies of the other person's perceptions.

3. There is a tendency to withhold feelings, which is frequently justified as "listening."

4. It is increasingly difficult to admit one's limitations or to admit not understanding what is being said.

Obviously, the successful utlization of significant others to demonstrate effective communication skills requires that these persons be taught how to be successful "helpers."

A successful interaction between a client and an effective helper or counselor requires that the helper possess and demonstrate the following identifiable characteristics: (1) sensitivity, (2) empathy, (3) positive regard, (4) respect, (5) warmth, (6) concreteness, (7) immediacy, (8) confrontation, and (9) genuineness. Each of these characteristics will now be described.

Sensitivity is not taught or acquired, it is felt and experienced. It involves awareness and understanding and is exclusive of judgment. It is interesting to note that formal counseling programs that have attempted to encourage the development of sensitivity in trainees have had negative results (O'Hern, 1969). In many cases, the levels of sensitivity in the trainees declined after the trainees completed the training programs.

Empathy should not be confused with sympathy. Empathy is seeing the client's world from the client's perspective. It is the utilization of the skills of reflective listening to hear the client accurately. It involves the use of influencing skills and the sharing of oneself and expertise, only as much as the client can absorb and within the client's frame of reference.

Positive regard is unconditional and involves selective attention to the positive aspects of the client's verbalization and behavior. It is the recognition of the client's assets.

Respect involves making enhancing, positive statements to the client and encouraging the client to move forward. It includes the honest appreciation of and toleration for differences.

Warmth primarily is expressed nonverbally. It is the use of vocal tone, posture, and facial expression to denote that the helper cares for the client. With low vision clients, these expressions must not be subtle or inconsequential.

Concreteness means being specific, obtaining details, and requesting clarification of facts and feelings.

Immediacy is responding to the client in the same tense (present, past, or future) that the client uses. Its effectiveness is often demonstrated when clients spontaneously start using all three tenses when talking about themselves.

Confrontation is meeting the client directly and pointing out differences, mixed messages, incongruities, and discrepancies in verbal and nonverbal behavior. Confrontation should not be seen as expressing a differing opinion, no matter how helpful the counselor thinks it may be.

Genuineness is being truly yourself in relationship with others, being spontaneous, and being sensitive to, without being engulfed by, the needs of the client.

The purpose of intervention with low vision clients is not only remedial. It should include the development of intentional functioning and the prevention of further problems. The psychoeducational model would be appropriate for low vision clients and significant others who express the desire to learn better communication skills, improve interpersonal relationships, or develop more effective coping strategies to obtain more reliable feedback from the environment.

Last, how should one approach "difficult" low vision clients or their parents? Or perhaps these clients should be called "dissatisfied" because the term "difficult" implies they are negative, hostile, uncooperative, and untreatable. Many low vision clients are dissatisfied, and their discontent is justified. The typical service to low vision clients and their parents often provides little or conflicting information or fragmented or infrequent information and advice and does not recognize or respond to their needs.

With the angry, distant, or verbally expressive client or parent, the helper should listen and respond not to their words but to their feelings, often not verbalized, of "I'm afraid," or "I fear." The helper should not delimit conferences with these clients or encourage them to discontinue receiving services. Rather, he or she should maintain regular and frequent contacts and use the just discussed skills, especially empathy, genuineness, immediacy, and confrontation.

References

Adams, S. *Seminar: Low vision.* Boston: Peripatology Program, Boston College, 1974.

Allen, D. Yet another minority. *Education for the Visually Handicapped,* 1972 4(1), 30-32.

Allport, G. W. Psychological problems of children with severely impaired vision. In B. Lowenfeld, *Psychology of Exceptional Children,* New York: Prentice-Hall, 1980.

Bateman, B. Sighted children's perceptions of blind children's abilities. *Exceptional Children,* 1962, **29,** 42-46.

Bauman, M. K. Group differences disclosed by inventory items. *International Journal for the Education of the Blind,* 1964, **13,** 101-106.

Bishop, L. As reported in Kelleher, D. *The effect of bioptic telescopic spectacles upon the self concept and achievement of low vision students in itinerant programs.* Doctoral dissertation, University of California, Berkeley, 1972.

Burlingham, D. Psychic problems of the blind. *American Image,* 1941, **19,** 95-112.

Cholden, L. S. *A psychiatrist works with blindness.* New York: American Foundation for the Blind, 1958.

Cowen, E. L., & Benham, F. G. *Adjustment to visual disability in adolescence.* New York: American Foundation for the Blind, 1961.

Davis, C. J. *Guidance programs for blind children.* Watertown, Mass.: Perkins School for the Blind, 1959.

Dennison, A. L. The eye report points the way. *Handbook for teachers of the visually handicapped.* Louisville, Ky: American Printing House for the Blind, 1974.

Faye, E. E. *The low vision patient.* New York: Grune & Stratton, 1970.

Freeman, E. Optometric rehabilitation of the partially blind—a case report on 175 cases. *American Journal of Optometry and Archives of the American Academy of Optometry, 1954,* 31(4), 230-239.

Freid, A. N., & Mehr, E. B. *Low vision care.* Chicago: Professional Press, 1974.

Glass, E. J. A working paper on psychosocial responses to low residual vision. In L. Apple (ed.). *Proceedings of the low-vision conference.* San Francisco: 1970.

Goldish, L. H. Severely visually impaired population as a marker for sensory aids and services. *New Outlook for the Blind,* 1973, **67.**

Jackson, R. M. Preliminaries in a theory of practice with low vision children and youth. Unpublished doctoral dissertation, Teachers College, Columbia University, 1978.

Jan, J. E.; Freeman, R. D.; & Scott, E. P. *Visual impairment in children and adolescents.* New York: Grune & Stratton, 1977.

Jervis, F. As reported by Davis, C. J. *Proceedings: Guidance programs for blind children.* Perkins School for the Blind Publication No. 20. Watertown, MA: 1959.

Jones, R. L., Lavine, K., & Shell, J. Blind children in classrooms with sighted children: A sociometric study. *New Outlook for the Blind,* 1972, **66,** 75-80.

Karnes, W., & Wollerstein, A. Report of the proceedings of the 1963 Council for Exceptional Children meeting. Washington, D.C.: National Education Association, 19.

Kelleher, D., Mehr, E. B., & Hirsch, M. J. Motor vehicle operation by a patient with low vision. *American Journal of Optometry and Archives of the American Academy of Optometry,* 1971, **4**(9), 773-777.

Lowenfeld, B. Psychology problems of children with severely limited vision. In W. M. Cruickshank (ed.). *Psychology of Exceptional Children and Youth.* Englewood Cliffs, N.J.: Prentice-Hall, 1980.

Maltz, M. *Psycho-cybernetics.* Englewood Cliffs, N.J.: Prentice-Hall, 1960.

McGuiness, R. A descriptive study of blind children educated in the itinerant teacher, resource room, and special school settings. *AFB Research Bulletin;,* 1970, **20**, 1-57.

Mehr, E. B. & Fried, A. N. *Low Vision Care.* Chicago, IL: Professional Press, 1975.

Mehr, H. M., Mehr, E. B., & Ault, C. D. Psychological aspects of low vision rehabilitation of the partially sighted. *American Journal of Optometry & Archives of the American Academy of Optometry,* 1970, **47**(8), 612-618.

Meighan, T. *An investigation of the self-concept of blind and visually handicapped adolescents.* New York: American Foundation for the Blind, 1971.

O'Hern, J. Consultation with author regarding her doctoral dissertation on sensitivity (1969).

The partially sighted person: A marginal man. Group 5. Western Michigan Conference.

Peabody, R. L., & Birch, J. W. Educational implications of partial vision—new findings from the national study. *Sight Saving Review,* 1967, **77**, 92-96.

Pearson, C. J. Application of guidance principles in a school for the blind. In Davis, C. J. *Proceedings: Guidance program for blind children.* Perkins School for the Blind Publication No. 20. Watertown, MA: 1959.

White, B. L. *Human infants: Experience and psychological development.* Englewood Cliffs, N.J.: Prentice-Hall, 1971.

CHAPTER 3

Psychosocial Aspects of Aging and Visual Impairment

SAM NEGRIN, M.S.W.

Older visually impaired people may have special problems that, in some cases, need more attention than the optical condition. Failure to recognize and respond to these problems may lead to frustration when trying to provide rehabilitation services to this population. This chapter first describes the general problem of aging, then relates these problems to visual impairment, and concludes with a discussion of services and impediments to service.

GENERAL PROBLEMS OF AGING

Growing old can be a dynamic life process in which meaningful new roles and goals are identified, anticipated or expanded, but old age (and visual impairment) can also be a condition of isolation, bewilderment, resignation, regression, and loss of health, status and dignity.

It is not true, as many would think, that most aged people are in nursing homes and other institutions. As research in the last few years has shown, only 4 percent of the persons above 65 and 14 percent of those aged 85 and older are in institutions. Where are the rest? Many aged people live in their own homes or with their extended family, or in other comfortable living situations. But many are neglected. There are now, in the United States, more than 21 million persons over age 65, and they are all struggling to find the answers to questions such as these: "Where will I live? How shall I live? What is in store for me in my remaining years?" The answers depend on a multitude of factors, including the state of their health, the amount of money they will have to live on, their goals for retirement, and most important, their attitudes about life.

Those who have met the challenges of life with determination and zest will greet retirement in much the same way; those who have been defeated by problems before, will, very likely, give way to depression, despair, and isolation. Philosophy of life is a strong determinant of whether older people drop out of the mainstream of life and become loners, remain in their homes and pursue their old habits and friendships, or pick up their worldly possessions and move across the country. Money is another. One can hardly relocate to Florida or Sun City when one is struggling to make ends meet on Social Security payments alone.

Yes, some public transportation is available to many older people, especially in the cities. However, even at reduced rates—even if it is provided free of charge—public transportation is not utilized because the elderly are afraid to leave their homes or to walk to the bus stop and wait for the bus. Fear of crime keeps many older people in their homes and isolated, virtually as prisoners.

Many homebound elderly persons (at least 15 percent) are deemed to be "functionally impaired," which means they must depend on others to cope with the normal demands of daily living. Research studies and surveys have found that a great number of elderly persons living at home suffer from physical and mental problems that are as severe as those of the institutionalized.

Another group of older people who are not part of the "mainstream" was recently described as "an aged population that resides in the heart of the city, yet lives on the fringe of society." These people are referred to as the invisible elderly" or, more officially, as "the single room onlys (SROs)." Little is known about these people, and there are no "experts" on this subject because only recently have social scientists begun to realize they exist. SROs live in the downtown, commercial, or other urban areas, generally in inadequate hotels or boarding houses that provide only a sleeping room, with no other amenities. The noteworthy aspect of the SROs is this: among the multitude of options available to many of them, they have chosen to live alone, in a world that consists of only a bleak hotel room and perhaps a few square blocks. They have, as one theoretician put it, disengaged themselves from life. As age advances, they have recognized difficulty after difficulty, diminution after diminution. Many have lost their hearing, both in the highest audible frequency and in the auditory threshold. They have experienced the loss of touch—a loss in the kinesthetic sense—a loss in time perception, a loss of strength and a loss in reaction time. They have lost teeth and the sense of smell, which accounts for major malnutrition problems in the aged. But, above all, they have experienced a visual loss: a loss of visual acuity, of adaptation to the dark, of accommodation. They have had serious losses in their field of vision or other severe losses, including the total loss of sight.

THE VISUALLY HANDICAPPED ELDERLY

And, what does aging have to do with visual impairment and blindness? The answer is simple: To a large extent, the problems of blindness *are* the problems of aging. Elderly blind people are elderly people who happen to be blind.

If being old and poor is a condition of double jeopardy, if being old, poor, and of ethnic minority status is a condition of triple jeopardy, then being old and blind (or having any other severe handicap for that matter) is to exist in a condition of multiple jeopardy. It is easy to realize that aging as such diminishes the capabilities and resources of any person, visually impaired or not, and that visual impairment or blindness limits the person even further. It may well be that visual decline or blindness does not create any more serious obstacles than would be created by other impairments of sensory abilities. It is clear, however, that the effects of visual incapacitation can be pervasive. It is not surprising, for example, to find that the blind residents of nursing homes tend to be the most inactive, lonely, fearful, and frustrated of all residents. The overall incapacity of visually handicapped people is further augmented by certain attitudes, inadvertent or not, on the part of staff in these homes and in many agencies serving the aged. Occasionally, a tendency to overprotect elderly blind residents or agency members results in their isolation or inappropriate exclusion from several of the activities at the facility or even, through some misguided although well-intentioned reasoning, to assignment to segregated activities that are designed for blind persons only.

Too often, workers with geriatric blind persons are myopic in their planning. They seem to think the life span is relatively short and, therefore, that many valuable services, such as vision screening, low vision services, and mobility and orientation programs, are not important. Therefore, geriatric blind persons frequently are denied such services.

It is true that many sighted elderly people suffer a loss of health, vitality, comfort, dignity, proximity with loved ones, and financial security. These indignities are extremely difficult to cope with, in themselves, but somehow, assisted by sympathetic families and caretakers, there is some hope. However, when blindness compounds these losses, the problems appear insoluble. Frequently, those elderly persons who have become recently blind seem to feel bitter toward all medical personnel and to members of the so-called helping professions, thinking that negligence has surely caused their suffering. Those who have been blind for years and are fairly well adjusted to blindness in their own homes, become devastated and traumatized by the prospect of unfamiliar surroundings and caretakers or agency staff who are unable to empathize with their losses. As a result, when they are consigned to a hospital or nursing home, blind aged persons usually are unable to recuperate *physiologically* from the disease or accident which necessitated hospitalization. In addition, the isolation caused by unfamiliar surroundings and strange caretakers frequently contributes to mental confusion, to resistance to services, and often to inappropriate aggressive behavior.

Since sight is deemed to be so important, and because most people bring into old age a lifetime of living with stereotyped thinking about the "tragedy of blindness," the incapacity to make a *psychological* adjustment to blindness seems greater than the ability to accept most other losses. Even with eye conditions such as glaucoma and cataracts, in which the individual has had a long time to adjust to potential blindness, the afflicted person may, as the ultimate loss of sight draws near, become hysterical and develop hyperactivity, belligerence, occasional combativeness, and suicidal tendencies.

We have caused elderly blind persons to feel cut off from society or loved ones. Elderly blind people experience a reduction of input and opportunity for communication; the consequence is that they turn their attention inward. This loss of input and the increased stress of internal psychological experiences helps to explain why individuals who have been "normal" and self-sufficient throughout their lives, may in later years become self-concerned and unmindful of the needs of others. Thus, one must also be aware that despite the difficult position that aging people are placed in today, they bring about some of the problems themselves. Many older blind people refuse to avail themselves of the wide variety of services that are available and do not continue with programs to which they have been introduced. From a psychodynamic standpoint, it may be said that some elderly people are in a masochistic situation in which they feel that they must be miserable to be happy.

The foregoing statement leads to another universal problem of aging that is compounded by the loss of sight: *depression*. This phenomenon deals with problems of a neurotic nature, the changes that attend the aging process, and the biochemical and physiological alterations that take place in older age, all of which are compounded by a feeling of powerlessness. Because they expect elderly people to be serious, many practitioners fail to detect these symptoms of depression and, consequently, the depression goes untreated and becomes progressively worse.

Father Carroll, in his book on blindness, described twenty losses that result from the advent of blindness. Just imagine the psychological impact of some of these losses as they affect the elderly blind and you can understand why depression can be such a prevalent factor: there is the loss of the feeling of personal worth and position as head of a family, there is the loss of privacy with the consequent loss of identity and individuality, and there is loss of security with the resultant feeling of helplessness.

SERVICES

It should be pointed out that elderly blind people often respond more readily and completely to good professional services and therapeutic procedures than do most other age groups. When service providers intervene in the lives of older people, they can correct things such as diet, depression, isolation, hostility toward family and society, and poor health conditions and experience a positive response from the older person. The older person, when treated properly, is thankful and appreciative and is glad that the helping professional has come into his life. It is often a mistake to take a social sentimental approach to the needs of the elderly by entering their lives with an abundance of services and programs when they really need something else. This is not to imply that these programs are not needed. Rather, it means that for many—or most—elderly blind people, services should be made available in places where they must go to get them instead of bringing everything to them. Many of the problems of the elderly blind are not necessarily the result of the attitudes of a hostile society but rather of the mistakes of agencies and professionals who foster dependence or misdiagnose the needs and problems of this population.

Helping professionals must encourage the psychological well-being of elderly blind people by preparing them to be psychosocially adequate. Rather than attempt to change character or bring about a reversal of psychoneurotic elements, they must work to dispel depression, offer social opportunities, and provide an atmosphere for belonging and identification by promoting activities to which one may have to travel in order to participate.

However, if services are ready to meet the needs of older people, they must meet the criteria of the four "As:" availability, accessibility, adequacy, and acceptability. Services to the blind elderly will continue to be inadequate and unacceptable until there is a system for all the elderly at the local level. Those concerned with the special needs of the blind must begin to recognize that the majority of blind people are elderly. They must, therefore, advocate a comprehensive coordinated service system that will provide for a continuity of services for *all* the elderly, including the blind. They must also ensure that the aging system responds to the special needs of the elderly blind, and indeed, when possible, prevents blindness as an additional handicap to that of being old and devalued.

As Father Carroll once said:

I believe that with any problem of life the main reaction must be to face it and then find how to overcome it. I believe that, for aged persons and particularly for aged blind persons, the only answer is *total* rehabilitation...a process whereby in varying stages of helplessness, emotional disturbance, and dependence, they come to gain a new understanding of themselves and of their handicap, the new skills necessary for their new state, and new control of their emotions.

CHAPTER 4

The Low Vision Rehabilitation Service

RANDALL T. JOSE, O.D.

This chapter outlines a model that can be followed in providing care for any person with low vision. It does not detail which professionals perform what tasks. It simply states what services should be provided for optimum care. The chapter gives the reader an overview of how an interdisciplinary low vision service functions and provides the basic information on what is entailed in establishing services. Actual clinical programs are discussed in Section V, Chapter 18.

"Low vision services" is a widely utilized term that describes a variety of services being offered to visually impaired people. The low vision field is developing as an area of expertise for many different disciplines that provide care within the blindness system. It is usually associated with a series of evaluations, training programs, and services to visually impaired persons that emphasize residual vision rather than visual loss or blindness. The number of professional disciplines involved in this field has created a confusing array of conflicting terminologies and professional philosophies of care.

As in any professional field, the scope of services provided within the profession varies from one practitioner to another, depending on the individual's experiences and geographical location, the area's resources, and the needs of patients. Although it is interesting to watch this exciting field of vision care grow, its unstructured growth, if left to its own design, will lead to interprofessional competition and a severe weakening of service programs. Given the continued increase in the development of new clinical programs, new professional school curricula, an increasing number of self-proclaimed specialists, and efforts to create a new type of professional trained solely for low vision work, there is a need to define terms and establish acceptable guidelines for low vision rehabilitation services.

The following are definitions of terms relevant to the field as used in this book: *Low vision specialist* is a specially trained professional (instructor or examiner) who contributes to the vision rehabilitation of visually impaired people. *Low vision care* is a philosophy, and *vision rehabilitation* is the service. Thus, the low vision field entails an interdisciplinary group of professionals who work with low vision persons toward the goal of enhancing their level of visual activity. The philosophy is geared toward making the visually impaired aware of their remaining visual capabilities so they do not dwell on their loss or impairment. The low vision rehabilitation service involves a specific series of diagnostic evaluations and instructional-training sequences that are designed to help low vision persons overcome the handicapping effects of their visual (or sight) impairment, function at an optimum level, and live a comfortable life-style. The service may concentrate on specific vocational, educational, recreational, or social tasks, but it must include a comprehensive look at all the individual's needs (vocational, educational, social, psychological, financial, optometric, and medical). Such a service mandates the interaction of several disciplines, and to be successful it requires the personal involvement of professionals from each discipline. Simply stated, low vision care is a philosophy that promotes the maximal use of vision, and the vision rehabilitation service is a commitment by an interdisciplinary group of professionals to help low vision persons fulfill that philosophy.

The concept of low vision care emphasizes a person's ability to function visually and does not entail a numerical classification system. The service is directed at solving problems created for individuals by the impairment of their vision. An *impairment* is the actual damage to the eye that results in an acuity or field loss. This impairment can be mild (20/40), moderate (20/200), or severe (20/800). The numbers attached to the impairment are clinical acuities; they are arbitrary and, for the purpose of a vision rehabilitation service, relatively useless. The handicapping effect of the acuity loss or field loss is the diagnostic finding that must be dealt with and not the notation of acuity or pathology. The identification of the pathology and the level of acuity help the professionals direct their services and monitor their efforts. However, the goal of the team of low vision specialists is to determine a person's *handicap* and then try to reduce the debilitating effects of that handicap for that particular individual. It is important that an impairment be differentiated from the handicap it creates. Two persons with the same impairment (retrolental fibroplasia with an acuity of 20/400) may have different handicaps. One person may be active socially, run track, make good grades, and enjoy life (a minimal handicap), while the second may have poor travel skills, do poorly in school, and have little, if any, social life (severe handicap). Thus, the same impairment resulted in different handicaps for the two individuals.

Technically, then, people with an ocular pathology and reduced acuities or fields, are referred to as visually impaired until they are seen in the vision rehabilitation service. At that time, problems are identified and the handicapping effect of the impairment is determined. Then the person can be labeled visually handicapped. Obviously, one can play with terminology forever, but the foregoing description best serves this concept of care.

This philosophy of low vision care has been promoted by Colenbrander (1977) and others in an effort to obtain new definitions of legal blindness or, more appropriately, to eliminate the term. New schemes for classifying individuals for services try to reflect functional levels of loss rather than the present system of using numbers such as 20/200 best correction or a 20-degree diameter of field or less (Genensky, 1976; Whitten, 1975). This type of system represents the necessary philosophical approach to low vision care as well as the changes needed in administrative/legislative supports to make the low vision services a meaningful and successful program for the low vision person.

If this philosophy of care is adhered to by all professionals involved in vision care, it will make it much easier to develop a low vision care delivery system (vision rehabilitation service). The delivery system must be able to meet the widely varying needs of low vision persons in a variety of situations. Flexibility in delivering services is essential. It is impossible to find one scheme of care that will meet the needs of one person with 20/1000 acuity who is functioning relatively independently and of another individual with 20/60 acuity who can legally drive during the day but is totally incapacitated by the impairment or fear of blindness. The difficulty in developing a vision-care program for these two types of low vision persons in one service framework is the reason for so much confusion in the field. Each member of the low vision specialist team looks at an individual with a biased professional eye and establishes his or her own set of priorities for rendering services. Usually, these priorities are not consistent with those of other members of the team. Thus, even though all the team members are trying to rehabilitate the visually impaired person, confusion is created, and a weakened, sometimes ineffective, service is provided. Therefore, the key to a successful program is intra-team communication and professional flexibility.

The two criteria just mentioned—communication and professional flexibility—are a strong foundation for the development of low vision rehabilitation programs. However, what are the parameters necessary for developing effective vision-care programs in the low vision field? The rest of this chapter describes a three-phase model of care (see Fig. 1) and outlines an optimum low vision service delivery system for the visually impaired (see Fig. 2).

PHASE 1 OF THE MODEL

In Phase 1, the low vision instructor must determine at which level of independence the low vision person is functioning. This evaluation is best done in a nonclinical setting and will be described in great detail in later chapters. Evaluation activities will be referred to as functional or environmental measurements, as opposed to clinical measurements. They can be performed entirely or in part by social workers, educators, mobility instructors, psychologists, rehabilitation teachers and counselors, nurses, occupational thera-

Figure 1. Model for the "Ideal" Low Vision Service

Preexamination Assessment

1. *Functional Evaluations*
   a. Motivation assessment
   b. Psychological set
   c. Functional acuity
      distance
      intermediate
      near
   d. Functional field loss
   e. Illumination problems
   f. Other handicapping
      conditions
   g. Family and peer reactions
   h. Mobility concerns

2. *Assessment of Needs*
   a. General environmental
   b. Vocational settings
   c. Educational settings
   d. Recreational setting
   e. Daily living problems

3. *Demonstration of Aids*
   a. Telescopic
   b. Microscopic
   c. Illumination control

4. *Other Pertinent Information*
   a. Teacher, parent, or employer
      concerns
   b. Rehabilitation teacher,
      counselor

Clinical Examination

1. *Case History*
   a. Compared with preclinic
      information
   b. Read functional reports

2. *Identified Needs*
   a. Primary needs as reported by
      patient
   b. Do they agree with previous
      reports?

3. *Motivation and Psychological
   Set of Patient*
   a. Clinician's impression
   b. Impressions of others

4. *Visual Acuities*
   a. Distance
   b. Near
   c. Intermediate

5. *Visual Fields*
   a. Peripheral
   b. Central
   c. Near

6. *Refractive Error*
   a. Spectacle Rx
   b. Contact lens
   c. Refract poor eye
   d. Objective tests

Postexamination Training

1. *Prognosis for Success with Aids*
   a. Based on examination data
   b. Based on in-clinic training

2. *Postfollow-up Revisit
   Examinations*
   a. In conjunction with training
      (success/failures)

3. *New or Previously Unidentified
   Real Problems with Prescribed
   Aids*
   a. New training problems
   b. New expectations

4. *New Problems*
   a. New needs
   b. New goals
   c. New adjustments to the
      lifestyle

5. *Satisfaction of Patient*
   a. Satisfied patient (verbally)
   b. All needs being met
   c. Will self-refer if needs change

d. Other professionals

5. *Medical Data*
   a. Obtain ophthalmological reports
   b. Determine need for additional medical consultation (one year)

a. Monocular
b. Binocular
c. Biocular

8. *Magnification Trials*
   a. Microscope
   b. Telescope
   c. Magnifiers
   d. Electro-optical
   e. Nonoptical
   f. Other services

9. *Illumination Control Assessment*
   a. Indoor
   b. Outdoor

10. *Prescription of Tentative Aids*

11. *Recommended Training*
    a. Estimated hours
    b. Types of problems
    c. Prognosis

12. *Other*
    a. Send letters to referral source
    b. Referral back to family eye specialist/physician
    c. Request other services for patient (e.g., mobility, activities of daily living)

Figure 2. The Vision Rehabilitation Service

The Low Vision Specialist Team
1. Community service groups and professional groups

1. Educators
2. Rehabilitation teachers/counselors
3. Orientation and mobility instructors
4. Social workers
5. Psychologists
6. Nurses
7. Occupational/physical therapists
8. Other related professionals

1. Optometrists
2. Ophthalmologists with Technicians
   Opticians
   Nurses
   Other formally trained staff

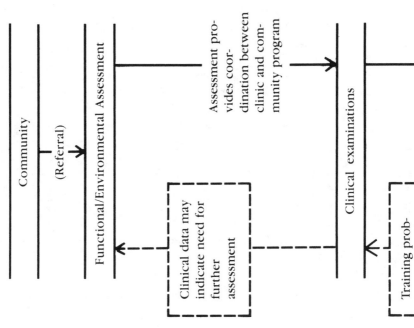

Community

(Referral)

Functional/Environmental Assessment

Assessment provides coordination between clinic and community program

Clinical data may indicate need for further assessment

Clinical examinations

Training problems related to the aid are immediately sent back to the clinic

Provided In House or by Community

Activities
1. Identify person as visually impaired and find services

1. Determine independence of life-style or self-sufficiency of low vision person
2. Functional measurements of vision
3. Establish priorities of problems to be resolved as indicated by the patient and the instructor
4. Obtain psychological, family, and social data as available
5. Consider:

Independent	Dependent		
20/20	20/200	LP	NLP

1. Discuss findings of the preliminary assessment
2. Evaluate pathology, acuities, fields, binocularity, refractive error, and so forth
3. Determine aids appropriate to solving identified problems
4. Set up training program for instructors

1. Same potential group as in-dicated in Functional/Environ-ment Assessment section

Training/Instruction

1. Develop patient's proficiency with aid
2. Assure use of aid in education/ rehabilitation program
3. Prevent frustration and determine new needs

NEAR: letter and word recognition, CCTV remedial reading skills, lighting, eccentric viewing, writing, typing, other uses of the aid, and hygiene

DISTANCE: Scanning, tracking fixation, field restriction problems, mobility, driving, viewing, localizing with aids, care of aids, increasing use of aids

SPECIAL TASKS: special vocational, educational, or avocational problems are addressed in coordination with other professionals involved with patient, e.g., classroom teacher

(optimum)

Community

The patient is returned to the community with a more normalized lifestyle pists, or other low vision personnel. For the purposes of this model, all the professionals functioning in a nonclinical setting will be referred to as low vision instructors.

The information gathered in the evaluation includes the individual's level of social activities; psychological adjustment to the impairment; travel skills; perceptual problems, including specific measurements of functional acuities, fields, color vision, recovery from glare, and photophobia; family dynamics; financial needs; access to medical care; and the person's report of his or her needs and goals. Obviously, it is impossible and even unnecessary to gather all these data on every person entering the service, but the low vision instructor must be prepared to provide services in all areas and to make at least a cursory evaluation of the potential problems. The extent to which these environmental measurements are obtained will depend on the needs of the particular low vision person and the resources and facilities of the service. Nevertheless, environmental measurements help the clinic's low vision team to determine a list of priorities to work with throughout the clinical low vision service and subsequent educational-rehabilitational training services.

Figure 3 helps one to visualize the responsibilities of the low vision instructor in the first phase of the low vision rehabilitation service. The diagram points out two important factors. First, legal blindness, 20/200 best-corrected vision, is situated on the independent side of the functional scale and demonstrates the significance of the statistic that 85 percent of the legally blind population has useful vision. It is vital that professionals do not stereotype a legally blind person as helpless. Second, total blindness is often associated with visual dependence in our society and 20/20 reflects a high level of visual independence. However, the field of low vision is steering away from that assumption. An evaluation of the *functional*/environmental measurements of a particular low vision person gives the low vision instructor some idea of the level of independence at which the person is functioning, regardless of acuity. Comparing this level of independence with clinically measured acuities provides a wealth of information with which to determine the extent of the visual handicap and gives an insight into possible factors, other than the ocular problems, that may affect the resolution of the handicap.

Functional Measurements (Environmental)	Visual Independence (1)					Visual Dependence (2)
					LP	NLP
Clinical Measurements	20/20	20/60	20/200	20/600		Total Blindness
		(2)			(1)	

Fig. 3. Two patients (1) and (2) are diagrammed on the scale according to their acuity and functioning.

As an example, compare the two patients graphed on the scale in Figure 3. Patient 1 has some object perception, owing to a traumatic accident as a child (<20/1000). The clinician would have to assume that Patient 1 was severely handicapped and would provide an exhaustive battery of clinical services. However, many low vision clinicians in an isolated noninterdisciplinary clinic would not even consider this patient worth seeing. Nevertheless, the evaluations of the low vision instructors indicated that Patient 1 leads a relatively normal business, social, and recreational life and that his self-image is that of a contributing member of society. Obviously, he has worked hard at decreasing the visual handicap and needs only a minimal program. Patient 1 will probably accept the limitations of the optical aids provided and the frustrations he may experience in the training programs. Patient 2 is an elderly man with beginning cataracts that have caused an impaired acuity of 20/60. The environmental evaluations indicate that he is functioning at a dependent level and considers himself blind. In fact, a 20/60 acuity was determined only by tricking him into seeing (he initially demonstrated 20/200 acuities). The low vision instructor, who was a social worker, finally determined the problem. Patient 2 is a wealthy man with a young, beautiful wife. His "blindness" keeps his wife at his side at all times. For him, the handicap is a convenience that he does not want rehabilitated. His wife enjoys caring for her "poor, blind" husband, and both are comfortable with this lifestyle. What looked like an easy clinical case turned out to be an impossible situation. If it was not for the low vision instructor (social worker), much clinical time and effort would have been wasted. Figure 3 shows how these clinical and environmental parameters compare.

This is the importance of Phase 1 of the vision rehabilitation service: *A thorough nonclinical description of the person is provided so the clinic's time is allocated in the most efficient way and the correct approach to problem solving for a particular individual is pursued.* The Phase 1 (functional/environmental evaluation) and its relationship to Phase 2 (the clinical evaluations) was demonstrated in the case of Patient 2 in which clinical acuity measurements were not obtained correctly until after the data from the functional/environmental evaluations indicated a sporadic level of functioning far greater than that indicated by the clinical data of 20/200. Without picking up an acuity chart, the low vision instructor was able to provide a more accurate assessment of "acuity" than the clinical measurements could. It is this sharing of information and confirmation of data from different settings that makes the clinical service a success. The low vision examiners need the information provided in the functional/environmental assessments to make the most effective use of the data gathered in the clinical evaluations.

PHASE 2 OF THE MODEL

Phase 2—the clinical evaluation—consists of making structured clinical assessments of acuity, field, refractive error, and magnification needs. A comparison of these data with data collected in the functional/environmental assessment allows the formulation of an ambitious and meaningful treatment plan. The formulation of this plan must:

1. Be done in conjunction with the low vision instructors. (The clinical data must correlate with the functional information.)

2. Be directed to meet the specific problems described by other professionals providing training in the field. That is, the plan should not concentrate on reading skills if the person's main problem is orientation and mobility.

3. Make sure the patient understands the treatment program and accepts the same priority of problem solving that the low vision specialist team has formulated. (If the patient's only desire is to read the newspaper, the plan should not concentrate on using telescopes to cross the street.)

PHASE 3 OF THE MODEL

Phase 3 of the vision rehabilitation service involves instruction and training. This phase is often the most neglected part of the service. Its purpose is twofold:

1. The patient is given the opportunity to use the aid and develop proficiency with it. Also complementary instructional programs, such as mobility and training in reading, may be offered in conjunction with the low vision services.

2. As problems arise in the instructional programs, further clinical evaluations may be arranged and the treatment program modified so levels of frustration are kept to a minimum. Also, as new problems are identified, the patient may be referred for further clinical evaluations and a new treatment program.

Although the service is described in three phases, it must be stressed that the service is actually a continuous loop and that parts of all three phases may be provided simultaneously. It should also be pointed out that specific techniques have not been described, professional roles have not been delineated, and the system is not rigid. There is no routine pattern of care. The specific mechanisms used to provide this service and the types of professionals involved will depend on the facility available, the population to be served, financial and professional resources, and myriad other factors. It is important to note that Phase 3 can be provided using community resources or it can be delivered in a private rehabilitation center, a mobile program functioning as an itinerant service, and in private practice, to name but a few types of settings (see Chapter 18). However, it cannot function in an isolated corner of a hospital or professional school because it requires interdisciplinary involvement.

The specific activities for each phase of the service will be presented in subsequent chapters. However, professional responsibilities are not assigned to each activity since there is too much professional overlap and too much variation in available resources from one setting to another. The service cannot be provided by one profession or professional, and the service will be successful only if the criteria of professional communication and flexibility are met. As the specific activities are outlined, the low vision specialist team will have to decide who is professionally trained to provide these activities or seek appropriate resources to perform them if the team members do not have the necessary expertise. If additional services are not sought, the vision care program will be inferior. It does not make any more sense to have an optometrist provide training in remedial reading skills or mobility instruction than it does to have educators or mobility specialists determine the treatment options. Although the optometrist may improve a person's reading skills and ability to travel, the person will not attain his or her optimum level of performance. Likewise, even though the educator and mobility specialist can probably prescribe the appropriate treatment for most low vision patients, these patients will not be afforded the opportunity of a comprehensive optometric workup. However, the educator and mobility specialist must have input into the final determination of treatment if the program is to be viable.

The most difficult aspect of keeping the program running smoothly is professional egos. With some experience, everyone feels they can handle everyone else's job. Instead of trying to do other people's jobs, the team members must concentrate on their own area of expertise and use it to make a meaningful contribution to the total service. They must remember that it is the final product that counts. The goal of the service should be to return people to the community as sight impaired—not visually handicapped.

References

Colenbrander, A. Dimensions of visual performance. *Transactions of the American Academy of Ophthalmology and Otolaryngology,* 1977, **83**(2), 332-337.

Genensky, S. Acuity measurements: Do they indicate how well a partially sighted person functions or could function? *American Journal of Optometry and Physiological Optics,* 1976, **53**(12), 809-812.

Jose, R. What is a low vision service? *Blindness 1974-75* (American Association of Workers for the Blind annual), 49-53.

Whitten, E. B. (ed.). *Pathology, impairment, functional limitation, disability: Implications for practice, research, program and policy development, service delivery.* Mary E. Switzer Memorial Series, No. 1. Washington, D.C.: National Rehabilitation Association, 1975.

SECTION II
ASSESSMENT

This section is designed to give the instructor an understanding of the type of information that should be gathered on a prospective low vision patient prior to a clinical examination. The difficulty in developing one basic assessment program is the variety of assessment activities that are needed, the wide range of people who need low-vision services (infants, children, adults, the aged, and the multiply handicapped), the various professional backgrounds of the assessors, and the amount of time various professionals have to do an assessment. These factors lead to the array of "assessments" being promoted across the country and the subsequent confusion about what is the correct system.

Generally speaking, there is no one correct system. The idea of the preclinic assessment is to get the instructors involved in the low vision service, prepare the low vision person for the clinical examination, and provide directions for the ophthalmologist or optometrist performing the examination. The basic goals of all assessments are to (1) promote the interdisciplinary service model and (2) open lines of communication between the clinician and the low vision instructors. These goals may be accomplished with a simple phone call in some settings or with complex and comprehensive assessments in other settings, depending on the working relationship of the professionals involved, the bureaucratic requirements, and the type of person being evaluated.

Chapter 5, "Minimum Assessment Sequence: The Optometrist's Viewpoint," by this editor describes the format of a minimal formal assessment (above a phone call) that should be done for each prospective patient. The sequence is general enough to serve, with minor modifications, as a basic evaluation for all populations. The new low vision instructor can use this format as a guide for the first few assessements and then build on it to develop a more individualized sequence that is specific to a particular population's needs and the resources of the agency.

In Chapter 6, "Comprehensive Preliminary Assessments of Low Vision," Mr. Carter outlines a more comprehensive evaluation that includes the demonstration (not the prescription) of optical aids. If there is enough time and the professional's skills are adequate, the assessment can be used successfully in settings where a clinical examination is not readily available. However, it is not a substitute for a clinical examination. It should be pointed out that Mr. Carter—a knowledgeable instructor on optics and the utilization of aids—would never provide patients with aids without a clinical examination, even though a clinic "prescribes" the same aid he has "demonstrated." This is the key to a successful interdisciplinary program. Mr. Carter concentrates his time on his own professional strengths (mobility) and the integration of his professional evaluations into clinical evaluations.

Some examiners do not want anyone but a doctor to touch an aid. This viewpoint is as ridiculous as an instructor who thinks that he or she can prescribe as well as any optometrist or ophthalmologist. Anyone can be taught to "dispense" aids successfully. It is the incorporation of the evaluations of all the disciplines into the decision about a particular aid that makes it a "prescription." It is hoped that this book will give all professionals a working knowledge of the total low vision service and how they can integrate their professional skills into the system. (The integration process is discussed further in Chapter 17.) Extensive assessments for the multiply handicapped are described in Chapter 15. As the instructor becomes familiar with the basic assessments, these additional procedures will become more valuable.

Randall T. Jose

CHAPTER 5

Minimum Assessment Sequence: The Optometrist's Viewpoint

RANDALL T. JOSE, O.D.

This chapter provides the instructor with an assessment sequence that can be utilized in almost any clinical setting. It represents the minimal input an instructor should have to be an effective member of the team providing low vision services.

The clinical examination of a person with low vision is the transition phase between the identification of a visual impairment in that person and the subsequent rehabilitation undertaken to minimize the handicapping effects of the impairment. The examination often is given too much importance in organizing services for individuals with low vision. It is a tool that the instructor can use to aid the development of a strong and effective low vision rehabilitation plan, that is, it is a resource. If the instructor keeps this concept in mind (and the examining doctor shares this philosophy), it becomes apparent that the preliminary assessment is significant for the overall success of the low vision service. Furthermore, rehabilitation becomes the responsibility of the instructor (as it should be)—not the clinician. The advantage is that the instructor takes an active part in the rehabilitation process. The disadvantage is that the instructor must assume responsibility for the services provided. Too often, when a referral is made to a clinic for a low vision examination, the expectation is that the clinic will prescribe a miraculous pair of glasses that will solve all the individual's problems and will give the instructor a successful educational/vocational closure. However, such a situation usually does not occur. Therefore, it is important to emphasize that the instructor will get out of the clinical examination what he or she puts into it. So let's discuss this input.

The clinician must make prescriptive judgments based on limited information gathered in the clinical setting. Unfortunately, clinical data are often misleading in that they do not truly indicate the person's ability or willingness to function visually. Frequently, a patient functions differently in a clinic and outside the clinic. In the clinic, a patient may deny problems, create problems he or she does not have, or mislead the clinician about the success or failure in using aids. For whatever reason, the patient gives the clinician the answers he or she thinks the clinician wants to hear, rather than the truth. This often results in an ineffective prescription and inaccurate clinical assessments of the individual's abilities as reported in the clinic's summary letter. These inaccuracies irritate the instructor who made the referral and the system breaks down.

It is obvious that the instructor has to provide sufficient information to the clinician to avoid the unfortunate situation just described. The pre-clinical information may be as simple as a brief letter or telephone call in which the instructor provides the following information:

1. How well does the patient utilize residual vision?

2. What specific problem areas are most important to address in the clinical examination?

3. What is the objective of rehabilitation that the instructor has set for the individual?

This information can be provided even by the busiest instructor and helps ensure coordintion of services. It opens up lines of communication and provides direction for the clinic. It prevents the prescription of a telescope for a person who went to the clinic for reading glasses.

LOW VISION REFERRAL FORM

If time permits, it is helpful to observe and evaluate the individual's ability to function visually in a variety of nonclinical settings. The format of the Low Vision Referral Form (page 77) can be followed for this evaluation/assessment. At first, the Low Vision Referral Form may seem to be a formidable assessment. However, it really is the basic evaluation because it covers most of the needs of the broad spectrum of people to be assessed. If the specific materials are reviewed, it becomes obvious that not all parameters need to be (or can be) assessed for each individual. Also, much of the report can be filled out through careful observation of the person being considered for low vision services. Yet, the form provides a structure for initiating some specific assessment activities if the instructor wants to become more involved with the evaluations.

Minimum Assessment Sequence: The Optometrist's Viewpoint

Low Vision Referral Form

Name: _____

Address: _____

Birthdate: _____

Grade/occupation: _____

Medications: _____

Other significant impairments: _____

Use of present prescription (conventional): _____

Use of optical aids (frequency, tasks): _____

Aid	Use
1._____	_____
2._____	_____
3._____	_____

Visual Posture/Behavior:

1. Is the person tactual/visual? _____

2. Does the person turn his or her head and body? _____

3. Is there a preferred eye? _____

4. Is there eccentric viewing?_____

5. Does the person squint? _____

6. Other observations: _____

Near Tasks: (nose to 16″ or 40 cm)

1. Working distance for gauges, and the like: _____

2. Working distance for reading: _____

Understanding Low Vision

3. Types of materials read: _____

4. Working distance for writing: _____

5. Hobbies: _____

6. Other near-point activities: _____

7. Near-point activities person has problems with: _____

Intermediate Tasks: (16″ or 40 cm to 3′)

1. Does the person type? _____

2. Does the person read music? _____

3. Does the person's hobby require intermediate tasks? _____

4. Does the person's job or school require intermediate tasks? _____

5. Other intermediate tasks with which the person is involved: _____

6. Intermediate tasks that the person has problems with: _____

Distance Tasks: (Beyond 3′)

1. Can the person make out facial details? _____

   At what distance? _____

2. Can the person see television? _____

   At what distance? _____

3. Can the person see movies? _____

   At what distance? _____

4. Does the person avoid objects while mobile? _____

   List the problems encountered: _____

5. Can the student work off a chalkboard? _____

   Distance requirements? _____

Minimum Assessment Sequence: The Optometrist's Viewpoint

6. Can the person see street signs, stop lights, and so forth? _____

7. Does the person travel visually (or is a cane or other aid used)? _____

   In familiar environments: _____

   In unfamiliar environments: _____

8. Other distance activities with which the person is involved: _____

   Vocational/educational: _____

   Social: _____

Illumination
  preferred _____

   night vision _____

Functional Assessment
Optional

General Ocular Motility Skills: (circle correct description)

1. Light/dark adaptation	Problem	No Problem	Unknown
2. Accommodation	Problem	No Problem	Unknown
3. Fixation skills	Problem	No Problem	Unknown
4. Tracking skills	Problem	No Problem	Unknown
5. Binocularity	Problem	No Problem	Unknown
6. Convergence	Problem	No Problem	Unknown
7. Scanning	Problem	No Problem	Unknown
8. Visual fields	Problem	No Problem	Unknown

Visual Perceptual Skills: (Circle correct description)

1. Visual-motor coordination	Problem	No Problem	Unknown
2. Figure-ground perception	Problem	No Problem	Unknown

3. Depth/space perception	Problem	No Problem	Unknown
4. Visual memory	Problem	No Problem	Unknown

Questions for the clinician and additional comments regarding the assessor's objectives for the patient:

_____

_____

_____

_____

_____

Assessor _____ Job title _____

Date(s) of assessment _____

Guidelines

The following guidelines may be used in filling out the form:

- *Use of Optical Aids.* It is important to know if a person has had failures with previous optical aids so these aids can be initially avoided in the examination. It is equally important to note if an individual is successfully using aids and for what purposes because the clinician can capitalize on these successes.
- *Light/Dark Adaptation.* Observe whether the person shields the eyes, wears sunglasses at all times, uses a wide-brimmed hat, avoids windows, and so forth. Does the person have to stop and adjust when going from light to dark or vice versa? Does the person squint in moderate levels of light?
- *Accommodation.* Look at the person to see if he or she seems to have difficulty when viewing objects held close to the eye. Does the person get headaches when working at near? Does the person report fluctuating vision when doing near work?
- *Fixation Skills.* The individual will have difficulty accurately moving his or her eyes from one object to another. The person will seem to wander before finally "finding" the object and lose place easily while reading.
- *Tracking Skills.* The individual will have difficulty following a moving object, especially when playing games and when watching sports events, movies, and the like.

- *Binocularity.* Difficulties in binocularity will result in the patient's reports of diplopia (double vision), missing objects when they are reached for, crossed eyes, the inability to bring the eyes together at a particular distance, or unusual tilts of the head to block out one eye.
- *Convergence.* The person may report double vision at near because he or she is unable to focus both eyes at the same time on a near object. This inability to focus both eyes results in avoidance of near tasks, frequent headaches when doing near tasks, unusual head or neck positions to block off one eye, inappropriate crossing of the eyes, and poor reading skills.
- *Scanning.* Scanning requires a coordinated effort of the head and eyes to develop a systematic search for objects in the environment. Too much head movement, taking an unusually long time to find an object (within the acuity level), and an inability to move the eyes without turning the head may be indications of problems in this area. Also, restricted fields often create poor scanning skills.
- *Visual Fields.* Observe whether the person consistently bumps into objects or trips over them. Does the person shuffle his or her feet or misjudge steps and curbs? In which situations does the person seem to have the most trouble? What is the size, location, and contrast of objects with which the person has difficulty? Unusual head postures or scanning movements may also be a tip-off to possible field losses.
- *Visual-Motor Coordination.** The individual with poor visual-motor skills will have difficulty in accurately pointing at objects; will seem to be clumsy in sports and other daily physical activities; will have poor writing, drawing, and cutting skills; and, in general, will have poor eye-hand coordination.

Information on the foregoing functions may be obtained through simple tests and good observations. However, the following functions may require more sophisticated tests.

- *Figure-Ground Perception.** Problems in this important area of vision will result in an inattentive and disorganized person who responds to many stimuli at the same time. The person will exhibit pseudo-scanning problems and have difficulty finding things right in front of him or her unless there is a clear background. Furthermore, the person will incorrectly label objects, and, in general, overlook details.
- *Depth/Space Perception.** Problems in space and depth perception are more difficult to evaluate. The person with such problems may have gross motor problems and seem clumsy; he or she will confuse verbal directions, have poor eye-hand coordination, and may exhibit improper sequencing of words and letters.
- *Visual Memory.** Loss of visual memory results in the inability to remember how an object looks after it no longer is visible. It can involve

---

*These components of the Assessment were derived from assessments developed by Dr. William Padula, Guilford, Connecticut.

short-term or long-term memory. It is most apparent in mobility situations in which a person will forget landmarks, get lost easily, become disoriented in new surroundings, and forget where objects are in familiar surroundings. The person will have difficulty with reading skills, especially in looking through a microscope. Telescopic training will be slow because of the disorientation that occurs from the fields of the telescope.

A number of clinical tests can be used to evaluate most of these functions. Hence, a diagnostic workup is not needed in each area. Rather, this brief discussion has indicated the typical behavioral observations that can be made. These behaviors may be clues to possible problem areas and can be followed up in the clinical evaluations. It is not necessary to do a perceptual workup; simply look for some of these behaviors and put the individual in a variety of situations that will demonstrate skills or lack of skills in each area.

The next six items can be evaluated through observation or by actually setting up activities in a structured environment to measure more accurately the person's ability to perform the indicated tasks. If time is pressing, the instructor may omit the foregoing activities and start the functional assessment at this point.

■ *Visual/Postural Behavior.** Observations of visual and postural behavior may be valuable in detecting all types of other motor, perceptual, acuity, and field-loss problems. It is important to know if the person is trying to use vision (or if he or she is still tactual) and how the vision is used (does the person turn the head or body, eccentrically view or look to the side of things, use a particular eye or switch eyes, and the like?). These observations should be made in a variety of settings with various lighting conditions and at different distances.

■ *Near tasks.* Observations of near tasks indicate how an individual functions visually within 16″ (40 cm). What is the optimum distance for the person to see games he or she plays and to read and write? Describe near-point tasks involved with a hobby or school- or job-related activities. The work distance, comfort, lighting requirements, and ancillary aids used by the person are the important parameters to record.

■ *Intermediate Tasks.* How does a person use vision to perform visual tasks from 16 inches (40 cm) to 3 feet? Tasks that usually are evaluated are typing, writing, and drawing skills. If a hobby or job- or school-related activity requires intermediate tasks, how well does the person perform these tasks? And, most important, does the inability to see at intermediate distances significantly affect the individual's personal goals or aggravate the accomplishment of present tasks? The foregoing question involves an area that will be addressed in the clinical examination.

■ *Distance Tasks.* How does a person use vision for a variety of distance tasks, such as mobility activities (recognizing faces, signs, lights, or store fronts and avoiding objects) and indoor activities (television or movie watching, and classroom or job tasks). Does the person depend on vision to travel or rely on other tools, such as canes, dogs, or sighted guides? Again, it is important to find out the activities with which the person is having difficulties and those that he or she can perform successfully. Changes in function with different lighting conditions will have a more significant impact on distance tasks than on other tasks, so special attention should be paid to levels of light, glare, and so forth.

■ *Illumination.* The importance of illumination in the assessment procedure cannot be overstated. It has an impact on all the skill areas mentioned so far. However, it may deserve repeating. This section can be used as a summary of the illumination levels preferred in general, glare recovery, or adaptation problems and night blindness if it exists. (A complete discussion of lighting is found in Chapter 16.)

■ *Questions for the Clinician and Additional Comments.* This section is the instructor's opportunity to have direct input into the examination. It allows the instructor to interpret the data collected and to indicate priorities for the problem areas uncovered during the assessment. Comments about the person's motivation and family or other support systems would be appropriate at this time. It is important to let the clinician know what services are being provided.

This format may result in a report that is a few paragraphs or volumes. It can take an hour or a few days to complete, depending on the situation. If time is scarce, the last six items should be dealt with first. If correctly managed, they will still provide answers to the three initial questions:

1. How well does this person utilize his or her residual vision?

2. What specific problem areas are most important to address in the clinical examination?

3. What is the objective of rehabilitation you (the instructor) have set for this individual?

The format presented is open ended and will need to be modified to suit individual needs. However, it does point up the important areas that will help the clinician to do a better job of interpreting the clinical data in more functional and individualized terms. Most important, it will facilitate coordination between clinician and instructor in their joint efforts to determine the optimum aid for the low vision person concerned.

CHAPTER 6

Comprehensive Preliminary Assessments of Low Vision

KENT CARTER, M.A.

This chapter provides guidelines for a more extensive environmental (nonclinical) assessment of a potential low vision patient. Such an assessment would be done primarily in areas that have no major clinical facility. Therefore, if a client has to travel far to get to a clinic, the more information the clinic receives initially in the environmental assessment, the fewer times the patient will have to return to the clinic and the more effective the clinic will be in resolving identified problems in a shorter time.

These guidelines will benefit the full-time low vision instructor who works with consulting optometrists and ophthalmologists in such settings as a rehabilitation agency, as well as the itinerant instructor or consultant. Although the guidelines are directed to the adult patient, they can be used with children if they are modified. Specific assessments for children are found in Chapter 7, and for the multiply handicapped, in Chapter 15.

There are numerous advantages in doing extensive preliminary assessments of low vision individuals before referring them to a low vision clinic. Many people feel that their physicians can say and do no wrong; therefore, if the physician has claimed, "This young man is not blind and should not receive any low vision services" or "Prognosis is poor and no further help can be provided," the low vision person is likely to assume that further clinical evaluations are a waste of time. Also, the person may be concerned that such an evaluation may offend his or her personal eye specialist. At-home initial assessments may help the individual realize that something further can be done without either building up the person's expectations of finding a "cure" or discouraging the person. Moreover, many patients must travel long distances for a clinical examination. However, if the proper assessment is provided and appropriate aids are *demonstrated,* the person may be motivated to travel to the clinic for a complete low vision clinical work-up. At a minimum, the results of the assessment may be shared with the doctor at the low vision clinic so that appropriate local resources can be tapped for care. This chapter first describes an actual case history of George E. and then describes the various elements of a comprehensive assessment.

CASE HISTORY

George had visited countless eye specialists all over New England to find a "miracle cure" for his rapidly progressive macular degeneration. He refused to attend a low vision clinic to which he was referred by the state vision re-habilitation agency. However, he finally agreed to talk with the instructor in his home. After a discussion of his past problems, he agreed to the preliminary evaluation. At the end of the first hour, he was shown how to hold and focus a 6X Selsi telescope and, with a few minutes' practice, he was able to locate the ski slope about a half mile behind his home. His exclamation of "There are people on that slope!" led him to realize that something could help him utilize his sight more efficiently even if only for his personal enjoyment. After the instructor explained that the telescope he had just used might not be the appropriate telescope for him, George agreed to undergo a thorough evaluation at the low vision clinic.

The instructor obtained a thorough case history about George from George, his family, his peers, his employers, his vision specialists, and others with whom he has had continual contact. The information gathered included the following: A thorough *medical history* including diagnosis, medications, present and past surgical treatments, current health status, similar medical problems, headaches, dizziness, and general observations of alertness. A psychological assessment of his attitudes toward visual impairment or of his peers, family, and others of immediate importance to him that is valuable if it can be obtained.

A *visual history* (onset of visual problems, present eye specialist, current eye treatment, best eye as indicated by George, cause of visual loss, recent changes in visual functioning, and prognosis). An up-to-date eye report (no older than one year) was obtained from George's personal eye specialist.

An *educational and employment history* included the educational level attained, vocational training, any special rehabilitation training already received (e.g., skills in activities of daily living, vocational counseling, and orientation and mobility), past and present employment positions, and future expectations for vocational education.

A *visual functioning assessment* determined if he could view television (with a black and white or a color set); if he could see billboards, building signs, crosswalks, mailboxes, street signs, and so forth (the instructor observed the distance at which each was recognizable); and if he could read newspaper headlines, large print, typed print, and classified ads (the instructor noted working distance of each task that allowed recognition of words or letters). The instructor also noted if glare caused major problems in reading, walking indoors or outdoors, and seeing colors and whether he recognized various color hues. Did he ever use optical or nonoptical aids? If so, of what kind and power, where were they obtained, and were they useful? Did walking about indoors or outdoors, in familiar or unfamiliar areas, cause any major problems for George?

Motivational factors are of primary importance for initial clinical evaluations in that they give direction to both the eye specialist and to the low vision patient. Knowing how the individual spends his average weekday and weekend from morning to night can provide invaluable insight into his present-day functioning. Likewise, having information about hobbies, sports activities, social functions, and community involvement can help the eye specialist zero in on useful motivational factors.

George, like any client, had specific visual needs and goals, but avoided describing what he feared were unrealistic goals or desires because he had often failed previously and did not wish to fail again. Therefore, the instructor explained that even though these goals seemed unrealistic, they should be explained to the low vision clinician and staff so that present and future possibilities could be explored. The instructor also obtained a list of George's needs that were observed by other involved parties; such information was helpful because these individuals reported needs other than those that George had mentioned.

Utility of the Case History
A thorough case history is useful for a number of reasons. For example, the medical and visual histories are useful to the doctor/clinician in deciding what was previously accomplished and what complications may be expected owing to other medical risks. The visual functioning list provides hints of major problems that require an in-depth analysis. The list of motivating factors and attitudes provides useful insight about the individual's personal frustrations and attainments. The questions on needs and goals help the examiner to make a positive first-time contact with the patient.

Various members of the low vision clinical staff each use information from the case history for a variety of purposes, such as determining whether distance or near training should be started first, building a rapport with George through a discussion of his personal interests, and assessing the need for involving other agencies.

The instructor doing the environmental assessment may use the case history to determine the appropriateness of a low vision referral, to update his or her understanding of the individual's needs, to change vocational training programs, and to develop stronger individualized educational plans.

It is important to obtain as much as possible of the information for the case history from the person in a comfortable, safe environment, preferably the person's home. The more relaxed the individual is, the more honest and direct will be his answers. Also, a home visit is an invaluable opportunity to observe how the person functions in his natural environment—a determination that cannot be made anywhere else. For example, the individual's verbal expression of visual capabilities and the actual visual capabilities and usage often diverge.

DISTANCE VISION MEASUREMENTS

Measurements of distance vision are taken to assess how the patient reacts to visual clues in the everyday environment. (All testing should take place in the individual's home, school, or place of work.) These acuity measurements will usually differ significantly from those of the clinical eye care specialists and, therefore, are not accurate for the doctor/examiner. However, they are utilized for comparisons between clinical and home tests. Visual acuities fluctuate according to many factors, such as eye fatigue, psychological tension, medication, pathological conditions, diet, lighting, and object-to-eye distance. These factors can be controlled in the clinic but not in everyday situations. That is why there is often a dramatic difference between clinical and nonclinical measurements, although both types of measurements and the differences between them are equally important.

With the nonclinical measurements, the clinicians have a baseline for starting their testing. This helps eliminate unnecessary familiarity with the patient's chart, the teaching of testing techniques during valuable clinic time, and overtiring the patient during each phase of clinical testing. In some cases, because of rapid pathological changes or the absence of eye specialists in rural areas, the clinical team may not receive an up-to-date ophthalmological report; therefore, the environmental measurements of distance vision may provide the team at least with some idea of the person's acuity.

There are several methods for measuring distance acuity. It should be stressed that the method chosen should be based on discussions with the entire low vision team so that all the team members can understand the environmental data and these data can be correlated with the clinical data.

Method 1

Environmental objects used to determine rough distance visual acuity:

Formula: $\dfrac{\text{The greatest height or width of an object in feet}}{\text{The distance from object to eye in feet}} \times 13760 = \dfrac{20}{\rule{2em}{0.4pt}}$

Example: An object that is 4 feet high and 2 feet wide and is first seen by the client at 50 feet would indicate a gross "visibility acuity" of _____.

$$\frac{4 \text{ ft}}{50 \text{ ft}} \times 13760 = .08 \times 13760 = \frac{20}{1101}$$

88

An object 12 inches high first seen at the same 50 feet would indicate a "visibility acuity" of roughly 20/275:

$$\frac{1 \text{ ft}}{50 \text{ ft}} \times 13760 = .02 \times 13760 = \frac{20}{275}$$

This method requires that any object used as the test target must be measured at its widest point or be equal on all sides. (See Table 1 for a chart of calculations.) It does not take into account such variables as detail vision, figure-ground, color, depth perception, lighting, surface glare, surface texture and contour, and the like. For these and other reasons, it must be considered to be a rough measurement of visibility acuity, unlike the "resolution acuity" usually performed in the clinical setting. These measurements can be useful with the same person during the low vision training program. They also help to determine the growth in visual usage and can be used for subjective comparisons of the clinical and environmental data on acuity. These measurements are perhaps most useful to the mobility instructor, as a nonstandardized

Table 1. Functional Distance Acuity Approximations

Gross Sizes (observable)		Minimum Sizes (separation)	
Overall Size of an item (in inches)	Snellen Equivalent	Detail Sizes (in inches)	Snellen Equivalent
$3/8$	= 20/20	$1/16$	= 20/20
$7/16$	= 20/25		
$1/2$	= 20/30	$1/8$	= 20/30
$3/4$	= 20/40	$3/16$	= 20/40
1	= 20/60	$1/4$	= 20/60
$1\ 1/2$	= 20/80	$5/16$	= 20/80
$1\ 3/4$	= 20/100	$7/16$	= 20/100
2	= 20/120	$1/2$	= 20/120
$2\ 7/16$	= 20/140	$9/16$	= 20/140
$2\ 3/4$	= 20/160	$11/16$	= 20/160
$3\ 1/4$	= 20/180	$1/46$	= 20/180
$3\ 1/2$	= 20/200	$13/16$	= 20/200
$4\ 1/4$	= 20/225		
$5\ 1/4$	= 20/300	$5/16$	= 20/300
$6\ 3/4$	= 20/350	1	= 20/350
$7\ 1/8$	= 20/400	$1\ 3/16$	= 20/400
$10\ 1/2$	= 20/600	$1\ 1/2$	= 20/600
12	= 20/700	$1\ 5/8$	= 20/700

Examples: A toy fork is 2 inches long = 20/120 @ 20 feet.
    A toy knife is 2 inches long = 20/120 @ 20 feet.
To see the difference between the fork and the knife at 20 feet requires 20/20 vision because the separation between the each fork prong is $1/16$ inch, assuming contrast and lighting are adequate.

assessment tool, for determining programs of outdoor visual stimulation (along with other initial observations and tests). If this method is utilized, it is helpful to carry an accurate optical tape measure during test periods, since the tape measure requires less footwork and allows the low vision instructor and the low vision person to remain together in the recognition phase of testing. (An optical tape measure is available from most engineering stores and major optical distributors.)

Method 2

Distance test charts may be used to determine visual acuities. The decision of which chart should be used to test distance acuities must be made jointly with the low vision clinical team since it is better to avoid using the same charts in the environmental and clinical settings. Memorization of a chart

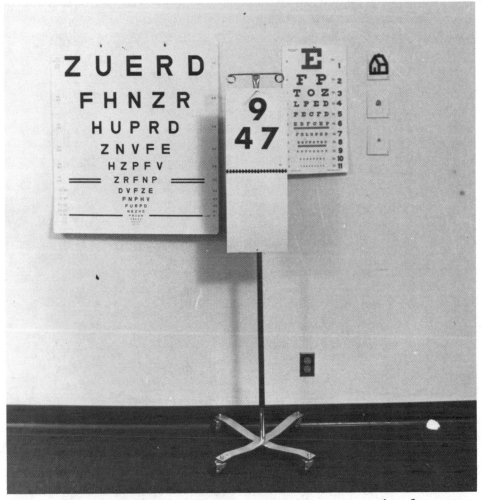

Fig. 1. There are a variety of distance acuity charts appropriate for assessment of visual acuity of low vision patients.

seems to be easy for many people, even young children. The Bausch & Lomb, American Optical, Feinbloom, Bailey, and New York Lighthouse charts seem to be most available (Fig. 1). The Feinbloom Distance Test Chart for the Partially Sighted has the added advantage of greater increments between the higher numerical values up to 10/700. One observation often noted is that the standard test charts in the offices of most general eye care practitioners do not test below the 20/200 acuity level. Therefore, eye reports often are returned as 20/200 –, which leaves other professionals uneasy about the actual acuity level of the person in question. Testing can be done at any distance, but the optimum distance for these charts is 10 feet.

Testing should be done in sequence starting with the better eye covered, then test the better eye, and then both eyes (with correction). Nystagmus will often increase rapidly with one eye covered; therefore, it may be necessary to avoid testing one eye at a time. Record this information for the clinical team. Begin the initial testing of each eye by moving within two or three feet of the person and showing the largest numeral or letter on the chart. If the low vision person responds with the correct answer, back away slowly until the person indicates it has faded away or you have reached the 10-foot testing distance. Proceed through the smaller and smaller numbers until the patient has missed several on a line or several pages in a row. The last recognizable target will indicate the person's acuity. Allow the individual to sit in a comfortable chair and to be as relaxed as possible with the head and eyes positioned as the person wishes. Note all the head postures and fixation positions. Each chart lists a number for that line, which is then written as the denominator, and the testing distance, from eye to chart, as the numerator (e.g., 10/250). Take a light meter reading of the reflectance on the chart and the overall room lighting (see Chapter 16). Do not attempt to change the home lighting conditions at this point because the purpose of the acuity assessment is to obtain a reading in the client's everyday environment. Continue the testing procedures as just outlined.

Method 3

In testing preschool or moderately multiplyhandicapped individuals, it will be necessary to utilize other charts and techniques, such as the New York Lighthouse Symbol Flash Cards, or determine at what distance the child can detect specific-size objects. Further testing procedures for the severely multiply handicapped are covered in Chapter 15. Occasionally, a child will respond best to colors on a test chart. These charts are available from numerous sources as "Kindergarten Charts in Color." The intent of all testing procedures is to build up the psychological self-worth of the individual. Therefore, when in doubt, use the largest test objects possible for all initial testing. The individual who has successfully recognized numerous letters or numbers in a row will push himself to see as much as possible during the session and later in the clinical setting. The added advantage of testing in the individual's environment is that he or she will know what is expected and what to expect from the doctors during clinical testing. Testing in the school, for instance, will indicate possible limitations of acuity. The ability to see at 10 feet, letters 1¾ inches high written with broad chalk on a well-lighted glare-free board, preferably a blackboard, would indicate 10/100 acuity. Many conditions can affect the clarity of chalkboard writing, but the acuities provide a starting point.

Method 4

To demonstrate distance telescopic aids, it is necessary to determine the appropriate telescopic magnification. Use the following procedure for this calculation, assuming that the goal is for the individual to achieve 20/50 acuity (which is adequate for most vocational and schoolwork at distance): If the person has tested at 10/100, multiply by two to get the Snellen equivalent of 20/200. Then divide the denominator (the individual's acuity) by the denominator of the level at which you wish him to read (e.g., /50), which, in this case, equals 4. Thus 4 is the times (x) magnification needed by this individual to reach a 20/50 level of acuity. The equation is as follows:

$$\begin{array}{cc} \textit{Individual's Acuity Level} & \textit{Desired Acuity Level} \\ 10/100 \ = \ 20/200 & 20/50 \end{array}$$

$$\frac{\text{denominator: acuity of individual (200)}}{\text{denominator: desired level of acuity (50)}} = (4x) \text{ magnification}$$

If in further evaluations the individual does not reach a 20/50 acuity with a 4 × telescope, then other factors may be interfering with the vision, such as refractive error or nystagmus. Because this method is only a rough assessment, it is essential that the low vision clinical team contribute to the decision about how much magnification the individual needs. In attempting to determine the appropriate telescopic magnification, other factors of concern are lighting conditions, the cosmetics of the aids, the individual's needs for magnification, and so forth. An instructor should never leave an aid with a client or student unless the aid has been prescribed by a doctor and all parameters of the visual system have been evaluated.

NEAR-POINT VISION MEASUREMENTS

Near-point vision may differ from distance acuity and should be accurately assessed in a variety of settings. The several methods for determining rough near-point acuities are listed here as a means of assessing the individual's visual abilities in the home, school, or workplace. Perhaps the most important aspect of near-point acuity is appropriate lighting. Accurate notes on how the person utilizes or fails to utilize effective illumination can be extremely helpful to the low vision clinical team. Such items as window shades, the distance between the light source and the task, and the location of windows in the room by compass direction should be observed carefully when using any of the following near-point methods of assessment.

Method 1

Near-point testing with environmental objects is the most functional measurement. Two formulas for assessment are these:

1. The formula for finding American Medical Association (AMA) notation at near-point for object acuity is:

$$\frac{\text{Height of lower case letters/object in mm}}{\text{Distance from print to eye in mm} \underline{\hspace{2cm}}} \times 9632 = \underline{14}$$

2. Formula for calculating the point size of print being read:

$$\frac{72}{\text{Number of lines in vertical inch}} = \text{Estimated point size of print}$$

These formulas may be used to determine an estimate of near acuity or the point size of print. When utilizing these methods, carefully note the lighting factors, the distance from the print to the eye in millimeters or inches, and the style of print being used as the best target (e.g., cursive writing is a poor target since the letters do not conform to standard specifications). Typewritten material can vary in vertical spacing. Printed materials, such as textbooks, paperbacks, and magazines, are the most appropriate.

The human eye has approximately 60 diopters of refracting power of which the lens contributes up to 12 diopters. Accommodative power is progressively lost in the lens as the individual ages. Therefore, adults may have much more difficulty than have children in focusing on print at close reading distances. This should be kept in mind during the near-point testing. In addition, the myopic individual may be able to remove prescription glasses and read comfortably at a close working distance. Up to 18–20 years, a child or young adult rarely needs bifocals. However, if the eye problem involves the macula, smaller print sizes may be impossible to read without high-add reading lenses.

Method 2

Near-point test charts may be used to determine visual acuities. Charts should be chosen and testing techniques developed jointly with the low vision clinical team. The New York Lighthouse near-acuity test, the Halifax School for the Blind Near Vision Test Card, the Keller Near Reading Cards, and the Sloan Reading Cards are all effective near-vision test charts. The New York Lighthouse Near Vision test-symbol card for young children can be useful for those who do not read or recognize configurations of letters (see Fig. 2). A matching game played with distance flash cards and the New York Lighthouse Near Vision Symbol Chart can help determine near acuity with individuals who have difficulty in verbalizing what they see.

NEAR VISION TEST
SYMBOLS FOR CHILDREN

			DISTANT EQUIVALENT	METER SIZE
umbrella	house	apple	20/400	8M
house	apple	umbrella	20/300	6M
umbrella	house	apple	20/200	4M
house	apple	umbrella	20/160	3M 27 Pt.
umbrella	house	apple	20/100	2M 18 Pt.
umbrella	house	apple umbrella	20/80	1.5M 14 Pt.
apple	umbrella	house apple	20/50	1M 9 Pt.
umbrella	house	apple umbrella	20/40	.8M 7 Pt.
apple	umbrella	house apple	20/25	.5M 4 Pt.

18 Point Large Type Grades 1 - 3
14 Point Average Book Print grades 4 - 7
9 Point Magazines, Paper Back Books, Typing
7 Point Newspaper

Distance equivalent calibrated for 40 cm (16 inches)

THE LIGHTHOUSE LOW VISION SERVICES
111 EAST 59th STREET, NEW YORK, N.Y. 10022

LHNV-3
©1970

Fig. 2. Use of symbols for near acuity optotypes will often provide responses when letter and number charts do not.

Near-point testing should be done in sequence beginning with the worse eye aided, as indicated by information in the case history, and the better eye occluded. If you are using one of the charts just mentioned , test at 40 centimeters (16 inches) from the eye to the chart and begin with the largest print available. If the individual is unable to see this line clearly at 40 centimeters, move the chart toward the eye until the person recognizes the configurations. Be sure to jot down the eye-to-chart distance. If the individual still is unable to recognize the configurations at three or four centimeters, further testing should be done with objects, and the person should be referred to the clinic. It may be necessary to block out other parts of the page so the intended image can be more quickly located and recognized. Viewing a magazine picture held at arm's length consists of ten or more fixations and lasts from three to five seconds before the total image is recognizable. Cutting down on the information available to the eye induces less scanning and quicker recognition. (If there is a marked increased in nystagmus, it may be necessary to skip monocular testing and move directly to binocular near-point testing.) Note any eye movements, head tilts, lighting problems, and so forth that may have helped or hindered the patient during the test. Jot down the smallest line recognized at 40 centimeters (or any other distance) and proceed with best-eye-aided and binocular-aided acuity. As previously mentioned, young children may be able to see small print at close working distances (e.g., 7-point print at 8–10 centimeters is not uncommon). However, the concern here is whether children can see their grade-level print (see Table 2) or the required reading material (see Table 3) at an adequate working distance.

A working distance that is too close to the eye will overburden the accommodative system and may cause a shortening of the duration of reading, watering eyes, and general eye fatigue. The low vision clinic will be able to determine if a near-add is needed to reduce eye-muscle fatigue and relax the accommodative system. In later years, the adult eye will not be able to focus on print held much closer than 25 centimeters (approximately 10 inches).

Table 2. Print Size of Various Reading Materials[a]

Type of Reading Material	Print Size	
Textbook for Grades 1–3	Book print size (average):	18 point print
Textbook for Grades 4–7	Book print size (average):	14 point print
Textbook for Grades 8–12	Book print size (average):	12 point print
College-level textbooks	Book print size (average):	9 point print
Telephone directory	(average):	6 point print
Want Ads	(average):	5 point print

[a] Developed by Sandra Ferraro, Educational Specialist, Low Vision Clinic, College of Optometry, University of Houston.

Table 3. Equivalent Visual Acuity Notations For Near[a]

Meters Equivalent	Snellen Equivalent	Usual Type Size of Text	Equivalent Reading Acuity
0.4M	20/20		
0.5M	20/25	Footnotes	Paperback/newsprint
0.8M	20/40	Paperback print	Magazines
1.0M	20/50	Newspaper print	High school texts
1.2M	20/60	Magazine print	Children's books
1.6M	20/80	Children's books	Large-print materials
2.0M	20/100	Large-print materials	
4.0M	20/200	Newspaper subheadlines	
5.0M	20/250	Newspaper headlines	
10.0M	20/500	½-inch letters	
20.0M	20/1000	1-inch letters	

[a] Developed by Randy Jose, O.D.; Richard Brilliant, O.D., Chief, William Feinbloom Vision Rehabilitation Center; and Gale Watson, M.A., Educational Specialist, Pennsylvania College of Optometry.

Method 3

To calculate the approximate magnification needed to recognize 1M (arbitrarily chosen as the near acuity that will allow one to perform most near-point tasks) print, use the following formulas:

$$\frac{\text{Print size client read (in meters)}}{\text{Distance from eye to chart (in centimeters)}} = \text{Diopters of add needed to read 1M print}$$

In this formula, you must convert the print size read from meters to centimeters to complete the process.

Example 1: $\quad \frac{2M}{40cm} = \frac{200\ cm}{40cm} = 5$ diopters of add needed to read 1M print

Example 2: $\quad \frac{4M}{10cm} = \frac{400cm}{10cm} = 40$ diopters of add needed to read 1M print

By dividing the diopter value by four (D/4), you will get the magnification you need to demonstrate a near hand-held or stand magnifier. To figure at what distance that much power would focus clearly on a page of print or a near-point task, use the following formula:

$$\frac{100}{\text{Diopters}} = \text{Focal point in centimeters (2.5 cm} = 1 \text{ inch)}$$

Example 1: 5D (1.25 magnification) of add would focus on 1M print at approximately 20 cm from the lens to the page.

Example 2: $\frac{100}{40D} = 2.5$ cm distance from the lens to the page

This formula will give you the lens-to-page focal point distance and does not affect the lens-to-eye distance.

Since many factors, such as accommodative power, refractive error, monocularity versus binocularity, and adequate working distance, will affect the individual's ability to perform visually at near-point tasks, the low vision clinical team should make the final decision about near-point magnification. In addition, it is unlikely that the instructor will have a full range of diopter and housing-lens configurations available. It is essential that the most effective power be prescribed for each low vision individual examined, since too much magnification will greatly reduce the person's working field of view and too little magnification may not allow the successful completion of the desired visual tasks.

VISUAL FIELD MEASUREMENTS

After the case history and environmental distance and near acuities have been determined, an assessment of the habitual visual field is necessary. In many situations, such an assessment can be more valuable before the measurements of acuity (e.g., in cases of retinitis pigmentosa, when effective magnification may be limited, and in cases of macular degeneration, when it may be necessary to teach viewing techniques before testing acuity). The examiner's or clinician's purpose in assessing the visual field is, of necessity, quite different from that of the instructor who is doing preliminary assessments. The clinical staff will wish to define more clearly the eye pathology, and accurate tests of the visual field will help by indicating the overall field of view, scotomas, color defects, and, most important, the progression of a disease over a long period. Environmental studies of the visual field will help the instructor determine training programs, more clearly define the individual's problem areas, and assist educational assessment teams to understand more thoroughly the patient's needs.

Method 1

Observational assessments of the visual field are most effective in determining the functional characteristics of the patient's use of vision. Body posture, the angle of head tilt, most numerous eye-fixation positions, changes in the position of the eye or head while viewing in situations of dim illumination and bright illumination, gait patterns, the way a person avoids objects, picture drawing, mistakes in detecting words or letters, and problems in recognizing contours and shapes are strong indicators of defects in the visual field. By watching for these clues, the instructor can formulate, often accurately, a theory about the extent of the restrictions on the individual's field. Further confirmation and clarification should be obtained from the low vision clinic through its peripheral- and central-field-testing techniques. In many cases, low vision clinics do not automatically do field tests of clients unless they are

97

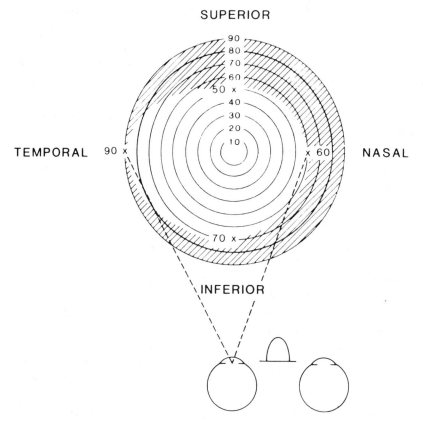

Fig. 3a. The normal full visual field is shown for the left eye.

specifically asked to or the eye condition mandates those tests. Some specific information about normal fields of view follows.

Normal Fields. Normal fields in each eye can see approximately 60 degrees to the nasal side (from dead center fixation point), 90 degrees to the temporal side, 50˙ degrees to the superior (up) and 70 degrees inferior (down) (see Fig. 3a and 3 b). Obviously, eye glasses will restrict the field, as will heavy eyebrows, a large nose, and bangs ofhair. The normal blind spot is approximately 18 mm in diameter when measurements are taken from a one-meter eye-to-the-screen distance. The blind spot is where the optic nerve leaves the retina to reach the cortex and is always on the temporal side of the fixation point regardless of which eye is being tested. It can be found about 25 centimeters from the fixation point when testing is done at one meter (10 inches or 16 degrees).

Hold this page at approximately 10 inches, close or occlude your left eye, fixate on the "X," and watch the figure "0" disappear (you may have to move the page closer or farther to achieve the effect). This is the location of the blind spot in your right eye.

X   0

To find the blind spot in your left eye, occlude your right eye, stare at the "0," and watch the "X" disappear when held at 10 inches. This is the same effect that a small scotoma would have on a person with a defective field of view, assuming that the scotomas were of equal size and location in each eye, since a normal field of view only in one eye is sufficient to suppress a small field loss in the other eye. The normal central field of view covers a diameter of 30 degrees from the fixation point.

Method 2

The Tangent Screen (central 30 degrees) and Amsler Grid (nearpoint 10 degrees) field tests are used clinically to determine defects in the central field, and the Perimeter (180 degrees) is used to assess defects in peripheral vision. With confrontation field assessments, you can obtain a rough peripheral

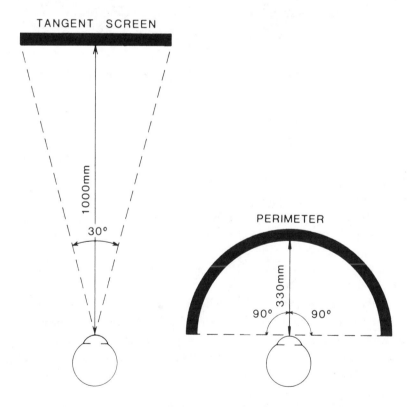

Fig. 3b. Tangent screen measures the central 30 degree of field while the perimeter measures 180 degrees.

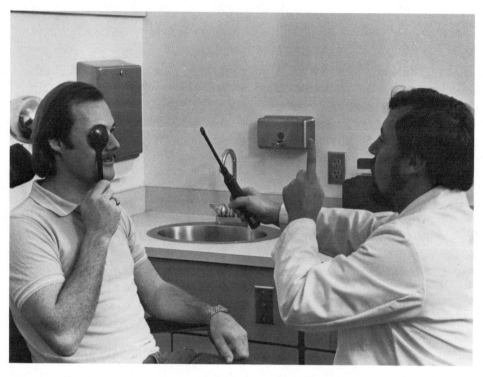

Fig. 4. An approximation of the visual field can be obtained with the confrontation technique.

field assessment without an expensive apparatus. To do a confrontation field test, occlude one of the patient's eyes and have the patient fixate on your nose (fixation object) as you sit one-third of a meter from his or her eye (see Fig. 4). Slowly move a target, such as a penlight, in a semicircular fashion from behind the patient's ear to in front of your nose and ask the patient to indicate when he or she first begins to see the light. (Remember to keep the target about 13 inches or one-third of a meter from the patient's eye at all times.) Make sure the patient continually stares at your nose and that the penlight is not aimed directly into his or her eye. The glow of the bulb should be used as the target, not the light beam itself; placing a clear plastic cap with the end occluded over the tip of the penlight can eliminate problems of glare from the light beam. If the eye flicks out toward the light, it may indicate (in a nonverbal child) that the patient recognized the target even though no verbal response was given.

Continue with the semicircular arcs around the perimeter of the patient's face until you are satisfied that the responses have been accurate. If the patient has given no response to the light until it reached a point slightly inside your face line, the patient may have a restricted peripheral field of 15 degrees or less. Other targets may include small finger puppets, toys, lollipops, magic wands, wiggling fingers on your hand, and the like. Use your imagination, but keep the target size no larger than about 10–20 millimeters.

Method 3

The chalkboard tangent screen can be used to determine whether there is a loss in the central field. On a large, clean blackboard, locate a fixation point with chalk, test the patient, and then measure the distance from the fixation point to the target recognition point (as marked by a fine tap of the chalk on the board when the patient says, "I see it coming."). Each 2½ inches (9 centimeters) will equal 5 degrees when testing is done at one meter from the chart to the eye. The targets can be made from a dull-white plastic string of pearls by gluing a straight pin through the hole of each pearl once it is removed from the string and pushing the pearl and pin into the end of a small dowel stick. The dowel should be painted a dull black to fade out of sight when placed in front of the chalkboard. Therefore, a crude tangent screen can be created for less than $10.00, assuming a blackboard or other dark background is available.

The testing procedure for chalkboard field assessments is as follows: occlude one eye, make sure the patient is fixating on the center dot (if large central losses are prevalent, a large "X" extending 10–15 degrees can be used; ask the person to fixate the eye on the point where he thinks the two stripes cross). With the selected target (find the smallest size the person can see with his or her perimacular vision), move the target slowly from a non-seeing area toward the fixation point and ask the patient to say, "I see it" when the target appears and, "It disappeared" if it fades away again. Make 14–16 passes from the outside to the center around the entire circumference of the board and mark each point of disappearance or appearance (the target will disappear when it goes through the blind spot). Follow the same procedure for the second eye. Remember to keep the distance at one meter from the eye to the center dot. If the target is moved too rapidly, fields smaller than actual will be reproduced. The opposite is true of slow target movement (ideally 5 degrees of movement per second). The patient with nystagmus may not be able to fixate one eye at a time; therefore, a rough overlapping field can be assessed by testing with both eyes open. To write down your information, measure the degrees to each mark and outline the overall configuration of dots on a piece of paper. Indicate the color of the target, its size in millimeters, and the distance from the eye to the chart in millimeters. 10/1000/W would indicate a 10-millimeter-size target in *white* with testing done at a distance of 1000 millimeters (one meter).

A functional near-point field test can be done if the tester uses graph paper (preferably a 1-millimeter square-grid pattern) held 14 inches from the client's eye. Follow the same procedures listed under Method 1, occluding one eye and then the other. The point of fixation can be a small mirror (one centimeter in diameter) or a dot or "X" placed on the page. Once a series of marks has been recorded on the page, measurements can be taken from the fixation point to the marks; however, in this case, each 5 millimeters equals 1 degree of field, or one inch equals approximately 5 degrees. Of even greater use is a textbook in a print size that the patient can see. Use of the textbook gives the tester a greater feel for the difficulties a field loss presents to the client while reading. In the clinical setting, this type of field testing is called the "Amsler Grid;" it is used in conjunction with other sophisticated methods of data collection to glean information about the patient's visual system (see Chapter 8).

None of these methods is used by the instructor for medical information. However, these methods are useful for determining a program design in visual stimulation, mobility, classroom seating, positioning of aids and material, and so forth.

OBSERVATIONS OF FUNCTIONAL VISION

Throughout the preliminary assessment process, observations of the patient will greatly help enhance or redirect information gathering. A few hints about what to look for are appropriate at this point.

Near-vision Clues
Some clues to problems in near vision are these: eyes turned in or out, reddened eyes, excessive tearing or blinking of eyes, headaches, frequent blurring of print, a short reading time, head turning as the patient reads across a page, the place lost often in reading, use of the finger as a line marker, a short attention span, omission of words or letters when reading, skipping of lines, complaints of seeing double, squinting, the closing or covering of one eye when reading, excessive head tilting, inability to stay on ruled lines, poor word spacing, avoidance of all near tasks, and abnormal or excessive fatigue. All these clues may indicate the need for further eye examinations. It must be noted that children with a normal visual system may exhibit some of these signs for other reasons.

Other near-vision clues are taking off glasses to see, looking over the top of the glasses, overreaching for objects, trouble in locating food on a plate, avoidance of playing visual games such as cards or scrabble, difficulty in selecting color-coordinated clothing, excessive wandering of eyes, a slow reading speed, and holding reading material up close.

Distance-vision Clues
Clues to difficulties in distance vision include the continuous adjustment of window shades or the contrast on the television screen; playing only in shaded areas, the viewing of television from far off to one side of the screen; the inability to distinguish between the lawn and sidewalk; collision with stationary or moving objects; the inability to recognize a person's features, to see traffic lights during the day or at night, to track moving cars, to see

curbs or crosswalks on the pavement, to see empty seats in a restaurant, to see the face or hands on a clock, or to identify various table utensils without touching them; and the ability to see certain size balls or toys but not others.

Assessments of the patient's need for lighting and the problems in using lighting, as indicated earlier, are important aspects of functional evaluations. Chapter 16 discusses how to assess lighting and the relationship between illumination and functional vision.

landmarks; the missing of steps and dropoffs; total reliance on auditory clues for recognizing traffic patterns; and excessive veering when walking. When noting observations to be presented to the low vision clinic, the instructor should list the approximate size (height and width), color, shape, and background color of the item, the lighting on the object and around the low vision individual, the distance from the person to the item, and the psychological stability of the person at the time of observation. These clues, taken together, help the clinical team to determine the patient's problems in visual functioning.

Assessments of the patient's need for lighting and the problems in using lighting, as indicated earlier, are important aspects of functional evaluations. Chapter 16 discusses how to assess lighting and the relationship between illumination and functional vision.

ADVANTAGES OF PRELIMINARY ASSESSMENTS

How much of the information from the environmental assessment is used depends on the scope of the low vision clinic, the area being served, and the professional personnel actively involved with low vision patients. Most educational and rehabilitation facilities in large urban areas do not provide low vision services in the home, school, or at work. Therefore, these facilities would find it helpful to receive sophisticated evaluative information about their patients. Programs that provide services in rural areas tend to rely more heavily on this type of information-gathering system because it paves the way for their eventual visit to the patient's home, school, or work site.

The overall advantages of the assessment are as follows:

■ Patients tend to be more open with the clinical team because they know what to expect and have been exposed to many of the testing techniques that will be used in the clinic or doctor's office.

■ If the patient has had success, no matter how limited, during the preliminary evaluation, he or she knows that a visual change for the better is possible. Therefore, the patient's motivational level is high when he or she enters the clinic.

■ If primary support groups of family members, friends, rehabilitation staff, and so forth have been included in the preliminary evaluations, the attitudes of these significant others about the patient's capabilities are usually much improved, which helps keep the patient motivated.

■ The referring party now has realistic expectations of the low vision service being developed for the individual and can prepare more appropriately to meet the person's needs.

■ Schools, teachers, parents, and others receive prompt recommendations in response to their urgent questions, such as whether to order large print or to begin braille instruction, and thus may proceed on a realistic course pending further clarification from the future clinical low vision evaluation.

■ The preliminary assessments unite many interested persons in their attempt to solve the visually impaired person's problems.

■ Use of the data obtained from the environmental assessment can greatly reduce wasted time for the clinical low vision team and allow more time to be directed toward meeting the individual's needs and solving his or her problems.

■ The low vision clinical team now has information to use as a baseline in each testing session so the patient will not become overtired.

■ The low vision clinic has data to compare the patient's functioning in the "real world" and in the structured clinical setting. This greatly enhances follow-up problem-solving sessions with the individual and other professional staff members.

■ Services that have been disjointed and, in many cases, overlapping in the past now can follow a step-by-step progression from the environment to the clinical setting and back to the environment for continuation of training activities.

In conclusion, it should be noted that some of the procedures may be unnecessary if the low vision clinic is designed to bring the eye-care team to the home, school, or work environment. The distance, near-point, field, and lighting assessments can be done by doctors or a clinical team if they are part of a mobile door-to-door clinic. However, the case histories and functional observations should still be obtained by a third person connected with the low vision team or by the referring party.

Bibliography

Bates, S. *Fundamentals for the optometric assistant.* Philadelphia: Chilton Book Co., 1970

Faye, E. *The low-vision patient.* New York: Grune & Stratton, 1970.

Freid, A., and Mehr, E. *Low vision care.* Chicago: Professional Press, 1974.

Harrington, D. *The visual fields.* 3rd. ed.; St. Louis, Mo.: C.V. Mosby Co., 1971.

Langley, B., and Dubose, R. Functional vision screening for severely handicapped children. *New Outlook for the Blind,* 1976, **10**(8), 346-350.

Larkin, M. Visual fields interpretation. *Journal of the American Optometric Association,* 1980, **51**(9), 837-842.

Newman, J. *A guide to the care of low vision patients.* St. Louis, Mo.: American Optometric Association, 1974.

Sloan, L. L. *Reading aids for the partially sighted.* Baltimore, Md.: Williams & Wilkins Co., 1977.

CHAPTER 7

Assessment of Children With Low Vision

TERESE HRITCKO, B.S.ED.

Implementation of the model presented in Chapter 4 and pursued throughout the book varies from setting to setting and with different populations. However, the three-phase objectives of the model can be realized in cities or in rural areas, with adults or children. The extent of the instructor's involvement depends on the setting and the instructor's ability to have an extended time with one child. The model described in this chapter was developed for the rural areas of New England, but it is applicable to itinerant teachers in other areas as well. It is a comprehensive evaluation that maximizes the clinical visits and develops strong ties of communication between the clinician and the instructor. The long distances sometimes needed for traveling to low vision clinics or practitioners necessitates this type of application of the model.

"A visually handicapped child's development of visual skills is directly influenced by visual tendencies (motivation), physical and mental characteristics, and environmental factors. Children have strengths and weaknesses in the visual modality which lead to the necessity of providing both a visual training and instructional program set up to match individual perceptual abilities, visual efficiency, and visual acuity" (Swallow, 1977, p. 10). Visual functioning relates to how well a child is able to use his or her remaining vision to perform everyday tasks. According to Barraga (1980, p. 93), visual functioning is a learned behavior, "primarily developmental;" the more visual experiences the child has, the more the pathways to the brain are stimulated, which leads to a greater accumulation of a variety of visual images and memories.

It is the role, then, of members of the low vision team (optometrists, ophthalmologists, itinerant low vision instructors, educational personnel, orientation and mobility specialists, psychologists, and others) and of parents to participate in the assessment of the whole child. Such an assessment should address the implications of the visual loss for the child's social, emotional, and cognitive development, with the goal being the development of a treatment plan to meet best the identified needs of the child and to promote the strengths of the individual. In addition to the formal optometric/diagnostic assessment performed in the clinical setting (Phase 2), it is particularly important that observations and functional assessments be done in the child's everyday environment (Phase 1). It is in the everyday environment that clinical information must be translated into practical application and used to develop an educational plan as well as a plan for low vision care.

In the area of education, the itinerant teacher/consultant, the resource teacher, or the home teacher often functions as a low vision instructor responsible for assessments. This allows for more effective communication between the classroom teacher and the itinerant teacher and ensures that the assessment will address the child's functioning in the classroom, the child's learning style and the classroom teacher's teaching style, materials used, the modifications needed and implications of the visual loss. The assessor's cooperation and interaction with the school personnel and understanding of educational methods are essential if the child and school personnel are to benefit from the evaluation. As O'Brien (1976, p. 230) stated, the assessor must have

> a thorough knowledge of visual development and the implications for those impairments which seriously affect visual efficiency. Parent counseling, early utilization and development of residual vision, basic concept and skill development, self-care, orientation and mobility, and perceptual, social, and emotional development must be [considered with regard to each low vision child].

What, then, is the role of the low vision instructor in identifying the needs and capacities of the visually handicapped? This chapter addresses the role of the instructor in determining the child's functional use of vision in a variety of settings, outlines procedures to be used, and describes how the information will be useful in everyday settings. As with material in the rest of this book, the information in this chapter is not meant to be followed rigidly. It is important that instructors identify and organize procedures that will be most valuable to themselves.

ROLES AND RESPONSIBILITIES

The instructor will be required to perform many roles and serve in a variety of capacities. Some of the responsibilities are as follows:

■ To arrange for and administer an assessment of functional vision. The results should provide additional information needed in programming and planning for the child and will be communicated to all persons involved with the child (eye-care specialists, school personnel, parents, and other service providers).

■ To interpret optometric and ophthalmological information in relation to the child's functioning at home or in school and its effects on the social and emotional development of the child.

■ After the assessment is completed, to help develop an individual education and low vision plan in relation to the visual loss. The low vision instructor recommends appropriate special evaluations and services e.g., orientation and mobility, low vision services, psychological evaluations, and vocational rehabilitation. Also, the needs for equipment and instruction in the utilization of residual vision, low vision aids, daily living skills, precane skills, taped materials, or nonoptical aids are identified.

■ To provide practical information to the home and school regarding what size materials the child is able to see, modifications of classroom materials and activities, and support of daily living skills at home.

■ To provide additional observations and follow-up to the clinician regarding the child's functional behavior in school and at home, the child's adaptive behavior (particularly with the multiply handicapped), and the child's visual needs (e.g., the need for increased working distance from the shop equipment). Keen observations may help the eye-care personnel determine an approximate visual acuity for the child.

With a new referral from a pupil evaluation team, an itinerant low vision instructor may be the primary (local) case manager and thus may be responsible for initiating the referral process to a clinic. Prior to the clinic visit, the instructor should complete a functional low vision assessment. For the assessment, the following materials are required from the home, the school, and medical personnel:

■ Current (within one year) medical (ophthalmological or optometric) information.

■ Report on the child's general medical status: current health, additional handicaps, medications, and restrictions on activities.

■ Previous low vision evaluation (if available).

■ Educational data (school, address, grade, years in school, contact person, reading and mathematics levels, the support services received by the child, and how frequently the services are provided.

■ A psychological evaluation (if available).

■ Specialty evaluation (e.g., occupational or physical therapy and an audiological evaluation).

■ Evaluation of orientation and mobility skills.

■ Reasons for referral (to be included by the referring agent). These can include an assessment of the child's functioning with regard to the increasing visual demands of higher grade levels, a yearly update and review of next year's materials with respect to the child's ophthalmological/optometric status, a change in visual status (increasing or decreasing visual acuity or field), the general need for practical and functional input to the home, school, and vocational rehabilitation agency to develop an appropriate program (functional assessment being one type of information collected).

By obtaining the data just mentioned, the low vision instructor, in addition to doing a general assessment of functional visual abilities, can gear the evaluation to the needs of a variety of people involved in the child's daily life. It is important that the instructor review the material carefully and note any specifics that should be observed or investigated further when the clinical and functional evaluations are completed.

The instructor contacts the child's parents to discuss the procedures to be used in assessing the child's functional use of vision as well as to note the parents' observations and concerns. The parents should be considered as invaluable members of the team and as a source of information about the child's development, daily interaction with the environment, peers, other family members, and so forth. Good communication is vital to developing a working relationship among the parents, educators, and other professionals; the parents will then perceive that those involved in the provision of services to the child are genuinely interested in supporting and promoting the child's growth and development.

A structured interview is a systematic way of gathering useful preliminary data on the child's overall development, as well as on how the child makes use of vision in the home. However, it should be cautioned that the format used for seeking information from parents often can jeopardize the early establishment of a working relationship. A checklist approach or emphasis on the child's abilities and limitations may be interpreted as pointing out negatives, may raise the parents' anxieties, or antagonize the parents by appearing to question their ability to deal with their child. Explanations are helpful so the parents understand the purpose of discussing the child's early and present development, interactions with the environment, and so forth. A general conversational approach with the parents is also nonthreatening; in this case, the instructor logs the data immediately following the interview.

Whatever the format, the following questions, asked of the parents during the interview or of the older child in a joint preassessment interview, will elicit important information:

- Does the child watch television—in black and white or color? How close does the child sit? What is the size of the set?
- Does the child enjoy reading? How often? Where does the child read? Describe the lighting. Fatigues when reads? After how long? Where does the child do homework? Does the child make use of additional lighting while doing homework? Does the child have a set time to do homework?
- What types of material does the child read: newspaper headlines, large print, typewritten matter, want ads? Note at what distance the child holds each type of reading matter.
- Does the child complain about glare? Prefer bright or overcast days?

Use sunglasses, a visor, or a hat? Does glare present difficulties in walking, reading, or identifying and seeing colors?

- Can the child read street signs, billboards, crosswalks, and house numbers? Note at what distance the child reads each object.

- Does the child make use of optical or nonoptical aids? If so, of what type and power? How long has the child had the aids? Are they useful? Where were they obtained?

- Is the child able to get around unaided, or does the child require a sighted guide? Is the child's approach visual or tactual? Does the child ever bump into things? If so, is there any consistency in the position or location of the obstacle? What is the child's reaction to a new setting either indoors or outdoors?

- Does the child like to play with other children? What is the child's favorite leisure activity, toy, or game? What gross motor activities does the child engage in (running, jumping, ball skills)? Describe the child's coordination.

- Is the child able to care for himself or herself? (Here it might be helpful to use a checklist type of format such as the Vision-up, Vineland Social Maturity Scale, Maxfield Buchholz, or daily living skills inventories, to serve as a reminder of the skills to question.) Note grooming, eating, and dressing skills.

- How much vision do the parents think their child has? Describe the parents' observations (e.g., child can identify and match colors, sees a four-inch object at five feet, or appears to prefer one eye).

- What are the parents' concerns? What is their understanding of their child's eye condition? Their expectations for their child? The history of visual conditions in the family?

- What is the name of the family's optometrist, ophthalmologist, and pediatrician? Does the child wear glasses? If so, for what activities.

- Describe the nature and severity of any additional handicapping conditions.

The assessor should also contact the child's classroom teacher to discuss the role of the low vision instructor and the procedure for a thorough assessment of functional vision. An appointment should be made to observe the child in a variety of classroom settings, performing various tasks. The low vision instructor should forward a list of activities to be observed, if at all possible. Such activities include the child in a reading group (observe oral and silent participation), tasks while seated (perhaps a workbook or worksheet activity), use of audiovisual equipment, running errands to the office (or showing the observer around the building), lunch time, recess, and specialty classes (physical education, industrial arts, instrument or music lesson, or home economics). The classroom teacher should be asked to save samples of the student's writing, workbooks, art, and the like, and to set aside time after the observation to discuss the following:

- What reading series is used with the child, and at what level does the child read? At what distance from the page does the child read? Does the child pick up or move close to the material? Use glasses? Use a workbook? Dittoes?

■ At what level of mathematics is the child working? Does the child have difficulty with any of the materials or concepts?

Table 1. Teacher's Observation Checklist: The ABCs of Visual Difficulty[a]

Appearance of the Student's eyes

1. Eyes crossed—turning in or out— at at any time, or eyes do not appear straight, especially when the child is tired.
2. Reddened eyes or eyelids.
3. Watery eyes.
4. Encrusted eyelids.
5. Frequent sties.
6. Clouding of pupils or pupillary opening.
7. Eyes in constant motion.
8. Drooping eye lids.

Behavioral Indications of Possible Visual Difficulty

1. A rigid body when reading or viewing a distant object.
2. Thrusting the head forward or backward while looking at distant objects.
3. Avoiding close work.
4. A short attention span.
5. Turning the head to use one eye only.
6. Tilting the head to one side.
7. Placing the head close to a book or desk when reading or writing; holding reading material excessively close or too far away.
8. Frowning or scowling while reading or writing.
9. Excessive blinking.
10. Tendency to rub eyes.
11. Covering or closing one eye.
12. Dislike for reading or inattentiveness during reading.
13. Unusual fatigue after completing a vision task or a deterioration in reading after lengthy periods.
14. Losing the place while reading.
15. Using a finger or marker to guide the eyes.
16. Saying the words aloud or lip reading.
17. Moving the head rather than the eyes while reading.
18. General reading difficulties: the tendency to reverse letters and words or to confuse letters and numbers with similar shapes (e.g., a, c; f, t; e, c; m, n; and h, n, r), frequent omission of words, or the attempt to guess words from quick recognition of a part of a word in easy reading material.
19. Stumbling over objects.
20. Poor spacing in writing and the inability to stay on or in a line. Reversal of letters or words in writing and copying.
21. Preference for reading versus play or motor activities or vice versa.

Complaints Associated with Using the Eyes

1. Headaches.
2. Nausea or dizziness.
3. Burning or itching eyes.
4. Blurred vision at any time.
5. Words or lines running together or grouped together.
6. Pains in the eyes.

[a] Adapted from the Vision Consultant to Educational Programs, Gerald N. Getman & George M. Milkia, American Optometric Association, St. Louis, 1973; Mainstreaming the Visually Impaired, Gloria Calovni (ed.). Illinois Office of Education, Springfield, IL (no date).

- What materials are used regularly in class: workbooks, dittoes, graphs, maps, a dictionary, an overhead projector, films, filmstrips, or television? Where does the child sit? Is the child able to get information from the black-board? Does the child need to have his or her seat changed to see the black-board?

- Does the child complain about glare? Have any difficulty adjusting to changes in illumination (e.g., when the lights go off for the use of audiovisual equipment, in a dim corridor, when the child goes from indoors to outdoors)? Does the child prefer dark or bright days? Does the child move toward or away from extra lighting?

- How does the child interact with peers? Does the child have any friends? Does the child participate in extracurricular activities or class jobs? Does the child establish eye contact when conversing?

- How does the child travel in the class, the building, the stairs, and the hallways?

- Does the child receive support services? If so, how frequently?

- What is the class schedule of activities? The class schedule helps the instructor to look at the demands placed on the child throughout the day and to schedule observations and assessments.

Table 1 lists additional observations to be made by the classroom teacher. By sending the list of questions to the classroom teacher before the observation, the instructor cues the classroom teacher as to which observations to make of the child's functioning in the class. Receipt of the list beforehand may also stimulate the classroom teacher to ask questions about the observations.

It may be necessary to schedule several days of observations depending on the child's and teacher's schedule and the number of areas of participation one wishes to observe before a formal, structured assessment. Each day's observations should be recorded for reporting purposes.

A nursery school, a day-care center, or the child's home provide excellent opportunities for observing the preschool child. The child's eating skills at meal or snack time, the child's ability to get his or her own snack, self-care activities, play time and interaction with peers, story time, arts and crafts activities, and independent and group activities are some examples of what can be observed.

OBSERVATION

Before using formal or informal assessment procedures, the instructor needs to observe the settings in which the child interacts daily. Information from the initial case history and a review of the data provide insight into the child's medical, social, and educational history. However, until the thorough observation, the instructor may make inappropriate assumptions and waste time deciding which assessment instruments should be useful to determine the child's level of visual functioning. As stated in earlier chapters, two children (or adults) with the same etiologies, acuities and chronological and mental age may function at different levels of visual efficiency (the functioning depending on lighting and the child's level of residual vision, attitudes, past experience, training, motivation, and so on). The observation must be as objective as possible, delineating observed behaviors and the context and climate in which they were observed.

It is crucial that each assessor develop a recording system that will serve as a quick, systematic way of recording data or that will outline behaviors to be remembered. In addition to recording the child's behavior, the assessor should record information regarding the child's environment.

Classroom and School Environment

In observing the classroom environment, the assessor should make specific notes of the following. A small schematic may provide one way of recording some of the information and will serve as a good reference.

- The type and placement of lighting (natural, such as light from windows, or artificial). It would be helpful to note the time of day, the lighting observed and the weather conditions.
- The color of the walls and the general arrangement of the room.
- The number of students.
- The location of the student—a description of the area (available storage, clear versus cluttered, and areas of glare).
- Location, position, quality (rutted, shiny, matte), color, and use of the chalkboard, maps, charts, bulletin boards, and audiovisual equipment.
- The child's desk: its surface (dull, glossy, color) and whether it is adjustable, and the child's seat (attached, adjustable, separate).
- The location of the room in the building.
- The number of grades in the building, the number of classrooms, the location of the cafeteria, locker, and gymnasium, and different lighting conditions.
- Activities (reading, mathematics, social studies, art, and so forth): Note the child's visual behaviors and posture as they relate to each subject area. Note the size and type of material or object viewed, the child's approximate distance from the object and whether the child uses one or both eyes, squints, or strains when using the object. Does the child use low vision aids or change glasses? Other factors to consider are the child's use of the hands (reference, exploration, or shielding), class participation, ability to copy and transfer materials, level of independence, and preferred writing distance. Does the child use an additional light source? How does the child's eyes adapt to different lighting conditions?
- *Indoor mobility.* Observe the child's ability to travel in the class, hallway or cafeteria and on the stairs. Does the child avoid obstacles in all planes? If not, note consistent areas of difficulty. Note the size of objects and the distance at which they are avoided. Is the child's approach to the en-

vironment visual or tactual? What are the child's posture, gait, and balancing abilities? In physical education, does the child prefer certain activities? Note the child's ability to see the instructor and follow directions as well as the child's motor coordination, and eye-hand and eye-foot coordination.

■ *Outdoor mobility.* Observe the child's ability to adapt to light and the time it takes for the child to adjust to light, the child's response to changes in the ground surface (texture—blacktop or grass, inclines—approach to curbs and markings). Does the child shuffle feet, step over markings, lose balance? At recess, note the child's use of the playground equipment, preferred activities, and the ability to locate peers and to particpate in activities.

■ *General Behavior and Appearance.* Note the child's behavior and appearance. Does the child cooperate (explain interactions)? What mannerisms are present? What is the child's appearance (height, weight, eye color, dress, and grooming)?

■ Observe the classroom teacher's style of instruction. Suggest possible modifications and techniques for use with visually handicapped students.

With preschool children, several additional observations may prove worthwhile in assessing and observing children in their home and nursery school environments. (See also Hammer, 1976; O'Brien, 1976.)

■ Do the child's eyes move in the direction of the stimulus, object, or people requiring his or her attention (e.g., if the child's name is called, can the child locate and focus on the person?) Note the relative coordination of these movements and use of the eyes.

■ Can the child go to a designated chair or area, independently, without tactual exploration?

■ Can the child recognize objects nearby and reach for them accurately, or does the child not indicate an awareness of the surroundings? Note the size of the object located and its distance from the child. Observe the child's ability to search for and locate visually. What types of materials are looked at? Are they colorful? What is their size?

■ Does the child examine objects visually, tactually, or both? Is the child able to transfer an object from one hand to another at midline? Does the child use other senses to acquire information about the environment?

■ What are the child's visual and postural behaviors?

■ Does the child demonstrate eye-hand coordination and reach for stationary and moving objects, stack objects, grasp objects (note use of the hands—pincer, palmar), and play ball?

■ How does the child move through and occupy space? Note the child's use of his or her body, balance, posture, and gait; motor planning; fitness; agility; and level of conceptual development in activities.

■ How does the child relate socially? Observe free play and determine the level or stage of play within which the child is functioning.

1. Is play isolated? (Isolated play is observable in the child's egocentric approach to people, objects, and the environment. The child sees objects

and people as items to be manipulated. The child begins to experience which behaviors are permitted and begins to understand causality.)

2. Does the child engage in parallel play? That is, although the child is aware of others, he or she is not interested in acknowledging their existence? The child may be performing the same activity, near the other children, but remains independent of them.

3. Is the child's play interactive? Does the child seek out others, share toys, and involve other children in a game?

In the conference following the initial observation, the low vision instructor should review the information gathered and provide some immediate feedback to the classroom teacher and parents. Any modifications discussed at this time should be included in the summary report for purposes of recording. Questions about consistent or inconsistent behavior observed in the child's functional use of vision could be posed at this time to the parents and teacher. If they are not able to answer specifically, the parents or teacher could make a point of observing the specific behavior between this observation and the next visit. The instructor could also assess behaviors in question at another time.

Samples of the child's work can be reviewed to note neatness, organization of the material, use of space, the child's ability to stay on or within lines, the ability to follow directions, and so forth. The classroom teacher sees the child's educational functioning in relation to other children and can assist the low vision instructor in noting whether the difficulty is age appropriate, a maturational problem, or a visual difficulty. Close cooperation among the low vision instructor, and teacher and parents is essential for organizing the assessment, for observations, and for developing programs. The low vision instructor should give the teacher a list of the assessment materials needed for the next session.

EVALUATING VISUAL FUNCTION

This evaluation portion of the assessment should be conducted in a quiet, uncluttered area with good, but controllable, lighting. It involves working on a one-to-one basis with the low vision child. The instructor should be organized and prepared so the child's interest and cooperation are not lost. This section of the full assessment may take more than one session to administer, depending on how easily the child tires, the child's attention span and motivation, scheduling, and additional factors. For each of the activities, describe the environment (lighting, room, and so forth). The instructor needs to be a keen observer, flexible in the administration and use of materials, and must record all the procedures used.

Table 2 is a sample reporting form that can be utilized for the low vision assessment. A discussion of the specific items of this report form follows. At the conclusion of the chapter, a completed assessment of a young student is

Table 2. Sample Reporting Format for Assessment of Functional Vision

Name: _____ Dates of Assessment: _____ School: _____
Date of Birth: _____ Date of Report: _____ Grade: _____
Address: _____ Evaluator: _____ Contact Person: _____

Eye Condition. Summary of eye report, description of what terminology refers to (e.g., photophobia—sensitivity to light), acuities, physician's name, and date of last examination.

Additional Handicapping Conditions. It is important to include the degree to which the individual is affected (e.g., mild retardation).

Medications. Record name of drug, the dosage, and the frequency of use.

1. *Ocular Functions.* Describe the child's response to each distance material used.
   a. Pupillary response
   b. Muscle imbalance
   c. Blink reflex
   d. Eye preference
   e. Tracking
   f. Convergence
   g. Shifting attention (gaze)
   h. Scanning

2. *Information on Functional Vision.* Include the names of the materials used. For distance and near vision, record data for each eye separately and both eyes together, with and without correction, and with low vision aids.
   a. Distance
   b. Near
   c. Field
   d. Color vision
   e. Lighting (present at the time of evaluation)

3. *Visual Perception.* Note the materials used for formal and informal observations.

4. *Educational Media.* Note all the factors in the physical environment and educational materials that affect the child's visual performance.

5. *Summary and Recommendations*

provided as an example of the actual types of information that can be derived from this extensive evaluation. In a rural area, the clinician will not be able to see the student for multiple visits, so these extensive evaluations by the low vision instructor are especially important.

Ocular Functions

A more detailed description of the activities in this section of the assessment is found in Chapter 15. In sum, the instructor should evaluate the following:

Pupillary Response. A change in the shape or size of the pupil when light is presented.

Muscle Imbalance. The tendency for the eyes to deviate (as observed in reflection of light).

Blink Reflex. Blinking in response to a hand or object moving toward the face.

Eye Preference. Changes in behavior as observed in the child's response (verbal or action) to the alternate patching or occluding of the eyes.

Visual Fields. (1) Central: The child responds to a light or an object presented in front of the face (i.e., the head or eye turns). (2) Peripheral: The child responds to a light or an object presented in outer areas of the face.

Tracking. The child's ability to follow a light or object with the eyes.

Convergence. The child's ability to follow a moving light or object as it moves toward him or her.

Shifting Attention. Shifting of visual attention is demonstrated when lights or objects are alternately presented.

Scanning. Searching in a line, from one object to another, as demonstrated in the response to three objects placed in front of the child.

Functional Vision Information (Distance)

Informal Observation Methods. In assessing each of the following, record the size of the object or toy, the lighting involved, the child's distance from the object, and whether the child uses one or both eyes. Note the child's ability to (1) locate a dropped object or toy, (2) identify or recognize symbols and objects, and (3) match toys and objects. The latter is assessed using two sets of toys that are the same except for their color. Record the child's ability to match the items at various distances.

Formal Charts (such as the Feinbloom Distance Test Chart for the Partially Sighted, Wall Distance Acuity Charts, and Lighthouse Flashcard/Symbol Cards). For near and distance, record room lighting, light near the student, reflectance from the chart, behavior (e.g. squinting or shielding the eyes), head tilts or turns (noting direction), position of the eye when fixating, the rate of nystagmus when the eye is occluded or if nystagmus increases with a decrease in the size of an object or decreases when the position of the head changes. Be aware of the condition of the assessment materials. Smudges and missing portions of symbols owing to wear influence the results.

Consider the background against which the material is presented so the child will not become visually distracted or have to deal with figure-ground elements. Angle the chart or card down slightly to avoid glare from overhead sources of light. It may be necessary to occlude portions of the chart if the child has difficulty fixating or localizing within a row or group of symbols. If this is the case, record the need for this adaptation; also, note if the child consistently misses one area on the chart. Record the accuracy of the identification, that is, whether the child seems to be guessing. Does the child appear to be using configuration?

With the Lighthouse Flashcard/Symbol Cards, introduce 20/200 size cards at a close range and have the child identify the symbols. Then increase the distance between the cards and the child to two feet and ask the child to identify the same cards while both eyes are open. If the child answers correctly, increase the distance to five feet and then to 10 feet. (It may be better to remain at five feet because younger children may not attend to the task with increasing distances.) At the preferred viewing distance, continue to test the child, testing each eye separately, both eyes together, and the eyes without and with correction. (See Brown & Brown, 1980.)

The parents or preschool teacher can be most helpful in training the child, assisting in the assessment, and interpreting the child's responses and behaviors. They may need to train the child to recognize the symbol cards because a consistent response (verbal or matching) is needed to assess visual ability with these cards. Two types of training activities follow:

1. Beginning at near, use two sets of cards. Using the largest symbol card, ask the child to match house to house. Then add one distractor (an apple or umbrella). When the child is consistent, add two distractors. The child should then be required to match his or her 20/200 set with decreasing acuity cards until he or she is consistent in matching even with the smallest set.

2. Move to distances of two, five, and 10 feet and record the child's responses and successes at each distance (for each eye, for both eyes, and without and with correction).

The cards are useful in the school to demonstrate to teachers how a visually handicapped child's vision compares with that of other children. By assessing the child in the classroom, it is possible to show how distractions in the environment affect functioning. The adequacy of lighting can be evaluated and visual functioning demonstrated when light from a window or artificial light is coming over the child's shoulder or directly into the child's face and when there is a difference in performance with and without light.

The opthalmological or optometric report may not have indicated for which tasks (near or distance) the glasses were prescribed. By assessing the child with the flashcards, one can observe whether the child's performance differs with or without glasses. With a telescope, one can assess and demonstrate the child's ability to locate, focus, and identify the symbol at various distances.

Screening Tests for Young Children and the Mentally Retarded. [National Foundation for Educational Research, Windsor, England, 1973.] These tests are useful with preschoolers and the mentally retarded. They are performed for each eye separately and both eyes together, without and with correction.

1. Miniature Toys Test. This test consists of two sets of 2-inch-high cars, planes, dolls, chairs, knives, forks, and spoons; two sets of 3¼-inch high knives, forks, and spoons; and one 5-inch-high doll. The child is shown the toys at a distance of three meters (10 feet) and is asked to identify them. If the child is unable to name the objects because of their distance, the assessor

moves closer and records the distance. If the child is unable verbally to identify the toys, the assessor uses the second set for matching purposes. Acuity translations are available in the manual.

2. Rolling Balls. This test involves a series of graded balls projected at a distance of 20 feet (in normally sighted children). The child is required to retrieve each ball after it is presented horizontally across the child's line of vision.

3. Letters. Cards can be used at a distance of five feet. Letters to be identified include capital T, H, V, X, and O.

Functional Vision Information (Nearpoint)

The nearpoint acuity is often left out of the eye report; yet, it is critical information to have in the functional visual assessment. Formal and informal measures follow.

Informal Assessment. In the informal assessment, observe which types of materials the child is able to see and read in the classroom or home, such as comic books, picture books, pictures, dictionaries, phone books, newspapers, and the like. Record the reading speed, work distances, and lighting required for each activity. This is the most valuable acuity assessment for the clinician.

Charts (such as the Lighthouse Near Acuity Card and the Near Vision Symbol Test discussed in Chapter 6, and the Sloan Continuous Text Reading Cards for Low Vision Patients). The Sloan Cards are 8″ × 10″ and contain a sentence or paragraph. The print simulates that of black typewriter type in an attempt to reproduce a lifelike situation. Information available on the cards includes the metric notation, acuity at 40 cm with equivalent distance acuity, the approximate number of diopters of addition required to read 1M print at a focal distance of selected add (the description is available in the card packet).

With the Sloan cards, note the child's posture, head and eye movements, fluency, rate of scanning, use of fingers as a guide and as a line marker, errors, the difference in performance when the size of the print is decreased, comprehension, and the difference in ability and performance with regard to single sentences versus paragraphs. It should then be remembered that reading ability depends on the child's level of skill and experience, the type size, illumination, available contrast, the density of the central scotoma or other field defects, and ocular-motor function.

The clinician does not strictly adhere to the acuity measurement obtained in such an assessment. However, the measurement provides a basis of comparison to that recorded on the eye report in that it adds to the data accumulated and contributes to an understanding of the visual functioning of the child. It also gives the parents, the teacher, and others insight into the child's response to high-contrast testing material in the home or at school, since the child may perform better in his or her natural environment. In reporting "acuity" results in an assessment report, it is just as meaningful to report the height or width of the smallest symbol identified, at a given distance, including lighting conditions, as it is to record 20/100. Copies of the charts are often attached so parents and others have a frame of reference within which to work.

Fields

Informal Assessment of Peripheral Fields. Two types of informal observations are used to assess the child's peripheral fields: confrontation and the nearpoint implications of the peripheral loss. To use confrontation, sit facing the child (approximately 35 centimeters [14 inches] away). Get the child to fixate on your nose by putting a sticker on your nose or blinking a penlight to hold the child's attention. Present a toy or light in different areas of the child's peripheral field (nasally, temporally, above, below and at angles) and ask the child to state when he or she sees the object. Watch for a shift in the child's eyes as a first indication that the object has been seen, since the child may be slow to respond verbally. You could also use a blinking light with additional light stationed at various positions. When the child fixes on the blinker, extinguish the light and switch on another light in the periphery. Stop the activity when the child is not fixating on your nose. Repeat the task, varying the distance and presentation of the object, and record the child's responses. Other modifications include using a parent to hold the child's attention, as well as to observe and record the child's response; attaching a small mirror to a wall at the child's eye level; and presenting the object or light while standing behind the child (see Chapter 6 for further discussion).

In evaluating nearpoint implications of peripheral loss, use an 8″ × 11″ "Word Search" puzzle of good contrast and mark the center letter with a large "X." Have the child fixate on the "X" and assess each eye separately. Bring in a contrasting object (possibly mounted on a pencil eraser) to record the information that the child is able to see at 16″ (40 cm). Vary the distance from the "X" and repeat with a new sheet, plotting areas of vision and blank areas. Record the size of the target used in each case. (A modified Amsler Grid is discussed in Chapter 6.) Another procedure is to scatter objects on a table surface and observe the child's ability to view and to count objects and the consistency in the areas that are omitted. Note the size and type of objects used and distance from the child's eyes.

Color Vision

Assessment of color vision may be formal, such as using the Farnsworth D-15 or Ishihara Plates, or informal, using color paint samples, blocks, cards, and yarn samples.

Procedure. Present each color separately in the following sequence: primary colors, secondary colors, and then shades of the colors. Record the child's ability to name the colors. If the child is unable to identify them, use two or more sets and ask the child to match his or her set to yours or to sort a shuffled group of cards. Record whether the child is relying on comparing contrast to identify or sort.

Lighting

Throughout the evaluation, the problem of lighting needs to be addressed. Lighting needs vary with each low vision individual in relation to the etiology of the eye condition and the task at hand. Factors that affect an individual's performance and lighting requirements include the type of task, the size of the material, the quality of the material, the viewing distance, the contrast of the material to the background environment, light adaptation, fatigue, and age. It is essential that the person has the proper level of illumination to minimize the possibility of visual fatigue and to promote optimal visual functioning. (See also Guth, 1971.)

In observing the child's environment and in direct assessment activities, it is important to note the following:

■ The type and source of lighting in the classroom or home (natural light from the windows or artificial light—flourescent or incandescent).

■ The placement and distribution of the source of light—overhead, the number of banks of lights, the location and number of windows, and the location of the room or rooms in the building (north, south, east, or west).

■ The level of brightness in the room. Is the room dark, dim, or bright? Consider the variability of light at different times of the day and with changes in weather. Observe whether the child is aware of the different levels of lighting. Does the child need to change his or her seat for more or less light? (Note the location of areas with better illumination.) Does the child prefer bright or dim light? For example, the child who has ocular albinism or aniridia seems to prefer lower levels of illumination because of sensitivity to light.

■ Brightness in the visual environment surrounding the task. Check such areas as the desk top; the chalkboard; the glossy quality of the classroom material (books, duplicated matter); the contrast between the color of the room, the floor, and the ceiling; and "hot spots" created by natural and artificial lighting.

■ Obstructions to lighting, such as room decorations, plants or mobiles.

■ The presence of glare should be eliminated or avoided because it causes visual fatigue, discomfort, and a decrease in the child's performance.

■ To determine whether glare is present, check the following:
Is the lamp shielded?
Where is a lamp placed?
Does the typoscope help functioning and decrease glare?
Are shades on the windows?
Are there shiny surfaces on the chalkboard, the floor, the desktop, the bookcase, and glass-covered pictures?
The quality of the paper: Is it glossy or matte?

Are charts, maps, or drawings hung near a window or close to a light source to create glare?

Does the teacher present demonstrations, show materials, and so forth near a window or with his or her back to a window? Such a practice requires the child to adapt to different levels of brightness.

■ Supplemental light sources. Where does the child place his or her light source? Ask the child to demonstrate where the light is placed and how it is positioned. The supplemental light source should not create a shadow from the arm while writing or reflect light directly into the child's eyes. Determine whether the increased light improves the contrast of materials, affects the child's reading speed, and lessens fatigue.

■ The child's adaptation time—in the building and outdoors. Does the child have difficulty going from a dim corridor to a bright classroom or when the lights are turned off for audiovisual presentations? Observe the child's adaptation time from light to dark areas and from dark to light areas.

■ The child's control of his or her individual lighting needs. Does the child wear a visor or sunglasses? Does the child move toward or away from a light source?

■ Materials commonly used in the classroom? (e.g., dittoes, workbooks).

■ The visual demands placed on the child, such as reading, writing, and fine discrimination.

In addition to observing the factors just mentioned, it is important to use a light meter to obtain specific readings of luminance. (These readings are explained in detail in Chapter 16). Measurements should be taken of the incident illumination and of the light source to task illumination (or light reflectance). Again, it may be valuable to assess the environmental lighting conditions at different times of the day and in different seasons because the illumination may vary significantly.

Visual Perception Skills

According to Barraga (1979), visual perception involves the processing, coding and interpretation of messages through the visual sense. It is a way of organizing the input so it will provide a data bank and basis on which future decisions and visual interpretations may be made. No one measure should be the sole determinant of the level of the child's development of visual perception. Observations of activities and the administration of standardized tools will help assess the level of the child's abilities in this area.

The development of visual perception is dependent on the areas of sensation, ocular-motor functioning, the child's intellectual capacity, and the child's experience, to name a few factors. One must determine, then, how the child has integrated the visual and motor experiences to derive meaning from his or her environment and how the child now responds to that environment.

An informal assessment, using activities and materials geared to the educational level of the child and considering the child's developmental age, the diagnosis of the visual loss, and earlier observations, "will provide an invaluable indication of the child's level of performance" (Efron & Duboff, 1976, p. 14). Table 3 contains a list of educational materials that may be used in observing the child's visual/perceptual abilities. This chapter cites a minimal number of materials that should be available to the functional vision specialist.

Table 3. Materials Useful in Assessing/Observing Visual Perceptual Functioning.

Stacking rings	Visual memory cards
Attribute blocks	Visual closure cards
Colored inch cubes and design cards	Spatial relationship cards
Parquetry (large and small) and design cards	Sequence cards (various levels)
Pegboard (beginning or primary, jumbo, small) and design cards	Pictured file (single object, with increasing complexity of background scenes, color, and black and white with various degrees of contrast, familiar to abstract)
Mitchell Wire Forms Kit	
Montessori materials (rods and graduated cylinders of various diameters)	DLM Eye-Hand Integration Exercises
Nuts and bolts	DLM Tracking Association Cards
Multivariant sequencing beads and cards	Single letter and sight word cards of various print sizes and styles
Lacing cards	Picture/word matching cards
Cuissenaire rods	Stencils
Nesting blocks	Coloring books
Shape cards (solid, outline, color, black, and white)	Mazes
	Dot-to-dot activities
Puzzles (form board, shape, flat wood, teacher made, or commercial object-picture-scene puzzles	Crayons, paints, pencils, markers
	Scissors
	Paste
	Paper

This portion of the assessment of functional vision serves as a screening tool of visual perception. In testing, it is important to record the child's approach to and analysis of the tasks (visual/tactual, systematic, organized, trial and error, and the like), eye-hand coordination; distance from the material; attention to shape, size, detail, and color; scanning abilities; and consistency of behavior with respect to earlier observations.

A sample of information activities to be observed in the child's performance of the activities follows:

■ The ability to perceive that an object, picture, or symbol has certain properties, such as color, size, shape, and position, and to note the similarities and differences between objects. Possible materials: inch cubes, attribute blocks, and discrimination flip books. Tasks: sorting, identifying, discriminating and sequencing.

■ The ability to copy a pattern or a design, specifically to imitate a three-dimensional pattern, to draw a line or a figure, and to copy a pattern on or off a card. Possible materials: inch cubes, parquetry, stringing beads, pegboard designs, and cards with lines, curves and shapes that can be copied.

■ The child's visual memory for objects, pictures, letters, numbers, and abstract symbols. Vary the complexity of tasks by increasing the number of items to be remembered and the span of time between the viewing and response or by requiring a motor response. Possible materials: visual memory cards, pictures, assorted objects, items to be copied from a chalkboard.

■ The child's ability to pick out a figure from the background, to note the spatial position of objects, and to identify overlapping figures. Possible materials: pictures with lines superimposed, pictures with perspective, parquetry, and puzzles.

■ Visual closure: the child's ablity to identify and recognize objects or symbols with incomplete representation. Possible materials: visual closure cards and dot-to-dot pictures.

■ Part/whole and whole/part relationships (piecing objects together to formulate a whole and analyzing the whole and breaking it down into parts). Possible materials: simple puzzles, pictures puzzles, and parquetry. Variation: requiring the child to complete an activity with and without a representation available for comparison.

■ Spatial awareness—the child's awareness of body parts in relation to the self or others, the body in relation to objects or pictorial representations, and an object in relation to another object. Possible materials: Hill Concept Inventory, Cratty "Body Image of the Blind Child," DLM Spatial Relations Cards.

■ Motor Skills. (1) General body movements and coordination (running, jumping, hopping, jumping jacks), (2) use of the body in space (running an obstacle course indoors or outdoors and the ability to walk on, along, or between a set path that has been delineated by ropes or other marked boundaries), and (3) eye-hand coordination: (a) gross use (throwing, catching, bouncing and catching, or throwing toward a target a bean bag or ball) and (b) fine-motor coordination (stacking blocks; placing blocks, beads, and the like in a container; stringing beads; doing puzzles, coloring; cutting; pasting; tracing; copying forms; drawing; and working with clay).

If it is determined from the evaluation that a formal assessment of perception and development is needed, the child should be referred to an educational, psychological, or optometric specialist. Some of the tests the specialist may use, and with which the instructor should be familiar, include the following:

Visual Efficiency Scale [American Printing House for the Blind (APH), 1965]. The purpose of the test is to assess the level to which each child has developed visual discrimination skills.

Diagnostic Assessment Procedure [from the Program to Develop Efficiency in Visual Functioning]. This procedure is used to evaluate visual development and skills in each of eight areas: the response to light and moving objects, movement of the self in a defined space, imitation of perceived movement and action, and discrimination and recognition of objects pictures, and symbols of decreasing size and increasing complexity. [APH, 1980].

Motor Free Visual Perception Test [Academic Therapy Press, 1972]. This test was designed for use by teachers, psychologists, and educational specialists who require a reliable and valid measure of a child's ability to process visual perceptions that is not influenced by the child's ability or inability to perform motor skills (see Hammill, 1972).

Developmental Test of Visual Motor Integration [Follett Educational Corporation, 1967]. As Beery and Buktenica (1967) noted, this test was "devised as a measure of the degree to which visual perception and motor behavior are integrated in young children" (p. 12).

Bender Visual Gestalt Test [American Orthopsychiatric Association, 1946]. This test was originally designed to evaluate visual-motor coordination and visual-motor integration. It provides an untimed, less structured method of observing a child's approach to a visual-motor test.

Diagnostic Reading Scales [McGraw Hill, 1972]. This series of tests is intended to provide a standardized evaluation of oral and silent reading skills and auditory comprehension. It has been found useful as a criterion referenced measure noting performance as print size decreases.

Slingerland Prereading Screening Procedure [Educator's Publishing Service, 1968]. This test was designed to note the strengths and weaknesses in visual, auditory, and kinesthetic functioning. It is primarily a screening device.

EDUCATIONAL MEDIA

Observations about educational media should be adapted, as necessary, to various grade levels and the visual demands placed on the learner. If the media are not observable during the low vision instructor's visit, they may need to be assessed on a one-to-one basis in a structured assessment.

Distance Tasks

Distance tasks should be observed in relation to the child's seating arrangement and the modifications needed. For the following media, note the child's distance from the material, the size of the material, the actual and required contrast, the size of image projected and the actual size (e.g., overlay copy), the position from which the material is viewed (above the chalkboard, near the window, and so forth), the quality of the material and its visual demands (e.g., to copy material), and the frequency of its use by the teacher.

1. Charts and wall maps.

2. Chalkboard material presented in manuscript and cursive, the size of the numbers and letters (actual and required); the areas of the chalkboard that are difficult to view; the child's ability to transfer information from the board; and the child's method for doing so.

3. Audiovisual materials: (a) an overhead projector (note the type of

overlays—diagrams, outlines, materials to be copied or read—the color of the ink, and the spacing of the material), and (b) a television set (note the size of the screen and whether it is a black-and-white set).

4. Demonstrations.

5. Environment (the child's ability to locate and read room numbers, labels, and the numbers on lockers and combinations, as well as the ability to locate objects, learning stations, and so forth in the environment).

Near/Intermediate Tasks

The low vision instructor should obtain the materials available to and used by the teacher and children in the school. Interpretations of observations should be made in relation to the child's eye condition, level of visual efficiency, the visual demands of the setting or grade, the child's learning style, the lighting, and the quality of materials.

Reading. It is important to assess the child's reading ability in nearpoint, as well as in intermediate and distance tasks. Some of the tasks involved include reading textbooks, reading materials that are specific to various subjects, reading reference materials, and reading miscellaneous types of materials delineated later.

In relation to *textbooks*, note the type style; the print size; the spacing between letters, words, and lines; the darkness and uniformity of inking; the color of the paper and ink; and the contrast between the ink and background (especially in primary books, diagrams, and maps). (The text can be compared to the tables in Chapter 6.) Note the child's posture, position of head, use of low vision aids and the prescription, and the lighting. Have the child read silently or orally for at least ten minutes and record how many words per minute the child can read. Does the child tire? What is the child's accommodative ability and its duration? Do the child's eyes tear? Are they red? Does the child complain of a headache? Has one eye slipped in one direction or another? What is the child's scanning ability? Does the child move his or her eyes, head, or material? Does the child use his or her finger as a line guide while reading? Note the areas of difficulty (loses place, skips lines, omits words or lines, reverses letters). Does the child understand what he or she is reading? Does the child comprehend the inkprint format: the organizing of the book, and its various parts (e.g., glossary, table of contents, index), type styles (bold face, italics), paragraph identation, and columns. Would the child benefit from nonoptical aids? If the child is using nonoptical aids, observe the amount of energy expended on the task of reading versus the reading itself. The system used may need changing.

In the spring of each school year, textbooks for the next grade level should be previewed with the child to determine whether the materials are the appropriate size, contrast, and quality. The determination of the appropriate print size depends on the child's visual acuity, visual field, type and power of the aid or prescription used, reading experience, reading rate, motivation, the bulk of material to be read, visual fatigue experienced, and additional handicaps. Based on all these factors, it may be necessary to consider low-vision aids, large print, recordings, or reader services for different subjects (these need to be ordered in the spring to assure delivery).

In observing the child's facility in reading *English and foreign languages*, note the amount of reading material, the child's ability to see accents and punctuation, and the child's library and reference skills. For *mathematics*, observe the child's ability to see and construct geometric drawings, metric measurements, and angle measures; to read and construct graphs, and tables; to set up problems properly and to see exponents, fractions, and decimals. In *science*, note the child's ability to read labels and formulas, to use measuring instruments, to log data in lab book, to dissect, to use a microscope, and to use safety procedures when completing independent experiments.

With *reference materials,* review the student's ability to use the dictionary, the encyclopedia, magazines, newspapers, and paperbacks to obtain needed information. Note the title of the book and the print size, the child's ability to see guide words and accents and to read headlines and want ads, and the child's knowledge of the inkprint format to assess the material.

With *miscellaneous* materials (dittoes—purple, black—mimeographed materials, workbooks, diagrams, maps, and graphs) evaluate their quality, the size of print, whether the material was typewritten or handwritten and its frequency of use in class. Is there adequate space in the material on which to write answers? Is the contrast improved with a filter? Is additional light required? Does the child use a prescription and low vision aid with the material?

Writing. Using the child's classroom paper and writing tool (pen or pencil), ask the child to write his or her name, the alphabet in manuscript and cursive, and upper and lower case letters, and numbers up to 10. It also may be helpful to dictate a sentence or have the child write a short story. Note the size, position, and spacing of the letters, words, and numbers. What is the grip of the tool used for writing? Is the hand motion smooth or shaky? What was the quality of the samples of work provided by the teacher? What is the child's working distance from the page? Have the child copy a mathematics problem from a book and a sentence from the chalkboard. How does the child transfer the material—letter by letter, word by word, or phrase by phrase? Is there a difference in the child's ability to transfer material near to near, as opposed to distance to near? How does the child keep his or her place? Again, note the spacing and the size, shape, and position of letters and numbers.

Assess the child's use of other writing papers available from the American Printing House for the Blind in Louisville, Kentucky, as well as a variety of pens and pencils to determine which tools provide the child with the optimum contrast, line size, and fluid movement. Note specifically what tools the child prefers (e.g., a BIC banana), the color of ink or the number of the lead pencil, and the width of the line produced.

Use of Low Vision Aids
Low vision aids should be observed in the context of the school environ-

ment. List all the aids, near and distance, used now and in the past. If the aids no longer are used, discuss why they are not used (cumbersome system? cosmesis? lack of training?) Such information will be useful for the team members. Observe and record which tasks the aids are used for, the size of the print or objects viewed, the child's ability to track and scan, the placement of the aid, the distance at which the material is viewed, grip, and the condition of the aids and how they are cared for. Does the child use or would the child benefit from any or all of the following nonoptical aids: (1) aids to control illumination (goose neck lamps, dimmers and filters), (2) aids to control contrast (papers, pens, typoscopes, filters), (3) aids to control physical comfort (reading stand, large print), and (4) tactual aids and educational models.

Observations of Special Classes

Special classes require different types of tasks and involve different environments in which to observe the child's functional use of vision, fine and gross motor skills, mobility, and levels of independence or dependence (see New Hampshire Educational Services for the Visually Handicapped, 1979). It is important to observe and record the child's approach to the task, the visual demands (e.g., manuals to be used, writing requirements, and near, intermediate, and distance tasks). The observations will be useful to the instructors, parents, vocational rehabilitation personnel, low vision staff, and the orientation and mobility instructor.

Industrial Arts. Describe the environment of the industrial arts class, including the ceiling height, the organization of materials, the obstacles, and the lighting.

In relation to the visual working distance, note whether all tasks are performed within a certain distance or whether the distance varies with each specific task and the size of an object. Also note the visual demands (reading, writing, and so forth). Observations of lighting should include the general lighting conditions, the variation in lighting from one area to another, the availability or need for additional lighting, and the presence of glare surfaces. To determine contrast and color note whether the tools are marked, whether floor markings are easily seen, whether the child is able to see and identify colors, whether increased contrast or any visual or tactual modifications are needed.

Other observations to be made in the industrial arts class involve the child's mobility, specific level of independence, and application of safety procedures and the teacher's instructional style. In relation to mobility, note whether the child is able to avoid obstacles, identify work areas, obtain his or her own materials, and see markings. Can the child orient himself or herself? Does the child use a visual or tactual approach? Also is the child able to complete a task in the specified time? Does the instructor give instructions orally or visually? Is audiovisual equipment used?

Home Economics. In the home economics class observe the following tasks: (1) reading a recipe on a box, in a book, or on recipe cards, (2) measur-

127

ing, (3) using the stove and oven (including identification of markings), (4) using other appliances, (5) using a sewing machine, (6) threading a needle, and (7) following a pattern.

Music. In the music class, is the child able to see and follow the director? Can the child read music? Note the distance required, the difference in the sizes of the score and text, and the illumination.

Physical Education. In physical education, indicate whether the child participates in activities. Which activities (indoor or outdoor) does the child prefer? Does the child use playground and physical education equipment and can he or she see the instructors and follow directions? Is the child able to identify boundaries and markings?

Business and Typing Courses. For business and typing courses, indicate the special formats required, and the timing of activities. Observe the child's ability to copy from a text (note size, distance, use of stand), to use a dictaphone, to operate office machines, to file, and to log data in ledgers and keep books.

SUMMARY AND RECOMMENDATIONS

The summary and recommendations section is the culmination of all the observations and formal and informal measures of assessing the child's use of vision. It should include a review of the available medical information, a translation of the eye condition into practical language, data gathered and observations made during the assessment, and materials used. The conclusions, if any, should cite examples to show how they were arrived at.

Recommendations for additional service and evaluations, modifications, programs needed, vision stimulation, and so forth should be made in accordance with the clinical recommendations and the information gathered on the child's functional use of vision. Such a report will provide useful information for the child, the family, educational personnel, other service providers, and members of the low vision team. If appropriate, the teacher may accompany the child to the clinical examination to help in the assessment or to ask questions about the child's functioning and visual status. The low vision instructor is available for consultation regarding the assessment of functional vision.

It is important to stress to those involved in the provision of services to the child that the assessment is ongoing and it is everyone's responsibility to stimulate and assess the child's continual use of vision in interacting with the environment.

SAMPLE REPORT

The following assessment of functional vision took two full days to complete plus the time involved in obtaining the initial intake materials before the first visit. This amount of time is not uncommon when assessing a new child. An assessment often will require that the instructor make more than one visit depending on the instructor's and the child's schedules, child's attention span, age, severity of visual loss, and fatigue. In this case, two consecutive days were used because of the great travel distance. The time needed for each task was as follows: (1) observation in the classroom and in special classes, 4 hours; (2) interview and consultation with the teachers, 2½ hours; (3) interview and consultation with the parents, 2 hours; (4) consultation with the principal, 1½ hours; (5) direct work with the child, 3 hours; and (6) report writing, 7 hours. It is often difficult for administrators and supervisors of programs and personnel to understand the need for a lengthy assessment and the instructor's use of time. It is hoped that this report will help them to understand the need for such a thorough workup.

Name: _____CT_____   **School:** _____

Date of birth _7/16/69_   **Grade:** _____

Address: _____   **Dates of evaluation:** May 29, 30, 1980

_____   **Date of report:** June 1, 1980

Eye condition: (according to the last available report from an eye specialist, 11/7/74): Albinism, photophobia (light sensitivity), nystagmus (pendular eye movement).

Visual Acuity (Distance)

	Without Correction	*With Glasses*
O.D. (right eye)	20/320-	20/200
O.S. (left eye)	20/320-	20/200
O.U. (both eyes together)	20/320-	20/200

Visual Acuity (Near)

	Without Correction	*With Glasses*	*With a Low Vision Aid*
O.D. (right eye)	10 pt. print	10 pt.	6 pt. print
O.S. (left eye)	10 pt. print	10 pt.	6 pt. print
O.U. (both eyes together)	10 pt. print	10 pt.	6 pt. print

Evaluation

CT was referred to this itinerant teacher for an assessment of her functional vision by her classroom teacher. I observed her at school on May 29 and May 30, 1980. The first observation was done in the classroom. The room was on the lowest level of the school; it was beige tone in color and contained two banks of flourescent lights and a back wall of windows. CT's desk was the second seat in the second row near the blackboard (located to her left). The room had a greal deal of light in the afternoon but did not appear to present

129

any difficulties. (A visit was also paid to next year's classroom for which specific recommendations are made later in this report.)

CT was able to maneuver around the classroom. During spelling, she used a large-print book without the reading glasses. (She stated later that periodically she uses her reading correction along with large print to see it more easily.) She followed along and answered questions correctly when called on. She did not pick up the material to view, but rested her chin on her hands (this may cause neck fatigue after a while). Head bobbing was noted at nearpoint tasks. She was three to six inches from her test paper when using her reading glasses.

CT was seen individually, and a variety of activities and materials were used in the assessment. From the Feinbloom Distance Test Chart for the Partially Sighted, the following information was obtained:

		With a
Distance Acuity at 10 feet	*With Correction*	*Low Vision Aid*
O.D. (right eye)	10/80 + (1½″ high numbers)	10/25-2 (½″)
O.S. (left eye)	10/80	
O.U. (both eyes)	10/60 (1″ high numbers)	

With her glasses on she was able to read the clock at 10 feet.

From the Lighthouse Near Acuity Chart, the following data were gathered:

Nearpoint Acuity (40 cm or 16″)	*Without Correction*	*With Regular Glasses*	*With Reading Glasses*
O.D. (right eye)	3M	—	—
O.S. (left eye)	5M (squinting observed) (½″ letter)	—	—
O.U. (both eyes)	3M (¼″ letter)	2M at 40 cm (1/8″) .8M at 4 cm (approx. 1/16″)	.8 M at 4cm (approx. 1/16″)

The Sloan Continuous Reading Text Cards were also used. With both eyes open and regular glasses, CT read 2.5M print and 2M print at 8 cm. When she reached the 1.5M print, she changed to her reading correction and read it at 11-12 cm. The 1M size also was read at 11-12 cm. CT appeared to be using her right eye most of the time for reading. She had little difficulty reading the smaller print sizes for five minutes, but after five minutes her eyes began to jump lines. The charts and testing materials, which have good spacing and excellent contrast, were used only to get a rough estimate of visual functioning. Samples of the Sloan cards are attached. CT reported she could read up to an hour at a time depending on lighting, contrast, and the size of spacing of the print. By covering one eye, she decreases the chance of jumping from line to line.

CT tracked by using a finger puppet. At midline, her left eye turned in while the right eye followed across. Midline, vertical, and circular tracking were smooth. CT was also able to shift her gaze quickly and accurately from left to right, diagonally and vertically.

The Visual Efficiency Scale, which CT completed in about 25 minutes, showed that her working distance averaged four to five inches with her reading glasses and three inches for smaller items. When a difficult item came up, CT shielded her eyes and rechecked her work, stating, "It took me a little longer." Also, she covered her right eye to look closely at small items. CT did not show inadequacies in any discrimination skills. Furthermore, the Motor Free Visual Perception Test did not indicate difficulties in that area. Also, CT did not have any problem in reproducing parquetry designs, although she initially placed the shapes on the design to verify them.

CT was given a page from the Perceptual Communication Skills, a listening series, as a way for this assessor to take an informal look at her ability to remember a given direction. I think she would benefit from work in this area to focus her auditory attention on what is being asked of her, since she did not look through all the choices before making a selection.

Adaptation to Changes in Lighting

CT and I went outside on a very bright day. She wore her photo-gray lenses, which darkened within three to five minutes. Although she grabbed on to the wall to give her a reference point and a solid surface for getting down the stairs she did not require assistance in moving around. On returning to the building, CT required a few minutes for her eyes to adjust and then proceeded down the stairs unaided. During a fire drill, a fellow student or teacher could assist her through the sighted guide technique, but this would be necessary only in an emergency. She maneuvers around the school well.

Evaluation of School Materials

Mathematics Book (regular print). CT was able to read problems that had been printed on a dark-green background using classroom lighting as the only source. She identified decimal points as they occurred, correctly interpreted a bar graph, and was able to read fractions and degrees on a small pictured protractor with her reading glasses at a distance of two inches from the page.

Social Studies (regular print). CT did not seem to have difficulty reading the material for short periods. Her working distance was 3½ to 4 inches with her reading glasses. She read quickly. Lengthy assignments would then be appropriate to listen to on tape. If maps are not cluttered and the boundaries and print are clear, CT should be able to handle them. She was able to read a map with one-eighth inch print and located capitals and rainfall amounts. CT functions best when materials have good contrast and even spacing. Visual clutter in materials and on the page may present problems for her periodically.

Paper. CT did not have difficulty using fine blue-line school writing paper. Bold-line paper has been ordered from the American Printing House for the Blind in case she prefers to use it.

Thorndike Junior Dictionary (regular print). CT was asked to look up a word and rewrite the definition. Although she was able to locate and read the definition, the print was small. She covered her right eye to scan along the line of print. A Merriam Webster large-print dictionary in a single volume is recommended.

Music Lessons. CT was observed during a clarinet lesson. She used a music stand, wore her reading glasses and read the music five to six inches from the page. As scores get more crowded and the print is smaller, large-print music may help considerably. Now, "punctuation" marks (such as a staccato mark or a slur) should be darkened or enlarged with a contrasting color so they will not be confused with quarter notes. CT should tell the music teacher to darken these marks or do so herself if necessary.

Recommendations

Psychoeducational Evaluation. Given the limited amount of information provided by CT's last educational placement and the absence of an itinerant teacher or consultant, it is recommended that a psychoeducational evaluation be done for CT by a psychologist with expertise in evaluating visually handicapped children. This evaluation should be completed as early in the school year as possible so baseline information will be available to the parents and the school that will indicate CT's best learning style, current level of functioning, and the modifications that may be needed. I think that this next school year will require preparation for an increasing amount of work in content areas, study skills, organizational skills, and so forth prior to CT's entrance into junior high school. A joint funding arrangement for a complete psychological evaluation should be pursued by the director of special education and the state supervisor/educational counselor for this upstate county. In the past, Dr. J. provided thorough assessments to several students in this area and informed the parents and the school of the results of his evaluations, which have been helpful in educational planning.

Educational Materials. The Division of Eye Care should provide the following materials for CT's use next year: (1) yellow filters (folder covers), (2) boldline paper (APH No. 1-0486 or smaller), (3) an APH tape recorder, (4) tapes for social studies and science, (5) blank staff paper for music, (6) a catalog for large-print music (to be provided to the music teacher), (7) a full series of blank large-print world maps, and (8) large-print copies of achievement tests (the school should forward information as soon as possible to Mr. A.'s office about the tests used, the form, and so forth. In addition the school should order a dictionary (available from G. K. Hall Co., 70 Lincoln Street,

Boston, Massachusetts 02111) and mail it to this assessor to be modified. The school should also provide the physical education teacher with *Movement Without Sight* by L. E. Kratz (available from Peek Publications, Box 11065, Palo Alto, California 94306.

Preferential Seating. CT should be allowed to sit in the first row, center seat, to see board work, filmstrips and the like. She should move up closer for demonstrations. CT was able to identify a 2-inch number at 10 feet. She should be able to see 2½ to 3-inch letters or words, if evenly spaced and clearly written, at 8–10 feet. These distances can be verified by having CT read from the board.

Glare. Glare should be avoided on all surfaces because CT is highly light sensitive. The shades on the first few banks of windows should be drawn to cut out extra light, and more shades should be drawn as needed (especially in the afternoon and during the winter when light is reflected off the snow). The teacher should not stand near a window or stand with his or her back to the window because that will require CT to look toward an area with a great deal of light.

Classroom Management. The following suggestions refer to various aspects of CT's work in the classroom.

- The teacher should speak as he or she writes on the board so CT and other students may get the information auditorially and visually.

- CT should have extra storage space near her desk for large-print books, a tape recorder, tapes, and the like. She should be helped to organize the materials on her desk so they are easily accessible.

- CT should remember to plug in the tape recorder overnight several times a week to maintain the charge on the battery pack.

- CT should receive the first copy of a purple ditto. To increase contrast, CT should place the yellow acetate folder cover over one copy and write the answers on a second copy of the worksheet. If she is to cut out any materials, CT may need to have the borders darkened with a wide black marker. Contrast is important when working with the visually handicapped.

- Large-print blank maps are being ordered. It would benefit CT to do several mapping exercises.

- If a great deal of reading is being assigned on a given night, perhaps CT should be assigned alternate numbers of mathematics problems rather than unnecessary drill work (if she demonstrates competence) to lessen her visual fatigue.

- Near-vision tasks should be alternated with distance-vision or oral-auditory tasks to lessen CT's fatigue. A child with nystagmus has difficulty holding a focus. If a test follows her reading for 30 minutes, the test could be dictated and CT could answer orally. A distance-vision task could be assigned after board work, a filmstrip, or other audiovisual presentations.

- CT should be encouraged to suggest or make her own modifications as appropriate; she needs to voice the difficulties she may have, but not to overindulge in this practice. Perhaps the teacher and CT could meet after the first month or so to see how things are working out.

▪ CT should be alert to assignments given in class and look them over when the teacher assigns them, to anticipate any questions she may have before she leaves school. In her assignment pad, she should note the assignments given. (Perhaps the teacher also could list the assignments in the corner of the blackboard).

▪ Time limits should be suspended on achievement tests because it takes about twice the time for a visually handicapped child to use vision. (This time span does not change the scores.) Also, more than one session should be considered because fatigue can lower the scores. Any such modifications in procedures should be noted. Large-print achievement tests can be ordered through Mr. A.'s office.

Physical Education. The book *Movement Without Sight* offers concrete suggestions for adapting physical education to the needs of the visually handicapped. CT should participate in the leadup skills but will be unable to see a small fast-moving object. She can participate in soccer if she plays a back position. She has volleyball skills, especially if a beach ball is used. Contrast can be added to materials with light tape, providing a beeper on a basket, and so forth.

Service Needs
CT should use a notebook for study. The notebook should contain pocket separators in which she can place worksheets each day after dating them, and the notebook should be divided into subject areas, each filled with looseleaf paper. Each homework paper should be dated and have her name on it in case the notebook is ever dropped. CT should list on a pad the subject, pages, and additional information necessary to do an assignment. When she completes an assignment, she should check it off. As far as the classroom routine goes, CT needs to anticipate classroom activities. As subjects change, she should have materials ready, her notebook out, and her assignment pad handy. The resource teacher may need to observe the classroom to ensure a carryover. Also, CT should request a makeup test or the receipt of assignments for days she has been absent (a regular classroom responsibility); she should complete this makeup work within two days.

Study Skills
CT should be helped to acquire the following study skills:

Knowledge of inkprint format: function of the table of contents, index, and glossary; use of boldprint to help locate answers to questions and of italics.

Answering questions: knowledge of what a question is asking for (who? what? when? where? and why?); such skills can be enhanced through the use of the Barnell Loft or Dexter and Westbrook *Specific Skill Series.*

Use of time: how to determine which homework assignments to do first and how to finish the work (doing either the easiest or longest assignment first).

Taking tests: CT should be sure to survey all choices before making a selection.

Reading questions: CT should read questions (in social studies, science, reading, or English) before reading or listening to a selection or assignment so she develops critical reading and listening skills and learns to cue into answers and the main ideas more readily. For example, the teacher should observe whether CT cues in to italicized and vocabulary words, the reasons why a certain event took place (how the facts fit together), the results of a certain event, important names and dates, and topic sentences.

Listening Skills: to improve CT's skills in understanding directions that are given auditorily and visually. The following series is recommended to enhance her skills in this area: *Perceptual Communication Skills Series,* Level 2, workbook and teachers handbook, by Dr. Selma Herr (available from: Edward S. Perry Distributors, 231 Norfolk Street, Walpole, Massachusetts 02081).

Recommendations regarding Low Vision

CT may require a special low vision evaluation. She needs glasses that have side and top shields and that cut out the infrared rays to lessen fatigue caused by glare, squinting or tearing. Since CT already has a telescope, the clip portion could be removed to allow her to use the telescope more efficiently in boardwork. It should be determined if the telescope is giving CT enough clarity or whether a 6–8X hand-held telescope should be considered as an alternative. A 6–8X hand-held telescope would permit her to follow visually a math or science problem, watch filmstrips, see material on an overhead projector or the like.

An in-service session should be held next year for the sixth grade. In that session, the American Foundation for the Blind's film *Not Without Sight* or the *Good Start* series of films could be shown and vision simulators and samples of low vision aids could be demonstrated to educate the child on the needs of the visually handicapped. In the afternoon, a similar in-service session should be given for the teachers.

Recommendations for the Home

CT should have a clear, quiet area in which to do her homework. She should have a set time to do her homework every night, preferably after dinner, so she has a chance to play or relax after school. She should do her homework on her own as much as possible, crossing off each assignment in her assignment book when it is completed. At the opening of the next school year, CT should have the following school supplies, (1) a three-ring notebook, (2) black pens, (3) No. 1 pencils (dark, soft lead), (4) an assignment pad, (5) a pencil case (to place in the three-ring binder), and (6) notebook dividers that have pockets (to be used for her worksheets and papers). These supplies are necessary for the resource room to begin addressing organizational and study skills. In addition, when she goes outside for physical education activities or recess, CT should be prepared with a hat, visor, or sunglasses and perhaps a light jacket or long-sleeved shirt that will help protect her from the sun's rays.

Summary

CT is an intelligent girl with a number of visual and intellectual strengths. In the next school year, she will need to improve her organizational, study, and personal management skills in preparation for increased academic demands. It is hoped that CT will become more independent and be given the room to grow both at home and at school. She is a child first, one who happens to have a visual handicap, and needs to be encouraged to develop to her fullest and to understand that everyone has successes and failures. I think she will benefit from a fairly structured environment. However, I do not think that she needs large-print material for all her subjects, although in the next school year, I recommend that taped materials be given further consideration.

This itinerant teacher remains available for consultation and to answer questions regarding this report.

References

Barraga, N. C. *Teacher's guide for the development of visual learning and utilization of low vision.* Louisville, KY.: American Printing House for the Blind, 1970.

Barraga, N.C. *Visual Handicaps and Learning.* Belmont, Calif.: Wadsworth, 1976.

Barraga, N.C., Collins, M., and Hollis, J. Development of Efficiency in Visual Functionning: A Literature Analysis *Journal of Visual Impairment and Blindness,* 1977, **71**(9), 387–391.

Barraga, N.C., & Collins, M. Development of efficiency in visual functioning: An evaluation process. *Journal of Visual Impairment and Blindness,* 1980, **74**(3), 93-96.

Barraga, N.C., & Collins, M. Development of efficiency in visual functioning: Rationale for a comprehensive program. *Journal of Visual Impairment and Blindness,* 1979, **73**(4), 121-126.

Beery, K. E., & Buktenica, N. A. *Developmental test of visual motor integration.* Chicago: Follet Educational Corp., 196 .

Brown, J., & Brown, L. Picture visual acuity cards: House, apple, umbrella. *National Newspatch,* 1980, **5**(1), 1-2.

Efron, M., & Duboff, B. R. *A vision guide for teachers of deaf-blind children.* Raleigh, N.C.: South Atlantic Regional Center for Services to Deaf-Blind Children, 1976.

Guth, S. Light and lighting for the visually handicapped. In E. Rex (ed.) *Proceedings of a special study institute: Methods and procedures for training low-vision skills.* Normal, Ill., Illinois State University, 1971.

Hammer, E. *Interaction of assessment and intervention for visually handicapped infants and preschool children.* Dallas: South Central Regional Center for Services to Deaf/Blind Children, University of Texas, 1976.

Hammill, D. *Motor free visual perception test (MVPT) manual*. Novato, Calif.: Academic Therapy Press, 1972.

Harley, R., & Allen, L. *Visual impairment in the schools*. Springfield, Ill.: Charles C. Thomas, 1977.

Holmes, R. History, philosophy, and research concerned with training techniques for utilization of low vision. In E. Rex (ed.). *Proceedings of a special study institute: Methods and procedures for training low-vision skills*. Normal, Ill.: Illinois State University, 1971.

Langley, B. and Dubose, R. Functional Vision Screening for Severely Handicapped Children. *New Outlook for the Blind*. 1976, **70**(8), 346–350.

New Hampshire Educational Services for the Visually Handicapped. *Functional Vision Assessment of School Age Children*. Nashua, N.H.: Author, 1978-79.

O'Brien, R. *Alive, aware, a person*. Rockville, Md.: Montgomery County Public Schools, 1976.

Scholl, G., & Schnur, R. *Measures of psychological, vocational and educational functioning in the blind and visually handicapped*. New York: American Foundation for the Blind, 1976.

Spungin, S. J., & Swallow, R. Psychoeducational assessments: Role of the psychologist to the teacher of the visually handicapped. *Education of the Visually handicapped*, 1975, 7(3), 67-75.

Swallow, R. *Assessment for visually handicapped children and youth*. New York: American Foundation for the Blind, 1977.

Swallow, R., Mangold, S.; & Mangold, P. *Informal assessment of developmental skills for visually handicapped children*. New York: American Foundation for the Blind, 1978.

Section III
Clinical Services

This section covers the activities, evaluations, and examinations that occur in the clinical setting. After data from the preliminary assessment are obtained, it is the responsibility of the clinical staff to provide diagnostic data to support or question these environmental observations and test data. Chapters 8, 9, and 10 include basic information about which services should be provided in and what data can be extracted from a well-organized clinical program. The discussion on aids gives the instructor a working knowledge of the parameters that a clinician considers when prescribing. This insight will help the instructor to develop an assessment or training program that is integrated more effectively with the clinical program. It must be emphasized that the protocols discussed in these chapters are based on this author's personal experiences (and biases) with a multidisciplinary program and may need slight modifications in different settings.

CHAPTER 8

Clinical Examination of Visually Impaired Individuals

RANDALL T. JOSE, O.D.

This chapter reviews the major components of a clinical examination. It gives the instructor an idea of what to expect from a low vision examination. It will be helpful in evaluating the effectiveness of a clinician and the clinician's understanding of the functional approach to low-vision rehabilitation in an interdisciplinary program.

This chapter reviews the main components of the clinical low vision examination performed by the ophthalmologist or optometrist (hereafter referred to as the clinician). It includes the social service and clinical history, as well as the examination techniques. It gives the low vision instructor an understanding of the basic low vision examination. Although the actual tests will vary from clinician to clinician and from patient to patient, almost every patient should benefit from such a clinical assessment.

The goals of the low vision examination are to improve the patient's use of residual vision and to help the patient to cope better with the demands of ordinary life and, hence, be independent. The examination should be success-oriented. That is, the typical low vision patient does not have to be convinced that his or her vision is poor; rather, the patient has to be convinced that he or she has vision worth using. The clinician and clinical staff must reinforce this idea throughout the testing procedures.

The desired end of the examination is the prescription of a low vision aid or services that will benefit the patient to some degree. Not every examination will result in a dramatic prescription and a feeling of "restored sight." The successful use of a low vision aid requires a hard and tedious program of training and often can be a frustrating and boring experience for the patient, the clinician, and other professionals involved. However, most cases are rewarding.

The examination should be done in a minimum of three visits (1) to assure that the pathological and refractive conditions are stable, (2) to avoid fatigue in the patients, and (3) to provide time for interdisciplinary communication among the clinician and the low vision instructors. During the first visit, patients should be instructed to bring their present optical aids, samples of materials they wish to read or work with, a list of tasks they wish to do, and a list of questions to which they desire answers. The low vision instructor can help make the examination successful by reminding patients to bring these materials to the clinic and by describing the low vision examination the patients will be receiving. Preliminary evaluations of the patients' present uses of aids and vision at home, in school, and at work are valuable. The clinician and instructor must discuss the results of these evaluations before the examination.

Every examiner will have his or her techniques for examining patients. However, it may be helpful for the low vision instructor to have an overview of a typical examination sequence. If the individual examiner varies from this model, the low vision instructor can question the variation. The discussion that follows can help the low vision instructor and the examiner to understand better the examination process. It is important to note that it is not mandatory to do every test on every individual. Knowing why a clinician eliminates a procedure from the examination will help the low vision instructor develop a better understanding of the importance of specific tests to the final prescription and subsequent training sessions. If an examiner deviates significantly from this model and offers no explanation or is defensive about the questions asked, it may be advisable to consult with another examiner. The components of a typical examination are (1) the case history, (2) ocular health, (3) acuities, (4) fields, (5) color vision, (6) refraction, (7) binocular vision, and (8) magnification. Each area to be tested or examined will be discussed separately.

CASE HISTORY

The case history is the first interaction the clinician has with the patient. The history must be extensive but it does not have to be done only by the clinician. A list of questions routinely asked of low vision patients before actually involving them in testing procedures is provided. This information may be gathered by the low vision instructor, a social worker, the clinician, a technician, or any combination of people. Some low vision instructors will gather most of these data; others do not have the time. It is not important who collects the data; what is important is that the data were collected and are available to the clinician before extensive testing is done. Often, the clinician will repeat questions already asked, because confirmation of answers is important. Whatever information is obtained before the examination should then be reviewed with the patient by the clinician. The case history should investigate the following broad areas:

- Family living situations.
- An explanation of the examination.

- Financial or transportation problems.
- Major concerns of the patient and the low vision instructor.
- Medical visual history (impairment).
- Present utilization of residual vision (handicap).

In relation to the patient's living situation, the case history should include the patient's marital status (whether married, single, separated, divorced, or widowed), number of dependents, sources of financial support (should be verified), and the involvement of other agencies.

Questions pertaining to the medical visual history are as follows:

When did you first notice trouble with your vision: OD, and OS? _____

What did you do when the problem first arose? _____

What is your understanding of the nature of your visual condition? _____

Have you had any operations or do you take any medications for your eyes?

_____

Does your vision fluctuate?_____

Do you ever have pain in your eyes? If so, what type of pain, how often, and in which eye? _____

Does anyone in your family have trouble with sight? If so, is the problem cataracts____, glaucoma____, diabetes____, or vascular____ or _____?

Do you have any other medical problems? _____

Do you take any medications? _____

Are you interested in genetic counseling? _____

Questions involving the patient's education should include the last grade completed in school, any special training (if the patient is still receiving special training, the nature of the progress, name of the teacher/counselor, the patient's favorite subjects, whether the level of vision hinders the patient in school, and the patient's educational/vocational plans). Job-related questions are as follows: Are you working, and at what? When did you last work, and at what? Did you retire because of your vision? Recreational activities should be probed as well. The patient should be asked about hobbies and whether he or she reads and makes use of radio services, talking books, braille, or large-print books. Other questions in this regard include these: Is there some activity you once enjoyed that your vision loss now prohibits? What is your greatest frustration in relation to your visual loss? What are your expectations from being seen at this clinic?

The following clinical questions are phrased for the patient. However, many of these questions may be answered more accurately by parents, a spouse, or other professionals. It is also informative to compare a teacher's answers to a student's, a parent's to a child's, and so forth.

How old is your prescription? _____ Does it still help? _____

Do you have any other optical aids? If so, where and when did you get them?_____

Can you read print with or without a prescription? What size print?_____

What gives you the most trouble with reading? _____

How long has it been since you read print?

Do you watch television? If so, is the television in color or in black and white? _____

Do you see the television or listen to it?_____

Do you have trouble with color perception? _____

Does bright sun or glare bother you? _____

Do you do anything special on sunny days? _____

Do you see better or sunny or rainy days?_____

Do you use any special lighting at home? If so, what? _____

How long does it take for your eyes to adjust to changes in lighting?_____

Do you bump into things more on one side than the other? _____

Do you have trouble seeing street signs and bus numbers? _____

Do you take public transportation? _____

Do you travel alone? _____ Do you have difficulty crossing streets? __

Do you move slower in unfamiliar territory? _____

Do you have problems with steps and curbs? _____

Do you have difficulty getting around your own home?_____

What causes you the most trouble with mobility? _____

Is there some activity you once enjoyed that your vision loss now prohibits?

When the low vision worker and the clinician have reviewed and compared all the data collected and have completed the case history, several problem areas that concern the patient will be identified. Record them in order of priority. Make statements brief and to the point. Be sure to cover potential problems in (1) vocational settings, (2) hobbies, (3) daily living (grooming, housecleaning, cooking, and so forth), (4) transportation and travel, (5) shopping, (6) social activities, and (7) educational settings. Record these difficulties even if it is improbable that they can be solved with optical aids or services.

The case history should provide two important pieces of information about the patient:

1. How well is the patient making use of residual vision? Is the patient functioning as a dependent or independent person for his or her level of acuity?

2. What specific problems should be concentrated on during the examination and in what order?

As was indicated before, the case history is the responsibility of all professionals involved with the low vision patient.

OCULAR HEALTH

This area of testing should indicate findings that require further medical attention. The clinician uses an ophthalmoscope to view the retina and other structures of the eye (see Fig. 1). The more anterior structures like the cornea and lens of the eye are investigated using the biomicroscope or slit lamp (see Fig. 2). The biomicroscope allows the clinician to look at the eye under high magnification to detect any structural changes that indicate an active pathology or other problem needing further attention. Often blood pressure and tonometry measurements are made at this point. At this point, the examiner also tries to describe the nystagmus and find a null point (direction of gaze where the nystagmus is minimal). Other problems with ocular muscles are noted as well, as is the impact of other motor-systemic problems on the ocular disorder. The more thorough the previous ophthalmological evalua-

145

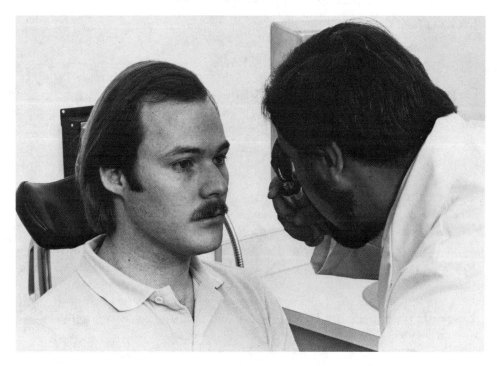

Fig. 1. The ophthalmoscope is used to examine the retina and other interior structures of the eye.

tions, the less time will be needed for this aspect of the low vision examination. Low vision services can be effective only when all types of routine medical-surgical intervention have been provided.

ACUITIES

Unaided distance and near acuities should be obtained in the first visit. When taking acuities, illumination must be considered; that is, illumination in the office should be set at an optimum level for the patient. The present prescription should be noted at every visit, or unaided acuities should be repeated if no prescription is habitually worn for distance or near vision. Acuities with present optical aids also are needed. The clinician should recheck unaided or current prescription acuities after determining the acuities from a tentative new prescription. Many patients "learn" to read the chart and will get much better unaided or current prescription acuities the second time around, thus decreasing the significance of the improvement in acuity with a new prescription. It is mandatory that the clinician record distances for near acuities (1M at 3 cm or .03/1M) (4 point at 10 cm). Near acuities have several notations. Table 1 is a comparative list of notations so both the examiner and the low vision instructor can better interpret the data collected. These acui-

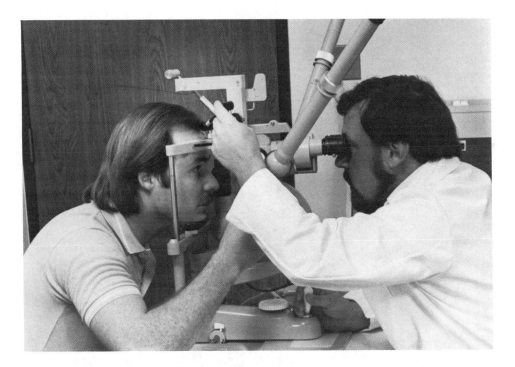

Fig. 2. The slit lamp (biomicroscope) is used to examine the anterior segments of the eye, especially the cornea and the lens.

ties also may be roughly compared to the noted text size for functional evaluations (see also Chapters 6 and 7). It is important to remember that there can be a tremendous difference between number and letter acuities and reading acuities; hence it is essential to know what kind of chart the clinician uses.

All acuity measurements should be checked for unexplained variations from setting to setting, from test to test, or from clinical to functional evaluation. It is not the clinician who decides what is a significant improvement in the patient's visual acuity; the patient should be given the opportunity to wear lenses in a trial frame indoors and outdoors to see if the subjective improvement in acuity is significant and corresponds with that found clinically. Some patients will subjectively refuse what seems to be a significant clinical increase in acuity, and others will dramatically accept changes that the average clinician would think are insignificant. In low vision, acuities are as much a subjective measurement as they are a clinical objective measurement.

To ensure success, the clinician generally uses book or wall cardboard charts so that high-contrast letters are presented to the patient (see Fig. 3). Furthermore, the patient usually is tested at 10 feet or less , which lets the patient ''see'' more letters and numbers on the chart and, therefore, puts the patient in a positive mood for the rest of the examination. This might have

Table 1. Approximate Table of Equivalent Visual Acuity Notations for Near[a]

Meters Equivalent	Snellen Equivalent	Jaeger[b]	American Medical Association Notation	Lower-Case Point	Approximate Height in Millimeters	Visual Angle In Minutes	Usual Type Text Size[c]	Equivalent Reading Acuity[d]
0.4	20/20		14/14	3	.58	5.00	Footnotes	Paperback and newsprint
0.5	20/25	J1-J2	14/17.5	4	.75	6.25	Paperback print	Magazines
0.8	20/40	J4-J5	14/28	6	1.15	10.00	Newspaper print	High school texts
1.0	20/50	J6	14/35	8	1.50	12.50	Magazine print	Children's books
1.2	20/60	J8	14/42	10	1.75	15.00	Children's books	Large-print materials
1.6	20/80	J9-J11	14/56	14	2.30	20.00	Large-print material	
2.0	20/100	J11-J12	14/70	18	3.00	25.00	Newspaper subheadlines	
4.0	20/200	J17	14/140	36	6.00	50.00	Newspaper headlines	
5.0	20/250	J18	14/175		7.50	62.50	½-inch letter	
10.0	20/500	J19	14/350		15.00	125.00	1-inch letter	
20.0	20/1000		14/700		30.00	250.00		

[a] There will be differences in the numbers presented in various published charts. These differences are indicative of the lack of standardization in charts and various clinical experiences.

[b] There can be as much as a 25-percent difference in the size of letters, words, and so forth from one Jaeger chart to another.

[c] This column refers to the comparison of letter size. It indicates the vision needed for reading labels and other short-term identification tasks.

[d] This column refers to the acuity needed by most patients to read the indicated materials comfortably. These equivalents were developed by Richard Brilliant, OD, William Feinbloom Vision Rehabilitation Center, Pennsylvania College of Optometry, and Randy Jose, OD, University of Houston College of Optometry, based on a review of clinical charts at the University of Houston and the Feinbloom Center.

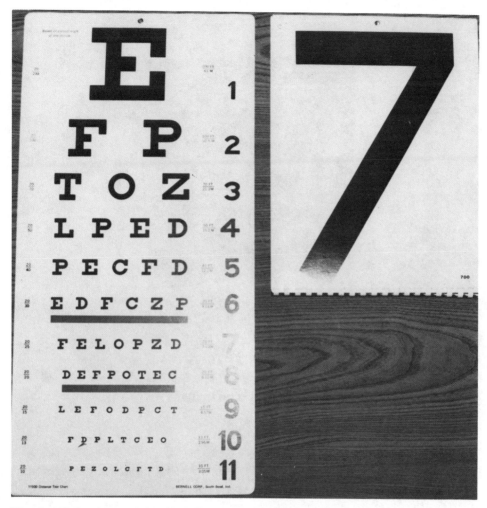

Fig. 3. High-contrast hand-held charts are used successfully in examinations of low vision patients.

been the first time a clinician examined the patient; it is gratifying to be able to respond to more than waving fingers, flashing lights, or a "Big E" (which the patient knew was there even if he or she could not see it). If the patient can see fingers at any distance, he or she can respond to a chart. It is much better psychologically to let the patient see symbols rather than fingers. A patient should rarely be given an acuity measurement of "finger count at 2 feet." If the patient can read several numbers from a low vision chart at five feet, it is a more reassuring way to develop a success-oriented rapport with the patient. The acuities should be recorded as follows:

NLP: no light perception (totally blind)
LP: light perception (can tell if light is present).
L Proj.: light projection (can tell the direction of light source).

149

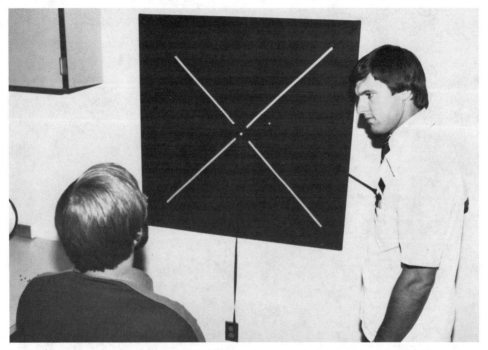

Fig. 4. A taped cross on the tangent screen helps low vision patients maintain fixation for tangent-screen tests.

HM: hand movement (rarely used; it means that a person can see motion, shadows, and perhaps some form vision).

FC: finger count (never used).

10/400:   Snellen Notation. This means that the test was done at 10 feet, and the patient saw a number that subtends 5′ of arc at 400 feet. It is equivalent to 20/800, which means the person sees objects at 20 feet that a person with 20/20 can see at 800 feet. (The 20/20 equivalent acuity is found by dividing the numerator into 20 [20 ÷ 10 = 2] and then multiplying both numerator and denominator by that number or [20/800] e.g., 5/50 = 20/200 [20 ÷ 5 = 4]).

Since these special charts and testing notations are intended to provide the optimum conditions for obtaining the maximal responses from the patient, better acuities than previously recorded are often found. Although these results may have a psychological advantage, they have a disadvantage as well. That is, the examiner must be careful not to deprive the patient of current services by finding an acuity better than 20/200 or some other bureaucratic cut-off. It may be beneficial to stamp all records to show that the acuities provided are "diagnostic only" and are not to be used in the determination of services. People with 10/60 (20/120) acuity, still have 20/200 acuity if tested on conventional charts. This concern will become especially important as more third-party insurance payments are permitted for low vision services.

FIELDS

Observations of the tangent screen, perimetry, Amsler-Grid, and functional field loss should be obtained for each patient. These can be done in the patient's environment or in the clinic, but it is necessary that some form of clinical test of the visual field be performed so there will be reliable baseline data on each patient. The tests of the fields done on low vision patients are not accurate because there are too many parameters to measure. Also, they are not as effective in determining the presence of an active pathology, as are tests of fields done on sighted individuals. The purpose of performing field tests is to determine if there is a major loss of vision in some sector of the patient's visual field. It is then up to the clinician to describe how the loss will affect the treatment options being considered or how it relates to the patient's reported or observed functional problems.

A tangent screen test measures the integrity of the central 25–35 degrees of the visual field. The patient sits one meter from a black screen and fixates on a buttonlike target or an "X" made of tape. (A large "X" or cross on the screen is used to help people with central field losses fixate centrally. They look where they think the lines of the cross meet.) (See Fig. 4.) The examiner brings a target in from the side and asks the patient to report when the target is seen. Most significant field losses will be picked up this way. It is important to observe the patients' posture and viewing technique during the test to get a more accurate and meaningful interpretation of the test results.

Perimetry is used when an extensive evaluation is needed that includes testing the periphery (90–100 degrees). For instance, in retinitis pigmentosa, the central field may be intact, but a large ring scotoma may surround the central area (see Fig. 5). A ring scotoma may extend from 15 to 65 degrees; beyond 65 degrees, however, there would be a ring of vision. This type of scotoma would be missed on the tangent screen because the screen goes only to a maximum of 35 degrees (usually 30 degrees). Therefore, without perimetry, an important piece of information about the patient would not be available to the clinical team, and it might not even be known by the patient. Once a ring scotoma is detected and the patient is trained to use the ring of remaining vision in a mobility program, the patient's level of functioning can be improved substantially without an aid. It is not unusual for a person with an island of vision in the periphery not to be aware of it or not to know how to use it without becoming confused. It is this type of person who can be trained to use two visual systems alternately but to process the information from each system simultaneously. The test (perimetry) is similar to a tangent screen test except that the test field is an arc or bowl that extends 90 degrees in every direction from the eye.

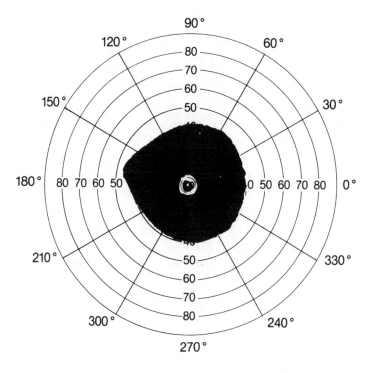

Fig. 5. A ring scotoma, like this one, can be missed if a tangent-screen test only is performed, in which case the patient will be diagnosed as having no peripheral vision.

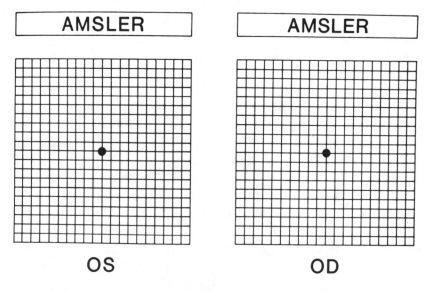

Fig. 6. The Amsler Grid is a near-point test of the visual field. It is valuable for determining the position and size of central scotomas.

152

The Amsler Grid is a nearpoint test of the central 10 degrees of vision. The test, which is in book form, consists of a white grid of small boxes on a black background (see Fig. 6). It is used to determine the location and extent of central scotomas. It helps the clinician develop a program for training in eccentric viewing that the instructor may use with the patient. Furthermore, the test gives the clinician an idea of the direction (and how much) in which the patient should view eccentrically, which eccentric viewing techniques the patient now uses, and if there are multiple central scotomas that will complicate training in the use of optical aids for reading and other distance and near tasks. If a patient moves the scotoma to the right, it will make reading difficult; therefore, the patient will have to be reinstructed to view superiorly. If there are two scotomas, the patient may try to use the 20/40 vision between the scotomas, leaving only a 2-degree field. It may be better to teach the patient to view farther out (inferior) where vision is 20/80 but where there is a larger field (see Fig. 7).

The purpose of all tests of visual fields is functional so that information on visual fields should be collected before a decision is made about the use of aids or services. For example, if the best area of vision is known, it is easier to teach the patient to develop consistent and reliable visual input about the environment. The better a patient uses his or her vision without aids, the easier

RIGHT

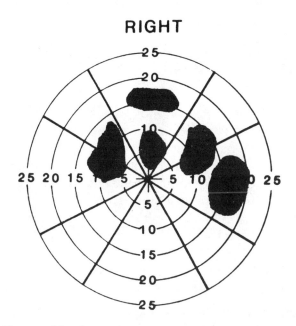

Fig. 7. According to this chart, the best acuity for this patient was found in the area between two of the central scotomas. However, the narrow field hindered the functional use of that area. Therefore, the patient was taught to use the inferior field with poorer acuity but larger fields.

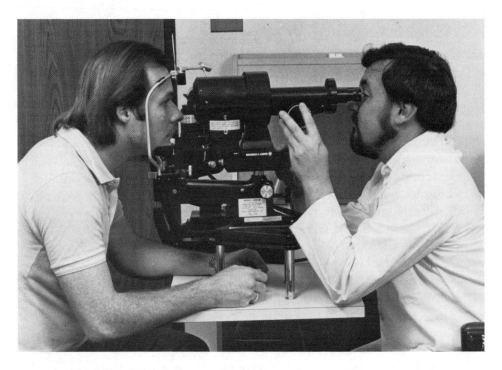

Fig. 8. The keratometer measures the curvature of the cornea to determine the presence of astigmatism and to evaluate the type of contact lenses that may be prescribed.

it will be to prescribe an optical aid that will be successful. The sequence in which these tests are done varies from clinician to clinician.

Color Vision
It is important that the clinical report indicate whether the patient is able to identify colors correctly. The preferred test for color vision is the D-15, which is 15 colored buttons that the patient must organize in matching colors. This test picks up significant color problems. Larger color chips can also be used if needed. If that test is not performed, at least a test of gross color discrimination should be noted. In addition to providing information about the pathology, the lack of color discrimination is of vital importance to professionals involved in the rehabilitation aspects of a patient's evaluation and instructional program.

REFRACTION

Testing for refraction is the most difficult part of the low vision examination, because of all the problems with the eye. Large refractive errors are frequently overlooked, especially in children. Testing for refraction is time consuming; thus it is often hurried or neglected. If the test is done correctly, substan-

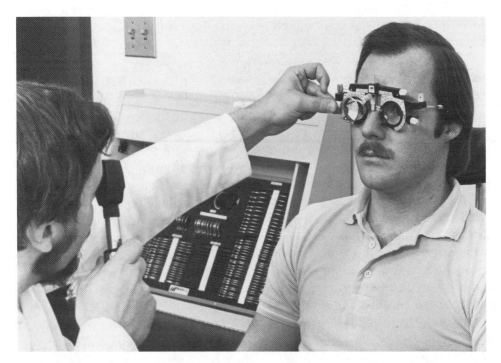

Fig. 9. To determine refractive errors, the clinician uses a retinoscope with a trial frame and hand-held lenses.

tial improvements in acuity can be realized with conventional lenses, and later options are increased in relation to prescribing optical aids because less magnification will be needed. Therefore, the importance of spending much time in testing refraction cannot be overemphasized.

Contact lenses often are of great value in improving the acuity of people with distorted corneas (the contact lenses and tears smooth out the irregular surface of the cornea and provide an undistorted retinal image) and with high refractive errors (more light and better optics increase the acuity). Contact lenses are particularly important for individuals with high refractive errors and small fields. Such people must scan to realize a meaningful functional field; if they scan behind a thick correction lens, they either suffer the distortion of the lens or scan with their head to maintain their visual field in the clear part (optical center) of the ophthalmic lens. The contact lens centers on the eye and moves with the eye; therefore, the patient can scan freely with eye movements and still enjoy the clearest optics.

The *keratometer* is often used to help the examiner determine the presence of refractive errors (see Fig. 8). This instrument measures the curvature of the cornea and gives the examiner insight into the presence of corneal distortions (a potential contact lens fit) and an indication of the presence of a large amount of astigmatism that may have been missed on previous tests. Some information can be obtained from this instrument even if the patient has nystagmus.

A *retinoscope* is used to determine refractive errors (see Fig. 9). A light is beamed into the patient's eye and is reflected off the retina back toward the examiner. By observing the movement of the light, the examiner can determine the presence of myopic, hyperopic, and astigmatic refractive errors. The test does not require any response from the patient and thus is valuable to use with children. By putting different lenses in front of the eye and observing the change in the movement of the light beam, the lenses needed to correct the refractive error can be determined. With low vision patients, the test is usually done in a trial frame with hand-held lenses, rather than with the phoropter (a big machine with lenses, routinely used to test refraction) because the examiner can watch the patient's head and eye movements during the test and such movements are important for determining reliable prescriptions. If the patient is hidden behind the phoropter, he or she may have to assume an unnatural posture of vision just to see through the instrument; hence unreliable findings may be obtained.

The *hand-held lenses* and a *trial frame* are even more important for a routine subjective examination. Most instruments are designed for the patient with macular or central vision. If the patient views peripherally, it will be difficult for the patient to give the clinician answers that reflect how he or she typically uses the eyes. Also, such instruments as the *phoropter* give the patient a choice of changes in small lenses. However, the patient with a low acuity may need a change in a large lens, and such a change can be given with the hand-held lenses. Hand-held lenses also decrease the chance of missing a large refractive error. The phoropter is probably responsible for more missed refractive errors than any other ophthalmic instrument.

Some clinicians perform a subjective examination while the patient is wearing a *telescope*. The telescope helps the examiner refine the final prescription and sometimes indicates that the correction needed with a telescope is different from what is needed with a conventional prescription. Such an indication is particularly important if a spectacle telescope is being considered as a possible treatment option.

BINOCULAR VISION

Binocular vision is often missed in the low vision evaluation. Because most low vision patients are monocular, the major part of the examination usually is spent working with the better eye. However, a patient frequently thinks that one eye is the better eye (from previous examinations) but the examiner finds that the other eye is better. That is, often the patient uses the better eye but does not know it or uses the worse eye simply out of ignorance. Therefore, the examiner must be careful to examine the potential of both eyes and not rely on the reports of patients.

Correcting an old refractive error in the worse eye (such as in cases of amblyopia or cataract surgery) may result in that eye becoming the better eye. The patient must then be trained to use that eye comfortably. If the acuities are relatively equal and not too severely reduced (i.e., if less than a 3X magnification is needed) it is possible that, with the appropriate correction and with compensation using a prism, the patient may enjoy binocular vision. However, most people need monocular corrections. When a monocular correction is prescribed, a person is usually required to wear a patch over the eye during the initial training period. The monocular prescription and the patch often create anxiety in the patient, who thinks that the eye which is wearing an eye patch will degenerate. This fallacy must be discussed with the patient before he or she leaves the office, or the fear of impending blindness will affect the success of the prescription and the training program. In addition, some people are bi-ocular; that is, they can use their eyes alternately, and thus require a reading lens for one eye and a writing lens for the other.

MAGNIFICATION

The examiner determines how much magnification is needed based on the best corrected acuities, the fields, and the tasks to be addressed. (A further discussion of magnification is found in Chapter 9.) The examiner should indicate the patient's acuity and subjective responses to several diagnostic optical aids, and should demonstrate to the patient how the calculated magnification can be provided, as (1) a microscope, (2) a telemicroscope, (3) a magnifier (stand and hand-held), (4) a projection magnifier (closed circuit television) or other non-optical aids, and (5) telescopes.

The pros and cons of each type of aid should be discussed with the patient. It should also be considered how each aid can be used to help solve the problems noted earlier in the history. The effects of illumination must be included with each demonstration. This part of the examination is the most "creative" for the low vision team. Close cooperation between the examiner and the training staff will allow for controlled experimentation and more flexibility in prescribing aids. The team should not get into a rut of prescribing the same aid to all patients as a matter of convenience rather than because a specific patient needs that aid. The treatment chosen should reflect the requirements of the instructional and rehabilitation professionals as well as the clinical data of the examiner. This type of interdisciplinary prescription is assured if a postexamination conference is held with the low vision instructor before a recommendation is given to the patient. However, the prescription still should be considered tentative (even after the conference) until the patient has had an opportunity to use a borrowed aid of the type the team thinks should be prescribed.

Table 2. Reference Outline of Typical Low Vision Examination[a]

I. The examination must be success oriented.

II. The following procedures should be followed:

A. The case history should be taken and nonclinical assessments reviewed.

B. Distant acuities with special charts are taken at distances of 2 feet to 10 feet. No "finger count" acuities are taken.

C. Retinoscopy—an objective measurement of refractive error in which a light is shone into the patient's eye and lenses are used to focus the light on the retina.

D. Keratometry—the measurement of the curvature of the cornea to detect the presence of refractive errors of astigmatism and to evaluate the type of contact lens that may be prescribed.

E. A subjective examination, in which the patient is asked which lenses are better or worse. This is usually done with a trial frame and hand-held lenses.

F. Field studies should be performed on most responsive patients. Either tangent screen or perimetry are done for distant fields, and the Amsler Grid is used for near.

G. Neutralization of all previous glasses and optical aids should be done so the clinician can be sure to build on or improve the design of these aids.

H. Telescopes may be demonstrated to the patient as a means of improving distance vision.

I. Near-point acuities are taken with special charts. The working distance and illumination used should be recorded.

J. Various near-point aids should be evaluated to determine their potential in resolving some of the problems identified in the case history.

K. A brief health evaluation is a part of every examination. The clinician evaluates the pupils, eye movements, pressures, and color vision. An ophthalmoscope is used to look at the retina and a slit-lamp (biomicroscope) is used to look at the cornea, the lens, and other anterior structures of the eye.

L. In appropriate cases, the clinician evaluates the presence of binocular or biocular vision.

M. Some in-clinic training is provided and an instructional regimen should be established with the patient, the instructor, or both.

N. An appropriate aid should be loaned to the patient to test it out.

O. A second visit is scheduled to evaluate the success and problems with the borrowed aid. Any diagnostic tests not completed should be finished and a prescription for an optical aid should be finalized.

P. Additional visits may be needed for extensive in-clinic structured training, for reinforcing the instructor's nonclinical training program, or to complete additional diagnostic tests.

Q. A final visit is scheduled for dispensing an aid and for establishing a follow-up program for the patient.

[a] This outline was developed from the lecture notes of Richard Brilliant, OD, Pennsylvania College of Optometry, Philadelphia.

The clinician should mention to the patient the potential problem areas observed in the examination. All instructions to the training staff should be written, at least until the team has had a chance to work together with several patients. The training staff will discuss the following with the patient. The first three items must be discussed at the clinic; the last two items may be discussed either at the clinic or in a future home visit.

1. How the borrowed aid will solve problems that the patient reported in the history.

2. Materials to be used for training.

3. Problem areas to be worked on at home (field of view, working distance, focusing, posture, lighting, localization and so forth).

4. Performance times, accuracies, scores, and the like that are expected by the next visit.

5. Reasons for changing a borrowed aid (after discussions with the clinician).

At least one member of the training staff will see the patient at all three visits—for the initial evaluation of how the patient is using the aid, the "progress" or second visit, and the dispensing visit. Most patients will benefit from additional training-progress visits as well. The more training that can be provided in the patient's environment, the fewer office visits will be needed. The clinician and low vision instructor should be in regular communication about the progress of each patient. The examination is not complete until all new problem areas have been identified and resolved and it is obvious that the patient is functioning at the maximum level of visual efficiency. An examination outline is included in Table 2, and a sample clinical record in Table 3.

Table 3. Case History Sheet

Date _____

_____

_____ Please Print _____

Name _____

Address _____

City _____ State _____ Zip _____

Telephone (H)_____ (O)_____

Sex_____ Birth ____/____/____

Ethnic Heritage _____

Understanding Low Vision

Marital Status: __ Dependents: _____ Accomp. by: _____

Referred by: _____

Visual History: _____

_____

_____

_____

_____

Eye Doctor OD or MD _____

Family History of Visual Problems _____

_____

_____

General health (medications): _____

_____

_____

Physician: _____

Education: _____

_____

Employment: _____

_____

Leisure Activities: _____

Eye Records Requested ( ) Yes   ( ) No   Received ( ) Yes

_____

Use of Current Prescription: _____

_____

Use of Current Aid: _____

_____

_____

Print—Current Ability and Needs: _____

_____

_____

_____

TV Hx _____

_____

Lighting Needs: _____

_____

Mobility Problems: _____

_____

_____

_____

Chief Complaint/Objectives: _____

_____

_____

_____

_____

_____

Comments: _____

_____

_____

_____

_____

_____

Preceptor _____   Preceptee _____

Treatment Sheet

Patient's Name _____   Age: _____

Date	Treatment

Optometric Evaluation

History: _____

_____

_____

_____

_____

Chief Complaint: _____

_____

Clinical Examination of the Visually Impaired

Acuity: VASC _____ (RX) _____ VAcc _____ (Aid) _____ VAcaid _____

(Dist)

OD _____

OS _____

(Near)

OD _____

OS _____

Use _____

Refraction: _____

OBJ: OD _____ VA _____

OS _____ VA _____

SUBJ: OD _____ VA _____

OS _____ VA _____

TS subj: _____

Binocularity: _____

_____

Low Vision Aids: _____

_____

_____

_____

_____

_____

Assessment: _____

_____

_____

Initial Training Plan: _____

_____

_____

_____ Initial Training Rx: _____

_____ (Pd) _____

Next Visit Concerns: _____

_____

Preceptee _____

Preceptor _____

4 HEALTH EVALUATIONS: _____

Externals: _____

	OD	Media	OS	
		Disc		
	_____	Cup/Disc H	_____	
	_____	Cup/Disc V	_____	
	_____	A/V Ratio	_____	
		Vessels (HR, AS)		
		Venous Pulse		
		Macular Area		
		Foveal Reflec		
		Other		

IOP _____   BP _____

_____   DRUGS_____

_____   _____

(   ) Direct Ophthalmoscopy   (   ) Indirect Ophthalmoscopy   (   ) Biomicroscopy

_____

Date - Initial Exam _____

_____

Color Vision: _____

_____

_____

Keratometry: OD _____

OS _____

_____

_____

_____

Near and Intermediate Distance Training

Patient_____   Date_____

Needs Assessment:

Reading   Writing

Homemaking   Hobbies, Crafts

Eccentric Viewing:

Reading:	1	2	
Aid _____			
Working Distance _____			
Illumination _____			
Skills:			
Focusing _____			
Localization _____			
Reading Skills:			
Scanning _____			
Locating next line _____			

Understanding Low Vision

	1	2	3
Speed			
Comprehension			

Materials Read:

Nonoptical Aids:

Reading Stand

Typoscope

Line Guide

Filter

Comments:

Writing:	1	2	3
Aid			
Working Distance			
Illumination			
Skills			
Writing Performed			
Nonoptical Aids:			
Writing guides			
Special pens/paper			
Stand			

Comments:

Other Activities:	1	2
Task Performed		
Optical Aid		
Working Distance		
Illumination		
Nonoptical Aids		

Comments:

Materials, Aids Loaned

Handouts, Information Given

Next Session

Instructor

REPORTS

Communication is a key factor in the success of any low vision service. Within the service, communication may be verbal, and the low vision instructor is encouraged to participate (not just observe) in all clinical sessions. However, written correspondence is necessary for funding purposes and to ensure the continuation of training services outside the low vision service.

After the examination services have been completed, the clinical data should be forwarded to the low vision instructor. Typically, a verbal report is given after each session, and a comprehensive written report is provided only on completion of the services. In other instances, short reports are forwarded after each visit to inform the low vision instructor of the significant information determined or for financial purposes. Even with this system, it is helpful to have the examiner complete a final and comprehensive report. In this section, samples of long and short reporting forms are provided for reference purposes. These can be modified to suit the specific needs of a particular low vision service.

The clinician's report should indicate the best conventional acuities obtained and when the glasses should be worn. It should discuss or show limitations in the visual fields and indicate their potential influence on the intended training program. Special lighting needs should also be indicated. The status of binocular vision or biocular vision, which is particularly important to know when prescribing a new aid, should be noted. Any significant anomalies in color vision should be reported. The aids to be used in the training program should be described in detail, and the intended uses and potential problem areas should be outlined. Ancillary filters, reading stands, and so forth should be indicated as well.

The report should provide enough information so the instructor can determine the patient's expected level of functioning with the aid, the specific tasks the aid was prescribed for, the areas of difficulty that can be expected, and the significance of other data on the impairment ascertained during the course of the examination. If other services or additional diagnostic data are being considered, these also should be indicated.

A report is no substitute for direct communications. Each group of professionals working together will devise its own system for communications. The following short and long letter formats have been used successfully in their several modified forms by a variety of clinical programs. One format will not work for all the patients seen, nor will it meet the requirements of every referral source. Therefore, these formats should be used only as guidelines.

Short Letter Formats

The following letter formats are used for brief communiques regarding the services provided for a particular patient.

1. Letter to Referral Source after a Patient's First Visit, Indicating Patient's Guarded Prognosis for Success Using an Aid

Re:_____

Dear_____

The above-named individual was examined at _____ on _____. The following were indicated by the patient as being chief problem areas related to the visual handicap:

1.
2.
3.

As a result of the initial interviews by our social worker and diagnostic evaluations by our optometric team, it is our impression that low vision services will be of limited value to this patient. Because of our experiences with the patient's reactions to the aids in this first visit, we think the patient has a guarded prognosis for success with low vision aids or acceptance of their limitations.

This is an initial impression, and we will need additional visits before we can come to a confident decision. It is obvious, however, from this first visit that many training sessions in our instructional program will be needed before we can successfully rehabilitate _____ to use low vision aids. As we continue our instructional sessions with our special education and mobility staff members, we will keep you advised of our progress.

We apologize for this form letter, but it allows us to expedite the transmission of our results. If you need further information or if your impressions significantly differ from our findings, please contact us at your earliest convenience so we can initiate a reevaluation. As you know, it is not easy to assimilate all data in a clinical setting, and we encourage and appreciate outside input.

A comprehensive report will be forwarded to you at the completion of our services. Thank you for your referral.

Sincerely,

cc: Attending Optometrist

2. Letter to Referral Source after the Initial Evaluation, Indicating the Patient's Suitability for Low Vision Services

Re:_____

Dear_____

The above-named individual was examined at _____ on _____. The following were indicated by the patient as being chief problem areas related to the visual handicap:

1.
2.
3.

As a result of the initial interviews by our social worker and diagnostic evaluations by our optometric team, it is our impression that low vision services will be of benefit to this patient. Services will be continued and a rehabilitative plan will be developed at the conclusion of our next session.

This is only our initial evaluation. Several additional visits will be needed with our instructional staff (special educator and mobility specialist) and social services staff in coordination with the optometric evaluations before services will be completed. When we are confident that _____ can successfully utilize the intended prescription, a formal recommendation for aids or services will be determined.

We apologize for this form letter, but it allows us to expedite the transmission of our results to you. If you need further information or your impressions significantly differ from our findings, please contact us at your earliest convenience so we can initiate a reevaluation. As you know, it is not easy to assimilate all data in a clinical setting and we encourage and appreciate outside input.

A comprehensive report will be forwarded to you at the completion of our services. Thank you for your referral.

Sincerely,

cc: Attending Optometrist

3. Letter to the Referral Source after the Initial Evaluation, Indicating the Patient's Unsuitability for Low Vision Aids

Re:_____

Dear_____

The above-named individual was examined at _____ on _____. The following were indicated by the patient as being chief problem areas related to the visual handicap:

1.
2.
3.

As a result of the initial interviews by our social worker and diagnostic evaluations by our optometric team, it is our impression that low vision services will not be of significant benefit to this patient. We were not able to find an optical or other low vision device that would enable the patient to improve his or her ability to function visually or to attain enough visual function to perform the tasks indicated above. No further evaluations will be pursued in the low vision unit. However, we have made the following recommendations for this patient:

1._____
2._____

We apologize for this form letter, but it allows us to expedite the transmission of our results to you. If you need further information or your impressions significantly differ from our findings, please contact us at your earliest convenience so we can initiate a reevaluation. As you know, it is not easy to assimilate all data in a clinical setting and we encourage and appreciate outside input.

Sincerely,

cc: Attending Optometrist

4. Short Preliminary Report to Referral Source of the Initial Evaluation

Dear _____

    On _____, 19__, _____ was seen at _____. Because our low service has a comprehensive multidisciplinary approach to the rehabilitation of the visually impaired, it includes examinations and evaluations by our social worker, faculty optometrist, low vision educational specialist, and mobility specialist. The following represents a preliminary report of the initial evaluation.

Visual Acuity	Old Unaided Prescription	New Prescription	Low Vision Aid 1	Low Vision Aid 2	Low Vision Aid 3
At Distance					
RE					
LE					
At Near					
RE					
LE					

Visual Fields (see attached field study).

RE _____ LE _____

_____These acuities/fields indicate that this patient is eligible for services pertinent to the legally blind.

_____These acuities/fields indicate that this patient is eligible for services pertinent to the visually impaired.

Low Vision Aids: Use

1. _____

2. _____

3. _____

4. _____

                                                       Sincerely,

5. Cover Letter for Patient's Status Record

The following individual _____ was seen at _____.

Since we are a referral service, it is important that we keep you abreast of our diagnostic and training activities. At regular intervals you will be sent an updated patient status record that briefly notes the total services offered this individual to date. A short commentary is also provided, regarding the staff's impressions of the potential for success in serving this patient or the need for further services and aids. Appropriate authorizations will be attached.

This communique is sent both to the referral source and to those individuals indicated by the patient as providing medical, educational. or rehabilitation services.

If further information or clarification of data is needed, do not hesitate to contact us. Your input is encouraged, either by return mail or by phone.

Sincerely,

_____
Patient

Referral source: _____

Distribution: _____

_____

_____

6. Patient's Status Record (Updated Periodically)

Name: _____   Sex: _____

Date of Birth: _____

Dates of Examination: _____

Attending Intern: _____   Supervisory Doctor: _____

Patient's goals or main objectives:

Summary of past surgical procedures and medical treatment:

Diagnosis:

Acuities: Distance   Near

    Unaided: R.E.
                L.E.

Conventional Rx: R.E.
                   L.E.

Rx: OD:
     OS:

Low Vision Devices and Acuity:

Fields:

Tonometry: R.E.   L.E.   Tonometer:

              Day: Time:

Other Tests:

Final Prescriptions:

Comments and Impressions:

Comprehensive Letter Formats

The following comprehensive letter formats are used to summarize all services that have been provided to a particular patient. They allow for a more detailed explanation of services from the multidisciplinary clinical team. They are usually sent at the completion of services. The format is written for optometric interns so they will have an idea of the type of information and statements needed in a letter. It can be easily modified for any type of program.

1. Low Vision Comprehensive Report Form

To: Counselor: _____

_____

Re: Patient: _____ Age:_____

Address: _____

Date(s) of Examination: _____

Clinical Data:
History: _____

_____

_____

_____

_____

Chief Complaint: _____

_____

Acuity:	Unaided Visual Acuity	Old Prescription	Acuity

Distance
OD _____

OS _____
Near
OD _____

OS _____

Visual Acuity with Present Aids (indicate which aids): _____

New Refraction: _____

Dist: OD _____VA _____

OS _____VA _____

Understanding Low Vision

Near: OD _____VA _____

OS _____VA _____

☐: No change in present distant prescription or use of conventional lenses is indicated.

Binocularity: Patient uses LE / RE   Patient is binocular at distance/near/both distance and near.

Patient is biocular using LE for   and RE for

Comments:_____

_____

Color Vision: Normal☐   Abnormal☐   Test Used

Comments:_____

_____

Date   _____

Amsler	Dist.

OS   OD

_____

Diagnosis and other ocular health data (tonometry, B.P., funduscopy):

_____

_____

_____

_____

_____

Low Vision Aids Evaluated (Illumination included)

Distance Aids   Intermediate Aids   Near Aids

_____

_____

_____

_____

Training (Tasks performed successfully and optical problems encountered):

_____

_____

_____

_____

_____

_____

_____   _____
Training   Examining OD/MD

Social Services (pertinent history, description of individual's self-concept, motivation and expectations, identification of other needs, support systems and prognosis for implementing prescriptive programs, follow-up services needed):

_____

_____

_____

_____

_____

_____

                                              _____
                                              Social Worker

Low Vision Mobility Evaluation (statement of patient's travel abilities, potential problem areas, utilization of prescribed aid or aids, additional training and instruction needed, discussion of tasks successfully performed with the aid and expected improvement in mobility skills, prognosis for solving patient's reported chief concerns, lighting needs):

_____

_____

_____

_____

_____

_____

_____

Orientation and Mobility Specialist

Low Vision Educational Evaluation (reading skills and performance, writing skills, optimum materials, nonoptical aids, lighting, other educational needs, relationship of fields to near-point performance, potential problem areas and successes with aids, resolution of chief concerns, prognosis):

_____

_____

_____

_____

_____

_____

Teacher for the Visually Handicapped

Low Vision Treatment Option Plan

1. Services provided in the initial diagnostic low vision evaluation:

☐ Social service intake   ☐ Low vision mobility evaluation

☐ Nonclinical evaluation   ☐ Low vision educational evaluation

☐ Clinical examination   ☐ Intermediate revisit

☐ Training session   ☐ Other _____

Total Fee _____

2. Aids and services recommended and anticipated benefits:

Treatment Option 1:_____

_____

_____

Cost_____

Clinical Examination of the Visually Impaired

Benefits: _____

_____

_____

_____

Additional Authorizations Needed:

☐ Brief revisits _____ ☐ Ophthalmological consultation

☐ Intermediate revisits _____ ☐ Psychological counseling

☐ Extended revisits _____ ☐ Educational instruction session

☐ Training session _____ ☐ Mobility instruction session

☐ Nonclinical evaluation _____ ☐ Other _____

Total Cost _____

Expected date of completion of services: _____

Treatment Option 2: _____

_____

_____

Cost _____

Benefits: _____

_____

_____

_____

Additional Authorizations Needed:

☐ Brief revisits _____ ☐ Ophthalmological consultation

☐ Intermediate revisits _____ ☐ Psychological counseling

☐ Extended revisits _____ ☐ Educational instruction session

☐ Training session _____ ☐ Mobility instruction session

☐ Nonclinical evaluation _____ ☐ Other _____

Total Cost _____

Expected date of completion of services: _____

Understanding Low Vision

Treatment Option 3: _____

_____

_____

Cost _____

Benefits: _____

_____

_____

_____

Additional Authorizations Needed:

☐ Brief revisits _____   ☐ Ophthalmological consultation

☐ Intermediate revisits _____   ☐ Psychological counseling

☐ Extended revisits _____   ☐ Educational instruction session

☐ Training session _____   ☐ Mobility instruction session

☐ Nonclinical evaluation _____   ☐ Other _____

Total Cost _____

Expected date of completion of services: _____

The treatment options described are based on the clinical and functional data obtained on this patient and will optimize the patient's chance to realize his or her vocational goals of _____

_____

Sincerely,

_____

Clinical Director

2. Low Vision Comprehensive Report Form

Dear _____

On _____, 19__, _____ was seen at _____. Since our low vision service has a comprehensive multidisciplinary approach to the rehabilitation of the visually impaired, _____ was evaluated by the following specialists on the following dates:

_____   _____

_____   _____

_____   _____

_____   _____

The following represents a categorized summary of the results of the aforementioned evaluations.

Visual Acuity

		Unaided	Old Prescription	New Prescription
At Distance	RE			
	LE			
At Near	RE			
	LE			

Visual Fields (See attached field study)

RE _____ LE _____

____ These acuities/fields indicate that this patient is eligible for services pertinent to the legally blind.

____ The acuities/fields indicate that this patient is eligible for services pertinent to the visually impaired.

History

1. A statement of the patient's age, the previous diagnosis of the visual loss, and a statement of the time of onset or duration of the loss, including changes in vision (stability).

2. A statement describing the patient's vision, including how the patient uses the vision (e.g., if he or she reads or how long since he or she has read, which eye sees better, what tasks he or she is able to do, what aids he or she now uses and what they are used for).

3. A statement regarding the patient's general health, including pertinent needs, and how health may or may not relate to the visual loss.

4. A brief statement describing the patient's psychological set (motivation, self-concept, acceptance of loss, and so forth). (Phrase statement as if the patient will receive the letter.)

5. Any other pertinent aspect of the social intake.

Understanding Low Vision

Objectives for the Patient (Problem list)

Ocular Health

1. A statement confirming or questioning the previous diagnosis. If questioning the previous diagnosis, give the new diagnosis; if confirming the previous diagnosis, write "Our findings are consistent with the previous diagnosis of. . . ."

2. If additional tests were performed, list them and give pertinent new findings.

3. Describe the prognosis (stable vs. progressive) of the ocular health problem and mention any recommendations for referring the patient to a medical specialist.

Tonometry/Blood Pressure

Intraocular pressures, as measured by _____ were RE _____mm
(type of tonometry)

and LE_____mm. These pressures are considered_____
(normal, borderline high, above normal)

Indicate if further attention is needed (e.g., "The patient was rescheduled" or "The patient was advised to have the pressure checked by his or her doctor." Blood pressure was recorded as _____/_____. This is [or is not] consistent with previous findings").

Color Vision

Color vision testing via the _____ revealed the following:
(instrument used)

1. _____ shows essentially normal color vision.
   (name)

2. _____ shows a _____ _____ color
   (name)   (partial/complete)   (protan/deutran/tritan)

defect. This type of defect can result in confusion of _____ and
(color)

_____. Indicate the importance of this defect to the patient's visual
(color)

tasks and discuss its ramifications for the patient's life (occupation, driving, and so forth).

Binocularity

_____ is _____, meaning
(name)   (a) binocular (b) monocular (c) biocular

1. The two eyes "team" together adequately.
2. The patient is essentially using only the _____ eye.
                                              (R/L)

3. The patient can use either eye independently, but because of _____
                                                                (XT, ET, vision, etc.)

the two eyes are not able to "team" or work together.
You may want to describe the relevance of the above.

Optical Aids/Acuity

Lighting Requirements

Indicate the need for special lamps and for such illumination control devices as sunfilters and visors. Mention when they should be worn and when they should not be worn. Indicate footcandles of light that are best for near and distance tasks. Discuss how the aid will be affected by not using correct lighting.

Sample phrases:

1. For _____ to function at his or her optimum level, a flex-arm or gooseneck lamp with a _____ watt bulb used at a _____ inch work distance will be required.

2. _____ indicated no special requirements for lighting to utilize successfully the low vision aids recommended or prescribed.

3. A _____ percent sunfilter was prescribed for _____ to be used when traveling outdoors under bright conditions. It will significantly decrease the glare recovery time now experienced.

4. _____ can read 5-point print at a rate of 50 words per minute if the correct lighting is provided. This was reduced to 10-point and 25 words per minute under less desirable lighting; 75 footcandles (a 50 watt bulb at 15 inches) should be used while using the 5X microscopic aid.

Rehabilitation Plan (Distant Vision)

1. State the individual's present travel abilities.

a. Patient reports no problems with mobility and our observations did not indicate any situations to question this statement. No further mobility services or evaluations are considered.

b. Patient reports no problems with mobility. However, we think the patient is not functioning at his [her] optimum level (explain why).

c. The patient reported the following difficulties with mobility (list them). We think these can [cannot] be resolved with the following aid or training program. (Discuss aids and training program.)

d. Our low vision mobility evaluations indicated the following problem area for this patient (list them). The intended distance aids that we believe will improve these situations are (list them).

2. Discuss the aids being considered as potential prescriptions.

a. The hand-held telescope was bound to be of optimum benefit for _____ to resolve the problem areas indicated. The aid was used in a variety of indoor and outdoor settings and _____ seems to have a thorough understanding of the uses and limitations of the unit, which are [describe them]. The patient successfully used the aid to [see the blackboard/street sign at a distance of. . . .].

b. The patient was evaluated with a variety of spectacle-mounted and hand-held distance aids and none was found to be of substantial *subjective* benefit to this patient. However, clinically we found the following improvements [list them].

c. Even though we found significant improvements in acuity clinically, the patient did not demonstrate this improvement in our instructional sessions. Thus, we have decided not to pursue distance aids further.

d. The patient shows moderate improvement in acuity and demonstrates adequate proficiency in the use of the telescope for a limited number of activities as demonstrated in the clinical and instructional sessions. The patient was advised that the telescope is to be used for the following tasks [list them]. The following problem areas were noted in the instructional sessions (an acceptable level of proficiency was demonstrated prior to prescribing the aid) and the patient was advised that attention will be needed in the following areas in continuing the training sessions at home (list the instructions).

3. The prognosis is [good, excellent, good if training regime is maintained, guarded, poor]. The aid will be used primarily for [elaborate]. Keep in mind the chief concerns and needs of the referral source.

Rehabilitation Plan (Nearpoint Vision)

1. State the individual's present skills.

a. Discuss the type of material that the patient can read now without aids or with old aids.

b. Discuss the patient's concerns about not being able to read newsprint or books or to sew, and so forth.

c. State how long it has been since the patient has been able to read.

d. List the difficult areas mentioned by the patient and indicate that we evaluated these areas and found:

1. No significant improvement could be attained.

2. A 2.5X bifocal was prescribed to allow _____ to read newsprint at 10M with 50 footcandles of lighting. He [she] read 55 words per minute under this clinical condition. His [her] subjective responses to this improvement were moderate enthusiasm. His [her] main concern was [the close working distance, field of view, slow reading speed, weight of lenses, and the like]. A reading stand was provided to help alleviate some of the areas of concern. With practice, he [she] will find his [her] objections to the lens system to be less significant and frustrating.

2. Discuss the aids prescribed and how the patient functioned with the aids (if not already stated). If problem areas exist, mention them and indicate why we prescribed in spite of them. As with distance aids, indicate that the patient had good clinical results but did not demonstrate these results in the instructional program. Thus we decided not to pursue the prescription of the _____.

3. The patient shows moderate improvement in acuity and demonstrates adequate proficiency in the use of the near aids for a limited number of activities, as demonstrated in the clinical and instructional sessions. The patient was advised that the near aids are to be used for the following tasks [list them]. The following problem areas were noted in the instructional sessions (an acceptable level of proficiency was demonstrated prior to prescribing the aid) and the patient was advised that attention will be needed in the following areas in continuing the training sessions at home [list the instructions].

4. The prognosis is [good, excellent, good if training regime maintained, guarded, poor]. The aid will be used primarily for [elaborate]. Keep in mind the chief concerns and needs of the referral source.

Prognosis

Reiterate the statements made in sections on distance and near rehabilitation. It is best to follow a pattern such as this:

1. Name the aid being prescribed and indicate the improvements in acuity when using the aid. List the activities that the patient can do with the aid and review potential problem areas. Be sure to list activities that are pertinent to the referral source. You do not need to indicate work distances, lighting, and so forth in this section. This is a review.

2. Request for additional visits, funding for aids, and the like.

The patient has successfully utilized the bioptic telescope in our instructional program and we are confident that he or she will substantially benefit from the aid for the indicated school-related (or work-related) tasks. We are requesting authorization for the following:

3.0X Ex. Field Bioptic	$800.00
Three Training Sessions at $25.00	75.00
14 percent NoIR Amber Filters	15.00
Total Authorization Request	890.00

This report has been an attempt to summarize, in a comprehensive manner, the pertinent aspects of the examination and rehabilitation of _____. We recognize that, as such, it may lack specific information that you may find necessary. If you have any questions or would like additional information, please contact us.

Sincerely,

Bibliography

Bailey, I. Refracting low vision patients. *Optometric Monthly,* 1978, **69**(8), 519-523.

Borish, I. *Clinical refraction* (3d. Ed.) Chicago: Professional Press, 1970.

Freid, A., & Mehr, E. *Low vision care.* Chicago: Professional Press, 1974.

Goodlaw, E. Assessing field defects of the low vision patient. *American Journal of Optometry and Physiological Optics,* 1981, **58**(6), 486-490.

Jose, R., & Atcherson, R. Standardization of near point acuity tests. *American Journal of Optometry and Physiological Optics,* 1977, **54**(9), 634-638.

Jose, R., & Springer, D. Optical aids—An interdisciplinary prescription. *New Outlook for the Blind,* 1973, **67**(1), 2-18.

Mehr, E., & Freid, A. The measurement and recording of vision at near test distances. *American Journal of Optometry and Physiological Optics,* 1976, **53**(6), 314-317.

Newman, J. (Ed.). *A guide to the care of low vision patients.* St. Louis, Mo.: American Optometric Association, 1974.

Rosenblum, A. Principles and techniques for examining the partially blind patient. *Journal of the American Optometric Association,* 1958, **29**(11), 715-718.

CHAPTER 9

Optics

RANDALL T. JOSE, O.D.

This chapter reviews the optics of lenses and lens systems as well as that of the eye. It discusses the relationship of the optics of the eye to that of aids and provides an overview of categories of magnification that are available for designing optical aids for individuals with low vision.

BASIC OPTICS

Before one can have knowledge about lenses, optical aids and the principles of magnification, one must be familiar with the way light rays travel through a lens. Light rays travel in straight lines parallel to one another and will not come to a focus unless a lens system is interjected in their path (see Fig. 1). Light rays must intercept one another at some point if an image is to be formed. This bending of the rays to make them intercept one another and come to a focus is done with a lens or combination of lenses. The shape of the lens, or combination of lenses used, will determine where all the light rays come to a focus and form an image point of the object from which they emanate.

The rays of light that are traveling parallel to one another and in a straight line, are labeled as having *zero vergence,* which means that they do not bend. Light rays coming from any object 20 feet or more from the eye or lens system

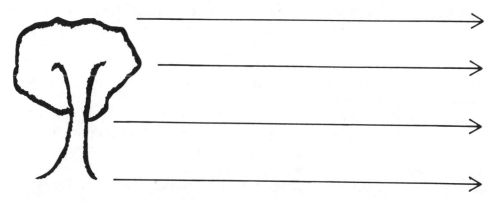

Fig. 1. Zero vergence (no image formed). Light rays emanating from an object more than 20 feet away from the eye travel in straight lines parallel to one another and will not come to a focus unless an optical system is interjected in their path.

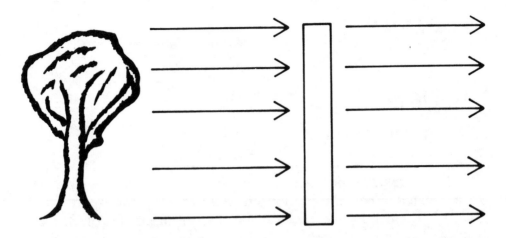

Fig. 2. Zero vergence through a thin plate of glass. When parallel rays of light strike a perpendicular surface, such as a thin plate of glass, no refraction of light occurs. This glass plate is considered to have zero bending power, or zero diopters. An image is still not formed and the light rays still have zero vergence.

are considered to be traveling as a parallel group of light rays and to have zero vergence—a situation often referred to as *optical infinity.* Optical infinity is the reason for testing patients at 20 feet for conventional prescriptions.

If the light rays of zero vergence pass through a thin plate of glass with its surfaces perpendicular to the direction of the light rays, the light rays will not change direction and will still have a zero vergence (see Fig. 2). The glass plate or lens will be considered to have zero diopter power (i.e., it does not bend light). When a convex (plus) lens is placed in the path of the light rays, each ray of light is bent toward the central ray, which is called the *optical axis ray* (see Fig. 3). The optical axis ray is the one ray of light from the object that passes through the optical center of the lens. The optical center of the lens acts like the parallel plate of glass and does not cause the light to bend. Because there always is an optical axis ray and it always passes through the lens without bending, it is used as the reference point when determining the bending power (diopters) of lenses.

All the other rays of light will cross the optical axis ray on the other side of the lens. Since all rays are converging at the same point (*focal point*) on the optical axis, the convex lens is referred to as a *converging lens* and given a plus (+) value when the bending power is converted to diopters. The thicker the lens (the more steeply curved it is), the more the light will be bent and the closer the focal point will be to the back surface of the lens, which gives the lens a greater diopter value (see Fig. 4). To determine the diopter value of the lens, the *focal distance* (in this case the distance between the back of the convex lens and the focal point) must be measured in centi-

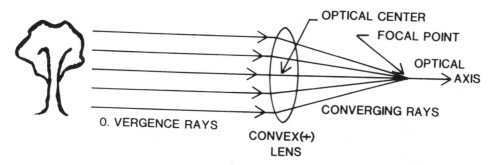

OPTICAL CENTER

FOCAL POINT

OPTICAL AXIS

CONVERGING RAYS

O. VERGENCE RAYS

CONVEX(+) LENS

Fig. 3. The optical axis ray. The optical axis ray strikes the perpendicular surface of the optical center of the lens and passes through the lens undeviated. The more peripheral rays are bent toward the optical axis (+ power) and converge to a specific point on the other side of the lens called the "focal point."

meters. The distance in centimeters is then divided into 100, which gives the diopter value (bending power).

If a concave lens is placed in the path of the light rays, the rays will bend away from the optical axis ray after they have passed through the lens (see Fig. 5). The concave lens is thus referred to as a *diverging lens* and is given a minus (–) value when the bending power is converted to diopters. Again, the thicker the lens (looking at the edge of the lens) and the more steeply curved it is (an inward curve in this case), the more divergence will occur or the greater will be the diopter value. The focal point of a concave lens is found on the front side of the lens. It is located at the point on the optical axis from which the rays of light seem to come as they diverge from the back side of the lens.

The focal distance in the case of a concave lens is the distance from the front surface of the lens to the focal point. Again the dioptric power (bending effect) of the lens is found by dividing the focal distance in centimeters into 100. In this case, it is given a minus diopter value.

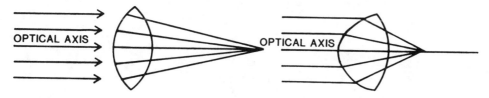

OPTICAL AXIS

OPTICAL AXIS

Fig. 4. Convex lens. The lens on the left has a moderately steep curve and the light rays are focused quite a distance behind the lens (long focal length). This is a weak lens with little bending power and it has a low diopter value. The lens on the right is steeply curved. The focal distance is shorter and thus the lens is considered to have a greater bending power and a high diopter value.

189

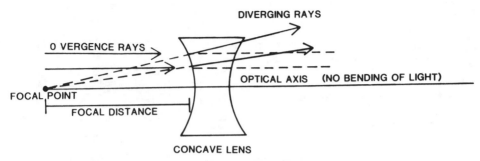

Fig. 5. Concave lens. A concave lens will bend light rays away from the optical axis. The focal point is that point in front of the lens from which the diverging rays "appear" to come.

To determine where light from an object will be focused (focal distance), use the following formula if the diopter value of the lens is known:

$$100/\text{diopters} = \text{focal distance (cm)}$$

With a 10-diopter lens (+ 10) the formula would be

$$100/10 = 10 \text{ cm focal distance (see Fig. 6)}$$

For a minus lens, the formula would be:

$$\frac{100}{-10} = -10 \text{ cm}$$

The minus means the focal point is one the same side of the lens as the zero vergence light rays (see Fig. 7).

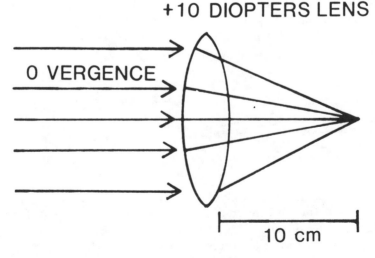

Fig. 6. + 10 diopter lens. Zero vergence rays entering a + 10-diopter lens will converge to a point 10 centimeters behind the lens.

190

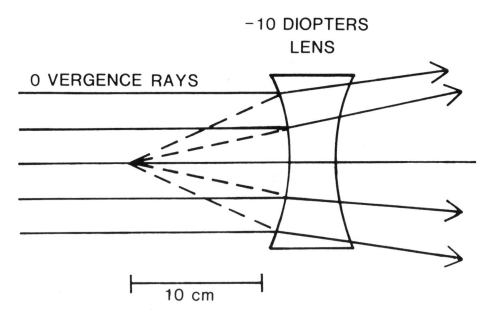

Fig. 7. − 10 diopter lens. Zero vergence rays strike a − 10-lens and diverge. The point from which these diverging rays seem to emanate is the focal point, which is located 10 centimeters in front of the lens.

Another important principle is the change of direction of zero vergence rays to diverging rays as an object comes closer to the eye than 20 feet. As the object is brought closer to the lens, the divergence of the rays increases (see Fig. 8). The diverging rays originate from every point on the object as a packet of rays. In the figures in this chapter, one sees the packet coming only from the object's point on the optical axis. To visualize the diverging rays, think of each of the vergence ray diagrams as being composed of three rays moving together, one ray of which is always the optical axis ray. These rays begin to diverge (except the optical axis ray) when the object is closer than 20 feet.

The amount of divergence of these light rays can be measured in diopters just as is done with a lens. The diopter value of the vergence of the rays of light is found by the following formula:

Diopters of Divergence
(Minus Value)
$$\frac{100}{\text{Distance of object from lens in centimeters}}$$

Thus an object located 50 centimeters from a lens will have the light rays from every point striking the lens with a divergence value of minus two diopters:

$$(-)\,D = \frac{100}{50\ \text{cm}} = -2D$$

191

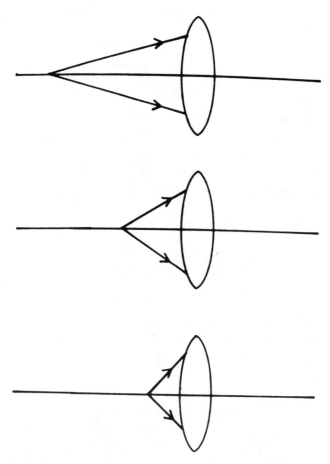

Fig. 8. The change of zero vergence rays to diverging rays. Rays of light will strike the surface of a lens with a divergent power when they emanate from an object that is situated closer than 20 feet from the lens. The closer the object is to the lens, the more divergent will be the rays.

If these rays pass through the + 10-diopter lens in Figure 6, the effective bending power of the + 10-diopter lens will be reduced and the point of focus will be varied. The lens will still bend 10 diopters, but the rays will not strike the lens with zero vergence. The lens will have a total bending effect of + 8-diopters. This is the combination of a − 2 ray with a + 10-diopter lens (see Figure 9).

The first two diopters of bending from the + 10-diopter lens brings the ray to a zero vergence position, leaving only 8 diopters of additional bending power. Now the image will be focused at

$$FD = \frac{100}{8D} = 12.5 \text{ cm}$$

192

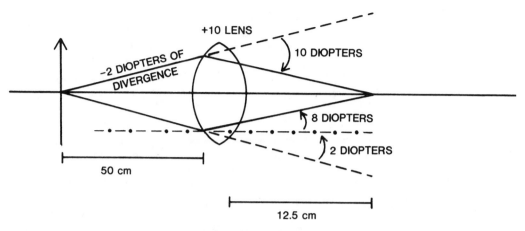

Fig. 9. Combination of a – 2 ray with a + 10 lens. The rays of light leaving the point on the optical axis of an object that is situated 50 centimeters from the lens strike the lens with – 2 diopters of divergence. The + 10 lens will converge the rays 10 diopters, as in the upper ray. This will consist of + 2 diopters of convergence to bring the ray to the zero vergence position of power still remaining. The rays will focus 12.5 centimeters behind the lens (acting like a + 8 diopter lens) instead of the 10 centimeters focal distance expected from a + 10 lens with zero vergence rays striking it.

A special situation arises for convex lenses when the object and the focal distance are the same distance from the lens. Now the rays of light diverge an amount equal to the converging power of the lens and the light rays leave the lens with a zero vergence or parallel (see Fig. 10). This is the manner in which microscopic lenses are used. To the eye, the object appears to come

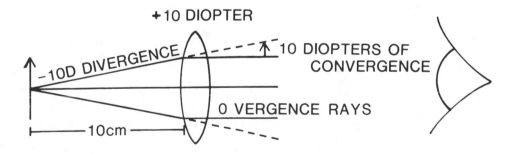

Fig. 10. Rays from an object located 10 centimeters from a + 10-diopter lens will strike that lens with a divergent power of – 10 diopters. If the – 10 diopters of divergence are now converged + 10 diopters by the lens, a zero vergence results, and the rays leave the lens parallel or with zero vergence. If reading materials are put in front of the lens at a distance equal to its focal distance, parallel light rays will enter the eye and no accommodation will be needed.

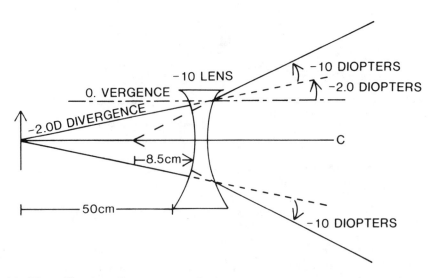

Fig. 11. The effective divergence of a concave lens. The rays of light from an object 50 centimeters from a – 10-diopter lens, strike the lens with – 2 diopters of divergence. The – 10 diopter lens diverges the rays another 10 diopters, for a total divergence of – 12 diopters. The imaginary focal point is located 8.5 centimetrs in front of the minus lens.

from optical infinity (20 feet or more); therefore, the low vision patient will not need to accommodate. For a more complete description of how the total image is formed from all the rays of light entering the lens, consult the publications listed at the end of this chapter.

For the concave lens, the effective divergence increases as an object is

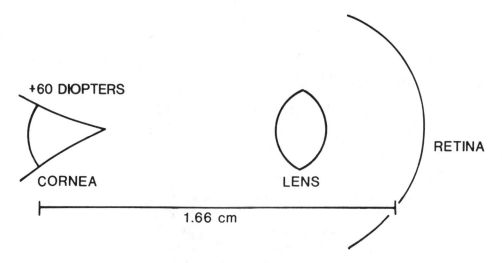

Fig. 12. Schematic drawing of an eye. In this drawing, the eye has a total bending power of + 60 diopters and a length of 1.66 centimeters.

brought closer (see Fig. 11). When the object is at 50 centimeters, the total divergence is − 2.0 diopters from the light rays and − 10 diopters from the lens to give a total divergence of the light rays of − 12 diopters. The focal distance of this system will be

$$FD = \frac{100}{-12} = 8.5 \text{ cm}$$

This focal distance in the front of the lens and is an imaginary point used as a reference to calculate the powers of a telescope lens and to correct refractive errors.

REFRACTION

The correction of refractive errors is the first step in the consideration of optical aids. Consider the eye as an optical system consisting of a cornea and lens and having a specific length of 1.66 centimeters (see Fig. 12). The cornea and lens have a dioptric value of + 60 diopters, and light is focused on the retina 1.66 centimeters away

$$\frac{100}{60D} = 1.66 \text{ cm.}$$

When the eye views an object 20 feet away, the light rays coming from that object and entering the eye will be light rays of zero vergence; they will be focused on the retina by the + 60 diopter optical system (see Fig. 13). Figure 13 is a simplified diagram but accurately depicts the optics needed for this discussion.

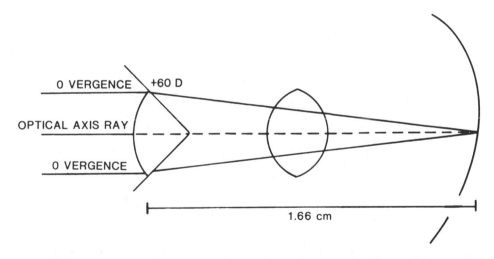

Fig. 13. Schematic drawing of normal eye. The zero vergence rays are focused exactly on the retina by the + 60-diopter normal eye. The focus is such that the image is on the macula for best vision in the normal eye.

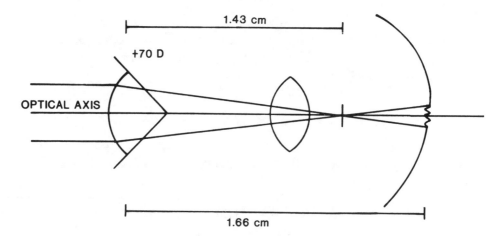

Fig. 14. The myopic eye. A myopic eye with a dioptric power of +70 diopters will focus light 1.43 centimeters from the front surface or cornea. The image will form in the vitreous and be blurred as it reaches the retina.

Myopia (nearsightedness) is created if the eye develops too strong a total power or if the eye itself is too long. When an eye has a steep cornea, it light with a greater convergence power and focuses the image closer than 1.66 centimeters, or in front of the retina. If the power of the eye was measured at +70 diopters, it would focus light (100/70), 1.43 centimeters

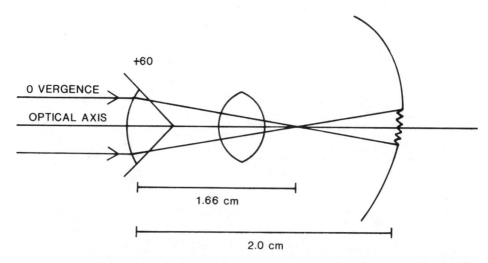

Fig. 15. The myopic elongated eye. In the myopic eye that is elongated, the optical system focuses at the correct distance of 1.66 centimeters but the eye is 2 centimeters long. Therefore, the image is formed in the vitrous and is blurred when it strikes the retina.

196

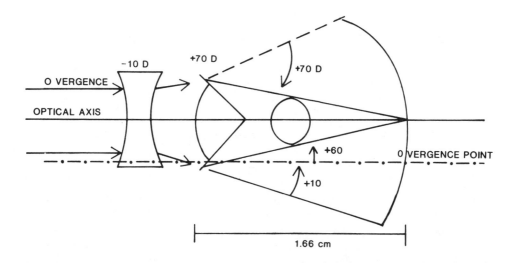

Fig. 16. Lens needed to allow a + 70 diopter myopic eye to see clearly. The zero vergence rays enter the – 10-diopter lens and the rays are diverged 10 diopters. These divergent rays enter the + 70-diopter myopic eye. The first 10 diopters of convergence are used to bring the diverging rays to zero vergence, which leaves + 60 diopters for converging. The rays will now be focused on the retina, 1.66 centimeters away, and the retina will receive a clear image.

from the cornea (see Fig. 14). If the eye is larger than normal without a compensating change in the power of the optical system (+ 60D), myopia can also occur (see Fig. 15). In most instances, the refractive error is a combination of both effects. In both cases, light is focused in front of the retina and the retina receives an image of the point that is spread out (blurred).

To get the retina of the eye in Figure 14 to receive an image of the point of light, that eye would have to have a power of + 60 diopters. Therefore, if a – 10-diopter lens is combined with the + 70-diopter eye, the optical system will be + 60 diopters, the light rays will focus on the retina, and the person with a good macula will again enjoy 20/20 vision (see Fig. 16).

For the elongated eye in Figure 15, the – 10-diopter lens combined with the + 60-diopter eye leaves a total bending power of + 50 diopters (see Fig. 17). This will focus the light 2 centimeters from the cornea or exactly on the retina:

$$FD \quad \frac{100}{50D} = 2 \text{ cm (the length of the eye)}$$

Another way of getting the person with myopia to see clearly is to provide minus power or divergence by bringing the object closer. If an object is

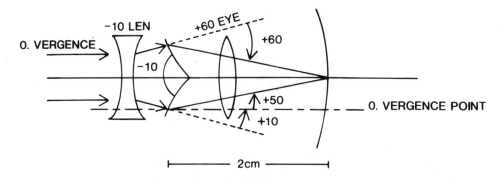

Fig. 17. Lens needed to permit an elongated +60 diopter myopic eye to see clearly. In the elongated myopic eye with a length of 2 centimeters, the −10-lens diverges the entering rays 10 diopters. These −10 diverging rays enter the +60-diopter eye and the rays are converged a total of +50 diopters. The first 10 diopters of convergence bring the diverging rays to zero vergence, and the remaining 50 diopters of the +60-diopter eye bring the light rays to focus 2 centimeters from the cornea or exactly on the retina.

brought 10 centimeters from the eye, the light rays will diverge with a diopter value of −10:

$$(-) \text{ divergence } = \frac{100}{\text{object-eye distance (10cm)}} = \frac{100}{10\text{cm}} = -10\text{D}$$

When the object is 10 centimeters from the eye, the light rays enter the

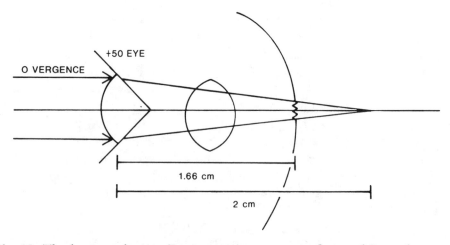

Fig. 18. The hyperopic eye. Zero vergence rays are focused 2 centimeters from the cornea or behind the retina in the +50 diopter hyperopic eye. As the light rays strike the retina, they still are not focused; thus, the retina receives a blurred image.

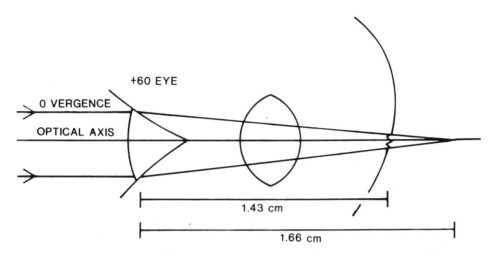

Fig. 19. The shortened hyperopic eye. The shortened hyperopic eye bends the zero vergence light rays to + 60 diopters and focuses them at 1.66 centimeters from the cornea or slightly behind the retina. Again, the image is blurred on the retina.

+70-diopter eye with a divergence of − 10 diopters. The combined bending will be + 60 diopters, and light will be focused on the retina. This is why myopia is called nearsightedness. The person with myopia can see clearer (or even correct the refractive error) if objects are brought closer to the eye. Thus, some low vision patients who are nearsighted will take off their glasses to read or do near work.

Hyperopia (farsightedness) exists when the power of the eye is less than + 60 diopters (see Fig. 18) or the length is too short (see Fig. 19). It is usually a combination of these two optical conditions. Light focused behind the retina will need more convergence to get it focused on the retina. If a + 10-diopter lens is added to increase the power of the + 50-diopter eye to + 60 diopters, the light will focus on the retina (see Figure 20). With the short eye, + 10 diopters are added to the + 60-diopter eye to get a total bending effect of + 70 diopters. This will focus light at 1.43 centimeters (the focal distance is 100/70), which is the distance to the retina.

Another way of correcting a hyperopic refractive error can be through accommodation. Accommodation, which is effected by to the crystalline lens changing its shape to a thicker, more steeply curved lens, increases the plus power of the lens and thus the refracting (bending) power of the eye (e.g., from + 50 to + 60) so that light focuses on the retina. Thus, a young farsighted patient can have 20/20 acuity; through accommodation the patient can correct his or her own refractive error. However, in older persons, the ability to accommodate decreases, and accommodation must be supplemented with lenses. For instance, an older person may accommodate 5 diopters and use a + 5-diopter lens.

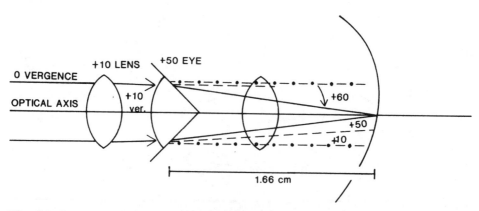

Fig. 20. Lens needed to get a + 50-diopter hyperopic eye to see clearly. The convergence of the + 10-diopter lens is added to the converging effect of the + 50-diopter eye, resulting in + 60 diopters of convergence. The rays are focused on the retina and a clear image appears on the retina.

What is the use of accommodation for objects brought near the eye? If an object is presented 10 centimeters from a fully corrected + 60-diopter eye, the total refracting power of the eye is + 50 diopters (– 10 diopters of vergence of light rays with + 60 diopters of refracting power), and light is focused behind the retina (see Fig. 21). The object is brought into focus

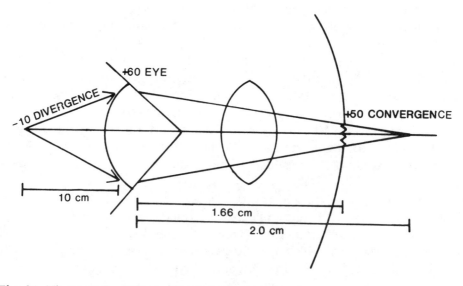

Fig. 21. The rays from the object placed 10 centimeters from the eye enter the eye with a divergence of – 10 diopters. The eye will bend these + 60 diopters for a total effect of + 50. (The first + 10 diopters bring the – 10 rays to zero vergence, and the remaining + 50 diopters are for convergence). The image of the object is 2 centimeters away, or behind the retina. The patient sees the object as blurred.

200

through accommodating 10 diopters (see Fig. 22A) or by providing the person with a +10-diopter lens over and above the distance correction (referred to as a bifocal) (see Fig. 22B). In either case, the total refractive power of the eye is brought to +60 diopters.

Since normal accommodation is +2.5 diopters and most children can sustain only 6 or 8 diopters without discomfort, a partial lens correction usually is prescribed. For –10 diopters of vergence the clinician may give a +6.0-diopter lens and allow the child +4 diopters of accommodation. For older low vision patients, most of the needed power is provided through lenses. For example, for the +70-diopter myopic eye with a –10-diopter spectacle lens, an object at 10 centimeters (–10 diopters of vergence) will be in focus if

1. A +10.0 diopter bifocal is added to the –10 diopter spectacle lens correcting the myopia.

2. The eye accommodates +10 diopters to neutralize the –10 vergence of rays from the object.

3. The –10 myopic correction is removed and replaced by the –10 vergence to maintain the +60-diopter eye.

Thus a person with a myopia of +65 diopters (–5-diopter lens) may remove the correction and be in focus at a viewing distance of 20 centimeters (focal distance = 100/5 = 20 cm). If an additional +5 spectacle reading lens

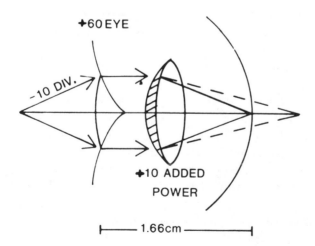

+60 EYE

–10 DIV.

+10 ADDED
POWER

1.66cm

Fig. 22A. How a near object is brought into focus through accommodation. The –10 diverging rays are converged +60 diopters for a total affect of +50 convergence. The lens increased its power an additional +10 diopters for a total bending power of +60, and the image is focused on the retina.

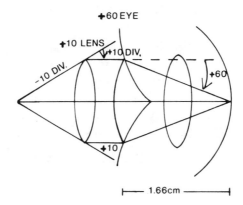

Fig. 22B. How a near object is brought into focus with a bifocal lens. This eye cannot increase its power through accommodation. Therefore, a +10-diopter lens must be added to neutralize the –10-diopter rays. The rays leave the lens with zero vergence, and the zero vergence rays are focused by the +60-diopter eye on the retina. The person sees the near object clearly.

is worn, the eye-lens system has a total bending power of +70 (+65 myopia and +5 spectacle lens). This represents +10 diopters over the normal +60-diopter eye and will allow the patient to read material clearly that has a vergence of –10 diopters or is at a distance of 10 centimeters from the eye (focal distance = 100/10 = 10 cm.). It is important to note that *uncorrected* refractive errors must be included in the determination of focal distance for a particular lens. In the case of the +5-diopter lens, there is a 10-centimeter focal distance in conjunction with 5 diopters of myopia. If the 5-diopter lens is used with an eye of +60 diopters (no refractive error), then the focal distance will be the expected 20 centimeters (focal distance = 100/5 = 20 cm). This also pertains to the eye with a refractive error that has been corrected to +60 diopters (think of a bifocal as a lens in front of the distance spectacle correction). If the +5-diopter lens is used with an eye of +58 diopters (+2.0 diopters of hyperopia), then +2 diopters of the +5-diopter lens will be used to correct the refractive error, leaving +3 diopters for near-point viewing. This means the focal distance will be 33.3 centimeters (focal distance = 100/3 = 33.3 cm).

To review: a +5-diopter lens can have three focal distances: (1) with –5 diopters of myopia (a +65-diopter eye), it will be 10 centimeters; (2) with no refractive error, it will be 20 centimeters; (3) with +2 diopters of hyperopia (a +58 diopter eye) it will be 33.3 centimeters. If accommodation comes into play, even these distances will vary. Therefore, it is important to consider the possibility that the patient is accommodating if the calculations of focal distance do not correspond to actual reading distances. Another reason for this discrepancy may be an uncorrected refractive error. Thus, these observations should be brought to the attention of the examining clinician.

ASTIGMATISM

The issue of astigmatism has little to do with understanding the optics of aids, which is the purpose of this chapter. Therefore, only a brief description of astigmatism will be offered, and the reader may pursue this topic further by consulting the bibliography at the end of this chapter.

In myopia or hyperopia all the rays of light are brought to a focus in front of the retina or behind it, respectively. The primary cause of astigmatism is that the cornea is shaped like a football in that the curve is flatter in one direction than the other. The flattest curve and the steepest curve are 90 degrees apart. If the steepest curve is vertical and the flattest curve is horizontal, then light rays traveling in a vertical direction will have a greater bending power and will be focused closer to the cornea than the rays hitting the horizontal curve (see Fig. 23). Thus, depending on the total power of the eye, the light can focus in several ways:

1. Both horizontal and vertical rays are focused behind the retina.

2. Both horizontal and vertical rays are focused in front of the retina.

3. One set of rays is focused on the retina and the other is focused behind the retina.

4. One set of rays is focused on the retina and the other is focused in front of the retina.

5. One set of rays is focused behind the retina and the other is focused in front of the retina.

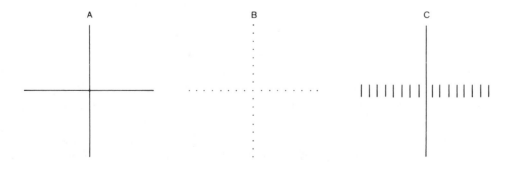

Fig. 23. Astigmatism. (A) A vertical and horizontal line; (B) Conceived as a series of point sources of light; (C) As imaged at the focus of the horizontal principal meridian by the astigmatic eye. The person sees the cross as blurred or distorted.

The net result of all these conditions is that when a person looks at a cross, one line of the cross will be in focus and the other will be out of focus. The steepest and flattest curves of the cornea are not always in a vertical (90 degrees) or horizontal (180 degrees) direction. However, they are, with rare exception, 90 degrees apart. In a prescription, the first number represents the lens needed to correct the myopia ($-$) or hyperopia ($+$); the second number, if it is present, represents how much difference there is between the steepest and flattest meridian or the astigmatism, and the third item is the axis or direction in which the steepest or flattest meridian occurs:

$$-4.00 = -2.00 \times 90$$
$$\text{(myopia) (2 diopters of difference)}$$
$$\text{or astigmatism}$$

The foregoing guidelines will assist the instructor in understanding the various ways in which patients will use their aids and in developing more astute observations of potential problem areas before they become too frustrating for the patient and the motivation to succeed is lost. The figures in this chapter are descriptive and may be technically incorrect in some aspects of optics. However, they reflect an accurate description of the functional parameters of optics.

MAGNIFICATION

Magnification is a method of increasing the size of the retinal image so that enough of the retina (retinal cells) is stimulated to send an impulse (detail or information) up the optic nerve to the brain allowing an object to be perceived (vision). The amount of magnification needed for a patient is determined only after the distance refractive error has been corrected. There are four ways of enlarging the retinal image or creating magnification: (1) relative-size magnification, (2) relative-distance (approach) magnification, (3) angular magnification, and (4) projection magnification.

Relative-size Magnification

In relative-size magnification, the actual size of the object is increased. In Figure 24 one can see how the retinal image size changes when an object is enlarged. If one looks at the optical axis ray and two limiting rays passing from the top and bottom points of an object, one can describe the size of the retinal image for that object. By taking the two limiting rays and passing them through the optical center of the eye (no deviation or bending occurs), one can actually draw the size of the object and image as shown.

As the size of the object is increased, the retinal image size increases. This relationship is such that if the size of the object is doubled, the retinal image size doubles and so on. Two examples are large-print textbooks or the use of a felt-tip pen instead of a ball-point pen for writing, which are simple techniques for providing magnification and should not be overlooked. However,

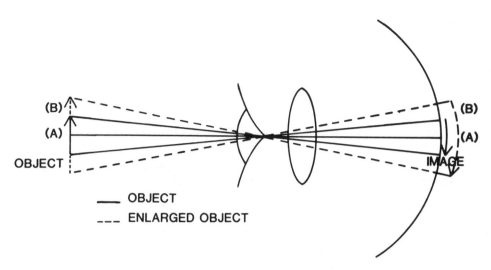

Fig. 24. Relative-size magnification. Relative-size magnification increases the size of the retinal image by enlarging the actual size of the object. Not enough retinal cells are stimulated by the small object (A) to send an impulse up the optic nerve to the brain. If the size of the object is doubled, (B), the image is double in size and twice the number of cells are stimulated. The cells now send an impulse to the brain and the visual information is perceived and the object is seen in detail.

they increase the size and weight of the materials duplicated and may be expensive, although reasonably priced services are available for reproducing material in large print. Sometimes this method of providing magnification is more acceptable to an individual, especially for reading because it allows a normal reading distance.

Relative-distance Magnification

Relative-distance magnification (approach magnification) simply means that as an object is brought closer to the eye, the retinal image becomes larger. The relationship is such that as an object is brought to one-half its present distance, the retinal image doubles. If the distance is increased by one-quarter or one-eighth, the retinal image size increases four or eight times, respectively (see Figure 25).

Note that one must arbitrarily assign some distance as being a reference point so it can be said that something is twice as big as something else. In this discussion, 40 centimeters will be used as the reference distance. Thus in Figure 25, "1X" is the image size of an object held 40 centimeters in front of the eye. When the object is 20 centimeters in front of the eye, the magnification is "2X"; at 10 centimeters, it is "4X"; at 5 centimeters, it is "8X"; and so forth. It is important to remember that the enlarged image occurred without

205

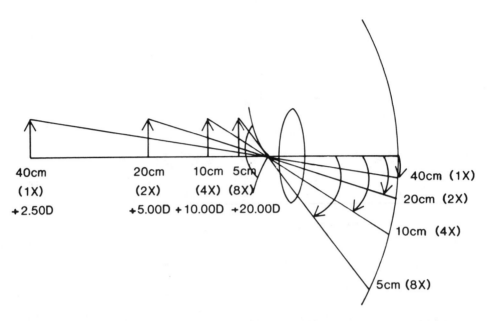

40cm   20cm   10cm 5cm   40cm (1X)
(1X)   (2X)   (4X) (8X)   20cm (2X)
+2.50D +5.00D +10.00D +20.00D   10cm (4X)
                                   5cm (8X)

Fig. 25. Relative-distance magnification. In relative-distance magnification, the image enlarges proportionately as the object is brought closer to the eye.

the use of microscopic lenses. Lenses do not create magnification; the decreased viewing distance does. Lenses are used to get a *clear* enlarged image. The object at 40 centimeters will have light rays entering the eye with a divergence of – 2.5 diopters (100/40 cm = – 2.50). To get this enlarged image focused on the retina, the eye must accommodate + 2.5 diopters, a + 2.5-diopter bifocal lens must be provided, or the patient must have 2.5 diopters of myopia. When the object is 20 centimeters in front of the eye, the magnification is 2X; that is, the retinal image of the object is twice as large as that of the retinal image of the object when the object was at 40 centimeters. Also, a + 5 -diopter (100/20 = 5) lens, 5 diopters of accommodation, or 5 diopters of myopia are needed to give a clear or focused image. For a chart of this distance magnification–lens power scheme, see Table 1.

From the table, one can see that every 1X magnification requires 2.5 diopters. Thus, for this system magnification can be determined with the formula $M = \dfrac{Diopter}{2.5}$. Thus the + 5 lens provides 2X magnification (5/2.5 = 2). Likewise, 2X magnification requires a total power of + 5 (2 × 2.5 = 5). This formula shows how much magnification is being provided by a specific distance. It is the distance that creates the enlarged image and mandates a specific lens power.

A distance of 25 centimeters is often used as a reference point in texts and

206

Table 1. Distance Magnification–Lens Power Scheme at a Reference Distance of 40 Centimeters.

Distance of Object (in centimeters)	Magnification	Lens Needed (in diopters)[a]
40	1X	2.5
20	2X	5.0
10	4X	10.0
5	8X	20.0
4	10X	25.0
2	20X	50.0
1	40X	100.0

[a]The necessary diopters may be provided by a lens or through accommodation or uncorrected myopia (or all three).

is the standard used to label many microscopic lenses. Table 2 shows the distance magnification–lens power scheme at 25 centimeters. These two schemes can be disconcerting because a 5X lens can be a + 12.50 lens with material held at 8 centimeters or a + 20-diopter lens with material held at 5 centimeters, depending on which system is referred to. This is why one works in diopters rather than magnification when describing aids. However, the knowledge that these two systems exist will prevent confusion when reviewing the literature of the field.

Table 2. Distance Magnification–Lens Power Scheme at a Reference Distance of 25 Centimeters.

Distance of Object (in centimeters)	Magnification	Lens Needed (in diopters)[a]
25.00	1X	4
12.50	2X	8
6.25	4X	16
5.00	5X	20
4.25	6X	24
3.30	8X	32
2.50	10X	40
1.00	25X	100

[a]The necessary diopters may be provided by a lens or through accommodation or uncorrected myopia (or all three).

The chief disadvantage of the use of relative-distance magnification is the close working distance and the field limitations of the lenses used. It is interesting to note that the limiting rays enter the eye along the same path when magnification is provided by doubling the size of an object at the reference

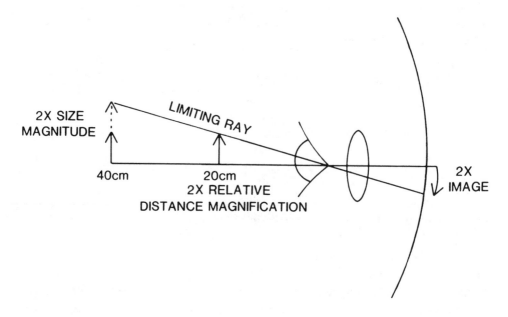

Fig. 26. The limiting ray that determines the image size of an enlarged object is the same both with relative-size magnification and relative-distance magnification.

distance or by bringing it to one-half the reference distance (see Fig. 26). The eye does not know the difference optically; to judge size, it responds only to the direction from which the limiting rays appear to come. Through other cues, it determines perceptually if the object was made 2X as large by enlarging the object or by bringing it closer.

Angular Magnification

Angular magnification is the magnification experienced when one looks through binoculars. It is created by a system of lenses in the telescope. However, it results in the same retinal image changes as the previous two systems of magnification. Angular magnification is needed when the object is too far away or too large to move closer or just too big to change its size. The telescopic lenses bend the lights rays so when they leave the telescope, they appear to be coming from the same direction as an object closer to the eye; thus, the object appears much larger. Think of the rays in Figures 27 and 28 as coming from a distant object, being bent as they leave the telescope, and then, because they are still parallel but traveling in a new direction, focusing on the retina. The eye ignores the telescope and, because the limiting rays are stimulating the same cells as in the previous examples, the brain interprets this to mean the object is twice as large as before. Since the brain knows the object was not enlarged, it assumes that it came closer; therefore,

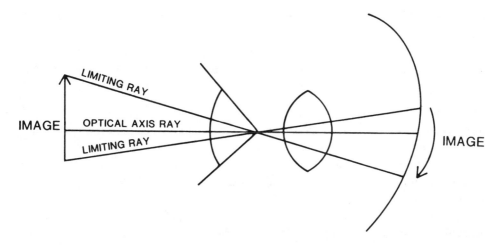

Fig. 27. This figure shows the limiting rays that determine the size of the image on the retina. If the image is not large enough to stimulate a visual impulse, then an enlarged image is needed. In this case a telescope will be interjected to bend the rays of light to stimulate a larger retinal area.

an object is perceived as being closer when one looks through binoculars or a telescope.

The telescope is useful for distance objects that cannot be enlarged or moved closer. However, it has a limited field of view (if the field of view were adequate, the telescope would be bulky like binoculars), it has motion parallax in that movement is exaggerated through the telescope, and an ob-

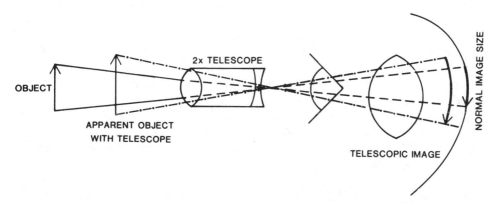

Fig. 28. The light rays enter the telescope, and instead of leaving in the same direction they entered and forming a normal image, the telescopic lenses increase the convergence of the rays and the rays enter the eye as though coming from an apparent object sitting much closer to the eye than the real object. Thus, the brain perceives the object as being bigger and closer and greater detail is seen.

ject appears to be closer than it really is. Thus, a telescope is used mainly to spot objects rather than for full-time wear. Furthermore, if we turn the telescope around and look through it, the optics is reversed and everything is minified. This characteristic will be elaborated on in the discussion of reversed telescopes for individuals with severe field losses (see Chapter 11).

Projection Magnification

The fourth area of magnification is projection magnification—the enlargement of an object by projecting it onto a screen, such as in films, slides, and so forth. The most familiar aid that utilizes this principle is the closed-circuit television system (CCTV). The magnification of the CCTV created by the projection on the screen (an electronic size increase) can be increased further by moving closer to the television screen. The Viewscan uses an array of fiber optics to yield a highly enlarged display.

Aids will create a magnified retinal image using one of the four magnification systems or some combination of the four. If one physically doubles the size of an object (2X) and then brings it from 40 centimeters to 20 centimeters (2X), a 4X magnification is created (i.e., the size was doubled and then that image size was doubled). When two types of magnification are combined, the total magnification is the product of the two systems. Thus, 4X projection magnification with 2X relative distance magnification produces a total magnification of 8X. Combinations of magnification systems will be discussed further in Chapter 10.

Bibliography

Bailey, I. Combining accommodation with spectacle additions. *Optometric Monthly,* 1971, **71**(6), 397-399.

Basic optical concepts. Southbridge, Mass.: American Optical Corp., 1976.

Browning, R. Lecture notes, University of Houston College of Optometry, 1981-82.

Byer, A. Magnification: The goal of low vision lenses. *Review of Optometry,* 1979, **116**(9), 47-50.

Duke-Elder, S., & Abrams, D. *Ophthalmic optics and refraction,* Vol. 4 of *System of ophthalmology,* St. Louis: C.V. Mosby Co., 1970.

Freid, A., & Mehr, E. *Low vision care.* Chicago: Professional Press, 1974.

Lenses, prisms, mirrors. Southbridge, Mass.: American Optical Corp., 1976.

Rosenberg, R. The optics of low vision lenses. In E. Faye (ed.), *Clinical low vision.* Boston: Little, Brown, 1976.

CHAPTER 10

Treatment Options

RANDALL T. JOSE, O.D.

This chapter is entitled "Treatment Options" instead of "Optical Aids," to emphasize the importance of the multidisciplinary approach to care and the relationship between the clinical and nonclinical aspects of care. Anyone can be taught to dispense aids. An effective program of low vision care utilizes optical aids as one component of the treatment plan for a particular individual. A telescope does not make a person an independent traveler. However, it may be the key to a successful mobility training program, and the telescope and the training program together may allow the individual to reach his or her educational or vocational potentials. This is how aids are presented in this chapter, which gives an overview of the various types of aids and discusses their advantages and limitations. Specific aids are not detailed, however, because they become rapidly outdated. To guide the reader through the variety of aids in the field, an extensive list of resources is given in Chapter 19.

Optical aids may be considered the "tools of the trade" in the field of low vision care. The following are three important points to remember about optical aids:

1. Optical aids are tools that are used to help the person with low vision and must be treated as such. Sometimes, they are the most insignificant part of the low vision service.

2. Optical aids are prescribed by a clinician based on information given and recommendations made by other professionals. This type of collaboration is necessary because of the sophisticated relationship between vision and the handicapped person. Any professional can dispense nonprescriptive aids to a person with low vision and thereby increase that person's acuity. However, only a prescriptive aid results in optimum levels of visual functioning and performance with the increased acuity.

3. It is as much of an abuse for a clinician to prescribe an aid for a visually handicapped person without input from other involved professionals as it is for the nonclinician to provide an aid to that person.

LEVELS OF MAGNIFICATION

Once the task has been identified that the patient wishes to achieve, the clinician must determine the level of magnification needed to accomplish it. The level of magnification, as well as the task, can dictate the type of aids to be considered or, in some cases, even the specific aid. The current technology regarding low vision aids is simple, and the options open to the clinician often are restricted.

Magnification is determined by assessing the acuity level needed to perform a desired task and relating it to the best-corrected acuity achievable with conventional lenses. The best-corrected acuity is needed to ensure that the patient's minimum needs for magnification are met, which results in greater options in the types of aids that may be used, larger fields, and longer working distances—factors that usually lead to greater success.

An estimate of the magnification needed is only a starting point. Typically, it is assumed that an acuity of 20/40 will suffice for most tasks. This estimate is an excellent starting point for most evaluations. However, it must be remembered that it is arbitrary and only a starting point. For example, a bookkeeper or computer programmer may require a final prescription that yields a 20/20 acuity, whereas a maintenance man may need a final prescription that produces a 20/70 acuity.

To illustrate the difficulties involved in determining the appropriate level of magnification for a particular patient, let us consider the case of an individual with an acuity of 20/400 that is improved to 20/200 with conventional lenses. To achieve the goal of an acuity of 20/40 (the arbitrary starting point), one would find the level of magnification needed by dividing 40 into 200, which would yield a 5X magnification.

$$20/200 \text{ to } 20/40 = 200/40 = 5$$

However, if the clinician missed the patient's refractive error or the instructor "prescribed" an aid without considering the refractive error, the case would be much more complicated. That is, without conventional glasses, the patient's acuity is 20/400, which means that the patient would need aids of 10X magnification (400/40 = 10X). Without the appropriate correction for the refractive error, the patient would have to tolerate the severe field and other restrictions of the distance and near aids. At near, a 5X-system requires a 5-centimeter working distance, and a 10X-system requires a 2.5-centimeter working distance and half the field of view. If the patient with 20/200 best-corrected acuity wanted to perform a task that required 20/20 vision, 10X magnification would be required (200/20 = 10X) for that task.

If a patient with 20/200 uses a 5X aid and gets a substantially better acuity or a significantly worse acuity than the expected 20/40, it is the clinician's responsibility to determine the optical, physiological, or psychological reasons for this unexpected performance. That is why it is so important for the clinician and the instructor to establish good communication.

Once the expected level of magnification is determined, appropriate aids of that power may be evaluated. The aid of choice will vary, depending on the power needed, the fields and working distances required, the patient's motivation, and myriad other factors. Because a discussion of the use of every aid in the field would be outdated before this book went to press, this chapter covers only the *categories* of aids that are available. Readers may familiarize themselves with specific aids by reviewing the current literature (see, e.g., Faye, 1976; Freid & Mehr, 1974; Genensky, 1969; Kelleher, 1979; Rosenberg, 1973; Sloan, 1977; Sloan & Habel, 1956; Turner, 1976) or by maintaining contact with the manufacturers of low vision aids, the large low vision clinics, or low vision organizations. For the purpose of understanding the nature and use of aids as they pertain to the instructional phases of the low vision service, the following categories of aids will be dealt with in this chapter:

1. Telescopes (including binoculars).
2. Telemicroscopes (near-point telescopes).
3. Microscopes (any spectacle-mounted device, such as a reading lens, a loupe, and a clip-on).
4. Magnifiers (stand and hand-held).
5. Projection-electronic magnifiers.
6. Nonoptical-accessory aids.
7. Field-utilization aids (prisms, minification, and so forth).

TELESCOPES

Telescopes are the only aids that assist a low vision person with distance tasks. These devices use angular magnification—the same principle involved in binoculars (see Chapter 9). The obvious inherent problems in the use of telescopes are the exaggerated movement of objects viewed through them, the apparent closeness of objects or the disruption of spatial judgments, and the reduced field of the smaller units or the bulk of the larger units with greater fields. The more magnification, the more important these problems become.

The instructor should know the following about the optics of the telescopic system:

■ An afocal telescope is focused for infinity. Thus, the low vision patient should view objects at a distance of 20 feet or more to be in clear focus.

■ Many telescopes have mechanisms that focus as close as 2 feet for a variety of distance tasks. The instructor should learn the focusing range of each telescope. Separating the elements of a telescope will usually result in added plus power to the system to compensate for the negative or diverging rays of the object closer than 20 feet.

■ Since any telescope can be set for infinity, the instructor or clinician should focus the telescope on the object to be viewed and then have the pa-

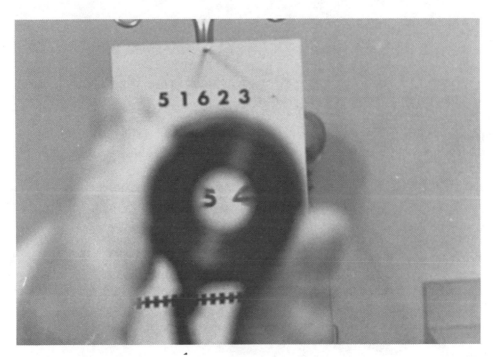

Fig. 1. A shows the view through a 2.5X telescope with a 5mm vertex distance and B shows the same view with a 10mm vertex distance.

tient look through the telescope. The patient should also report whether the object is in focus. If the patient has to make much of a change in the focusing system to see the object clearly, then the patient may have an uncorrected refractive error. The instructor should report this information to the low vision clinician for further evaluation.

■ The patient should wear any significant refractive-error correction when using a telescope, or have it incorporated into the telescopic device. Some telescopes will allow the patient to hold the telescope closer to the eye and enjoy a larger field of view (see Fig. 1). Refractive errors must be evaluated to assure optimum use of the telescope. The instructor should check with the clinician about the need for correcting a refractive error when the patient uses a particular telescope.

■ An exit pupil is the optical window through which the patient views when using a telescope. It is smaller than the ocular lens of the telescope (the lens toward the eye). The higher the magnification, the smaller the exit pupil. This fact is important to remember when working with patients who have poor fixation or localization skills. If these patients are having problems, the low vision clinician can provide a telescope of a different design to enlarge the size of the exit pupil (a Keplerian telescope has a larger exit pupil than a Galilean telescope), or a telescope with less magnification can be used as a training aid to develop fixation or localization skills.

■ It is important to remember that telescopes lose light; thus, in a training program, greater success will be achieved if adequate lighting and contrast are provided on the instructional targets and objects.

■ With Keplerian telescopes you can have the patient look at a light source with the telescope. The image of that light source can be viewed on the patient's iris. By adjusting the telescope until the image is located in the pupil, sometimes you can find the patient's line of sight (the direction in which the patient normally turns the eye to view objects) and get him or her to "see" an object. Many patients with poor fixation cannot find the exit pupil, and report seeing black, until the telescope is properly aligned.

■ Generally, hand-held telescopes are found in powers of 2.5X, 2.8X, 3X, 4X, 6X, 8X and 10X. Spectacle telescopes are found in powers of 2X, 2.2X, 3X, 4X, 6X, and 8X.

The instructor should be familiar with the following parameters of the telescopes being used in the low vision service:

1. The powers available.
2. The field of view.
3. The focusing range.
4. The weight.
5. The potential for mounting spectacles.
6. The loss of light.
7. The possibility that refractive-error corrections can be included.
8. The depth of focus.

215

The basic categories of telescopes are hand-held, clip-on, full-field spectacle, bioptic spectacle, and binoculars. A few comments on the functional uses of the different systems are offered below.

Hand-Held Telescopes

The hand-held telescope is designed for spotting distance objects or for other short-term distance tasks. It is small and can be kept in a pocket or purse or hung around the neck when not being used. Some uses of telescopes by patients are as follows:

1. To enhance independent travel by allowing the patient to see stop lights, street signs, store signs, bus numbers, and so forth.
2. To watch television for short periods.
3. To see who is coming up the front walk or who is at the front door.
4. To watch birds and squirrels in the back yard.
5. To view flowers in a garden.
6. To find a newspaper that has been thrown in the front yard.
7. To see a ball game or a play.
8. To sight-see while riding as a passenger in the family car.
9. To see the blackboard in school.
10. To see the activities of employees.
11. To watch children in another room without disturbing them.
12. To see pins and scores when bowling.
13. To see street names, house numbers, and so forth from the car.
14. To watch other people.
15. To use on hikes, in parks, and other nature-related activities.

Most hand-held telescopes are monocular and are used with the preferred eye; they have a focusing ring to make the image as clear as possible. Many telescopes will not focus for objects closer than five feet, so check each telescope. The stronger the power of a telescope, the smaller the field of view when looking through it.

Clip-On Telescopes

Clip-on telescopes usually are monocular. When a telescope is needed, patients simply take out the clip-on telescope, slip it over the top rim of their glasses, and focus on the object with the focusing ring. Often they will have better results if they patch the eye that does not use the telescope during the initial stages of training; plastic clip-on patches are often used for this purpose. Clip-on telescopes are useful for short-term telescopic needs when patients need their hands free for a specific task. For example, a student can look at the blackboard with the clip-on telescope over one eye and use the other eye for near tasks, such as writing, although the acuity must be almost the same in each eye for this type of biocularity to be successful. The clip-on telescope also can be used for watching television or a movie or any other type of distance viewing. As with the hand-held telescope, the increased magnification of the clip-on telescope will reduce the field of view.

As with any low vision aid, the clip-on telescope is maximally effective only after a person practices viewing through it. Since it covers the entire eye, it cannot be used when the person moves around. (For this reason, it should be considered in the same category as a full-field telescope.)

Bioptic Telescope

When a person needs a telescope for constant use and yet is always moving about, a bioptic telescope must be prescribed. This type of telescope uses conventional plastic ophthalmic prescription lenses in a frame; a small hole is drilled in the top part of the lenses and a miniature telescope is mounted in each hole. The conventional lenses are used for general viewing and the bioptic telescope is used for seeing distance objects in detail. To use the bioptic telescope, the person lowers the head and raises the eye to look through the telescopic portion (see Fig. 2). When he or she no longer needs the telescope, the person raises his or her head and continues on, looking through the conventional lens (see Fig. 3). A clip-on telescope can be prescribed, but it must be inserted and removed for each visual task. It (or any telescope)

Fig. 2. The patient lowers his head to view through the telescopic portion of a bioptic system.

217

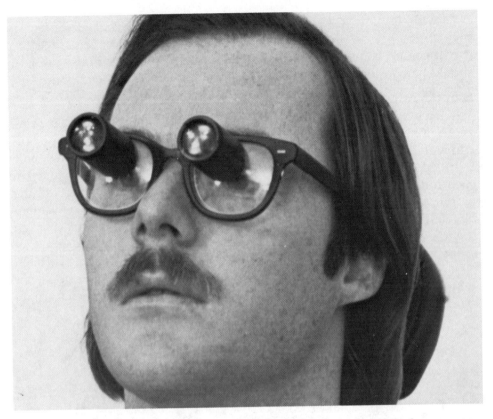

Fig. 3. The bioptic design allows the patient to look through the conventional lens while walking around.

cannot be used when the person is mobile because it magnifies the image and reduces the field of view; thus, objects seem to be closer and to be moving faster than they really are.

The major disadvantage of the bioptic telescope is that it is miniaturized so the field of view is even smaller than in hand-held or clip-on telescopes and this makes spotting objects through it more difficult. Training should follow a step-by-step process similar to that used with the hand-held telescope. Because the bioptic telescope is difficult to learn to use, patients should be cautioned not to become frustrated if their progress is slow. With training, individuals learn to overcome or adapt to the problems of small fields, speed smear, and spatial-distance judgments. Once patients learn to use the bioptic telescope effectively, they find it valuable in vocational and educational settings.

Full-Field Telescope

The full-field telescope covers the entire lens in the frame (see Fig. 4). Although it gives a larger field of view than the bioptic telescope, it is used only for visual activities that may be accomplished while standing or sitting

Fig. 4. A full-field telescope does not allow the patient to look around the telescope. This is the ocular view through a 2.5X clip-on telescope.

because learning to walk with this type of lens is difficult and should only be attempted in the presence of an experienced low vision instructor. A patient must receive specific instructions on how and when to use the full-field telescope. This type of telescope is prescribed for unique vocational or recreational needs and is not used often.

A unique full-field telescope is the contact-lens telescope (see Fig. 5). A high minus-power contact lens serves as the ocular of the telescope and a plus-spectacle lens (cataract like lens) is worn as the objective of the telescope. Up to 2X magnification can be obtained with this system. Because it is worn full time, some adaptive training is needed.

Binoculars

Even though they are large and cumbersome, binoculars provide high magnification with large fields and are excellent as an adjunct to smaller systems or for patients who have problems with the smaller systems. Binoculars can be used for short-term tasks (the weight makes it difficult to stabilize for long periods) when a large field of view is needed. A tripod can be designed if the

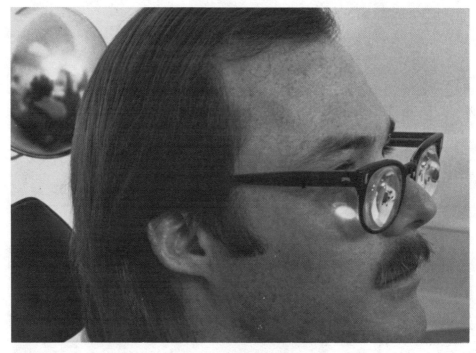

Fig. 5. The contact lens telescope utilizes a high minus contact lens for the ocular and a cataract like lens for the objective.

binoculars are needed for a longer time. If the patient is monocular, one scope can be used for distance and the other for near.

TELEMICROSCOPES

As indicated earlier, telescopes are focused for a distance of at least 20 feet. However, as an object approaches the eye closer than 20 feet, the rays of light reaching the eye (or telescope) have a negative power (see Chapter 9). The eye accommodates or reading glasses (plus power) compensate for these negative vergence rays. A telescope cannot accommodate, and it alters the light rays so that the negative vergence is increased in proportion to the square of the magnification of the telescope. This means that even with low-powered telescopes, the eye cannot accurately focus on near objects without help. At 10 inches, an object will need 25 diopters of accommodation when viewed through a weak 2.5X telescope. Since most people can accommodate only 8–10 diopters, telescopes are useless for near tasks unless they are adapted. Some telescopes are designed so the ocular lens can be moved outward, creating plus power to focus on near objects. A telemicroscope is simply a telescope with a reading cap incorporated into its front (objective) lens. The power of the reading cap dictates the working distance. Since the goal is to have zero vergence rays entering the telescope, the material must be placed at the focal point of the reading cap. By dividing the diopter power of the lens into 100, one can determine the working space (from the front of the telescope to the object) in centimeters. Thus a +2 reading cap will require the person to hold the material to be viewed at 50 centimeters, or 20 inches. The term working distance is different from the working space; it is from the spectacle plane (or cornea) to the object being viewed. It is always longer than the working space because it includes the working space plus the length of the telescope (see Fig. 6).

It is important to note that the magnification changes with different reading caps. For example, with a +4 cap, the magnification of the telemicroscope is equivalent to the power of the telescope. A 6X Selsi with a +4 cap will provide 6X magnification at 25 centimeters. Reading caps stronger than +4 will increase the magnification (decrease the working distance), and powers less than +4 will decrease the magnification (increase the working distance). The magnification can be determined by the following formula:

(Power of telescope) × (diopters of cap/4) = power telemicroscope

Telemicroscopes provide greater working distances than do microscopes but they sacrifice the field of view. A 4X increase in working distance may result in as much as a 4X decrease in the field of view. The new Feinbloom terrestrial spectacle-mounted bioptic telescopes provide an increased working distance but minimize this field loss. The instructor should compare equivalent telemicroscopic units (6X telescope with +4 cap) and microscopic units (24-diopter lens) to visualize the relationship between the working distance and field of view (25 centimeters versus 4.1 centimeters). Telemicroscopes also have a much more critical depth of focus than do comparable microscopes.

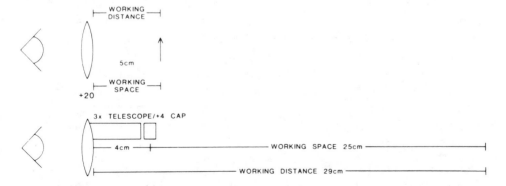

Fig. 6. The working distance of an optical aid is the distance from the eye or spectacle to the object. The working space is the distance from the front of the optical system to the object.

Because the telemicroscope has an exit pupil, training activities must acknowledge the size of the exit pupil if problems arise. The exit pupil should be aligned with the patient's normal line of vision. Starting with a hand-held telescope or a low-power telescope may improve the chance of success in difficult training cases because the exit pupil is larger in these systems.

To be binocular, telemicroscopes have to be designed for a specific working distance. Once the distance is established, they are angled inward and downward to point at the object to be viewed. This alignment process is difficult and critical. In systems that utilize only one distance (known as near-point or reading telescopes), reading caps usually are incorporated into the front of the telescope and the system always is used at a fixed distance. If a reading cap is placed over the system, the patient will be monocular because the telescopes will be pointed at one distance and focused at another. Occasionally, a minus cap is used so the person can view objects at a distance. The minus cap neutralizes the plus lens added to the system for near.

With telemicroscopes (as with telescopes) refractive errors must be corrected and usually are incorporated into the system. The examiner will help determine the best technique for this. Any major deviations from the correct working distance may indicate a refractive error and should be referred to the examiner. The focal point is also critical. The stronger the system, the more important it is to hold the material at the exact focal distance. This is why individuals with poor motor control find it difficult to use these systems. The low vision instructor should, therefore, experiment with the depth of focus of the particular patient's telemicroscopic system.

The spectacle telemicroscope can be designed as a full-field system in which the telescope either is so large it takes up the whole frame or it is mounted in the center of the frame (see Fig. 7). This system does not allow mobility or distance viewing (unless the caps are removed). A telescope that is clipped onto a person's spectacles is considered a full-field system because the person cannot "look around it."

In a reading telescope, the telescopes are mounted in the lower part of the frame so the person looks through them in the normal reading position and can look over the frame through the conventional prescription lens to see distant objects. Reading telescopes may be monocular, binocular, or biocular. With a biocular reading telescope, a person can use the right eye to type with a +3 cap (33 cm) and use the left eye to read the small manuscript at 25 centimeters with a +4 cap. The caps may be built in if the working distance is always the same, but if the working distance varies, a different cap should be provided for each new task.

Prescription Options

If a person uses a telescope for distance and near, either a bioptic telescope or a hand-held telescope with caps must be used. If a person has only occasional intermediate distance or near tasks (spotting), then a hand-held telescope with appropriate reading caps is the best solution. If the object of the

Fig. 7. Full-field telescopes can be large aperture telescopes (left) or small centrally mounted telescopes (right).

prescription is to provide the person with optimum vision for long-term tasks entailing five or six hours a day, then a bioptic spectacle telescope with caps is the prescription of choice. In bioptic spectacle telescopes, the telescopes are mounted in the upper portion of the frame; thus, the person can look below the telescopes to use his or her normal vision for mobility. By dropping the head or raising the eyes, the person can look through the telescope and get the magnification needed for seeing distant objects in detail. Because the telescopes are aligned for distant binocular use, they will have to be used monocularly (one cannot turn the tubes inward to point at the near object) or biocularly at near (each tube has a different power cap for different working distances). Some people read with one eye until they tire and then switch the cap to the other eye and continue reading. They think this type of biocular use of the telescopes significantly increases their reading time.

In working with telescopes, it should be noted that it usually is easiest for a patient to adapt to the full-field position, probably because this position most closely approximates the person's normal line of sight. If a patient has difficulty fixating through a bioptic mounting, start with a centrally mounted telescope and move it slowly upward as the patient begins to find the object through the telescope. Sometimes this can be accomplished by starting with a hand-held telemicroscope so the patient can find his or her own line

223

of sight. Holding the telescope also provides kinesthetic feedback to help fixation and localization. Another point to consider is this: When patients try to read printed material held in a normal reading position, they will have to use exaggerated neck and head movements to view the materials (or point the telescopes correctly). They will have to look down farther than they think they should to find the print. Sometimes looking at their own fingers gives them better feedback.

MICROSCOPES

The microscope is a plus lens that utilizes the principle of relative-distance magnification. All aids that are head borne or frame mounted are arbitrarily included in this category for convenience. Reading material is brought closer to the eye, and the microscope creates a clear enlarged retinal image. The closer the object is brought to the eye, the more divergent (minus power) the rays of light (see Chapter 9). Thus, the eye has to increase its focusing power greater than the normal 60 diopters. Young children can do this by accommodation; they bring the book closer to get an enlarged image and then use accommodation to clear up the enlarged image. (Because of their ability to accommodate, visually handicapped children should be allowed to hold their book up to their nose if necessary.) The examiner sometimes can provide microscopes that will slightly increase the working distance of or at least reduce the fatigue experienced by the child who has to sustain such large accommodative efforts. Although microscopes will not improve the acuity (letter sizes seen), they may increase the child's attention span and reading duration.

Persons with severe myopia have a "built in" microscope. By taking off their glasses, they have extra plus-focusing power to see magnified objects clearly. A myopic eye has too much plus power (70 diopters instead of 60 diopters). The extra plus power is corrected by giving the light rays negative power with glasses or by moving the object closer (it does not make any difference to the eye). In most cases, encourage the myopic child to read without glasses if the reading performance increases. As usual, a thorough examination will determine the best system to use.

Advantages of Use

One advantage of microscopic correction is that it allows both hands to be free. Microscopes also provide a large field (relative to telescopes and magnifiers of the same power) because they are worn close to the eyes and do not have the multiple lenses of the telescopes. This makes them more convenient to use for such tasks as (1) long-term reading sessions, (2) writing tasks and signatures (with adequate work space), (3) making out checks and balancing books, (4) needlework, (5) gardening tasks, such as inspecting plants for insects, (6) reading shipping invoices, receipts, and other small-print items.

Disadvantages of Use

The higher the magnification, the shorter the working distance and obviously the more limited the number of tasks that can be accomplished easily. If a person must hold material at 10 centimeters to see it, then a + 10-diopter lens is being used (unless the person has myopia or is using accommodation). Likewise, if the examiner determines that 5X is needed (+ 20 diopters), then the working distance will be 100/20 or 5 centimeters. A 2X microscope (+ 8 diopters) allows a 12.5-centimeter working distance. Thus, it is important to determine the minimum magnification needed to provide the greatest working distance. The close working distance is the greatest obstacle to the successful use of microscopes because

- The close working distance is too conspicuous.
- The new position of the arms, neck, and shoulder muscles results in quick fatigue.
- The kinesthetic feedback to the eyes is altered and confuses the reading task.
- Head and arm movements are required instead of ocular movements, and this new coordination of head-arm-ocular muscles is difficult to learn.
- Reading speed is slower than before the problem occurred.

Another difficulty is that the strength of the lens interferes with mobility because a person's distance acuity is severely blurred by the microscope (some people become nauseous when they try to look in the distance with a microscope). The blurring of distance acuity is a particular problem with full-field microscopes, since the patient cannot look around the lenses. Geriatric patients especially should be warned not to walk around with the lenses on because they may become confused or dizzy and fall. A bifocal has its mobility setbacks as well. Even though the person can look over the microscopic bifocal, the bifocal acts as a lower field loss. This type of loss can be a serious obstacle for children and older persons and in specific vocational endeavors.

Optics of the Microscope

The optics of the microscope are straightforward. The higher the magnification, the smaller the field and the shorter the working distance. By designing a multilens microscope (Feinbloom, Nikon, or Keeler lenses) the field of view that is free of distortion can be substantially improved in the higher powers. The decision to design such a microscope will be made by the examiner, but it can be verified through performance evaluations by the instructional staff.

The working distance can be determined by dividing the diopter of the lens into 100. (Usually every 4 diopters equals 1X, so 4X equals 4 × 4 diopters or + 16 diopters.) The refractive error affects the diopter power of the lenses. If a + 16 microscope (4X) is put on a person with + 6 diopters of hyperopia, the power of the microscope is really + 10 diopters (6 diopters used to correct the hyperopia, and +10 diopters are left over for magnification). The person will hold the material at 10 centimeters (100/10 = 10 cm). If the microscope is put on a person with −6 diopters of myopia (+6 diopters from the myopic eye and +16 diopters from the lens), the working distance is 4.5 centimeters (100/22 = 4.5 cm). If the person has no refractive error, is not accommodating, wears contact lenses, or is putting the microscope over the conventional glasses, then the material will be held at the expected distance of 6.2 centimeters (100/16 = 6.2 cm). Thus, it is important to measure the person's working distance to determine if a greater or lesser distance will give better results, especially if the person is reporting problems. However, it should be noted that many optical factors can vary this distance. If you find a discrepancy, report it to the examiner so a logical explanation can be given or the aid can be modified.

The depth of focus of the microscope is critical, especially at the higher magnifications. The person must be taught to move the head to read or move the paper perpendicular to the center of the microscopes. If only eye movements are used, even the small change in distance between the eye and the end of the page will cause a significant blur when reading.

Binocular vision is typically limited to 3X magnification or less. The correction must include prisms to help reduce fatigue from having to converge the eyes for such close working distances. The muscles move the eyes inward in a coordinated fashion so both eyes are aligned with the object being focused on. Many patients must wear a patch or receive monocular corrections to reduce confusion from images being received by the poorer eye. (Most people automatically suppress the poorer eye and do not even realize they are monocular.) It is important to counsel these patients beforehand because many patients are afraid that the poorer eye will go blind if they do not use it. Therefore, they must be convinced that, in their situation, the monocular status is functionally better and will help improve vision in the better eye. In all cases, peripheral vision is still being used (even behind the patch), so the eye will not degenerate or lose vision.

Design of the Microscope
The microscope may be designed as a full lens (reading glasses). This design gives the largest field and is best used when a person is performing a near task while stationary. If the person is mobile, a bifocal system can be used. The microscope may be designed to cover a majority of the total lens if the person needs only occasional distance vision and does not walk around with the glasses on. If the person must walk around but still needs a large field, the bifocal can be made wider and set as high in the frame as possible so the person can still look over the bifocal for mobility. Sometimes a clip-on loupe works well too. The loupe covers most of the lens when placed in front of the eye, thus affording a large field, and can be flipped up and out of the way for greater mobility. The person can then walk around with a full distance

lens. If the person uses the microscope only for short spotting tasks while mobile, a button-type bifocal can be designed that will give the maximum field for distance vision and yet have the convenience of a bifocal microscope. Loupes and clip-ons can fall down and blur distance vision, which can cause a hazard in vocational settings; thus a bifocal is the preferred prescription in this type of setting. Sometimes the bifocal can even be put in the top part of the lens so the lower field is free and undistorted for mobility. As in other situations, the exact design of the aid will depend on the instructor's evaluations and determination of needs and the clinician's examination findings. The better the coordination of these evaluations, the more functional will be the design of the microscope.

MAGNIFIERS

Magnifiers are designed to help the low vision patient with short-term spotting tasks at near. They may be either mounted on stands or held in the hand. For some individuals, a magnifier is the primary aid of choice because it solves all their reported problems (either all their desired tasks are short-term or they are able to use the magnifier for extended periods). The magnifier also is an excellent secondary aid; for example, a person may use a spectacle microscope for reading but rely on a hand-held magnifier for checking prices while shopping.

Typical uses of magnifiers (stand and hand-held) are as follows:

- To read a newspaper for a short time or to scan the large print (headlines, titles, subheadlines) in books or newspapers before reading the smaller print with microscopes.
- To read labels and prices while shopping.
- To see dials, gauges, and other controls on ovens, grills, ranges, and other appliances.
- To read recipes.
- To look up phone numbers and addresses.
- To read mail.
- To see measuring tapes, dials, gauges, and so forth in a workshop or other vocational setting.
- To read labels on medicine bottles.
- To proofread manuscripts or other typed materials.
- To thread a needle on a sewing machine.
- To check the hygiene of contact lenses.
- To read maps and bus or train schedules.
- To read a menu in a restaurant.
- To verify checks that have been made out by another person.
- To verify correct denominations of currency.

The examiner works in conjunction with the instructor to determine if the most appropriate solution to the patient's problems is the prescription of a telescope, telemicroscope, microscope, magnifier, or a combination of the optical treatments presented so far (see Faye, 1976; Freid & Mehr, 1974; Kelleher, 1979).

The Hand-held Magnifier

The hand-held magnifier probably is the most common aid. Often people purchase several magnifiers before they seek a low vision evaluation. Thus, it is important to find out what power magnifiers they used, what they used them for, the problems they encountered, and how long ago they stopped using them. This information will allow the clinician to prescribe a more appropriate aid based on the patient's previous experiences. The hand-held magnifier also can be used as a training aid for patients who resist the close working distance of a microscope. Because the more customary working distance of the hand-held magnifier makes the patient physically and psychologically more comfortable, the patient will make greater use of the aid. Some hand-held magnifiers are illuminated. They serve as an excellent ancillary aid for situations in which lighting is impossible to control (in restaurants, and in night or evening activities). These magnifiers follow the same optical principles as the nonilluminated magnifiers.

The object to be viewed should be held at the focal distance of the magnifying lens. Thus, if a 5X (+ 20-diopter) lens is used, then the object should be held 5 centimeters (100/20cm = 5cm) from the magnifier. At this distance, light rays leave the magnifier with zero vergence (see Fig. 8). This means the individual can hold the magnifier at any distance from the eye and still enjoy the same level of magnification; no accommodation is needed. Many patients who have received a magnifier as a training aid or initial prescription will return to the examiner or instructor using the magnifier held against or close to the eye because they enjoy an increased field of view at the closer distance. Although they initially favored the magnifier because of the greater working distance it affords, after using the aid for a while, they realize that the field of view is larger when they hold the magnifier closer to the eye. Many will eventually ask for a magnifier they can "attach" to their glasses and have their hands free. They have trained themselves to use a microscope (perhaps even the same one they rejected at the initial examination). The need for a large field usully outweighs the discomfort of a close working distance.

The field of view also depends on the power and design of the magnifier. The greater the magnification, the smaller the field of view. If the magnifier is designed to be small, like a pocket magnifier, the field also will be reduced. Most people want a magnifier that covers the whole page. Although some Fresnel page magnifiers (approx. 1.5X) and Edna Lite stand-mounted magnifiers cover large areas, the patient usually must contend with the smaller fields.

The Stand-mounted Magnifier

Many people prefer the stand-mounted magnifier because it is relatively easy to use: thus, it is a good training aid. The stand automatically sets the magni-

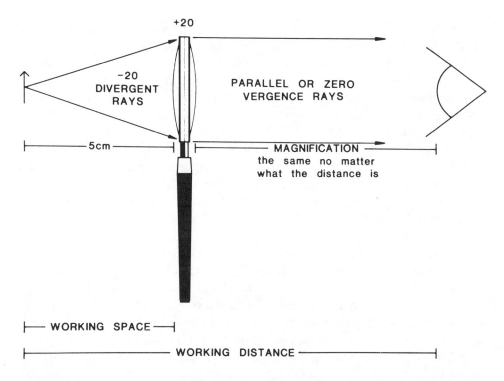

+20

−20
DIVERGENT
RAYS

PARALLEL OR ZERO
VERGENCE RAYS

5cm

MAGNIFICATION
the same no matter
what the distance is

WORKING SPACE

WORKING DISTANCE

Fig. 8. When an object is held at the focal distance of a hand-held magnifier, the light rays leave the magnifier at zero vergence.

fier at the correct distance from the reading material. This factor is important for individuals with tremors or other motor-control problems who cannot maintain the exact focal distance required by the hand-held magnifier (or microscope). The stand-mounted magnifier can be focusable or nonfocusable, illuminated or nonilluminated. It usually is more bulky and less convenient to carry.

The focusable units can be used to correct simple refractive errors. By moving the lens closer to the page, the light rays leave the magnifying lens with minus vergence and will correct a myopic refractive error. If the patient has hyperopia, moving the lens farther from the page (separating the elements) will cause converging rays (plus power) to leave the magnifying lens, which will correct the refractive error. If the instructor sets the focus of the lens, the patient may accommodate because of the "nearness" of the reading material, and an inaccurate setting may result, especially for the geriatric patient. It may be best to have the patient view the reading material at several different settings to find the most appropriate one for continued use. The examiner can help the evaluator determine the best setting for each patient.

An illuminated system can be provided for the stand magnifier that will concentrate light on the reading material without creating glare that sometimes occurs with external sources of light. Like the illuminated hand magnifier, the illuminated stand-mount magnifier is an excellent adjunct aid to full-field microscopes and other nonilluminated systems. In some cases, it can be attached by a spectacle frame (Keeler) for unique uses.

The nonfocusable stand-mounted magnifier usually is designed for hobbyists. It is inexpensive because it has a market greater than just the low vision population. It is used with children as an initial aid or as a training aid for patients who have problems with working distance or who have motor difficulties. Two important factors to remember when working with a nonfocusable stand-mounted magnifier are these:

1. Its actual power is usually less than that stated on the box or label.

2. Geriatric patients experience optimum magnification when they use a bifocal in conjunction with it.

The nonfocusable stand-mounted magnifier usually is designed with legs that are shorter than the focal length of the lens because the edge distortions of the lens are reduced and it is easier to market a lens with a clear periphery. The result is that the reading material is held too close to the lens and diverging rays leave the magnifying lens. This means the young patient must accommodate to get a clear, magnified image on the retina and the geriatric patient must use bifocals or reading glasses to obtain maximum magnification. The diverging rays leaving the lens of the stand-mounted magnifier cause the magnifier and accommodation/bifocal to act like a thick lens (Sloane, 1977), which results in the total effective power (the actual magnification enjoyed by the patient) being less than that written on the box. Thus, if a patient can see with a 5X microscope or hand-held magnifier but rejects the aid for other reasons, the examiner must evaluate the patient with a 7X high-power stand-mounted magnifier because it has an effective power of 5X (power comparable to the 5X microscope and hand-held magnifier of 20 diopters).

To determine the effective power of a particular stand magnifier, it is advisable to contact the examiner. Let the examiner know which stand magnifier is being used, the distance from the lens to the eye, and the spectacle correction the patient is wearing. These data can be calculated to determine the exact magnification the individual is using. A list of stand magnifiers and the effective power under various conditions may be found in Sloan (1977), Sloan and Habel, (1956), and Rosenberg (1973). It is important to remember that the magnification which the patient experiences (in diopters) is not equivalent to that marked on the box of most stand-mounted magnifiers.

As with all optical aids, the stronger the magnification of the stand-mounted magnifier, the smaller the field. Thus, with the higher power when there already is a small field, it is advisable to train patients to hold the lens as close to the eye as they will tolerate. At 8X magnification, it is probably necessary to hold the lens at the spectacle plane to appreciate a reasonable functional field of view.

PROJECTION AND ELECTRONIC MAGNIFICATION

Slide projections are an excellent example of projection magnification. In slide projections, the object is made larger (a 2″ x 2″ slide is magnified to the size of the screen), but at the expense of less resolution to the picture and loss of light. Also slide projectors are not portable.

An overhead projector can be used effectively to present materials to visually impaired students. Some children with serious impairments (e.g., severe retrolental fibroplasia) can look at figures drawn directly on the glass writing plate. The intense background illumination of the overhead projector creates a high contrast. This excessive illumination (the average person cannot even look at the light because it is so strong) can be the initial stimulus to vision and to the development of object-form recognition. However, such a drastic step should be taken only after consultation with the examiner.

The variety of rear-projection systems available have limited value in most low vision settings. They are not portable, they do not provide high magnification levels, they lose light, and they create contrast problems for the objects projected. Furthermore, only objects of a certain size can be placed under the projection lens system. However, at times they are the aid of choice, and should be considered when determining options. Some new fiber optic systems are being developed that may overcome some of these problems (e.g., Viewscan).

Closed Circuit Television

Closed circuit television (CCTV) is an example of electronic magnification (see Fig 9). In the CCTV, a video camera is directed at an object and the image of this object is projected on a television monitor screen. The camera can be modified for use in a variety of vocational settings at distance and near. Furthermore, the CCTV offers some flexibility in its use. For example, contrast can be increased electronically and through reversing polarity (white letters on a black background). There is a wealth of literature on the mechanics of and training techniques for using the CCTV in a variety of educational and vocational settings (see, e.g., Genensky, 1969; Goodrich, Mehr & Darling, 1980; Turner, 1976).

The CCTV is an excellent aid to use in training a patient to improve fixation and localization skills. Since the individual needs only to focus on the screen and then move the letters and words by moving the platform on which the reading material rests across the screen, there is less need for coordinated head-eye motor movements. The patient with central scotomas can find the eccentric viewing position and then "hold" it while the reading materials are presented to this retinal area by operating the moving platform and moving the reading material on the screen. As this area is reinforced with continued practice, the patient can be taught to move the eyes and head slowly across the screen to simulate a reading posture and movement

Fig. 9. The closed circuit television provides high contrast and high magnification.

that is used with optical aids. Eventually, the patient will be able to use optical aids such as magnifiers and microscopes if this training is continued.

Since the reading material (or other objects) is presented to the individual's field of best acuity and the patient does not have to seek the reading material by moving the eye and neck muscles, it is substantially easier to learn to read with the CCTV than with a comparable optical aid. Therefore, it may be better for the low vision patient if the initial aid is an optical device. Although such an aid will necessitate more extensive training than will the CCTV, it will allow the patient to adapt to its limitations. If a patient is trained first on the easier CCTV, it is usually more difficult to accept the limitations of a microscope or other aid. Thus, the total rehabilitation plan can be hampered if the patient really needs to use a portable optical device for maximum visual efficiency. The CCTV essentially makes the patient lazy during the initial stages. Why should the patient struggle to read with a microscope when it is much easier with the CCTV?

The CCTV is an excellent *primary aid* for the following types of patients:

- Patients whose needs are resolved with the television system.
- Patients who have failed to adapt to optical aids.
- Patients whose vision is so low that the CCTV is the only way to get a reasonable functional response (usually about 12X magnification and above).
- Patients (children or adults) with no history of having used their vision and who appear to have some level of acuity.
- Patients who have small 5-degree fields and for whom optical aids have not been successful.
- Patients whose primary problem is reading endurance.

The CCTV is an excellent *secondary aid* for vocational and educational settings in which portability is not a factor. If the person already has learned to use an optical aid for daily activities and if he or she can set up a schedule for utilizing the various aids outside the physical location of the CCTV, a combination of optical aids and the CCTV will often result in enhanced visual functioning for the active and contributing low vision patient. A fiber-optic system called Viewscan provides the acuity improvements of the CCTV with the added feature of being very portable.

BINOCULAR TECHNIQUES

The importance to a patient of using two eyes cannot be overestimated. As was indicated previously, it is difficult (if not impossible) to obtain binocularity with a microscopic aid over 12 diopters (3X magnification). If an aid is prescribed that has a lens or telescope before one eye only, then the rationale for this should be explained to the patient before dispensing the aid. The patient must be informed that because of differences in acuity, changes in blind spots, the strength of the lenses, the inability of the muscles to turn the eyes in, or suppression, the two eyes are not able to work together with the actual aid. However, because the patient uses the eyes without the aid (and even with the aid) for much of the day, the patient still has peripheral binocular vision (simultaneous perception). Thus, no atrophy or degeneration of the other eye will result from the prescription. In most cases, the use of optical aids for a short period will cause a subjective improvement in conventional vision.

Some clinicians prefer to prescribe binocularly to avoid the foregoing issue, even though they know one eye will be suppressed. This is a legitimate approach to the problem. It can be coupled with instructions to occlude the good eye twice a day and to view such materials as large print through the lens or telescope with the other eye. This technique makes the patient comfortable because he or she believes the weaker eye is being strengthened.

233

Some patients will not suppress the weaker eye and require a patch over that eye during the initial training until they learn to do so.

If possible, the individual should be given a biocular correction so that each eye can be used independently. Different corrections or the same correction can be placed in each eye. Either the person can work at different tasks with each eye or possibly work longer at one task by alternating eyes to reduce fatigue.

Whatever the system, careful Pd (pupillary diameter) measurements (positioning the aid exactly to the patient's line of sight) are important to the successful binocular prescription. The Engleman Unit (red filter strips and green card, available from Designs for Vision) is most acceptable for measuring Pds in low vision patients because the unit measures the line of sight actually used by the patient who has lost portions of the macular area.

CONTACT LENSES

Contact lenses are an important prescriptive option for all low vision examiners. They are particularly significant for patients with refractive errors of ±10 diopters or more. Contact lenses offer better optics or fewer distortions, a wider field of view, more light, and better fixation than do comparable power-spectacle corrections. If the patient has a small field (10 degrees or less) in conjunction with the high refractive error, contact lenses are the correction of choice. The patient's ability to scan behind a spectacle prescription is limited by the peripheral distortions and the physical limitations of the lens. However, with properly fitted contact lenses, the best optics are centered on the eyes and move with the eyes while scanning. Thus, the individual will show significant improvements in functional vision with contact lenses. A patient with retinitis pigmentosa who has had cataract surgery is severely incapacitated with aphakic lenses. The magnification of the lenses decreases the actual field size, prevents scanning, and distorts spatial perception. A contact lens can alleviate most of these problems.

If the clinician discovers corneal distortions, contact lenses should be prescribed. A good physiological fit can often result in dramatic increases in conventional acuity. Contact lenses should not be overlooked when prescribing telescopes. The improved optics will make it easier for the individual to fixate through the telescope and usually result in better acuity. Also, they can increase the field of view by decreasing the vertex distance almost to the corneal plane because, as was already explained, the closer the telescope is to the eye, the greater the field of view through it.

A contact-lens telescopic system can be designed for special patients (Ludlam, 1960). It can provide magnifications up to 2X and allows for a large field of view; by pulling the spectacle lenses down the nose, it can be used as a telemicroscope for near work. The system consists of a high-powered (difficult to fit) contact lens with an aphakic or cataract-like lens worn over it. Patients should be told how the two types of lenses will look because many patients think that the contact lens telescope will be cosmetically appealing and are disappointed when they see the thick cataract lenses they must wear.

Contact lenses also are used to occlude eyes, serve as artificial pupils, partially correct high refractive errors, possibly slow nystagmus, and provide cosmetic improvements. This latter feature is as important to the visually handicapped young adult as to the sighted.

NONOPTICAL AND ACCESSORY AIDS

Nonoptical aids often enhance the use of vision with or without optical aids. Generally, nonoptical aids increase illumination, increase contrast, or provide greater physical comfort (Courtwright, Mihok, & Jose, 1975; Mehr, 1969; Sicurella, 1977).

Illumination

Proper illumination is essential for the low vision patient. Light should be adjusted on the printed material and should not shine in the eyes (glare). Illumination can be thought of as light that strikes the material to be viewed and bounces back directly into the eye. This light increases contrast or increases the difference between the light coming from the object viewed and the light level of the background of the object. Glare is light that is not useful; it comes from oblique sources and enters the periphery of the eye, thus increasing the background illumination and decreasing contrast. Because glare decreases contrast and causes fatigue and strain, it is important to consider illumination-control devices with all optical aid systems.

A goose-necked lamp or a flexible arm lamp can be of tremendous benefit in that it can be positioned so the illumination is optimum for the individual task. However, not all patients need much light. Therefore, the examining clinician should be consulted as to the most comfortable level of light for the patient.

Pinholes. Pinholes, although an optical system, are mentioned here because they also control illumination. Placing a pinhole aperture before an eye will help reduce blur owing to uncorrected refractive errors, corneal distortions, light scatter, and fixation anomalies.

Sunfilters. A functional evaluation involving indoor and outdoor activities should be performed to determine the extent of a person's illumination-glare problems. The major factors to look for are comfort in a variety of illumination levels, the time it takes to adapt when going from a sunny area to a dark area (dark adaptation), and the time it takes to adapt when going from a dark area to a well-lighted or sunny area (light adaptation time). Some people report being "blind" for as much as five minutes when going from one level of illumination to another. This adaptation time can be decreased and comfort increased with the following aids, optical and nonoptical:

- Tint in a spectacle prescription (filterwelds, dyes for plastic lenses, especially yellow and Polaroid).
- Visors (caps).

235

- Sunfilters like OLO and NoIR lenses that fit over a spectacle and provide excellent protection from above and from the side.
- Clip-on or slip-behind devices to be used with conventional lens or sunfilters.
  - Tinted contact lenses.
  - Polaroid lenses that can be varied (Polamatic).

The NoIR and OLO sunfilters will be most helpful to patients with severe illumination problems (such as retinitis pigmentosa, achromatism, albinism, and some cataracts). They are wrap-around sunfilters that provide protection from strong light entering from the side and from the superior field of vision. The NoIR lenses also provide additional protection from ultraviolet and infrared light if this is desired. Contrast can be enhanced by using special tints such a yellow hunter's lenses or yellow clip-on filters, a reddish tint like that found in some target-shooting lenses, or utilization of the Polamatic lenses—a variable Polaroid spectacle lens. An excellent overview of sunfilters is found in McGillivray (1979). New devices and aids are constantly available, so the instructor should maintain an updated list of available filters and lenses. and lenses.

Contrast

Contrast, which is necessary for reading printed material, can be enhanced by using black felt-tip pens instead of blue ball-point pens. With a felt-tip pen, one can also write larger to give a magnified image. Another effective way to enhance contrast is to place yellow filter paper over the print or yellow clip-on filters over spectacles, because yellow filters tend to make print, especially mimeographed materials, look blacker.

A typoscope, which is a piece of black cardboard with a slit in it, has two general uses. Because it blocks out all but the line of print viewed through the slit, it helps the patient keep his or her place while reading. Also, when a single line of print is framed by black, that line tends to stand out better and appear blacker, thus increasing contrast. Paper with bold lines will increase contrast and makes it easier both to write and to read.

Physical Comfort

The purpose of a reading stand is to hold the reading material in a comfortable position so the patient can maintain a close working distance without straining the neck and back muscles or tiring the arms. Many people find a comfortable chair, a reading stand, and an adjustable lamp helpful when reading, especially for extended periods. However, good functional reading stands are difficult to find on the commercial market or do not have the features needed by most patients. Figures 10 and 11 illustrate two designs that can be made locally.

These are just some general categories of the types of devices used in a low vision program. From these basic units, a host of special systems can be designed to meet the unique needs of a visually handicapped patient. There

Fig. 10. Reading Stand No. 1:[a] This wooden stand is simple to make. It has four height adjustments and can extend over the desk or table top to accommodate short working distances. A weight balances it on the table. The reading platform angle is adjustable. The platform is on dowel tracks and allows the patient to move the book right to left for easier reading. Although the stand is not made for writing, it can be modified for that purpose. Other modifications can be made upon request.

[a]Designed by Randy Jose and Sandra Ferraro. Available from Richard (Dean) Jose, 1156, 1901 Dayton Road, Chico, California 95926.

are far too many aids to list them all, but consideration should be given to nonoptical aids to assist the patient with common tasks, such as writing, sewing, cooking, games, medical devices, and large-print reading materials. Agencies listed in Chapter 19 should be contacted for updated information on specific nonoptical aids that provide solutions to problems in each of these areas of concern.

FIELD UTILIZATION AIDS

Patients with severely reduced peripheral fields or hemianopsias (blindness in one-half of the visual field) require special consideration in designing treatment options. For the purposes of this discussion, individuals with 20-degree visual fields and greater are not considered to be in need of special prescriptions or training. For persons with 10-degree to 20-degree fields, all the treatment options discussed previously are useful, and the field loss is a

READING STAND PLANS #2

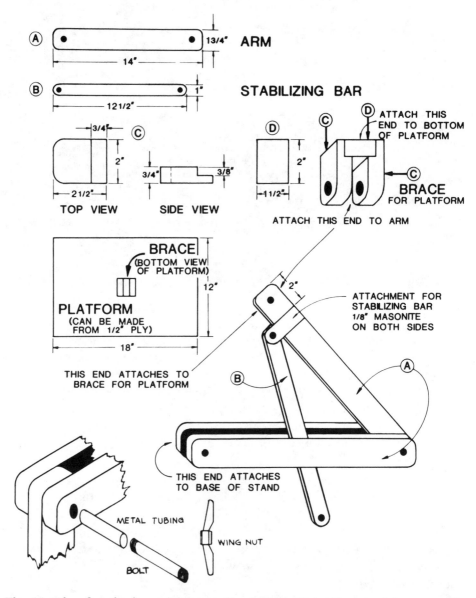

Fig. 11. Plan for the low vision reading stand #2.* All materials are made from ¾ " plywood, except for the platform itself, which can be made from ½ " plywood. For smoother movement of the arms and platform, it is suggested that metal tubing (supplied by local hardware store) be put into the moveable joints. The bolts used in locking the stand in a stationary position should be as large as possible (approximately ⅜ " to ¼ " wide). This will both help the patient to set up the stand and to keep the stand in a stationary position. Large size washers are used on the outside of the move-
*Initially designed by Dr. Thomas Milok

238

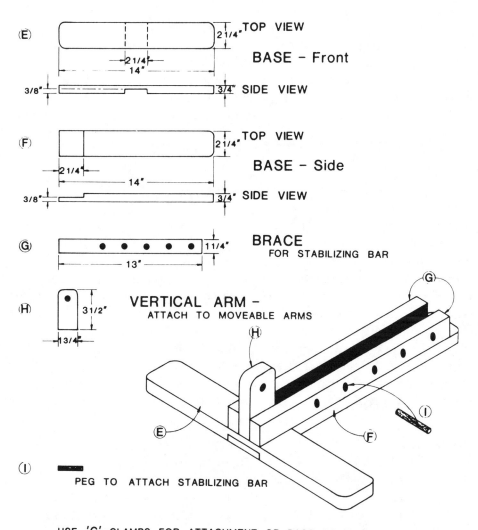

(E) TOP VIEW
BASE – Front
2 1/4"
2 1/4"
14"
3/8" 3/4" SIDE VIEW

(F) TOP VIEW
BASE – Side
2 1/4"
2 1/4"
14"
3/8" 3/4" SIDE VIEW

(G) BRACE
FOR STABILIZING BAR
1 1/4"
13"

(H) VERTICAL ARM –
ATTACH TO MOVEABLE ARMS
3 1/2"
1 3/4"

(I) PEG TO ATTACH STABILIZING BAR

USE 'C' CLAMPS FOR ATTACHMENT OF BASE TO TABLE

able joints. This helps to tighten down each joint. A spring approximately ½ " wide and 8" long is used to stabilize the system. It can be adjusted for any angle of the reading platform and can extend over the table for patient comfort with close working distances. It clamps to the table or desk a person is working on; he or she can also write on it.

Available at William Feinbloom Vision Rehabilitation Center: The Eye Institute, 1201 W. Spencer, Philadelphia, PA 19141. Can be made locally by retired patients with woodshops, high school woodshop projects, etc., by following these plans.

consideration only in that a mobility evaluation should be provided to determine if there are any specific problems that may be alleviated by mobility instruction. However, individuals with 10-degree to 5-degree fields are in need of special attention. Even with 5-degree fields, they can utilize as high as 10X magnification if they have good scanning skills and a good visual memory. The combination of smaller fields and higher magnification needs will require more training for the successful use of an aid, and, as was indicated earlier, the use of a CCTV may be considered.

Training

Training essentially requires patients to relearn whole-part or gestalt concepts. The telescope or microscope presents an even smaller field than the 5 degrees they are used to. They must learn to move this reduced field more systematically. Usually, the aid requires that they use head and neck movements to scan, rather than eye movements. (This may be contrary to their mobility lessons, in which they are encouraged to scan more with their eyes. Careful coordination between the two training programs will prevent confusion.) As the patients learn to scan systematically, to develop better whole-part concepts, and to improve their visual memory, the pieces of the picture are put together in a meaningful concept, and the patients experience an enhanced level of vision. These concepts are difficult to learn, and require substantial practice. The more that patients used their vision before the severe field losses, the easier it will be for them to develop new viewing techniques or perceptual skills.

Magnification

Magnification is difficult when the fields are 5 degrees or less because the retinal image is simply magnified onto dead tissue. Thus, all magnification does is to reduce the amount of the object seen at one time, although the portion of the object seen is seen in great detail. Most people will report this as a decrease in acuity or vision even though the magnification provides more detail. They may see their friend's eye clearly, but not recognize it as an eye because they have no concept of looking at a face when looking through a telescope. Until they learn how to scan through a telescope, using neck and head movements; view the nose, other eye, hair line, and mouth; and put together a composite picture of a face, they will not be able to appreciate magnification. The CCTV is most effective with small fields because it allows adjustment of magnification over a continuous scale so that minimum magnification (the maximum field) is utilized. The eye can hold its position and the materials can be presented to the eye for easy localization and tracking. Only a limited number of patients will have the visual perception skills necessary to work with magnification and fields of less than 5 degrees. However, the instructor should not assume it cannot be done (a scientist with 3-degree fields is utilizing a 24X telemicroscope daily for his computer work). In all cases of field loss, patients should decide what they can and cannot do. The instructor must understand the perceptual problems that are created with magnification so he or she can help them adapt at their own pace or understand why the initial prescription is not providing the hoped-for success.

Prisms

For mobility purposes, a 30Δ (this is an arbitrary power for the prism) fresnel prism can be attached to the outer edge of a patient's spectacle (Gadbaw et al., 1976; Jose & Smith, 1976). The prism is placed on the spectacle as close to the center of the lens as possible without interfering with normal scanning vision. (Each individual has different scanning patterns or amplitudes to compensate for the reduced fields.) Normally, if the person wishes to see an object in the periphery, he or she will move the eyes approximately 20 degrees and then turn the head. This is a slow and inefficient way to process information. By placing the prism on the spectacle, the person makes a small eye movement into the prism and the peripheral objects are displaced from the periphery toward the center of the prism. This means that the patient can sample which objects are located in the periphery by making small eye movements in and out of the prism instead of making exaggerated eye and neck movements.

Adaptation to such a device with the two visual-world presentations, displacements in space, and optical distortions requires an extended training period. In addition to allowing the individual to be more "aware of" objects in the periphery (note the term "see" was not used), the prism provides a stimulus for the patient with severe field restrictions to start scanning more efficiently. Most patients will ask to have the prisms moved more temporally as the training program proceeds because their normal scanning pattern has increased in amplitude and they constantly look into the prism. They will complain of blurred vision, of double vision, or simply of feeling closed in by the prisms. A further discussion of specific training techniques is found in Section IV: Training and Instructional Services.

Cane Techniques. Most people with 5-degree fields or less who are candidates for prisms also should be taught how to travel with a cane. However, they usually resist cane travel because they think it is a sign of blindness and dependence. Prism training can sometimes be used to get the person involved in initial cane training techniques. The individual is told that the eyes will tend to look downward as long as the lower field is unprotected. If cane techniques are utilized, the person can raise the eyes to a primary gaze and start utilizing the prisms to expand the useful field of vision. Once the person becomes comfortable with cane travel in the training program, he or she frequently will keep using the cane and view it as an aid for independence rather than for dependence.

Prognosis for the Successful Use of Prisms. Caution should be used when deciding whether to start prism training. Many patients with retinitis pigmentosa have substantial areas of peripheral vision that will interfere with the use of prisms. Thus, the instructor should make sure that extensive perimetry was performed and that no major islands of peripheral vision exist. If an island of peripheral vision is found, mobility training should be begun to teach the person to use that area of vision. Many patients are not even aware that they have islands of peripheral vision until the clinical team tests for it, plots it, and teaches them to use it.

If the central acuity is less than 20/100, the prognosis for using prisms is guarded. The instructor should make no preconceived judgments about success until a functional evaluation has been performed (one patient with 20/400 vision was able to use prisms successfully). A temporal prism is used first. If the patient learns to use the temporal prism, then additional prisms may be added slowly for the lower field, the nasal field, and the superior field, if necessary.

Fresnel prisms are not a cure-all for individuals with severely constricted peripheral fields. For some they are a great asset, and for others it is a disappointing technique. In general, the following points should be kept in mind when selecting candidates for this treatment option:

▪ Patients with visual fields or 10 degrees of less will generally be more successful than patients with larger fields. The smaller the field of view, the greater the chance of success. Patients with fields larger than 10 degrees usually will benefit more from training in scanning techniques.

▪ The sharper the acuity, the better the chance for success. Patients with an acuity of less than 20/200 will generally not benefit from prisms.

▪ The more recent the loss, the better prognosis for acceptance, because the patient has not developed good scanning skills and the prism will be more efficient than their present system of processing information.

▪ Patients with hemianopsias of recent onset are the most successful candidates. Again, it is a matter of the efficient processing of information. The person with a recent loss of the right peripheral field will have little or no scanning skills; use of the prism is a way to view peripheral objects.

▪ Patients will "outgrow" this treatment option. The successful prism cases are those who throw the prism away in a couple of months because they have developed such enhanced amplitudes of scanning and improved their information processing so much (visual memory and understanding of whole-part concepts) that they no longer need the prism to view peripheral objects. At that point, their eye movements are more efficient than their prism system.

Minification Systems

One way to combat the problem of a constricted field is to reduce the size of objects to be placed in that field. This is the principle of reversed telescopes, which minify objects being observed by the patient (Ricker, 1978). The technology of reversed telescopes still is primitive. For the most part, telescopes available on the market are used. The patient simply looks through the "wrong end" of the telescope. Another minification device is a conventional door "peep hole" that is mounted in a lens. A few more sophisticated designs have been developed by Dr. William Feinbloom at Designs for Vision. These designs are bioptic in form; they allow the patient to view through the minification lenses and then look under them with the normal fields.

Success with reversed telescopes has been limited primarily because of the peripheral distortions of most lenses and because the small apertures of the telescopes prevent scanning. Thus, the person with 3-degree fields who scans is used to having about 15 degrees of functional field. With a 3X expander, the field is increased to 9 degrees but with no scanning. The person's first impression of the system in a static setting is that it is excellent (i.e. "My fields increased from 3 degrees to 9 degrees"). However, as training progresses and the patient uses the reversed telescope in a dynamic setting, he or she is disappointed (i.e., "My 15-degree fields were reduced to 9 degrees"). Also the threefold loss of acuity makes viewing through the system impractical. That is, the person sees more but does not know what he or she is seeing more of.

Persons who have a specific area they want to view (a desk top, a refrigerator, or a tool bench) have the most success with reversed telescopes. A hand-held device is sufficient for this purpose. Minification systems will probably be more successful when they can be designed so they are free of peripheral distortions, have 1.3X or 2.0X minification, and include an aperture that will allow a degree of scanning. If such a system is designed in a bioptic form, it may allow for continued daily use. Much research is still needed in the area of minification.

BIOPTICS AND DRIVING

Driving is an important activity that many visually handicapped people cannot perform. Some visually handicapped people can drive if they are fitted with a bioptic telescope. However, extensive evaluations and consultations must be made before considering this treatment option. Clinicians must be careful not to prescribe bioptics indiscriminately for this purpose even though patients may exert pressure on them and other staff members. Clinicians must stay within and build on the present guidelines for prescribing until more data can be obtained on the visual input to safe driving. Today, two states (New York and California) allow individuals to drive with acuities of 20/120 and 20/100, respectively, with conventional corrections if they have an acuity of 20/40 through the bioptic telescope. Although the statistics are constantly being reevaluated, it appears that the safety records of these drivers have been comparable to those of nonvisually impaired drivers.

There are many arguments for and against driving with bioptics (Jose, Carter & Carter, 1983; Feinbloom, 1977; Jose & Butler, 1975). However, it should be noted that the same arguments have been used for 10 years, and no research has been undertaken to resolve some of these issues. Thus, one must assume that clinicians have been arguing more from their feelings than from scientific evidence. Until solid and convincing research has been completed, clinicians must follow their feelings, state regulations, and some practical guidelines. At the William Feinbloom Vision Rehabilitation Center and the Low Vision Clinic, University of Houston College of Optometry, driving with bioptics is not presented as an option unless the patient requests it. Patients must demonstrate acuities of 20/40 or better with telescopes, conventional acuities of 20/160 or better, excellent travel skills in the mobility evaluation, and proficiency with the aid in all aspects of the training program (distance and near) and perform adequately behind the wheel in the initial evaluations. If they meet all these criteria, they are put on a three-to-six-month training schedule* and are advised to take a drivers' training course utilizing bioptics. During the training period, patients are encouraged to ride in the family car as passengers and try to anticipate or locate potentially hazardous situations, or to ride a bicycle with bioptics. If clinicians, instructors, and patients behave responsibly, driving with bioptics can be a rewarding treatment option that can be pursued successfully and safely.

VISION STIMULATION

Vision stimulation is another treatment option that the clinician may consider even though it probably will be conducted, in large part, by the instructional staff. Essentially, vision stimulation means helping a person to develop maximal use of residual vision. It may mean teaching some people to use visual instead of tactual cues or teaching others to use their vision more efficiently. It can even be used to teach individuals to use their optical aids. Vision stimulation (or whatever you wish to label these activities) will raise the visually impaired person's level of visual awareness and efficiency.

PERCEPTION

"Perception" is an often-misunderstood term. It conjures up all sorts of vague treatment options and unusual therapy sessions. Actually perception is simply the brain's interpretation of the images or messages sent to it from the retina. The cortex must take these coded messages and make meaningful use of them. This interpretive skill can be improved through structured experiences. For instance, if while watching television the pictures becomes snowy, you can barely see the figures on the screen because of the poor back-

---

*A very specific series of training activities has been developed by Mr. Kent Carter for use in teaching his clients to drive with bioptics in Maine. A 20-page compilation on this training program and that developed by Dr. William Feinbloom is available by contacting Dr. Jose or Mr. Carter.

ground (poor figure-ground separation). If you continue to watch television with a poor figure-ground separation for a few weeks the picture does not appear as confusing as it did at first. The brain has learned to ignore some of the snow, and the figures on the screen are easier to discern. This type of perceptual adaptation can occur with the use of optical aids. Although the foregoing was a simplified explanation of a complex process, it may serve as a model for investigating new training techniques to determine potential problem areas. For example, a patient may see a blurred object in the distance with the conventional lens and then by quickly viewing it through the bioptic may recognize and correctly label it. The patient then looks at the object through the conventional lens; because the object is known, the brain is able to "see" or "perceive" it more accurately. The comparison of objects through the blur of the conventional lens and the detail of the telescope, in many cases, results in improved interpretive skills with the conventional lens. Although the acuity remains the same, the person reports that his or her vision has improved. This may be considered a perceptual adaptation.

Telescopes also can work in a negative way. The reduced field, spatial distortions, speed smears, and the like that are experienced by the telescope user, will distort the typical retinal images sent to the cortex. Although there will be increased detail, perceptually these other changes in the cortical input will confuse the perceived image. Until the person learns to adapt to these perceptual disturbances, he or she can have 20/20 vision through the telescopes but not understand what is seen. Such an individual must be trained to develop better whole-part, systematic tracking and visual memory skills. The acuities are a retinal activity; awareness of the meaningfulness of improvements in acuity is, in large part, a perceptual activity. Fortunately, most people adapt to changes in acuity with minimal problems. However, some "difficult" cases may be having problems with perception that the clinician is overlooking. Also, if clinicians pay attention to cortical activity as well as to retinal activity in their evaluations, they may be able to raise the level of utilization of aids and vision even in successful cases. The area of perception is an extension of the previously discussed areas of vision stimulation or visual efficiency. It may be considered a clinical approach to these same problem areas and instruction programs.

CONCLUSION

It is more important for the instructor to understand the functional aspects of aids than to memorize the names of a few aids. Such an understanding will keep the low vision clinical team from continually prescribing the same few "favorites." It will also help to eliminate simple problems in the training program before the patient becomes frustrated. The only way truly to become familiar with aids is to purchase them and work with them to exper-

Table 1. List of Suggested Equipment for a Low Vision Service ($5,000-$6,000)

S. Walters
412 West Sixth Street
Los Angeles, Calif. 90014
    Walters   10x2
    Walters   8x20
    Walters   6x16
    Walters   8x50
    Walters   3X
    Walters   4X

New York Association for the Blind (Lighthouse)
Optical Aids Service
111 East 59th Street
New York, N.Y. 10022
    Handy Glass 4x30, No. 226 (LH)
    Sportglass 2.8X, No. 229
    Selsi monocular 2.8X, No. 229B
    Selsi clip on 2.5X, No. 148A
    Selsi monocular 6x/8X, No. 162
    Agfa 8X, No. AG-8
    Ary Loupe Trial Set, No. LH-A
    +6, +8, +10 half-eyes, No. LHS-1-power
    +12 Aspherics, No. LHS-2-12
    Jupiter Standlupe, No. 402
    Cataract stand mag. 20D, No. 5428
    Cataract stand mag. 28D, No. 5123
    Cataract hand mag. 20D, No. 5460
    48mm hand mag. (+11D, No. 5247
    Easi-view mag. (chest mag), No. 5178
    Selsi Bar mag. (phone book), No. 377
    Yellow filter glasses (yellow clip-ons), No. LH-14

Designs for Vision
120 East 23rd Street
New York, N.Y. 10010
    2.2X full diameter telescope with +2, +4, +6, +8 caps
    2.2X bioptic I wide angle in Yeoman Frame (64 PD)
    4.0X expanded field telescope in trial ring mounted as a bioptic
    (+2.50, +4, +6, +8 caps)
    Selection of Yeoman G frames
    10X, 12X, 16X full diameter microscopes
    Designs for Vision distant chart and near chart

Recreational Innovations Inc.
P.O. Box 159 South Lyon, MI 48178
    Selection of NoIR sunfilters

Bernell Corporation
422 East Monroe Street
South Bend, Ind. 46601
   2.2X Aloe reading telescope
   E.F. trial lens clip
   Bernell clip occluders

American Optical Co.
Low Vision Aids Service, Dept. 3401
PO Box 1
Southbridge, Me. 01550
   AO Basic microscopic trial set

Keeler Optical Co.
456 Parkway
Broomall, Pa. 19008
   LVA 9 illuminated set with transformer

Nikon, Inc.
Instrument Division
623 Stewart Avenue
Garden City, N.Y. 11530
   Subnormal vision aids diagnostic set

Carl Zeiss, Inc.
One Zeiss Drive
Thornwood, N.Y. 10594
Att: Low Vision
   Selection of telemicroscopes

---

[a] Represents the equipment needed for a minimum kit of low vision aids.

ience the optical and functional parameters discussed in this chapter.

Chapter 19 lists manufacturers and distributors of aids and a few other resources to whom interested readers may write for information about specific aids. Table 1 is a practical list of suggested aids with which new clinicians may begin to equip themselves. The list is comprehensive enough for clinics to be able to manage low vision cases with these aids. The advantages and disadvantages of each aid must be compared in relation to focal distance, fields of view, depth of focus, cost, illumination factors, weight, distortions, possible modifications, and so forth. Such a comparison can be made only by using the lenses or each aid in a variety of settings. If the instructor has a thorough grasp of these factors, training will be much more effective and rewarding both for the instructor and for the patient.

Finally, it must be remembered that the low vision service is not exclusive of other rehabilitation services. Thus, it is not uncommon for a person to be working with low vision aids and receiving instruction in mobility, activities

247

of daily living, and braille. Various means of communication must be opened up for the individual, and all techniques that will assist the person to become more independent are compatible with low vision services.

References

Courtwright, G., Mihok, T., Jose, R. Reading stands: A nonoptical aid. *Optometric Weekly*, 1975, **66**(16), 449-452.

Faye, E. *Clinical low vision*. Boston: Little, Brown & Co., 1976.

Feinbloom, W. Driving with bioptic telescopic spectacles. *American Journal of Optometry and Physiological Optics*, 1977, **54**(1), 35-42.

Freid, A., & Mehr, E. *Low vision care*. Chicago: Professional Press, 1974.

Gadbaw, P., et al. Parameters of success in the use of fresnel prisms. *Review of Optometry*, 1976, **113**(12), 41-43.

Genensky, S. Some comments on the closed circuit television system for the visually handicapped. *American Journal of Optometry and Physiological Optics*, 1969, **46**(7), 519-524.

Goodrich, G. L., Mehr, E. B., & Darling, N. C. Parameters in the use of CCTVs and optical aids. *American Journal of Optometry, Archives of the American Academy of Optometry*, 1980, **57**(12), 881-892.

Jose, R., & Butler, J. Drivers training for partially sighted persons: An interdisciplinary approach. *New Outlook for the Blind*, 1975, **69**(7), 305-311.

Jose, R., Carter, K., & Carter, C. A training program for clients considering the use of bioptic telescope for driving. *Journal of Visual Impairment & Blindness*, 1983, **77**(9), 425-428.

Jose, R., & Smith, A. Increasing peripheral field awareness with Fresnel prisms. *Review of Optometry*, 1976, **113**(12), 33-37.

Kelleher, D. Orientation to low vision aids. *Journal of Visual Impairment and Blindness*, 1979, **73**(5), 161-166.

Ludlam, W. Clinical experience with a contact lens telescope. *American Journal of Optometry, Archives of the American Academy of Optometry*, 1960, **37**(7), 363-372.

McGillivray, R. (ed.) Review #1—Sunglasses. *Aids and Appliances Review*, 1979, **1**(1), 1-10.

Mehr, E. B. The typoscope by Charles Prentice. *American Journal of Optometry, Archives of the American Academy of Optometry*, 1969, **46**(11), 885-887.

Ricker, K. S. Visual field wideners: A personal report. *Journal of Visual Impairment and Blindness*, 1978, **72**(11), 28-29.

Rosenberg, R. A survey of magnification aids to low vision. *Journal of the American Optometric Association*, 1973, **44**(6), 628-635.

Sicurella, V. G. Color contrast as an aid for visually impaired persons. *Journal of Visual Impairment and Blindness*, 1977, **71**(6), 252-257.

Sloan, L. *Reading aids for the partially sighted*. Baltimore: Williams & Wilkins, 1977.

Sloan, L., & Habel, A. Reading aids for the partially blind: New methods of rating and prescribing optical aids. *American Journal of Ophthalmology*, 1956, **42**(6), 863-872

Turner, P. J. The place of the CCTV in the rehabilitation of the low vision patient. *New Outlook for the Blind*, 1976, **70**(5), 206-214.

SECTION IV
Training and Instructional Services

This section covers activities involved in the actual instruction of visually impaired persons in the use of the aids. It is the responsibility of the clinician to prescribe the optical or nonoptical system to resolve the individual's reported problems and ensure that the person can use the aid before he or she leaves the examination room.

The actual training and instructional activities can take place in the clinic or outside the clinic as indicated in the model of services presented in this book. The information in Chapter 11 is based on the experiences of John and Sandra Ferraro in developing a training program for the low vision clinic at the College of Optometry, University of Houston. It is designed as an overview for the new instructor with minimal experience in setting up a low vision program.* More specific training techniques for distance and near are offered in Chapter 12 by Rachel V. Berg, Randy Jose, and Kent Carter, and in Chapter 13 by Gale Watson and Rachel V. Berg. The techniques presented in those chapters can be used in any sequence as problem-solving tools. Unique training programs have been developed for individuals with restricted fields; they are presented in Chapter 14 by John Ferraro and Randy Jose.

Training is not a separate entity in the low vision service. It permeates the assessment and clinical phases of the vision care programs as well as all the other services and programs in which the visually impaired person is involved. The purpose of training is to develop the person's efficiency in using prescribed aids so that, along with other services, they can help to normalize the individual's life through enhancing his or her ability to use vision in daily tasks.

---

*In this section the service provider is referred to as the instructor and the visually impaired individual is referred to as the student. These two terms best describe the relationship of the two in this phase of low vision service.

249

CHAPTER 11

Establishing a Training-Instructional Program

SANDRA FERRARO, M.A., AND JOHN FERRARO, M.A.

Because the field of low vision care is so new, more and more professionals with limited experience are being called on to initiate low vision services. The task of deciding where to start and what materials are necessary in preparation for this responsibility can be anxiety-producing, if not overwhelming. This chapter provides the new low vision instructor with the information needed to address these issues. However, since training can take place in many different settings and may be only one part of the professional's responsibilities, the suggestions in this chapter can be modified to specific settings. The purpose of training is to help the visually impaired person to utilize prescribed aids efficiently. The aids and other services, then, can be instrumental in normalizing the individual's lifestyle because they enhance the ability to use vision in performing daily tasks.

PROFESSIONAL PREPARATION

The nonclinical low vision instructor needs to become familiar with the body of knowledge associated with low vision services and to become part of the professional community that provides these services. This section deals with ways in which these goals can be obtained.

Professional Reading

There are many books and literally hundreds of journal articles that address low vision. As with any area of knowledge, one must choose some basic texts and articles to establish a foundation of information. At the time of writing, this is the only book specifically designed for the nonclinical low vision instructor and, as such, is an excellent starting point. The following selected annotated bibliography of other texts and journal articles covers the major areas and philosophies of low vision services. Other bibliographies throughout the book list many other sources. The point is not to attempt to read everything that has been written about low vision but to establish a broad base of knowledge to be supplemented with additional readings related to the specific population with which you are working and your areas of interest.

Texts

Bäckman, Ö., & Inde, K. *Low vision training.* Malmö, Sweden: Liber Hermods, 1979.

This book gives the visually impaired student information on the function of the eye, the functional effects of eye diseases that cause low vision, optical aids, and visual training. The information is basic and well written, and the emphasis is on reading. The book also includes a number of exercises for increasing visual functioning and reading ability.

Cholden, L. S. *A psychiatrist works with blindness.* New York: American Foundation for the Blind, 1958.

This volume contains selected papers presented by Dr. Cholden. It is one of the best resources for understanding the psychological and sociological problems associated with visual impairment.

Faye, E. E. *Clinical low vision.* Boston: Little, Brown & Co., 1976.

This comprehensive book on low vision is designed for the clinical ophthalmologist and optometrist. The chapters on defining low vision, identifying the patient, the functional classification of eye diseases, and children with low vision are particularly helpful. Information on training is brief.

Mehr, E. B., & Freid, A. N. *Low vision care.* Chicago: Professional Press, 1975.

This text is also written for the optometrist and ophthalmologist. It emphasizes the examination, aids, and prescriptions. The chapters on illumination, psychological and sociological implications, contact lenses, and sources of optical and nonoptical aids are particularly useful for the nonclinical low vision instructor.

Manuals

AO Vision Series: (1) *Basic optical concepts,* (2) *Lenses, prisms, mirrors,* (3) *The human eye,* and (4) *Normal and abnormal vision.* Southbridge, Mass.: American Optical Corp, Optical Products Division, 1976.

These four manuals are programmed instruction courses. They are useful as introductory or review material in the four subject areas.

Quillman, R. D. *Low vision training manual.* Kalamazoo: Western Michigan University, College of Health and Human Services, Department of Blind Rehabilitation.

This manual discusses training procedures and techniques and includes a number of near training exercises in various print sizes.

Journal Articles

Barraga, N. C. Learning efficiency in low vision. *Journal of the American Optometric Association,* 1969, **40**(8), 807–810.

This article discusses visual functioning, visual training, visual efficiency, and the stages of visual perceptual development; a chart on visual discrimination and the sequence of activities is included. This article provides a good background for determining the need for and sequencing of training activities.

Barraga, N. C. Utilization of low vision in adults who are severely visually handicapped. *New Outlook for the Blind,* 1976, **70**(5), 177–181.

This article emphasizes visual functioning rather than visual acuity; it is primarily concerned with the use of residual vision for all aspects of a person's life. It also discusses the possible reorganization or development of visual perceptions that may need to occur after visual loss.

Cross, H. E. Genetic counseling and blinding disorders. *Blindness* (American Association of Workers for the Blind annual), 1974–75, 29–41.

Written for the genetic counselor, this article includes basic information on genetic diseases and emphasizes the presentation and interpretation of information in counseling.

Faye, E., & Hood, C. Low vision services in an agency: Structure and philosophy. *New Outlook for the Blind,* 1975, **69**(5), 241–248.

This article is a comprehensive description of the New York Lighthouse Low Vision Service. It includes that agency's philosophy of the most appropriate setting for low vision services.

Goodrich, G. L., & Quillman, R. D. Training eccentric viewing. *Journal of Visual Impairment & Blindness,* 1977, **71**(11), 377–381.

This article discusses the functional problems associated with central scotomas and describes four techniques for the long-term training of eccentric viewing.

Goodrich, G. L., Mehr, E. B., & Darling, N. C. Parameters in the use of CCTVs and optical aids. *American Journal of Optometry & Physiological Optics,* 1980, **57**(12), 881–892.

This article presents comprehensive data from a two-year study of 96 veterans who used closed-circuit television; 48 of the subjects also used an optical aid for near tasks. The findings have implications for prescribing and training with CCTVs.

Hoover, R. E. Toward a new definition of blindness. *Blindness* (American Association of Workers for the Blind annual), 1964, 99–106.

253

This article includes an interesting discussion of the need to develop definitions that relate to visual functioning and personal needs and suggests that the legal definition of blindness may keep people from services. It contains a list of the definitions of blindness that are used in 24 countries.

Israel, L. CCTV reading machines for visually handicapped persons: A guide for selection. *New Outlook for the Blind,* 1973, **67**(3), 102–137.

This article presents general information on CCTVs and the characteristics and personal needs to be considered when evaluating various systems.

Jose, R. T., Cummings, J., & McAdams, L. The model low vision clinical service: An interdisciplinary vision rehabilitation program. *New Outlook for the Blind,* 1975, **69**(6), 249–254.

This article describes a low vision service as part of a rehabilitation agency. It emphasizes the total integration of the low vision clinic with the services of the agency.

Jose, R. T., & Smith, A. J. Increasing peripheral field awareness with Fresnel prisms. *Optical Journal & Review of Optometry,* 1976, **113**(12), 33–37.

This article presents information on the placement and power of prisms, the selection of patients to use prisms, and training. It discusses how prisms are used to increase awareness in the visual field.

Jose, R. T., Smith, A. J., & Shane, K. G. Evaluating and stimulating vision in the multiply impaired. *Journal of Visual Impairment & Blindness,* 1980, **74**(1), 2–8.

This article describes a functional visual evaluation, recommended examination procedures, and a vision stimulation sequence that includes 17 visual tasks. It contains good information for developing assessments and training multiply handicapped children.

Mehr, E. B. The typoscope by C. F. Prentice. *American Journal of Optometry & Archives of the American Academy of Optometry,* 1969, **46**(11), 885–887.

This article is a reprint of an original paper written by Prentice in 1897 with introductory notes by Mehr; it concerns the physiological principles of the typoscope.

Rosenberg, R. A survey of magnification aids to low vision. *Journal of the American Optometric Association,* 1973, **44**(6), 628–635.

This article discusses the methods of magnification and how they are achieved through various optical aids, the advantages and disadvantages of aids as to field, working distances, available powers, and lighting.

Sicurella, V. J. Color contrast as an aid for visually impaired persons. *Journal of Visual Impairment & Blindness,* 1977, **71**(6), 252–257.

This article contains a good overview of the use of color contrast as an aid to increased visual functioning; practical suggestions for each area of the home are presented.

Sloan, L. L., & Habel, A. Reading speeds with textbooks in large and standard print. *Sightsaving Review,* 1973, **43**(2), 107–111.

This article presents data from a study of the reading speeds of 22 legally blind children using large and standard print; the study was part of an investigation into the advantages and disadvantages of large-print textbooks.

Watson, G., & Jose, R. T. A training sequence for low vision patients. *Journal of the American Optometric Association,* 1976, **47**(11), 1407–1414.

This article describes a long-term training program in a rehabilitation facility. It presents a sequence of materials for training students in reading with optical aids; the training is based on task analysis and success-oriented philosophy.

Low Vision Aids

It is one thing to know intellectually the focal distance, the effective magnification, and the advantages and disadvantages of a particular optical low vision aid and another thing to understand what it is like to read with a 6X microscope or to try to fill out a check using a bioptic telescope with a near cap. One of the best ways to understand the type of problems that students have when using an aid is through first-hand experience. The following activities can be done with or without patches or goggles that simulate low vision.

Reading. The following activities can be performed with a variety of aids to compare functioning with different types and amounts of magnification and various fields and working distances. A representative selection of aids includes a stand magnifier, a hand magnifier, + 6.00 half-eyes, a 4X microscope, an 8X microscope, a full-field telescope with a reading cap, and a closed-circuit television (CCTV).

1. Take one-minute timed readings of various reading materials. Note the differences in speed when reading with various aids and in different print sizes.

2. Compare functional fields by counting the number of words or letters that you can see clearly at one time.

3. Check the motion effect caused by various aids when you scan.

4. Compare the ease with which you can locate the next line of print when using various aids.

5. Determine the benefits of using nonoptical aids (such as the typoscope,

the reading stand, and filters) and of varying the levels of illumination for reading.

6. Look up an address and phone number in a telephone book.

7. Read the recommended dosage on a bottle of aspirin.

8. Determine the current amount due on a utility bill.

Writing. Attempt the following activities with a variety of optical aids: + 6.00 half-eyes, a 4X microscope, an 8X microscope, full-field and bioptic telescopes with + 2.50 and + 4.00 caps, and CCTV. Note particularly the functional effect of the fields and the difficulties in eye-hand coordination associated with depth perception.

1. Fill out a check with and without a check-writing guide.

2. Address an envelope.

3. Fill out a job application form.

4. Copy a paragraph from a book.

Other activities. Evaluate the effectiveness of various optical aids for completing the following near and intermediate activities:

1. Thread a needle with and without a needle-threading device.

2. Sew on a button.

3. Play a card game and a board game such as Scrabble.

4. Paint a picture.

5. Type a paragraph from a book.

6. Pound in a nail; replace a screw in a small appliance.

Obviously it would consume a great deal of time to work with many different aids and complete all the activities listed. Instead, select activities that seem to be most appropriate for the specific population with whom you will be working. The underlying value of doing these activites is not to evaluate the use of a specific aid for a specific task for a specific student but, rather, to understand visual functioning with optical aids and the difficulties encountered in order to work more effectively with students during training.

Observation of Examinations

Observing a routine low vision examination is an effective way of making sense of the technical data, notations, and instruments involved in low vision services. It is important to understand why special charts and instruments are used in the examination. Although reading about them is helpful, observing their use in an examination adds the real-life dimension of how the procedure can be related to a specific student and how the student acts during the examination. The following are areas that the low vision instructor should particularly note during the low vision examination: information gained through the case history; special techniques for doing refraction; charts used for distance acuities; procedures for testing fields; presentation of optical aids; the determination of a tentative prescription; and suggestions for training.

The instructor also should become thoroughly familiar with the testing equipment and instruments. For example, administer the D-15 color test; read through the Amsler Grid manual; look through various distance and near acuity charts. Knowledge of how data are obtained enhances the use of the data for more productive training.

Of course, observations should not be limited to eye examinations. One should be familiar with all phases of a particular low vision service, including social services, other training, specialized assessments and evaluations, and any other services provided by clinic and agency personnel. To know how and why all the components of the low vision service are performed is to be able to integrate the near and distance training components effectively and hence to provide the best service possible to the student.

Local and State Resources

To be of maximum benefit to the students, the low vision instructor should be aware of and in contact with local and state resources for visually handicapped individuals. Such knowledge is important not only for giving information to students but for becoming part of the community serving the needs of visually handicapped individuals. The following list contains general resources about which instructor should be knowledgeable and suggests where specific names and addresses may be found.

State rehabilitation services. Every state has a structure of rehabilitation services that are supported by state and federal funds. Rehabilitation services are provided through rehabilitation counselors, teachers, and caseworkers and may include home teaching as well as residential rehabilitation facilities. Sources of these services can be obtained through local offices of the state vocational rehabilitation service; also consult the American Foundation for the Blind (AFB) *Directory of Agencies Serving the Visually Handicapped in the U.S.* (see Chapter 19 for the address).

Agencies for the visually handicapped. Lighthouses for the blind and private rehabilitation agencies offer many services for visually handicapped persons and may be a local source for some nonoptical aids, particularly large print. Consult the AFB directory.

Agencies for older individuals. Most communities have a number of agencies that serve older adults, such as visiting nurses, recreational programs, and homemaker services. Consult the local telephone book, a United Fund directory, or a directory of social services.

Special education services. Delivery systems, referral and placement procedures, and auxiliary educational services vary from state to state and sometimes from school district to school district. State-level information can be found in the AFB directory; also consult special education departments of local school districts, colleges, and universities.

State library for the blind and physically handicapped. To locate the nearest state or regional library, consult the AFB directory, local agencies serving visually handicapped individuals, or the National Library Service for the Blind and Physically Handicapped (see Chapter 19 for the address).

Radio information services [formerly Radio Reading Services]. In some areas, special radio programs for visually impaired individuals are available through special receivers; they usually include the reading of major local newspapers. Consult the AFB *Directory of Radio Reading Services* or the reference circular *Directory of Local Radio Reading Services* from the National Library Service for the Blind and Physically Handicapped.

Other low vision services. The AFB directory has a special low vision section that lists the name, address, contact person, and available services of the major low vision services in each state. Information also may be obtained from local professional groups for optometrists and ophthalmologists who provide low vision care through private practice.

TRAINING ROOM, EQUIPMENT, AND MATERIALS (NEAR)

Depending on the particular facility in which you work, you may find that there are equipment and materials for near and intermediate distance training, or that the training room, equipment, and materials are inadequate or excellent. This section deals with suggestions for the instructor who is setting up a training program for the first time as well as for the instructor who is becoming familiar with an existing system and attempting to inject his or her personal and professional character into the program. The itinerant instructor will need to be particularly flexible and creative in organizing facilities and materials.

Training Room (Near)

Although training often takes place in rooms that have been designed for other purposes, a room must fulfill certain requirements for effective training. The room must be large enough (no less than 12 by 15 feet) to hold the work space, training equipment and materials, the student, one or two people who may accompany the student, and the instructor. The room should have good overhead lighting—no less than 100 foot-candles. It is helpful if the lighting can be adjusted to 50 foot-candles for photophobic students.

The work space should be a table or counter that is about the normal height of a desk or table (about 28 to 30 inches high); this height should accommodate most wheelchairs. The table area should be large enough to hold a reading stand and other training materials and should be near an electrical outlet so the extra lighting source is easily accessible. It is helpful if the table is away from the wall so the instructor can work across from the student when observing eye and head movements as well as next to or behind the student. Chairs should be adjustable to accommodate students of various heights and should be on wheels so the student can move easily. A second work space is necessary if there is a CCTV in the training room.

The training room should have adequate space for storing equipment and materials. Vertical desk-top files keep single-page training and reading materials categorized and accessible. A large bookcase can be used for storing most other training materials from books and periodicals to sewing and knitting materials.

In arranging the training room, accessibility is a key factor. Equipment and materials used in most training sessions (such as the typoscope, reading stand, stopwatch, light meter, and ruler) should be kept next to the work space. Special materials, such as blueprints, music books, and cookbooks, should be arranged so they are easily found. The best training session can be ruined if the instructor must constantly walk around the room to locate equipment, or spends 10 minutes trying to find the large-print Bible.

If the room can be equipped with one-way observation windows, it allows the clinician to check on the progress of the training without interruption if the training is occurring in the clinical setting. It is also a convenient way for other interested professionals to observe without interfering with the training program.

Training Equipment (Near)

A certain amount of equipment is needed for training. The following list is the minimum equipment that should be available in the instruction room. Suggested sources for the starred equipment can be found in Chapter 19.

- A flex-arm floor lamp, 50-, 75-, and 100-watt bulbs.
- A 15-cm ruler or Pd stick.
- A 30-cm ruler.
- A yardstick.
- A light meter.
- *Straps for eyeglasses.
- *Clip-on occluders.
- *Filters.
- *A typoscope.
- *Reading stands.
- A penlight.
- A clipboard.
- *A check-writing guide.
- *A signature guide.
- *A needle-threading device.
- A stopwatch.
- *A CCTV (optional). A CCTV is an excellent diagnostic and training tool as well as a possible prescriptive aid. Sometimes it is possible to arrange to use a CCTV through a manufacturer's regional sales representative.

Training Materials (Near)

One major reason for near training is to develop specific visual skills vital to the reading process. Some students learn to scan quickly and are able to substitute head or material movements for eye movements. Other patients have a difficult time dealing with the reading problems created by high magnifica-

259

tion, closer working distances, or central scotomas. An instructor must have a variety of materials that have been designed to assess and train individuals in visual and reading skills. Sources of the starred materials may be found in Chapter 19.

General Reading Ability
*■ Feinbloom Subnormal Vision Reading Card, by Designs for Vision.
*■ Sloan Reading Cards for Low Vision Patients, by the Lighthouse Low Vision Service.
■ Dolch word lists.
■ Exercises in *Low Vision Training*, by Bäckman and Inde (see the section on professional reading in this chapter).
*■ Reading exercises in *Low Vision Training Manual* by Quillman (see the section on professional reading in this chapter).
■ Reprinted paragraphs from texts or magazines in various print sizes.

Reading Speed
The instructor can use printed paragraphs that are about 150 words long and that have a cumulative word count on each line in the margin. Vary the print size (18 point, 14 point, and 10 point cover a good range) and have available reading materials of various grade levels so the reading material can be suited to the specific student.

Scanning
For the purpose of this and subsequent chapters dealing with reading and other near point activities, the term "scanning" will be used to refer to two types of visual skills: (1) moving from left to right across a line of printed material, and (2) finding a particular point on a page of print, a picture, and so forth.
■ Pages with lines, symbols, letters, or words that require the student to scan in a straight line from left to right. (Figures 1–5 are examples of the kind of scanning exercises that can be prepared. The print size used in these exercises can be varied, as can the thickness of lines and the spacing. Figures 1–5 present exercises in an ascending order of difficulty.) Some of the exercises in *Low Vision Training* by Bäckman and Inde are excellent for scanning. The Ann Arbor Tracking Program also includes exercises to increase scanning skills. It is available from Ann Arbor Publishers, P.O. Box 7249, Naples, Florida 33940.

Visual Perceptual Skills
Any of the basic visual perception assessments such as the "Test of Visual Analysis Skills" is helpful in evaluating possible perceptual problems in reading, particularly with children and stroke victims. If problems are suspected, more thorough evaluations should be administered by appropriate specialists.

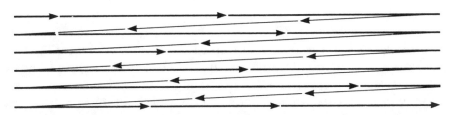

Fig. 1. The student is to practice scanning these lines as an aid to learning the appropriate skills for reading. Numbers can be added to check the students' correct scanning movements.

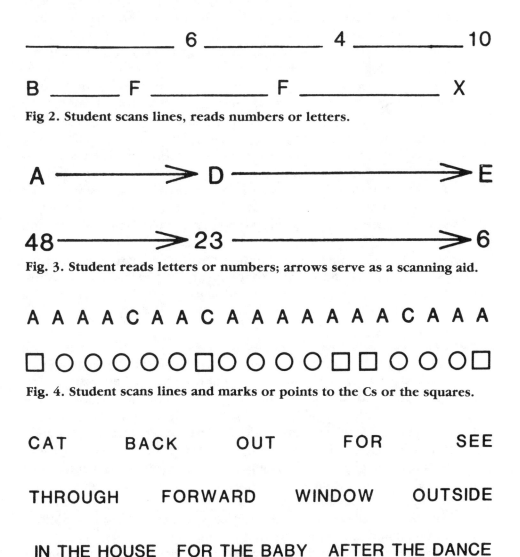

——————————— 6 ——————— 4 ————— 10

B ——— F ——————— F ——————— X

Fig 2. Student scans lines, reads numbers or letters.

A ——————→ D ——————————→ E

48 ————→ 23 ——————————→ 6

Fig. 3. Student reads letters or numbers; arrows serve as a scanning aid.

A A A A C A A C A A A A A A A C A A A

□ O O O O O □ O O O O O □ □ O O O O □

Fig. 4. Student scans lines and marks or points to the Cs or the squares.

CAT   BACK   OUT   FOR   SEE

THROUGH   FORWARD   WINDOW   OUTSIDE

IN THE HOUSE   FOR THE BABY   AFTER THE DANCE

Fig. 5. Student scans lines of words; vary word length and move into short phrases.

261

Reading Materials to be Used with an Aid

Another major reason for training is to help students become efficient *and feel comfortable* while using low vision aids for specific activities. The training room or area is the place where students can read magazines, books, labels on cans, or blueprints instead of reading charts and test cards. Most of the following materials can be obtained easily and cover the common needs of students in relation to near and intermediate distance activities. Sources for the large-print materials are listed in Chapter 19.

Religious materials, regular and large print; news magazines; home magazines; technical magazines; children's magazines; large-print editions of *Reader's Digest;* large-print editions of the *New York Times Weekly;* newspapers; hard cover books, regular and large print; paperback books, adult and teenage level; cookbooks, regular and large print; music, regular and large print; catalogs of home products and technical materials; telephone books; foreign-language materials, depending on the needs of the student population; blueprints; checks; bank statements; utility bills; job application forms; television guides.; income tax forms and instruction books; handwritten letters; junk mail; computer printouts; school textbooks of various grade levels; comic books; school workbooks of various grade levels; coloring books; purple dittoes; menues; instructions for assembling toys; warranty and assembly instructions for home appliances; an assortment of food containers (soup cans, cereal boxes, coffee jars, and so forth); medicine bottles with over-the counter and prescription labels; writing tools: ballpoint pens, pencils, felt-tip pens, and crayons; sewing supplies: spools of thread in several colors, fabric, and needles; knitting and crocheting supplies: knitting needles, crochet hooks, and yarn; hobby supplies: model kits, stamps, coins, and embroidery or needlepoint kits; tools for general repairs, e.g., hammers, nails, screwdrivers.

Near Practice Materials

When an aid—especially a reading aid—is lent to a student, practice materials should be included. If, for example, a student receives a 4X microscope that allows him or her to read 1.5M print, it would be disastrous if the student tried to practice with that aid by reading the newspaper (.5M Print). Such a situation can occur if the student is not given a structured training program with materials. Practice sheets can be printed, typed, or handwritten. Paper and printing should be of good quality: these sheets are designed to teach good visual skills, not to introduce students to the reality of poor-quality newsprint or glossy magazine pages. As with training materials, practice sheets should be available in various print sizes, sentence lengths (one sheet, for example, could have sentences that completely fit into the cut-out of a typoscope), reading levels, and languages. Some of the pages in the sources mentioned for training materials make good practice materials. (The authors of these materials must give permission before you can reproduce them.)

Nonoptical Aids (Near)

Most students will be able to utilize nonoptical aids to enhance the performance of an optical aid or to carry out a specific task such as threading a needle. Displaying these nonoptical aids allows students to evaluate them first-hand, rather than through descriptions in catalogs. Sources of the following aids are listed in Chapter 19:

- Needle-threading guides.
- Self-threading needles.
- Low vision playing cards.
- Magnetic padlocks.
- Large dominoes.
- Flex-arm lamps.
- Writing pens with a light.
- Writing guides (signature, check, letter, envelope).
- Bold-line paper.
- Large-number telephone dials and push-button-phone attachments.
- Reading stands.
- Typoscopes.
- Filters.
- Clocks and watches with large numbers.

Handouts (Near)

The following list of handouts covers a wide variety of information for visually impaired patients, family members, teachers, and counselors. If copies of such pamphlets, catalogs, and application forms are available, the student can take the material home rather than having to order it. Addresses for the sources of the starred materials can be found in Chapter 19.

Catalogs

*■ "Aids and Appliances for the Blind and Visually Impaired" (Independent Living Aids).

*■ American Bible Society.

*■ CCTV information: contact the national address for the regional representative. (Manufacturers: Apollo Lasers; Pelco; Visualtek.)

*■ "Print-A-Log" (Science for the Blind).

*■ "Products for People with Vision Problems" (American Foundation for the Blind).

Pamphlets

■ "A Closer Look at Low Vision Aids," by Marybeth Dean, is designed for school age children (available from the Connecticut State Board of Education and Services for the Blind, 170 Ridge Rd, Wethersfield, Conn., 06109).

*■ Short pamphlets discussing the conditions and effects of common refractive errors and eye diseases (American Optometric Association).

■ "A Teacher's Guide to Low Vision Aids" (available from the University of Alabama at Birmingham Low Vision Clinic).

*■ "When You Have a Visually Handicapped Child in Your Classroom: Suggestions for Teachers" (American Foundation for the Blind).

Application and Ordering Forms

■ Handicapped user applications for exemption from directory assistance charges (available from the local offices of the telephone company).

*■ Large-type *Reader's Digest.*

*■ Large-type *New York Times Weekly.*

*■ *New York Times* large-type crossword puzzles.

*■ Applications for radio reading services (check AFB "Directory of Radio Reading Services").

*■ State Library for the Blind and Physically Handicapped (addresses of regional libraries available from the National Library Service for the Blind and Physically Handicapped (see Chapter 19).

TRAINING ROOM, EQUIPMENT, AND MATERIALS (DISTANCE)

When one considers distance aids, the most common impression is of a person using a binocular or monocular telescope to see a street sign or pedestrian control device in a mobility situation. However this characterization is often the culmination of a successful distance training program and it is not these activities that lead to success. In order to assure that an individual can utilize a distance aid, he or she must first learn the unique properties of the aid and the tasks essential to maximize its use. These can best be learned in a quiet indoor area, free from distraction, where the student can be monitored or controlled by the instructor.

It should be noted that the concept of the distance training room is the "ideal" situation. In many instances, such as itinerant teaching or a community based rehabilitation program, such a room is impractical. The following information however, provides the concepts, equipment, and materials to facilitate training individuals to use distance aids.

Distance Training Room

Since most distance aids have varying focal distances of 3 feet to optical infinity the training room should be large enough to accommodate optimal focusing of the aid, normally considered to be 20 feet. An optimum situation is a rectangular room measuring 25 feet long by 10 feet wide, thus allowing for activities at varying distances that will require periodic changes in focus. It is also useful to have various distances, such as 10 feet and 5 feet, marked either on the floor or along a baseboard should the need arise to move a student closer or further away from an activity.

The walls of the room should be relatively free from distracting material. It is best if an activity can be set up and then removed to avoid confusion on the part of the student. A chalkboard placed at one end of the room is most useful for conducting many of the training activities (see chapter 6) as well as real life situations such as copying material from the board.

The lighting in the room should be about 100 foot candles, and it is advisable that it can be controlled for various individuals. It is important to note that the lighting at the sides and end of the room where activities take place should be consistent. In many situations the optimum lighting is at the center of the room and greatly reduced at the outer perimeter. A light meter will quickly give you an indication of the amount of light available in a particular activity area.

The room should contain ample storage space so that equipment or materials that are not being used do not create distractions. However, these same items should be close at hand.

Distance Training Equipment

2 Flexible arm floor lamps (60 watt bulb)
1 Chalk board
1 Feinbloom bioptic driving chart
2 Flickering lights (1 Red, 1 Green)
1 Light socket and 10' extension cord
1 Penlight
1 Adjustable height table (hospital type)
1 Slide projector
1 Clip-on occluder
1 Paddle-type occluder

Distance Training Materials

Cardboard tubes of various sizes
Kaleidoscope
Felt washers
Elastic Velcro Straps
20' length of rope
Colored ball (8" diameter)
Assorted signs

Telescopic Aids

2.5X Sportglass
2.5X Hand held Selsi
2.5X Clip on Selsi
2.8X Sportglass
2.8X Hand held Selsi
2.8X Clip on Selsi
3X Walters
4X Walters
4X30 Handy Glas
6X Selsi
6X Walters
6X/8X Selsi
8X Selsi
8X20 Walters
8X50 Walters
10X Selsi
10X Walters

TRAINING SESSIONS

Near Training Sessions

As with other components of a low vision service, training sessions must be based on the individual's level of functioning and needs. In designing an individualized training session for near and intermediate-distance tasks, one can, however, start from a basic pattern. This section deals with developing that basic pattern in terms of preparation, sequencing, and recording.

Preparation for a Near Training Session

To maximize the quality of training, the instructor, the student, the room, the materials, and the aids must be ready. The following should be done before the start of a training session. Some of this information, such as the review of the case history, is covered in greater depth in other chapters.

Case history. Review the student's file, including medical history (general and eye), living environment, vocation, leisure-time activities, problems and needs, and expectations.

Examination data. Review data obtained by the examining optometrist or ophthalmologist, including acuities, fields, refraction, special diagnostic tests, low vision aids presented, and initial training plan. When possible, confer with the examining optometrist or ophthalmologist about the data as well as about the student's apparent motivation.

Previous training data. Review notes and data from previous training sessions.

Aids. Review the characteristics of the aids to be used, their advantages and disadvantages, and the common problems associated with their use. If an aid is unfamiliar or to be used for an uncommon task, try out the aid to become familiar with its properties.

Materials. Review and assemble the training materials best suited for the specific aids being used and the tasks to be accomplished.

Students. If the student is going directly from an examination to a training session, it may be helpful to suggest a short break; a person who is tired or hungry is not going to get the maximum benefit from the training session.

Sequencing a Near Training Session

The low vision instructor should develop a sequence that can be followed during *all* training sessions. Such a sequence should cover all aspects of near and intermediate-distance tasks and include the concepts of assessment and instruction. What is most important is that the sequence should be flexible to meet the needs of each student. Table 1 is an example of a training sequence. This sequence may require more than one session to complete.

Recording a Training Near Session

The development of forms on which to record training information can be an excellent way to organize one's thoughts about training and the parts that need to be recorded. A good recording form helps the instructor remember

Table 1. Outline of Training Sequence for Near and Intermediate Tasks

   I. Observe the student
  II. Social conversation
 III. Student's objectives
     A. Discuss those already noted
     B. Add to the list
     C. Establish priorities
 IV. Eye condition
     A. The student's concept
     B. Discuss the functional implications, especially as they affect specific tasks
     C. Discuss implications for the student's health
  V. Eccentric viewing
 VI. Reading
     A. Discuss the aid
        1. Name
        2. Monocular or binocular
        3. Focal distance
        4. Advantages and disadvantages
        5. Successes and problems in the clinical examination
     B. Assessment
        1. Timed reading
           a. Use reading stand
           b. Use assumed appropriate lighting
           c. Have the student read aloud
           d. Note print size
        2. Determine the best physical setting
           a. Reading stand or clipboard
           b. Lighting—intensity, direction
           c. Discuss posture
         3. Ability to focus
        4. Ability to localize
        5. Ability to scan
           a. Left to right across a line of print
           b. Patterned search of a full page
     C. Begin instruction based on the assessment
        1. Practice based on strengths and weaknesses
        2. Use of nonoptical reading aids
     D. Second timed reading
 VII. Other near tasks
     A. Discuss the aid
        1. Name
        2. Monocular or binocular
        3. Focal distance
        4. Advantages and disadvantages
        5. Success and problems in the clinical examination
     B. Assessment
        1. Determine the best physical setting

         a. Height of table or working space
         b. Reading stand, clipboard, other stands
         c. Lighting—intensity, direction, type
         d. Discuss posture
     2. Ability to focus
     3. Ability to localize
     4. Ability to fixate
     5. Ability to scan
  C. Begin instruction based on the assessment
     1. Practice based on strengths and weaknesses
     2. Use of nonoptical aids
VIII. General discussion
  A. The student's understanding of how to use the aid
  B. The student's questions about the training session
  C. The student's feelings about the success of the aid in reaching stated objectives
  D. Instructions to the student

---

to cover pertinent areas during the training session. Careful recording can make letter and report writing easier and aids the instructor in reviewing a case before a subsequent training session. Table 2 is an example of a form for recording a training session. In the case of children, a separate recording form that emphasizes classroom activities and materials can be useful; Table 3 is an example of such a form.

Table 2. Near and Intermediate Distance Training

Student _____   Date _____

Assessment of Needs	
Reading	
Writing	Vocational
Homemaking	Hobbies, Crafts

Eccentric Viewing

Reading	1	2	3
Aid			
Working distance			
Illumination			
Skills			
Focusing			
Localization			
Reading Skills			
Scanning			
Locating next line			
Speed			
Comprehension			
Materials Read			
Nonoptical Aids			
Reading stand			
Typoscope			
Line guide			
Filter			

Comments

Writing	1	2	3
Aid			
Working Distance			
Illumination			
Skills			
Writing Performed			
Nonoptical Aids Writing guides			
Special pens and paper			
Stand			

Comments

Other Activities Tasks Performed	1	2
Optical Aid		
Working Distance		
Illumination		
Nonoptical Aids		

Comments

Materials and Aids Loaned

Handouts and Other Information Given

Next Session

Instructor

Table 3. Clinical Assessment of Visual Functioning: Classroom Materials and Activities

Name _____   Date _____

Reading

Materials Read	1_____	2_____	3_____	4_____
Print Size				
Optical Aid				
Working Distance				
Illumination				
Nonoptical Aids				

Skills

Speed				
Comprehension				
Comments				

Other Activities	1_____	2_____	3_____	4_____
Optical Aid				
Working Distance				

Illumination
Nonoptical Aids

Skills

Comments

Chalkboard Work
Optical Aid

Distance from Board

Size of Board Material

Illumination

Copying from Board
Skills

Comments

Distance Training Session

As with near training, distance training must be individualized to meet the needs and specific tasks of the students. A basic pattern must be established for all distance training sessions (see Table 4). The following section deals with the preparation, sequencing and recording of distance training sessions.

Student Practice Sessions

Once a student has achieved a minimum level of proficiency he or she is usually given a loaner aid. In most cases the aid is the same level of magnification as the prescribed aid; in some cases it will be of lower magnification. The concept is that individuals begin to incorporate the aid in their daily

Table 4. Distance Training Sequence

  I. Informal Conversation
 II. Patient Objectives
     A. Those previously noted
     B. Any new items identified
III. Eye Condition
     A. Patient's concept
     B. Functional implications
        1. Acuity
        2. Fields
 IV. Telescopic Aid
     A. Name
     B. Magnification
     C. Field
     D. Advantages and disadvantages
     E. Type of mounting
  V. Assessment
     A. Ability to focus the aid
     B. Field of view through the aid
     C. Acuity with the aid
     D. Ability to localize through the aid
     E. Ability to spot through the aid
     F. Ability to scan through the aid
     G. Ability to track through the aid
 VI. General Discussion
     A. Student's understanding of the aid
     B. Student's feeling about the assessment
     C. Questions concerning the training session
     D. Instructions to student
VII. Evaluation
     A. Determine the appropriateness of the aid to student's objectives
     B. Determine how aid is to be utilized (hand-held or spectacle mounted)
     C. Planning future training sessions

routine. The first step is to develop a short period (anywhere from five to ten minutes) every day during which the person uses the aid. The activity might be viewing television or observing pedestrians from the front window. It is useful if the person develops a list of things that he or she can do with the aid, and bring the list to the next training session. Another useful activity is for the student to note times or situations where he or she could have used the aid. A review of the list (at the next training session) helps to demonstrate how useful the aid is in a daily regimen.

Preparation for Distance Training
A short preparation time prior to training allows the instructor to devote his or her full attention to the patient and insures that necessary equipment, ma-

273

terials and aids are readily available during the next session. Review the case history including medical, vocational and/or educational information, leisure activities, problems, goals, and expectations before each training session.

Examination Data: Review data regarding acuities, field problems, refraction recommended aids, and initial training objectives.

Previous Training Data: When a patient is seen for subsequent visits, information from prior sessions is helpful in determining what aspects of distance activities need to be addressed. This also aids in developing a short review session to determine if any previously learned skills need attention.

Aids: A brief review of the characteristics of the aids will be helpful in determining if the student is having more problems than are usually anticipated and adjusting the training session accordingly.

Materials: Assemble materials suited to the tasks to be accomplished. A good rule of thumb is to have some materials that are simpler to use as well as some of higher complexity.

Patient: Inform the student of what you are trying to achieve in a given session as this lets him or her understand what you wish that individual to accomplish during the session. A quick review of previously learned skills will offer you the opportunity to assess the student's effectiveness with the aid and prepare him or her for the selected task of that training session.

Recording Distance Training Sequence

Keeping accurate records of what has taken place during a training session is essential for making a final decision regarding an aid. To insure that all aspects of the aids and all skills have been assessed, it is important that the instructor use a form or checklist. It is most helpful if the form can be brief with small comment sections throughout. It is best if the form is filled out as the training session progresses and not left until after the student has left.

Table 5 is a sample recording sheet which can be used as a baseline for developing one which will fit the specific situation.

Table 5. Distance Training Recording Sheet

Patient _____   Date _____

Type of Session: ____Evaluation   ____Training   ____Instruction

Major Complaint: _____

_____   Attending O.D._____

AIDS

EYE USED:	1	2	3
TYPE OF AID			
Hand Held			
Spec. Mt.			

MAGNIFICATION: _____

MODIFICATION _____

COMMENTS_____

_____

FIELD COMPARISON

HAND DRAWN	1	2	3
Distance	@ ′	@ ′	@ ′
Width	cm	cm	cm
Height	cm	cm	cm
Sample			

COMMENTS_____

_____

FIELD CHART _____

ACUITIES THROUGH
AID _____

O.S. _____

O.D. _____

O.U. _____

_____

_____

FOCUSING: ____Excellent   ____Requires Additional Training
Comments: _____

_____

SPOTTING: ____Excellent   ____Requires Additional Training
Comments: _____

_____

SCANNING: ____Excellent   ____Requires Additional Training
Comments: _____

_____

TRACKING: ____Excellent   ____Requires Additional Training
Comments: _____

_____

ILLUMINATION
EVALUATION   Tint Preference ____Amber ____Green ____Grey Green

_____

NoIRs: ____201   ____111   ____101   ____107   ____108
    ____202   ____112   ____102   ____109   IBD____%

_____

Olo: Tint Preference   ____Amber   ____Green   ____Grey Green

_____

    10% G 8% A 4% A 2% G/ 1% D/G I B D

_____

Present filter   ____YES   ____NO   LIGHT TRANSMISSION_____%

MOBILITY EVALUATION_____

RECOMMENDATIONS_____

LOANER AID_____

NEXT VISIT_____

_____

CHAPTER 12

Distance Training Techniques

R. VICTORIA BERG, M.A.
RANDALL T. JOSE, O.D.
KENT CARTER, M.A.

This chapter presents some of the more common problems encountered by individuals when trying to become proficient in the use of telescopic aids. It explains why problems may occur so the instructor will be able to find solutions for each individual. A few problem-solving techniques are offered as examples, but their importance is only to help the reader understand the underlying prinicples of why they work.

Training and instruction in the use of prescribed aids is the most challenging aspect of the low vision service. A successful program involves professional cooperation, flexibility, and ingenuity. The program consists of instruction and training. The "instructional" phase of the program is the review of pertinent data, the establishment of immediate goals for the visually impaired student, and the setting of the sequence of activities to reach those goals. "Training" is the practice part of the program. Once a particular technique is determined to be necessary for reaching specified goals, then repetitive practicing of that technique must be pursued until proficiency is attained (training).

BASIC CONCEPTS

To establish a successful training and instructional program, attention should be given to the following basic considerations:

■ To work with an aid, the instructor must be familiar with all its optical parameters, limitations, and modifications.

■ To understand the frustrations involved in learning to use the aid, the instructor must be thoroughly knowledgeable about the physiological and functional characteristics of visual impairment.

■ The instructor must know personality, motivations, goals, self-concept, support services being received, history, and so forth of the visually impaired student because all these factors affect the way a student approaches the use of an aid.

■ The instructor must know the student's expected level of performance with the aid, as indicated in the data from the clinical examination. Without

277

such information, the instructor will be guessing about the student's ability to attain expected levels.

■ Experience with other students having similar problems and goals is advantageous because it helps the instructor determine just how much the student can be pushed to accomplish specific tasks with or without the aids.

The following are some general concepts and considerations that are the foundation of a successful training program. Specific activites can be developed around these concepts.

Meaningful objectives. All activities in which a student engages must be related to the student's goals, and the student must be aware of the relationship.

Simple to complex. All activities must start with the simplest visual tasks and targets. Targets with high contrast, adequate acuity, and a minimum of detail are best; a one-block symbol on a white background is the simplest figure-ground discrimination task. As the program progresses to more detailed and confusing visual tasks, the student will begin to have difficulty, which can be alleviated by removing some of the figure-ground complications from the task.

Static to dynamic. The first phase of the sequence is static in that the student is sitting and the object is stationary. It is the least confusing and the most successful situation. In the second phase, the student sits and works with moving targets. In the third phase, the student moves and observes stationary targets. Finally, the student observes moving targets while mobile. The static to dynamic concept is similar to the simple-to-complex concept except that motion is a parameter instead of the figure versus the ground.

Reducing magnification. If the student is having problems with a particular activity that utilizes a high-power telescope, reduce the power and make appropriate changes in the size of the target. Think of the telescope as having a small window (exit pupil) through which the student must look. The lower the power of the telescope or the larger it is physically, the larger is the window. The increased size of the window allows the student to view through the telescope and begin to appreciate magnification. It slowly accustoms the student to speed smear, the apparent closeness of objects, and the small fields of telescopes. Use of the weaker telescope makes it easier for the student to adapt later to the stronger telescope. In difficult cases, students may first have to look through an empty paper towel tube to try to find objects; practice with the tube helps them develop motor control and directionalization.

All-or-nothing viewing. If a student is having trouble with localization and fixation and has generally poor visual skills, the all-or-nothing concept may be helpful. If the student is working with a monocular telescope for the right eye, the instructor should completely occlude the student's left eye and patch the right eye so the student is able to see light only through the telescope. It is best if the telescope is positioned centrally in front of the right eye. If the student does not wear glasses, the rubber shields that come with

278

some telescopes should be used as occluders. By occluding all light except what comes from the telescope, the instructor makes it easier for the student to find the window and maintain fixation through it. As soon as the student's fixation wanders, he or she sees darkness. Because there is only one source of light (the telescope), it is easier for the student to relocate the window and regain fixation. With practice, the student develops the sensory feedback and motor control necessary to maintain fixation with the optical system. This concept is important for all aspects of distance and near training.

Comfort increases proficiency. The more physically comfortable and relaxed the student is, the more productive he or she will be. Comfortable chairs, adjustable tables, good lighting, and pleasant surroundings greatly facilitate the early completion of a training program. Informal talk about the examination before starting the training session also is an invaluable tool in developing rapport with the student and in strengthening the student's confidence in the instructor's ability to help.

Knowledge of the student's visual diagnosis. Before working with a student, the instructor should review the clinical low vision evaluation, study the prescribed aids, and perform the tasks that the student will be asked to perform. These activities will give the instructor some insight into the nature of the tasks and potential problem areas.

Determining goals. Some students are motivated to learn to use an aid and have specific goals for its use. The instructor should examine these goals and discuss them with the student to determine whether they are realistic. Knowledge of the student's visual diagnosis and motivation helps the instructor make a decision. Students who do not have preconceived goals will need assistance in forming them.

Length of instructional periods. Initially, instructional periods should be short and success-oriented. Students who have not used their vision for some time will need to work in short sessions to prevent fatigue.

INFORMATION FROM THE CLINICAL EXAMINATION

The low vision instructor should obtain as much information as possible from the clinical low vision team and its report before and while working with the visually impaired student. This information can be gathered more easily if the instructor accompanies the student to the low vision evaluation. Clinical information that will help the instructor understand the student's functional use of vision includes the cause of visual impairment, the student's age at the onset of the eye condition, near and distance acuities, the prognosis, the size and shape of visual fields, characteristics of the student's vision, and the student's tolerance of various lighting conditions.

The low vision instructor also should obtain the following information about each prescribed telescopic aid: (1) name and type of aid, (2) the power and focal distance of the aid, (3) which eye is to be used with the aid, (4) whether the student should use regular prescription glasses when using the aid and whether an occluder lens should be added, (5) for what tasks or situations the aid is being prescribed, (6) the visual acuity achieved with the aid, and (7) the optimal lighting conditions designated in foot candles for distance or foot lamberts for near. If the telescopic aid also is to be used for reading, the clinician and the instructor should discuss the initial print size that should be used during training and the print size with which the student should be able to read following training. If, after a period of training, the instructor's expectations of the student's visual functioning (based on information from the clinical team) are not being met, the instructor should contact the clinic. The clinical staff may offer additional suggestions or may schedule a follow-up appointment for the student and the instructor.

Before training is begun, the instructor should discuss the results of the clinical evaluation with the visually impaired student. Some students have questions they either did not wish to ask the clinician or have thought of since the evaluation. The instructor should make sure that the student understands the cause and extent of the visual condition and how it may change in the future. In addition, the instructor should ascertain whether the student has realistic expectations of the aid and understands that he or she will have to learn how to use it effectively and efficiently. Some adults and most children need assistance not only to understand their visual impairment and its implications but also to explain it to others. Role playing may be used to help children find words to convey their abilities and disabilities.

INSTRUCTION IN DIFFERENT SETTINGS

Clinical Setting

The type of setting in which instruction is given will, to some degree, affect the instructional procedures. Instruction in a clinical setting will facilitate interaction among the student, the instructor, and the clinician. Students should begin to learn to use an aid immediately after it has been prescribed, when motivation is usually highest. In the clinical setting, if they do not seem to be functioning effectively with one type of aid, another can be prescribed. Furthermore, students who reject an aid when it is introduced often can be encouraged to try it with the instructor for a suitable trial period in the clinical setting. If the aid still is not satisfactory after that period, another aid can be tried. It is advisable for students to leave the aid with the instructor and to use it only at the clinic for as many instructional periods as are necessary until they are proficient in its use. Some students will require only one period of instruction; others will require many. Three training sessions are the average. If they attempt to use the aid before having mastered the basics of its use, they may fail, become discouraged, and doubt their abilities. The success experienced when using the aid correctly, with the proper print size and illumination, is usually worth waiting for.

Non-clinic Setting

When students are prepared to take the aid from the clinic or use it without direct supervision in the non-clinic setting, the instructor should provide directions for its use to serve as guidelines for practice. Directions can be recorded on a tape or can be in a readable print size. If a family member or friend observes the instructional sessions, the students will have an additional resource when practicing at home. This person should be one who will provide support and motivation. Every effort should be made to assist students to transfer skills and abilities to their home, school, and workplace. Continuation of the training sequence in the home after the initial clinical training is best.

Rehabilitation Center

Students in rehabilitation programs should incorporate residual vision and low vision aids into as many courses and daily activities as possible unless contraindicated by the training plan. By doing so they will be better able to transfer the skills they have learned to the home, school or workplace after they leave the program. Often new goals and objectives are identified in the home, school or workplace owing to the success enjoyed in the rehabilitation training program. Therefore, follow–up will be needed after the student leaves the training program. In addition to direct teaching of the use of vision and low vision aids, the low vision instructor can serve as a resource for other vocational instructors.

Home and School

Before working with students at home or in school, the instructor should review the clinical evaluation, the prescribed aid, and any necessary nonoptical aids. In addition, the instructor should discuss the students' visual impairment and low vision aids with the students, their family, their teachers, and their counselors. The understanding of these significant others will facilitate the successful use by students of their residual vision and low vision aids. Furthermore, the instructor can help establish a practical and supportive environment at home and in school. At home, the instructor can assist the student and family to set up a reading-study corner with proper illumination, supports for the telescope, supplies, and so forth. At school, the instructor can give teachers ideas for applying the aids, proper illumination and seat assignments, and appropriate board work.

Workplace

If visually impaired students are having problems in transferring their visual skills to and using aids in the workplace, the instructor should anaylze the visual requirements necessary to complete the work and consider whether further instruction at the place of employment is needed. If the aids do not permit the completion of a required task, the instructor may recommend the evaluation of other aids. If these alternatives do not ameliorate the situation, the possibility of changing the method in which tasks are performed or changing the tasks themselves should be investigated.

DEVELOPMENT AND PRACTICE OF SKILLS

The room chosen for instruction should be a quiet and visually simple area with natural and artificial illumination. The walls should be painted a light color with a flat, not glossy, paint. There should be several large, bright objects or pictures on the walls, grossly visible to the student's naked eye but with details that can be examined only with the telescope. A table or desk should be available for the student to rest elbows on during beginning exercises.

It is important for the instructor to follow a logical sequence so the student masters simple skills before undertaking complex ones. The student should practice focusing on an indoor target before trying to focus on a moving target indoors. If the student has been prescribed more than one low vision aid, he or she should work first with the lowest power aid. the intructor should evaluate the student in each skill area. If a student is able to demonstrate proficiency with an aid or has had previous experience with a telescopic aid, instruction in that skill sequence may be eliminated.

The teaching area and objects used during lessons should also follow a sequence of progressive complexity. Environmental factors that affect the level of complexity include the quality, intensity, and position of light sources; the level of visual intricacy (visual clutter); the student's familarity with the environment; the predictability of the environment; and the stress level of the environment. The instructor should also control the following variables pertaining to the object being viewed by the student: its size and shape, its distance from the student, its position with respect to elevation and azimuth; its complexity (figure-ground); its texture and reflective qualities (hue, brightness, and saturation), the length of time a moving object is present; the contrast between the object and its surroundings, and the student's familiarity with the object. The instructor's awareness of all variables and concomitant levels of difficulty makes control of the task possible. Each of the environmental and object variables encompasses a range of complexity, e.g., shape (regular to irregular), position (in front of the eye to high oblique), and duration (permanent to transitory). A controlled increase in the complexity of any one variable affects the degree of difficulty of the entire task. An example of a task in which simple levels of each variable are required is as follows: focusing on a stationary piece of 12-inch black construction paper with a circle affixed, at the student's eye level, to a dull off-white uncluttered wall that is six feet from the student and perpendicular to the student's facing direction, in a familiar classroom with the student's optimal lighting conditions. Once the student has mastered incresingly complex levels of the environmental and object variables, he or she will be able to deal effectively with a relatively uncontrolled task, such as reading the destination sign of an oncoming bus in a busy, urban area.

282

During the skill-development period, the instructor should keep a record of the student's progress, noting the date and length of the lesson, the student's level of skill, the appearance and illumination of the teaching area, which objects were viewed and the distance and position of the objects. Lessons should include instruction and practice in problem-solving with realistic, meaningful situations that the student will encounter in the future. This practice should be geared toward helping the student incorporate the aid into daily activities, discover further applications for use of the aid, and deal more effectively with problems when no longer working with the low vision instructor.

In addition to observing how and where the student is looking when using the telescope, the instructor should ask the student to describe what he or she sees through the aid. Before beginning each lesson, the student should check the aid to make sure it is clean and in good repair. Inspection of the aid at every lesson ensures that the student will consider such an activity routine after completing instruction. When the student has mastered the basics of focusing he or she should begin to take the aid home between lessons. In addition to assigning tasks that specify the skill or activity to be performed and the length of time to be spent, the instructor should ask the student to list applications of the aid in educational, vocational, and recreational activities. Making a list can help motivate a student to discover new applications of the aid and to practice between lessons.

Many students encounter problems during this phase, most of which involve a reduced field of view. Learning how to focus a telescope mounted on a tripod may help because of the increased field and stability. If a student has difficulty locating a specific object with a hand-held aid, the instructor may substitute an object such as a radio, a ticking clock, or a beeper ball, that can be located auditorially as well as visually. Auditory clues should be phased out when they are no longer needed. If difficulties persist, the instructor should consult with the low vision clinic about the possibility of the student's working with an aid of the same power but with a larger objective lens or an aid with lower power but a larger field of view. The larger field will provide more visual information and make it easier for the student to determine when the object is in focus. If the instructor thinks the student's lack of progress with the aid is due to poor accommodation, fixation, binocular integration, or convergence, the student should be referred to the low vision clinic for a complete evaluation of visual skills. If the student needs to work on basic visual skills, this should be done before continuing instruction.

CHARACTERISTICS OF TELESCOPIC AIDS

This section presents a brief review of some of the main characteristics of telescopes with which the instructor should be familiar before developing activities for training visually impaired students to use telescopic aids. Telescopic aids are prescribed to give visually impaired persons a larger image of an object. Many telescopes used by visually impaired students are Galilean telescopes because they produce an erect image and are generally smaller and lighter than terrestrial telescopes, which need a large prism to produce an erect image. However, new designs are making the terrestrial telescope more compact while maintaining the advantage of the larger fields of view that this design offers.

The components of a telescope are the *ocular* (the lens nearer to the eye), the *objective* (the convex or plus lens that is nearer to the object), and the *housing,* which is usually of metal or plastic. Other lenses and prisms may be found between the ocular and objective, but they do not affect this discussion.

A telescope is labeled to indicate its power and field of view. For example, a notation of 6 x 30 with a field of 7.5 degrees indicates that the aid forms an image of an object that is six times larger than the actual object and has an objective lens that is 30 millimeters in diameter. The maximum field of view that can be seen through this telescope is 7.5 degrees. The field of view of some telescopes is noted as x feet at 1,000 yards. A telescope with a field of 7.5 degrees permits a person to see the entire width of an object that is 394 feet wide and 1,000 yards away from the viewer (if the person's pupil size permits that wide an angle of view). To compare the fields of two telescopes, one of which is designated by degrees and one by feet, multiply the number of degrees by 52.5 (the number of feet in 1 degree at 1,000 yards). The field of view generally decreases as the magnification increases. For example, the Selsi monocular telescope with interchangeable objective lenses has an 11-degree field with the 6X objective, but only an 8.2 degree field with the 8X objective.

The brightness of the image produced varies from one telescope to another. One measure of light transmission may be determined by dividing the diameter of the objective lens by the power of the telescope. For example, a 6 x 30 telescope enables a 5-millimeter area of light rays to reach the eye. A 6 x 18 telescope permits only a 3-millimeter area of light rays to reach the eye. If a visually impaired student's pupil is 5 millimeters in diameter, the student would receive a brighter image when looking through a 6 x 30 telescope than through a 6 x 18 telescope. If the pupil is only 3 millimeters, the student would receive an image of the same brightness when using either telescope. Different levels of illumination may affect the size of a person's pupils. As Mehr and Fried (1974, p. 76) stated: "A patient who is in need of a bright image who has a 2mm pupil in daylight but a 5mm pupil at night would find a 6 x 15 telescope satisfactory in daylight, but a 6 x 30 better at night. However, a 6 x 50 would not further improve the image brightness for him." For this reason, it is important that students identify tasks for which they would like to use a telescope before the aid is prescribed. The size of the exit pupil (viewing window) of the telescope can be found by dividing the power of the telescope into the diameter of the objective lens. For example, the size of the exit pupil in the 6 x 30 telescope is 5 millimeters

(30/6). If the student has trouble localizing through an 8 x 20 monocular, which has a 2.5-millimeter exit pupil, then an 8 x 50 monocular (with an exit pupil of 6.25 millimeters) should be used because, with that telescope, the student will have a window that is 2½ times larger. This is the same parameter that determines brightness.

The range of focus of telescopes varies slightly from person to person and is different for each telescope. However, many telescopes can be focused so objects that are 2–12 feet away can be seen clearly. If a person must see an object at a closer distance through a telescope, a reading cap will be needed for the telescope. By moving the objective lens outward (making the tube larger), the telescope will focus on near objects.

The vertex distance (the distance from the eye to the ocular lens of the telescope) is important in determining the student's field of view through the telescope. The instructor should be aware that the closer the eye is to the telescope, the larger will be the field of view. Depth of focus is also critical in telescopes. Therefore, the instructor should be familiar with the depth of focus for each unit used in the training program. Refractive errors, especially astigmatism, must be corrected in the telescope by putting the correcting lens behind the ocular lens. Sometimes, the field of view has to be sacrificed because spectacle corrections for the refractive errors must be used to obtain good acuity with the telescope. The spectacle lenses necessitate holding the telescope further from the eye (a greater vertex distance), which decreases the field.

Telescopes will exaggerate movement and create a speed smear when used in a dynamic situation. (Students describe this movement as "bouncing.") The stronger the telescope, the more the small tremors and movement of the student are magnified. This phenomenon seems to occur primarily while students are adapting to the telescope and fades after they have used the lenses for a short time.

FAMILIARIZATION WITH THE AID

The student should examine the aid that has been prescribed, locate the ocular, objective, and housing, and develop some technique for knowing which end to hold up to the eye. If the aid is cylindrical, the student may have difficulty distinguishing between the two ends. The instructor can paint a thin band of contrasting color around the housing to indicate which end should be held up to the eye.

The instructor can discuss the optics of the lenses if the student is interested and can understand this information.

Higher functioning students will be able to discover many of the optical principles of the aid through guided investigation. For example, the instructor could focus the aid so a poster on a wall six to eight feet directly in front of the student is in focus. The student could be asked to look through the aid and tell the instructor what he or she has found out about the magnification of the aid. (Most students will answer that the picture looks closer or bigger.) The student could then compare the field of view with and without the aid, and the instructor could then guide the student to discover that the widest field of view through the aid is achieved when the aid is closest to the eye.

If the student wears eyeglasses for distance and has an astigmatic cylinder correction of less than 2.00 (the amount of cylinder is the number found after the equal sign on the student's eyeglass prescription) he or she should try looking through the telescope without the eyeglasses. To do so, the student probably will need to change the focus to correct for his refractive error. If the student must wear eyeglasses when using the aid, and the aid does not have a flexible rubber collar around the ocular end of the housing, the instructor should glue a rubber washer or small circular felt pad on the ocular end of the housing. Then the student will be able to hold the aid against the eyeglasses without scratching the lens. Many students who wear eyeglasses while using a telescopic aid prefer to hold the aid with both hands to steady the aid. Also, using the cross-body technique with a long cane allows the person to support the elbow of the arm holding the aid on the cane. The following optical principles should be explored in a similar manner: focal length and working distance, depth of focus, increase of speed of motion, and motion parallax.

Most students will not be able to absorb all this information in one lesson. All students should, however, immediately learn how to care for and safely store their telescopic aids. (Information about maintenance is given later in this chapter.) It is also helpful if they can describe how they feel about the aid and about using the aid. Many students feel conspicuous about using something that is "different." This can be a significant problem in spite of the enthusiasm for the aid expressed in the clinical examination. If students seem to be rejecting the aid for this reason, the instructor can ask that they first learn to use the aid in the privacy of their own home and then make a more informed decision about whether they will use it at school, at work, and for recreational activities.

The remaining sections will cover training in the skills of localization, fixation, spotting, bracing, tracking, scanning, and integrating the various skills that have been learned. Exercises to be used in training students in each skill appear at the end of the respective sections when appropriate.

LOCALIZATION

Positioning the Aid
To reduce the chance of breaking the aid by dropping it, students should attach to the telescope a small strap that can be slipped onto the wrist. Some children prefer to attach a longer strap that can be worn around the neck.

Securing the aid in this manner is particularly important when the aid is used outdoors in the winter and gloves or mittens are worn. Also during the winter, a light coating of windshield "de-icer" will help prevent the ocular lens from fogging. Students should hold the aid with a firm, comfortable grip as near the eye as possible to maximize the field of view. Most students find it easier to hold the aid with the hand that is on the same side of the body as the eye being used. The aid is gripped by wrapping the fingers and thumb around it. The circle that is formed by the index finger and thumb should be placed against the face to steady the aid and to block out all ambient light.

The aid should be supported firmly to minimize movement. When sitting, students may rest their elbows on a table. If the table is too low for comfort, books may be placed on the table to raise the elbows or the case that houses the aid may be placed on the thigh, and the elbows can lean on the case. When standing, students may steady the aid by holding their upper arms against their body or by supporting the elbow of the arm holding the aid with the palm of the opposite hand. At first, students may want to lean against a stable surface so they can concentrate on the aid rather than on keeping their balance.

Frequently, students with cerebral palsy, multiple sclerosis, advanced diabetes, or those who are elderly or have had a stroke have problems in motor control and hence find it difficult to hold the aid steady, manipulate it, and develop localization skills. A support system must be designed to stabilize the aid. It may be as simple as bracing the arms on a table or against the chest or mounting the telescope on a tripod or other similar stand if the aid is to be used only for one task (e.g., taking notes from a chalkboard or watching television). More specific suggestions for working with students with special problems appear in the section on special problems at the end of this chapter.

It may be necessary for students with motor-control problems to return to the clinic to try a different aid of the same power. For some students, a larger monocular telescope or a pair of binoculars is easier to control. Those with hand tremors sometimes find that a heavier aid produces a heavier grip and hences reduces unwanted movement. Larger and lower powered telescopes also increase the size of the exit pupil and thus may be used by students who cannot easily localize with the lighter and higher powered aids. They may serve as a transition in that by using them students will have a better idea of what to look for in the stronger telescopes and will develop a better feeling for localizing.

Spectacle-mounted or clip-on head-borne aids may be the best compromise. If the weight of a clip-on monocular telescope causes the eyeglasses to slide down, an elastic Velcro strap may be attached to the back of the temples and worn behind the head to secure the glasses, or the clinic may prescribe spectacle frames with temple pieces that wrap around the back of the ear (comfort cable).

Directing the Aid

Some students experience difficulty controlling the direction of the aid. If students with no scotomas report that the image seen through the aids (especially through spectacle mounted aids) is oval rather than circular or that they see flashes of light, a silver-moon effect, or a dark band, the aid probably is misaligned and should be returned to the clinic with the student for proper alignment or for replacement of displaced internal lenses. If the problems persist with hand-held devices, the telescope is not being held correctly in front of the eye; its position should be changed to obtain a better alignment. Working in a dimly lit room with a brightly lit object at the other end of the room may help overcome these problems. With terrestrial telescopes, the instructor can get some indication of the alignment of the optics of the telescope in relationship to the pupil of the eye by looking for the telescope's image of the brightly lit object on the cornea.

Locating the Instructor

Training in localization should take place initially in a room with few visual stimuli. The instructor should stand in front of a blank field and focus the aid at 10 feet. Then the instructor should walk to a position that is 10 feet in front of the student and ask the student to try to look at him or her; auditory clues may be helpful. If the student cannot locate the instructor, he or she should tell the student which way to move the aid until it is pointing directly at the instructor. This exercise may have to be repeated several times until the student understands how to get the full field of view.

Students with scotomas. Students with a central scotoma must learn how

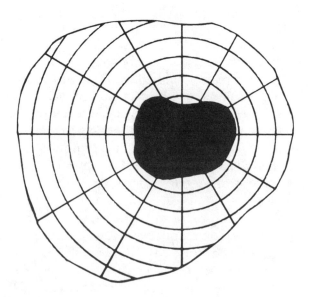

Fig. 1. Large central scotoma.

288

to eccentrically view without the aid before using the aid. Students with multiple scotomas will find that an object appears, disappears, and reappears in the field of view as its image passes through the several scotomas on the retina. Sometimes the scotomas are so confusing that students cannot localize even without the aid. In the case of students with multiple scotomas who have adequate acuities, it may be helpful to patch the eye except for a two-centimeter hole in the patch that is placed where the clinician or instructor thinks the line of sight (best vision) should be. This is an all-or-nothing procedure; as the eye wanders behind the patch it will receive a visual input only when it passes the aperture. This procedure reinforces the ocular muscles to develop a sense of directionalization to visual stimuli and, in time and with effort, students develop localization skills.

When working with a student who has a scotoma or an unusual visual field, the instructor should identify the part of the student's field that has the most acute vision. Most low vision clinics evaluate visual fields with the Amsler Grid, a tangent screen, or an arc perimeter. The results usually are reported on a diagram. In Figures 1 and 2, the part of the retina with which the student can see is not darkened. The area of most acute vision is found in the fovea, which is in the center of the retina. The potential for visual acuity decreases from 20/20 in the fovea to light perception in the periphery of the visual field. In Figure 1, the most acute vision is most likely above the central scotoma, and the student will need to direct his or her gaze down approximately 20 degrees to have the most distinct vision directed forward. In Figure 2, the student will need to direct his or her gaze up and to the right approximately 40 degrees to have the most acute vision directed forward.

Fig. 2. Small island of peripheral vision.

If results of a visual-field examination are not found in the clinical report and are not obtainable, the instructor may gain information by researching the etiology of the student's visual condition and by observing or testing the student. Many ocular pathologies have a characteristic field loss, and information about the student's pathology may help the instructor find evidence of abnormalities in the field. The instructor may observe the student holding his or her head in an unusual position or directing the gaze in a consistently eccentric direction when attempting to examine an object closely. To determine more precisely the location of the student's most acute vision, the instructor may conduct a confrontation field test on the student (see Chapter 6) or carry out the following procedure:

■ The instructor and student should sit facing each other, six to eight feet apart. The instructor should hold a card with a large number on it in front of his or her face. The student should begin to scan slowly with the eyes (holding the head stationary) on a horizontal line to the left of the instructor's face. The student should stop at any point where the image of the number is becoming clearer. When the student no longer can scan any further to the left, he or she should slowly return the eyes to the central position. This scanning should be repeated to the right, above, below, and then along four diagonal lines away from the instructor's face, with the student stopping to examine any position in which the most acute vision is directed toward the instructor. The instructor can check the student's perception and help the student make an accurate comparison by holding cards with numbers, letters, or shapes of different sizes and assisting the student to locate the position in which the smallest figure can be identified.

Once the instructor has ascertained the direction of gaze that puts the most acute vision in a forward position, he or she should discuss this information with the student, using graphic or tactile drawings to illustrate the explanation. The student should practice this position by turning to face various objects in the room and then shifting the gaze to the most appropriate position. When the student can do this independently, he or she is ready to combine eccentric viewing with the use of the telescope. An exercise for doing so appears at the end of this section on localization.

In review, localization skills are developed by

1. Teaching students to align the aid with the eye's line of sight and to view eccentrically.

2. Using support systems if the aid cannot be stabilized.

3. Using appropriately sized targets and keeping the target background free of clutter.

4. Keeping activities related to the particular goals of students.

5. Using lower powered telescopes when students cannot localize with their prescribed telescope.

6. Considering spectacle-mounted or clip-on head-borne full-field telescopes as an initial training aid to develop localization skills.

7. Familiarizing students with what they are supposed to see through the telescope before they actually use it; this can be done by starting with lower powered telescopes, by moving targets closer to students, or by describing targets the way they are to be seen (e.g., "You will see only a part of my face when you look through the telescope.").

8. Always focusing the telescope for the students.

9. Utilizing patching techniques when necessary.

Exercises

Exercise 1. The aim of this exercise is to hold the aid steadily and securely.

■ The instructor first sits where the student will be sitting and focuses the aid on an eye chart, or another high-contrast target, that is 8 to 10 feet away and directly facing the chair. Then the student sits in the chair and places the strap of the aid around the wrist or neck. The student should attempt each of these two techniques for holding the aid while reading from the chart:

1. After identifying which eye will be used to look through the aid, the student should wrap the fingers and thumb of the hand on the same side as that eye around the ocular end of the aid. The student should place the circle formed by the index finger and thumb on his or her face to steady the aid and to block out all ambient light.

2. After positioning the hand as just described, the student may place the free hand around the housing at the objective end of the aid to steady it.

The student should then practice supporting the aid by resting one or both elbows on the table (or on books placed on the table if the table is too low for the elbows to rest comfortably) or by placing the aid's case on the thigh and resting the elbow on the case.

The next step is to practice holding the aid while standing 8 to 10 feet from the chart. Two techniques for steadying the aid while standing should be practiced:

1. Holding the aid with one or both hands and placing the upper arm or arms agains the body.

2. Holding the aid with one hand and supporting the elbow on the same side with the palm of the opposite hand. At first, the student may prefer to lean against a stable surface, such as a desk or wall, to avoid losing balance.

The student and instructor should discuss the student's accuracy and comfort with each of the techniques and decide which seem to work best. More than one technique should be mastered because the choice of which technique to use will depend on the environment, the size of the object being looked at, and how long the student is looking at the object.

Exercise 2. The goal of this exercise is to hold the aid as near to the eye as possible.

■ The instructor places a number line (a bold horizontal line with sequential numbers at 3-inch intervals drawn on poster board, chalkboard, or another type of erasable board) 8 to 10 feet in front of and directly facing the student's chair. The instructor then sits in the chair and focuses the telescope on the number line. (See Figure 3.) The student replaces the instructor in the chair, holds the aid four inches from the eye, and reads all the numbers he or she can see without moving the aid. The student repeats this activity while holding the aid two inches from the eye, and finally, as near to the eye as possible. By noting the difference in field size, the student can recognize which position is most advantageous. If necessary, the exercise may be repeated using the instructor's face as a visual target. The student can compare how much of the instructor's face can be seen when he or she holds the aid at different distances from the eye.

Exercise 3. The aim of this exercise is to align the aid without verbal assistance from the instructor and to develop the concept of projection.

- The student holds a 5-inch diameter cardboard tube with both hands and looks through it with both eyes at the instructor's face. (The instructor's face should be well illuminated and near the end of the tube.) The student first describes whether the instructor is smiling or frowning. If the student cannot do so, the instructor asks the student to identify the color and shape of a geometric figure on a card held near the end of the tube and to follow it visually as it is moves slowly in a horizontal direction. When the student is successful, the instructor decreases the diameter of the tube, in stages, to two inches and then begins to work with the telescope. If the student continues to have difficulty, the instructor should refer the student back to the low vision clinic for an aid with a lower power and a larger field of view. The initially prescribed aid should be reintroduced later in the instructional sequence.

Exercise 4. The goal of this exercise is for students with scotomas to combine eccentric viewing with the use of a telescopic aid.

- The student sits 6 to 8 feet away from and facing the instructor. After directing the gaze so the area of most acute vision falls on the instructor's face, the student should move the aid (which the instructor has focused for the specific distance between them) in front of the better eye without changing the position of the head or eyes. The instructor can monitor the stability of the student's head and eye positions while providing verbal directions on how to manipulate the aid to align it between the student's eye and the instructor's face. The student should continue to practice this exercise until he or she can align the aid independently and hold it securely as near to the eye as possible.

FIXATION

Once localization skills have been established, the training program can proceed to fixation skills. Fixation skills allow the student to identify the object whose position was found through the use of localization skills.

Teaching Focusing
Focusing a telescope changes the distance between the ocular and the objec-

Fig. 3. Bold horizontal line with numbers spaced 3 inches apart.

tive. To focus on a nearby object, the distance between the lenses must be increased; the distance must be decreased to focus on an object father away. Initially, the instructor focuses the aid to show the student what an in-focus target is. To teach focusing, the instructor stands at the same distance from the target as the student (about 6 to 8 feet) and turns the ocular all the way around in one direction. The student then turns the ocular with a slow, smooth motion until the image of the object is clear; next, the student turns past that point until the image begins to blur and then turns back to the point of clearest focus. For maximum magnification, the instructor starts with the objective and ocular lens moved furthest apart.

The instructor frequently checks the student's focusing ability by looking through the aid at the same object on which the student has focused and at the same distance. If the student seems to be consistently inaccurate and is wearing distance prescription glasses, then either the student or the instructor may have a refractive error and should consult the clinician for a more accurate prescription. If the student is not wearing distance prescription glasses and is focusing inaccurately, the student either is using some of the power in the telescope to compensate for a refractive error (which may be acceptable) or does not understand the concept of focusing for a clear image.

To give the student practice in focusing the aid, the instructor stands in front of the student and asks the student to focus clearly on the instructor's face. This exercise is repeated at various distances. During the focusing exercises, the instructor may assist the student in determining the focal range of the aid and should give directions for moving the aid if the student cannot locate the instructor. Once the student has learned the closest distance he or she can be to an object and still focus on it, the student will not be frustrated by trying to focus on an object that is too close. To develop this understanding, the instructor can ask the student to identify and practice looking at objects that are far enough away to focus and at those that are too close.

Some students, usually those who have congenital low vision, do not appear to understand the concept of clear focus. The instructor can teach this concept by working with the student to fine tune a radio for the clearest sound and to focus a slide projector to achieve the clearest image. Once the student understands the concept of focusing through these analogies, the instructor can help the student transfer the concept to focusing a telescopic aid. If the student has difficulty holding the aid while learning to focus it, the instructor can hold the aid while the student focuses it. A clip-on telescope or a flip-down loupe will be most effective if it can be focused while it is attached to the spectacle frame.

Some students cannot learn to focus telescopic aids. They may be referred to the clinic to investigate the possibility of their using afocal telescopes. Setting or making a focusable telescope for a particular distance may be a beneficial alternative in the case of a low-functioning student who needs an aid only for one task and who is always the same distance from the object to be viewed. The instructor can set the aid at the proper foucs and paint a line along the entire length of the telescope's housing; if the aid goes out of focus, it can be reset easily by rotating the housing until the two ends of the line meet. Different colored lines could be used for different distances. Those individuals with poor motor control who cannot use a pincer grip to focus the telescope may be helped by the following special adaptions: (1) wrapping cloth or tape around the focusing unit or (2) putting a handle on the focusing ring so focusing can be done with a pushing movement rather than a pincer grasp. Physical or occupational therapists can advise the instuctor about other modifications for specific physical impairments.

The focusing range of telescopes may be as little as 12 inches away or as much as 12 feet. The instructor should check the range of each unit so the student can be advised of the telescope's range. Because of refractive errors, pupil size, accommodation, and other optical considerations, the exact ranges may differ between the student and instructor but they should be reasonably equivalent.

It is important that the student focuses slowly. Small turns can make a great change in some of the higher powered telescopes. The student should practice blurring and clearing the image as often as is necessary.

Exercises

The objective of all the exercises in this section is as follows: when presented with two large targets, one 8 feet away and one 15 feet away, the student will focus on the near object and describe or read it; then focus on the distant object, using a slow smooth movement, and describe or read it; and finally refocus on the near object.

Exercise 1. The aim of this exercise is for the student to determine the minimal focal point of the aid.

■ The instructor adjusts the focus on the telescope so the objective and ocular lenses are as far apart as possible. After placing an eye chart on a wall at the student's eye level when standing, the instructor finds the nearest point to the chart where a clear focus can be maintained. This is the minimal focal distance of the aid.

The student stands in the same place and looks at the chart through the aid (with the strap of the aid around the wrist or neck). While holding the aid with one hand and turning the focus with the other, the student notes how the image of the chart goes out of focus. Then the student refocuses on the chart by turning the focus all the way in one direction and reads the smallest possible line on the chart.

294

The next step is for the student to step backwards 2 feet and locate the chart through the telescope. While looking at the chart, the student turns the focus slowly and smoothly until the image is clear again, continues turning past the clear point until the image is out of focus, and then returns to the clear focus and reads the chart. As a check, the student next returns to the original position and refocuses the aid.

Exercise 2. The goal of this exercise is to practice how to focus.

■ The instructor stands the minimal focal distance from the student and holds a card with a letter on it similar to one of the letters on an eye chart. The student focuses the aid on the card and reads it. The instructor then moves away from the student while the student watches the instructor without the aid. The student realigns the aid, focuses it on a new card (with another letter on it) that the instructor is holding, and reads the card. The instructor continues to change positions, making sure that he or she always is in front of the student. After assuming each new position, the instructor shows the student a different card. If the instructor takes a position that is too near for the student to focus on, the student should try to recognize that the instructor is too close and check by looking through the aid.

During this exercise, the instructor periodically checks the student's focusing accuracy (as already described), observes whether the student is focusing slowly and smoothly, and notes whether the student is learning to anticipate which direction to turn the focus when the distance between the student and the instructor decreases or increases.

Exercise 3. The aim of this exercise is for the student to understand the importance of the viewing angle.

■ The instructor repeats Exercise 2 but occasionally turns so he or she is not facing the student directly. The instructor assesses the student's ability to focus and to determine when he or she will have to move to read the card with the aid because the viewing angle is incorrect.

Exercise 4. The goal of this exercise is to determine the student's preferred type, level and angle of illumination.

■ In a quiet indoor area with natural illumination controlled by shades or venetian blinds and overhead fluorescent lights, the instructor attaches an eye chart to a wall at the student's eye level so the light from a window is falling on the chart from the side. The instructor asks the student to focus on the chart and to read it. Then the instructor reduces the amount of light and compares the student's reading performance. This procedure is repeated with a standing gooseneck incandescent lamp regulated by a rheostat and with overhead fluorescent lights. The instructor determines whether the student can read the chart more easily from the window side of the room or from the opposite side. The student should apply this information to indoor activities involving the telescopic aid, such as reading notes from a chalkboard, watching television, reading menus posted behind counters in fast-food restaurants and so on.

SPOTTING

Spotting is the result of localization and fixation skills. It involves finding an object without the aid, raising the telescope so it is aligned between the eye and the object, and focusing the aid until the image is as clear as possible. If the object is not visible to the student without the aid, the procedures described later in this chapter should be followed to scan for the object.

At the beginning of training, the student should be seated facing a wall that is 6 to 8 feet away. On the wall should be the objects, such as numbers, letters, and words that are large enough (at least 50 percent larger than the best clinical acuity with the aid) and bright enough to be located without the aid. The student should describe what he or she is seeing through the aid. As the student develops spotting skills, the size of the print can be reduced, the distance from the object can be increased, and the illumination level can be varied. After this skill is mastered in a sitting position, the activies are repeated while the student is standing.

The student should also practice this skill on objects in the environment. If the student cannot see a word or sign through the telescope clearly enough to read it, he or she should attempt to guess the word from its configuration and from contextural clues. For example, a round red sign located on a corner in an urban area is probably a stop sign. With practice, a student who is waiting for a bus and knows that the particular bus is the only one at that stop with a two-word destination can identify the desired bus by recognizing that there are two words in its destination sign.

Some students will have difficulty maintaining their viewing directions while raising the aid. The student could practice this skill using a hollow cylinder whose circumference is larger than the aid. The student could also practice with a lower power or larger telescope that has a wider field of view.

The instructor should make sure that students are using a slow, smooth movement when they raise the aid. Students who have difficulty doing so often change head or eye positions as they raise the aid in front of their eye. For students who have vision in both eyes, this problem can be amelioriated by their keeping both eyes open as they raise the aid and closing the non-dominant eye only when the aid is aligned between the dominant eye and the object to be viewed. The instructor could also try using a target that produces sound, such as a radio or metronome; students could then use auditory information to augment visual information about the spatial position of the target.

If these procedures are not effective, the instructor should contact the low vision clinic to see if an aid with a larger objective, larger field, or lower power should be tried.

Students who use a bioptic telescope often will have difficulty spotting an object through their aid if they do not first center the object in their visual field. To do so, they must (1) locate the object through their prescription lens, (2) place the object directly in the center of their visual field, (3) drop their head to spot the object through the bioptic telescope, and (4) continue to look at the target while moving their head.

If a student is centering the object but is still having problems, the instructor should check the position of the bioptic in the carrier lens. The bioptic should be directly above the student's pupil when the student is looking straight ahead at an object that is more than 20 feet away.

In review, the instructor helps the student develop fixation skills by

1. Insuring that localization skills have been mastered.
2. Teaching the student to focus the telescope correctly.
3. Teaching the student the focusing range of the telescope.
4. Teaching the concept of clear versus blurred images to congenitally impaired students.
5. Stabilizing the student's optical system with tables, stands, and so forth.
6. Changing to telescopes with larger fields of view as needed.
7. Controlling the size of the target and other variables.
8. Teaching the student to spot with a telescope.

Exercises

The objective of the exercises in this section is for the student to locate an object without the aid, raise the telescope so it is aligned between the eye and the object without changing head or eye positions, and focus the aid until the image is as clear as possible, controlling for glare when necessary.

Exercise 1. The aim of this exercise is to develop spotting skills in a controlled environment.

■ The exercise is performed in a quiet well-illuminated room with at least one blank wall painted a flat, light color. The instructor cuts from colored paper (that is light enough to contrast with the wall color) various geometric shapes that are large enough to be seen from a distance of 8 to 10 feet without using the aid. With a dark felt-tipped pen, the instructor writes a number on each shape. The number should be small enough so the student cannot read it without the telescope but large enough so it can be read with the telescope. After the instructor has attached several shapes to the wall at the student's eye level, the student spots the shape without the aid, guesses the shape and color, raises the aid, confirms the shape and color, and reads the number. As the student develops spotting skills, the instructor slowly decreases the size of the numbers, replaces the numbers with words, increases the student's distance from the wall, and varies the illumination. In addition, the instructor may vary this practice by asking the student to read numbers and words on digital or dial clocks, on scoreboards at ball games, or drawn on a chalkboard.

Exercise 2. The goal of this exercise is to develop spotting skills in a less controlled environment.

■ In a shaded outdoor area with a variety of objects, such as a playground or a parking lot, the instructor selects an object from the environmental and object variables described in Chapter 6. The instructor describes the object in general terms so the student can locate it without the aid. (For example, the student could be asked to locate a large red sign about 15 away). After the student has located the object, he or she should raise the telescope slowly and smoothly, focus on the object, change position, if necessary, and read or describe the object. Objects of increasing difficulty should be selected. This exercise should be repeated in an area that is unfamiliar to the student.

Exercise 3. The aim of this exercise is to control glare when using a telescope.

■ In a sunny outdoor area with a variety of objects and signs at different heights, the student spots and examines a series of street and store signs with the telescope while experimenting with the following techniques for controlling glare:

1. Students should try different types of sunglasses (from the least absorptive to the most absorptive), preferably those that block light from above, from the sides, and from in front. The best sunglasses will be those that reduce the maximum amount of glare while allowing the maximum visual acuity. Students with slow light-to-dark adaption may wish to close their eyes while changing from one pair of sunglasses to another. After allowing their eyes to adapt to the level of light transmission of each pair of sunglasses, they should describe what they can see. After selecting two pairs that seem best, the student should compare their effects while looking through the telescope and describe what can be seen. (To avoid scratching the plastic sunglass lenses, students should follow the suggestions described earlier in this chapter for regular glasses.) The student's preference and the instructor's assessment of the student's visual performance should determine the final selection of sunglasses.

2. Students should try various broad-brimmed hats or baseball caps positioned so the eyes and the objective end of the aid are shaded from the sun.

3. The student should experiment with different types of visors, including one with an adjustable strap that goes around the back of the head and one that can be attached to spectacle frames.

4. The instructor can make a sunglass cap for the student's aid from a plastic cap to a bottle or film canister that fits snugly over the objective end of the aid and a pair of sunglasses or a filter that can be cut to fit the cap. First a circle is cut from the sunglass lens or filter, the diameter of which is slightly smaller than the inside diameter of the cap. Second, a circle, which is slightly smaller than the sunglass or filter circle, is cut out of the top of the cap. Third, the lens circle is glued into the cap. The student can use this sunglass cap to reduce glare and can easily remove it when in the shade or indoors.

5. The student can use the free hand to shield his or her eyes and the objective end of the aid from the sun.

6. The student can change position so he or she is standing in the shade or with the source of glare behind rather than in front.

At this point, the student is able to find a specific target in the environment and examine it for detail so as to identify it. However, if the target is much larger than the telescope's field of view or it is not stationary, then movement of the telescope is required. This is the next phase of the training program, which involves tracing and tracking.

TRACING

Tracing is the intermediate task between fixation and tracking. It involves visually following a stationary line in the environment and is similar to tracking a line with a pencil. It is one of the simplest skills because the student has control over the speed of movement. After locating a line without the aid, the student raises the aid so it is aligned between the eye and the line being viewed. After focusing the aid on the line, the student moves his or her head (not eye) with a slow, smooth movement while following the line. Some students who are able to maintain a good adjustment of the eye, aid, and object while focusing and spotting lose the alignment when they begin to move their head to trace a line. The instructor should make sure that such students are moving their head and the aid as a unit. If not, they should be encouraged to modify their grip on the aid so the index finger and thumb are placed against the face. In using this grip, they will not have to move their hand or the aid because both will move as the head moves.

The student can practice tracing by visually following lines the instructor has drawn on a large piece of posterboard with a wide marker of contrasting color or on a chalkboard. (If the student is unable to see the lines or numbers, the instructor should draw them larger in a color that contrasts more sharply with the background.) When the student can trace straight, horizontal, vertical, and diagonal lines, geometric shapes may be presented that the student should trace and identify while looking through the aid. Next, curved lines should be introduced. To evaluate the accuracy of the student's tracing, the instructor can place numbers, which the student should read aloud, beside the curved line. On a chalkboard or on another piece of posterboard, the instructor may replace the numbers with signs commonly found on the street. As the student's skill develops, the boldness and contrast of the line should be decreased. The instructor should observe the smoothness of the student's movements and the speed and accuracy of tracing.

After the student has mastered the tracing of lines that lie in a plane perpendicular to the direction being faced, he or she should begin tracing lines that project away from him or her. This task will require the student to change the focus while tracing with the aid. The lines of a hopscotch game may be used, or the instructor could put tape of a contrasting color on the floor and place numbers, words, or signs at intervals along the line of tape. (For more detailed instructions, see the exercises at the end of this section.)

For additional practice, the student could trace the lines formed by a chalkboard, door frame, or corner of a room, or the instructor's extended arm to examine a sign the instructor is holding. Some students will enjoy the application of tracing in recreation. In a bowling alley, for example, a student may use a telescopic aid to trace along the gutter to the far end of the lane to count the standing pins. While watching a baseball game, a student may trace the lines between the bases to find out who is on base.

A student who has difficulty with the slow, steady head movements required for tracing can practice tracing tactually by following with a finger a raised line with braille numbers or tactile symbols superimposed on it. The student will inadvertently skip over some symbols of the tracing movement if the student's finger is not slow and thorough. After proficiency has been gained in tracing tactually, the student should begin tracing visually with the aid, bringing the line to be traced as close to the face as necessary to see the line and the numbers beside it. When the student is able to trace a line accurately without an aid, then it is time to learn to trace with the aid.

Students who are measuring success by speed, rather than by accuracy, should be encouraged to slow down. It usually takes more time to retrace a line to locate omitted numbers than it does to trace slowly and accurately the first time. Students with poor motor control may find that leaning the back of their head against a wall or the back of a chair and moving their head while it touches the wall or chair will help them move more smoothly. If they have more control in their torso than in their neck, students could rotate their upper body and neck together as a unit instead of moving just their neck.

Some students with nystagmus have one eye position or direction of gaze called the null point in which oscillation is reduced. If such students have trouble using the telescope, they should receive a clinical low vision reevaluation in which their null point is identified. The instructor also can determine the null point by noting differences in the amount of nystagmoid movements as the student shifts his or her gaze from one direction to another. Frequently, the null point is in a temporal gaze of the dominant eye. When a student is looking at an object and an eye is at its null point, the telescope should be aligned between the dominant eye and the object being viewed even if the student is not facing the object. Any tendency to move the aid as the eye moves should be discouraged because such movement will cause the student to lose the alignment of the aid with the object. Instead of moving the aid, the student should hold the aid in place and wait for the eye to return to its previous position. A student with nystagmus may appreciate the increased field of view available in a telescope with a large objective lens. If the field of view seen through a telescope is larger than the student's pupil,

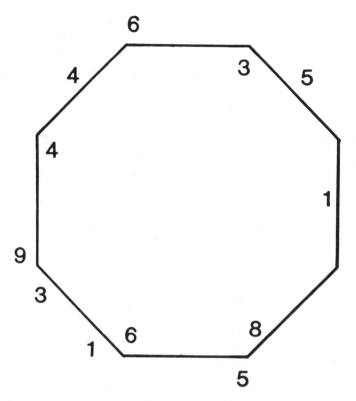

Fig. 4. Geometric figure with numbers.

there will be a margin of room for the eye to oscillate and still receive an image of the object being viewed.

Exercises

Exercise 1. The goal of this exercise is to trace a line that is perpendicular to the student's facing direction.

■ The instructor draws a straight horizontal line on a chalkboard or paper and then places randomly selected numbers about six inches apart and just above the line. The numbers should be small enough so the student cannot read them without the aid. The student spots the line or one of the numbers, raises the aid, and visually traces the line, reading each number in turn. (The head, not the eyes, should be moved while tracing.) The instructor observes the smoothness of the student's head movements and the accuracy of tracing as evidenced by the student's reading every number in order. When this task is mastered, the student goes on to tracing a vertical line and then a horizontal line.

■ The instructor draws several large geometric shapes on the chalkboard or paper, such as the one illustrated in Figure 4. The student visually traces each shape with the aid and names the shape or draws it. The instructor

301

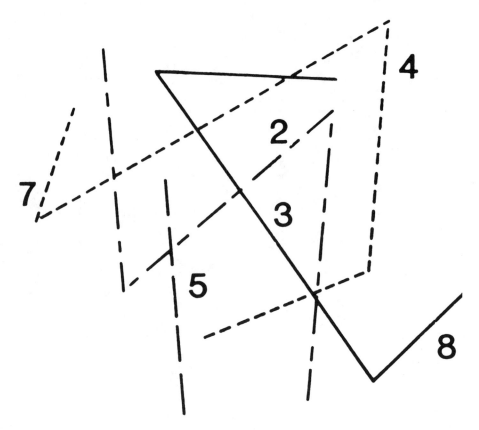

Fig. 5. Irregular lines with numbers.

observes the student's smoothness of movement, accuracy, and level of kinesthetic awareness of the point at which tracing began. If the student is not tracing thoroughly, the instructor places numbers beside the lines of each figure that the student then reads. In this way, the instructor can monitor the student's thoroughness and observe the circumstances that present problems.

■ The instructor draws figures (using several colors of chalk or pen) that do not have identifiable shapes (see Figure 5 for one example). After placing numbers beside the lines, the instructor asks the student to find the number 7 and to identify the color of the line that is nearest to the number. When the student is able to do so easily and accurately, the instructor draws designs with one, and then several curved lines (such as the design shown in Figure 6). As the student's skill increases, the instructor decreases the boldness of the line, the size of the numbers, and the contrast of the numbers against the background and replaces the numbers with words. At each step, the instructor should observe the smoothness of the student's movements and the accuracy and speed of tracing.

302

Exercise 2. The aim of this exercise is to trace a line that projects away from the student. Two indoor areas are required for this exercise—one having a floor with a uniform color and one having a multicolored floor.

■ With colored tape or rope that contrasts with the color of the floor, the instructor makes a straight line on the floor, that projects away from the stu-

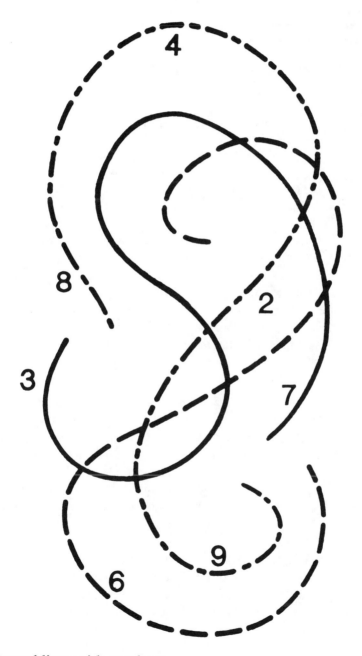

Fig. 6. Curved lines with numbers.

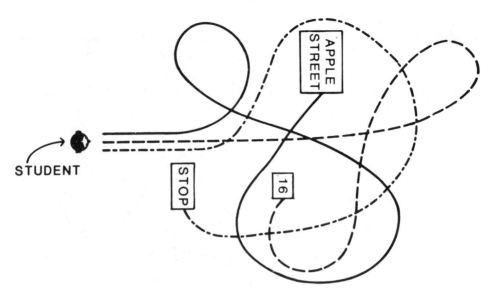

Fig. 7. Layout of room used for training telescopic skills.

dent. Cards with numbers, letters, and words are then placed beside the line to form a design (see Figure 7). The student begins tracing at the end of the line nearest him or her and reads each card as it is passed. The student refocuses the aid as he or she traces. The instructor observes the student's accuracy and speed of tracing and increases the complexity of the designs when the student masters the simpler ones. Complete the exercise on a floor with uniform color first and then repeat the exercise on a multicolored floor.

TRACKING

Tracking is the ability to follow visually a moving object in the environment. It is more difficult than tracing because the students cannot control the speed of the target. To track accurately, the students must move at a speed determined by the object being tracked. When students are tracking an object with a low vision aid, they should move their head (and body, if necessary) slowly and smoothly; they should not move their eyes. Central field losses will complicate this task because it requires students not only to view eccentrically to find the target but to maintain that eccentric position while moving the head.

Persons with peripheral field losses will find the task even more frustrating. They have learned to use quick scanning movements for mobility and may even be involved in an orientation and mobility (O&M) program to learn how to move the eyes systematically. The telescope requires them to move their head—a trait that is ususally discouraged in the O&M program. Such students often are confused by the demands of the telescope. Their

304

reports of the object disappearing or fluctuating and the presence of arcs of light are indicative of this inability to move the head, eye, and aid as one unit. If these problems persist, and the instructor observes the eye movements, a retraining program is needed. The instructor should explain to the student what is happening so the student will be more conscious of the need for moving the head while tracking. It may help to start some exercises. For example, using a patch with a 2–5-centimeter aperture will help eliminate eye movements and encourage head movements for tracking an object without the telescope. Practicing tracking activities with a long paper-towel tube will encourage head movements. Since the student may need good eye movements without the telescope for general mobility, the low vision instructor should make sure that the O&M instructor is aware of this training activity so the patient is not confused by contradictory training activities.

As with all phases of training, if difficulties exist, the instructor should start the student in a seated position with a low-power telescope and a simple figure-ground environment. The low-power telescope allows the person to pick up a moving target more easily and provides a large-enough field in front of the moving target so that changes in direction and speed can be anticipated.

When students are learning to track, the instructor should select objects that are visible without the aid. Students should practice tracking objects moving in a straight path in the following sequence:

1. An object that is perpendicular to the student's facing direction and is moving horizontally.

2. An object that is perpendicular to the student's direction and is moving vertically.

3. An object that is parallel to the student's facing direction and is moving away from the student.

4. An object moving diagonally away from the student.

5. An object moving diagonally toward the student.

6. An object moving toward and parallel to the student's direction.

7. An object that is moving in curved paths.

Throughout the exercises to practice tracking, the instructor should control the environmental and object variables, as described in the section on tracing. The student should begin by tracking the instructor's moving head, an object in the instructor's hand, or a basketball being rolled slowly across the floor. The instructor may also stand facing the student and hold a word or letter card in the palm of the hand so the back of the card is toward the student. The student traces up the instructor's arm to locate the card, identifies the color of the card, and then tracks the card as the instructor moves it. An added task is to read the word on the card when the instructor flips it over. If the student can read the word as soon as it is revealed, then he or she has been tracking it accurately.

The student also can practice tracking in the environment. Such exercises include determining at which floor an elevator in a glass shaft is stopping, visually following an animal as it moves, and tracking actors or dancers in a theater or children in a playground. To prepare for the analysis of intersections, a student may track vehicles moving through an intersection and indicate which way they have turned. During a ping-pong or tennis game, a student with a wide-angle telescope could attempt to track a ball that has been painted in a color that contrasts with the background. The type of activities in which the instructor can involve the student are endless. To review, the instructor can help the student develop tracking skills by:

1. Making sure the student has adequate ocular-motor control and can track large objects without a telescope.

2. Training the student to make head movements instead of eye movements while tracking with a telescope.

3. Teaching the student to move the neck or head, the eyes, and the telescope as a fixed unit while tracking.

4. Beginning with the simplest task (student seated, using low-power telescope, and looking at high-contrast targets with no figure-ground confusion).

5. Using a patch with a small aperture to teach head and neck tracking without a telescope.

6. Working with the student on tracing skills before attempting tracking activities.

7. Identifying null-point position of gaze for students with nystagmus.

8. Beginning with simple targets with predictable movements and progressing to more complicated environments with targets that move erratically.

Some students can only track objects that are moving slowly. They should return to a controlled indoor environment where the instructor can manipulate the speed of targets. The instructor should reintroduce a target with a sound source so the student can gather information through two sensory systems. The speed of the target should be increased gradually, and all other variables should be controlled. Then the speed of the target should be held constant, the complexity of the other variables should be increased slowly. The instructor should try to duplicate some of the elements of the situation in which the student first had difficulty (e.g., illumination, background noise, distinguishing the figure from the ground, and familiarity with the target), and then reintroduce the actual situation. If the student is bothered by the "swimming effect" of a moving image seen through a high-power telescope, he or she should work temporarily with an aid of a lower power and gradually increase his or her tolerance. There is a direct correlation between the power of an aid and the apparent "swimming" motion of the image.

Students must understand, however, that some objects are difficult to track because of their speed or the unpredictable nature of their course. They should learn through experience which objects they can effectively and efficiently track visually and which they can track more effectively and efficiently through auditory rather than visual stimuli.

Exercises

Exercise 1. The goal of this exercise is to track an object that is moving perpendicular to the student's facing direction.

■ In a quiet indoor area with various amounts of illumination and visual clutter, the instructor stands about 10 feet in front of the student and holds two cards back to back. At first, the instructor should stand before a bare wall. After the student focuses on the card by either spotting the card or by tracing along the instructor's arm to the card, the instructor slowly moves his or her hand in an arc over his or her head. At some point in the arc, the instructor stops and flips the hand so the card that was hidden is revealed. Later, the instructor can flip to the hidden card while his or her hand is still moving. If the student can read the card as soon as it is revealed, the student probably has tracked accurately. As the student's accuracy increases, the instructor can increase the speed of movement and move to a position in front of a wall with increased visual clutter.

Exercise 2. The aim of this exercise is to track an object that is moving toward or away from the student. This exercise uses the same materials, environment, and procedures that are used in Exercise 1.

■ Starting about 20 feet in front of the student, the instructor walks slowly toward the student and, at some point, flips the cards in his or her hand. If the student maintained a good focus on the card as the instructor walked toward him, the student should be able to read the new card as soon as it is revealed. The instructor should move slowly at first but speed up when the student's accuracy increases. The instructor can then walk in paths that are oblique to the student's direction and, eventually, in curving paths. The student always should be able to see one card so he or she can maintain a clear focus despite the changes in distance between the student and the instructor.

Exercise 3. The objective of this exercise is to learn tracking skills in a plus-shaped intersection that is controlled by a traffic light and a button-activated pedestrian walk–don't walk sign and that has a large volume of traffic on each street.

■ The student stands 15 to 20 feet from the intersection and tracks vehicles as they move through it. The student describes the action each vehicle takes (e.g., "blue van, left turn") so the instructor can monitor his or her accuracy. The student looks for evidence of unusual traffic patterns such as a delayed green light for one lane of traffic or a yellow directional arrow. The student also can practice tracking in a playground or pack and in a theater or sports arena.

SCANNING

Once the individual is able to track with a telescope, scanning activities must be pursued. Scanning is the most difficult but the most valuable task that will enhance the student's visual efficiency and normalize the student's lifestyle.

Scanning is searching the environment for an object that cannot be located without the aid.* Students should use a scanning pattern of straight, overlapping swaths to cover the entire area instead of quick, random movements. They should have an environmental reference point or utilize kinesthetic awareness to determine the length of the swaths; for instance, when looking for a specific object on a visually cluttered wall, students should not scan beyond the point where the wall meets the next wall. Furthermore, if scanning in an open space with no environmental reference points, (such as the point where the floor meets the wall), students should be aware kinesthetically how far they have turned their head or body so all swaths will be approximately the same length and the students will scan the area completely.

Students who do not use kinesthetic awareness to limit the length of their swaths should be encouraged to move their torso as well as their head when scanning. Because there is less flexibility in the torso than in the neck, some students are better able to judge the length of the swath by the amount of muscular tension in their torso. Students who continue to have difficulty should be told to scan too far rather than not far enough. Another helpful technique for developing a systematic search pattern is to have students verbalize what they see through the telescope while scanning.

The instructor should try to determine why a student leaves gaps in scanning rather than covering the entire area. Is it a lack of motivation, conviction or understanding that is causing this problem? If the student is not motivated, the instructor should try to design an exercise to which the student will be more likely to pay attention. For example, a young sports fan may scan a bulletin board covered with baseball cards to locate a designated player more thoroughly than he would scan a chalkboard to locate a designated number. If a student is not convinced that using a thorough scanning pattern is more efficient than a random search pattern, the instructor should time the student's efforts to locate a dropped object with each technique.

Developing a thorough search pattern with a low vision aid is difficult for most students because there are few guidelines to follow in the environment. To practice this skill, a student can face a chalkboard on which a horizontal scanning pattern has been drawn (see Figure 8). With the aid, the student can trace the lines and read aloud numbers that have been placed beside the lines. When the student has successfully reviewed this exercise, the instructor may draw the same pattern using short broken lines rather than one continuous line. Then, the length of the dashes may be decreased and the space between them increased. In the final step of this exercise, the student scans a chalkboard on which only numbers have been placed in a random fashion. As the

---

*This definition is slightly different from the one used in Chapter 13 ("Near Training Techniques"). In distance training, reading across a line of print is considered a tracing activity, not scanning.

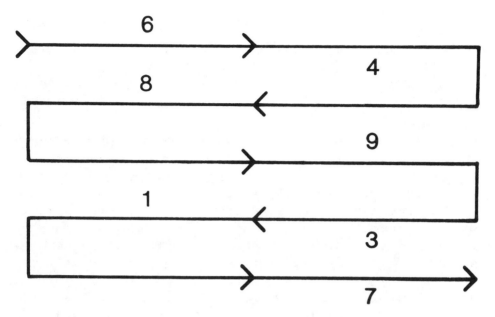

Fig. 8. Diagramming a scanning sequence.

student reads the numbers, the instructor can assess the thoroughness of the student's scanning pattern by the completeness of the response. The student is advised to find the corner of the board and begin a systematic scanning of the entire board from there. When the student can scan horizontally, he or she should practice scanning vertically, repeating as many of the exercise steps as necessary. As the student's skill develops, the instructor can increase the complexity of the task by increasing the student's distance from the board, decreasing the size of the numbers, varying the illumination, and so on.

After these techniques are mastered, students should apply scanning skills in the environment. For example, they can scan an intersection to locate a traffic light, a department store directory to determine where a desired product is sold, a sidewalk or corridor to check for obstacles after turning the corner, or a floor to locate a dropped object. Students with advanced skills can scan to locate kites or birds in the sky, sailboats in a race, or a friend in a crowded room.

The most difficult aspect of scanning is to overlap the visual swaths completely. A student can experience this skill in a tactile mode by scanning a tray of metal shavings with a magnet. If the sweeps of the hand are not overlapping, there will be metal remaining after the student has finished scanning the tray. In a similar way, a student can scan a chalkboard with an eraser or a dirty window with a cloth. If a student appears to be scanning thoroughly but misses numbers or objects that should be found, it is possible that he or she is scanning too fast.

INTEGRATING SKILLS

Students can use a combination of spotting, tracing , tracking, and scanning to locate specific information and environmental landmarks. They can also use the skills to orient themselves to unfamiliar areas, to plan routes, and to negotiate congested areas. This is the instructional phase of the program.

Street Signs

Reading street signs requires a combination of skills. Street signs are located at the intersections of two or more streets and are parallel to the street they identify. If students cannot spot a desired sign or a sign pole without the aid, they should use the telescopic aid to examine the corner on which they are standing, the two adjacent corners (localization), and the diagonally opposite corner until they find the street-sign pole. After facing the corner they wish to examine, they should *scan* across the sidewalk to the edge that is farthest away and then *trace* the line horizontally from where the far edge of the sidewalk meets the grass or a building to the pole. Thus, the sign pole, usually located on the sidewalk or on the grass strip between the sidewalk and the street, will be between them and the line being traced. Once the pole is found, they should visually trace up the pole to *locate* (fixate on) the sign. If the sign is not on the pole, they should trace back down the pole and continue to trace the sidewalk edge until they locate another pole. If they have located the street sign but cannot read it, they should move closer (*focusing*), which, in some cases, will mean crossing the street, especially if the street is wide or congested. If possible, however, students should examine all four corners from their original position; unnecessary street crossing is inefficient, can cause orientation problems, and may be dangerous.

If students have difficulty reading street signs, they may need to return to an indoor, more controlled, area for practice. The instructor can make lettered or numbered signs of various sizes and levels of contrast that represent street, building, and store signs. The instructor may also purchase from Developmental Learning Materials functional signs (e.g., exit, telephone or restroom signs), survival signs (e.g., police, fire escape, high voltage signs), and international signs and symbols (e.g., directional and traffic signs). In some cities, the department of public works or the safety department makes actual street signs and traffic lights available for instructional purposes.

Traffic Lights

Traffic lights may be located on poles at the corner of an intersection or may be suspended from a horizontal support bar on a pole or from wires over the center of the intersection. The following techniques can be used to locate a traffic light on a pole at the corner of an intersection:

- Spotting the traffic without the aid.
- Scanning to the sidewalk across the street, tracing the sidewalk edge to the pole and tracing up the pole to the traffic light.

■ Standing on the curb, turning around, and spotting the traffic light that is on the same corner as the student and that is facing the street the student wishes to cross. Although in this last procedure, the angle that must be used to view the traffic light is unfavorable, the viewing distance is substantially reduced. This procedure also offers an alternative to viewing a light from across the street when the sun is rising or setting near the pole.

Lights that are suspended from horizontal support bars may be located by the same techniques. When tracing up the pole with the telescope, the student should look for the horizontal bar on the side of the pole that is nearest to the intersection and trace it to the traffic light.

Traffic lights that are suspended from wires are more difficult to locate. These techniques may be helpful:

■ Spotting the light without the aid and raising the aid to examine it.

■ Tracing up the pole to the wire and then tracing across the wire to the suspended light. (The wire, however, is too thin for most students to see even through a telescope.)

■ Facing the diagonally opposite corner, the student imagines that two vertical lines are extended straight up from the adjacent corners and uses these vertical lines as boundaries for a horizontal scanning pattern. The student should look through the aid at one of the imaginary boundary lines, scan horizontally to the other line, raise the head and aid slightly, scan back to the starting line, and continue in this manner until the traffic light is located.

Many students find it inefficient to locate traffic lights with their telescope aids, preferring instead to listen or to watch traffic patterns. Telescopes are useful, however, in enabling the student to see the "walk" and "don't walk" lights. These lights are the most reliable source of information for determining the beginning of the walk cycle. Students crossing the street during the walk cycle who are not able to use the walk lights must rely on the completion of a traffic cycle, as indicated by the cessation of traffic movement or the beginning of pedestrian movement. The accuracy of pinpointing the beginning of the walk cycle is decreased if traffic is late in clearing the intersection or if pedestrians cross at times other than the walk cycle. If students cross the street just as the "walk" light comes on, they will have the full cycle in which to cross. Students who cannot see the "walk" light go on (it is usually white), can sometimes see the "don't walk" light go off and can use this clue instead. Students may locate pedestrian walk lights with the procedures used to locate vehicular traffic lights.

Store Signs

Store signs also may be located with the telescope and a combination of skills. Most store signs are positioned either perpendicular or parallel to storefronts. Those that are perpendicular to store fronts and are not obstructed by other signs are best viewed from 10 to 20 feet away on the same side of the street. The student should spot the door of the store without the aid, raise the aid, and scan up the store front until the sign is located. If necessary, the student should move closer to read the sign. A sign positioned parallel to the storefront is best seen from the curb in front of the store or from across the street. A student who has located a store sign from across the street with the telescope should select a landmark near the sign that he or she will be able to see without the telescope after he or she has crossed the street and is looking for the store. The landmark could be a large or brightly colored object in the store window, a mailbox, an awning, or so forth. When the student has crossed the street and is walking toward the store, he or she can look for the landmark without the aid. The instructor should present a sequence of store signs of increasing difficulty with respect to environmental and object variables. O&M lessons with stores as destinations can give the student the practice needed to locate all types of signs in the future.

House and Building Numbers

House and building numbers usually are more difficult to locate than are store signs because their placement is less uniform, the numerals are smaller, the type styles are more varied, they contrast less with the background, and they often must be viewed from a greater distance. House numbers may be placed on the front door, the door frame, the porch, the top rise of the front steps, or a pillar on the porch. Before beginning to look for a house number, the student should know that the odd-numbered houses are on one side of the street and even-numbered houses are on the other side, that house numbers increase as one moves away from the city center, and that not all numbers are used. To locate a particular house number, a student should first find any house number to determine if he or she is on the correct side of the street. Finding the number of the next house will help determine how many numbers were omitted from the sequence and will indicate whether the numbers are increasing or decreasing. The student can then estimate how many houses are between that house and the one to be located. The student should periodically check the numbers of the houses being passed to make sure that he or she has not gone too far. The student also may find a pattern to the numbers (e.g., 50 numbers per block) that can help in estimating the location more accurately. If the student cannot find a number on a house, he or she either can walk down the sidewalk closer to the house or can go to the next house and find that number.

Other Tasks

Most students have difficulty reading the route number and destination sign on a moving bus. Before a bus approaches, the student should focus the aid for distance by bringing the ocular and objective closer together. As a bus approaches, the student should spot the top of the front of the bus, where the sign is located, and raise the aid to read the sign. It will be necessary to continue focusing the aid as the bus approaches. A student will most likely need repeated practice to become proficient at this task. It helps if the student is positioned 10 feet or more past the bus stop area to perform this task.

Unfamiliar areas

Telescopic aids can assist students to familizarize themselves with a room, a store, a building, a shopping mall, a campus, and so on. After entering an unfamiliar room, for example, the student can step to the side of the doorway and scan with or without the aid to determine the general layout of the room, its size, and the location of the large pieces of furniture and other objects. If the shape of the room is unusual or difficult to determine, tracing the perimeter of the ceiling with the aid may make the shape more apparent. From this position beside the door, the student can scan the walls at head height to determine whether there are any protruding objects to be aware of before walking into the room. Then the student can move about the room and examine it in more detail. A student may locate the elevator, emergency exit, bathroom, drinking fountain, mail chute, ash tray, and office numbers in an unfamiliar office building with the telescope.

Congested areas

Many students find telescopes helpful in negotiating congested areas. In a supermarket, for example, a student can scan horizontally about eight feet above the floor to find an aisle opening and then scan vertically to find the sign that lists the types of products shelved in that aisle. If bothered by glare when looking up at the sign in the aisle, the student can try reading the other side of the sign. (In some stores, the lighting fixtures are shaded on one side.) In a department store the student can scan the walls near the main entrance or near the elevators to locate a store directory. In an elevator, the telescope can be used to monitor the floor on which the elevator is stopping.

In an airport or bus terminal it can be used to locate the desired ticket window, concourse, and gate by reading the directional signs posted on the walls or on the ceilings of hallways. In a fast-food restaurant, the student can locate the counter where one places an order, menus that are posted on the wall behind the counter, the condiment table, an available seat, and the exit. A student who feels pressured to keep moving in stores, restaurants, and other public areas may be more relaxed if he or she stands out of the path of pedestrian traffic and leans against a wall or pillar for support while aiming, focusing, and looking through the telescopic aid. A student can select a landmark to facilitate the return to a car parked in a large parking lot. This landmark could be the store nearest the car or a sign on a lamp post used to designate locations in the lot.

OTHER CONSIDERATIONS

Students who are using monocular aids will not be able to judge distances with binocular clues. Although everything seen through a telescope appears to be closer than it really is, a student can use monocular clues such as interposition, upward dislocation, linear and textural perspective, relative size, and movement parallax to help perceive distances. The student quickly adapts to the apparent closeness of objects and, in a short time, can make reasonably good judgments of distance through the telescope.

Psychosocial Problems

The instructor should also be aware of a hidden problem that can result in a variety of difficulties throughout the training program—the psychosocial aspects of using telescopes. Often students do not speak of their inhibitions about using telescopes, instead, they express their feelings through repeated failures or problems with all phases of the program. These students do not want to be identified as visually impaired or refuse to be seen in public with an optical device. They want a "normal" looking pair of glasses for distance vision and do not yet understand or believe the technological impossibility of providing such a lens system. Even those who do use a telescope in public may have unrealistic expectations of the improvement in vision they think it should provide. Their disappointment is expressed in their marginal success with the various tasks in the training program. Other people lack motivation to use aids because they simply have not accepted their visual loss. If the instructor is aware of these problems at the onset of the training program, he or she can modify the training sessions. That is, the instructor can help students build self-esteem, eliminate external pressures, and create an atmosphere in which students are willing to work with an aid.

Elderly People

For elderly or physically handicapped students, the instructor can use the procedures discussed in this chapter. However, certain modifications are needed to address the followng problems:

Quick fatigue. Fatigue is handled by using comfortable arm chairs, reading stands, and aids that are easy to manipulate. Short training sessions are essential. Sessions can be lengthened as a student's endurance increases.

Physical impairments. Arthritis, stroke, circulatory problems, Parkinson's disease and advanced diabetes are a few of the disorders that result in (1) tremors (2) the inability to maintain close working distances or to sustain clarity of vision with an aid that has a small depth of focus, (3) the inability to grasp an aid to focus and position it, (4) the inability to hold an arm in one position for any length of time, (5) discomfort when moving arms, the neck, and so on, (6) partial paralysis or weakness of the limbs, (7) the inability to concentrate for adequate periods and (8) poor hand-eye coordination. These problems are best managed by short sessions; modifying aids to minimize the use of fine motor movements, and selecting high-back chairs with arms, tables, and reading stands that provide good support, simple large-print targets, and other materials that allow the student to perform successfully.

Lack of specific goals. Elderly students may have given up all their previous activities. Most likely, they will have unrealistic goals, such as wanting to "see better." The only solution to this problem is for the instructor to have patience. The instructor should work with such students on simple activities, have frequent discussions with them, and try to find an interest that may be realistic considering their present level of visual skills and potential for enhancing these skills.

Frustration. These problems just mentioned exacerbate the feeling of many students that they "can't do anything." Hence, they may become easily frustrated. Again, the best technique is for the instructor to be patient, advise the student that these seeming failures are normal, and revert immediately to a task the student can do. In addition, if the instructor has kept records and has data on how long it took the student initially to perform a task or the acuity performance when the student started, the instructor will be able to substantiate the student's progess in the program and thereby counteract the feelings of frustration.

In general, a successful training program for elderly students will include the following components:

1. Short sessions.

2. High-back armchairs, tables of an adequate height, and reading stands to ensure good posture.

3. Simple large-print targets.

4. The provision of tactile reinforcement, such as a pipecleaner attached to the eye-glasses to establish the correct working distance.

5. An emphasis on gross motor tasks, including the use of a cork to hold a needle for threading, tape or cloth on telescope, and so forth.

6. The provision of auditory feedback (letting the student know he or she is correct) and a relaxed environment.

7. Modify aids to minimize the use of fine motor movements. For example, a tripod with a large telescope is preferable to a small hand-held or spectacle-mounted telescope.

Geriatric students can be rewarding to work with because of the tremendous changes that can occur in their personality and attitudes as a result of training. However, because training elderly students is an arduous undertaking (as it is with all students who have problems other than visual impairment), instructors reach their tolerance more quickly. Thus, it is preferable to alternate instructors. That is, as one professional reaches the point of intolerance, another professional (with a new set of tasks) takes over. For example, in the clinic the O&M instructor could take over from the educator. Even if the new person only goes through routine placebo-like evaluations, this break will work wonders both for the instructor and for the student. The turnover must be done in a positive manner if the rapport between the instructor and the student is to be maintained.

Deafness

Deafness is another impairment that complicates a training program. To work with a deaf student, the instructor must establish a good communication system. To facilitate communication, the instructor must break down the instructions for activities into their simplest form. Working with others who have had experience with the person also helps. For example, even if the instructor knows sign language, it is easier to utilize an interpreter with whom the student has signed before. To ensure that the student understands the instructions or that the interpreter is giving the correct instructions, the instructor should have the student demonstrate the technique discussed. If the student lip reads, the instructor should be in a favorable position for best contrast and should not exaggerate his or her speech.

Mental Retardation

Students who are mentally retarded will have difficulty understanding and remembering instructions. Repetition is the key to success. Tasks should be broken down into the most basic, simplest activities that are possible. The instructor should set or reach goals only in conjunction with other professionals involved in other types of training programs. The two instructional programs—for mental retardation and for visual impairment—may not be compatible, and so, will confuse the student. Using short sessions, simple tasks, and a behavior modification approach will increase the chances for success.

Reference

Mehr, E., & Freid, A. *Low vision care*. Chicago: Professional Press, 1974.

Additional Reading

Davidson, T. A survey of developments in a new field: O&M for the low vision person—Part II. *Low Vision Abstracts,* 1973,(4), 1–100.

Margach, C. D. Optical characteristics of focusable ophthalmic telescopes. *Optical Journal and Review of Optometry,* 1974, **111**(8), 12–16.

Mehr, E., & Freid, A. *Proceedings of the workshop on low vision mobility.* Washington, D. C.: Department of Medicine and Surgery, Veterans Administration, August 1976.

Yohey, R. An evaluation of telescopes as low vision aids. *Optical Journal and Review of Optometry,* 1972, **110**(22), 33–40

CHAPTER 13

Near Training Techniques

GALE WATSON, M.ED.
R. VICTORIA BERG, M.A.

This chapter organizes instructional activities to develop a student's proficiency in using vision with near aids. The reader will note that many of the techniques and suggestions for developing strategies in near training are similar to those described for distance training in Chapter 12. Therefore, Chapters 12 and 13 are meant to complement and reinforce each other.

Training the visually impaired student to use prescribed aids for near tasks (those tasks performed at arm's length or closer) involves a unique set of factors. The nature of the visual impairment, the personality and motivation of the student, the student's best mode of learning, the advantages and limitations of the aids, the environment in which the aids will be used, the creativity and expertise of the interdisciplinary team, and the team members' relationships with the student are some of the factors taken into consideration when designing an instructional program.

Instruction enables students to make the transition from the clinical setting to the environment where vision must be used for specific purposes. As with many desirable behavioral changes, understanding and ability are not always equal to the task. Therefore, the role of the instructor is to analyze tasks and provide explanations, support, and encouragement until the students can function independently. A major goal of instruction is to enable students (along with significant others) to review and set specific, realistic objectives for the use of vision and aids. The clinicians and counselors will have helped them decide what tasks they want to perform and which optical aids will ameliorate their visual impairment for those tasks. The instructional program allows students to explore the efficacy of the use of aids and vision for the task.

The instructional program helps students learn the level and usefulness of their remaining vision. Often students have been counseled on what they *cannot* accomplish with vision. The functional implications of the particular visual impairment and its unique nature will be discussed and explained at appropriate times during the program. Encouraging students to verbalize what, where, and how they see and presenting tasks that are developmental

317

will provide the instructor with "teachable moments" in which to understand and discuss the students' level and use of residual vision.

Solving specific problems encountered when using vision and low vision aids is another major goal of instruction. Difficulties in achieving and maintaining fixation and focus, glare, lights that are too dim, poor-quality print or other inappropriate materials, fatigue and stress, and perceptual or motor problems lend themselves to creative problem solving. Certain difficulties encountered routinely by many students over the years during low vision examinations and training have resulted in the development of strategies for teaching visual skills for specific tasks. Some of these strategies are presented in this chapter; readers are invited to use them as a springboard for their own ideas.

Any near task can be enhanced by aids. Reading, writing, arts and crafts, shop and homemaking activities, games, collecting stamps and coins, reading sheet music while playing an instrument, gardening, personal management, and other academic and vocational activities are some of the visual tasks that may be performed with aids. Because aids are task specific, a student who wishes to be as visually active as possible may use many aids.

A suggested sequence for planning a training program follows. It is designed so that novice instructors may use its external structure to begin training. As they become more experienced, instructors will want to use a more fluid approach, such as teaching visual skills without an aid only after a student has difficulty with an aid. The suggested sequence is not designed to lock instructors or students into a rigid approach, but to be a jumping-off point for the uninitiated. Creative instructors will soon amass their own repertoire of special techniques. They may find that experimenting with an aid and trying to perform with it a task that students wish to accomplish, often leads to understanding the task better, leads to some new techniques for teaching it, and enables them to compare experiences with the students.

SUGGESTED SEQUENCE FOR TRAINING

I. Preparation for Training
    A. Assembling information about a student
    B. Making a tentative outline for training
    C. Preparing the environment
    D. Gathering materials
II. The Initial Encounter: Discussion
    A. Establishment of objectives for the use of aids and priorities among them
    B. Current level of performance of tasks
    C. Present use of aids
    D. Student's understanding of vision and its functional implications
    E. The clinical examination
    F. Preferred illumination

III. Presentation of Low Vision Aids
    A. The student examines the aids tactually and visually
    B. The instructor describes the aids, their uses, advantages, limitations, and how to take care of them
IV. Efficient Use of Visual Skills without Aids
    A. Fixation
    B. Eccentric viewing (if necessary)
    C. Localization
    D. Scanning
    E. Tracking
V. Efficient Use of Visual Skills with Aids
    A. Focal distance, field of view of the aid
    B. Localization
    C. Scanning
    D. Fixation, eccentric viewing
    E. Tracking
VI. Performing Specific Tasks with an Aid
    A. Establish a performance baseline with and without the aid
    B. Analysis of tasks
    C. Problem solving
      1. Determine the problem
      2. Explore the options for treatment
VII. Termination of Training
    A. The student reaches the desired goal
    B. The student reaches a level where the goal can be pursued through practice without the instructor
    C. The student reaches a plateau; further instruction is not helpful
VIII. Follow-up
    A. The student is telephoned or visited
    B. The student returns to the instruction site where skills are demonstrated with aids
      1. Skills are satisfactory
      2. Skills are not satisfactory
IX. Returning to Training
    A. A problem is identified with which instructor can help
    B. The student has a change in vision or a change in goals or new aids.
    Repeat sequence, if necessary.

PREPARATIONS FOR TRAINING

Assembling Information

The utilization of residual vision encompasses all facets of a student's life: personality, intelligence, type of vision loss, education, vocation, peers, family, and the community. Each component contributes to the achievement of or the failure to achieve visual goals. The probability of amassing copious amounts of information in each of these areas is slim. However, the wise instructor will be on the lookout for information about the student in each of these areas. The first places to look for such information are the records or reports of other professionals. The types of information that may be found are as follows:

Vision loss. The type and severity of the vision loss and the actual disease, disorder, or anomaly will suggest certain functional information. For example, macular degeneration usually is accompanied by central scotomas, while retinitis pigmentosa frequently causes restricted fields. The visual acuities obtained will suggest what size target may be seen at what distance.

Refractive error. Students who are hyperopic or myopic may need to wear eyeglasses to correct their condition. Students who are myopic often can view near tasks at a close distance with greater ease if they take off their glasses. This "built-in" magnification will not harm the eyes; if it is strong enough, it will be more convenient than using an optical aid with the spectacle correction. If the built-in magnifiction is not enough, the optometrist or ophthalmologist probably will prescribe additional magnification. Myopic students will need to wear prescription glasses for distance tasks. The presence of hyperopia and myopia will change the focal distance of an optical aid unless the prescription for the refractive error is incorporated into the aid.

Cylindrical correction. Students who require cylindrical correction may need to wear this correction in a pair of eyeglasses. If the correction is extensive, it may need to be incorporated into the optical aids for a clear image.

Onset of the visual impairment. If the onset is recent, students may have psychosocial problems that outweigh the optical problems. Generally, the more long-standing the vision loss, the more ready the student is for visual education and rehabilitation. Students with a severe congenital visual loss may experience some delay in conceptual and perceptual development.

Level of general health. The training program may need to be modified to avoid fatigue or other specific problems, depending on whether a student has other physical impairments.

Medications. Blurred vision, fluctuating vision, and photophobia are side effects of medications that may affect the student's ability to use vision. The *Physician's Desk Reference* includes useful information on the visual side effects of medications.

Education. Generally, the more education and experience a student has, the more specific the student will be in establishing goals and in communicating.

Employment. The desire to obtain or remain in a job can lead to specific goals and often is a source of motivation.

Leisure activities. Hobbies and social and recreational activities are indicators of a high quality of life. These activities also can lead to specific goals, are a source of motivation, and provide opportunities to use residual vision in a more relaxed atmosphere.

Previous use of low vision aids. If a student is using low vision aids successfully, then the student has demonstrated a desire and ability to maximize vision. If previous attempts to use low vision aids were unsuccessful, it is imperative to prescribe aids and design a program that increases the chances for success by taking this into consideration.

Present level of skills. If the student is performing a desired task even to a minimal extent, it shows a strong desire to remain visually active. It also may be an indication of refined visual skills and the easy acceptance of low vision aids.

Environmental considerations. A student's use of vision may be inhibited by some aspect of the environment, such as insufficient illumination, which the student is unable to control.

Psychosocial considerations. Consultation with a counselor, social worker, or psychologist may reveal insights into the student's motivation for using vision. Psychosocial problems may inhibit the effective use of vision in some students but they may spur other students to achieve.

Clinical data. The results of the clinical evaluation with an optical aid will give the instructor an idea of the student's ability to use residual vision. For example, a 4X magnifying lens that gives only a 2X increase in acuity may indicate the need for training in eccentric viewing, a change in illumination, or a lack of motivation to achieve. Whatever the difficulty, a well-designed training program can help discover and solve it. The clinical report indicates the position of the field loss or scotoma and thus allows the instructor to predict potential problem areas. It also describes the type, size, magnification, focal distance, and objectives of the optical aids that have been prescribed for or lent to the student and indicates whether a regular spectacle correction improves the student's vision and when and under what circumstances it should be worn. Answers to the following questions may be found in the clinical report as well: Does the low vision aid prescribed by the clinician meet the student's expectations? Why did the clinician prescribe the needed amount of magnification in the chosen design (i.e., a telemicroscope versus a microscope)? Is it necessary to patch the eye not being used? Which target and of what size did the student see with the aid? What type of material (letter, number, word, paragraph, symbol) did the student recognize? What were the clinician's recommendations for teaching the use of the aid?

Preparing the Environment and Gathering Materials

Training takes place in various environments. Some students receive training in the clinical setting in which the optical aid was prescribed; others work at home or in a school, vocational, or other setting. Wherever training takes place, the instructor should be able to control the illumination, provide postural comfort, and have available a variety of optical and nonoptical aids and other materials that are needed to complete tasks and maintain uninterrupted sessions.

Illumination control may be provided by draperies or shades on windows; rheostats on overhead lights; a variety of flex-arm or goose-neck lamps with incandescent, fluorescent, and high-intensity bulbs; colored filters; tinted lenses; visors; temple and forehead shields for spectacles; and pinhole patches. A light meter should be used to measure the light preferred by the student. This preferred lighting should be noted and duplicated at subsequent training sessions.

THE INITIAL ENCOUNTER

In the first session, the instructor introduces himself or herself and, in general, tries to make the student feel comfortable. Then the instructor asks the student and family about the student's goals for near training. Although these questions may seem redundant, they will help the student to be more specific and to establish priorities among multiple goals. Thus, even though the student may have been prescribed aids for reading and writing, he or she will need help in deciding the specific tasks to be performed and in determining which tasks are most important. *For example, reading grocery-item prices is a different task from reading a newspaper, and signing one's name on a check is different from writing a letter.*

The instructor also asks about which tasks the student is currently performing and at what level, whether the tasks were performed in the past, and, if so, how long ago they were performed. The purpose of these questions is to establish a point of entry into training. The appropriate entry point allows the student to achieve success in a task, yet is difficult enough to present some challenge. If the entry point is too easy, the instructor will move forward quickly; if it is too difficult, the instructor will drop back to an easier level.

The clinician's examination is the next topic of discussion. When appropriate, the instructor and student should discuss the student's acuity, fields, pathology, and prescriptions. (The instructor may have to translate the technical terms into more commonly understood language for the student. In addition, the instructor may compare the functional implications of acuities and fields with what the student feels about his or her condition. However, *the instructor must make sure that his or her descriptions are consistent with those of the clinician.*)

The involvement of family members and peers in explanations, discussions, and training can be helpful. These persons provide an excellent support system and can assist the student to practice at home and in school. They often hear and remember what the student does not. If there is tension between the student and significant others, however, the student should work alone.

The next topic of discussion is illumination. The instructor should find out if the student prefers bright or dim light and under what circumstances. The instructor should also determine whether the student's lighting needs fluctuate from day to day or from morning to afternoon and if the student is bothered by glare and in what places. If training does not occur in the environment in which the aid will be used, the instructor should question the student about the lighting in the actual environment.

GENERAL GUIDELINES FOR TRAINING

In developing an instructional program, the following general guidelines should be observed. First, the training environment should be as relaxed as possible. The instructor should look for signs of stress, fatigue, or withdrawal in the student. Clenched fists, shallow breathing, confusion, stammering, nervous laughter, sighing, tight shoulder or neck muscles, slumping, and mumbling are indications that the student is tense and not ready to begin training. Gently calling attention to these signs of stress may help alleviate them, but, in some circumstances, pointing them out may make the student more tense. The instructor may decide to shorten the session, work on easier tasks, delay the session until another time, or consult with other professionals if the student's level of stress does not abate.

Second, the initial tasks should be easy enough for success and challenging enough to hold the student's interest. Visual tasks with high contrast and little or no figure-ground confusion are the best types of task in the beginning. Thus, modification of activities to meet the needs of the student is always necessary.

Third, the training sequence always should be flexible enough to meet the demands of the individual student. For example, physical disabilities that may inhibit the performance of a task should be identified, and the task should be altered so success can be achieved. For example, a student with cerebral palsy who has hand tremors may have great difficulty maneuvering a stand magnifier for reading. Use of a microscopic spectacle with a reading stand will minimize the involvement of the hands in this task.

Fourth, shorter sessions interspersed with periods of discussion are helpful. As the student becomes more proficient, he or she will be able to view comfortably for longer periods and with less fatigue.

Fifth, frequent communication with other members of the low vision team will enable all team members to lend their expertise fully at key times. A knotty problem with a student's use of vision or aids is best solved when the team works together.

PRESENTATION OF LOW VISION AIDS

Low vision aids fall into two main categories—optical and nonoptical. Optical aids, such as hand-held and stand magnifiers, have lenses to enable a target to be seen more clearly. Nonoptical aids, such as large-print books, a reading stand, or a special lamp, are devices that help students to achieve a task but that do not have lenses. Often nonoptical and optical aids are used together for a task because certain aids complement each other. For example, a student may use a marker under a line of print (nonoptical aid) while reading with a microscope (optical aid) to overcome problems with scanning imposed by a small field of view.

There are three types of optical aids for near tasks: stand and hand-held magnifiers, microscopes, and telemicroscopes. Each type of optical aid has characteristics that are useful for students with particular conditions and with certain tasks. In the following sections, the three types of optical aid are described, including their advantages and disadvantages.

Hand-held and Stand Magnifiers

Hand-held magnifiers. Hand-held magnifiers are convex (plus) lenses that increase the size of a retinal image and bring the image into focus. A hand-held magnifier provides maximum magnification when positioned at its focal distance with respect to the material to be recognized. The focal distance (the distance between the magnifier and the page) in centimeters is determined by dividing the dioptric power of the aid into 100. Thus, a +4.00 diopter magnifier should be held at 25 centimeters, or about 10 inches from the page. As long as the magnifier is held that distance from the page, magnification will remain the same whether the aid is 3 or 50 centimeters from the eye. However, the nearer the magnifier is to the eye, the larger the field of view seen through the aid and the smaller the apparent distortion. The times power of a magnifier is designated by a number followed by an "X" indicating its strength and magnification. It is found by dividing the diopters of the lens by 4. For example, a 32 diopter lens will magnify an object eight times and is written "8X." The stronger the diopters of a magnifier, the more magnification it provides. A stronger magnifier decreases the focal distance, the depth of focus, and the field of view.

Hand-held magnifiers are readily available and are relatively inexpensive. Because they are widely used, they may be more acceptable cosmetically than the same amount of magnification in spectacle form. In addition, they can be held away from the eye (a smaller field of view is the only penalty) and thus the working distance may be easier for students to deal with in the beginning. If a student begins to hold the magnifier closer to the spectacle plane as practice progresses, he or she may be indicating a readiness for microscopes. Most hand-held magnifiers are portable; therefore, they are convenient for shoppers, students, and technicians who need an aid for spotting rather than for the continuous reading of textual matter.

Often students appreciate that when they look up from reading, their surroundings are in a normal perspective and are not blurred as they would be when viewed through a microscope. Furthermore, reading with a hand-held magnifier may require less accommodation than it would with a stand magnifier or microscope and both eyes may be used together, if desired. Magnifiers are also helpful for specific tasks that require students to move their head close to the object to be seen, such as reading the dials on a stove.

Hand-held magnifiers present some problems, however. The farther away a magnifier is held, the smaller its field of view. The field of a + 10-diopter lens is approximately 4 times smaller at 10 inches from the eye than at one inch from the eye. Moreover, unless a reading stand is used, the student must hold the magnifier and the material with both hands. Some students find it difficult to hold the magnifier parallel to the reading material and to maintain the focal distance. Effective use of the hand-held magnifier requires developing good eye–hand coordination.

Stand magnifiers. Stand magnifiers are convex lenses mounted in a stand that fixes the distance of the lenses from the page. The lower rim of the stand rests on the page and is moved across the page, maintaining contact with the page or material to be recognized. The lens is mounted in the stand at a slightly shorter distance than the actual focal distance, which decreases aberrations in the periphery of the lens and means that the actual power of the stand magnifier is less than that of its lens. Because of this difference in distance, the image seen through the stand magnifier is not in focus unless the student can accommodate for the divergent light rays (about 2.5 diopters) or wears a pair of reading glasses. Use of a focusable stand magnifier can alleviate this problem. By focusing the lens closer or farther away from the page, the student can induce a correction for myopia and hyperopia.

An advantage of the stand magnifier is that it can set its own focal distance when it touches a page on all sides. It can be the aid of choice for students with hand or arm tremors or those who cannot develop necessary eye–hand coordination for the hand-held magnifier. The disadvantages of the stand magnifier include the difficulty in illuminating the material being read, the need to utilize both hands for most tasks, and the problem encountered by the necessity to accommodate for clear vision unless illuminated and focusable models are used.

Microscopes

Microsopes are plus (convex) lenses mounted in a spectacle frame. Because they are mounted close to the eye, the material to be recognized must be held at a closer distance to the face to be in focus than with other near aids. As with magnifiers, the focal distance of a microscope may be determined by dividing the dioptric power of the lens into 100. For instance, the focal distance of a 6X microscope (which has a + 24-diopter lens (1X = 4 diopters) is approximately 4 centimeters.

Microscopes are available in a wide variety of strengths and lens designs, and some are illuminated. With most microscopes, students may use each eye separately (if there is usable vision in each eye) but not both eyes together. Half-eye glasses with spectacle microscopes, which allow students to look over the top of the glasses with their regular vision, may incorporate enough prism in the lower powers (+ 12 diopters or less) to allow students to use both eyes together if the students are binocular without the aid.

The advantages of a microscope for near tasks are that it does not require students to use their hands to hold the aid and that it widens the field of view. The microscope generally allows the fastest, easiest reading of all the optical aids. A microscope's disadvantages are its close focal distance and the student's inability to view the surroundings with normal vision while wearing them. In higher powers, which require closer focal distances, a microscope may require special illumination techniques.

Telemicroscopes

Telemicroscopes, also known as reading telescopes or surgical telescopes, are distance telescopes that have been modified for use at closer working distances by the placement of a reading cap on the objective. They allow students to perform tasks at the distance they are usually performed and to have the freedom of a head-borne aid. Changing to a cap of a different power creates a different working distance, which gives the student great versatility for a variety of objectives. For example, students can use the telescope for distance tasks, such as watching television and viewing the chalkboard, and then place a cap on the objective so they may read, write, or play music.

There are certain drawbacks, however. Telemicroscopes usually are more difficult to use because of their smaller field of view, critical depth of focus, and the apparent displacement of the material to be viewed. Because of angular magnification, the student's depth perception changes; in addition, vertical displacement occurs because of the length of the telescope's tube (the student must lower the head more than seems necessary to find the target). In higher powers, this sytem also exaggerates head movements and causes the target to appear to "bounce" with each movement.

The total magnification of telemicroscopes is the power of the telescope times the power of the reading cap. A + 4-diopter cap on any telescope results in a total power of a telemicroscope equal to the power of the telescope (a 6X telescope with + 4-diopter cap equals a 6X telemicroscope). Such a system will have a focal distance of 25 centimeters, since the focal distance of a telemicroscope is figured and measured from the reading cap alone.

If the cap is increased in power to 8 diopters, or 2X, the focal distance is decreased to 12.5 centimeters (100 divided by 8 diopters = 12.5 cm.), and the power of the telemicroscope is increased to 12X (6X $\times$ 2X = 12X).

Taking Care of Aids

Optical aids should be cleaned first by blowing grit and dust from their surfaces and then by wiping them with a soft, clean cloth or optical-quality tissue. If necessary, magnifiers and some spectacles may be washed with a pure film-free soap and dried with a soft lint-free cloth. Telemicroscopes should *never* be submersed because droplets may leak into the lens system and cause blurring and distortion. Instead, a small amount of soap or cleaner should be applied to a cloth and then wiped onto the lens. Lenses should be maintained free of residue and fingerprints so that vision is optimal. Magnifiers and spectacles should be placed in a sturdy case when not in use so they do not become scratched or broken. Spectacles should never be placed with the lenses on a surface because the lenses will be scratched. Spectacle frames should be checked periodically for loose fit, misalignment, and loose screws.

NONOPTICAL AIDS

Many nonoptical aids enable students to function more independently and increase their quality of life. Three main categories of nonoptical aids are described in this section, and some agencies and companies from which nonoptical aids may be ordered are listed.

Illumination-control Aids

Each student needs a particular amount of illumination, and many aids have been designed to control illumination. The student's preference and objective assessments of the student's visual performance determine the optimal lighting conditions for a student. The environment in which a task is to be performed must be assessed in terms of the lighting it provides. Natural or artificial light, incandescent or fluorescent lighting, reflectance of surrounding surfaces, placement of the student in relation to the lighting source or reflecting surface, glare, and contrast are subjects of scrutiny in assessing illumination. Some students will require greater amounts of lighting than the environment allows. For them, additional lighting in the form of lamps or illuminated optical aids will be helpful. Lamps usually should be shaded, have flexible or goose-neck arms, and be capable of a range of illumination (with a dimmer or rheostat). To determine whether incandescent or fluorescent bulbs should be used, the instructor and student should test both types of bulb with the actual task to ascertain which helps most. (Some students prefer the brightness of a fluorescent bulb while others are dazzled into discomfort.) Bulbs should be replaced and cleaned frequently because they lose intensity toward the end of their use, and lighting efficiency is reduced as much as 50 percent if dust is permitted to accumulate on them.

The lighting source should be positioned so there is no shadow or glare on the materials. Usually, lamps are placed near the same temple as the eye being used, equidistant from the page and from the head and slightly higher than both. The light should fall more on the materials than on the face without causing glare if the materials are reflective. For writing, a lamp should be to the front and opposite the hand being used, to avoid shadows.

The intensity of lighting for a particular task often will be specified by the clinical low vision team. A light meter may be used to duplicate recommendations. For most students, an increase in the intensity of light will increase acuity only up to a point; too much intensity or improper placement of light will cause glare.

For reading, the page should be as evenly illuminated as possible and there should be adequate illumination throughout the room. If the illumination in the room is less than one-third of the illumination of the task, the student may experience fatigue from the continuous need to adapt (Kaufman & Christensen, 1972).

Some students prefer and perform better in dim illumination. They may be photophobic (light sensitive) or they may simply appreciate the increase in pupil size and therefore the field of view caused by dim illumination. These students are afforded greater comfort by absorptive lenses, such as NoIR or Olo, or by slip-in sunlenses. Some students appreciate visors or side shields on their spectacles or a combination of these two illumination-control devices. Dimmer switches on lamps and overhead lights, and draperies or blinds on windows may be helpful. Often experimentation is necessary until optimal comfort and relief are obtained.

Glare should be prevented for all students because it causes discomfort and decreases visual ability. Highly reflective surfaces, such as glossy paper, shiny desk tops or work surfaces, and dirty chalkboards, must be avoided whenever possible. Colored acetate filters, typoscopes (flat black cards with a window cut-out placed over a line of print), and absorptive lenses may reduce glare on reading or other near tasks. Shading windows or changing the position from which a target is to be viewed may relieve glare on other tasks.

Contrast

Providing appropriate contrast for tasks can make their execution easier. The typoscope also can provide contrast in the reading task. Yellow acetate filters turn blue or purple ink to black on mimeograph and ditto sheets and clear the washed-out effect of poor-quality newspaper print. Yellow lenses may be clipped onto spectacles for a similar effect. For household tasks, a dark background for viewing light-colored materials and a light background for seeing dark materials enable students to perform more accurately. For example, pouring milk into a glass on a dark countertop is easier than pouring it into a glass on a white countertop. Bold-line paper and felt-tip pens make writing less difficult.

Print

The print chosen for a student depends on a number of factors—including the student's motivation and interest, visual acuity and fields of view, and reading experience and ability; the type and power of the low vision aids; lighting; and accessibility of print. In some cases, students may alternate among several different print sizes and styles and may supplement print reading with recorded materials, readers, and braille, depending on the situation. For example, a college student may write and read class notes in braille; depend on recordings for literature; read large-print mathematics books; read regular print on bills, mail, personal correspondence, and other materials; and utilize a reader for library research. The student also may find a variety of optical aids helpful for regular-print reading, large-print reading, writing, and shopping because printed materials of different sizes require different powers of magnification.

The legibility of print may be affected not only by the size of the print but by the boldness of the line; the uniformity of inking; the contrast among letters in words and among words themselves; the width of margins; the size of gutters; the spacing between letters, words, and lines; and the styles of type, which vary from plain to embellished.

Whether a student should use regular-print or large-print materials if both are recognizable should be given careful attention. Both types of materials have advantages and disadvantages, and there are situations in which each can be helpful. The advantages of large print are that (1) it is more comfortable and easier to read because of the wider spacing (not necessarily the larger print), (2) it is usually produced on nonglare paper, (3) it offers a less-restricted field of view compared to a magnifying lens and regular print, and (4) it has a greater working distance. Regular-size print has these advantages: (1) a wider range of materials is available in regular print, particularly high school and college reference works, vocational materials, and bills, mail, and correspondence, (2) the student is able to read what peers are reading, (3) it avoids the problem of using large print as a crutch, which makes switching to regular print difficult, (4) regular-print materials cost less, (5) books printed in regular print are smaller and hence portable, and (6) reading regular print does not require a total sweep of the head and so may be faster. The decisions on when to read large print and when to read regular print should be made by the student, the student's teachers, the parents, and the low vision team. Comparisons of performance in both print types should include (1) the rate of oral and silent reading, (2) comfort while reading, (3) the number of skipped and miscalled words, (4) comprehension, and (5) the duration of reading before fatigue.

Other nonoptical aids also may be used. For example, reading stands often enable the student to read more comfortably with better posture for longer periods. Stencils may be utilized for writing letters and checks and for addressing envelopes. Large-print educational aids, including globes, atlases, maps, and models, enhance learning. Large-dial watches, clocks, and timers and large-print dials allow more independence and aid punctuality and the use of appliances. Measuring aids, such as tape measures, rulers, yard or meter sticks, and insulin gauges are available with enlarged numbers. Large-print typewriters and labelers permit writing and labeling with ease.

Sources of Equipment
American Printing House for the Blind
P.O. Box 6085
Louisville, Kentucky 40206

Reading and music stands, large-print checks, bold-line and raised-line paper, bold-line graph paper, and other large-print and tactile aids.

American Foundation for the Blind
15 West 16th Street
New York, New York 10011

Large-print telephone dials, large-print cards, large-eye needles, writing guides, check stencils, needle threaders, sewing machine threaders, notched-hem gauges, and other tactile and visual aids and appliances.

Designs for Vision, Inc.
120 East 23rd Street
New York, New York 10010

Typoscopes and subnormal vision reading cards.

Bernell Corporation
422 East Monroe Street
South Bend, Indiana 46601

Eye patches and lense patches.

New York Association for the Blind (the Lighthouse)
111 East 59th Street
New York, New York 10022

Sloan reading cards, yellow filter lenses, absorptive lenses, and visorettes.

Independent Living Aids, Inc.
11 Commercial Court
Plainview, New York 11803

Sewing, writing, large-print, and other nonoptical and tactile aids.

Recreational Innovations
P.O. Box 159
South Lyon, Michigan 48178

NoIR absorptive lenses.

Olo Products, Ltd.
P.O. Box 613
Manhasset, New York 11030

Olo absorptive lenses.

Vision Corporation of America
70 State Street
Westbury, New York 11590

   Velcro Glas-Straps for spectacles.

The New York Times
229 West 43rd Street
New York, New York 10036

   The New York Times Large-Type Weekly.

Reader's Digest
Pleasantville, New York 10570

   Reader's Digest Large-Type Edition.

Carroll Center for the Blind
770 Centre Street
Newton, Massachusetts 02158

   Aids and Appliances Review.

Mrs. Betty Jo Keitzer
1129 Peninsula Drive
Lake Wales, Florida 33853

   Keitzer checkwriting guide.

Theatrical supply stores

   Colored filter sheets (ask for "theatrical gels").

Athletic supply stores

   Stopwatches.

Camera shops

   Light meters.

Department stores and artist supply stores

Flex-arm incandescent architect's lamps.

Feinbloom Vision Rehabilitation Center
The Eye Institute
1201 West Spencer Street
Philadelphia, Pennsylvania 19141

Plans for building an adjustable reading stand.

Richard Jose
1901 Dayton Road
CMCC #156
Chico, California 95926

Customized reading stands.

CLOSED-CIRCUIT TELEVISION SYSTEM

Closed-circuit television (CCTV) provides electronic magnification. It usually consists of a camera, a monitor (screen), and a movable platform on which the material to be viewed is placed. A variety of sizes with different options are available from several companies. (Most CCTVs are purchased directly from the company that manufactures them; thus, the student purchases a service as well as a product, because the system will need maintenance and the replacement of parts from time to time. Instructors who teach CCTV techniques should be familiar with the various models and the sales representatives in the geographic areas because they often are called on to make recommendations.)

Most CCTV monitors operate like regular televisions. The contrast and brightness of the image can be controlled. Many have reverse polarity options that show material in negative (i.e., black print on a white background appears as white print on a black background). Some models have electronic line markers that isolate the line the student wishes to read and thus have the same effect as typoscopes.

The camera is mounted above the movable platform; it controls the amount of magnification produced. A focus mechanism is also a part of the camera, as is an aperture control for the correct amount of lighting that is provided by a high-intensity bulb usually mounted behind the camera.

The movable tray is an option that permits the easy scanning of material. It can be shifted horizontally and vertically to allow all areas of the material placed on it to be viewed on the monitor. Margin stops, similar to those on typewriters, are on each side of the tray for reading long periods in the same book. A friction brake prevents the shifting of the tray too rapidly in the beginning and so avoids skipping parts of the area to be viewed.

The amount of magnification provided by the CCTV can be as much as 65X in the larger models. Students may establish their own distance magnification by moving closer to the screen. The total amount of magnification being used is calculated by the following formula:

$$\frac{\text{TV print size in centimeters}}{\text{Actual print size in centimeters}} = X$$

$$\frac{25 \text{ centimeters}}{\text{Working distance in centimeters}} = Y$$

Total magnification $= X \cdot Y$

The print is measured from the height of the highest ascender (e.g., "H") to the depth of the lowest descender (e.g., lower case "g").

The advantages of the CCTV are its greater amount of magnification, its reverse polarity that can provide greater contrast, and its wider field of view. In addition, the student can use head and body movements for eccentric viewing, it provides its own illumination, and some models can be used for static distance viewing if appropriately mounted, for typing, and for other tasks.

One disadvantage of the CCTV is its lack of portability. A small, approximately 40-pound, model is available but that model sacrifices magnification, field of view, and options for portability. Another disadvantage is that it is more expensive than most other near low vision aids, although some of the sophisticated telemicroscopes can be just as costly.

If copious amounts of reading and writing are to be done, the CCTV allows for the fastest speed and greatest ease. For students who are not responding to optical aids because of a need for greater contrast, more magnification, or problems with eccentric viewing, the CCTV may be the choice for beginning skills. Students may wish to transfer to some other low vision aid when their level of skills increases.

EFFICIENT USE OF VISUAL SKILLS WITHOUT AIDS

The efficiency with which a student is using vision can be a predictor of future success with aids. That is, students who utilize more vision without an aid find it easier to incorporate aids into the performance of visual tasks. However, some students compensate so well with their visual skills that they may, at first, be slowed down by the optical aid or consider it to be too much "trouble." Some students hardly use their vision; because they have encountered environmental or psychosocial difficulties or never have learned certain visual skills, they rely on other modalities or on sighted helpers. If the instructor is familiar with the student's visual skills without optical aids, he or she will be able to understand and resolve difficulties that might occur with the aids, plan a more precise program for the use of low vision aids, enable the student to increase awareness of how he or she is using vision, and increase the student's efficiency without aids. Some excellent drills in the use of visual skills for reading may be found in two manuals on low vision training, by Bäckman and Inde (1979) and by Quillman (no date). Also see the section on Performing Specific Tasks in this chapter.

The visual skills needed for near tasks are as follows:

1. Fixation, or "fixing" the target in the area of clearest vision so it can be recognized with the greatest detail.

2. Localization, or finding the target by shifting the area of clearest vision to the area where the target appears.

3. Scanning, or shifting the area of clearest vision back and forth in an established pattern to find a target or identify rows of targets.

4. Tracking, or following a moving target.

Fixation

Fixation is difficult for students who do not have foveal vision and must move a scotoma or blind spot to one side to use the area of clearest vision. The difficulty arises when the student attempts to "see" with the foveal area but notices the targets on either side of the scotoma, missing the one in the middle. A student often has this problem if he or she skips and miscalls letters and small words when attempting to read. To teach the student what portion of the field of view to use, the portion *not* to be used must be taught first. Some students who experience problems with this field of view are often unaware of the central scotoma and must be made aware of it by using the following demonstration of eccentric viewing:

- The eye not being used should be patched.
- The instructor's face should be appropriately illuminated.
- The instructor tells the student to look without moving the eye, at the instructor's face directly in front and approximately 1½ feet away.
- The instructor says: "When you look at my face, some portion of it will appear unclear or missing. Can you tell me which area?"
- The student's response will be subjective. The instructor should note where his or her reflection fell in the student's eye. If the reflection fell in the center of the student's pupil, the student will probably report that some part of the instructor's face was unclear or missing. If the reflection fell in some quadrant of the pupil, the student may report no unclear or missing areas because he or she already was viewing eccentrically; in such a case, the instructor should ask the student to repeat the task and this time to center the face.
- After the student notices what part of the face is missing, the instructor asks the student to move the eye in different directions to clear the face (i.e., look to the right ear, to the left ear, to the top of the head, and to the chin of the instructor).
- The instructor directs the student to shift only the eye (not the head or body) to see the instructor's face most clearly. (This type of shifting will be

necessary to look through the optical center of the lens of a low vision aid.)

■ Students whose widest field of view is vertical rather than horizontal (e.g., those with hemianopsias, scattered scotomas, or central scotomas in combination with restricted fields) always find eccentric viewing with a head movement easier than with an eye movement. Tilting the head and cyclo-rotating the eye can widen the horizontal field of view and make the target easier to localize and scan. It may be helpful for these students to tilt the target in the appropriate direction and keep their head in an upright position or use some type of low vision aid that permits the head to stay erect.

■ The skills learned in the previous steps may be transferred to viewing a symbol printed in a recognizable size on an index card. The student should repeat the procedure used with the face and compare the area of vision used to view the symbol with the area used to view the face. Was the same area used to view both targets? If not, the student should repeat these tasks to find out why.

■ Students with central scotomas and restricted fields, scattered scotomas, or only a small off-foveal area of vision may not be able to hold the area of clearest vision long enough to perform these tasks. For the eye being tested, the instructor provides a patch with a small aperture (2 to 5 cm) to be placed over the eye and tells the student to move it into the position where the symbol on the card can best be seen through the aperture. Because the aperture is placed close to the area of clearest vision, any wandering eye movements will cause all vision to blur or blank out. This all-or-nothing technique provides the student with reinforcement for holding the eye in the correct position. The instructor should record with a stopwatch how long the student can maintain the target image through the aperture. As practice progresses, the student may show a dramatic increase in the length of fixation. Eventually the aperture can be made larger; it can be removed when the student habitually maintains the correct gaze.

■ Increasing the size of the target also helps the student to fixate.

Localization

Localization is necessary for finding the beginning of a page and for reading an article or diagram. Other tasks that require localization include searching for key words such as those at the top of a page of a dictionary or telephone book, the price of a grocery store item, or the amount to be paid on a telephone bill, and picking up a dropped stitch in crocheting or knitting. These exercises may be helpful in checking a student's localization skills:

■ The instructor gives the student a page of recognizable single letters, numbers, or other symbols and asks the student to find the top-left symbol, the bottom-right symbol, a symbol close to the middle of the page, a symbol in each quadrant of the page, and so forth. The instructor checks the student's directionality. Does the student mix up left and right or top and bottom? When looking at the middle, is the student off center? Does the student use the upper-left and bottom-right corners and margins as guides to find symbols in those corners?

- If the previous task was too difficult, the instructor places several rows of small objects on a table top and asks the student to perform the same exercise with these objects.

- In both these exercises the instructor observes the student's posture and the position of the body, the head, and the eyes and provides the optimal illumination and contrast.

Scanning

Scanning is used for reading one or more lines of print, for checking the front of an appliance for controls, and for searching a telephone book for a particular name. It requires the student to maintain consistent fixation by holding the eye as steady as possible and moving the target in the appropriate direction, or holding the eye and the target steady and moving the head. Students with restricted fields and no central scotomas who are not using optical aids may prefer to scan with eye movements only. The following procedures may be used:

- The instructor notes the pattern in which the student reads the numbers, letters, or symbols. Is it left to right or top to bottom? Did the student skip any letters or lines or miscall letters or confuse similar-looking letters? How did the student find the next line? Did he or she scan back to the left side of the page on the line just read, on the line below, or on a slant between the two lines?'

- If the foregoing task could not be performed, the instructor should place several rows of small objects on a table top and ask the student to scan them, naming all the objects.

- The instructor should observe the position of the student's body, head, and eyes when performing these tasks. Optimal illumination and contrast should be provided.

Tracking

Tracking is required for following the movement of a pen across a page when writing or following the movement of a needle when sewing. Many shop and craft activities require good tracking skills as well. To check the student's tracking, the instructor should do as follows:

- Move a small recognizable target from left to right, top to bottom, and in circular motions in front of the student and note his or her ability to follow the target by using head and eye movements, then only eye movements.

- Gradually decrease target size and note the student's response.

- Have the student move the target. Note the student's eye–hand coordination. Is the student able to maintain fixation on the target as it moves? Does the student use head and eye movements or just eye movements? Tell the student to use head movements only and keep the eye steady if optical aids are to be tried.

EFFICIENT USE OF VISUAL SKILLS WITH AIDS

This section discusses training students to use visual skills with aids and the techniques to be used with students who have difficulties with specific skills. The skills covered in this section are (1) focal distance, (2) localization, (3) scanning, (4) fixation, and (5) tracking. Table 1 presents a succinct summary of the problems that may be encountered in various areas, including visual skills, and the techniques that may be tried to ameliorate them.

Focal Distance

■ Patch the eye not being used if the student is monocular. The student should be advised that patching will not cause the eye to atrophy—a common concern of most students with this condition.

■ Instruct the student to view through the center of the lens.

■ Position the target (symbol or word on an index card) at the appropriate distance until the student recognizes it. Remember to have high contrast to distinguish between the figure and the ground.

■ Demonstrate the depth of focus by moving the card too close or too far away so the student notices the differences in depth.

■ Have the student hold the card at the appropriate focal distance for a clear image and then blur the image.

■ Measure the working distance and compare it with the focal distance. It should be noted that the working distance may be different from the focal distance because of the student's refractive error, accommodation, or blur interpretation. Make certain the card (and all reading materials) is held on the same plane and at the approximate height as the lens used for reading.

Difficulties. If the student has problems with focal distance, the following techniques may be helpful:

■ Use a reading stand.

■ With a microscope or telemicroscope, attach a pipe cleaner to the temple of the frame so it protrudes the appropriate distance; the pipe cleaner must touch the page.

■ With a microscope or telemicroscope, cut a piece of stiff cardboard to the appropriate length; position one edge at the page and the other edge resting on the frame of the glasses.

■ For difficulty with the focal distance of a hand-held magnifier, use a stand magnifier of the same power (the clinician may need to add a plus-lens to the spectacle for accommodation).

■ Touch the page to the student's nose or to the end of the lens and move it away slowly until the print is clear.

Table 1. Problems in Various Areas and Their Possible Solutions

Category	Problem	Possible Solution
Visual Skills ■ Localization (pg. 335, 342)	*The student may* ■ Exhibit erratic eye and head movements. ■ Verbalize the inability to see anything. ■ Verbalize the inability to see things clearly (objects are foggy, smoky, or blurred. ■ Hold hand-held magnifiers too far from the eye.	*The instructor could* ■ Move the target so it appears in the student's best viewing area. ■ Hold the student's head or the target steady. ■ Use a typoscope, pointer, or marker. ■ Isolate the area to be viewed. ■ Instruct the student to move the eye, head, or target more slowly. ■ Use a pen light to check the alignment of the lens. ■ Manipulate the pupillary distance or panascopic tilt of the lens. ■ Change to a larger target with wider spacing. Increase the contrast of the target. ■ Manipulate the lighting. ■ Consult the examining clinician.
■ Focal Distance (pg. 337)	■ Move the head or target too quickly. ■ Resist moving the page or target close enough. ■ Verbalize discomfort with a close focal distance. ■ Compensate for incorrect eccentric viewing (blurred image) by moving the page in and out.	■ Check the student's eccentric viewing techniques and train the student separately in these techniques. ■ Check the distance by holding the target at the correct focal distance and then moving it in and out to demonstrate blur. ■ Attach pipe cleaner to the temple of the lens for short focal distances and use small dowels for longer distances. ■ Use a reading stand. ■ Try to lower power magnification and larger print.
Visual Skills ■ Scanning	*The student may* ■ Lose a line.	*The instructor could* ■ Instruct the student to hold the head

ments.
- Verbalize the inability to find lines ("words skip around").
- Read only part of a line.

beginning of the line just read.
- Use colored markers in margins as visual cues.
- Use a typoscope, paper clip, or finger as a marker to point out the beginning of a line.
- Use a colored filter strip in margins to provide feedback.
- Instruct the student to look for empty spaces at the beginning and end of margins.

- Double Vision (pg. 334)
  - Verbalize seeing two images.
  - Verbalize the presence of a "light" in the field of view if the eye not being used has light perception only.
  - Exhibit general reading difficulties if the eye not being used is not patched.

- Occlude the eye not being used if the student's aid is monocular.
- Check the pupillary distance if the aid is binocular.
- Consult the examining clinician.

Recognition of Letters and Words (pg. 335)
- Confuse similar-looking letters.
- Miss the top, bottom, or either side of letters and words.
- "Guess" words or substitute words with the same beginning or ending letters.
- Report that the middle letters of words are missing.
- Verbalize the "crowding" or "blending" of words.
- Spell words but not pronounce them.

- Provide larger print, more contrast, and more spacing between letters and words.
- Instruct the student in the skills of eccentric viewing.
- Require the student to spell words before pronouncing them.
- Devise letter-recognition drills for those letters that the student confuses.
- Check the student's past reading experiences.
- Instruct the student to look for wider spacing between words.
- Consult a reading specialist.

Table 1. Problems in Various Areas and Their Possible Solutions (cont.)

Category	Problem	Possible Solution
Visual Skills Reading Comprehension (pg. 335, 336)	■ Read slowly. ■ Forget what has been read. ■ Read isolated letters but not words.	■ Instruct the student to pause after every sentence to recall what was read. ■ Tell the student to read paragraphs twice. ■ Time the student's reading in words per minute to show improvement (or lack of improvement) in speed. ■ Discuss the student's expectations. ■ Refer the student to a reading specialist if the student's comprehension has not improved after reaching the visual-skills plateau.
Optical Aids (pg. 344)	■ Verbalize discomfort because the aid is too heavy. ■ Be unable to adjust to the focal distance. ■ Object vehemently to the appearance of the aid. ■ Be unable to view through the center of the lens because of pupillary distance, panascopic tilt, or the angle of eccentric viewing. ■ Be unable to adjust to the strength of magnification.	■ Consult with the examining clinician and the social worker.
Physical or Psycho-social Set (pg. 321)	■ Tire easily. ■ Experience headaches or nausea. ■ Appear frustrated, unmotivated, unhappy, withdrawn, nervous, or sad. ■ Verbalize expectations that cannot be	■ Provide postural support (e.g., a high-back chair with arms and wheels, or a reading stand). ■ Shorten the training sessions, provide breaks, and allow the student to

- distant objects or look around the room with near aids. Instruct the student to look directly through the center of the lens.
- Instruct the student not to relax tension in the head, neck, and shoulders.
- Instruct the student to move the head, eyes, and target more slowly.
- Consult with the clinician, social worker, physical therapist, and family members.

Physical Movement, Restrictions, and Motor Difficulties (pg. 343)

- Be unable to hold the head steady.
- Verbalize that the target "bounces."
- Be unable to hold the head, body, and hands in the correct position.
- Exhibit problems with directionality.

- Consider head-borne aids for hand tremors
- Consider training with a less sophisticated aid.
- "Pattern" the correct position of the head, body, and target by positioning the student and moving the target correctly (the instructor places his or her hands over the student's hands).
- Provide tactile clues for directionality during training (e.g., when instructing the student to scan to the right, touch the right temple; when instructing the student to scan to the left, touch the left temple).
- Consult with the physical or occupational therapist, the optometrist or opthalmologist, the learning disabilities teacher, or the visual training clinician.

Localization

■ Have the student hold the target or place the target on a reading stand with his or her finger on the target. Preferred illumination is essential.

■ Have the student find the target through the lens and position it at the correct focal distance.

Problems. If the student has problems with localization, these techniques will be beneficial:

■ Use a typoscope or cutout to make localization easier. Position the cutout around the target and instruct the student to find the "window."

■ Increase the contrast between the target and the background.

■ Have the student position the target in the area of clearest vision without the aid and then move the lens into position in front of the eye and focus on the target.

■ Have the student follow his or her arm down to the hand and the finger or locate the finger and then shift to the target.

■ Have the student use a systematic searching pattern to locate the target (i.e., from top left to right, back to left and down, and so on).

■ With a bioptic telemicroscope, have the student sight the target through the carrier lens, position the barrel of the telescope directly above the target, and move the eye up into the telescope. While viewing through the telescope, the student should slowly lower the head until the target is sighted. Apparent displacement occurs because of the upper mount of the bioptic. Explain this displacement and instruct the student to lower his or her head more than seems necessary.

■ With a paper clip, attach a red filter sheet on top of the page above the line to be read and a green filter sheet on the lower portion of the page below the line to be read. Instruct the student to find the line that is neither red nor green. The color that the student reports the page to be will indicate where he or she is looking.

■ For reading, have the student place a finger at the place where reading should begin by viewing the place without the aid (the headline or the top-left corner of the page), then move the lens into position, focus on the finger, and shift to print.

■ For reading, have the student get the page of print into focus with the lens, scan left to the margin, and then follow the line edges up to the top of the page.

If the problems persist, consult with the examiner about having the student change to an aid with a lower power or one that will give the student a larger field of view. If the student learns to localize with a lower-power aid, the student may be able to localize through the aid that was prescribed initially.

Scanning

■ Instruct the student to use a systematic scanning pattern to find the target or the inner detail on the target.

■ For reading, tell the student to read slowly from left to right, to scan back to the first word of that line, and then shift to the line below.

Difficulties. Techniques to overcome difficulties with scanning are as follows:

■ Instruct the student to use a typoscope or a marker under the line.

■ Tell the student to position his or her finger at the beginning of the line, scan back to the finger, and then move the eye and finger down together.

■ If reading is the goal and scanning is difficult, a scanning exercise may be practiced. Use the dark lines and large numbers in a pattern, such as the one below:

1_____2

3_____4

5_____6

7_____8

9_____10

The student is instructed to look from 1 to 2, back to 1, down to 3, and so forth. Words, rather than numbers, may be used at the next level. Then intersperse the words and numbers on the lines.

Fixation with an Aid

The student must regain fixation each time the eye is shifted in scanning. Regaining fixation is especially necessary to achieve consistency in recognizing print. If fixation is difficult, targets or details of targets will be skipped over while scanning.

Problems. If the student has problems with maintaining fixation with an aid, the instructor should try these techniques:

■ Increase the size of the target.

■ Consult with the clinician to experiment with increased or decreased magnification.

■ For students who must view eccentrically, isolate the target with a cutout or use a pointer. Move the pointer or cutout in the scanning direction that the student must cultivate. The student learns fixation for scanning by tracking a pointer or cutout and noting the details or the targets seen.

■ Use short, simple words and large print for reading.

■ Hand print or type exercises that are simple enough to master.

■ Increase contrast.

■ Increase the size of the target or the spacing between details.

Tips to Ensure Success

■ Observe the student's particular strengths and weaknesses during training as well as the expressions of the student's satisfaction and dissatisfaction.

- Note the student's understanding of how to use the low vision aid. It is helpful to have the student verbalize what the aid is used for, how she or he will practice with it at home, and so forth. Clear up any misconceptions before the student leaves the training session.

- While using optical aids, some students experience headaches, eyestrain, dizziness, nausea, and tension in the back and neck muscles. Explain the commonality of these symptoms and do the following: (If the symptoms persist, consult the clinician.)

1. Instruct the student not to look around the room or in the distance with near aids. The student must be seated and view only the target.

2. Decrease the length of each training session and increase the number of sessions.

3. Tell the student to relax the facial, neck, back, and arm muscles and to breathe deeply.

4. Patch the eye not being used (unless the student is binocular) to prevent facial muscles from tightening or the unused eye from squinting or shutting.

5. Choose a time for the training session when the student is calm and alert, not tired or upset.

6. Make sure the student looks through the center of the lens and not at the distortion at the edges. It may be helpful to patch the periphery of the lens.

PERFORMING SPECIFIC TASKS

Virtually any task performed at arm's length or closer can be accomplished visually with the use of low vision aids. In this section, the tasks that students most often cite as desirable objectives will be used as examples in the presentation of techniques for training and the suggestions for materials.

Reading, which is necessary for communication and maintaining independence, is the task that most students state they would like to begin, improve, or return to. Writing, household tasks such as sewing, recreational tasks such as card playing or playing a musical instrument, and vocational tasks such as operating machinery also allow students to function in the mainstream.

Some students with good visual skills may need only a short lesson with a specific aid. Such students practice the specific material they want to see and are ready immediately to integrate the aid into their life-styles. Other students may need to build the necessary visual skills slowly, combine their visual skills with the motor skills required to operate the low vision aid, and then intertwine these skills to perform the specific task. For these students, each component of the task must be taught separately; after one component is learned, the student moves on to the next, more complicated, component until all the components are mastered.

Reading

Optical Aids Used

A hand-held magnifier, a stand magnifier, microscopes (full field, bifocal, trifocal, and half eye), telemicroscopes (full field, bioptic, and surgical).

Nonoptical Aids Used

A typoscope or marker, a reading stand, colored filter sheets, large print, and illumination controls.

Training Tips

- Always gear training for success. Never allow a student to continue struggling with print he or she cannot recognize consistently. Replace that print with a sample of material in a larger size print or with more spacing and contrast until the student achieves greater perception. A suggested sequence for training materials is this:

1. 20–24-point print (5M) newspaper headlines, large Sloan reading cards, hand-printed materials, and the first paragraph of a Feinbloom reading card.

2. 14–18-point (2–3M) large-print materials (such as the large-type *Reader's Digest, New York Times Weekly),* large-type texts or library books, and material typed on a large-print typewriter.

3. 8–10-point (1–1.5M) clear typed print with good contrast. For some students, spacing and contrast are more important than the size of the print. To maintain clarity, use a new typewriter ribbon.

4. 8–9-point (1M) regular book print in good clear print on opaque, off-white paper (not paperback books).

5. 7–8-point (1M) magazine print similar to newspaper print but with better contrast; if the glossy paper creates glare, use a filter sheet.

6. 7–8-point (.08M) newspaper print, paperback book print, and other materials printed on poor-quality paper and on which the ink is blurred, making reading difficult. Teach the student to localize the headline without an aid and then add an optical aid. Also, teach the student to notice the spacing between columns so the student does not read all the way across the page.

7. 4–5-point (.05M) very small print (found in want ads, stock market quotations, dictionaries, small Bibles, and telephone books). Use a marker or typoscope under the line of type in a telephone book or dictionary. Teach localization of the name or word by using the key name or word at the top of the page. Show the student how to skim occasional words in alphabetical order to find the desired word or name.

- Success also may depend on how difficult the print is and the style of the type. The easiest material will have good spacing between lines and good density. Look for several different type styles: serif, sans serif, capitals and lower case, all capitals, bold face, italic face, and regular face.

- Practice material should be of several column widths.

■ Reading material should be appropriate to the comprehension level of the student. At first, use material with an easy vocabulary of short words. Gradually increase the complexity of the material until it is commensurate with the student's level of understanding, whether fourth grade or postdoctoral. A suggested sequence is as follows:

1. Recognition of letters.
2. Recognition of short words (two to three letters).
3. Introduction of longer words. If longer words are not recognizable, ask the student to spell or sound out the words phonetically.
4. Reading of sentences.
5. Reading short paragraphs (anecdotes, jokes, quotations, and sayings).
6. Reading short stories.

■ If the student continues to have problems with reading comprehension, the instructor may refer the student to a reading specialist.

■ Reading forms, bills, statements, computer printouts, and the like.

1. Instruct the student to scan the face of the form to become familiar with how the form is organized into columns.
2. Show the student how to find headings for the columns.
3. With two markers or typoscopes, teach the student to place the edges down and across appropriate columns to find the desired entry.

Writing

Optical Aids Used

Microscopes in powers of 4–5X or less, magnifiers, and telemicroscopes.

Nonoptical Aids Used

Felt-tip pens, bold or raised-line paper, a script board, and stencil guides.

Training Tips

■ Instruct the student to find the place where he or she wishes to begin writing.

■ Have the student move the tip of the pen into the field of view and keep the tip in the field of view as it moves across the line.

■ The student should follow the same pattern as for reading: from left to right, to the left on the same line, and down to the next line.

■ Writing script is usually easier than printing because it does not require lifting the pen as often as does printing. The student may need to draw lines or make loops simulating handwriting until he or she is able to keep the focal distance, coordinate the eyes and hands, and so on.

■ With a bioptic telemicroscope, instruct the student to do as follows:

1. Locate, through the carrier lens, the place where writing will begin.
2. Move the pen into the position where writing will begin and place the tip on the page.
3. Locate the tip of the pen through the telescope.
4. Focus.

5. Begin writing, keeping the tip of the pen in the field of view.

▪ For writing checks, instruct the student to

1. Scan the face of the check to locate all entry lines and become familiar with their positions.

2. Place a finger to the left of each entry line and write in the appropriate entry, making sure to start writing at the *beginning* of the line to prevent the insertion of other words or numbers by others (fraud).

In writing mathematics problems, it is helpful to use regular or bold-line graph paper or a marker from the top to the bottom of the page to keep the columns straight.

Needlework
Optical Aids Used
Microscopes in lower powers (especially half eye and bifocal) a chest magnifier, and a telemicroscope. (These tasks are difficult to perform with microscopes in higher powers or with bioptic microscopes.)

Nonoptical Aids Used
For embroidery, self-threading or large-eye needles, needle-threaders, embroidery thread, and an embroidery hoop on a floor stand. For crocheting and knitting, a large size hook and large knitting needles.

Training Tips
The instructor should teach the student to do as follows:

▪ Prop his or her elbows on a high arm chair for stability and to maintain the focal distance.

▪ Initially, use the largest needles available and thread in a color that contrasts with the material being used for practice.

▪ Place a towel in a solid contrasting color on the lap to provide good background contrast to the thread or yarn.

▪ Stick a sewing needle in a cork for easier threading; this also makes the needle easier to find if it is dropped.

▪ Because a change in depth perception and in the depth of focus makes needle threading difficult, the student should practice touching the needle with the thread and make successive approximations until he or she is able to judge the distance and depth for threading. The student should position the needle so the needle's eye is facing him or her, not sideways.

Practice making large stitches and decrease the size of the stitches gradually until the preferred size is reached.

Card Playing
Optical Aids Used
For cards in the hand: a chest magnifier and microscopes in lower powers (especially half eye and bifocal).

Nonoptical Aids Used
Jumbo and low vision playing cards.

Training Tips
■ To see cards on a table with a bioptic telemicroscope, the student should
   1. Locate the cards using the carrier lens.
   2. Place the appropriate cap on the telescope to get the focal distance.
   3. Scan to see all the cards on the table. It may take practice to remember all the cards seen.

Training with CCTVs

Task
Familiarization with the characteristics, advantages, and disadvantages of various CCTVs.

Techniques for Training
■ If possible, provide the student with access to several CCTV units and compare their characteristics as follows:
   1. The size of the screen (field of view).
   2. Magnification.
   3. Portability.
   4. Expense (if this is a consideration).
■ If access to CCTV units is impossible, describe the systems and show pictures, if possible, so the student knows they are available. Contact the local CCTV representatives for a demonstration of the units.

Task
Demonstrate and familiarize the student with the controls of the CCTV.

Techniques for Training
■ The instructor demonstrates and has the student operate the following controls:
   1. The on-off switch.
   2. Reverse polarity.
   3. The magnification control.
   4. The focusing mechanism.
   5. The aperture control.
   6. Contrast.
   7. Brightness.
   8. Other controls inherent to the set being demonstrated (e.g., the electronic line marker and the split screen).
■ After demonstrating each individual control, the instructor should have the student name and operate each control to ensure that the student understands them.
■ The instructor should demonstrate, and have the student operate, con-

trols that are dependent on each other. For example, after changing the magnification, one must reset the focus; after changing the polarity, one must adjust the contrast and brightness.

Task

Determination of the student's magnification needs.

Techniques for Training

■ The instructor should do the following to determine the student's magnification needs:

1. Use recognizable print or symbols.

2. Zoom to very large print and have the student move as close to the screen as is necessary to name the symbols.

3. Slowly decrease the size and instruct the student to verbalize when he or she no longer is able to discriminate the print.

4. Increase the print size slightly until the student is able to recognize consistently the printed symbols.

■ The student's preferred magnification is calculated by this formula:

$$X \cdot Y = \text{magnification}$$

$$\frac{\text{CCTV print size (in centimeters)}}{\text{actual print size (in centimeters)}} = X$$

$$\frac{25 \text{ centimeters}}{\text{working distance (in centimeters)}} = Y$$

As the student's perceptual skills and eccentric viewing improve, the student's magnification needs may decrease.

Task

Use of the X–Y platform (the movable table under the camera onto which the target material is placed).

Techniques for Training

■ The instructor demonstrates the features of the X–Y platform—its movement, margin stops, friction brake, and so on.

■ The instructor demonstrates movements on the screen using printed symbols.

■ The instructor places his or her hands over the student's hands and shows that left movement brings the right side of the page into view and vice versa, that "away" movement brings the bottom of the page into view, and that "toward" movement brings the top of the page into view.

■ The instructor tells the student to keep the print in the middle of the platform and the hands on the edges to avoid moving the page.

■ A plexiglass sheet may be placed over the material to keep it flat and smooth.

■ For a book that curves near the binding and changes the focal distance, slip a thinner book under the thin side to raise it to the level of the other side.

Task
Fixation.

Techniques for Training
- The student may use head or body movements for eccentric viewing, if necessary; instruct the student to keep consistent fixation and not to shift constantly.
- Binocularity may be achieved with the CCTV if the acuities are equal, the fields of view allow it, and there is no muscle imbalance or suppression.
- For a student who has difficulty, it may help to patch part of the screen to show how one line or one letter, or to use an electronic line marker or construction paper for that purpose.
- If fields of view in two eyes conflict, causing double vision or a constant shift from one eye to the other, the instructor should patch one eye.

Task
Localization and scanning.

Techniques for Training
- The instructor first manipulates the platform to position symbols on the screen, which the student identifies.
- The instructor moves the platform in the appropriate scanning sequence, and the student scans the information as it moves across the screen (the lines of shapes, letters, symbols, and words).
- The student begins to control the platform with the instructor's hands over the student's. The student does simple scanning from left to right and from top to bottom. The student learns to locate the first line by scanning to the left of the page and up to the beginning line.
- The student then scans simple formats without guidance from the instructor.
- The student scans and reads paragraphs, noting their indentation, and develops the ability to use contextual clues and visual closure.
- The instructor demonstrates the part–whole relationships of newspapers, forms, bills, statements, diagrams, charts, and schedules, setting the magnification for as much of a field of view as is possible and then zooming into specific areas for detail.
- The student masters the part-to-whole relationship and uses it with other materials (such as poetry, forms, and graphs) to recognize their format.
- The student uses a systematic scanning pattern to find and review information in a variety of formats.
- The instructor demonstrates "skimming" skills for locating a specific section in a book, scanning headlines, lines in a telephone book and dictionary, and so on.
- For long sessions of reading, it may help the student if magnification is increased slightly to prevent fatigue.

Task
Lighting and contrast.

Techniques for Training
- Some students avoid fatigue by switching from white print on black to black print on white when reading.
- The room in which the student is reading should have some background lighting to avoid eye fatigue. However, the instructor should make sure that the room lights are not creating glare on the CCTV screen.
- Some students are bothered by glare from the CCTV light. To avoid this glare, the instructor should make a shield for the light out of dark construction paper and place it high enough so reading material may be slipped onto the platform.

Task
Writing.

Techniques for Training
- The instructor demonstrates writing skills by standing behind or beside the student and placing his or her hands over the student's hands.
    1. Position the area where writing is to begin onto the screen by moving it under the camera and using the heat from the light as a clue to placement.
    2. Move the tip of the pen into the field of view.
    3. Place the tip of the pen on the page and begin to write, keeping the tip of the pen in the field of view.
- It may be easier for the student first to make straight and curvy lines until the techniques are familiar.
- It may help to use bold-line paper and felt-tip pens for writing.
- Writing is performed in the same left-to-right, top-to-bottom sequence as is reading.
- After the student demonstrates mastery of these techniques, he or she may attempt to:
    1. Mark appropriate areas on a form.
    2. Sign and fill in checks.
    3. Fill out forms that require short answers.
    4. Take notes.
    5. Do mathematics problems (graph paper is helpful for columns).
    6. Fill in a checkbook register and ledger sheets.

Further Comments
1. In the beginning, use the least amount of detail, the greatest contrast, the most comfortable print size and magnification level, the simplest format, the most orientation clues, and the slowest speed. Gradually, these variables are changed and a variety of materials are introduced, depending on the student's needs.

2. Other attachments for the CCTV are available, including a typing attachment and a CRT terminal attachment. Ask the CCTV representative to demonstrate these attachments.

3. The CCTV is an excellent device to train students in reading skills, especially students who have difficulties with fixation or whose lowered acuities make the initial use of optical aids difficult. Fixation, scanning, and perceptual skills for reading can be taught on the CCTV and then transferred to an optical aid with a similar power.

4. For reading, the CCTV gives the greatest magnification and field of view of any low vison aid. Students who must do copious amounts of reading for vocational or educational reasons may use it to supplement other optical aids for the greatest ease and speed in reading.

5. The CCTV may be used for a variety of tasks other than reading and writing around the home, shop, or office; one enterprising CCTV user even used it for dissecting in a college biology course.

6. The CCTV can be used to determine a student's interest in reading. A student who reports that he or she wants to read but is not progressing with optical aids can be evaluated on the CCTV. A student's reading skills can be measured more easily on a CCTV because the problems in visual skills inherent in optical aids do not exist with the CCTV.

HOME PRACTICE

Whenever possible, the student will be lent the low vision aid for practice and training at home. The true success of an instructional program is whether the student can use the aids as well in his or her own environment as in the training environment. It is essential that the instructor give the student comprehensive easy-to-read-and-follow instructions for utilizing the aids in the milieu for which they were prescribed. The instructions should be provided in a format best understood by the student if possible (e.g., tapes, braille, or large print). The basic elements to be covered in the instructions include the following:

1. The name, brand, type, and power of each aid.

2. The purposes of the aid and what it can and cannot do. Specific instructions for each component of a multifunctional aid, such as a telemicroscope, must be given.

3. The suggested length and time of practice sessions, based on the student's abilities in the training session (for example, 10 minutes four times a day, with breaks between sessions).

4. Practice material and nonoptical aids should be provided, if possible, such as letter drills and large print.

5. Specific safety precautions. *(continued on p. 362)*

Fig. 1. General Information/Cover Sheet Accompanying Instructions on Individual Aids for Home Use.

The aid you are being loaned is a _____

The working distance of the aid is _____

You should practice these activities with this aid: _____

_____

_____

    Call the clinic at _____ if you have any questions about your eye examination or the use of the aid you have been lent.

    Use the aid only for its specific purpose. Do not try to walk around while wearing reading glasses. Do not try to read while wearing a distance aid.

    Create the best setting for using the aid. Sit or stand in a comfortable position. Use good lighting when inside. Make sure the aid is focused correctly or that you are the correct distance from the object or material you are viewing.

    Start by practicing just for five to 10 minutes several times a day. When you feel more comfortable using the aid, increase the amount of time per session. If you are very tired or feeling discouraged, take the day off; things will be much brighter the next day!

    One of your eyes may be covered with a patch (occluded). The purpose of patching is to allow you to concentrate on what you are seeing with your other eye. Keep the covered eye open so your facial muscles are relaxed. The covered eye will retain its normal functioning.

    A few people may experience tearing, blurring, or nausea while practicing with the aid. If you do, just remove the aid, sit back, and relax for a moment while your eyes and head clear. Then continue to practice. These symptoms are occurring because you are exercising your eyes in a new way. *You cannot lose vision by using low vision aids.*

Fig. 2. Information on Stand Magnifiers for Home Use

Description

1. Your vision aid is a stand magnifier.

2. The power of your magnifier is _____ X (makes objects _____ times bigger).

3. When the material is against the base of the stand, it is automatically in focus.

4. You should be able to read _____ size print or larger with this magnifier.

Directions for Use

1. Place the stand on the material.

2. View through the center of the magnifier.

3. Hold your head at a comfortable distance from the magnifier. Remember that the closer you are to the magnifier, the wider your field of view.

4. Move the magnifier across the page as you read.

5. If you wear bifocals, look through the bifocal (bottom portion of the lens) when using the stand magnifier.

Hints for the Best Use of Your Aid

1. Use good lighting (a flex-arm lamp is best). The light should come from the side so it can shine directly on the material under the lens.

2. Place your finger at the left edge of the material to keep your place when reading.

3. Hold the material in a vertical position to avoid strain caused by leaning over. A reading stand or clipboard may help you keep the material steady.

4. Always keep the stand flat on the material.

5. Start by using your aid for five to 10 minute sessions, several times a day. As you become more proficient, increase the amount of time at one sitting.

Care of Your Aid

1. To clean your aid, use a soft, damp, lint-free cloth (no tissues).
2. Do not immerse the aid in water.
3. Do not set the aid down so the lens touches a hard surface because doing so may scratch the lens.

Possible Additional Uses

Some people have found they were able to use this aid for the following activities. Your use of the stand magnifier for these activities depends on the design and power of your lens as well as your needs. Some possible activities include these:

1. Reading labels and prices while shopping.

2. Checking a bus or train schedule.

3. Reading a television schedule.

4. Reading labels on medicine bottles.

5. Verifying currency denominations.

6. Reading menus.

7. Locating addresses and numbers in the telephone book.

8. Reading return addresses on envelopes.

9. Reading amounts on bills.

Fig. 3. Information on Microscopes for Home Use

Description

1. Your vision aid is a microscope; it is a high-plus (very strong) lens mounted in a spectacle frame.

2. The power of your aid is _____ X (makes objects _____ times bigger).

3. The working distance of your aid is _____ (distance from the lens to the material).

4. You should be able to read _____ size print or larger with these microscopes.

5. The microscope is for your _____ eye only. You should [should not] wear a patch over the other eye.

Directions for Use

1. Put the reading material close to your face (almost touching your nose).

2. Slowly move the material away from your face until the words are clearly focused. This should be about _____ away.

3. Move the material or your head, not your eyes, as you read.

4. Always view through the center of the lens.

5. Do not stand or walk around while looking through these glasses.

Hints for the Best Use of Your Aid

1. Use good lighting (a flex-arm lamp is best) and have the light shine directly on the material.

2. A typoscope, line guide, or your finger can help outline the words you are reading and help you keep your place.

3. Hold the material in a vertical position to avoid the strain caused by leaning over. A reading stand or clipboard may help you keep the material upright.

4. Start by using your aid for five to 10 minute sessions several times a day. As you become more proficient, increase the amount of time at one sitting.

5. If you have been given a head strap, adjust it so the spectacle frame is snug against your nose.

Care of Your Aid

1. To clean your aid, use a damp, soft, lint-free cloth (no tissues).

2. Do not immerse the aid in water.

3. Do not set the aid down so the lenses touch a hard surface because doing so may scratch the lenses.

4. Do not try to adjust the frames.

Possible Additional Uses

Some people have found they were able to use this aid for the following activities. Your use of the microscope for these activities depends on the design and power of your lens as well as your needs. Possible activities include these:

1. Reading for extended periods.

2. Reading prices and labels while shopping.

3. Reading gauges, dials, and other controls.

4. Reading labels on medicine bottles.

5. Threading a sewing machine.

6. Verifying currency denominations.

7. Reading menus.

8. Locating addresses and numbers in the telephone book.

9. Knitting, crocheting, sewing, or doing other needlework.

10. Looking for insects on plants while gardening.

11. Identifying playing cards.

12. Reading amounts on bills.

13. Writing for short periods (making out checks, signing documents, and so forth).

14. Reading recipes.

15. Reading the time on a wristwatch.

Fig. 4. Information on Focusable Hand-held Monocular Telescopes for Home Use

Description

1. Your vision aid is a focusable hand-held monocular telescope.

2. This telescope has a power of _____ X (makes objects _____ times bigger).

3. By focusing the telescope, you can see objects at _____ or further away.

Directions for Use

1. Locate (spot) the objects you wish to see first without looking through the telescope.

2. With your _____ hand, bring the telescope up in front of your _____ eye, and point it at the object. Hold the telescope as close as possible to your eye or glasses.

3. Focusing: With your _____ hand, turn the focusing ring out until the objects are blurred. Then turn the ring in the opposite direction and stop as soon as the object is clear; this will give you the largest clear image.

4. Scanning (looking at an object that is bigger than the field of view of your telescope, for example, reading a wide sign or looking around a room):
   - Spot the object and focus the telescope as described above.
   - Move your head and the telescope together as you scan.
   - Do not try to look around by moving your eyes.
   - Always move slowly since the telescope will make things appear to pass by very quickly.

5. Tracking (following a moving object, for example, watching the path of a car or watching a person walk by):
   - Spot the object and focus the telescope as described above.
   - As the distance between you and the object changes, you may need to refocus.
   - If you need to move to follow the object, move your head and the telescope together slowly.
   - Do not try to follow the object by moving your eyes.

6. Do not try to walk around while looking through the telescope.

Hints for the Best Use of Your Aid

1. This telescope is small and can be kept in a pocket or purse or hung around the neck when not in use.

2. When standing, hold your arm against your body or support it with your other hand to help keep the telescope steady.

3. When sitting and using your telescope, rest your elbow on a table or arm of a chair to help hold the telescope stand and avoid fatigue.

4. Start by using your aid for short sessions (five to 10 minutes) several

times each day. As you become more proficient, increase the amount of time per session.

Care of Your Aid

1. To clean your aid, use a soft, damp, lint-free cloth (no tissues).
2. Do not immerse the aid in water.
3. Do not set the aid down so the lens touches a hard surface since doing so may scratch the lens.

Possible Additional Uses

Some people have found they were able to use this aid for the following activities. Your use of the telescope for these activities depends on the design and power of your lens as well as your needs. Some additional activities are these:

1. Spotting and identifying street signs, bus numbers, traffic lights, and so on.

2. Watching television for short periods.

3. Identifying a person coming up the front walk or at the front door.

4. Locating the newspaper in the yard.

5. Viewing the blackboard.

6. Identifying the brand on cattle.

7. Locating the entrance to a building.

8. Monitoring children in another room.

9. Sight-seeing while riding in a car.

10. Seeing people's faces more clearly as they enter a room.

Fig. 5. Information on Focusable Spectacle-mounted Telescope.

Description

1. Your vision aid is a focusable spectacle-mounted telescope.

2. This telescope has a power of ____ X (makes objects ____ times bigger).

3. By focusing the telescope, you can see objects at _____ or farther away.

Directions for Use

1. Locate (spot) the object you wish to see first without looking through the telescope (raise your glasses or view with your other eye).

2. Look through the telescope to see the object clearly.

3. Focusing: With your _____ hand, turn or pull the focusing ring out until the objects are blurred. Then move the ring in the opposite direction and stop as soon as the image is clear; this will give you the largest clear image.

4. Scanning (looking at an object that is bigger than the field of view of your telescope, for example, reading a wide sign or looking around a room):
   - Spot the object and focus the telescope as described above.
   - Move your head and the telescope together as you scan.
   - Do not try to look around by moving your eyes.
   - Always move slowly because the telescope will make things appear to pass by very quickly.

5. Tracking (following a moving object, for example, watching the path of a car or watching a person walk by):
   - Spot the object and focus the telescope as described above.
   - As the distance between you and the object changes, you may need to refocus.
   - If you have to move to follow the object, move your head and the telescope together slowly.
   - Do not try to follow the object by moving your eyes.

6. Do not try to walk around while looking through the telescope.

Hints for Best Use of Your Aid

1. Start by using your aid for short sessions (five to 10 minutes) several times a day. As you become more proficient, increase the amount of time per session.

2. If you have been given head straps, adjust them so the spectacle frame is snug against your nose.

3. When focusing, it may be helpful to hold the telescope with one hand and turn the ring with the other hand.

Care of Your Aid

1. To clean your aid, use a soft, damp, lint-free cloth (no tissues).

2. Do not immerse the aid in water.

3. Do not set the aid down so the lens touches a hard surface since doing so may scratch the lens.

4. Do not try to adjust the frames.

Possible Additional Uses
Some people have found they were able to use this aid for the following activities. Your use of the telescope for these activities depends on the design and power of your lens as well as your needs. Some additional activities include these:

1. Viewing the blackboard.

2. Identifying the brand on cattle.

3. Locating an entrance to a building.

4. Monitoring children in another room.

5. Sight-seeing while riding in a car.

6. Viewing objects of art in museums and art galleries.

7. Looking at the tote board at the race track.

8. Watching television for extended periods of time.

9. Viewing sporting events, concerts, or lectures.

10. Seeing people in a room clearly.

11. Watching movies in the theater.

6. Suggestions for optimum illumination.

7. Postural support and relaxation during practice.

8. How to care for and clean the aids.

9. Special instructions for family members, or others who will be aiding the student in practice.

10. The name and telephone number of the office where the instructor can be reached for questions or further assistance.

Figures 1–5 illustrate the information that should be provided to students for the at-home use of their aid in the form of individual student-information sheets. These information sheets were developed by Sandra Ferraro of the Low Vision Clinic, University of Houston College of Optometry. They are an invaluable tool for reminding students of what is expected in home practice and for educating family members and significant others about the prescribed aids. Sheets such as those in the figures can be made up for each clinical-instructional program.

References

Bäckman, Ö., & Inde, K. *Low vision training.* Malmö, Sweden: Liber Hermoöls, 1979.

Goodrich, G., & Quillman, R. Training eccentric viewing. *Journal of Visual Impairment and Blindness,* 1977, **71**, 377–381.

Jose, R., & Watson, G. Hope for the hopeless. *Optometric Weekly,* June 26, 1975, 9–13.

Kaufman, J. E., & Christensen, J. F. *Lighting handbook.* (5th Ed.). New York: Illuminating Engineering Society of North America, 1972.

McGillivray, R. (Ed.). *Aids and Appliances Review.* Newton, Mass.: Carroll Center for the Blind, July 1972.

Physician's desk reference for nonprescription drugs. Oradell, N.J.: Medical Economics Co., 1980.

Quillman, R. D. *Low vision training manual.* Kalamazoo: Department of Blind Rehabilitation, College of Health and Human Services, Western Michigan University, no date.

Watson, G. Training with near and intermediate distance optical and nonoptical aids. In M. Belivea & A. Smith, *The interdisciplinary approach to low vision.* (Manual for the National Training Workshop in Low Vision, Chicago, August, 1980).

CHAPTER 14

Training Programs for Individuals with Restricted Fields

JOHN FERRARO, M.A.
RANDALL T. JOSE, O.D.

The individual with severely restricted fields (10 degrees or less) is a difficult person to manage in a low vision program. Often the psychosocial implications of the impairment are more significant than the actual loss of vision. Furthermore, technology for the design of optical systems for this population is in its infancy, and magnification can be more dehabilitating than rehabilitating if it is not properly prescribed. In this chapter, training programs for the few treatment options available to the clinician-instructor are offered as well as a general discussion of the significance of reduced fields to all training activities.

The measurement of visual fields is important clinical information that should not be overlooked in the clinical evaluation. The size, location, and extent of field losses will influence which low vision aid is prescribed and the subsequent training programs.

TESTS

As suggested in Chapter 8, three types of field studies can be undertaken:

Perimetry. Perimetry tests the 180-degree field of view for scotomas. It is not routinely performed but is important when scotomas have been plotted on other tests or a disease has involved the periphery (for example, retinitis pigmentosa, glaucoma, and atrophy of the optic nerve).

Tangent Screen. The tangent screen test investigates the central 25–35 degrees of the visual field. Blind spots in this area are most destructive to acuity and mobility and often are indicative of additional problems in the periphery.

Amsler Grid. The Amsler Grid is a nearpoint study of the central 10 degrees of vision. It is mainly used to test for the existence of blind spots in the macular area.

Although all students do not need all three field studies, the low vision clinician should make some attempt to describe a student's intact visual field and the presence of blind spots or distorted areas of the retina. That is, the clinician should provide the instructor with more accurate fields than "confrontation"—especially confrontation fields utilizing fingers or lights for targets. The confrontation test should be used for uncommunicative students, such as multiply impaired children.

It is generally believed that individuals with severely reduced fields will not be able to use low vision aids. This belief has not been confirmed by clinical experience. Although persons with severely reduced fields may need some special considerations, they can benefit from appropriately prescribed aids.

DEFINITIONS

For the purposes of this discussion, the following definitions of field restrictions will be used:

Mild field restriction. Individuals with mild field restrictions exhibit a loss of peripheral vision such that only 20–40 degrees of the central field remain. The field loss is probably secondary to the acuity loss in this case and is given only some attention in prescribing for and training the individual. This level of field loss does not interfere with the prescription of magnifying devices, does not make localization and other visual skills more difficult, and does not contraindicate the use of telescopes. Usually, such persons need an orientation and mobility (O&M) evaluation and may need to be taught to scan more efficiently.

Moderate field restriction. When the central field is reduced to between 10 and 20 degrees, then some special considerations have to be given to the prescription of aids and the recommendations for training. Such persons must first be evaluated by an O&M instructor to determine their ability to scan to compensate for the loss in the peripheral field. Up to 8X magnification can be accepted by the retina with no major problems; spectacle, as well as hand-held, magnification devices can be used, as can telescopes. However, problems with localization and tracking will complicate the training program.

Severe field restriction. When the central field is 10 degrees or less, much special attention must be given to the design of optical systems. All prescriptions for aids, distant or near, must be prescribed in coordination with an O&M program. The person's perceptual skills (especially part-whole recognition and visual memory) will determine how much magnification can be prescribed; scanning skills will determine the person's potential success with the aid as well as its design. When the fields are 5 degrees or less, special field-enhancement aids should be used.

The degrees of usable vision listed in the three definitions should not be

364

rigidly observed; they simply are guidelines. Acuity level, physical disabilities, age, intellectual or emotional problems and motor difficulties are but a few of the factors that will alter the previous definitions. Functionally, individuals with 20 degrees in the central field can have other problems that will further complicate their mobility and other daily living activities. The purpose of the definitions is to encourage the prescription of aids and services for individuals with severe field losses.

Functionally, the loss of peripheral fields inhibits the information-processing abilities of the visual system; thus, not enough information can be taken in at one time. To compensate for this defect, the individual must learn systematically to scan the environment to obtain meaningful information. The person sees only a small portion of the environment at a time; thus, seeing is like trying to figure out a puzzle from one piece of it. The success in completing such a task depends on the person's ability (1) to pick up each piece and identify what it is a part of (whole-part concepts), (2) to remember all the pieces that have been picked up (visual memory), and (3) to put all the pieces into a composite picture (percept). The task is made easier if

- The person has some preconceived notion of the puzzle.
- The puzzle is picked up systematically, one piece at a time, and put back into its correct position (i.e., the puzzle was not dumped on the floor; it was still together). (This illustrates the importance of scanning.)
- Each piece of the puzzle contains some meaningful information so it can be identified and remembered (visual memory).
- The person does not have to hurry or is not under pressure (life-style). The foregoing probably is a poor analogy, but it gives one a feel for the visual task facing the individual with severely impaired fields. The obvious solution to the problem is to increase the size of the fields (which is impossible) or to improve the person's information-processing system. The latter is the goal of the various field-enhancement devices, such as prisms and reversed telescopes, which will be discussed later in this chapter, as will night-vision goggles and ancillary lighting systems.

Types of Scanning

Before initiating treatment for reduced fields, the instructor and clinician should evaluate the person's present strategies of information processing. Individuals with 10-degree fields or greater should be given O&M instruction and regular aids. Those with 10 degrees or less in the central field, no islands of vision in the periphery, an acuity of about 20/100, realistic expectations, and patience are potential candidates for prisms and reverse telescopes (Ferraro, 1982). However, the instructor and clinician must also determine how these persons are scanning and whether the type of scanning lends itself to the introduction of prisms. The following are some possibilities:

Efficient scanning. Individuals who scan efficiently will not be good candidates for prisms because they already can process information in the periphery with quick eye movements. Therefore, prisms probably will be more confusing than useful to them. Such persons will reject reverse telescopes because the reverse telescopes eliminate the ability to scan and reduce the functional or dynamic field. Individuals with a static field of 3 degrees and good scanning skills will have a dynamic field of 15 degrees or more. The 15 degrees continuously are sampled through scanning movements, and information about the central 15 degrees always is available to these people for functional purposes.

Erratic scanning. Persons who scan erratically have poor scanning skills and no systematic approach to their environment. Prisms will help such people develop better scanning skills, but reverse telescopes will create difficulties in adaptation.

Head scanning. Individuals who scan with their heads may be considered to have the "frozen eyeball" syndrome. All their visual information is obtained through head and neck movements. These movements are not as efficient for information gathering as eye movements. Thus, head scanners are not able to assess their immediate surroundings quickly and are poor travelers. They are good candidates for prisms since the placement of prisms on a spectacle correction will require them to move their eyes. When prisms are first introduced, such people show a dramatic improvement at first in non-mobile situations. However, many revert back to the frozen eyeball syndrome as soon as movement is introduced. They usually require mobility and scanning lessons to overcome this problem. Reverse telescopes also may be helpful for specific tasks.

Shoe gazing. Persons who are termed "shoe gazers" refuse to use a cane and spend all their visual energy looking at their lower field for drop-offs, objects, and so forth. They have to be convinced that a cane will provide them with protection and confidence for the lower field so they can raise their eyes for other uses. Under the pretense of giving them instruction in the use of prisms, the instructor also can teach them how to use a cane. When they learn to walk with a cane, training in the use of prisms for the peripheral field can be initiated. If they refuse to use a cane, they will never look up to use the prisms, so it is not worthwhile to pursue this treatment option. Prisms placed in the lower field may help these individuals move their eyes to the upper field; however, the prisms usually confuse these persons more than help them. Thus, the best course is for the instructor to demonstrate the prisms and then let these persons think about their use for a while. When these individuals become aware that they are shoe gazers and are wasting their vision on the ground when it could be used for other areas, they may reconsider. They will begin to realize that the cane symbolizes independent travel — not dependence. Because they do not have organized scanning movements, these persons also may be good candidates for reverse telescopes.

Head and eye scanning. Individuals who scan with their head and eyes are good candidates for prisms. Because they already utilize all their skills to process information efficiently, the prism will allow them to become more adept at scanning the periphery by allowing small eye movements into the prism to replace the less efficient head-neck scanning movements. However, reverse telescopes will impede scanning for these people and probably will be rejected by them.

Hemianopsias. Since persons with hemianopsias still have peripheral vision in some quadrants, they have not learned to organize their eye movements to compensate for the loss of a particular field, and thus their information processing in that field is inefficient. Prisms usually create a dramatic improvement in these individuals, who generally have high success rates with prisms. Reverse telescopes cannot be used with these persons because vision still remains in half the field.

The foregoing are the main characteristics of people who are potential candidates for prisms or reverse telescopes. It is essential that candidates for prisms or reverse telescopes realize that either system helps to increase their efficiency of information processing with reduced fields and is not a device to expand the fields.

FRESNEL PRISMS

Fresnel prisms will initially be placed on the outer edge of both spectacle lenses (base out) so the individual can make small eye movements into the prism to check for objects in the periphery (65 to 85 degrees); this eliminates the need for inefficient neck movements to accomplish the same task. The person becomes more "aware" of objects in the periphery once he or she learns to scan systematically into the prism (Jose, 1976; Finn, 1975; Weiss, 1972).

Measurements

Instructions for determining the position of the fresnel prisms on the spectacles are as follows:

- Have the individual fixate on a distant target monocularly with the spectacle correction on a plano (0 power) demonstration spectacle.
- Move a 3x5-inch card from the outer edge of the lens toward the center until the person reports seeing the card, mark this point, and repeat the measurement several times (see Figure 1).
- Repeat the foregoing procedure to measure the other eye.
- Cut and tape the 3 x 5-inch card to the spectacles about 2 millimeters outside the average of the points marked (see Figure 2).
- The person walks around with the cards on the spectacles to see if the cards encroach on his or her ability to scan. If the individual does not notice the cards, set them closer to the center of the lens. If the person notices the cards, move them closer to the outer edges of the spectacles. These adjustments are continued until the person can walk around without noticing the cards. The cards should be placed as close to the edge of the "dynamic field" as possible without interfering with normal scanning (see Figure 3). One of

367

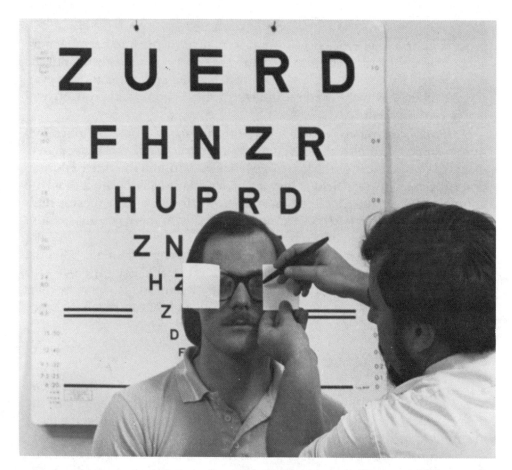

Fig. 1. While the patient fixates a distant target, a 3x5 card is moved from the outer edge of the spectacles until the patient reports seeing the edge of the card. This point is marked on the lenses and represents the static field at the spectacle plane.

the disadvantages of the fresnel prisms is that the person always will see the card when attempting to look to the right or left. When the person wants to look into the periphery, he or she must look around the prism with exaggerated head movements.

■ Once the proper position of the cards is determined, cut and place a $30^\triangle$ fresnel prism base out on the surface of each spectacle lens. The use of a $30^\triangle$ prism is based on clinical experience. This type of prism gives the largest displacement, which makes it the most efficient but also the hardest to adapt to. You may wish to experiment with other powers but start with $30^\triangle$.

■ Cut the prisms to the shape of the spectacle lens and apply by submerging the lens and prism under water and pressing the prism to the lens. Squeeze all the air bubbles from under the prism while it is under water. Let it dry for about 10 minutes. (Most clinicians will be able to mount the prisms.) Make sure the prism is oriented base out and that the central edge is cut straight.

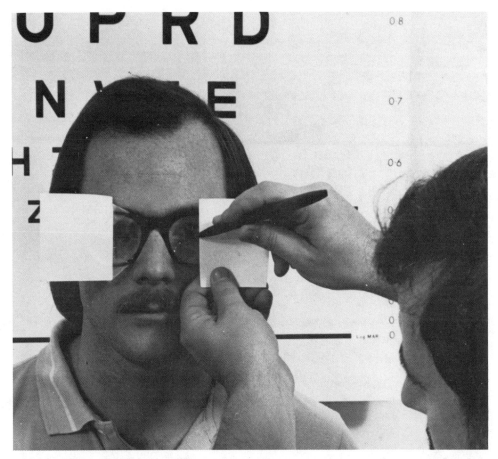

Fig. 2. The card is cut and taped to the spectacles 2mm temporal to the point marked on the lenses. This allows for scanning and represents the dynamic field at the spectacle plane.

Exercises

Prism blur. The instructor demonstrates prism blur to the student while the student is wearing spectacles. The student looks at a picture through the conventional lens and then through the prism. He or she will notice a decrease in clarity (acuity) in the picture when it is viewed through the prism; the acuity loss varies from person to person.

Displacement. The instructor shows the student what displacement is like by having the student view through the prism an object that has been placed in the periphery and then reach out to touch the object. The object will appear to be more central than it is so the student will point centrally away from the object (see Figure 4). While the student is still pointing in the same direction, the instructor asks the student to turn his or her head to see the object through the lens and to check how far off he or she was when pointing at the object. This exercise should be practiced a few times with the ob-

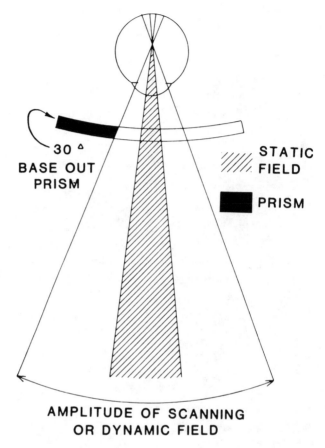

**30 ᵃ
BASE OUT
PRISM**

**STATIC
FIELD**

PRISM

**AMPLITUDE OF SCANNING
OR DYNAMIC FIELD**

Fig. 3. The diagram represents the points measured in Figs. 1 and 2. The prism should be placed as close to the edge of the dynamic field (or scanning amplitude) as possible for maximum efficiency.

ject in various locations about 16 inches away. The person should start pointing in the correct direction through the prism in about five minutes.

To help confirm adaptation to displacement of an object by the prism, the instructor asks the seated student to hold the object with one hand, look at it through the prism, and point at it with the other hand. The student's kinesthetic awareness or feedback will help him or her adapt to the displacement. The next step is for another person to hold objects in the student's periphery to which the student points with a finger and then with a small stick or pencil (in this way, kinesthetic awareness is eliminated). The student always confirms the accuracy of his or her pointing by looking through the conventional lens.

The targets then can be moved farther away—2–30 feet. The same procedure is followed: the student locates the object through the prism while seated, points at it, and then confirms his or her accuracy. Because linear dis-

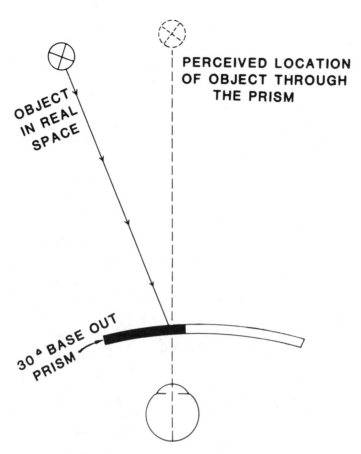

PERCEIVED LOCATION OF OBJECT THROUGH THE PRISM

OBJECT IN REAL SPACE

30° BASE OUT PRISM

Fig. 4. The prism will displace objects centrally as indicated in this diagram. *Initially,* **the patient will point to objects as though they were located more centrally than their real location.**

placement is greater the farther away an object is, the student should be taught that "poorer" aiming at distance is normal and is a result of the optics of the prism—not the student's lack of ability. Objects should be placed at various degrees in the periphery as well as at different distances.

Functional use of prisms. The next demonstration is to have the student stand in a room without wearing the prisms and look straight ahead. The instructor walks past the student from behind, and the student reports when he or she first notices or sees the instructor (the student is allowed to move the eyes). Usually, the student sees the instructor when he or she is two to three feet in front. The instructor repeats the exercise while the student is wearing the prisms. Most of the time, the student will see the instructor almost at the side or just slightly in front. Again, the instructor asks the student to point out where he or she thinks the instructor is and then to confirm this position with the conventional lenses.

Outdoors. After the student masters the foregoing exercises, it is time to practice out of doors and to move around various outdoor environments. The purpose of the ativities is to give the student additional experience with the spatial displacement of objects and to help him or her develop a system for scanning into prisms while walking. The student must be taught to "sample" the periphery with eye movements into the prisms and learn to respond only to important stimuli. Often students fail in the use of prisms because they are put into a complicated environment too quickly and they are confused by the two visual inputs. Students require a great deal of practice wih frequent visual and tactile reinforcement of the placement of objects before they cari negotiate a complicated environment.

Difficulties with Prisms
Students may encounter the following problems when using prisms:

Blur. Some students cannot tolerate prism blur and must discontinue using prisms. Before they give up, the instructor should remount the prisms to eliminate dirt and air bubbles, change the position of the prism slightly on the spectacle lens, tint the spectacle lens slightly; try sunfilters, such as NoIR, over the system, or increase the base curve of the spectacle lens. If these adjustments do not work, the instructor may have to consider other options.

Confusion. Some students report that they get confused when they wear prisms. Their confusion means they have not had enough training in structured settings. Often students say that wearing prisms in crowds is particularly annoying. Those who experience this problem may have to remove the prisms while in crowds because confusion cannot be alleviated; crowds move in all directions, and it is difficult to separate which of the continuum of masses is in the prism and which is seen through the conventional lens. The instructor should forewarn students of the complications of a crowd and give them lots of training before sending them out on their own. If a student reports that he or she is confused, the instructor should revert to a structured training program.

Confusion of images also can be caused by the existence of islands of vision in the periphery. It is possible that islands of vision will become functional from the stimulation of awareness in the periphery that is part of the prism training program. Because of this possibility, it is important to test the perimetric fields prior and during prism training.

Double vision. Double vision is reported for two reasons: (1) the student is looking through the edge of the prism or (2) the student does not suppress the other eye when one eye is looking through the prism. For example, if the right eye looks to the right, the left eye will be looking through the nasal edge of the left spectacle lens without a prism. Double vision results unless the brain suppresses the image of the left eye. In the first instance, the problem will be corrected by cutting the prism back slightly to the outer edge of the lens. In the second case, the problem can be solved by putting a base-in prism on the nasal edge of the lens on the left eye to match the base-out prism on the outer edge of the right eye. If the two types of prisms can be matched, single vision may be restored, although it is difficult to do so. Another solution is to put a small patch on the nasal lens of the left eye, which eliminates double vision in some cases without severely disrupting normal scanning.

Double vision also may be eliminated by having the student engage in more training activities involving hand-eye feedback to the prism displacement. These activities will help the visual system attend to the object displaced by the prism and ignore or suppress the image from the other eye. Putting a red or green filter paper over the area of the lens of the eye without the prism will aid the cortex to identify which of the images should be attended to.

After students successfully have used prisms for a time, they will report that the prisms are not as effective as they were at first or that they occasionally experience double vision. Because their scanning has improved and the amplitude of their eye movements has increased, they scan in and out of the prism. (The dynamic field has increased.) This problem is corrected by cutting the prism smaller and moving it closer to the outer edge of the lens. It may be advisable to try the 3 x 5-inch cards again and find the new position from scratch.

The foregoing are the basic steps in helping students become comfortable with fresnel prisms as field-awareness devices. As the clinician and instructor become more familiar with the uses and problems of these prisms, they will be more accurate in their selection of candidates and more creative in solving the problems related to prisms. The best problem-solving technique is to get back to the basics of hand-eye coordination and simple environments. It should be remembered as well that some people do not think prisms are worth the effort or meet their expectations. Such people usually will not express their feelings outright; rather, they will develop problems. The instructor must determine which problems are real and which problems are masking a dislike for the prisms. As with all aids, even if the clinician and instructor think the person should be successful, the person may decide that prisms are not beneficial or successful for his or her purposes.

REVERSE TELESCOPES

Reverse telescopes are a new treatment option, and hence there has been little experience in applying them. The concept of reverse telescopes is that if images are minified, more information can be seen at one time in the same field. An individual with 5 degrees of vision in the central field can see two chairs and an end table across the room. If a 2x reverse telescope is used, the size of objects is cut in half, and twice as much is seen in the same retinal field. The major disadvantage of these telescopes, however, is that since the objects are twice as small, detail is lost. Even so, students with 5-degree fields and 20/20 vision may find them useful because the students will still have 20/40 vision in the 10-degree field. However, those with 5-degree fields and 20/80 vision will have 20/160 acuity in the 10-degree field, and the trade-off may be more debilitating than helpful.

Because most reverse telescopes are designed with small ocular lenses, students cannot scan when looking through the telescope unless they scan with head and neck. Scanning in this way decreases efficiency, so the students usually reject the aid. A person with 5-degree fields can easily scan to maintain a 15-degree field. However, the dynamic field is cut to 10 degrees with a reverse telescope. Therefore, many people actually lose functional fields with reverse telescopes. In addition to causing a loss of acuity, reverse telescopes make all objects look twice as far away as they really are. This spatial distortion is difficult to adapt to; most students find it is impossible to adjust. Thus, reverse telescopes cannot be worn full time and must be mounted on bioptic spectacles or held in the hand.

There is no structured training program because the use of the system has been minimal to date. Therefore, if a reversed telescope is prescribed, the instructor should observe the student using the telescope in as many settings as possible and record the student's reactions. When problems occur, they will have to be resolved by the clinician and instructor on an individual basis.

The literature (Rickeo, 1978; Holm, 1970; Ciufredda, 1972) indicates the major use to be spotting objects in specific areas, such as a desk top, a workbench, or a refrigerator. The reverse telescope allows the students who are familiar with what they are looking for (and do not need acuity to locate it) to find more quickly a particular object on a desk or in the refrigerator (when working at arm's length so tactile awareness of distance eliminates the reverse telescope's distortion of space and distance). Since it is used for short spotting tasks, the reverse telescope does not affect mobility.

The ideal reverse telescope would allow an individual to scan in the telescope. A small 1.5X minifier with a rectangular ocular lens mounted as a bioptic would allow the student to scan in the telescope at 1.5X the efficiency outside the telescope; there would be a minimal loss of acuity, and the student could revert to a spatially undistorted view of the environment by looking underneath the reversed bioptic and through the conventional lens.

NIGHT-VISION AIDS

Many students with restricted peripheral fields also have problems with night vision. The only available solutions to this problem are these:

Cane travel. The instructor should teach the student to use a folding cane for going out at night.

Wide Angle Mobility Light (WAML). The WAML is a headlamp with belts that can be strapped to and worn around the waist. It throws a wide, bright beam of light that allows sufficient light for the individual's central vision.

Another supplementary light that can be used for mobility at night is the camper's flashlight; for indoor use, small penlights or flashlights are handy, as are pens with built-in lights for writing in dark areas.

Night-vision scope. A night-vision scope is a light-intensification unit that allows a person to see detail at night. Small amounts of light are intensified 750 times or greater and provide enough light on the retina to stimulate central vision. The night-vision scope is used like a monocular telescope and is most successful when used in conjunction with cane travel. It has its optimum application in rural areas. (Jose, 1976; Coursey, 1972; Berson, 1973, 1983; Morrissette & Goodrich, 1983a; Morrissette & Goodrich, 1983b). Information on its availability and cost (approximately $3000) can be obtained from the National Retinitis Pigmentosa Foundation.

As is obvious, the technology for rehabilitating night blindness is not advanced. However, the foregoing options should be explored for those individuals who are seriously handicapped by this condition.

CONCLUSION

Loss of peripheral fields can complicate the prescription of aids and subsequent training programs. If the instructor understands the functional implications of small central fields, individualized instructional programs can be developed to overcome many of the problems experienced in learning to use aids efficiently. Field expanders, field enhancement devices, and the like are just tools to improve a person's ability to process information through the visual system. A thorough knowledge of a person's present skills at processing information is required before decisions about prescribing prisms and reversed telescopes can be made.

References

Berson, E. et al. Advances in night vision technology. *Archives of Ophthalmology,* 1973, **90** (12), 427–31.

Berson, E. Night vision aid. *Journal of Visual Impairment & Blindness,* 1983, 77(3), 121.

Ciuffreda, K. J. Retinitis pigmentosa–An overall view and approach. *Optical Journal and Review of Optometry,* 1972, **109**(20), 38–46.

Coursey, T. Night viewing goggles for night blind travelers. Publication of the Western Blind Rehabilitation Center, Veterans Administration Hospital, Palo Alto, Ca., 1972.

Ferraro, J., Jose, R. and McClain, L. Fresnel prisms as a treatment option for retinitis pigmentosa. *Texas Optometry,* 1982, **38**(5), 13–17.

Finn, W. A., Gadbaw, P. O., Kevorkian, C. A. and De L'Aune, W. R. Increased field accessibility through prismatically displaced images. *New Outlook for the Blind,* 1975, 69(10), 465–467.

Hom, O. A simple method for widening restricted visual fields. *Archives of Ophthalmology,* 1970, **84**(5), 611–612.

Jose, R. and Smith, A. Increasing peripheral field awareness with fresnel prisms. *Optical Journal and Review of Optometry,* 1976, **113**(12), 33–37.

Jose, R., Echols, C. and Davidson, B. The development of the Generation II as an aid for patients with retinitis pigmentosa and night blindness. *American Journal of Optometry and Physiological Optics,* 1976, **63**(2), 27–29.

Morrissette, D. L. and Goodrich, G. L. The night vision aid for legally blind people with night blindness: An evaluation. *Journal of Visual Impairment & Blindness,* 1983a, **77**(2), 67–70.

Morrissette, D. L. and Goodrich, G. L. Rejoinder. *Journal of Visual Impairment and Blindness,* 1983b, **77**(3), 121–122.

Rickers, K. Visual field wideness: A personal report. *Journal of Visual Impairment and Blindness,* 1978, **72**(1), 28–29.

Weiss, N. An application of cemented prisms with severe field loss. *American Journal of Optometry and Archives of the American Academy of Optometry,* 1972, **49**(3), 261–264.

Other Readings

Bailey, I. Prismatic treatment for field defects. *Optometric Monthly,* 1978, **69**(14), 99–107.

Drasdo, N. Techniques, instruments, cases: Visual field expanders. *American Journal of Optometry and Physiological Optics,* 1976, **53**(9), 464–467.

Gadbaw, P. O., Finn, W. A., Dolan, M. T. and Del'Aune W. R. Parameters of success in the use of fresnel prisms. *Optical Journal and Review of Optometry,* 1976, **113**(12), 41–43.

Hoeft, W. The management of visual field defects through low vision aids. *Journal of the American Optometric Association,* 1980, **51**(9), 863–864.

Krefman, R. Reversed telescopes and visual efficiency scores in field restricted patients. *American Journal of Optometry and Physiological Optics,* 1981, **58**(2), 159–162.

SECTION V
Special Considerations

This section brings together some of the general information already presented and applies it to real-life situations. The authors of these chapters are relating their experiences in working with special populations, such as multiply handicapped individuals, or with special concerns, such as lighting and role modeling. In addition, the chapters on resources and the annotated references are presented to stimulate and guide further reading in the field of low vision care.

CHAPTER 15

Assessment of the Multiply Handicapped

KAREN SHANE COTE, M.S., AND AUDREY SMITH, M.A.

This chapter deals with the educator's assessment of individuals with multiple handicaps, especially those that involve the severe loss of vision and some mental retardation or delayed learning. Although the chapter describes the evaluation of children, most of the techniques are applicable to multiply handicapped adults as well. The assessment is designed to help the educator become aware of the individual child's functional vision. It also serves as a tool to facilitate the evaluation of the eye care specialist.

If educators are to plan successful vision stimulation programs, they must first observe, evaluate, and record all information that indicates a child's functional level of vision. Much can be learned about a child's level of functioning by observing the child in a variety of situations, such as in the classroom, at play, or while eating.

OBSERVING THE CHILD'S BEHAVIOR

The purpose of the evaluation is to increase the educator's observational skills and to decrease assumptions. For example, if the child consistently turns the right eye in the direction of stimuli, you record that the child views primarily with the right eye turned in the direction of the stimuli. Do not assume, for instance, that there is no vision in the left eye, because the child could be exhibiting this response for a number of reasons, such as attempting to eliminate double vision, achieving binocularity, or stilling nystagmoid movements. Assumptions should be eliminated; although subjective observations are considered in the evaluation recording form, the goal of the evaluation is for the educator to be as objective as possible.

First, observe whether the child exhibits a change in behavioral response

The information in this chapter was developed mainly at the Center for the Blind, Upsal Day School for Blind Children, Philadelphia, Pennsylvania, under Grant No. 300-76-0352 from the then U.S. Department of Health, Education, and Welfare.

to any stimuli—auditory, visual, or tactile. Then look for indications of whether the child is functioning visually. Examples of behaviors to observe are as follows:

Movement Patterns
1. Does the child move with ease and speed?
2. Does the child exhibit a smooth range of movement?
3. Does the child shuffle his or her feet?
4. Does the child walk with the head downward?
5. Does the child consistently avoid or bump into objects?
6. Does the child bump into objects that are waist high, to one side, or below knee level?

Sensory Responses
1. Does the child exhibit such behaviors as light gazing and flicking?
2. Does the child bring objects to the mouth for exploration?
3. Does the child explore objects primarily with the fingers and hands?
4. Does the child demonstrate more awareness of sounds?

Postural Responses
1. Does the child exhibit neck and facial straining?
2. Is the child tilting his or her head?
3. Does the child exhibit compensatory body adjustments?
4. Does the child squint?

The items covered in this evaluation represent samples of visual sensation, and visual-motor and visual-perceptual skills. To obtain an accurate and comprehensive picture of the child's visual functioning, record more than just the presence or absence of the response. For example, when an object is presented to the child, describe the illumination in the room, the type and size of the object, and the distance at which the child sees it. If the task, distance, or position of the child is changed in any way, indicate the change on the evaluation form. Then answer the following questions about the child's responses:

1. Are both eyes being used?
2. Does the child perform independently or require assistance?
3. What behaviors are demonstrated when the child is responding to the evaluation items?

The child's responses may not "look like" what you had expected. The postural and behavioral responses of children who have adapted to their visual impairment (or to any other type of impairment) may seem "strange." However, any response the child exhibits should be noted, because the child may be responding within a repertoire of adaptive behaviors.

When working with a severely impaired child, you may need several sessions to complete the evaluation. Such a child may require more time to respond or need assistance from the evaluator in responding. At times during the evaluation, additional stimulation may be necessary just to motivate the child. When attempting to elicit responses, it is important to communicate on the child's level of understanding.

EVALUATION OF SPECIFIC VISUAL CONDITIONS

The following section outlines the techniques that are helpful in eliciting various types of responses to test whether children have certain eye conditions. Materials that are useful in this evaluation include penlights, flashlights, flicker lights, translucent and transparent colored filters, familiar objects in the child's environment, bubbles, balloons, puppets, blocks (different sizes and colors), squeeze toys, small musical instruments, bells, and food, such as cereal, raisins, and pretzels.

Pupillary Response

A pupillary response occurs when the pupil of the eye changes shape or size when light is presented. It should be noted that there are abnormal conditions such as "hippus"—a continual constriction and dilation of the pupil—or "fixed pupil"—a pupil that will not constrict or dilate regardless of the amount of stimulation.

Techniques. The following techniques will help the evaluator observe whether the child exhibits a pupillary response.

1. Observe the condition of the pupil without stimulation.

2. Direct a light into the child's eyes from approximately 12 inches away and notice whether the pupils constrict, dilate, or remain unaffected.

3. Observe the pupils when the child emerges from a dark room after an extended period.

4. Measure changes in the size of the pupils with an "optistick" (a millimeter ruler).

5. Use a brighter light source or turn off the room lights to provide greater contrast.

6. Present a light in different areas of the visual field, not only directly in front of the child.

7. Vary the child's position and repeat steps 1–6.

Muscle Imbalance

A muscle imbalance may be suspected if light is not reflected in corresponding places in both eyes, that is, if the light reflection is off center or if it differs from one eye to the other. With some conditions, such as aniridia and leukokoria, it may be difficult to see a reflection.

Techniques. The evaluator should shine a light into the child's eyes from approximately 30 inches away and record where the light is reflected in both eyes. If any deviation in reflection is noted, the evaluator should consult an eye-care specialist.

Blink Reflex

With the blink reflex, blinking occurs automatically when a hand or any object moves toward the face.

Technique. With the fingers spread out, the evaluator moves a hand toward the child's face. It is important not to create wind by moving the hand too quickly; if wind is created, the child may blink in response to the wind, rather than to the visual stimulus.

Different Visual Behaviors

Different visual behaviors include flicking and light gazing. Although these behaviors are considered socially unacceptable, they may often be the only indication that the child is using vision—that at least light projection and shadow projection exist.

Eye Preference

Eye preference is indicated when behavioral changes are demonstrated in response to alternate patching of the eyes. If the child does not resist having one eye patched, this does not necessarily mean that one eye is preferred. Resistance may be a result of tactile defensiveness.

Techniques. The following techniques may be used to determine whether a child prefers one eye.

1. While holding a light or small object 12 to 18 inches in front of the child's eye, alternately cover each eye and record if the child demonstrates any change in behavior.

2. To avoid touching the eye, block vision by holding the thumb in front of the child's pupil or ask the child to cover one eye.

Visual Fields—Central

A response in the visual fields may be noted if the child turns his or her head or eyes when light is presented in front of the child's face.

Techniques. The evaluator may detect a response in the visual fields by using these techniques:

1. Shine a light from approximately 12 inches in front of the child's face.

2. Shine a light slightly above, below, to the left and to the right of the child's face. Record the areas of response and nonresponse.

3. If no response is demonstrated, move the light closer, blink the light, or use a different type of light or a colored light.

4. If a response is demonstrated, repeat Procedures 1 and 2 using small objects instead of a light.

5. Vary the child's position and repeat the field test.

Visual Fields—Peripheral

A response in the peripheral fields may be detected by shining a light in the outer areas surrounding the face. It is important to maintain a consistent arc of distance from the child's face and to vary the movement and speed of the light with each child. Be aware that the child's reaction may be to the evaluator's arm (auditory or olfactory responses) rather than to the light. Note any eye movements because they will cause a shift in visual fields and result in inconsistent information.

Techniques. Responses in the peripheral fields may be noted while using the following techniques:

1. While positioned behind the child, slowly bring a light into the child's field of view from above, from below, from left to right, and from right to left. Record the areas of response and nonresponse.

2. If a response is demonstrated, repeat the procedure using small objects instead of a light.

3. Lights or objects may be held by the evaluator or suspended from an "invisible" string.

4. Another person may be positioned in front of the child to observe eye movements.

5. Vary the child's position and repeat the procedures for measuring the peripheral fields.

Visual Field Preference

A visual field preference means that the child demonstrates a preference for lights or objects presented in one area of the visual field, as opposed to another. If the child pays attention to one object, rather than to both, consider that the child may be demonstrating a preference either for the object or for the visual field. Also, the child may be ignoring one area of the visual field rather than not seeing objects presented in that area. Even when you get a positive response, set up the test under different conditions (a new room or new targets) to confirm your initial responses.

Techniques. The evaluator may find these techniques helpful in detecting such a preference:

1. Find two identical lights or objects to which the child responds.

2. Simultaneously present both lights or objects to corresponding areas of the visual field (upper and lower, right and left). Record whether the child responds in both areas of the visual field or demonstrates a preference in one area.

Tracking

Tracking is evidenced when the child follows a moving light or a moving object with his or her eyes or head. Multiply impaired children, it should be noted, have difficulty tracking across the midline.

Techniques. To determine if the child is tracking, use the following techniques:

1. Use lights, toys, puppets, or whatever small objects will attract the child's attention.

2. Hold a light or object within the child's range of vision. Move the light or object slowly to the right and left, up and down, and circularly. Record whether the child follows the movement with his or her eyes or head and the length of the child's attention span.

Table 1. The Educator's Evaluation Recording Form

Item	Date	Present or Absent	OD, OS OU	Distance of Light or Object	Illumination	Type and Size of Light or Object	Description Independent and Dependent-Subjective Comments
Pupillary response							
Muscle imbalance							
Blink reflex							
Different visual behaviors							
Eye preference							
Central fields							
Peripheral Fields							
Visual field preference							
Tracking							horizontal, vertical, oblique, circular, head, eyes, head and eyes, jerky, smooth.
Shifting attention							
Scanning							
Reaching or moving toward lights and							In front, to the right, to the left, above eye level, and below eye level.

3. Present lights and objects to all areas of the visual field.

4. Note if the child follows with the head, the eyes, or both and describe the type of tracking (smooth or jerky, with one or both eyes).

5. Vary the child's position and repeat the foregoing procedures.

Shifting of Visual Attention

Shifting of visual attention is demonstrated when lights or objects are presented alternately. It should be noted that some children experience difficulty with motor coordination and need additional time to respond.

Techniques. The evaluator may use these techniques to detect a shifting of visual attention:

1. Hold two familiar lights or objects in front of the child. Shine, blink, or shake one of them. Pause, then repeat the actions with a second light or object. See if the child will shift his or her attention from the first light to the second light.

2. Vary the position of the lights or the objects presented.

3. Vary the child's position and repeat procedures 1 and 2.

Scanning

Scanning—searching in a line from one object to another—is demonstrated as a response to three objects placed in front of the child.

Techniques. The following techniques may help the evaluator determine if the child is scanning:

1. Place three objects in front of the child or in the child's functional field of view. Note the child's ability to search in a line from one object to the next.

2. Vary the position of the objects and repeat the procedure.

3. Vary the child's position and repeat procedures 1 and 2.

Reaching or Moving Toward Lights

Reaching or moving toward lights or objects includes extending an arm, swiping, or any type of body movement.

Technique. Place lights, toys and other visually stimulating objects at various levels and in different directions from the child. Note whether the child reaches for, swipes at, or moves his or her body toward the light or object.

For children who are capable only of prone, supine, and other stationary positions, place lights and objects within reach. For example, hang lights or shiny objects from the ceiling but have them low enough so they are at eye level.

Observations can be recorded in a format similar to that shown in Table 1. To probe further into individual evaluation items, one may use the format shown in Table 2. Information such as the best time of day, which type of light or object to use, the most appropriate position and the best type of illumination may be included. The information gained from these observations can be shared with the participating clinician and other professionals involved with the child. Round-table discussions of the confirmation of those observations of visual behavior from the team will be instrumental in designing appropriate modifications to the basic vision stimulation program discussed next.

Table 2. Investigation of Individual Evaluation Items

Item	Time Date	Present Absent	OS/OD OU	Description of Lights or Object	Position	Illumination	Response

VISION STIMULATION SEQUENCE

The following sequence of vision stimulation activities may be adapted for a range of children, from multiply impaired children to those whose only impairment is low vision. In using this sequence, it is of utmost importance to consider the individuality of each child's approach to learning. Therefore, it should be noted that the sequence offers adaptations in each step and is aranged to permit the teacher to be creative and flexible in relation to the child's behavior. If the sequence is followed rigidly, learning will be hindered for both the teacher and the child.

Generally, a sequence means that the activities progress in an orderly pattern. However, a child may be able to perform an activity that comes later in the sequence even though he or she could not perform a task that came earlier in the sequence. Thus, it is recommended that each child start the sequence from the beginning. Starting from the beginning eliminates the assumption that the child is functioning at a certain level and permits the discovery of developmental lags, which may later result in visual perceptual problems.

The sequence assumes that each child is beginning at Day One of visual development, even though visual responses may not be demonstrated. At this point, as in early infancy, visual stimulation may be received by the eyes and other sensory receptors and may reach the brain. However, because of probable neurological damage, multiply impaired children often cannot organize visual information. The sequence concentrates on visual sensation and visual motor activities. It is designed to arouse the visual system and to

386

facilitate searching and looking, thus providing a strong foundation for the child's beginning visual development.

Considerations

Before instruction begins, the following considerations need to be reemphasized:

Motivation. Motivation is the key to successful programming. However, motivating multiply impaired childen is often the most difficult component of the program. Even so, careful observation in a variety of situations will reveal the appropriate motivation for the child.

Adaptive behavior. By the time you begin stimulating the child's vision, the child may have already integrated such adaptive behavior as a head tilt to compensate for field programs. Therefore, with the aid of eye-care and other specialists, determine the child's adaptive behaviors and decide whether they are useful or detrimental to the child.

Movement. Movement is the key to learning. The more one moves,the more one learns of the body in relation to space and the more the other sensory modalities become stimulated. If movement is combined with visual stimulation, the child has a greater chance to integrate learning more fully.

Length and timing of each lesson. The length of each lesson, the time of day, and which day in the week are important for determining the appropriate amount of stimulation to be given and for encouraging a child to be as open as possible. Special consideration should be given to timing the lesson in relation to when a drug has been administered, since a particular drug may affect the child's ability to learn.

Positioning. In many instances, it may be useless to attempt to stimulate a child visually if the child—especially the multiply impaired child—is positioned inappropriately. The correct positioning that will help the child achieve sensory integration should be determined through consultation with occupational and physical therapists. Attainment of the correct position ensures a nonstressful situation and facilitates a balance under which the child can more effectively receive stimulation.

Observation. As was mentioned in the section on evaluation, observational skills are essential. For this reason, the following procedures for observation are reemphasized here:

1. The activities best suited for observation are those day-to-day activities in which the child is normally involved, such as eating, toileting, playing, working with other teachers, and so forth. Moreover, observation need not involve the use of special materials; common materials used throughout the day are the most appropriate.

2. Notice changes in the child's behavioral response to any stimulus. Then observe whether there is a visual response for anything that creates a doubt.

In relation to postural changes, notice (1) head tilts, which may mean that the child is using the best part of the visual field or is seeing better with one eye or is hearing better with one ear, (2) facial straining, which usually indicates that the child is attempting to use vision, although it may result from a neurological problem, and (3) compensatory body adjustments (forward extension of the neck or lifting one shoulder or one hip to compensate for the loss of balance produced by the head tilt).

In observing the child's gait, check whether the child moves with ease and speed or avoids or bumps into obstacles. Bumping may indicate a lack of visual attention or a loss in the visual field. Thus, you should note the position of the obstacles that the child bumps into. Are the obstacles head high, waist high, or low lying? Does the child bump one side or area of the body more consistently than another?

In detecting sensory functioning, it should be remembered that the use of vision or other sensory behaviors (e.g., groping, licking, or sniffing, may indicate which sense the child is most accustomed to using). This is important because exploration usually occurs through the sense that the child is most comfortable with. Furthermore, behaviors such as light gazing, light flicking, and eye poking are often the only indications that the child is receiving visual stimulation.

The various aspects of the vision stimulation program are organized in the following format:

I. Name and explanation of step
   A. Procedure
   B. Activity 1
      1. Materials
      2. Explanation
      3. Comments
   C. Activity 2
      1. Materials
      2. Explanation
      3. Comments
   D. Activity 3
      1. Materials
      2. Explanation
      3. Comments

Awareness of Any Stimulus

Use any stimulus (an object, sound, light, smell, or temperature change) and observe whether the child displays a consistent change in behavior (smiling, crying, cessation of rocking, or any pattern of behavior) when the stimulus is presented.

Procedure

Choose a stimulus to which the child seems to respond favorably, since it may be necessary to pair it with a visual stimulus later in the sequence. For example, if the child is overstimulated by the feeling of powder being rubbed on the arm, powder should not be chosen as a stimulus because when later paired with a visual stimulus, it would cause the child to make an unpleasant association with that stimulus. Remain aware that any response may be a result of stimulation you are *not* controlling. For example, if a child cries when a light is shone, consider that the response may be caused by the postural insecurity of the child's present position, rather than by the light. It is crucial to observe carefully and to experiment in a controlled manner to avoid over-or understimulating the child by creating multiple environmental stresses.

Activity 1

Materials. Aluminum foil, Christmas lights, light-reflecting ornaments and objects, string, and electrical wires (safety).

Explanation. Place the child in a small, darkened room whose walls have been lined with aluminum foil. Place the child in an appropriate position, as determined by the occupational therapist and the physical therapist. String up blinking and nonblinking Christmas lights and suspend from the ceiling mobiles and objects that reflect light. In a small room, position the child to face a corner. Line the corner with aluminum foil and suspend the same lights and objects from the ceiling. Darken the room for additional contrast.

Comments. Check with a neurologist to determine if it is advisable to use blinking lights with some seizure-prone children. Keep detailed seizure charts.

Activity 2

Materials. A large therapy vibrator with adjustable speeds and foam-rubber encasements.

Explanation. Touch the child with or allow the child to touch a foam-rubber-encased vibrator. Guide and encourage the child to manipulate the vibrator.

Comments. If using tactile stimulation, consider the child's degree of tactile defensiveness. Proceed slowly and manipulate the environment (e.g., change positions, control ambient noise, and so forth) to avoid surpassing the child's tolerance.

Activity 3

Materials. Garlic, salt, vanilla extract, chocolate, lemon juice, Tabasco sauce, mint, and so on.

Explanation. Allow the child to taste various substances by placing them on the child's tongue.

Comments. Check any possible allergic reactions before using these substances.

Attention to Any Stimulus

Once a stimulus has been found to which the child seems to respond, try to elicit a consistent response each time the stimulus is presented.

Procedure

Repeat the procedure from the previous step but require a longer period of concentration.

Activity 1
Continue the *favorable* activity used in the previous step.

Activity 2
Materials. Musical instruments.

Explantion. Shake a bell, tambourine, or rattle near the child. Find an instrument to which the child consistently attends (e.g., turns the head, reaches for the instrument, or moves his or her body toward the sound).

Activity 3
Materials. None.

Explanation. Place the child on your lap and slowly rock the child from side to side, circularly, or forward and backward. Observe if the child responds to the rocking in a consistent manner (e.g., is calmed, makes spontaneous sounds, opens eyes).

Comments. With more severely impaired children, there is no consistent pattern to the attention span involved in responding to stimuli. Thus, one child may attend for long periods while another may have a short attention span.

Since the child's response may be elicited only under certain circumstances, (e.g., the child will smile when touched by a soft cloth, only when in a beanbag chair, after lunch, or when Ms. Jones is the caregiver), consider that along with each change of circumstances comes a new set of responses. This variety of responses is desired to ensure the generalization of the response to different situations.

Pairing a Light with a Positive Stimulus
Light is presented in conjunction with a previous stimulus to which the child has favorably responded. It may be necessary to darken the room for contrast.

Procedure
Each time you present the stimulus to which the child previously responded positively, introduce a light source as well. Continue the light for as long as the child pays attention. The purpose of this pairing of stimuli is to help the child to become more aware of light and to associate a positive stimulus with eventual attention to light.

Activity 1
Materials. Sponges, a wash cloth, waterproof wind-up toys, a self-contained light (waterproof).

Explanation. During water play, observe if the child responds to an object or wind-up toy that produces sound or moves through water. Attach a self-contained light to the toy and allow the child to manipulate it. When the toy stops, turn off the light.

Activity 2
Materials. A bolster, a light, and a mirror (if the caregiver needs to be behind the child).

Explanation. Position the child over a bolster. While rocking the child, present the light source. When you stop rocking, turn off the light.

Comments. Avoid consistently placing the light source directly in front of the child, since this may not be the area of the child's functional vision. Attempt to place the light in various areas of the child's visual field.

Activity 3
Materials. Baby powder, baby oil, and a light.

Explanation. Rub the child's body parts with the powder or baby oil. Each time you rub, shine the light. Turn off the light when you stop rubbing.

Comments. One stimulus, such as the sound of a shaking tambourine, may not be enough to elicit a response from a child. For example, if the tambourine is shaken, the child may exhibit no response. If a light is shone, again there may be no response. However, if the tambourine is shaken as the light is shone, this may cause the child to respond. Often it may be necessary to provide a combination of stimuli to reach the child's threshold for responding. In some cases, however, the use of more than one stimulus may cause the child to be overstimulated. Often responses from the child are not as noticeable until you reach the step when a previous positive stimulus is paired with a light.

Awareness of a Light Stimulus Alone

Remove the original stimulus and encourage the child to pay attention only to the light.

Procedure

Intermittently shine the light source without pairing it with the original stimulus. Note whether the child gives the same behavioral response. Monitor the child's response to the light (e.g., whether the child turns to avoid the light, pushes it away, constricts the pupils, reaches for the light, or stares or gazes at the light) and proceed slowly by experimenting with different types of lights. Placing different colored filter paper in front of the light source, using flickering colored lights, and shining lights through a transparent or translucent surface are examples of various types of light sources and ways of presenting them. Note the area of the visual field in which the child consistently does or does not respond to the light.

Activity 1
Continue to use the favorable light sources and activities found in the previous step and remove the original stimulus.

Comments. If the child's pupils do not constrict, do not assume that the child has no visual functioning. The size of pupils can be affected by several conditions, such as nerve damage, hippus (continual constriction and dilation of the pupil), fixed pupils, and aniridia, as well as medications.

Penlights or flashlights may be inadequate stimulation for some children.

Flicker lights and red and yellow filters are preferable and often elicit a more consistent response.

Attention to a Light Stimulus Alone
Each time a light is presented, the child will demonstrate consistent visual attention.

Procedure
Gradually decrease pairing the light with the other stimulus until the child consistently responds to the light source alone.

Activity 1
Continue to use the favorable light sources and activities discussed in previous steps.

Comments. In some instances, it might not be evident that the child is visually attending because the child's eyes may not seem to be directed toward the stimulus. The inability to direct the eyes toward a stimulus may be caused by various factors such as a loss in the visual field and eccentric fixation. Therefore, when presenting a light, observe how consistently the child's eyes move in one direction, as opposed to always expecting the child to look "directly" at the light.

Awareness of Light in Various Areas of the Visual Field
The child finds a stationary light when it is placed in all areas of the visual field. This step allows the educator to discover how the child functions in each area of the visual field.

Procedure
A light is presented in all areas of the visual field. Note the child's behavioral reaction (e.g., if the child turns the head or moves a body part toward the light). Notice where the child is physically able to localize the light. For example, if the child is in a spastic position, it will be necessary to hold the light where the child's head is facing. If the child is positioned differently, the area of localization may vary. Be aware that the child should not be in a stationary position only. If, for example, the child walks toward a light, encourage this response. The more the child purposefully moves, the greater the amount of sensory input is experienced, and the more the child learns about the body in space. Thus, the child can more fully integrate learning.

Activity 1
Materials. A flashlight and an adaptive chair.
Explanation. With the child seated in an adaptive chair, shine a flashlight in all areas of the visual field and note the child's reaction in each area.
Comments. It is crucial to vary the child's position to facilitate activity and to avoid surpassing the child's tolerance for stress. If necessary, the room should be darkened to heighten the contrast.

Activity 2
Materials. A hammock and a light.

Explanation. Swing the child in a hammock (after consultation with the physical therapist or the occupational therapist). Place a stationary light above the child and require the child to localize it while swinging from side to side.

Comments. Any time a light is used that is not self-contained, place a piece of plexiglass between the child and the light source to reduce heat and eliminate the possibility of an accident. Note the child's preference for different types of lights. A variety of lights should be used (different colors and intensities, translucent and transparent filters, and so forth).

Activity 3
Materials. Light.

Explanation. Shine a light on different parts of the child's body. Require the child to look at, touch, and name the body part on which light is shone.

Comments. Creating a gamelike atmosphere may increase the child's motivation and attention.

Attention to Light in Various Areas of the Visual Field
Once the child responds to a light presented in various areas of the visual field, efforts should be made to elicit a consistent response each time the light is presented.

Procedure
Repeat the procedure of the previous step but require a longer period of concentration.

Activity 1
Continue using the favorable light source, as discussed in the previous steps.

Activity 2
Materials. Light.

Explanation. Shine a light in various parts of a small darkened room. Require the child to locate the light either by looking at it or by touching it.

Comments. Although the child may attend consistently to light in most areas of the visual field, there may be areas in which the child never exhibits a response. This lack of response may or may not be indicative of a field loss.

Observe these areas and take into account the following:

1. The position of the child. Does the field problem change as the child is moved? This may suggest that the field problem is a result of a motor problem.

2. The type and intensity of light. Does the child exhibit field problems with some types of lights and not others?

3. Does the child show different field problems at different times? This may suggest that fluctuating vision is a result of the pathology of the eye.

Activity 3

Materials. Soap bubbles, food dye, and light.

Explanation. Blow colored soap bubbles near the child's face. Shine a light behind one bubble at a time and ask the child to point toward or put a finger through the bubble on which the light is shining.

Comments. If necessary, first demonstrate the activity and physically assist the child in breaking the bubbles.

Visual Tracking: Saccadic Eye Movements

Saccadic, or short, choppy, eye movements are indicative of an underdeveloped visual-motor system. As the child gains control of the motor system, the child also is better able to control his or her eye movements, which facilitates smooth visual tracking.

Procedure

Blink a light slowly along a line and require the child to follow the light. Present the blinking light in a horizontal, vertical, oblique, and then circular sequence. Gradually increase the pace of blinking along a line (e.g., blink, wait for the child's eyes to "catch up," blink, and so on until the child is following a rapidly blinking light. Increase the pace of blinking until the child tracks along a solid (nonblinking) line of light.

When teaching visual-motor skills, observe the following sequence (the sequence of these steps may be individually determined):

1. *Head-movement tracking:* the child moves the head alone or the head and eyes together. Observe the child's ability to utilize the neck and head muscles.

2. *Eye-movement tracking:* the child isolates eye movements from head and neck movements. Observe the child's ocular mobility.

3. *Head-and-eye-movement tracking:* the child moves the head and eyes in a coordinated manner. Observe the child's ability to coordinate head and eye movements.

Activity 1

Materials. Cardboard, paint, translucent and transparent filters, and light.

Explanation. Punch half-inch holes along a line on a piece of cardboard. Outline the holes with paint. Slowly move a light behind the cardboard. Experiment with various colors and transparent and translucent filters. Require the child to look at the light as it moves from hole to hole, to touch the hole through which the light is shining, and to name the color surrounding the hole.

Comments. Instead of starting a light at the far left, far right, or midline, begin presenting the light from whichever direction the child is looking. Then move the light toward the midline or side.

Activity 2

Materials. A xylophone and a light.

Explanation. Hold a xylophone at the child's eye level with the keys facing the child. Start moving the light from whichever direction the child is looking and move it across the back of the xylophone. Require the child to look at or touch the light as it moves between the xylophone keys. If the child is physically capable, encourage the child to press the keys as the light passes between them.

Comments. As the child tracks across the midline, observe eye movements and behavioral reactions. Does the child lose the light or experience such difficulties as blinking, sudden nystagmoid movements, jerking, or crying when attempting to track across the midline? If the child's position is changed, can the child still track across the midline? Consultation with the occupational therapist or physical therapist is essential to establish a working position for the child that facilitates bilateral integration.

Activity 3
Materials. A circular multicolored Christmas light fixture.
Explanation. Using a circular multicolored Christmas light fixture, with moving or sequenced lights shining behind color filters, require the child to watch the lights as they pass behind each color.

Visual Tracking: Smooth Eye Movements
The child, barring impairments in the motor system or the visual field, smoothly tracks a line of light in all directions.

Procedure
Present a moving light source horizontally, vertically, obliquely, and circularly and require the child to follow the movement of the light. When teaching this skill, observe the preceding sequence in the procedure.

Provide physical assistance, if necessary. At first, move the child's head in the direction of the light source. To facilitate eye movement that is independent of head movement, it may be necessary to hold the child's head. During the initial stages of tracking, the skills combine vision with the child's other senses. Allow the child to hold the light source as it moves and give verbal cues as to the direction of the movement. Gradually, remove these additional sensory cues and require the child to track by visual cues alone.

Activity 1
Materials. A record player and a light.
Explanation. Attach a light to the turntable of a record player. Turn on the record player and require the child to follow the moving light. Encourage the child to pick up the light.
Comments. If the child does not respond either independently or with physical assistance, present the activity in another way. For example, change the child's position and present the activity again.

Activity 2
Materials. A light or a light projector.
Explanation. Shine a light along a wall of a darkened room and require

the child to follow or touch the reflection of the moving light. Encourage the child to keep a hand or another body part on the reflection. Allow the child to shine the light on the wall and to move it in various directions; require the child to pay attention to the patterns made by the moving light.

Comments. Provide the child with appropriate light sources to encourage as much independent manipulation as possible.

Activity 3
Materials. Day-glo tape and a ''black'' light.

Explanation. Place a line of day-glo tape on the floor. Darken the room and shine a black light on the tape. Require the child to walk along the glowing line.

Comments. For some children, this activity may be a test of general motor abilities rather than of the ability to follow a light.

Awareness of Whether a Light is On or Off
At the beginning of the sequence, it was assumed that although the child was receiving visual stimulation, that stimulation was unorganized and meaningless. Therefore, no assumptions were made that the child knew what or where the light was. Previous steps in this sequence have dealt with the sensation or awareness of light. When the child was asked to localize the light, the concept of where the light was or was not, a dark or a light place, or the presence or absence of light was introduced. In this step, the concept of on and off is brought to the child's attention.

Procedure
A light source is presented and then blocked with an opaque material. Observe the child's behavioral response. Does the child visually search or reach out for the missing light, either independently or with guidance?

Activity 1
Materials. A light box (a wooden box with a translucent cover containing lights controlled by a dimmer switch) and opaque materials such as a carpet remnant, cardboard, cloth, and so forth.

Explanation. Place the child next to the light box and verbally or physically direct the child's attention toward the light. Then block the light by placing the opaque material over it. Allow the child to touch the material.

Comments. Light boxes such as those used by photographers are expensive. However, a light box can be made at relatively little cost.

Activity 2
Materials. A nondiffuse light source.

Explanation. Instead of a light table, use a nondiffuse light, such as a tensor lamp or shielded light. In a dark room, shine the light and ask or help the child to assist in covering the light completely. Then remove the cover and repeat the activity.

Activity 3

Materials. A light and containers with lids.

Explanation. Place the light in a container. Require the child to block the light from view by placing the appropriate lid over the container. Repeat the activity using containers of different sizes.

Comments. When teaching this concept, verbalize or sign "on" and "off" with each activity.

Attention to Whether Light is On or Off

As the light is repeatedly presented and blocked, require the child to demonstrate consistent visual attention.

Procedure

Repeat the activities described in the previous step but require longer periods of attention. Refinement of this step is necessary if the child is to integrate the concept of objects as blockages of light. By varying the size of objects, the environment, and the intensity of illumination, you can reinforce this concept. The step is further divided into three sections, which are treated as separate steps:

1. A gradual decrease in the size of objects blocking the light source.
2. A gradual decrease in the background illumination.
3. A generalization of activities with a variety of materials and in a variety of environments.

Gradual Decrease in the Size of Objects Blocking the Light Source

The light source is partially blocked, and the child is required to locate the object that is blocking the light. The size of the object is gradually reduced, requiring the child to demonstrate finer visual discrimination. The discrimination of contrast as a method of detecting objects is stressed.

Procedure

Partially block a nondiffuse light source with opaque material. Gradually reduce the size of the opaque material, which creates a concomitant increase in the area of light. Require the child to locate the object that is blocking the light. Allow the child to explore the object by touching it. Having sensory experiences with objects enables the child to integrate a more meaningful concept into the blockage of light and facilitates a beginning awareness of objects.

Activity 1

Continue the favorable activities used in the previous steps, and gradually reduce the size of the opaque material used. Note when the child begins to have difficulty locating an object. To require the child to locate an object beyond that point may be testing beyond the child's threshold of visual capability. Identify which is the minimum-sized object that the child still is able to locate. The minimum size is one of the clues to the child's functional visual acuity.

Activity 2
Materials. A nondiffuse light source, carpet remnants, and sandpaper.

Explanation. Partially block the light source by using the decreasing sizes of the soft carpet remnants and of the sandpaper. Provide tactile reinforcement by allowing the child to place and remove the remnants.

Comments. Stress additional sensory discrimination to enhance the awareness of objects.

Activity 3
Materials. A nondiffuse light source, cardboard, large puzzle pieces, small boxes, and cookies.

Explanation. Block the light source by using a variety of objects of decreasing size. Allow the child to touch, taste, and smell the objects, thus providing sensory reinforcement while reducing the size of the blockage of light. Be discriminating in the use of food as a primary reinforcer for visual activity. In some instances, food may not be the appropriate reward.

Gradual Decrease in Background Illumination
The intensity of the light sources should vary. Since there is a variety of contrast between an object and its background illumination in everyday life, the child needs to experience more realistic lighting conditions.

Procedure
Repeat the activities in the previous steps, but substitute light sources of decreasing intensity. If working on a light table, use a large carpet remnant to block the bright light. Gradually decrease the illumination. Then, use a smaller carpet remnant with greater illumination and gradually decrease the illumination until the child has difficulty localizing the blockage of light.

Activity 1
Continue the favorable activities used in the previous steps and gradually decrease the intensity of light. Note at which level of background illumination the child begins to have problems distinguishing objects, because a further decrease in illumination may be testing beyond the child's visual ability. Be aware of the lowest intensity of illumination at which the child is still able to locate the object or blockage of light. Knowing the lowest intensity of illumination and the smallest sized object gives you a more realistic idea of the child's functional visual acuity.

Activity 2
Materials. A nondiffuse light source, light bulbs of various wattages, and opaque material.

Explanation. When using a nondiffuse lamp, begin with a 150 watt bulb, then replace it with a 100 watt bulb. Continue to substitute bulbs with lower wattages (75 watts, 50 watts, 30 watts, 15 watts). Require the child to locate the opaque material partially blocking each light.

Comments. Use plexiglass between the light source and the child. Darken the room if further contrast is necessary.

Activity 3
Materials. Light and objects of various sizes.

Explanation. Present a variety of objects in various light sources of decreasing intensity (a photographer's light, a tensor light, a lamplight, a flashlight, then more diffuse light such as a room light). Require the child to locate objects in different conditions of gradually decreasing background illumination.

Generalization of Activities
To ensure the transfer of learning of this skill, make sure that the child experiences a variety of environments and materials to avoid a splintering of skills. For example, if the child is trained only in one activity such as finding a cookie on a light box and cannot locate other objects or cookies in different illumination, the child has not fully integrated the concept of an object as a blocker of light.

Procedure
Present a variety of objects (not necessarily of decreasing size) under a variety of indoor-and-outdoor-illumination conditions. Observe and note the child's awareness of or behavioral response to each situation. Does the child reach out, touch, walk toward, or smell objects presented?

Activity 1
Materials. An eating utensil.

Explanation. Hold the child's eating utensil up to a light. Require the child to retrieve it.

Activity 2
Materials. Balloons.

Explanation. Throw one or more different-colored balloons in the air and ask the child to retrieve or walk toward them.

Comments. Encourage the child to move and to interact more with objects. The more movement the child is encouraged to initiate, such as rolling, crawling, and scooting, the more the child will learn from the experience. Be aware that those children who cannot walk need to be placed in the most facilitative position and to have objects and lighting situations manipulated for them.

Activity 3
Materials. A bolster, balls, and blocks.

Explanation. Rock the child in a prone position over a bolster. Require the child to touch a ball or block while being thrust forward.

Comments. Use a variety of objects to broaden the child's frame of reference through experience with different objects.

Tracking Objects

The child with motor or visual field difficulties smoothly tracks objects in all directions.

Procedure

Present a moving object horizontally, vertially, obliquely, and circularly and require the child to follow the direction of the object with his or her eyes. Follow the same sequence listed under "Visual Tracking."

Activity 1

Materials. A transparent plastic tube (12–18 inches), oil, and marbles.

Explanation. Drop one marble at a time into a transparent tube filled with oil. Require the child to follow the marble as it moves through the tube. Then move the tube in a variety of directions, requiring the child's attention to the direction of the movement.

Comments. Efforts should be made to involve the child's other senses in the tracking activities (i.e., allow the child to manipulate the tube independently and, if applicable, to verbalize in which direction the marbles are moving).

Activity 2

Materials. Balloons and string.

Explanation. Suspend balloons at various levels and positions in relation to the child. Require the child to track the moving balloons and attempt to swipe them with a hand or a stick.

Comments. Vary the complexity of this task by changing the child's position (i.e., kneeling, supine, prone, sitting, and so forth). For children with limited motor ability, choose a position that will facilitate their postural security. Remember to provide contrasting background colors to avoid figure-ground confusion.

Activity 3

Materials. Wind-up or friction toys.

Explanation. Help the child to start moving the wind-up or friction toy and require the child visually to follow the moving toy.

Comments. Some children may rely only on auditory cues to determine the location of the toy. Encourage consistent visual attention.

Exploration of Objects with Movement

Once the child is attending to and tracking objects, efforts should be made to encourage further interaction with objects in space.

Procedure

Reaching for and moving toward light and objects is encouraged throughout the next activities. At this point, specific emphasis is placed on purposeful movement and manipulation of objects for the refinement of eye-body coordination.

Activity 1

Materials. An obstacle course with objects such as chairs, tables, mats, tunnels, slides, steps, barrels, and blocks.

Explanation. Guide the child through the obstacle course. Encourage the child to attend to colors, sizes, shapes, shadows, and the like. Emphasize the child's proprioceptive feedback while learning spatial concepts such as over, under, around, between, and through.

Comments. It may be necessary to help the child physically through the obstacle course. Continue to direct the child's visual attention to each object in the course.

Activity 2

Materials. A large box and large and small objects.

Explanation. Place the child in the large box filled with objects of various sizes. Encourage the child to move independently and to interact with the objects in this confined setting. Remove the box and gradually increase the play area (i.e., from a closet to a small room to a large room to outdoors) until the child generalizes the interaction with objects in a variety of everyday settings.

Comments. By at first playing in a more confined setting, the child is able to experience the control of close boundaries as well as the control of objects within those boundaries.

Activity 3

Materials. A variety of balls (e.g., a "cage" or large canvas ball, a playground ball, a volleyball, and small rubber balls).

Explanation. Roll a ball to the child and require the child to touch the ball and to return it using various body parts (e.g., hit the ball with the elbow, kick it with a foot). Repeat the exercise with each type of ball.

Comments. Initially, the child may need physical guidance to perform the correct movements because efficient eye-hand and eye-foot coordination are learned activities. Hand and foot movements should be directed into the child's functional field of view.

CONCLUSION

When the vision stimulation activities are completed, the child will be ready for visual efficiency activities. Once the child is able to track objects, the next task is to develop tracking skills with smaller targets as objects. These skills have to be integrated into the development of good scanning habits, which will allow the child visually to process information about the environment in an efficient way. As indicated earlier, the techniques described in this chapter may be applied to the evaluation of severely impaired adults. Assessments for the higher level child are discussed in Chapters 6, 7, and 17. Similar programs with recording forms can also be obtained from the "Functional Vision Inventory" by Langley (1981).

Bibliography

Bernstein, G. Integration of vision stimulation in the classroom. Part 1: Individual programming. *Education of the Visually Handicapped,* 1979, **11**(1), 14–18.

Bernstein, G. Integration of vision stimulation in the classroom. Part 2: Group programming. *Education of the Visually Handicapped.* 1979, **11**(2), 39–48.

Bernstein, G. Integration of vision stimulation in the classroom. Part 3: A total approach. *Education of the Visually Handicapped,* 1979, **11**(3), 80–84.

Ficociello, C. Vision stimulation for low functioning deaf-blind rubella children. *Teaching Exceptional Children,* 1976, **8**(3), 128–130.

Jose, R., Smith, A., & Shane, K. Evaluating and stimulating vision in the multiply impaired. *Journal of Visual Impairment and Blindness,* 1980, **74**(1), 2–8.

Langley, M. B. *Functional vision inventory.* Paper presented at the International Conference of the American Association of Workers for the Blind, Toronto, Canada, July 19, 1981. (Available from the Euclid Center of the Department of Education for Exceptional Students, 101 S Tenth Avenue North, St. Petersburg, Fla. 33705.)

CHAPTER 16

Assessment of Lighting

KENT CARTER, M.A.

Lighting is important to all aspects of the low vision service. This chapter reviews the principles of lighting and color vision. Incorporation of such information into the understanding of an individual's functional vision is discussed.

According to electromagnetic theory, light moves as a wave outward from its source like ripples in a pond. Moreover, visible light can be measured. Measurements of the length of each wave range from 360 nanometers (nm) to 760nm on the electromagnetic spectrum. (A nanometer equals 15 billionths of an inch in length; thus, if a light wave took one inch in space to make its complete rise and fall ripple, it would equal 15 billion nm.) Each receptor in the eye will accept a different wave length of light; for example, some cones may accept only a light wave measuring 550nm while others may accept only a 380nm light wave. Since three are over 125 million rods and 7 million cones in each eye (Lindsay, 1977), the eyes have the capacity for receiving countless millions of light waves of various lengths at any one time.

COLOR VISION

Hue or color vision is dependent primarily on the length of the light waves striking the cone receptors. The primary colors of *light* are red, green, and blue. In combination, they can produce all other colors. Any two colors that produce gray when mixed are complementary colors. Each color is produced by a certain wavelength of light. For example, when a blue light measuring 450nm and a green light measuring 540nm enter the eye and strike their respective cones simultaneously, one sees a mixture of the two colors, or a bluish-green. Each cone has a pigment that responds to these light waves. The red-orange pigment is called erythrolabe, and the yellow-green pigment is called chloralobe; although research has not proved their existence, blue pigment cones probably exist as well. A light source will appear to be white if it emits radiant energy that contains several visible wavelengths; an object will appear to be black if it reflects no wavelengths. Color judgments are based on the *mean* (average) wavelength of all the energy waves striking the cones simultaneously; therefore, the perception of color can be different from any one wavelength. Even though the lens of the eye disrupts various wavelengths, so many cones are responding at any one time that most people have no difficulty matching and remembering hues. There are various levels of color sensitivity in the human eye. As a person passes from higher to lower light levels, blue objects appear brighter than equally pigmented red objects (the reverse is true as the light levels increase). One study indicated that red was the most readily perceived color by all the persons tested (Geruschat, 1976). Thus, it can be surmised that the study was done in higher levels of light. The human eye finds color matching easier than identifying one color at a time, because identification requires preconceived perceptions and memory, whereas matching colors is a cone pigment response.

Color Vision Defects

Most individuals with color vision defects either have less sensitivity in the cones in general or lack pigment in certain cones. The lack of one color pigment type causes few problems in everyday life because most environmental hues are rarely pure in nature (e.g., green grass reflects some yellow and blue wavelengths of light along with the green wavelengths). However, the loss of two pigment types will leave the individual with only one color range and, therefore, everything will appear to be different shades of the same color.

As was mentioned previously, identification of colors is more difficult than matching colors. Therefore, in testing a visually impaired person for color vision defects, it is more effective to ask the person to match 10–15 different hues covering the length of the color spectrum than to name specific colors. Using dull paint chips of adequate size (2–3 inches square) or heavy, colored nonglare paper, the instructor can determine basic color vision information about the visually impaired person.

The Farnsworth D-15 Color Panel test, which requires the individual to arrange 15 different hue disks in a sequence through the entire color spectrum, is an effective clinical color vision test. Both the color-matching system just described and the Farnsworth test are best given in direct sunlight or under a daylight fluorescent lamp (the Macbeth easel lamp), since the full range of reflected light from 360nm to 760nm must be available to the eye for the appropriate cone pigments to respond. (Incandescent lights tend to emphasize the red end of the spectrum and to suppress the blue end.) In addition, figure-ground and contrast problems should be minimized by placing a dull black cloth on the testing surface to absorb unnecessary light waves.

Certain common physiological problems in the eye may affect the assessment and function of color during the evaluation process. For example, cataracts tend to act as a separate light source by scattering light in the eye. Once a lens has been removed, ultraviolet light (light waves beyond the normal visible spectrum in the range of 350nm) is no longer absorbed by the yellowish pigment of the lens and therefore enters the eye. Thus, a person whose lens has been removed may see ultraviolet light as a violet color and can easily see a test chart illuminated by an ultraviolet light in a room that appears totally dark to an individual whose lens is intact.

As a person ages, the yellowish color of the lens deepens, and visible light at the lower nanometer levels (from 380 to 480nm) is restricted from entering the eye so that violets and blues are not seen, which may be the reason that aging artists tend to use less blues and more reds in their paintings. If, in testing, it appears that an individual cannot match blues and violets, the low vision instructor should note this observation in the color vision assessment report so that the clinical low vision team is alerted to approaching cataract problems. Although the inability to perceive blue-violet hues tends to decrease dramatically by the high school years, it is important to recognize the potential problems of this lack of pigment response and to alert school personnel to restrict their use of "purple smudge" dittos for *all* children, not just visually impaired children. These studies also indicate that mimeographed black print on white paper or black print on yellow paper is the most effective material for all schoolage children to use in nearpoint tasks and that chalkboards should be black and writing should be done with broad white or yellow chalk (McCambridge, 1974).

ADAPTATION TO DARK AND LIGHT

As was already mentioned, the cones primarily are receptors of light that is converted into a hue by cone pigment reaction. The function of the rods is to increase the sensitivity to light or brightness. The cones adapt quickly to darkness but are not as sensitive to low levels of light as are the rods. For example, when a person enters a darkened movie theater from the outdoors, the cones will respond to the change in the level of light during the first few seconds or minutes by allowing spots of color to be seen and then to fade away as the rods take over and adapt during the next 10–15 minutes (McBurney, 1977). After about 10 minutes, the rods will reach a plateau in their adaptation process; during the next 20 minutes, they will fully adapt to the darkness. After the final adaptation to darkness, the cones no longer react intensively. Therefore, one can no longer recognize colors or distinct contours or discriminate lines; one can only recognize forms.

When a person returns to a lighted environment from a dark environment, he or she should be able to adapt rapidly (usually in about two to six minutes for the normal eye) because the cones respond and the rods become bleached out and therefore less sensitive to light. The light wavelengths of around 650nm (red light) do not seem to bleach the rods as much as other wavelengths. Therefore, goggles with red lenses that are put on before a person enters a dark room will allow the rods to react to the decrease in the intensity of light at the same rate as cones when a person returns to a brightly lit environment. For the same reason, the individual who has only useful peripheral vision may wish to put on red tinted glasses a few minutes before going out at night so the rods will adapt more quickly and the person will not have to rely on the long adaptation of the rods. Restricting light entering the eye to the level of 550 nm will reduce the bleaching of the rods and may help to mitigate the effects of glare and the intensity of light. The NoIR model 109 dark-green sunglasses can help the person who is extremely light sensitive to see more clearly with less sensitivity to glare because they decrease rod flare and allow a quicker response by the fovea (the rodless area of the retina) to images at other levels of light.

ENVIRONMENTAL ILLUMINATION ASSESSMENT

It is important to know what kind of lighting exists in the student's work or home environment. The assessment of the types of lighting used by the client for differing tasks is an environmental illumination assessment.

Just as the nanometer is the measure of light wavelengths, the lumen is the measure of the quantity of light a source provides, or its intensity, as expressed in footcandles of power. However, the eye does not react to direct light; it responds to reflected light expressed in foot lamberts. Brightness is another term for luminance.

Glare can be controlled by limiting the amount of light emitted in the direction of the eye (blinking or closing an eye) or by spreading the amount of light over a larger area. Reflected glare may be controlled by removing or reducing the materials causing the glare or by changing the characteristics of the glare-producing object.

Contrast is another factor that must be considered when doing an environmental illumination assessment. The Illuminating Engineering Society (IES) suggests that the eyes are most comfortable when the task is only slightly lighter than the surfaces that immediately surround it; however, this standard may not be acceptable to low vision individuals with certain types of eye conditions and pathologies.

Measurements of Brightness

A "footcandle" is defined as the illumination produced on a surface all points of which are one foot from a uniform point source of light of one candle and that is equal to one lumen per square foot. The footcandle is a measure of incident illumination, or the amount of light arriving on a surface. To obtain a footcandle reading on any surface, place the bottom of any light meter that has readings in footcandles against the surface so that the light strikes the cell filters or the meter eye. In taking such readings, make sure that the meter dial is either vertical or face up and that the multiplier switch is in the correct position for either high- or low-level readings. Also, do not allow shadows to fall on the meter eye. The light meter will provide information about illumination from the light source to the task.

To determine the illumination from the task to the eye (light reflectance), another procedure must be used. The procedure will be described after the following explanation. As was indicated previously, reflected light is measured in foot lamberts. A foot lambert is a unit of brightness equal to surface reflectance at the rate of one lumen per square foot. Therefore, the average foot lamberts on any surface are the product of the footcandles reaching that surface from a light source multiplied by the percentage of reflectance of that work surface. IES recommends the following reflective percentages for major surfaces in the home: ceilings, 60–90 percent; floors, 15–35 percent; and walls, 35–60 percent (see Table 1). To measure the brightness or reflecting quality of a surface or object, place the light meter at a distance where the reading remains constant (roughly 2–5 inches from the

Table 1. Recommended Percentages of Surface Reflectance

Area	Surface	Range of Reflectance (in percentages)
General		
	Ceilings	70–90%
	Walls	40–60
	Floors	25–45
Offices		
	Ceilings	89–90
	Walls	40–60
	Furniture	25–45
	Office equipment	25–45
	Floors	20–40
Residences		
	Ceilings	60–90
	Large curtains and draperies	35–60
	Walls	35–60
	Floors	15–35
Schools		
	Ceilings	70–90
	Walls	40–60
	Chalkboards	up to 20
	Floors	30–50
Industry		
	Ceilings	80–90
	Walls	40–90
	Equipment and desk tops	25–45
	Floors	20

SOURCE: Kaufman, J. E., & Christensen, J. F. *Lighting handbook*. 5th ed. New York: Illuminating Engineering Society, 1972.

surface). This reading is in foot lamberts. Divide the foot lamberts by the previously measured footcandles (from source to surface); the result will be

Table 2. Minimal Task Lighting[a]

Area or Task	Footcandles on Task
Food Services	
Cashier	50
Dining area	15–30
Quick service type	50–100
Food displays	50–100
Service Garages	
Repairs	100
Active traffic area	20
Storage areas	5–10
Hotels	
Bathrooms	10–30
Bedrooms	10–30
Front office	50
Libraries	
Reading area	30
Study area	70
Book stacks	30
Card files	100
Nursing Homes	
Corridors and ramps	20
Stairways	30
Lobby	50
Recreation area	50
Occupational therapy rooms	30
Dining area	30
Offices	
Accounting offices	150
General offices	150
Private offices	150
Conference rooms	150
Residences	
Dining room	15–20
Grooming	50
Ironing	50
Kitchen duties	150
Laundry	50
Reading and writing	70
Sewing	100–200
Studying	70

Area or Task	Footcandles on Task
Schools	
Reading printed material	30
Spirit duplicted material reading	100
Drafting	140
Lip reading	150
Chalkboard reading	150
Sight-saving rooms	150
Corridors and stairways	20
Home economics activities	70–150
Lecture rooms (general)	70
Shops	150
Study halls	70
Typing rooms	70
General Nearpoint Tasks	
Handwriting in pencil	70
Typing on white paper	20
Reading magazine print	35
Reading newspaper print	70
Taking shorthand notes	100
Bookkeeping	140
Reading a telephone directory	200
Medium grade assembly	250
Seeing white thread on black cloth	360
Seeing black thread on black cloth	1400

[a] Absolute minimum lighting for an individual aged 20–29 years with 20/30 vision.
SOURCE: Kaufman, J. E., & Christensen, J. F. *Lighting handbook.* 5th ed. New York: Illuminating Engineering Society, 1972.

the approximate percentage of reflectance. If a desk top has 100 footcandles falling on it and reflects 70 foot lamberts, the desk surface is approximately 70 percent reflective. Similar methods may be used to determine the transmission percentages of tinted and untinted lenses; however, since most manufacturers list the transmission percentages of their sunglasses, the methods for that type of measurement will not be discussed here.

With the foregoing information and a copy of IES's recommended illumination levels for tasks (see Table 2), the instructor can assess the environmental-illumination-per-task arrangement in which the visually impaired individual has been operating. For example, if a student has been assigned a seat for reading in which the average illumination above the surface is 10 footcandles and the IES has recommended 30 footcandles as a minimum for that task, then the instructor will need the clinical low vision team's opinion as to whether the student needs greater light on the task or some type of adaptive system for that task (e.g., reduction of luminaire to task distance, a yellow tint to increase contrast, or shading of the eyes). It must be remembered that IES's rcommended levels of illumination for tasks are only the minimal amounts; they do not take into account an individual's pathology and current eye condition (see Table 3).

Table 3. Luminance Needs of Visually Impaired Clients[a]

			Actual Tested Luminance Needs	
Patient[b]	Eye Disease	Lighthouse Functional Luminance Needs[c]	Foot-candles	Foot Lamberts
1	Juvenile macular degeneration	Average or dim light preferred	8–10	22
2	Senile macular degeneration	Bright, average, or dim light preferred	10	20–30
3	Senile macular degeneration	Bright, average, or dim light preferred	18–20	30–40
4	Senile macular degeneration	Bright, average, or dim light preferred	20	70 +
5	Senile macular degeneration	Bright, average, or dim light preferred	15	40 +

[a] Charted by general and specific luminance needs methods. Macular degeneration is used as the charted eye disease.
[b] Taken from actual case studies of the Maine Region IV Low Vision Services Program, Orono.
[c] E. Faye, MD. *A worker's guide to characteristics of partial sight* (a descriptive code). New York: Lighthouse Low Vision Research Division, 1978.

A useful tool in any assessment of nearpoint lighting is the *inverse square law:*

$$\frac{\text{candle power of source}}{\text{source to surface distance}^2} = \text{illuminance on the task}$$

If a light meter is not readily available, the instructor can take a footcandle reading by finding the lumens of power produced by a particular light source. (The lumens are usually printed on the light bulb package, or see Table 4.) One lumen equals one footcandle; therefore, if a 75 watt bulb produces 1180 lumens when new and the bulb-to-surface distance is 6 feet, then:

$$\frac{1180}{6^2} = 33 \text{ footcandles of luminance on the task.}$$

How does the low vision instructor translate this information in work with a specific visually impaired patient? The following will serve as an example. Suppose a visually impaired male patient works in the salesroom of a service station, for which work IES recommends at least 50 footcandles of overall light. However, the optometrist or ophthalmologist has indicated

Table 4. Incandescent Light Bulb Lumens[a]

Type of Bulb[b]	WATTS	LUMENS
Soft white bulbs	15	120
	25	190
	40	440
	60	855
	75	1170
	100	1710
Standard bulbs	40	455
	60	870
	75	1190
	100	1750
Soft white three-way bulbs	30	280
	70	1035
	100	1315

[a] One lumen equals one footcandle of illuminance at the bulb filament.
[b] Based on new General Electric bulbs.

that the lighting for the task should be increased. How can the light be increased? The choices are as follows:

1. Change the bulb to a higher lumens output bulb.

2. Reduce the task-to-bulb distance by lowering the light to four feet, thus producing 72 footcandles of light on the task area. This tends to be the best overall method if conditions allow it.

3. Provide supplemental lighting through portable lamps or illuminated optical aids.

4. Change the background so that contrast appears to change the level of illumination (percentage-of-reflectance method). For example, paint the countertop in a color that contrasts with the color of the sales slips the patient fills out.

By using the previously discussed foot-lambert measurements to substitute a better reflective surface through the percentage-of-reflectance method, effective illumination can be achieved. For instance, painting dark green walls a light cream color will change the percentage of light reflected in the room from 7 percent to 75 percent. Contrasts in nearpoint surfaces also can be helpful; for example, black on yellow provides roughly a 60 percent return of the source of light, whereas black on white reflects nearly 80 percent. Furthermore, although shiny surfaces provide a great amount of light reflection to the eye, they may need to be changed to control reflected glare.

Luminaires

Most low vision clinics recommend the use of 60–75 watt incandescent cool-shielded lamps or high-intensity reading lamps for nearpoint tasks. Incandescent lamps are best fitted with an inside frosted bulb because the so-called soft white bulbs diffuse the light too much and produce a substantially lower overall output of light than do inside frosted bulbs. When selecting an incandescent lamp, be sure that the shield is an air-cooled, double-layered type, since low vision nearpoint tasks often require the face and the lamp to be in close proximity. For nearpoint tasks, the lamp should be placed on the opposite side of the working hand or at the same side as the best eye. The bottom of the shade should be level with the reader's eyes unless the nose casts too great a shadow on the page or the amount of illumination needed requires a close bulb-to-page distance. High-intensity lamps tend to produce colored light that may be disturbing to some individuals, and their overall output of illumination is not as great as that of incandescent lamps.

Fluorescent lamps tend to produce stroboscopic effects when the eye is looking at an object illuminated by a single tube (McBurney & Collings, 1977). This effect can be eliminated when two lamps are used as a series-sequence circuit. The individual who is severely irritated by the flickering of fluorescent bulbs can wear red or pink tinted lenses, which tend to relax the periphery of the retina. Fluorescent lamps also tend to be noisy and cannot be dimmed as easily as can incandescent sources. Thus, it is preferable to use other types of lighting sources whenever possible. However, newer fluorescent bulb mixtures provide a balanced spectrum of light, particularly "Deluxe Phosphor Mixture" bulbs, whereas older bulbs tended to provide a stronger blue and green tint.

Taking light-meter readings in situations in which the photophobic individual indicates that the light is optimal can lead to the charting of ideal levels of illumination. The prescription of sunglasses that then restrict the transmission of light to the optimal footcandle level is the job of the low vision clinic.

OUTDOOR ENVIRONMENTAL LIGHTING ASSESSMENTS

Since outdoor lighting during daylight hours is usually adequate for visually impaired individuals in performing most tasks, the important aspects to observe are these:

1. The effects of glare on the patient's functioning (both direct and reflected types of glare).

2. The techniques used by the individual to combat excessive outdoor illumination.

3. The problems caused by rapid reductions in outdoor lighting.

4. The contrast and shading problems that deter recognition of environmental dangers.

5. The individual's functioning in dim illumination, as assessed during the evening hours.

Observing how the individual reacts to glare, such as a reflected window pane or a metal surface light, split-second reflections, water, snow, and so forth, will help the low vision instructor determine if outdoor illumination control devices are necessary. Does the individual utilize such light-deterrent techniques as selecting the shaded side of the street, shading the eyes with the hands, using an alternating sequence of inferior eye rotation or of alternating eye usage if binocular, maintaining close proximity to nonglare surfaces such as grass shorelines, or relying on nonoptical illumination control aids? Is veering a problem in situations where illumination changes rapidly? Do blended curbs, sidewalk pavement contrasts, and irregular shorelines cause excessive problems? Does the patient properly align the sunlight before looking at an object? Is the person utilizing too much tint for the situation at hand, or eccentric viewing or eye blinking under conditions of excessive glare? The clues are virtually endless, but each one presents a problem that can be solved or dramatically reduced through appropriate outdoor illumination control devices and training of the patient. Timing the individual's period of response to visual clues can be helpful because low light levels require a longer response to distinguish fine visual details than do high light levels, especially when the objects being observed are in motion (objects appear to move slower under low levels of illumination). If the person responds much more quickly and accurately to visual details under low light levels than under high light levels, the instructor should alert the clinical team so the team can carefully check for rod-cone dysfunction or visual field loss.

Light-meter readings are as useful in outdoor lighting assessments as they are in indoor assessments. Jotting down the patient's reactions and lighting measurements can lead to the prescription of appropriate sunglasses or other lighting control aids. Often the individual has taken it for granted that nothing can help reduce outdoor lighting problems, and will say little about this or other concerns unless faced with a difficult situation.

Data on outdoor illumination can best be obtained during the orientation and mobility evaluation phase of the overall low vision assessment. Additional information about outdoor low vision mobility evaluations is covered in Chapter 17.

References

Geruschat, D. *The effect illumination and color combinations have on the preferred viewing distance of partially sighted adults.* Kalamazoo, MI: Unpublished paper, Western Michigan University, 1976.

Kaufman, J. E., & Christensen, J. F. *Lighting handbook.* 5th ed. New York: Illuminating Engineering Society, 1972.

Lindsay, P., & Norman, D. *Human information processing: An introduction to psychology.* 2d ed. New York: Academic Press, 1977.

McBurney, D., & Collings, V. *Introduction to sensation-perception.* Englewood Cliffs, N.J.: Prentice-Hall, 1977.

McCambridge, S. Efficacy of color cominations on perception of educationally handicapped children. Greeley, CO: Unpublished dissertation, School of Special Education and Rehabilitation, 1974.

Nuckolls, J. L. *Interior lighting for environmental designers.* New York: John Wiley & Sons, 1976.

Scientific American, *Perception: Mechanisms and models.* San Francisco: W. H. Freeman, 1972.

Skoff, E., & Pollack, R. Visual acuity in children as a function of hue. *Perception and Psychophysics,* 1969, **6,** 244-246.

Stieri, E. Electricity in the home, 1962.

Zaha, M. A. Shedding some needed light on optical measurements. *Electronics,* 1972.

CHAPTER 17

Role Model for an Orientation and Mobility Instructor and a Teacher for the Visually Handicapped

CONNIE CARTER, M.A. AND FRANK JOHNS, ED.D.

This chapter shows how the information offered in this text can be used by an orientation and mobility instructor and an itinerant teacher. Some case histories are presented, along with a discussion of what services were provided and how they were delivered within the confines of the professions described. There is significant overlap in the low vision services provided by the two disciplines, so an arbitrary division of services will be represented in this chapter. For distance evaluations the O & M professional's responsibilities will be discussed, and the itinerant teacher will be the responsible professional for the classroom and near vision activities. The authors are aware that this is an unrealistic representation of the actual delivery of services. It is known that O & M instructors must often do classroom evaluations and itinerant teachers must perform some outdoor evaluations. Thus both professions can peruse the material offered in this chapter and use those suggestions pertinent to their professional training and service delivery responsibilities.

It is hoped that team members from other disciplines will identify with the principles of functional evaluation described here and will recognize the importance to the functioning of the entire team of these two professionals—as well as professionals from all the other disciplines involved. That is, an O & M instructor cannot adequately teach an individual with a low vision aid to travel independently unless the clinician informs the instructor of the function of the aid and why it was chosen for that particular person. Likewise, the itinerant teacher may have trouble understanding the reluctance of a child to use a new magnifier in class until the social worker informs the teacher of the child's high-risk home environment.

It is hoped that the ideas and their applications will be useful to all practitioners in the field of low vision, both in direct work with visually impaired patients and in the development of new programs and techniques that will ultimately improve low vision services. It should be noted that the sections on mobility are intended for use with both children and adults. The sections on the itinerant teacher, although obviously written about work with children, contains many ideas and situations that can easily be adapted for use with adults.

EVALUATION

Before starting a training program, visually impaired patients should be given a thorough low vision assessment and evaluation. The low vision workup should be both functional and clinical, and a variety of disciplines should be involved because normal acuity may vary, depending on visual conditions and environmental circumstances. The performance of visually impaired individuals in an O & M or educational program will be affected by many factors: visual condition, vocational status, physical condition, psychological set, family attitudes and so forth. Therefore, not only is it necessary to have a functional evaluation from the low vision instructor, but it is also essential to have the results of a clinical evaluation and information from the social worker, the rehabilitation counselor or special educator, the psychologist, and the family.

This section concentrates on the development of a thorough functional evaluation and discusses how information from other disciplines contributes critical insight into the establishment of the O & M or educational program. The following concerns will be addressed:

1. What needs to be considered in a functional evaluation?
2. When should the evaluation be done?
3. Where is the most appropriate setting for the evaluation?
4. What should be done with the evaluation data once they have been collected?
5. How does the O & M instructor plan an O & M training program or the itinerant teacher an educational program based on the evaluation data?

Since a complete mobility training program involves travel in various environments, distance evaluations also should be done in several settings—indoors and outdoors and in familiar and unfamiliar places, depending on the functional level of the individual. It is not necessary to evaluate persons in an area to which they never intend to go. Such an assessment would create anxiety and demonstrate that the evaluation had not taken the individual into account. Thus, it must be emphasized that the needs and functioning of the individual must be the key guideline in developing an evaluation.

Case History

Before the functional evaluation is begun, a case history is started. A case history includes data on the person's educational background, vocational status, living conditions, past and current health status, type of visual impairment and any other impairments, onset of the visual condition, medication and other forms of treatment, surgery, which is the better eye, lighting preferences, preferred viewing distances for near and far objects, current use of visual aids, self-perception of the ability to travel indoors and outdoors and in familiar and unfamiliar settings, motivation to use vision, and specific travel needs. (See Chapter 6.)

It is also important to include information from teachers, counselors, family, employers, and other involved personnel to determine the attitudes of these people toward the visually impaired person and what the person will have to confront as he or she attempts independent mobility. Such information helps establish a balance between the visually impaired person's view of himself or herself and the view of others. The case of JL may serve as an example:

JL, a man in his forties, seemed an ideal candidate for low vision service. He had been forced to leave his job operating heavy machinery two years before because of failing vision caused by cataracts (aphakic O.D., inoperable cataract O.S.). With his glasses, JL had an acuity of 20/400 O.D., but he had rejected the glasses as "not helping." JL was married and the father of three children in their late teens and early twenties all living at home. He had told his rehabilitation counselor that he would like to return to work, but that he could not see well enough to get to a job or to move around the work site once he was there. The counselor referred JL for a low vision work-up and recommended the investigation of a distance aid, especially a telescopic system, that would allow him more independent mobility.

After a case history was taken, a different picture of JL began to surface. JL talked about how much he enjoyed doing the household chores—cooking, laundry, and cleaning — while his wife worked outside the home. He felt as if he were really taking care of his family and they, in turn, took care of him by taking him for rides in the car, walks, and other excursions. This was, apparently, a side he had been reluctant to reveal to his vocational rehabilitation counselor, with whom he thought he should feign an interest in working outside the home.

In the environmental assessment, a Selsi 8X telescope was demonstrated. That telescope did not improve his acuity, but he was referred for a thorough examination to the low vision eye care specialist. The specialist could find nothing physical that would keep JL's vision from being improved with a telescopic device; however, JL's vision still did not improve beyond 20/400. During the examination, JL talked more about helping his family and how they took such good care of him. This input, combined with the information from the case history, made it clear that JL was afraid that a low vision aid would deprive him of his family's attention and force him back to work outside the home—something he felt he should do, but did not want to do. This information changed the direction of JL's rehabilitation program. The focus now was on helping JL and his family to adjust emotionally and functionally to JL's visual condition and helping JL become happier working at home.

Functional O & M Evaluation

With due consideration to the information obtained from the case history, the functional evaluation is started. If the person needs to be evaluated in various areas—residential, a college campus, business, indoors, outdoors, or a rural or urban environment—the evaluation is scheduled for several sessions to avoid overfatigue. A formal evaluation is done even if the O & M instructor has been working with the individual previously. Observations of previous travel situations can provide helpful support for the findings of the current evaluation. However, it is important to have a new functional evaluation that is as unbiased as possible and concentrates on the aspects of low vision. It is essential that the evaluation is done at night as well as during the day, especially if the person's visual condition fluctuates with different lighting. Certain behaviors are observed in all settings and under all lighting conditions:

Distances for identifying and avoiding objects. Note the size, colors, texture, and distance of objects that the individual identifies and then avoids. Can the person identify moving objects or only stationary objects? Is it easier for the individual to identify smaller or larger objects or objects on a particular side? Does the person try to identify objects tactually or auditorially before using vision? Does the person avoid objects smoothly or seem startled by them? Does the individual consistently bump into objects of a particular color more easily than objects of another color?

Determination of movement. At what distance is the individual able to detect the movement of traffic, pedestrians, and so forth? Can the person determine the direction of movement? Can the person identify the color, size, and other characteristics of a moving object?

Scanning patterns. Does the individual scan vertically or horizontally? Are the scanning techniques systematic or does the person jump from one area to another? Does the individual tend to scan more to one side than to another? Does the person set boundaries for scanning patterns, such as a window frame or that of a building?

Fixation. Does the individual look directly at an object or the side or slightly above or below the object (eccentrically view)? Does staring at an object cause nystagmus?

418

Landmarks used for orientation. What clues and landmarks does the person use for orientation? Are the clues primarily visual, auditory, olfactory, or kinesthetic? If the person uses visual landmarks, do they have a common characteristic—the same size, color, relative location, and so forth?

Posture and body movements. Is the individual's posture arched back or leaning forward? What seems to cause this type of posture—vision or another impairment? Does the person lead with a particular side of the body when moving forward? Does he or she walk slowly or fast? Is the person hesitant in certain situations—while climbing stairs, crossing streets, or moving in crowded areas? Is there a balance problem?

Head position. Does the individual's head tilt to one side or the other? Does he or she tend to look down all the time? Does the person constantly move his or her head in a particular pattern?

Viewing patterns. Does the individual always veer to one side? Does veering occur toward a visual landmark or in open space? Is the person able to use environmental aids to keep from veering (e.g., the grassline, crosswalk lines, building fronts, and traffic sounds and patterns)?

Use of color. Is the individual able to identify colors and shades of colors? Does he or she identify a particular color more easily than other colors? Is the person able to use color clues while traveling? How does lighting affect the ability to identify and use colors? Can the individual see certain colors at greater distances than other colors?

The actual routes on which the visually impaired person is taken depend on the areas available to the O & M instructor. No matter what routes are chosen, some type of indoor residential and business routes should definitely be established. The indoor route used in this case includes identification of objects in a room from a set point such as the door, objects of various heights, and stairs; a description of hallways; negotiation of doors; and navigation around objects in a room and in crowded areas. It is important to note lighting conditions and any of the behaviors just described.

Outdoor routes may be divided into residential and business areas. Again, lighting and any of the previously mentioned behaviors should be noted. Residential routes should be designed to allow for identification of shorelines, sidewalks, streets, curbs (note distances), discrimination of buildings, the location and use of street and building signs, and navigation of open spaces. The overlap of tasks performed on indoor, residential, and business routes, such as the identification of objects and the avoidance and negotiation of crowded areas, allows for good comparisons, especially if the tasks are done on different days when the person may be in a different frame of mind or when the eye condition may be at a different stage. The business route used includes movement in crowded areas, the use of traffic light-controlled intersections, the recognition of crosswalks and walk-don't walk signals, the use of public transportation, and the identification of moving vehicles and traffic patterns. In all three situations, the O & M instructor notes if

419

and under what circumstances the person is using a low vision aid, a cane, or other mobility aid; the ability to use sensory clues other than visual ones; and the use of depth perception and recognition of objects and landmarks while the person is moving.

In night evaluations, it is sometimes found that even though the individual seems to be using little vision during the day, he or she actually relies heavily on visual input when traveling at night. Furthermore, the O & M instructor should not forget to evaluate how the visually impaired person functions at near, such as in shopping and reading bus schedules and menus. Situations for evaluating functional near-point vision should be included as part of the evaluation routes.

Although it is not necessary for the low vision evaluation to be instructional, the O&M instructor may wish to give some limited instruction to determine how well the visually impaired person responds to it and to estimate how much time should be allocated for low vision and mobility training. The functional evaluation is done before the low vision clinic's examination. Therefore, the O&M instructor will be able to inform the clinical staff of the findings and perhaps aid the clinician in determining the appropriate optical system. If the instructor is present during the examination, he or she will be able to compare the person's performances in the clinic with the person's performance in everyday situations. Such a comparison may help prevent the prescription of aids that are doomed to failure because of the way the visually impaired individual functions outside the clinic.

With proper instruction and supervision, the O&M instructor may wish to do a low vision screening (this process is described in Chapters 5 and 6). The information gained in such a screening allows for an even better comparison between the clinic and the home or work environments because near and distance acuities and lighting conditions can be compared. It is by no means mandatory for the O&M instructor to gather these data. Moreover, low vision screening should not be attempted unless the instructor has had special training to do so and works closely with a low vision clinic.

The case of LF illustrates what is learned in a functional evaluation:

LF—a 15-year-old high school student—had Lawrence Moon-Biedl Syndrome and her visual condition was characterized by 3–4 degree fields, a 20/30 acuity in each eye, and poor night vision. She had requested mobility instruction because she had difficulty traveling at night. LF's itinerant teacher referred her for mobility instruction and recommended a low vision work-up.

A functional evaluation was done to determine which needs should be addressed in LF's O&M program and to gather pertinent information to share with the low vision examiner. LF was asked to give the O&M instructor a tour of her school and to locate various sections in a large department store for the indoor part of her evaluation. She was found to travel well indoors; she scanned effectively and remained visually oriented in unfamiliar areas. She exhibited a slight hesitancy on dimly lit stairways, but otherwise her travel was slow but safe and efficient. The outdoor evaluation was done by walking through the woods (since she lived in a rural area) and in the business area of the closest town. LF traveled well through the woods and had no problem with the actual visual negotiation of the town business area. Her difficulty was in a lack of conceptual knowledge of street and traffic patterns, traffic lights, the use of assistance from passers by, and the use of public transportation. Her scanning and obstacle avoidance were excellent. An additional night evaluation was done; LF was found to have adequate vision to travel well except in dimly lit areas.

From the information gathered in the functional evaluation, LF's mobility program was developed to emphasize travel concepts and night travel. She was taught to make maximum use of visual clues that she gathered as she scanned her environment and to use a cane only if she felt a need to do so. The low vision clinic considered this information and decided that her scanning patterns were so effective that she would not be a good candidate for field-expansion devices and that her night travel was adequate enough for her not to try the ITT scope. Thus, owing to a thorough functional evaluation and the O&M instructor's share of information with the whole low vision team, LF was given a low vision service designed for her and saved the frustrations of learning techniques she did not need and of using devices for skills she was already performing effectively.

MOBILITY TRAINING

After clinical and functional data are collected, the O&M instructor develops a mobility training program. Many aspects of a standard O&M training program may be included, but certain specific procedures and techniques should be incorporated for the visually impaired individual. This section discusses those particular areas and will assume that the reader is familiar with traditional O&M training programs.

The first step in establishing a low vision mobility training program is to teach the individual to use residual vision without low vision aids. Visually impaired persons need to develop several skills (scanning, blur interpretation, and tracking) to use their vision effectively. Although this step may take considerable time, it will make teaching the use of a low vision aid much easier and will be less frustrating for the individual. It also is essential for the visually impaired person to know how to use lighting conditions to the maximum benefit. Moreover, learning to know where things are supposed to be (such as street signs, traffic lights, and building numbers) is a slow process, particularly if the individual has never used residual vision. In essence, the person must develop a system by which he or she visually approaches the environment.

Another skill to be learned is the use of other sensory clues and information for deciding visual puzzles. For example, if the person smells the aroma of hamburgers and sees large yellow letters, he or she can be certain of having found McDonald's without deciphering each letter. Thus much time can be saved by knowing the environment and piecing together segments of information to help identify a location. Still another skill to be learned is how to find the viewing point best suited to the individual's eye condition and particular situation (eccentric viewing).

It would be ideal if these skills could be isolated and taught one by one until each has been mastered. Unfortunately, many of the skills overlap and thus must be learned simultaneously. For instance, it does not really benefit a person to know how to scan if the person does not understand his or her best viewing point or is unfamiliar with a visual approach to the environment. Therefore, the O & M instructor or itinerant teacher can concentrate on teaching a skill and providing information about how to approach the world in a visual manner. There are, undoubtedly, numerous ways to teach these skills; what follows here are the authors' guidelines to approaches and activities.

Visual Awareness

The first step in training is to help the individual become visually aware. This step may not be necessary for people who have been using their vision extensively, but, for most individuals, it is crucial. The itinerant teacher or O&M instructor stimulates visual awareness by presenting various targets at a distance at which the individual can comfortably see them with maximum clarity, and then gradually increasing the distance and reducing the size and contrast of the targets until viewing is less clear. Activities are provided that allow the person to learn to attend to (or be aware of) an object, to detect the movement of an object, and to fixate on an object. The instructor must be able to detect the development of those skills by critical observation. If, for example, a child becomes quiet when a large red circle is placed in front of him or her, the child probably is attending visually even though he or she may not actually fixate the circle. Presentation of such targets, especially ones that may have meaning for the person (a favorite fruit, shape, toy, piece of clothing and so on) will motivate the person to become visually aware and then to fixate on and identify objects.

With independent travel the goal, several environmental objects—such as stop signs, traffic lights, and building or product signs—may be used for identification. Although these objects may at first be presented in picture form, the individual is exposed to the real item as quickly as possible so he or she does not develop a log of misrepresented objects in the visual memory. As the person begins to build a large repertoire of identifiable objects, the instructor increases the distance at which these objects are presented and teaches the person how to interpret the relative blur seen at the new distance. For example, the person may learn what a stop sign looks like and be able to identify it while traveling, not by seeing it clearly but by equating it with what is seen— the red color with a white section in the middle or by a relatively round red-and-white sign. The ability to think about the environment and the types of objects that may be found will prove helpful in developing the skill of interpreting blurred objects; for instance, one is not likely to find a red-and-white Coca-Cola sign at an intersection; therefore, the sign must be a stop sign.

Identifying Objects and Symbols

As the visually impaired person becomes more visually aware, he or she learns to identify objects and then representations of objects (symbols); after these skills are mastered, the individual eventually develops a visual memory and has visual closure skills. During this process, the instructor observes the scanning patterns used to identify objects and teaches more effective techniques, if necessary. For example, the person may require a program that teaches him or her how to pinpoint the identifying characteristics of objects until the person is able to do so independently. The instructor starts off by presenting solid shapes of various colors and pointing out their distinguishing characteristics, such as the four corners of a square and the round ends of a cylinder with a tall portion between the ends. Once this skill has been mastered, the person can transfer it to identifying shapes in the environment —the square front of a building, a telephone pole, a mail box, and the like.

The second step is to learn to identify the representations of objects. Thus, the person will move from identifying an object to identifying a picture of the object. At first, the instructor presents outlines of the objects used in object identification—e.g., octagons, triangles, outlines of parking meters, mailboxes, cars, and buses. Then, the size and density of the objects are diminished and more inner detail is included in the representations. For example, the instructor may start with the solid shape of a house, progress to the outline of the house, and then add a door, windows, and so on. Finally, the size and density of the picture are diminished until the object is barely identifiable. It is important that these pictures have meaning for the individual. The rural inhabitant will be more inspired to learn to recognize a tractor than a city bus. Although it is important to expose him or her eventually to such urban objects, it is critical to begin the program with those objects that will prove most motivating. The third step is to identify pictorial figures and scenes depicting situations and actions. Again, scanning patterns and a knowledge of the visual environment and how it is generally represented are important. If the individual is congenitally visually impaired and has not been visually oriented to the environment and travels, it is helpful to begin with a tactile representation of a scene. The Chang mobility kit may be used for this purpose. With the kit, a cross-type intersection may be represented which the person can explore tactually and visually; then a picture of the intersection. In learning to identify the intersection, the person can begin to look for inner details—a street sign on one corner, a grass shoreline, crosswalk lines, and so forth. The same exercise can be done with a variety of scenes—a room, a hallway, a T-intersection, a department store, and a rural road. The individual should know how to analyze the scene depicted in each picture to gain the necessary information.

It may be easier for one person to identify things by shape and another to do so by color. What is important is that the person has some system for scanning the environment whatever system is chosen.

In helping the person develop a scanning system, the O&M instructor should teach the basic purpose of scanning—to view a total desired area in a systematic manner. One system is for the person always to be the initial reference point and then to scan from left to right because it is easy for an individual to remember to start consistently with himself or herself. However, other patterns may be better for certain individuals or in certain settings. The O&M instructor may prefer the person to start scanning doorways at the bottom left corner when looking for house numbers or always to start on the northeast corner of an intersection when trying to locate a street sign. Whichever system is eventually chosen, the O&M instructor should develop a variety of approaches to scanning the visual environment and teach the visually impaired individual how to scan.

The fourth step is to learn to identify the movement of people and vehicles in a picture. This step returns to the first developmental level of awareness when the person first became aware of movement. Now it is important to identify the movement and transfer it to the environment. Again, the need for a system arises. First, the person looks for movement while scanning the environment; then, if movement is found, the individual must determine how it will affect him or her. Is the movement toward the person? Is the individual on a collision course with the moving object? Is there a route that will avoid a collision? Is there a pattern of movement into which the person must fit? Is the observed movement extraneous to the path through the environment? What is the speed of the moving object? Such questions teach the individual to analyze scenes and actions. The O&M instructor can teach these skills by presenting the individual with increasingly difficult scenes to assess and negotiate. However, initially, the person should not be overloaded with details. The instructor should first present a room with only a few objects. Then increase the number of objects, then move to the hallway and to the rest of the building, and then move outside to basic residential travel. By asking the same question about movement in every situation, the O&M instructor teaches a system of approach. This allows the person to become familiar with areas so he or she will not have to rely on the assistance of sighted people in every new setting.

Solving Objects and Picture Puzzles

Internal representation of an object (visual memory) is a gradual process. One identifies an object or a place by assembling its components. For example, it is not necessary to see all the New York City skyline to identify it. Most eyes go quickly to the outline of the Empire State Building or the United Nations building and know the skyline is New York City. Certain features of an object, person, or scene yield the most information and thus are used for identification. The visually impaired person needs to be able to scan an intersection or a building line and identify the location by a particular sign, display, or window pattern. This skill permits more independent travel in new areas.

To develop this skill, the O&M instructor shows part of a simple sign or a picture of one object or building, such as a mailbox, a stop sign, a public telephone, and a parking meter. Slides of objects, some of whose parts are occluded, are a good training tool. Once the individual can identify objects in this manner, the instructor presents parts of larger areas—the person's room or office, a familiar building front, a classroom, a workshop—again in slides with a portion of each picture concealed. The instructor then teaches the identification of areas in the same way, by showing partly blocked-off pictures of an intersection, blocks, backyard, an office building and surroundings, a school yard and the like. Finally, the training proceeds to the real setting, where special emphasis is given to thorough scanning and to lighting. In the real setting, people tend not to scan the entire scene, especially after viewing pictures that allow a smaller scanning area. Thus, it is critical for the O&M instructor to observe the person's scanning patterns and to discuss the scanning boundaries needed to develop wide-area scanning. Particularly when outside, visually impaired students must learn to place themselves so the lighting will be advantageous to their viewing.

Lighting

Generally, visually impaired persons are taught to arrange the light source so it comes over the shoulder on the side of the better eye. The individual should be taught to arrange his or her environment to keep this lighting position both indoors and outdoors. If this is not possible, they learn how to shade their eyes with their hand. While this skill is being practiced in the environment, the settings should be kept simple with a few definite characteristics; as the person progresses, the settings can be made more complicated. Thus, the instructor starts indoor training in a small room that contains one brightly colored piece of furniture or a distinctive row of windows and moves gradually to larger rooms with more objects. With outdoor training, the instructor begins with one block that has a particular type of sidewalk (such as a grass pattern), a special kind of housing, or certain shrubbery. Training progresses to a simple, but distinct, intersection and then to more crowded and complicated areas. The pattern is much the same as an O&M training program for the totally blind except that instruction in visual skills is substituted for or added to training in auditory, kinesthetic and olfactory skills.

Identification of Abstract Symbols

The final step is the identification of abstract symbols—letters, words, and sentences. The adventitiously visually impaired person will no doubt have progressed to this step before O&M training, but it is still important to present tasks requiring this skill until he or she has successfully passed through the previous stages. The congenitally visually impaired individual probably will need to start with the basics in this area—discriminating shapes of letters, then progressing to recognition of one letter, to grouping letters together, and finally to reading.

The whole sequence of visual development, but especially this skill, should be closely coordinated with instruction at near point. Training can be done with slides, with a chalkboard, or with large contrasting posters. The itinerant teacher first teaches the discrimination of simple symbols, such as a line of "O"s with one "1" and proceed to more difficult symbols, such as "bbdb" or "cccee." The individual is taught certain letters—perhaps starting with those in his or her name and progressing to letters that will help in travel. After the person learns letters (visually), groups of letters are presented for identification; eventually the person learns to read words. (For maximum effectiveness, reading should be taught in conjunction with a reading specialist.)

The itinerant teacher should coordinate the teaching of reading with instruction in the use of context and environment in reading. That is, visually impaired persons should not have to read the walk sign to know that it is safe to cross a street. They should be taught to see "WA" and to combine those letters with the knowledge of where they are (location) and know it is safe to cross the street. In so doing, they have more time to cross the street because they spend less time at the curb trying to decipher the whole word. Once they are familiar with an area, they can apply the same concept to street signs, billboards, building signs, and so on.

This approach to the development of useful vision is most successful when the visually impaired individual goes through the same sequences in O&M and classroom training in other areas of rehabilitation, such as vocational training and personal management. Once again, the importance of the team approach cannot be overemphasized, and it must be noted that the most important member of the team is the visually impaired individual; without the person's motivation to learn, all training will be ineffective and frustrating. The following case example illustrates the entire evaluation and training approach for an O&M instructor or itinerant teacher:

> MS, a boy of 12, had been considered blind his whole life. All teaching methods, eye reports, parent conferences, and types of assessment had labeled him blind. When low vision and mobility services were introduced to his classroom, it became apparent from observation that MS was using many visual clues to travel and function

in the environment. For example, he always reached directly for whatever he wanted and never felt for steps. He knew no letters, numbers, or colors because he had always been taught as if he were totally blind. All the staff members who were involved with MS decided he might benefit from a vision stimulation program. The program began by developing MS's awareness of objects and of movement in the environment. At the same time, the counselor began to work intensively with MS on what was perhaps the most critical aspect of the program—whether he wanted to be considered sighted or blind. MS also was taught by his itinerant teacher object identification, scanning patterns, tracking, blur interpretation, symbol learning, color and letter identification, and eventually reading words and traveling simple residential routes.

There was close communication among all team members, and every member of the low vision team played an important role; for example, the parents relied only on what the low vision examiner said, and MS trusted only his counselor and would claim he could not see something with his O&M instructor that he had seen with the itinerant teacher. With much coordination, MS learned to interpret such blurs in the environment as water fountains (a white blur on the school wall), Coca-Cola signs (red and white signs in business areas), stop signs, and McDonald's golden arches. He also learned to use the Sonicguide™, which helped him to be aware of many more objects in the environment, to scan more thoroughly, and to define more exactly the parameters of his visual world. MS became excited about using his vision and being independent instead of using his blindness to manipulate others. He is now ready to undergo another low vision examination and, if it is prescribed, to learn to use a low vision aid to help him define his visual world even more clearly and to use it more efficiently.

USING A TELESCOPE

After visually impaired people have been trained to use vision without low vision aids, they may be trained to use an aid if it has been prescribed by the low vision clinic. Ideally, the instructor should be knowledgeable about the use of near and distance aids because many travel and classroom situations require both types of vision. However, this section will deal only with the use of the telescope—a distance aid.

Basic Information
The first step in training a person to use the telescope is to explain thoroughly how the device operates, what it is designed to do, what its limitations are, and the basic care and repair of the aid. Ideally, the person should receive this information at the low vision clinic. However, owing to time, the situation, or the type of facility, this does not happen and thus the full responsibility for this part of the training falls to professionals outside the clinic. Furthermore, even if the client has received such information, the O&M instructor should repeat the instructions to clarify any questions the person

may have and to be certain that he or she remembers and understands the functions of the aid. Usually, visually impaired people are too excited by their visit to the clinic and by being able to see objects at a distance that they do not really hear the explanation of how such a magical device functions. The O&M instructor should know the purpose for which the aid was prescribed and should try out the aid with the same tasks that the person will be performing. In this way, the instructor will come to understand some of the problems, benefits, and limitations of the aid before training begins.

How the telescope operates. First, the O&M instructor explains that a telescope moves objects closer to the person by enlarging the retinal image. The same effect could be accomplished by making the actual object larger or by moving closer to the object. A telescope is the only optical method to improve distance acuity when standard spectacles are unsuccessful. The telescope has a restricted field of view that usually increases with greater magnification (a 2.5X telescope placed 12 millimeters from the eye allows an 8–10 degree field). Therefore, the telescope should be used primarily as a spotting device because its spatial-distortion characteristics make full-time viewing difficult. The instructor then shows the range of focus for the particular device and tells the person that the aid should not be used to view near objects. The instructor also demonstrates how to focus the telescope and which end of the scope should be held next to the eye. It is helpful to give both visual and tactile information so the individual can choose the easier way (e.g., the rough edge is what you turn to focus or the bumpy ring goes next to the eye).

Next, the O & M instructor explains that the device should be cleaned with a soft dry cloth, not tissue paper, to avoid scratching. Children especially may find it helpful if a rawhide shoelace or lanyard strap is attached to the telescope so it can be hung around the neck and hence can be more accessible.

Holding the telescope. The visually impaired person is then taught how to hold the telescope properly. The individual is encouraged to sit next to a table or other support for his or her arm so the device can be kept steady; there will be no unnecessary movement of the object being viewed, and fatigue can be avoided. The instructor uses the clinically measured visual fields to determine the position that will best utilize the person's maximum vision (e.g., central foveal focus, eccentric utilization, null point of fixation for nystagmus, and so forth). Sometimes it is helpful if the instructor paints a white ring around the aperture of the aid to allow the individual to locate the opening more easily. If the person is using the telescope and spectacles simultaneously, a thin circle of felt or a small circular pad used for corns on the feet, when placed around the aperture, will prevent the glasses from being scratched by the telescope. The instructor tells the individual to fit the device into the palm of the hand, using the thumb as a support and wrapping the fingers over the top. The telescope should be held as close to the eye as possible to black out extraneous light and to procure the best field; the hand on the same side of the body as the better eye is used to hold the telescope, and the elbow is kept close to the body to allow for firm support.

Introduction to the classroom. First, it is important to try the device in the classroom when there are no other students around, such as before or after school, during recess, or at lunch time. In this way, the student is free to move around the room and discover best viewing positions for various tasks (blackboard viewing, flash cards, overhead projectors, and so on). The itinerant teacher informs the classroom teacher of these positions and lighting factors and encourages the teacher to take the telescope home for a night to use it and thus gain an understanding of the functioning and frustrations of the device. When the child is ready to use the device consistently in the classroom, the itinerant teacher and the child should discuss the best method for introducing the aid to the child's classmates. The child may prefer just to appear with the telescope and handle the questions as they arise or to have the classroom teacher explain the telescope; a young child may wish to include the aid in "show and tell." What is important is that the child is comfortable with the way the device is introduced.

Because of regularly scheduled teaching sessions, the itinerant teacher is in a unique position to develop and institute a sequential training program to promote comfortable and effective use of the optical aid. A good working relationship between the itinerant teacher, the student, parents, and school personnel helps to provide direction, support, and realistic goals for the training. In addition, Table 1 lists a number of activities that can be easily incorporated into the classroom. It is imperative that the teacher be alert to any possible problems which would necessitate a re-evaluation of the child or follow-up services. The case of DB illustrates the need for classroom intervention:

> DB, a fourth-grade student, had a visual acuity of 20/200 and a diagnosed eye condition of marked myopia and astigmatism. A 6X-8X monocular telescope was prescribed for distance tasks, but DB was given no training in its use. DB was still not using the telescope a year after it was prescribed. The itinerant teacher found that although DB seemed excited about the aid and said it was useful in a variety of settings, his teachers reported that he was not using it in school. The itinerant teacher discovered that the telescope was not working properly; DB did not know that; he thought the aid was working "just fine."
>
> A training program (three 45-minute sessions per week for three weeks) was initiated with the support of DB's teachers, parents, and classmates. After he completed training, DB became proficient with the telescope and used it for chalkboard work, travel situations, and the operation of an athletic scoreboard.

Introduction to the work environment. As with the classroom, the telescope should first be used in the work environment when no other workers are around so the individual may experiment freely without being embarrassed or interfering with the work being done. If the device has allowed the person to move to a different position or to begin employment in a new setting, the initial training for the task may be done in a simulated environment. Once the individual feels comfortable in performing the task with the device, the employer should be briefed on how the telescope functions, especially how it helps the visually impaired employee to perform the task he or she was hired to do. This may be done by the visually impaired individual, by the itinerant teacher, the O & M instructor, by the counselor, or by whoever the visually impaired person chooses and in a way that is most comfortable for the person. If possible, the device should be explained to the other workers, who may wish to try it so they understand better how it helps the employee to do the job.

To focus the device, the person uses his or her free hand to reach over the device and grasp the focus knob from above. Minute changes can be made quickly in this manner. On the first lesson, the instructor focuses the device first so the individual does not become frustrated by a blurred image. The student may need to make minor changes to obtain maximum clarity, but the image should be basically in focus.

Training in the use of any low vision aid is essential because without directed practice, the frustration of using an aid too often causes the aid to be discarded. The specific verbal and printed information that is provided when an aid is dispensed does not seem to be enough; success seems to be dependent on frequent contact with and intervention from knowledgeable personnel, particularly at the time of a problem. Experience has shown that frequent training within the first few weeks (at least two times per week) will give maximum support for both the psychological and technical aspects of using an aid.

Indoor Training

Training begins indoors, and the initial tasks are designed to generate immediate success. The first sessions are short so the person does not tire or become discouraged. Three-to-five-minute sessions, followed by a half-hour rest period, have proven to be the best time span at first. As the individual develops greater endurance and the use of the telescope becomes more habitual, the length of sessions is increased.

Setting. A 12-by-15-foot room that is sparsely furnished makes a good beginning training setting. The individual is seated at an angle that allows the best light on the object being viewed; that is, the light is above and behind the person at a 45-degree angle on the side of the better eye. If direct lighting on the target is necessary, a high-intensity lamp is placed a short distance away and is directed on the target.

Target. A target with a dull-white background and good contrast is chosen. One often-used target is a large poster board with an object painted in dull black outline. The size of the target should represent one line above the last line seen on the eye chart to be certain that the individual will be able to see it; thus, if the person saw the 10/20 line on the clinical chart, training should begin with the 10/25 line. Possible targets and their relative sizes include playing cards (10/20), jumbo playing cards (10/30), and shuffle book cards (10/25). Training is begun at 10 feet with a stationary target. The person is taught to spot the target with the naked eye, to hold it in view, to then bring the aid to the eye, and then to read the target. At first, it is helpful to use a target with an auditory clue, such as a beeper ball, a radio, a goal locater, or a ticking clock to help the person locate the target more easily. When the individual can identify targets at 10 feet, the instructor flashes targets while moving around him or her at various angles and distances. This activity requires continuous spotting and focusing. The person locates the instructor and the target with the naked eye, brings the telescope up to the eye (or lowers the head if using a bioptic system), focuses the scope, and reads the target. As the individual becomes more skilled in this activity, the instructor varies his or her position and the target size so the person has to move to obtain the best lighting and viewing conditions. With children, this level of training is presented as a game; points or tokens are awarded to the child for each correctly identified target; for each target the child names incorrectly, the instructor receives a point.

Tracking skills. Once the individual is able to locate and identify stationary targets, the instructor begins to teach tracking or shorelining skills. Instruction in tracking initially involves two stationary targets that are placed at an equal distance from the visually impaired person and about four or five feet apart. Between the targets should be a shoreline, or border, that contrasts sharply with its background. Appropriate shorelines include wainscotting, the top of a couch, white adhesive tape on a dark wall, or dark tape or ribbon on a light wall, and the eraser shelf of a chalkboard.

The first tracking exercise is to (1) locate one target with the naked eye, (2) view it through the telescope, (3) follow the shoreline with the naked eye to the other target, (4) bring this target in view, and (5) spot it through the telescope. The person learns to move the head (not the eye) because eventually the shoreline will be followed through the aid. The second tracking exercise involves seeing the target with the naked eye and then through the telescope and following the shoreline with the telescope to the next target. These two tracking exercises use a left-to-right movement, which is the pattern used for reading and thus is probably the most familiar to the individual.

The next step in tracking is to follow a moving target. The instructor holds the target and walks slowly from left to right; the visually impaired person watches the instructor through the aid. The instructor should talk while moving to give an auditory clue to the individual who may temporarily lose sight of the target as it moves. At first, the instructor should move in a circle so the focus can remain set and the person only has to be concerned with following the target and not with focusing the aid. Once this skill is perfected, the instructor moves backward and forward, gradually increasing his or her speed and varying the distance from the individual; this type of movement requires the person to focus the aid while tracking. After that skill is mastered, the advanced student practices identifying changing moving targets; the instructor changes the target (from playing cards, to pictures, to flash cards, and so on) as he or she walks across the room, and the individual is required to identify each moving target.

Proficiency in these skills usually can be achieved in two weeks if the training is done every day, although the time may vary, depending on the individual. The person must understand how the telescope functions and be competent in its use before he or she is allowed to use it unsupervised in the setting for which it has been prescribed. If the individual is not proficient in its use, embarassing and discouraging situations may arise. For example, the person may be asked by friends or family members to perform a task with the telescope of which neither the person nor the aid is capable. A child may be asked to identify an object that is too close to be viewed through the telescope, or an adult may be asked to tell what the referee of a football game is doing before he or she has learned to spot or track a moving target. Thus, it is best for the O & M instructor to work daily with the individual and to teach the person to use the aid only during lessons or when practicing the skills worked on during the lessons. With children, it may be best for the instructor to keep the device until they are able to use it proficiently.

As part of the initial training, the instructor should explain the telescope's functioning, repair, and care to the person's family, teachers, supervisors, counselors, and employers. Since these people will praise, criticize, and help motivate the individual in the use of the aid, the more knowledge they have about it, the more supportive they can be as the person incorporates the aid into daily activities. The following situations merit a special discussion of the ways in which the telescope can be integrated into the individual's life.

Outdoor Training
Outdoor training follows the same sequence as indoor training. Even though the skills of spotting and tracking already have been developed, the new environment is vast and should be approached slowly and systematically. In presenting the initial target, the instructor should start with a solid background, such as a building wall or a house. A target held against an open space will be much more difficult to pinpoint. Presentation of targets appropriate for outdoor travel will allow the individual to become familiar with them before actually encountering them in the environment. Therefore, street signs, house numbers, license plates, trash cans, and people all make good targets. In addition, targets that can be recognized by shape alone, such as fire hydrants, yield signs, and stop signs, help reinforce blur-interpreta-

tion skills. The lettering on street signs is approximately 20/200 and usually provides good contrast.

In establishing proper viewing distances, the instructor should remember that an average street is about 40 feet wide. Once the individual feels capable of locating and identifying targets and tracking moving targets outdoors, the instructor can teach the basic skills that are pertinent to travel in the environment: the identification of street signs, house numbers, street lights, traffic lights, bus numbers, and so forth. As in indoor training, the outdoor settings for use of the telescope move from the simple to the more complicated. Thus, the instructor starts training in the location and reading of street signs in the person's residential area. If the individual's vision is adequate, he or she should stand on a street corner and scan the intersection (all four corners) with the naked eye to locate poles and street signs. If the person cannot see well enough to do so, he or she should use the telescope for scanning, being certain that the arm is held close to the body to provide maximum stability of viewing through the scope. The training sequence is designed so the pole initially is on the same corner as the individual, to make location easier. Then the street sign is moved to the opposite corner, to the side corner, and eventually to the diagonal corner. Although the person may not be able to read the diagonally opposite street sign because of the greater distance, he or she may at least locate it and travel to that corner to read the name of the street. After the pole is located, the individual can follow it to the top and move the telescope into position for viewing. (If the itinerant teacher initiates this training, it is best if it can be in consultation with the student's mobility instructor.)

Locating the pole. Several techniques can be used to locate the pole. For example, the person may scan the shoreline between the curb and the street for a pole—a particularly good technique if the curb and street are of contrasting colors. If the pole is on another corner, the individual may follow the crosswalk lines to the appropriate corner and then scan for the pole. In a business area, the person can lean against the building edge and scan the building line to look for the sign. As they begin to travel more extensively, visually impaired students are instructed to look for patterns in placement of street signs that will make it easier for them to locate the signs, e.g., the street signs are always on the northeast corner or are always in front of the stop sign. Knowledge of these patterns will save time and, particularly in busy areas, prevent unnecessary interference with pedestrian traffic.

Locating house numbers. The individual must first understand that each house has its own number, that even and odd numbers are on opposite sides of the street, that house numbers are sequential in ascending and descending order, and that house numbers are grouped in blocks by tens, one hundreds, and so forth. The student should also be familiar with the possible position of house numbers on a house, such as on either side of the door frame, above the door, or just below the top step.

The next step is for the instructor to choose a house whose number is clear. (Before selecting a house to be used as a training location, the instructor should ask the inhabitants for permission to use the house so they will not become alarmed and call the police to report "peeping Toms.") The visually impaired person then stands in the middle of the front of the house and uses the grassline or path to the house to locate the door visually with the naked eye, if possible. Once the door has been found, the individual systematically scans around the frame, always starting in one spot on the frame, e.g., the bottom left, and always proceeding in the same sequence—whatever sequence is chosen—until the number is found. One such procedure is first to scan the frame, then the door from left to right and from top to bottom, and then the step area. If all else fails, the person should look for any shiny objects (a metallic house number) and sight it through the telescope.

Traffic lights. A method similar to that used for locating street signs is used to locate traffic lights and walk–don't walk signs. The individual first finds the traffic-light pole, paying special attention to its color. Then, he or she scans up to locate the light. If the person is unable to tell which light is lit at the time, he or she views the light until a change occurs. The walk–don't walk signs are located by continuing downward past the traffic lights. Once these are located, the individual maintains fixation to be able to detect when the sign changes; valuable time will be lost if the person lowers the telescope and then raises it to again find the sign when he or she suspects it is the correct time to cross. The person also should learn to use and listen to traffic patterns when crossing streets as a back-up check of the telescopic system.

Bus numbers. Before the individual is taught to locate and read bus numbers with the telescope, he or she must be proficient in tracking moving objects. Therefore, the O&M instructor begins outdoor training in this skill by teaching the person to follow people who are traveling at a slow speed. This activity is first done in an isolated area and gradually moves into more crowded areas. It is important to instruct the student to pick an identifiable characteristic, such as an orange coat or a wide hat, to view and track through the telescope. The principles involved in tracking people are then applied to tracking cars and buses. To locate and read a bus number, the person stands at a fixed location, such as against a post or building, where the arm that is holding the telescope can be supported. The individual looks through the telescope at a landmark about 60 degrees from the curb and just above the traffic—a height that is approximately that of the bus sign. The person then listens for the bus, keeping the focus at infinity. As the bus comes into view, the individual tracks it until he or she has read the number or name of the bus. Obviously, only a sophisticated telescope user can acquire this skill. Those who do not reach this level or who do not like to track buses may prefer to ask a pedestrian for help or the driver of each bus. Thus, although the individual is exposed to the visual method, he or she does not have to use it in this case.

Hints for Effective Viewing

Becoming familiar with a room, viewing a concert, looking out a window, watching television, and obtaining visual information as a passenger in a car are just a few of the many tasks that can be performed with a telescope. Since all the tasks cannot be covered here, the following general hints for viewing through a telescope are provided that can be applied to all situations.

Viewing is most effective from a stationary position.

- The O&M instructor and the student should discuss how a route is planned and how the plan is put into practice. For both indoor and outdoor travel, the person should assess lighting characteristics, viewing positions, negotiation of crowds, and other pertinent factors as he or she plans a route from one point to another. For example, because of the sunlight, it may be better to walk on one side of a corridor or street in the morning and the other side in the afternoon.

- As with any mobility or vision stimulation program, the person must be encouraged to think about the objects that may be found and their possible location in the environment.

- If an individual's vision is severely limited, outdoor training should begin with large signs and move to smaller objects as training progresses.

- The telescope may be used to check for a clear path during travel by scanning from wall to wall or building line to street and back at the beginning of the corridor or block and again at the midpoint.

- To become proficient in using the telescope, the individual must practice a great deal.

- The O&M instructor should encourage the person to use the telescope and should help the person to think of new ways to use it.

The case of DL shows the effects of telescope training on the life of a visually impaired person:

DL, a 23-year-old woman with retrolental fibroplasia, was a braille reader and had functioned as blind all her life. When a low vision service was introduced into her area, the vocational rehabilitation counselor referred her for an evaluation. The evaluation found that with a good and thorough refraction and 8X microscopic glasses, DL was able to read regular typewritten print. With a 4X Huntscope her C.F. 2-feet acuity was improved to 20/80. DL underwent several sessions of training at nearpoint from the clinic staff and made excellent progress in reading. She even made arrangements with the local library to keep books longer than the usual two weeks without paying a fine. However, DL received no training with the telescope. Several months later, when asked by the O&M instructor if she found the device useful, she replied that she never used it because it seemed too much of a bother and she did not think she needed it.

DL began an O&M training program that incorporated a vision stimulation program. As she became better able to use her vision at distance, training with the telescope was begun. After several sessions, it became apparent that the 4X telescope was not strong enough for the tasks for which DL needed and wanted it: reading street signs, reading house numbers, reading signs in grocery store aisles, and so forth. Therefore, she returned to the clinic and received a 6X telescope that, with training, has allowed her to read street signs from the opposite corner and house numbers from the sidewalk. She is also able to read signs above the aisles in a large discount supermarket so she is no longer dependent on the high-priced local small grocery store. With training she has become as motivated to use her distance vision and aids as she has her nearpoint visual system.

Near Point Activities

The itinerant teacher should ensure that the child's reading habits do not interfere with the placement of the aid. The types of aids that may be used for nearpoint activities are:

1. Stand magnifiers. Either the fixed-focus or focusable types should be placed directly over the object being examined. They rest on the page and can be viewed at a normal viewing distance except in cases of high magnification when the viewing distance is reduced to obtain a maximum field. Increased illumination is generally needed.

2. Hand-held magnifiers. They should be placed over the object or against

Table 1. Nearpoint and Distance Games and Activities

Tic-tac-toe
Crossword puzzles
Flash card bingo
Dot-to-dot
Mazes
Matching of likenesses and differences
Puzzles
Riddles
Object lotto
Picture lotto
"What's missing?"
Story cards
Sequential picture cards
"Hidden objects, pictures"
Peg board
Reproducing patterns
Parquetry blocks

Near Point Games at a Distance
Cards
Tic-tac-toe on the chalkboard
Letter recogniton on the chalkboard
Crossword puzzles on the chalkboard
Dot-to-dot on the chalkboard
Mazes on the chalkboard
"Hide and seek"
Flash card bingo
"What's missing"
Object identification

the eye. The lens should be held steady and parallel to the object, and the eye should look through its center. Resting one's arm on a desk and keeping the wrist stiff and the side of the hand resting on the desk will help to steady the magnifier. The magnifier should be moved off the material to that point which gives good magnification but no distortion. Increased illumination is rarely needed.

3. Spectacle magnifiers. They may be desirable in that they free one's hands and provide a wide field of view. They are particularly suited for prolonged reading. Material should be held parallel to the face, at a distance that will allow a clear image. Increased illumination may be needed. A clip-on occluder will prevent interaction.

As with telescopic aids, trainingshould proceed in a sequence:

Spotting

1. With the naked eye. Have the student identify individual letters, shapes, and pictures within a border on a card. The purpose is not to locate objects but to identify them; therefore, objects should be within the viewing area. (Assistance may be needed.)

2. With the aid. Begin by having the student spot objects and symbols that are directly in the viewing area. The objects should be large enough so they can be seen clearly, yet not so large that they cannot be seen in their entirety without moving the aid. Individual letters, pictures, shapes, and objects can be used. The purpose is to help the student understand the aid's characteristics and the correct operating techniques.

Tracking and Scanning. When the student is able to operate the aid properly and spot objects, tracking, and scanning techniques should be taught.

1. With the naked eye. Begin by having the student follow a line of good contrast (with a shape, letter, or object at either side) from left to right. Games may be played that incorporate this technique, such as Spot the Dog (lefthand margin) and the Show Me the Way to the Dog House (righthand margin). Gradually increase the number of lines per page and vary the activities. Teach students logical search patterns that will enable them to view the complete page. Instruction in left-right movement, the scanning of margins, and the format of a printed page (margin, paragraph design, location of page number, type of print) will increase adequate page coverage. A difficult but worthwhile exercise is to cut a printed page into pieces and have the student assemble the page based on clues derived from a knowledge of the format. Teach the student techniques that will help him or her locate succeeding links. At first, it may be necessary to have the student mark each line after it is read. Numbering lines in sequence may also help the student to locate succeeding lines, as will a finger, a line marker, or a typoscope.

2. With the aid. With the aid, have the student perform the various activities completed without the aid. If the magnifier being utilized is strong (8X plus), make sure the student arrives at a proper working distance and moves the book or page rather than the eyes or head. Especially with spectacle aids,

it is important to maintain a constant working distance and keep eye and head movements to a minimum.

Interpretation. After the student has mastered the previously mentioned areas, concentrate on activities that involve the interpretation of what is being viewed. These activities should relate to the student's overall goals. If the student's goal is to be able to read standard-size print, initiate a reading program.

In this instance, the training program will necessitate that the itinerant teacher work closely with classroom teachers and possibly with the school reading specialists because the reading skills for the student low vision training program should concentrate on the recognition of words utilizing content clues, not with developing reading skills. Print sizes should gradually be diminished, and a variety of types included. If the student's goal is to be able to read the card catalog in the library, make up sample cards. Initially, introduce large letters, words, and numbers. Instruct the student in format of catalog cards to help him or her locate the needed information. Gradually reduce the size and increase the amount of information on each card until actual catalog cards are introduced.

SOME QUESTIONS ABOUT TRAINING

The following discussion raises and answers three questions that frequently come up during O&M training.

Use of the Long Cane

Should an O&M instructor encourage a person with residual vision to use the long cane? This question cannot be answered generally because whether such use should be recommended depends on the amount of vision an individual has, how well the person uses information from the other senses, and how the person feels about vision and use of the cane. If the instructor thinks that a cane will interfere with the individual's use of vision, perhaps it is better for the instructor to concentrate on the person's vision and to introduce the cane later when the individual feels comfortable about using vision. However, if the individual feels insecure about relying on vision for safe travel, the O&M instructor should encourage the person to use a cane so the person will be relaxed enough to use vision in a supplementary way. In some cases, it may be appropriate for the person to use a folding cane only in certain situations, e.g., approaching steps, at street crossings, in department stores, and the like. The list of possibilities and exceptions is endless. There is no rule except that at all times the person's dignity and safety must be top considerations.

Blindfolding

Should a visually impaired person be blindfolded at some point in training? An O&M instructor usually blindfolds a student if he or she thinks that the individual's vision is interfering with the ability to travel and use information from the other senses. However, it does not make sense to blindfold a person who is losing vision or who has recently lost it because blindness is that person's greatest fear. Furthermore, once the blindfold has been removed, a visually impaired person cannot ignore vision and use the other senses as efficiently. Since people receive 80 percent of their information visually, the phenomenon of visual override occurs when the blindfold is removed; thus vision will, once again, become dominant and make other sensory information confusing.

A much better approach is to teach the individual how to utilize information from the other senses while he or she is seeing. In this case, the process will be integrated in the learning stage. It will not be learned in isolation and then have to be relearned later to achieve sensory integration.

The Sonicguide™

How can the Sonicguide™ be used in vision stimulation and training? The Sonicguide™ is a head-mounted electronic sensing device that probes the environment of the user with an ultrasonic beam, receives feedback from the beam, and translates it into an auditory message. Although the device has not as yet been used extensively in O&M training, it is theorized that the Sonicguide™ can help to train individuals to use their residual vision more efficiently by providing feedback about the types of objects found in the environment, their distance from the user, and their relative positions in space. It may help a student learn to localize, to align his or her body, and to approach an object at an appropriate distace for viewing, thus eliminating the unnecessary stop-and-start system utilized by most visually impaired persons. The Sonicguide™ may also be used to develop an individual's straight-line orientation, to provide protection from low overhangs, and to give a person concrete information about the environment. The Sonciguide™ has been found helpful in improving scanning techniques and increasing the general awareness of objects and light in severely visually impaired children. The theory seems sound, and it is hoped the potential functions of the device will be explored further.

CHAPTER 18

Delivery Systems

KENT CARTER, M.A.

This chapter shows you how to implement the ideal model for a low vision service that was presented in previous chapters. It includes tips for success; how to design a program, including the strengths and weaknesses of various types of services; how to plan a budget and obtain funds; how to establish procedures; and suggestions for documenting what has been accomplished.

The low vision service model presented in this book is, in many respects, an ideal; as a total service unit, it cannot be found in the United States today. What, then, is one to do when trying to find appropriate low vision services for one's clientele? A closer look at the model may provide some answers.

The ideal model, as diagramed in Chapter 4 of this book, involves a three-step continuum from preclinical through clinical to postclinical (follow-up) services. This process has been used for years, although perhaps in less distinct forms. For example, in "Standards for Providing Eyeglasses and Visual Services" (1970) the U.S. Department of Health, Education, and Welfare outlined the procedures that lead to the successful rehabilitation of low vision citizens. Under the "range of visual services" was included "examination and training services necessary for the prescription and provision of conventional lenses, contact lenses, telescopic and microscopic devices and other special aids as prescribed by a physician skilled in diseases of the eye or by an optometrist" (Sec. 6, No. IV E). These standards also contained a statement, based on the experiences of agencies in the previous decade, of the need for low vision instructors, which it terms aides:

> To make the most effective use of subnormal vision aids, usually there is need for a special training aide to supplement services provided by the ophthalmologist or optometrist. After prescription and fitting, the special aide should work with the client to make certain he is able to make maximum use of the special lenses. This is within the scope of visual services and, therefore, qualifies for federal financial participation (Sec. 6, NO. IV E)...[as is] the analysis of visual function at various working distances to evaluate visual efficiency (Sec. 6, No. IV F).

These few lines represent the federal government's recognition of and justification for the ideal model of low vision services—preclinical information such as analysis of visual functioning, clinical data such as special aids prescribed by an eye specialist, and follow-up training, which "usually" is necessary as an adjunct to the clinical data. As may be noted, then, the field is behind in its efforts to establish these services, especially in sparsely populated areas. What can be done to improve this situation?

Although it is frustrating to know that a client needs a professional service which is not available in a particular area, that is no reason to take the unprofessional and perhaps disastrous step of providing the service from a portable low vision aids kit. Is it true, as Emery (1979) noted, that there are "people in the hills of Arkansas and Virginia who are hundreds of miles from a low vision clinic" and that there is no other solution except to provide care without clinical input? These views often have been expressed by low vision professionals. However, there are resources and methods to eradicate these problems. It is the job of low vision professionals to ensure that the methods and resources are found now that will benefit the clients we serve.

STEPS TO SUCCESS

The ideal model can be used in any number of settings with any number of professionals as long as the various parts are utilized. The agency or professional who indicates that the ophthalmologist or optometrist *is* the low vision service is just as remiss and uninformed as the person who professes to solve all problems with an aids kit. What is required are two (or more) interested, determined, and dedicated professionals such as a rehabilitation professional and an eye care specialist. With these two professionals alone, it is only a matter of time before low vision clients receive the high-quality services they want, need, and deserve. The steps leading to success are essentially the same in all settings, as follows:

- Locating interested counterpart professionals with whom one can work.
- Trust, understanding, and cooperation among the various professionals involved.
- Development of a timetable and plan that itemizes what is needed to reach the goal.
- Contact with the authorities who have the ability and desire to help (professional resources).
- Arrangements for appropriate and thorough training for each professional in his or her respective profession, with special emphasis on low vision work.
- Development of a service delivery model that meets the needs of the population to be served.

442

- Contacts with authorities who can provide the necessary, even if limited, financial aid.
- Development of procedures or guidelines for implementing the services, even if on a limited basis at first.
- Documentation of the successes and failures of clients and an assessment of the needs of the general population in the target region.

Professional Cooperation

The essential ingredient of a successful low vision service is cooperation among the professionals involved. The initiator, either the rehabilitation professional or the eye care specialist, must seek a partner from the other profession with whom he or she can have an open exchange of ideas and information. Both partners must be willing to suppress the feelings and professional conflicts that may destroy or hinder the progress of clients. Thus, the seemingly ongoing jealousy among professionals from similar disciplines—ophthalmologists versus optometrists, physical therapists versus occupational therapists, or any number of other counterpart occupations—must not be allowed to interfere with the needs of the low vision clients. These conflicts can be handled best in an initial straightforward, face-to-face discussion between the two professionals in a neutral, calming atmosphere. If, at that time, they cannot reach agreement about how to work together, then perhaps each should seek another partner. If both are truly concerned with their clients' needs, they will be able to reach a compromise. Once a solid working relationship has been established, the other steps can be taken either jointly or as assigned endeavors. Frequently, the initial meeting will be between professionals from an established low vision clinic and a professional field worker, which will greatly reduce the number of future steps needed to reach the goal of service delivery.

Developing a Timetable and Plan

In this step, the professionals write down the specifics of each of the next six steps and assign duties. It should take no more than six months to obtain all the necessary information; action, based on the raw data, should be taken within one year. The age-old thought "but my client needs help *now*" may require compromise. That is, limited service may be given to a few low vision individuals whose need is great, while the working plan moves forward. This type of limited service involves give and take by both professionals and may mean that the clinician provides free clinical evaluations while the rehabilitation teacher seeks one-time financial resources to furnish aids. However, it is important that the developed plan must not be allowed to erode simply because a quick "fix" has been found. If anything, the plan must be moved along so it is completed as early as possible. The service must not be so restricted by the plan that it is not allowed to change as information is gathered. Frequent meetings of the professionals who designed the plan will assure that it grows in a positive way.

Contacting Appropriate Authorities

To find out what is and is not being done for low vision individuals in a state or region, the professionals should design a letter requesting information about low vision services—where they are provided, by whom, and how often; whether services are included in clinics; referral information; costs; and the like. This letter should be sent to the major hospitals in the area, especially teaching hospitals or university-connected hospitals, and to the nearest college of optometry. A similar letter should be sent to the various agencies that provide services to the visually impaired within the geographic area. Most of these agencies are listed in *Directory of Agencies Serving the Visually Handicapped*, published by AFB. The state agency charged with providing low vision services should be contacted and asked how it is meeting the needs of low vision clients in the state. If no response is received, the professionals should write again, perhaps requesting additional information on how the agency acted on "Standards for Providing Eyeglasses and Visual Services" (1970).

Finding Interested Counterpart Professionals

The blindness professional seeking a partner in the eye care field should phone or write a low vision center and ask for the names of professionals who are working in that geographic area and who have shown an interest in the field of low vision. (When requesting information by mail from any source, enclose a brief, open-spaced form and a self-addressed, stamped envelope.) The William Feinbloom Center, Philadelphia, Pennsylvania; the New York Lighthouse for the Blind, New York City; and University of Houston, College of Optometry, Houston, Texas, are among the resources one should contact. However, it is important to contact staff in the low vision programs at these centers to obtain the latest information. The American Foundation for the Blind's national consultant on low vision services also is a good contact for locating university-connected resources.

The eye care specialist seeking a counterpart in the blindness profession will find an excellent resource in the American Association of Workers for the Blind (AAWB) Low Vision Division No. VII. [Contact AAWB at Alliance for Education and Rehabilitation of the Visually Impaired, Inc., 206 North Washington St., Alexandria, VA 22314.] Ask for the name and address of the chairperson of the national interest group or the regional chairperson, who should be able to refer you to interested local staff. When all the information is received, try to condense it into useful items and persons who may be of further use as the plan evolves.

Obtaining Low Vision Training

The more experience and knowledge in low vision a professional has, the more likely the professional is to provide extensive service in that area. As Apple, Apple, and Blasch noted (1980, p. 201): "It appears that the more basic content knowledge the mobility instructor has, the less likely he is to cut the training program short. He is able to recognize the client's needs based on depth of understanding.'' This statement also appears to be true with respect to low vision. Where is such knowledge to be found?

Universities. Most university programs provide minimal information about low vision, usually in the form of one or two courses. However, their primary interest is to develop a well-rounded program for students in a professional blindness program, and they cannot be expected to provide all the necessary specialized information. Therefore, blindness workers may find universities useful only for refresher courses in the summer or during special sessions.

I believe that a new program leading to a master's degree in low vision work would help the field grow.* (A suggested university program outline is found in Appendix 1). Many university programs are now establishing operating agreements with extensive low vision service clinics to allow the placement of their students as interns at the clinics. These placements usually are for 10 to 12 weeks. This design is a step in the right direction for the low vision field.

Low vision clinic in-service programs. These programs offer a viable option for blindness professionals and eye care specialists in upgrading their skills. Such programs are given at the University of Houston College of Optometry, Houston, Texas; William Feinbloom Vision Rehabilitation Center, Philadelphia, Pennsylvania (part of the Pennsylvania College of Optometry); and the New York Lighthouse for the Blind, New York City. (An outline of the University of Houston program appears in Appendix 2.) Costs run from $25.00 to $100.00 per day; the fees are lower for month-long attendance.

National workshops. National workshops, such as the Low Vision Mobility Conference in Kalamazoo, Michigan, in 1975, and the AFB-sponsored low vision conference in Chicago in 1980 can be useful tools for developing expertise and expanding one's knowledge base. The national and local offices of the AAWB and the Association for Education of the Visually Handicapped (AEVH) periodically run programs that emphasize services to low vision citizens. These programs can be useful for gathering information and establishing professional contacts. An example of such programs was the two-day joint AAWB-AEVH New England Region Workshop held in Boston in 1980, which dealt exclusively with low vision services for New England. Letters of suggestion to local chapters may initiate programs on low vision services for other geographic areas.

Local workshops. Professionals who have neither the time nor the money to attend one of the above-mentioned training sessions should interest their local or state blindness agencies in holding low vision workshops at the state level. Again, contact low vision clinics that provide continuing education courses for help in designing a proposal to be submitted to local or state

---

*A Master's program was developed at the Pennsylvania College of Optometry in 1982—after this chapter was written.

authorities. Three to four days of extensive instruction by two or three experts will cost at least $3,000, but the advantage of providing training to many workers will far outweigh the additional costs.

Eye care specialists who specialize in low vision during their professional education spend about the same amount of time on the topic as do blindness professionals in university programs. Certainly their time is (and should be) spent studying the clinical aspects of service rather than peripheral concerns such as training. However, without further extensive in-depth study by clinical and rehabilitation professionals, it is unlikely that a thorough and complete service for low vision clients will develop. Thus, personnel must be willing to sacrifice time and perhaps money so that future clients will receive the best possible service. Views vary as to whether clinical and rehabilitation personnel should attend a lengthy program together or visit different settings. The choice should be decided by the professionals involved.

Once all the personnel have attended a two- or three-week in-service program at a comprehensive center, they must confer and share the knowledge they have acquired. By comparing notes and expressing feelings, they will be able to prepare an outline of the type of service needed in a specific locale — and, in essence, decide on their interpretation of the ideal model presented in this book.

DEVELOPING A SERVICE DELIVERY MODEL

After the program designers have a clear understanding of what the comprehensive low vision service model entails, they are ready to design the program. Careful attention must be paid to the type of delivery that will provide optimal service to the low vision individual. At this point, it is necessary to disregard financial concerns, since the aim is to provide optimal service. The financial impact of such services will become important later, but, at this stage, thinking about costs will only limit ideas and inhibit creativity. All low vision clinics are based on one or another form of the ideal model. Each type of clinic is briefly described in this section, along with its possible strengths and weaknesses.

University-Affiliated Clinics: Strengths
- Usually, both ophthalmological and optometric services are provided.
- Generally, frequent weekly clinic times are scheduled.
- Loans to clients for low vision aids are commonplace (sometimes a borrower's fee is required).
- Diagnostic equipment is almost always superior and of the latest design, which leads to more accurate evaluations.
- Often, other related services, such as social work or intake processing, are provided as a part of the low vision service.
- New ideas and techniques frequently are part of the clinical design because of the research performed in university settings.

446

- Participation by outside professionals who work with clients is usually encouraged.
- Reports are generally thorough, and thought is given to making the information useful to other professionals.

University-Affiliated Clinics: Weaknesses

- Sometimes training is slighted, and no specific training staff are provided for training in the clinic.
- Preliminary functional data from the field may or may not be used by the clinic staff.
- Examination time may be too limited owing to heavy caseloads. (A minimum of two hours is usually recommended for the patient's first visit with the clinician.)
- Eye care specialist interns may be used extensively and may not be closely supervised by experienced clincians.
- Many of the clinical tests (e.g., thorough peripheral field taking, color-vision assessment, or illumination control assessments) may be glossed over if the examination time is limited.
- The sterile atmosphere of the clinic may induce inaccurate visual functioning responses by clients. (Visits by the clinician to a client's home, school, or job often can be enlightening and helpful in solving specific problems).
- Diagnostic aids tend to "disappear" in low vision clinics, which means that clients may not receive the optimal aid for the task requested unless an adequate stock is maintained.

Blindness Agency or Center Clinic: Strengths

- Clients usually have immediate access to professional staff such as orientation and mobility specialists, communication teachers, home and personal management staff, and counselors.*
- Preliminary field data on the functioning of clients usually are readily available either from an agreement with staff from other agencies or from the clinic program of home visiting before clients come to the clinic.
- The lending of low vision aids is commonplace, although a fee may be required.
- In-house training is usually provided by the low vision instructor, who may or may not act in other capacities. If the low vision instructor is acting in another capacity, his or her scheduled time per low vision client should be examined to assure the allocation of adequate training time.
- Clients usually are allotted the optimal examination time unless the agency's budget limits the amount payable to the clinician.

---

*The reader should note that Veterans Administration (VA) medical centers are included in this category, rather than in the next category (medical center or hospital clinic) because low vision services at VA medical centers are provided in much the same way as they are at blindness agencies or center clinics.

■ Reports are usually thorough; their emphasis is on the utility to other professionals serving the low vision clients.

Blindness Agency or Center Clinic: Weaknesses

■ Ophthalmological consultations may not be readily available during the clinic's hours.

■ Appointment times may be limited to fewer than one or two days per month.

■ Only the simplest diagnostic equipment may be available; such diagnostic tests as globe perimetry, ophthalmoscopy, and retinoscopy may not be given during the clinic's hours.

■ Research usually is not conducted.

■ Many tests and evaluations may be glossed over if the examination time is not adequate.

■ The clinicians or training staff may not visit clients at home, at school, or at work.

■ Financial concerns may limit the quantity of low vision aids kept in stock; therefore, the best aid for a specific task may not be available or even known.

Medical Center or Hospital Clinics: Strengths

■ Diagnostic equipment usually is superior.

■ Medical professionals other then eye care specialists are on hand, which is a strong consideration for those with fluctuating disease processes.

■ Health insurance for the cost of the low vision services usually is more easily arranged.

■ Intake services by social workers usually are part of the low vision service.

Medical Center or Hospital Clinic: Weaknesses

■ Optometric consultations may not be readily available.

■ The clinic's hours may be limited to less than a half-day per week.

■ The examination time may be restricted to less than a half-hour per client; many tests may be performed superficially or may be considered "unnecessary."

■ Training may be provided by a nonprofessional aide, or by a clinician who spends only a few minutes on an explanation, or it may not be done at all.

■ The "sterile" atmosphere of the hospital may not stimulate realistic visual responses from clients.

■ Low vision aids generally are limited in number and type, which reduces the chances for success, and clients may not be able to borrow aids to try out at home.

■ Participation by outside professionals may not be encouraged or allowed.

■ Owing to the limited time devoted to services to clients, reports frequently are sketchy and superficial.

■ Home, school, or work visits by the clinic staff in the preclinic or postclinic phases are unlikely.

Mobile Service Unit: Strengths

- Usually, the services of other types of professional staff are obtainable in a given period (e.g., one week to ten days).
- Home, school, or work evaluations are made as part of the service so that real problems are observed as they occur.
- Preliminary field data before the client's visit to the clinic are available from the local blindness agency or low vision service staff acting as field evaluators.
- The service goes to the people rather than the people coming to it, which is a psychological advantage because it shows that the clients' needs are foremost. Moreover, these units permit the establishment of regional clinics as well as provide person-to-person services.
- The lending of low vision aids is commonplace (fees may or may not be charged).
- Training usually is provided by the instructor, whose schedule follows that of the mobile unit and whose work is done at the client's home, school, or place of work.
- Services to severely impaired or immobile clients are easily provided.
- The optimal examination time per client is feasible unless travel time is restricted because of budgetary considerations or poor itinerary planning.
- Reports usually are thorough; emphasis is on their usefulness to other professionals serving low vision clients.

Mobile Service Unit: Weaknesses

- Other professionals, such as social workers and psychologists, may not be available.
- Consultation with an ophthalmologist may not be available.
- Diagnostic equipment may be limited because of the size and configuration of the mobile unit.
- The clinic's time may be restricted by regional rotation, which may limit access for a specific client by as much as six weeks.
- Participation by outside professionals during the examination may be limited by the seating space in the unit and by budgetary constraints.
- Training may be delayed by as much as a week until the instructor is able to include the new client in a daily travel schedule.

Private Practice Clinic: Strengths

- Usually, the location of such clinics is accessible to most clients, and the appointment hours are convenient.
- Diagnostic equipment generally is adequate if not superior to that of an agency.
- Eye care specialists, such as optometrists or ophthalmologists, generally are accessible.
- The time allocated for examinations frequently is optimal.
- Participation by outside professionals may or may not be encouraged.

Private Practice Clinic: Weaknesses

- In-house functional evaluations often are not made or sought.
- Other professional services, such as social work, orientation and mobility, and rehabilitation teaching, frequently are available only by referral.
- Training usually is provided by a nonprofessional aide or by a clinician who gives a short explanation.
- Research generally is not conducted.
- Only a limited number and type of aids is available, and aids usually are not loaned to clients.
- The allocation of professional time may be limited by financial constraints and thus many tests may be glossed over or eliminated.
- Clinic reports are likely to be superficial.

The strengths of the various types of low vision clinics just described may be combined to fit the needs of the staff and the needs of the target population. People who live too far from services may require a new type of delivery unit to meet their needs. A mobile unit working out of a clinic located 100 miles away could provide the appropriate clinical service in conjunction with the training services of the low vision worker. Severely handicapped children in far-reaching corners of a region could also be served by a mobile clinic. In a medium-sized city, an eye care specialist near the inner city could be contacted to provide low vision services. An optometrist who is new to an area may attempt to work out a reciprocal agreement with a blindness agency in which the training staff of the agency becomes an adjunct to the optometrist's private practice. The possibilities depend on two things: the desire to provide the best services and money.

ESTABLISHING A BUDGET

The task of developing a budget to fit the service model one chooses may be as simple as setting clinician's fees or as complex as a line-item budget for a grant proposal. First, a few important points should be considered about the costs per client outlined by low vision clinics and agencies serving the blind.

To figure costs and thereby establish a baseline budget, one should carefully weigh information about the budgets of regional, state, or national low vision clinics. Over the years, the tendency has been to underestimate how much it costs to provide adequate low vision services. In general, fees for clinic services range from $50 to over $2,000 per client, although the average fee is $75 to $100. However, it is important to examine which services these fees cover and if they accurately reflect *all* the service costs. If a clinic in a major metropolitan area is charging $60 for a complete low vision service, is it likely that this fee represents the true costs? If it does, is it equally likely that comprehensive services are being provided? The answers are difficult to obtain but are necessary if this information is to be used in formulating a service plan.

450

The easiest way to determine the actual costs of a service is to add up all the money spent in one year and to divide the total by the number of clients served. However, the answer is not an accurate reflection of which services were received by which individuals. Some items to look at in figuring costs are these:

- Salaries of all staff (even part-time or limited-time personnel).
- Fringe benefits for all staff (including withholding taxes, retirement, health benefits, workmen's compensation, vacation, and sick leave).
- Travel money (if appropriate).
- Telephones.
- Office supplies.
- Major equipment purchases (costed out for a five-year life expectancy).
- Inventory of low vision aids.
- Copying equipment and supplies.
- Postage.
- Professional and liability insurance.
- Travel to conferences.
- Electricity.
- Water fees.
- Sewage disposal fees (if appropriate).
- Trash disposal fees (if appropriate).
- Cost per square foot of clinic-office space (either rental fee or the percentage of the mortgage).
- Equipment rental fees.
- Office furnishings and furniture (costed out over ten years).
- Office equipment (e.g., typewriters, stamp machines, and the like).
- A percentage of the total for administrative services (e.g., bookkeeping and public relations).

Other items may be added or some of the items listed may be subtracted, depending on the type of service and its location. In the example of the metropolitan low vision service mentioned previously, it is doubtful that the actual cost per client is as low as the $60 fee charged when all the twenty items are added up and divided by the number of clients served. More likely, certain budgetary items are eliminated because of donated space and furniture, endowment money given to the agency, fees charged to other organizations for professional consultation, and low-cost staff such as student interns. The nonprofit agency that houses such services often has many options for discounting certain costs as tax-deductible public donations. However, these options usually are not available to the beginner who is designing a low vision program.

The start-up year for a low vision service in rural Maine may serve as another example. According to the cost analysis of that service, which examined the cost per client and the cost per service unit, the entire first-year budget was $34,980 to serve 48 clients, or roughly $492 per client. However, at the end of the first year, the total number of clients served was 72, and thus the cost per client was reduced to $485. Although rural services tend to be more expensive than urban services because of travel time and money that must be allocated in providing itinerant care, the cost per client of the Maine service was far below the $1,000 per client often cited as the cost for providing rural low vision service.

The most expensive part of a comprehensive low vision service is the training costs. This is perhaps one reason why many agencies that provide low vision service do not include training. The cost per unit of time provided by clinicians during examinations is more than double the cost per unit of training and coordination. However, less clinician time is needed than training time—five to six hours of clinical examination time versus 10 direct-service hours of training time. Thus, when an agency or service provider must cut costs, it usually eliminates training services because their elimination provides the maximum amount of savings.

The necessity of including the complete service unit must be recognized. If cuts must be made in the low vision service model, they should be made by equally paring down all service components. Thus, the number of clients served per year must be reduced rather than the effectiveness of the services they receive. The end result of providing high-quality services to fewer clients is far better than poor-quality services to more clients.

OBTAINING FUNDS

Once a plan and appropriate budget are made, what happens next? The next steps depend on the program design and how extensive are the costs.

If the intent is to locate funds for low vision aids and the basic equipment listed in Chapter 10, Table 1, then local groups are the most likely resources. The local Chamber of Commerce will provide a list of local clubs and organizations that provide funds for needy projects. Each organization listed should be sent a neatly typed personal letter describing the project and the needs of the population to be served. The letter should be followed by a telephone call about a week later. If you are soliciting help from several organizations, indicate this at your meeting with the group. Clubs often like to take on yearly projects so their entire efforts can be devoted to one cause. Make sure you have permission to mention the agency or practice where the services will be housed so that no misunderstandings occur. If the need for monetary assistance is much larger than a few thousand dollars, a well-documented proposal for establishing a low vision clinic may be presented to the local or state agency for the blind. Application blanks and guidelines for writing a grant proposal are available from the state rehabilitation services agency. (Federal domestic assistance bulletins from the Office of Management and the Budget, Washington, D.C., may provide insights into likely prospects within the federal system, such as research and demonstration programs.) Some useful tips on filling out the applications follow:

■ Seek out the state agency employee or employees who handle the paperwork for the blindness department. That person will have certain priorities or will be concerned about specific handicaps. Find out what they are and use them to your benefit or find another agency through which to apply.

■ Talk with the directors and the commissioners directly connected with the blindness field, but do not be too specific about the plan at this point. Simply seek information about what concerns them in other projects or their future desires for programming.

■ Talk with others who have submitted proposals to an agency. Find out what "games" are played. Sometimes all decisions have been made prior to the formal acceptance of an application.

■ Find out if the persons who review grant applications like elaborate grant proposals with exaggerated claims or concise proposals that specify the project's objectives.

■ Use the application blanks to help organize the project before writing begins.

■ State and federal grants are awarded for two periods: July 1 to June 1 and June 1 to June 30. Grants awarded for for July 1 to June 1 require a great amount of detail and have many restrictions. Grants awarded for June 1 to June 30 are quick allocations of leftover money (wash-out funds); they usually require proposals that are simple in design and low in cost. The two grant periods are in flux because the federal government has changed the fiscal year to October 1 to September 30, which means that, in the future, September may be the most likely period to obtain wash-out money.

■ The grant should start with a statement of goals, which is a broad statement of the philosophy of the project. This statement is followed by a concise list of objectives and by a list of management "steps." Find out what the particular agency requires in the way of accountability for time and money and write it in.

■ Other items of concern are procedures for execution, the results expected, foreseen constraints, the acceptable degree of success, and how the end results will be evaluated. The evaluation phase should be extensive and should include a review of the program's content, the input obtained (e.g., dollars, activities, consultations, and so forth), the process or activities, and the end product or results (how many clients are now successfully using their vision and aids).

■ Take time to learn the jargon of grant proposals and note which words are appreciated and which are not. Also, make sure the project leans toward the agency's philosophy and intent, as stated in its legal charter, which may be found in the state law library.

■ Try to sum up the entire project in the introductory paragraph so that overworked bureaucrats will be able to digest the major points in a few minutes of reading and will be enticed to read further.

■ Keep the budgetary information concise. The days of extensive financial padding have disappeared. Today, a lean budget is appreciated. Find out if the agency has certain restrictions on grants, such as not allowing money for attending conferences. Perhaps slightly inflating the travel budget will cover attendance at some conferences.

If governmental agencies reject the proposal, private philanthropic foundations are other possible funding sources. Some resources include the following:

1. The Foundation Center, 888 Seventh Avenue, New York, N. Y., 10106, provides services to members, including a listing of previous grants and funding sources in various fields. The center also publishes the bimonthly journal *Foundation News,* and *Foundation Grants Index: Subjects.* Overall, the center is an excellent resource for finding state or regional organizations that are interested in services to blind persons.

2. The Robert Wood Johnson Foundation, P.O. Box 2316, Princeton, N.J., 08540, has funded programs all over the country that deal with "ready access to personal health care" and "improving performance of health care systems."

3. The resources developed during the initial requests for data from low vision clinics can provide information about where and how to seek support money.

DEVELOPMENT OF PROCEDURES

This phase of planning is done when a proposal is submitted to funding agencies. All the professionals involved must divide the services offered. Some tasks, such as the clinical examination, the medical diagnosis, or mobility training, are readily discernible. Other tasks, such as coordination, report writing, use of a data bank, or overall administration are not as easily identified. Care must be taken not to allow stereotypes to interfere with the logical assessment of each task. For example, several articles have been written on the advisibility of designating the ophthalmological consultant as the program administrator; however, in most cases the best administrator is the person who has competence in administration. The person who has the most managerial experience, related business education, and overall ability in this area will probably be the best choice for the administrator, whatever his or her profession. It also is important to develop some clear-cut job descriptions that will also help clarify role relationships (see Appendix 3). Each design for a service delivery system will necessitate variations in responsibilities and roles. In one setting, the ophthalmologist may act as the medical consultant, the examiner, and perhaps the administrator; in another setting, the ophthalmologist may perform different roles.

Additional information on setting up a low vision service may be obtained from the low vision consultant at AFB and from the evaluation study guides for self-assessment of agency low vision services published by the National Accreditation Council for Agencies Serving the Blind and Visually Handicapped, 79 Madison Avenue, New York, N.Y. 10016.

DOCUMENTATION

Before the project begins, the personnel should have a clear understanding of the potential clientele for low vision services. The 1977 statistics from the National Center for Health Statistics indicate that 6.6 out of every 1,000 persons and 44 out of every 1,000 persons over age 65 experience a severe loss of vision. Thus, to determine how many people in your area may require low vision services, divide the population of your area by 1,000. This will provide a rough estimate on which to base the program plan.

Once the project is under way, carefully record all actions taken, including telephone consultations. At the end of the year, it is important to be able to show not only how many people were helped but other data as well, such as the following:

- The number of clients who have each type of eye disease.
- Which aids are prescribed most often.
- The advantages and disadvantages of nonoptical aids for persons with each type of eye disease.
- The average number of training visits.
- The average number of clinical visits.
- Which illumination-control devices have been most effective for the various pathologies.
- The time spent ordering and tracing equipment.
- The number of clients who needed extensive counseling services.
- The average length of the initial examination.
- The number and variety of problems expressed by low vision individuals.

Obviously, a small computer would be useful for recording and evaluating the data if the budget can afford it. Be careful to track *all* expenditures and account for every penny. It is usually helpful to designate all aids that are loaned to clients and that cost less than $100 as "expendable supplies." This expedites accounting and allows for the rapid purchase of additional aids if the initial year's supply runs low. Moreover, a carefully followed evaluation plan will make the next year's plan clear and easy to develop.

Appendix 4 contains a brief description of a program developed by the Virginia Commission for the Visually Handicapped. By training an optometrist, an ophthalmologist, and a teacher in each district of the state, the program has assured that every visually impaired child in Virginia had reasonable (within 50 miles) access to interdisciplinary low vision services. There were problems in Virginia, just like any other state, but with organization and a few dedicated people, Project LUV came into existence. It serves the needs of the children in the state and certainly meets the objectives of the model. One final thought: "Don't give up." Often the process just presented takes from one to two years before a true start is made. However, once the project begins, dedication and effort may allow for the quick delivery of services to low vision clients.

Bibliography

Apple, M., Apple, L. E., & Blasch, B. Low vision. In R. Welsh & B. Blasch (Eds.), *Foundations of orientation and mobility*. New York: American Foundation for the Blind, 1980.

Carter, K., & Carter, C. Itinerant low vision services. *New Outlook for the Blind,* 1975, **69**, 225–260.

Directory of agencies serving the visually handicapped. New York: American Foundation for the Blind, 22nd Edition 1983. [Updated periodically.]

Faye, E. E., & Hood, C. Low vision services in an agency: Structure and philosophy. *New Outlook for the Blind,* 1975, **69**, 241–248.

Jose, R., Cummings, J., & McAdams, L. The model low vision clinical service: An interdisciplinary vision rehabilitation program. *New Outlook for the Blind,* 1975, **69**, 249–254.

Olshansky, S. Some comments on the delivery of services. *Rehabilitation literature,* 1973, **34**(7), 203–206.

Standards for providing eyeglasses and visual services. Washington, D.C.: Rehabilitation Services Administration, U.S. Department of Health, Education & Welfare, March 20, 1970.

Appendix 1
Low Vision Instructors
Proposed Degree Program

Subject*	Optimal Number of Hours
I. Overview of the team approach in low vision: Client, assessment, clinical, training, follow-up, assessment, closure	2
II. Light A. Theories of light B. Measurement of light C. Effect of light on vision	6
III. Functions of the Human Eye A. Structure of the eye B. Theories and facts on the functioning of the eye C. Pathological characteristics related to low vision functioning D. Vision classification systems	20
IV. Visual Perception A. Retinal image (light) B. Eye movement (muscle) C. Cortical reception D. Effects of contrast, texture, brightness, and so on, visual recognition and perception	16
V. Physiological Optics A. Refraction of light	12

*A degree program following this basic outline is offered by the Low Vision Research and Training Center at the Pennsylvania College of Optometry, Philadelphia, Pennsylvania.

		Subject	Optimal Number of Hours

B. Characteristics and measurement of the lens

C. Design of microscopic and telescopic systems

D. Optical effects on the human eye

VI. Psychosocial Issues Pertinent to Extreme Visual Loss   20

A. Overview of counseling theories in rehabilitation work

B. Recognition of behavioral patterns in low vision clients

C. Use of psychological evaluations and inventories

VII. Low Vision Environmental Assessments   20

A. Observational factors

B. Case history

C. Environmental assessments

   1. Distance

   2. Near

   3. Illumination

   4. Color

   5. Visual field

   6. Magnification effects

   7. Equipment needed

D. Psychosocial factors

E. Assessment formats

VIII. Clinical Low Vision   20

A. Procedures performed by the optometrist or ophthalmologist

   1. Uses of equipment: lensometer, ophthalmoscope, retinoscope, and the like

   2. Refraction

   3. Field assessment

   4. Near and distance evaluations, including aids

   5. Illumination concerns

   6. Extraneous evaluations: reverse telescopes, fresnel lenses, and so on

B. Prescription and lending of aids

   1. Many versus few aids

   2. Initial instruction of the client in the use of an aid or aids

Subject	*Optimal Number of Hours*

3. Aid to meet specific needs
4. Systems for lending aids
C. Reports and recommendations
    1. Written, decipherable reports
    2. Recommendations for training
    3. Referrals to other agencies
    4. Other services to be provided to the client by the low vision team

IX. Low Vision Aids   10
A. Microscopes: advantages, disadvantages, and styles
B. Telescopes: advantages, disadvantages, and styles
C. Telemicroscopes: advantages, disadvantages, and styles
D. Closed-circuit television, fresnel prisms, ITT scope, others

X. Training without Aids   20
A. Visual efficiency measurements
B. Theories on advancing the use of visual perception
C. Training program designs
D. Procedures for near-vision training
E. Procedures for distance-vision training
F. Proper timing of visual efficiency training—before or after the clinical process?

XI. Training with Aids   20
A. Writing individualized training programs
B. Procedures for near-vision training, including reading-instruction techniques
C. Procedures for distance-aid training
D. Incorporating the use of aids into the client's everyday life
E. What to do when problems arise

XII. Follow-up Services   4
A. Client feedback processes
B. Problem-solving hints
C. Reassessment procedures
    1. Psychosocial

459

	Subject	*Optimal Number of Hours*
	2. Field of vision	
	3. Distance vision	
	4. Near vision	
	5. Illumination	
	6. Use of aids	
	D. When to refer the client back to the clinical team	

XIII. Clinical Setups   12

    A. Equipment needs
    B. Low vision aids and systems for lending aids
    C. Accounting procedures
    D. Client referral procedures
    E. Paperwork and minimizing red tape
    F. Program designs to meet the needs of a population
       1. Rural versus city
       2. Daily service versus other types of service
       3. In-house versus primary environ clinics

XIV. Funding Needs   8

    A. Grants (federal, state, and private)
       1. Available types
       2. The basics of writing grant proposals
       3. Justifications for service
    B. State special education funds
    C. State vocational rehabilitation funds
    D. Funding by private organizations

XV. Duties of the Low Vision Therapist   8

    A. Variations depending on the therapist's position, the type of clinic, and overall design of the program
    B. Review of the team-approach model

XVI. Internships

    A. Schools of optometry
    B. University vision programs
    C. Schools for the blind
    D. Itinerant programs
    E. Vocational rehabilitation programs

                             Total   198
plus the hours spent on internship

Appendix 2
Curriculum for Low Vision Educational
Intern Program
University of Houston College of Optometry
Low Vision Clinic

JOHN FERRARO, MA
SANDRA FERRARO, MA

UNIT 1: PHYSIOLOGICAL STRUCTURE AND FUNCTION OF THE EYE

Input	Process	Output
Students (non-O.D., M.A. level)	The student will complete a section on the physiological structure and function of the eye.	Upon completion of this section the student will be able to:
Rehabilitative Optometry Faculty: Optometrist, Low Vision	Information will be presented through one hour of lecture and discussion and assigned readings.	Identify the parts of the eye from a schematic drawing.
Lecture Room (4–6 people)		State specific visual functions performed by the parts of the eye.
Assigned Readings Mehr, E. B., & Freid, A. N. *Low vision care.* Chicago: Professional Press, 1975. Chapter 4.	Evaluation will be through written test.	State specific visual functions performed by specific areas of the retina.
The Human Eye. Southbridge, MA: American Optical Corporation, 1976.		Identify hemispheres of vision and ocular mobility.

UNIT 2: DISEASES OF THE EYE AND FUNCTIONAL IMPLICATIONS

Input	Process	Output
Students (non-O.D., M.A. level)	The student will complete a section on diseases of the eye and functional implications of the diseases.	Upon completion of this section the student will be able to:
Rehabilitative Optometry Faculty: Optometrist, Low Vision	Information will be presented through one hour of lecture and discussion, slide presentation, and assigned readings.	List main characteristics of major eye diseases.
Lecture Room (4–6 people)		Identify physiological and ocular effects of systemic disease processes.
Fundus slides depicting eye diseases	Evaluation will be through written test.	List functional effects of eye diseases.
Slide Projector		Classify eye pathologies according to field defects.
Assigned Readings Faye, E. E. *Clinical low vision.* Boston: Little, Brown & Co., 1976. Chapters 17–21, 24, 26, 27.		

UNIT 3: MEDICAL AND SURGICAL INTERVENTION

Input	Process	Output
Students (non-O.D., M.A. level)	The student will complete a section on medical and surgical intervention.	Upon completion of this section the student will be able to:
Rehabilitative Optometry Faculty: Optometrist, Low Vision	Information will be presented through one hour of lecture and discussion and assigned readings.	Identify in lay terms surgical intervention procedures for common eye disease processes.
Lecture Room (4–6 people)	Evaluation will be through written test.	Identify in lay terms surgical intervention procedures for correcting ocular motility problems.
Assigned Readings Faye, Chapters 22, 23, 25. Krefman, R.A. Surgical Treatment of refractive errors. *Optometric Monthly*, September, 1981, 35–38.		State physiological and functional effects of drugs used to control common eye disease processes.

Input	Process	Output
Students (non-O.D., M.A. level) Rehabilitative Optometry Faculty: Optometrist, Low Vision Lecture Room (4–6 people) *Assigned Readings* *Basic Optical Concepts.* Southbridge, MA: American Optical Corporation, 1976.	The student will complete a section on basic optics. Information will be presented through one hour of lecture and discussion and assigned readings. Evaluation will be through written test.	Upon completion of this section the student will be able to: State the two major theories of light transmission. Identify the components of the light spectrum. Define the following terms: reflection, refraction, absorption. Describe convergent, divergent and parallel light.

UNIT 5: REFRACTION

Input	Process	Output
Students (non-O.D., M.A. level) Rehabilitative Optometry Faculty: Optometrist, Low Vision Lecture Room (4–6 people) *Assigned Readings* *Lenses, Prisms and Mirrors.* Southbridge, MA: American Optical Corporation, 1976. *Normal and Abnormal Vision.* Southbridge, MA: American Optical Corporation, 1976.	The student will complete a section on the refraction of light and refractive errors of the eye. Information will be presented through one hour of lecture and discussion and assigned readings. Evaluation will be through written test.	Upon completion of this section the student will be able to: State the effect of plus and minus lenses on light rays. Compute dioptric power and focal point through standard formulas. Write a definition of the following terms: diopter, convergence, divergence, concave lens, convex lens, focal point, accommodation, optical axis ray. Identify the parts of the eye which have refractive powers. State the refractive errors of the eye and how they are corrected. Identify when and how refractive errors can affect the use of low vision optical aids.

UNIT 6: MAGNIFICATION

Input	Process	Output
Students (non-O.D., M.A. level)	The student will complete a section on magnification.	Upon completion of this section the student will be able to:
Rehabilitative Optometry Faculty: Optometrist, Low Vision	Information will be presented through one hour of lecture and discussion and assigned readings.	Write a definition of the term magnification.
Lecture Room (4–6 people)	Evaluation will be through written test.	Describe magnification as a ratio.
Assigned Readings Faye, Chapter 3. Mehr and Freid, Chapter 5.		Identify types of magnification and list ways in which they are achieved.
		State the mathematical relation between diopters and magnification according to the 40 cm and 25 cm reference distances.
		Given specific pathologies, state the effect of magnification on the diseased eye.

UNIT 7: TRAINING

Input	Process	Output
Students (non-O.D., M.A. level)	The student will complete a section on basic principles of training patients in the use of low vision aids.	Upon completion of this section the student will be able to:
Rehabilitative Optometry Faculty: Low Vision Educational Specialist Orientation and Mobility Specialist	Information will be presented through one hour of lecture and discussion, observation, practicum, and assigned readings.	List eight objectives which can be achieved through training.
Lecture Room (4–6 people)	Evaluation will be through written test, and faculty review of completed observation forms and practicum sessions.	List four basic learning principles which can be applied to training.
Low Vision Clinic Facilities: Near Training Room Distance Training Room		Demonstrate use of a creative problem-solving approach when working with a patient.

464

responsibility. *Optometric Weekly*, 1975, **66**(24), 655-657.

Identify sources for long-term training programs.

UNIT 8: THE LOW VISION EXAMINATION–PRELIMINARY

Input	Process	Output
Students (non-O.D., M.A. level)	The student will complete a section on the preliminary components of the low vision examination.	Upon completion of this section the student will be able to:
Rehabilitative Optometry Faculty: Optometrist, Low Vision	Information will be presented through a one-half hour of lecture, one hour of lab, observation, and assigned readings.	List case history information obtained by the optometrist.
Lecture Room (4–6 people)	Lab: the student will be given an eye examination and complete the lab worksheet.	Identify methods commonly used to determine distance acuity of low vision patients, including specific charts, distances, and lighting.
Low Vision Clinic Facilities: Examination Room	Evaluation will be through written test, and faculty review of completed lab worksheet and observation forms.	Identify methods commonly used to determine near acuity of low vision patients including specific charts, distances, and lighting.
Assigned Readings		Compare data obtained through measurement of letter, line, and reading acuities.
Bailey, I.L. Refracting low vision patients. *Optometric Monthly*, 1978, **69**(8), 519-523.		List the three visual field tests commonly used in low vision; write a description of each procedure and indicate which part of the field is being measured.
——. Specification of nearpoint performance. *Optometric Monthly*, 1978, **69**(12), 895-898.		State the procedure for objective and subjective refraction.
——. Visual acuity measurement in low vision. *Optometric Monthly*, 1978, **69**(7), 418-424.		Identify information obtained through retinoscopy, tonometry, biomicroscopy, D-15, and Worth 4 Dot.
——. Visual field measurement in low vision. *Optometric Monthly*, 1978, **69**(7), 697-701.		
Faye, Chapters, 3–6.		

UNIT 9: THE LOW VISION EXAMINATION—MAGNIFICATION EVALUATION

Input	Process	Output
Students (non-O.D., M.A. level)	The student will complete a section on the magnification evaluation, prescription, and dispensing components of the low vision examination.	Upon completion of this section the student will be able to:
Rehabilitative Optometry Faculty: Optometrist, Low Vision		Compute magnification required to obtain a desired acuity through both distance and near acuity methods.
Lecture Room (4–6 people)	Information will be presented through a one-half hour of lecture and discussion, observation and assigned readings.	Write a basic order for presenting low vision aids to a patient including a rationale for that order.
Low Vision Clinic Facilities: Examination Room	Evaluation will be through written test, and faculty review of completed observation forms.	List four factors which must be considered before making a tentative low vision aid prescription.
Assigned Readings Faye, Chapters 7 and 9.		Given magnification required and specific tasks to be accomplished, list at least two optical aids which could be used.
		Given optometric data from a low vision examination, write a training plan and list possible problem areas.
		Identify the following instruments and indicate what they measure: slit lamp, phoropter, retinoscope, opthalmoscope, keratometer, Goldmann tonometer, lensometer, Mackay Marg tonometer.
		State information obtained through the following tests and procedures: fundus photography, contrast sensitivity, preferential looking, visual evoked response or visual evoked potential, elec-

UNIT 10: DATA NOTATION, INSTRUMENTATION, AND SPECIAL DIAGNOSTIC TECHNIQUES

Input	Process	Output
Students (non-O.D., M.A. level)	The student will complete a section on optometric data notation, instrumentation, and special diagnostic techniques.	Upon completion of this section the student will be able to:
Rehabilitative Optometry Faculty: Optometrist, low vision experience	Information will be presented through one hour of lecture and discussion, observation, and assigned readings.	State the meaning of the following notations: VAsc, VAc, VAcaid, OD, OS, OU, Rx, Hx, TS, MS, EFTS, TMS, FDMS, WNL.
Lecture Room (4–6 people)		
Clinic Facilities: Low Vision Examination Room	Evaluation will be through written test and faculty review of completed observation forms.	Given a typical refractive error prescription, state the meaning of each component.
Assigned Readings Kleinstein, R. N. Contrast Sensitivity. *Optometric Monthly,* 1981, **72**(4), 38-40.		Translate 10/120 into its approximate Snellen equivalent.
		Given the near acuity .04/.8M, state what the patient performed.

UNIT 11: OPTICAL AIDS

Input	Process	Output
Students (non-O.D., M.A. level)	The student will complete a section on optical and functional characteristics of optical low vision aids, advantages and disadvantages, and resources for aids.	Upon completion of this section the student will be able to:
Rehabilitative Optometry Faculty: O.D., experience with optical low vision aids		Compute the focal point of a given aid.
Lecture Room (4-6 people)	Information will be presented through one hour of lecture and discussion, four hours of lab, observation, practicum, and assigned readings.	Determine the power in diopters of a given aid and the magnification according to the 40 cm and 25 cm reference distances.
Low Vision Clinic Facilities: Examination Room Conference Room		Define the terms chromatic aberration and spherical aberration.
Complete array of low vision optical aids	Labs: The student will measure field, focal point, and working distance of a variety of near and distance optical aids, and do various activities while using the aids; the student will complete four lab worksheets.	State the properties of low vision aids which affect field of view and working distance and state how they are affected.
Assigned Readings Berson, E. L., Rabin, A. R., Mehaffrey, L. Advances in night vision technology: A pocketscope for patients with Retinitis Pigmentosa. *Archives of Opthalmology*, 1973, **90**(12), 427-431.	Evaluation will be through written test and faculty review of completed lab and observation sheets.	Identify the following low vision aids: microscope, telemicroscope, magnifier, loupe, telescope, half-eyes, surgical spectacles, bioptic telescope.
Drasdo, N. Visual field expanders. *American Journal of Optometry and Physiological Optics*, 1976, **53**(9), 464-467.		State the correct method for care and cleaning of low vision aids.
Faye, Chapters 8, 15, 16, Appendices 1, 3.		Given a specific optical aid, list a variety of tasks for which it may be used.
Ludlum, W. M. Clinical experience with the contact lens telescope. *American Journal of Optometry*		Given a specific optical aid, list two of its advantages and two of its disadvantages.
		Given a case history, compare two aids as to which would best meet a patient's

vision aids.

Given several low vision aids, state basic prices and ordering processes.

Identify expertise required for prescribing and ordering optical low vision aids.

H. K., Goodrich, G. L. Low Vision monocular field study. *Optometric Weekly,* 1976, **67**(44), 1202-1205.

Rosenberg, R. A survey of magnification aids to low vision. *Journal of the American Optometric Association,* 1973, **44**(6), 628-635.

UNIT 12: NON OPTICAL LOW VISION AIDS

Input	Process	Output
Students (non-O.D., M.A. level)	The student will complete a section on types, uses, and resources of non-optical low vision aids and materials.	Upon completion of this section the student will be able to:
Rehabilitative Optometry Faculty: Low Vision Educational Specialist Orientation and Mobility Specialist	Information will be presented through one hour of lecture and discussion, two hours of lab, observation, practicum and assigned readings.	Classify nonoptical aids and materials according to purpose.
Lecture Room (4–6 people)		List several nonoptical aids which could enhance performance of the following activities: reading, writing, cooking, personal grooming, walking outside.
Low Vision Clinic Facilities: Near Training Room Distance Training Room	Labs: the student will complete a variety of activities using non-optical aids, use a closed-circuit television, and complete lab worksheets.	Assess a patient's need for use of a nonoptical aid.
Closed-Circuit Television	Evaluation will be through written test, faculty evaluation of completed lab worksheets, observation forms, and practicum session.	Assess lighting needs of a patient.
Array of nonoptical low vision aids and materials		Operate a CCTV.
		List visual and motor skills required for reading and writing with a CCTV.
Assigned Readings Faye, Chapter 10.		List print size in point and M system of the following materials: elementary textbooks, large print, paperbacks, college texts, magazines, newspapers, phone books.
Goodrich, G. L., Mehr, E. B., Darling, N.C. Parameters in the use of CCTVs and optical aids. *American Journal of Optometry and Physiological Optics*, 1980, **57**(12), 881-892.		Identify resources, prices, and ordering information for nonoptical aids and materials.
Israel, L. CCTV reading machines for visually handicapped persons: A guide for selection. *New Outlook*, 1973, **67**(3), 102-110, 137.		
Lehon, L. H. Development of lighting		

McGillivray, R., ed. *Aids and appliances Review*, Issues #1 (January 1979), Issue #2 (July 1979), Issue #3 (January 1980). Newton, MA: Carroll Center for the Blind.

Mehr, E. B. The typoscope by Charles F. Prentice. *American Journal of Optometry; Archives of the American Academy of Optometry*, 1969, **46**(11), 885-887.

Sicurella, V. G. Color contrast as an aid for visually impaired persons. *Journal of Visual Impairment & Blindness*, 1977, **71**(6), 252-257.

Verma, S. B. Non-optical aids. *American Journal of Optometry and Physiological Optics*, 1974, **51**(10), 758-764.

UNIT 13: DISTANCE TRAINING

Input	Process	Output
Students (non-O.D., M.A. level) Rehabilitative Optometry Faculty: Orientation and Mobility Specialist Lecture Room (4–6 people) Low Vision Clinic Facilities: Distance Training Room *Assigned Readings* Finn, W. A., Gadbaw, P. D., Kevorkian, G.A., De l'Aune, W. R. Increasing field accessibility through prismatically displaced images. *New Outlook*, 1975, **69**(10), 465-467. Jose, R. T., Smith, A. J. Increasing peripheral field awareness with fresnel prisms. *Optometric Journal and Review of Optometry*, 1976, **113**(12), 33-37. Wiener, W., Vopata, A. Suggested curriculum for distance vision training with optical aids. *Journal of Visual Impairment & Blindness*, 1980, **74**(2), 49-56.	The student will complete a section on training low vision patients with optical aids for distance tasks. Information will be presented through one hour of lecture and discussion, observation, practicum, and assigned readings. Evaluation will be through written test and faculty review of completed observations and practicum sessions.	Upon completion of this section the student will be able to: Write a general sequence for a distance training session. Define the following visual skills as they apply to distance tasks: spotting, focusing, tracing, tracking, scanning. List three specific training techniques for use of a telescope for the following skills: tracking, scanning. Develop and conduct an individual training session for distance activities. Write an evaluation of a distance training session in terms of patient management and skills presented and taught. Produce distance training materials. Identify degree of field restriction which best lends itself to use of fresnel prisms. List steps for training a patient to use prisms.

UNIT 14: NEAR TRAINING

Input	Process	Output
Students (non-O.D., M.A. level)	The student will complete a section on training low vision patients with optical aids for near- and intermediate-distance tasks.	Upon completion of this section the student will be able to:
Rehabilitative Optometry Faculty: Low Vision Educational Specialist		Write a general sequence for a near training session.
Lecture Room (4–6 people)	Information will be presented through one hour of lecture and discussion, observation, practicum, and assigned readings.	Define the following visual skills as they apply to near tasks: localization, focusing, fixation, and scanning.
Low Vision Clinic Facilities: Near Training Room	Evaluation will be through written test and faculty review of completed observation forms and practicum sessions.	List three specific training techniques for each of the following aids: microscope, telemicroscope, hand-held magnifier.
Assigned Readings		Develop and conduct an individual training session for near- and intermediate-distance activities.
Inde, K. Low vision training in Sweden. *Journal of Visual Impairment & Blindness*, 1978, **72**, 307-310.		Write an evaluation of a near training session in terms of patient management and skills presented and taught.
Jose, R. T., Watson, G. Increasing reading efficiency with an optical aid/training program. *Optometric Journal and Review of Optometry*, 1978, **115**(2), 41-48.		List 20 commercially produced reading materials for near training: The list should represent a variety of reading interests and age levels.
Kurpis, J. S. People with low vision can distinguish paper currency. *Journal of Visual Impairment & Blindness*, 1977, **71**(2), 75-77.		Produce near training materials.
Watson, G., Jose, R. T. A training sequence for low vision patients. *Journal of American Optometric Association*, 1976, **47**(11), 1407-1415.		

UNIT 15: COMPREHENSIVE MULTIDISCIPLINARY LOW VISION SERVICE

Input	Process	Output
Students (non-O.D., M.A. level)	The student will complete a section on the philosophy and implementation of a comprehensive multidisciplinary low vision service.	Upon completion of this section the student will be able to:
Rehabilitative Optometry Faculty: O.D., experience in a multidisciplinary low vision service		Write a description of a low vision service model which includes components from various professions.
Lecture Room (4–6 people)	Information will be presented through one hour of lecture and discussion and assigned readings.	List members of a clinical low vision team and describe their individual roles.
Low Vision Clinic Facilities: Interview Room Examination Room Near Training Room Distance Training Room Staffing Room	Labs: The student will view the videotape *Low Vision, The Team Approach,* and complete the lab worksheet; the student will attend a low vision staffing, and summarize data presented.	Present training information at a staffing.
Videotape: *Low Vision, The Team Approach*	Evaluation will be through written examination, and faculty review of completed lab worksheet, staffing summary, completed observation forms, and practicum sessions.	List several methods of follow-up (after the clinical service) and identify outside resources which can help complete such follow-up.
Assigned Readings Davis, L. Community resources—why should we use them? *Journal of American Optometric Association,* 1976, **47**(11), 1445-1448. Faye, Chapter 12. Faye, E. E., Hood, C. M. Low vision services in an agency: Structure and philosophy. *New Outlook,* 1975, **69**(5), 241-248. Jose, R. T. What is low vision service? *Blindness 1974–75,* AAWB Annual,		

Olshansky, S. Some comments on the delivery of service. *Rehabilitation Literature*, 1973, 34(7), 203-206.

UNIT 16: THE ROLE OF SOCIAL SERVICES IN A MULTIDISCIPLINARY LOW VISION SERVICE

Input	Process	Output
Students (non-O.D., M.A. level)	The student will complete a section on the role of social services in a multidisciplinary low vision service.	Upon completion of this section the student will be able to:
Rehabilitative Optometry Faculty: Social Worker	Information will be presented through one hour of lecture and discussion and observation.	Identify six major areas of information covered in a social service case history.
Lecture Room (4–6 people)	Evaluation will be through written test and faculty review of completed observation forms.	List three roles of the social workers in a multidisciplinary low vision service.
Low Vision Clinic Facilities: Interview Room		Given a case history, identify patient needs which should be addressed through social services.

UNIT 17: ORIENTATION AND MOBILITY IN A LOW VISION SETTING

Input	Process	Output
Students (non-O.D., M.A. level)	The student will complete a section on assessing and training orientation and mobility skills for the low vision patient in a clinical setting.	Upon completion of this section the student will be able to:
Rehabilitative Optometry Faculty: Orientation and Mobility Specialist		List orientation and mobility skills to be assessed as part of a low vision service.
Lecture Room (4–6 people)	Information will be presented through one hour of lecture and discussion, observation, practicum, and assigned readings.	State factors which would indicate need for orientation and mobility training before a distance aid should be prescribed.
Low Vision Clinic Facilities: Distance Training Room		
Full array of NoIR and Olo spectacles	Evaluation will be through written test, and faculty evaluation of completed observation forms and practicum sessions.	List resources for long-term orientation and mobility training.
Assigned Readings		List three pathologies which restrict a person's ability to travel.
McGillivray, R., ed. *Aids and Appliances Review*, Issue #1, (January 1979), Newton, MA: Carroll Center for the Blind.		Assess a patient's need for special filter lenses such as NoIR's or Olo's.

UNIT 18: ECCENTRIC VIEWING

Input	Process	Output
Students (non-O.D., M.A. level)	The student will complete a section on assessment of and training for effective eccentric viewing.	Upon completion of this section the student will be able to:
Rehabilitative Optometry Faculty: Low Vision Educational Specialist		Define the following terms: Absolute scotoma, relative scotoma.
Lecture Room (4–6 people)	Information will be presented through one hour of lecture and discussion, observation, practicum, and assigned readings.	Given a completed Amsler grid, identify the functional effect of the scotoma(s) for near and distance activities.
Low Vision Clinic Facilities: Near Training Room	Evaluation will be through written test, and faculty review of completed observation forms and practicum sessions.	List several techniques for assessing a patient's eccentric viewing.
Assigned Readings		List several methods for training eccentric viewing.
Goodrich, G. L., Quillman, R. D. Training eccentric viewing. *Journal of Visual Impairment & Blindness*, 1977, **71**(9), 377–381.		Identify eye pathologies which, due to functional effects, require use of eccentric viewing for best efficiency.
Holcomb, J. G., Goodrich, G. L. Eccentric viewing training. *Journal of the American Optometric Association*, 1976, **47**(11), 1438–1443.		Compare a patient's eccentric viewing skill with his or her ability to perform near and distance activities.
		Assess and train a patient's ability to view eccentrically.

UNIT 19: PSYCHOLOGICAL AND SOCIOLOGICAL ASPECTS OF VISUAL LOSS

Input	Process	Output
Students (non-O.D., M.A. level)	The student will complete a section on the psychological and sociological aspects of visual loss, including patient goals and motivation, and counseling.	Upon completion of this section the student will be able to:
Rehabilitative Optometry Faculty: Social Worker		List major psychological and sociological aspects of a visual loss.
Lecture Room (4–6 people)	Information will be presented through one hour of lecture and discussion, observation, and assigned readings.	Identify social systems which influence a person's ability to cope with a visual loss.
Low Vision Clinic Facilities: Interview Room Examination Room Near Training Room Distance Training Room	Evaluation will be through written test and faculty review of completed observation forms.	Write an assessment of a specific patient's psychological set.
		List guidelines for determining need for referring a patient to counseling services.
Assigned Readings		Identify outside sources for various types of counseling.
Cholden, L. S. *A Psychiatrist Works with Blindness.* New York: American Foundation for the Blind, 1958.		
Adams, G. L., Pearlman, J. T., Sloan, S. H. Guidelines for the psychiatric referral of visually handicapped patients. *Annals of Ophthalmology,* 1971, 3(1), 72–81.		
Mehr and Fried, Chapter 3, Chapter 8 (105–106, 116–118).		
Schein, A. Counseling issues in Retinitis Pigmentosa. A.A.R.T., Spring 1976, 9–14.		
Welsh, R. L. The use of group strategies with the visually impaired: A review. *Journal of Visual Impair-*		

UNIT 20: LOW VISION—HISTORY AND DEMOGRAPHICS

Input	Process	Output
Students (non-O.D., M.A. level)	The student will complete a section on low vision history, demographics, and defining the low vision individual.	Upon completion of this section the student will be able to:
Rehabilitative Optometry Faculty: Low Vision Educational Specialist	Information will be presented through one hour of lecture and discussion and assigned readings.	Write a definition of the term low vision.
Lecture Room (4–6 people)	Evaluation will be through written test.	Write a brief history of low vision services.
Assigned Readings Faye, Chapters 1 and 2. Hoover, R., Kupfer, C. Low vision clinics: A report. *American Journal of Ophthalmology*, 1959, **48**(2), 177–187.		Compare several functional definitions and classification systems for low vision.
Kleen, S. R., Levoy, R. J. Low vision care: Correlation of patient age, visual goals, and aids prescribed. *American Journal of Optometry and Physiological Optics*, 1981, **58**(3), 200–205.		Name resources for statistics on low vision individuals and available services.
Unruh, D., Barraga, N. C. Data synthesis: Alternative approaches to research with low incidence populations. *Journal of Visual Impairment & Blindness*, 1981, **75**(8), 317–320.		

UNIT 21: GERIATRIC LOW VISION PATIENTS

Input	Process	Output
Students (non-O.D., M.A. level)	The student will complete a section on the geriatric low vision patient.	Upon completion of this section the student will be able to:
Rehabilitative Optometry Faculty: Optometrist, experience with geriatric low vision patients	Information will be presented through one hour of lecture and discussion, observation, practicum, and assigned readings.	List changes in visual functioning due to the normal aging process.
Lecture Room (4–6 people)	Evaluation will be through written test, and faculty review of completed observation forms and practicum sessions.	List the major eye diseases which affect the geriatric population.
Low Vision Clinic Facilities: Interview Room Examination Room Near Training Room Distance Training Room		Identify psychological and sociological problems which are specific to the older low vision patient.
		List five community resources to which the older low vision patient may be referred.
Assigned Readings Andriola, M. J. When visual disturbances are linked to neurological disorders. *Geriatrics*, 1976, **31**(3), 109–112.		Given specific pathologies, indicate lighting requirements for best visual acuity and functioning.
Carroll, T. J. A look at aging. *New Outlook*, 1972, **66**(4), 97–103. Crouch, C. L. Lighting needs for older eyes. *Sight Saving Review*, 1965, **35**(4), 213–215.		List three functional effects of cataract surgery and adaptation problems experienced by patients.
Donahue, W., MacFarland, D. C. Aging and blindness. *Blindness 1964*, AAWB Annual, 85–98.		Given a specific case history, assess the effect of a stroke on the visual functioning of that patient.
Faye, E. E. Visual function in geriatric eye disease. *New Outlook*, 1971, **65**(7), 204–208. Kotulak, J. C., Brungardt, T. Age-related changes in the corner. *Iour*		Conduct a training session demonstrating an understanding of the special needs of a geriatric low vision patient.

American Optometric Association, 1967, **38**(12), 1034–1036.

UNIT 22: THE MULTIPLY HANDICAPPED LOW VISION PATIENT

Input	Process	Output
Students (non-O.D., M.A. level)	The student will complete a section on the examination of multiply handicapped low vision patients.	Upon completion of this section the student will be able to:
Rehabilitative Optometry Faculty: O.D., experience in examining multiply handicapped low vision children	Information will be presented through one hour of lecture and discussion, one hour of lab, observation, and assigned readings.	List five pieces of information to be gathered through the case history which are specific to multiply handicapped patients.
Lecture Room (4–6 people)	Lab: The student will view the video-tape *Optometric Examination of the Multihandicapped* and complete the lab worksheet.	Given a case history, list areas of concern which should be addressed in the examination for that particular patient.
Low Vision Clinic Facilities: Interview Room Examination Room		List the four basic areas assessed in an optometric examination of a multiply handicapped low vision patient.
Videotape: *Optometric Examination of the Multihandicapped*	Evaluation will be through written test and faculty review of completed lab worksheet and observation forms.	Identify six adaptive techniques which can be used in the examination of a multiply handicapped low vision patient.
Videotape Playback Equipment		
Assigned Readings Deckard, D. K. Adapted visual efficiency scale: A comparison of performance obtained by multiply handicapped children. *Education of the Visually Handicapped,* 1979, **11**(3), 75–80.		
Yarnall, G. D., Dodgion-Ensor, B. Identifying effective reinforcers for a multiply handicapped student. *Education of the Visually Handicapped,* 1980, **12**(1), 11–21.		

UNIT 23: PATIENT MANAGEMENT

Input	Process	Output
Students (non-O.D., M.A. level)	The student will complete a section on patient management.	Upon completion of this section the student will be able to:
Rehabilitative Optometry Faculty: Social Worker Orientation and Mobility Specialist	Information will be presented through one hour of lecture and discussion, a one-half hour of lab, observation, and practicum.	List four patient management skills which can be used effectively during a low vision examination.
Lecture Room (4–6 people)	Lab: The student will complete a lab on using sighted guide techniques.	Analyze any part of a comprehensive low vison examination in terms of effective patient management.
Low Vision Clinic Facilities: Interview Room Examination Room Near Training Room Distance Training Room Conference Room	Evaluation will be through written test, faculty review of completed observation forms and practicum sessions, and practical exam covering sighted guide.	Guide a patient using correct sighted guide technique.
		Identify four patient management skills specific to training sessions.
		Conduct a training session using effective patient management skills.

UNIT 24: VISION STIMULATION

Input	Process	Output
Students (non-O.D., M.A. level)	The student will complete a section on vision stimulation.	Upon completion of this section the student will be able to:
Rehabilitative Optometry Faculty: Optometrist and Educational Specialist, experience with low functioning visually impaired children	Information will be presented through one hour of lecture and discussion, one hour of lab, and assigned readings.	Write a definition of the term vision stimulation.
		List a continuum of visual skills which can be addressed through vision stimulation.
Lecture Room (4–6 people)	Lab: The student will view the videotape *Consider Me Seeing* and complete the lab worksheet.	Given a specific visual skill, such as "attending to light," list three training activities designed to improve that skill.
Videotape: *Consider Me Seeing*	Evaluation will be through written test and faculty review of completed lab worksheet.	Identify resources and personnel for a long-term vision stimulation program.
Videotape Playback Equipment		Prepare materials to be used in a vision stimulation program.

Assigned Readings

Ficociello, C. Vision stimulation for low functioning deaf-blind rubella children. *Teaching Exceptional Children*, 1976, **8**(3), 128–130.

Langley, B., Dubose, R. F. Functional vision screening for severely handicapped children. *New Outlook*, 1976, **70**(8), 346–350.

"Vision stimulation sequence." The Upsal low vision team.

483

UNIT 25: VISUAL FUNCTIONING

Input	Process	Output
Students (non-O.D., M.A. level) Rehabilitative Optometry Faculty: Low Vision Educational Specialist Lecture Room (4–6 people) Visual Assessment Kit, based on the Ficociello-Gates materials. Program to Develop Efficiency in Visual Functioning. Louisville, KY: American Printing House for the Blind, 1980. *Assigned Readings* Barraga, N.C. Utilization of low vision in adults who are severely visually handicapped. *New Outlook*, 1976, **70**(5), 177–181. Barraga, N. C., Collins, M., Hollis, J. Development of efficiency in visual functioning: A literature analysis. *Journal of Visual Impairment & Blindness*, 1977, **71**(9), 387–391. Morris, O. F. Teacher assessment of visual functioning. *Education of the Visually Handicapped*, 1981, **13**,(2), 42–50.	The student will complete a section on visual functioning, assessing visual functional skills, and developing visual efficiency. Information will be presented through one hour of lecture and discussion, one hour of lab, and assigned readings. Lab: The student will review the Program to Develop Efficiency in Visual Diagnostic Assessment Procedure and the Visual Assessment Kit and complete the lab worksheet. Evaluation will be through written test and faculty review of completed lab worksheet.	Upon completion of this section the student will be able to: Write a continuum of visual functional skills which can be used as a base for assessment. Write a definition of the following terms: Visual functioning, visual efficiency, visual perception. State the interaction between visual functioning and visual efficiency. Assess visual functioning of a low vision individual. State the effect of magnification on visual functional skills.

UNIT 26: EDUCATIONAL CONSIDERATIONS

Input	Process	Output
Students (non-O.D., M.A. level)	The student will complete a section on	Upon completion of this section the

of materials and/or environmental adaptations.

Clinically evaluate a low vision student's ability to perform classroom activities.

Screen a child with low vision for possible visual perceptual difficulties.

Identify functional implications of a specific eye condition as related to classroom activities.

State factors to be considered when determining the extent to which a low vision child can participate in physical education activities.

Outline a functional visual assessment to be used outside a clinical setting.

---

vation, practicum, and assigned readings.

Evaluation will be through written test, and faculty review of completed observation forms and practicum sessions.

Lecture Room (4–6 people)

Low Vision Clinic Facilities: Near Training Room

Assigned Readings

Arensman, D. The role of the teacher for visually handicapped in vision assessment. *Education of the Visually Handicapped*, 1975, 7(1), 5–8.

Bateman, B. Mild visual defect and learning problems in partially seeing children. *Sight Saving Review*, 1963, 33(1), 30–33.

Corn, A. L. Optical aids in the classroom. *Education of the Visually Handicapped*, 1981, 12(4), 114–121.

Fridal, G., Jansen, L., Klindt, M. Courses in reading development for partially sighted students. *Journal of Visual Impairment & Blindness*, 1981, 75(1), 4–7.

Sloan, L. L., Habel, A. Reading speeds with textbooks in large and in standard print. *Sight Saving Review*, 1973, 43(2), 107–111.

Swallow, R. M. Fifty assessment instruments commonly used with blind and partially seeing individuals. *Journal of Visual Impairment & Blindness*, 1981, 75(2), 65–72.

Sykes, K. C. Print reading for visually handicapped children. *Education of the Visually Handicapped*, 1972, 4(3), 71–75.

UNIT 27: VISION TRAINING

Input	Process	Output
Students (non-O.D., M.A. level) College of Optometry Faculty: Optometrist, expertise in vision therapy Optometrist, low vision Clinic Facilities: Vision therapy examination room Lecture Room (4–6 people) *Assigned Readings* Brod, N. Visual development and reading. *American Journal of Optometry*, 1969, **46**, 96–102. McKee, G. A. The role of the optometrist in the development of perceptual and visuomotor skills in children. *American Journal of Optometry*, 1967, **44**(5), 297–310. Rosner, J. Perceptual skills with development in children with learning disabilities. *Pediatric Opthalmology*, Boston: Buttersworth, 1982. Weber, G. V. Visual disabilities—their identification and relationship with academic achievement. *Journal of Learning Disability*, **13**(6), 301–305.	The student will complete a section on vision training and visual skills related to perceptual activities. Information will be presented through a one-half hour of lecture and discussion, one hour of lab, and assigned readings. Lab: The student will observe a vision therapy session and write a one-page summary. Evaluation will be through written test and faculty review of the observation summary.	Upon completion of this section the student will be able to: List functional characteristics which indicate visual perceptual difficulties. Define the following visual skills: Binocularity, tracking, stereopsis, convergence, accommodation. Describe procedure for assessing binocularity, convergence, and accommodation. Define saccades and visual pursuit. List three activities for developing tracking and binocularity.

Input	Process	Output
Students (non-O.D., M.A. level)	The student will complete a section on driving with bioptic telescopes.	Upon completion of this section the student will be able to:
Rehabilitative Optometry Faculty: Optometrist, experience in fitting and prescribing bioptic telescopes for driving	Information will be presented through one hour of lecture and discussion, observation, practicum, and assigned readings.	List telescopic systems which can be used for driving.
Orientation and Mobility Specialist		List minimum field and acuity requirements for driving with a bioptic telescope.
Lecture Room (4–6 people)	Evaluation will be through written test, and faculty review of completed observation forms and practicum sessions.	Define spotting, scanning, and tracking skills used in driving with a bioptic telescope.
Low Vision Clinic Facilities: Examination Room Distance Training Room		Write a sequential outline for a program to train a patient to drive using bioptic telescopes.
		Compare the major arguments for and against low vison individual's driving with bioptic telescopes.

Assigned Readings

Burg, A. Vision and driving: A report on research. *Human Factors*, 1971, **13**(1), 79–87.

Fonda, G. A bioptic telescopic spectacle: Advantages and limitations. *Sight Saving Review*, Fall 1978, 125–128.

Jose, R. T., Butler, J. H. Driver's training for partially sighted persons: An interdisciplinary approach. *New Outlook*, 1975, **69**(7), 305–311.

Kelleher, D. K. Driving with low vision. *Journal of Visual Impairment & Blindness*, 1979, **73**(9), 345–350.

Korb, D. R. Preparing the visually handicapped person for motor vehicle operation. *American Journal of Optometry Archives of the American Academy of Optometry*, 1970, **47**(8), 619–628.

UNIT 29: CONTACT LENSES

Input	Process	Output
Students (non-O.D., M.A. level)	The student will complete a section on contact lenses and the use of contact lenses for low vision patients.	Upon completion of this section the student will be able to:
College of Optometry Faculty: Optometrist, expertise with contact lenses, experience in using contact lenses with low vision patients	Information will be presented through one hour of lecture and discussion.	List the types of contact lenses and the major physical properties of each.
Lecture Room (4–6 people)	Evaluation will be through written test.	State advantages and disadvantages of the various types of contact lenses.
Assigned Readings Gasson, A. New materials and designs in contact lens practice. *Ophthalmic Optometry*, 1981, April 11, 250–262.		Identify functional advantages of contact lenses for the low vision patient.
		List symptoms experienced by the contact lense wearer which indicate need for immediate referral to an eye care specialist.

UNIT 30: GENETICS

Input	Process	Output
Students (non-O.D., M.A. level)	The student will complete a section on genetics and genetic counseling.	Upon completion of this section the student will be able to:
Rehabilitative Optometry Faculty: Optometrist, experience in low vision and genetics	Information will be presented through one hour of lecture and discussion, and assigned readings.	Identify common eye diseases which may be inherited.
Lecture Room (4–6 people)	Evaluation will be through written test.	Write a definition of the following terms: Autosomal dominant, autosomal

75, AAWB Annual, 29–41.
Faye, Chapter 28.

List resources for genetic counseling.

UNIT 31: THE ROLE OF OPTOMETRY IN THE HEALTH CARE FIELD

Input	Process	Output
Students (non-O.D., M.A. level)	The student will complete a section on the role of optometry in the health care field.	Upon completion of this section the student will be able to:
College of Optometry Faculty: O.D., expertise in the historical development of the Optometry profession	Information will be presented through one hour of lecture and discussion, and assigned readings.	Write a brief outline of the development of optometry as a health care profession.
Lecture Facilities (4–6 people)	Evaluation will be through written test.	Identify primary, secondary and tertiary levels of health care delivery systems.
Assigned Readings Di Stefano, A. F. Rationalizing the delivery of eye care. Part I. *Journal of the American Optometric Association*, 1976, **47**(2), 216–221. Part II. *Journal of the American Optometric Association*, 1976, **47**(4), 489–494. Part III. *Journal of the American Optometric Association*, 1976, **47**(5), 627–632.		Identify the accreditation systems for clinical and educational optometry programs.
		Identify the procedure for membership in the Low Vision Diplomate section of the American Academy of Optometry.

UNIT 32: OBSERVATION

Input	Process	Output
Students (non-O.D., M.A. level) Rehabilitative Optometry Faculty: Optometrist, Low Vision Orientation and Mobility Specialist Low Vision Educational Specialist Social Worker Low Vision Clinic Facilities: Interview Room Examination Room Near Training Room Distance Training Room	As part of the activities for the completion of this curriculum, the student will observe all facets of the multidisciplinary low vision service. These observations will total approximately 30 hours including two intake interviews, two exit interviews, four optometric examinations, and 18 training sessions (minimum 6 each near and distance). The 30-hour requirement includes time spent reviewing case histories with faculty and independent review of case files. Evaluation will be through faculty review of completed observation sheets.	Upon completion of these observations, the student will have achieved relevant objectives from sections in this curriculum.

UNIT 33: PRACTICUM

Input	Process	Output
Students (non-O.D., M.A. level) Rehabilitative Optometry Faculty: Orientation and Mobility Specialist Low Vision Educational Specialist Low Vision Clinic Facilities:	As part of the activities for completion of this curriculum, the student will work directly with patients in all facets of the training procedure (assessment, instruction, staffings, and follow-up) for near and distance training. This practicum will total approximately 30 hours with a minimum of 8 sessions each for near and dis-	Upon completion of the practicum, the student will have achieved relevant objectives from sections in this curriculum.

490

Full array of nonoptical low vision aids
Full array of training materials, near and distance.

Evaluation will be through written assessment of the training sessions.

Upon completion of this project, the student will have achieved relevant objectives from sections in this curriculum.

UNIT 34: PROJECT

Input	Process	Output
Students (non-O.D., M.A. level) Rehabilitative Optometry Faculty:* Optometrist Orientation and Mobility Specialist Low Vision Educational Specialist Social Worker	As part of the activities for completion of this curriculum, the student will complete one to three projects of his or her choice relating to low vision services. Such project(s) will be approved and supervised by a member of the Rehabilitative Optometry Faculty.	Upon completion of this project, the student will have achieved relevant objectives from sections in this curriculum.
Clinic Materials:* Optical Aids Nonoptical Aids Training Materials	The student will give a formal presentation of one of his or her projects at a seminar which may include faculty and other students in low vision.	
College of Optometry Library*	The student will write a review of the completed project(s).	
*The specific faculty and materials required will depend on the project(s) chosen by the student.	Evaluation will be through written assessment of the project(s) by the appropriate faculty member.	

491

Appendix 3
Job Descriptions for Low Vision Service Specialists

Low Vision Clinical Specialist

Definition. The low vision clinical specialist is the professional person who is responsible for providing eye examinations to clients.

Educational qualifications. The low vision clinical specialist must meet all requirements for appropriate certification as an optometrist or ophthalmologist. In addition, the specialist shall have extensive training in the field of low vision by a recognized school of optometry or by an ophthalmology program with equivalent training.

Experience required. At least one year of experience in the provision of low vision examinations and low vision services to clients is necessary. In addition, application for recognition as a fellow in low vision by the American Academy of Optometry or membership in the low vision section of the American Optometric Association or membership in the Low Vision Clinical Society shall be pending or completed.

Personal qualifications. The low vision clinical specialist shall be mature and dependable; have initiative, sound judgment, a positive attitude toward low vision rehabilitation or habilitation, and a desire to work effectively with professionals from related disciplines; and be in good physical and emotional health.

Responsibilities. The responsibilities of this position include but are not limited to the following:

1. To provide thorough low vision clinical examinations to all clients referred.

2. To seek appropriate medical information from the program's medical consultant when necessary.

3. To provide complete written reports on all aspects of evaluations of clients.

4. To make appropriate and sound recommendations on low vision services to individual clients.

4. To refer clients to an eye specialist when further medical treatment is indicated or "normal" eye care services will solve their visual problems.

6. To participate in designing or obtaining specialized low vision devices to fit the needs of individual clients.

7. To attend appropriate staff meetings of the low vision program.

8. To evaluate objectively the quality of low vision services provided on a client-by-client basis.

9. To accept and perform other duties as assigned.

492

Medical Consultant to the Low Vision Program

Definition. The medical consultant is the professional person who is responsible for providing guidance to the program staff of the low vision program regarding the need for additional medical treatment of eye diseases on a case-by-case basis.

Educational qualifications. The medical consultant must meet all requirements for practicing the specialty of ophthalmology in the State of Maine.

Experience required. Experience in treating a wide variety of eye diseases and complications is necessary. A basic understanding of the principles involved in the subspecialty of low vision is preferred; however, it is not essential.

Personal qualifications. The medical consultant shall be mature and dependable; have initiative, sound judgment, a positive attitude toward low vision rehabilitation or habilitation, and a desire to work effectively with professionals from related disciplines; and be in good physical and emotional health.

Responsibilities. The responsibilities of this position include but are not limited to the following:

1. To provide medical consultation on the client's overall eye condition and health-related problems.

2. To make appropriate and sound recommendations about low vision services for individual clients.

3. To be available for diagnostic examinations of clients at low vision clinics when medical questions arise.

4. To attend appropriate staff meetings of the low vision program.

5. To evaluate objectively the quality of low vision services provided on a client-by-client basis.

6. To accept and perform other duties as assigned.

Staff reporting relationships. The medical consultant is responsible to the coordinator-instructor of the low vision program for the direct-service components of the program. This is usually a contract position.

Coordinator-Instructor of the Low Vision Program

Definition. The coordinator-instructor is the professional person qualified to organize, supervise, direct, and provide low vision services to the visually impaired. These services will help the visually impaired persons obtain or maintain appropriate employment, education and other daily living skills, visual skills, and positive attitudes toward life through visual rather than nonvisual means.

Educational qualifications. The coordinator-instructor shall have a minimum of a master's degree in one or more of the following areas: teaching the visually handicapped, orientation and mobility, social services and rehabilitation teaching of blind or visually impaired people (or comparable training).

Experience required. The coordinator-instructor shall have a minimum of one year's experience in a low vision clinical or rehabilitation program in di-

493

rect work with visually impaired individuals.

Personal qualifications. The coordinator-instructor shall be creative, mature, and dependable; have initiative and sound judgment; be in good physical and emotional health; and be able to communicate orally and in writing and to work effectively with professionals from related disciplines.

Responsibilities. The responsibilities of this position include but are not limited to the following:

1. To assess the visually impaired individual's visual functioning and visual environment to determine the need for further diagnostic evaluations at a low vision clinic.

2. To work compatibly and effectively with the program's medical and evaluative personnel.

3. To develop and implement effective visual training programs for each visually impaired client.

4. To provide ongoing consultation with referring personnel regarding each client's progress and the results of the low vision service.

5. To identify and stock appropriate and necessary equipment for the low vision program.

6. To participate in the development and maintenance of appropriate program data, both research and daily records.

7. To provide appropriate and timely follow-up services as indicated by other involved program personnel.

8. To participate in the establishment and implementation of goals.

9. To be an advocate for the blind and visually impaired.

10. To accept and perform other duties as assigned.

Appendix 4
Virginia Commission for the Visually Handicapped Education Services: Project LUV

The Education Services Department of the Virginia Commission for the Visually Handicapped is implementing a low vision service component of its program of total education services. The program, called Project LUV (Learn to Use your Vision), emphasizes maximizing each child's remaining vision by providing a total program of vision-sensory stimulation matched to each child's level of readiness for full perceptual development, or visual efficiency. A management advisory team, consisting of an administrator, educator, orientation and mobility specialist, optometrist, and ophthalmologist, will administer the project. Each project optometrist and ophthalmologist will participate in a training program that will describe the program and set the project's procedures and requirements.

An essential component of the project will be a thorough low vision examination. The low vision examination will include a pre-examination conference with the appropriate educator, the project's low vision examination, and the postexamination conference with teacher, parent, and child. Each visually impaired child will be scheduled for a low vision examination within three weeks of the teacher's referral to the examiner; the referral will be based on an eye examination given within the preceding year.

An itinerant teacher of the visually handicapped and education specialist, and an education consultant or an orientation and mobility specialist will schedule the child in a nearby Project LUV office. For the most part, each educator knows the visually handicapped children in his or her area of responsibility and will stress the necessary vision-stimulation program. With this information, the teacher will schedule an examination; transport the child and family to the examiner's office, if necessary; review with the examiner the findings and information before the examination; observe the examination; participate with the child, family, and doctor in the postexamination conference in which the use of prescriptions is demonstrated and described; return the family to the community; and provide the crucial follow-up support and training. A mandatory follow-up examination with the same examiner will be scheduled within four to six weeks of the first examination.

Again, the teacher will schedule the examination, accompany the family, and participate with the family and the doctor in the follow-up examination in which the prescriptions and the child's progress are reviewed. Training and support will continue throughout the program. Since the child is being referred to a Project LUV examiner for this low vision service, the primary care practitioner will be kept fully informed of the child's referral and the examination results.

Certain low vision diagnostic equipment will be lent to each examiner, and prescriptive material will be made available to each office for lending to the children. The equipment, plus the examination fee, will be funded by the project. There will be no fee charged to any child for the low vision examination or for the loaned aids.

The project stresses an interdisciplinary approach. Educators, optometrists, and ophthalmologists work closely to maximize a child's functional vision with or without aids. The intense low vision stimulation programs plus a pertinent functional vision evaluation by the teacher will give the low vision examiner important information. Using the information, the examiner can then examine and prescribe, if appropriate, and utilize the expertise of the teacher for a follow-up program; thus, the interdisciplinary team has an optimal impact on the child.

CHAPTER 19

Resources

SANDRA FERRARO, M.A.

Company or Organization	Services for Adults	Services for Children	General Information	Telescopes	Projection/Electronic Magnification	Microscopes	Magnifiers	Contact Lenses	Writing Aids	Reading Aids	Leisure-Activity Aids	Large Print	Illumination Controls	Homemaking Aids	Additional Aids and Services
Albert Aloe Co. 141 No. Meramec #23 St. Louis, Mo. 53105 (314) 726-2727				●											2.2 X clip-on reading loupe, 3 X clip-on telescope.
American Association of Workers for the Blind 206 No. Washington St. Alexandria, Va. 22314 (703) 548-1884			●												National membership organization with a low vision interest group.
American Bible Society 1865 Broadway New York, N.Y. 10023 (212) 581-7400												●			Religious materials; also available on cassettes.

Company or Organization	Services for Adults	Services for Children	General Information	Telescopes	Projection/Electronic Magnification	Microscopes	Magnifiers	Contact Lenses	Writing Aids	Reading Aids	Leisure-Activity Aids	Large Print	Illumination Controls	Homemaking Aids	Additional Aids and Services
American Council of the Blind 1211 Connecticut Ave., N.W. Suite 506 Washington, D.C. 20036 (202) 833-1251; 1-800-424-8666	●	●	●												Membership group organized for visually impaired individuals; state affiliates.
American Diabetes Association 2 Park Ave. New York, N.Y. 10016 (212) 683-7444			●												
American Foundation for the Blind 15 West 16th St. New York, N.Y. 10011 (212) 620-2000			●						●	●	●		●	●	Catalogs and publications: *Products for People with Vision Problems; Directory of Agencies Serving the Visually Handicapped in the United States; Sensory Aids for Employment of Blind and Visually Impaired Persons: A Resource Guide; Directory of Radio Reading Services; Journal of Visual Impairment & Blindness.*

Low Vision Aids, Dept. 3401
Southbridge, Mass. 01550
(617) 765-9711, x3269

American Optometric Association
600 Maryland Ave., S.W., Suite 400
Washington, D.C. 20024

Public Information pamphlets on common refractive conditions and eye diseases.

American Printing House for the Blind
1839 Frankfort Ave.
P.O. Box 6085
Louisville, Ky. 40206
(502) 895-2405

Publications: *Program to Develop Efficiency in Visual Functioning* and *Materials on the Utilization of Low Vision*, both by Natalie Barraga; catalogs for large-print materials and aids; nonoptical aids, including bold-line paper and reading stands.

American Thermo-Ware Co.
16 Warren St.
New York, N.Y. 10007
(212) 267-1126

Prisms, loupes.

Apollo Lasers
6357 Arizona Circle
P.O. Box 45002
Los Angeles, Calif. 90045
(213) 776-3343

Closed-circuit televisions.

Association for Education of the
    Visually Handicapped
206 No. Washington St.
Third Floor
Alexandria, Va. 22314
(703) 836-6060

National membership organization.

Company or Organization	Services for Adults	Services for Children	General Information	Telescopes	Projection/Electronic Magnification	Microscopes	Magnifiers	Contact Lenses	Writing Aids	Reading Aids	Leisure-Activity Aids	Large Print	Illumination Controls	Homemaking Aids	Additional Aids and Services
Bausch & Lomb 1400 North Goodman Street Rochester, N.Y. 14602 (716) 338–6000							●								Sunglasses, safety glasses, loupes, GlasStrap, Velcro spectacle bands.
Benson Optical Co. 10900 Red Circle Dr. Minnetonka, Minn. 55343 (612) 933–6616						●									Aphakic lenses.
Bernell Corp. 750 Lincolnway East South Bend, Ind. 46618 (219) 234–3200				●		●	●						●		Sun visors, sunglasses, clip-on occluders, spectacle loupes, magnifying mirrors, fresnel lenses, page magnifiers, D–15 color tests.
Best Visual Products Ltd. 65 Earle Ave. Lynbrook, N.Y. 15563 (516) 593–1135					●										

Supplier	Notes				
1753 DeSales St., N.W. Washington, D.C. 20036 (202) 347-4010					
Clovernook Home and School for the Blind 7000 Hamilton Ave. Cincinnati, Ohio 45231 (513) 522-3860					
Coburn Optical Industries 1701 South Cherokee, Box 627 Muskogee, Okla.	COIL Distributor	●		●	
Colonial Optical Co. 8415 South La Cienega Blvd. Inglewood, Calif. 90301 (213) 776-0777			●	●	
Copeland Extralens 129 East 61st St. New York, N.Y. 10021 (212) 988-9452	Copeland ColoReader Copeland Cone + 10.00D stand magnifier.				
Corning Glass Works Medical Optics Dept. MP21-2 Corning, N.Y. 14831	Tinted lenses for indoor and outdoor wear.				●

Company or Organization	Accessory Aids						Optical Aids					Services			Additional Aids and Services
	Homemaking Aids	Illumination Controls	Large Print	Leisure-Activity Aids	Reading Aids	Writing Aids	Contact Lenses	Magnifiers	Microscopes	Projection/Electronic Magnification	Telescopes	General Information	Services for Children	Services for Adults	
Council of Citizens with Low Vision c/o Dr. Elizabeth Lennon 1315 Greenwood Ave. Kalamazoo, Mich. 49007												●			National membership organization represents the interests of partially sighted persons through promotion of public and professional education, technical developments, and service agencies for the partially sighted.
Covington Plating Works 331 Pike St. Covington, Ky. 41011		●						●							
Delta Gamma Foundation Delta Gamma Executive Offices 3250 Riverside Drive Columbus, Ohio 43221													●	●	Service group with major interest in visually impaired; has local chapters.
Department of Education Special Education Programs 400 Sixth St., S.W. (Donahoe Bldg.) Washington, D.C. 20202													●	●	Main federal agency for administering governmental programs, grants, and research related to education of handicapped children.

vision Reading Cards, sunglasses, Velcro straps, special lens designs.

Binocular headband magnifiers, flexible-arm table magnifiers, loupes.

20/200 low vision playing cards.

Spectacle loupes, binoculars, colored filters, fresnel lenses, page magnifiers.

Aphakic spectacles, plano absorptive spectacles, binocular headband magnifiers.

Nitewriter illuminated pen, magi-mirror—2X magnification.

120 East 23rd St.
New York, N.Y. 10010
(212) 674-0600 or toll free
(800) 221-3476

Donegan Optical Co.
15549 West 108th St.
P.O. Box 5217
Lenexa, Kans. 66215
(913) 492-2500

Duffner and Sutton
3203 West 83 Terrace
Leawood, Kans. 66206
(913) 383-1894

Edmund Scientific Co.
101 E. Gloucester Pike
Barrington, N.J. 08007

Ednalite Corp.
200 North Water St.
Peekskill, N.Y. 10566

Edward Marcus
Moor House
7 Moorfields
London, EC2Y 9AE England
01-638 0390

Electro-Optix
Hy Farber Associates
391 Grand Ave.
Englewood, N.J. 07631

Company or Organization	Homemaking Aids	Illumination Controls	Large Print	Leisure-Activity Aids	Reading Aids	Writing Aids	Contact Lenses	Magnifiers	Microscopes	Projection/Electronic Magnification	Telescopes	General Information	Services for Children	Services for Adults	Additional Aids and Services
Gambit Corporation 174 E. Bellevue Dr. Pasadena, Ca. 91105 (213) 681-7437															
Goodlite Manufacturing Co. 7426 West Madison St. Forest Park, Ill. 60130 (312) 366-3860															Acuity charts, reading cards.
G. K. Hall 70 Lincoln St. Boston, Mass. 02111 (617) 423-3990			●												Has large-print book club with a list of best sellers.
Theodore Hamblin 15 Wigmore Street London W1 LAN 4343 England								●	●		●				

Loupes, acuity charts, Munsell color tests.

Low vision watches and clocks, absorptive lenses, magnetic padlocks, medical devices, telephone dials and push-button phone attachments, needle threaders, illuminated pens, writing guides, playing cards, catalog.

Wide Angle Mobility Light (WAML)

Service group whose major interest is in visually impaired; local chapters.

11 Middle Neck Rd.
Sands Point, N.Y. 11050
(516) 944-8900

House of Vision
135–137 North Wabash Ave.
Chicago, Ill. 60602
(312) 346-0755

Independent Living Aids
11 Commercial Court
Plainview, N.Y. 11803
(516) 681-8288

Innovative Rehabilitation Technology
375 Distel Circle
Suite C-4
Los Altos, Calif. 94022
(415) 965-8102

International Association of Lions Clubs
300 22nd St.
Oak Brook, Ill. 60570
(312) 986-1700

John Curley & Associates
P.O. Box 37
South Yarmouth, Mass. 02664

Company or Organization	Services for Adults	Services for Children	General Information	Telescopes	Projection/Electronic Magnification	Microscopes	Magnifiers	Contact Lenses	Writing Aids	Reading Aids	Leisure-Activity Aids	Large Print	Illumination Controls	Homemaking Aids	Additional Aids and Services
Keeler Instruments 456 Parkway Broomall, Pa. 19008 (215) 353–4350				●		●	●								Clip-on occluders, binoculars.
Keitzer Check Writing Guide 1129 Peninsula Drive Lake Wales, Fl. 33853 (813) 676–1805									●						
Low Vision Reading Stand c/o Richard Jose CMCC 1561 1901 Dayton Rd. Chico, Calif. 95926										●					Adjustable wooden reading stand.
Luxo Lamp Corp. Monument Park Port Chester, N.Y. 10573 (914) 937–4433							●						●		Lamps, stand magnifiers with built-in illumination.

Column groups: Services — Services for Adults, Services for Children, General Information. Optical Aids — Telescopes, Projection/Electronic Magnification, Microscopes, Magnifiers, Contact Lenses. Accessory Aids — Writing Aids, Reading Aids, Leisure-Activity Aids, Large Print, Illumination Controls, Homemaking Aids.

100 Jefferson Park
Warwick, R.I. 02888
(401) 467-3000

Fresnel lenses and prisms, post-operative cataract spectacles.

Mentor O&O, Inc.
20 Industrial Park Rd.
Hingham, Mass. 02043
(617) 749-8215

Narcissus Medical Foundation
1800 Sullivan Ave., Suite 506
Daly City, Calif. 94015

Tinted and painted contact lenses, soft and hard.

National Accreditation Council for Agencies Serving the Blind and Visually Handicapped
15 W. 65th St.
New York, N.Y. 10023
(212) 496-5880

Administers programs of accreditation for agencies, schools, and services for the blind and visually handicapped; sets standards for low vision services.

National Association for Parents of the Visually Impaired
3329 Northaven Rd.
Dallas, Tx. 75229
(214) 358-1995

Provides support for families of visually impaired children; national clearinghouse of information and services.

National Association for the Visually Handicapped
305 East 24th St.
New York, N.Y. 10010
(212) 889-3141

Book stand.

Company or Organization	Homemaking Aids	Illumination Controls	Large Print	Leisure-Activity Aids	Reading Aids	Writing Aids	Contact Lenses	Magnifiers	Microscopes	Projection/Electronic Magnification	Telescopes	General Information	Services for Children	Services for Adults	Additional Aids and Services
National Federation of the Blind 1800 Johnson St. Baltimore, Md. 21230 (301) 659-9314												●	●	●	National organization of blind individuals; has state groups.
National Genetics Foundation 250 West 57th St. New York, N.Y. 10019 (212) 759-4432.												●			Clearinghouse for counseling and treatment centers in the United States.
National Institute of Rehabilitation Engineering 97 Decker Rd. Butler, N.J. 07405 (201) 838-2500		●													Night vision aid.
National Library Service for the Blind and Physically Handicapped Library of Congress 1291 Taylor St., N.W. Washington, D.C. 20542			●									●	●		Materials in large print; cassettes and talking books available from regional libraries reference circulars, magazines in special media; reading, writing, and other communication

...ials in large type; directory of local radio services for the blind and physically handicapped.

Research, public education programs, national registry of individuals with retinitis pigmentosa; night vision aid; has local organizations active throughout the United States.

Public and professional research, education, industrial and community services.

Absorptive lenses, lamps, Sloan continuous text cards, low vision textbooks, clip-on occluders, typoscopes, loupes.

National Retinitis Pigmentosa
  Foundation
8331 Mindale Circle
Baltimore, Md. 21207
(301) 655–1011; TDD (301) 655–1190

National Society to Prevent Blindness
79 Madison Ave.
New York, N.Y. 10016
(212) 684–3505

New York Lighthouse Optical Aids
  Service
36-02 Northern Blvd.
Long Island City, N.Y. 11101
(212) 937–9338

New York Times Large Type Puzzle
  Collection
229 West 43rd St.
New York, N.Y. 10036
(212) 556–1234

New York Times Large Type Weekly
229 West 43rd St.
New York, N.Y. 10036
(212) 556–1234

Company or Organization	Accessory Aids						Optical Aids					Services			Additional Aids and Services
	Homemaking Aids	Illumination Controls	Large Print	Leisure-Activity Aids	Reading Aids	Writing Aids	Contact Lenses	Magnifiers	Microscopes	Projection/Electronic Magnification	Telescopes	General Information	Services for Children	Services for Adults	
Nikon Instrument Division 623 Stewart Ave. Garden City, N.Y. 11530 (516) 222–0200		●									●				Spectacle-mounted telescopes with reading caps.
Nu-Vue Visor Co. P.O. Box 757 Fairhope, Ala. 35632															Visors, sunshades.
Ocutech Low Vision Aids Vision Development Enterprises 3803 Tremont Dr. Durham, N.C. 27705 (919) 493–7456								●	●		●				Telescopes, minifiers, telescope clips, and television magnifiers.
Olo Products P.O. Box 613 Manhasset, N.Y. 11030 (516) 487–8576		●													Absorptive lenses

Absorptive lenses.

Main federal agency for administering programs, grants, and training facilities related to the rehabilitation of visually impaired individuals.

Street signs and other road information signs.

Full-page magnifiers, lamps, adjustable spectacle sports band, playing cards; catalog.

Binoculars, table magnifiers, spectacle loupes, high-intensity lamps.

Gardena, Calif. 90248
(213) 321-5591

Reader's Digest Fund for the Blind, Inc.
Large-Type Edition, Large Type Reader
Pleasantville, NY 10570

Recreational Innovations Co.
Medical Products Division
P.O. Box 159
South Lyon, Mich. 48178
(313) 769-5565; (800) 521-9746

Rehabilitation Services Administration
Bureau for the Blind and Visually
Handicapped
330 C St., S.W.
Washington, D.C. 20201
(202) 245-0918

Safety Lights Co.
6813 Dixie Dr.
Houston, Tex. 77087
(713) 644-7379

Science for the Blind Products
Box A
Southeastern, Pa. 19399
(215) 687-3731

Selsi Co.
40 Veterans Blvd.
Carlstadt, N.J. 07072
(201) 935-0388

Company or Organization	Accessory Aids						Optical Aids					Services			Additional Aids and Services
	Homemaking Aids	Illumination Controls	Large Print	Leisure-Activity Aids	Reading Aids	Writing Aids	Contact Lenses	Magnifiers	Microscopes	Projection/Electronic Magnification	Telescopes	General Information	Services for Children	Services for Adults	
Siebe Norton, Inc. 2000 Plainfield Pike Cranston, R.I. 02920		●													Safety glasses, tinted glasses.
Stanwix House 3020 Chartiers Ave. Pittsburgh, Pa. 15204 (412) 771-4233			●												
Swift Instrument Co. 952 Dorchester Ave. Dorchester, Mass. 02125 (617) 436-2960								●			●				Binoculars.
Sensory Aids Corporation Suite 110, White Pines Office Center 205 West Grand Ave. Bensenville, Ill. 60106 (312) 766-3935 Distributor: Telesensory Systems, Inc.										●					Viewscan electronic reading aid.

Sponsors recreational activities for legally blind individuals; local, state, and regional chapters.

Publishes *Coping with Sight Loss: The Vision Resource Book*, by F. Weisse and M. Winer; and "Vision Inventory List."

Closed-circuit television; local representatives available.

A fee-for-service agency

Binoculars.

Clip-on binocular loupes and telescopes, flex-arm stand magnifiers.

New York, N.Y. 10001
(212) 563–7796; 1–800–223–7610

U.S. Association for Blind Athletes
55 West California Ave.
Beach Haven Park, N.J. 08008
(609) 492–1017

Vision Foundation
2 Mt. Auburn St.
Watertown, Mass. 02172
(617) 926–4232

Visualtek
1610 26th St.
Santa Monica, Calif. 90404-4077
(213) 829–6841

Volunteer Transcribing Services
205 East Third Ave.
Room 207
San Mateo, Calif. 94401-4077

S. Walters
412 West Sixth St.
Los Angeles, Calif. 90014
(213) 622–0744

Wingate Opth. Co.
1418 E.88 St.
Brooklyn, N.Y. 11236
(516) 378–4473

CHAPTER 20

Selected References

SANDRA FERRARO, M.A.
KATHLEEN E. FRASER, O.D.

GENERAL REFERENCES

Barraga, N. C. *Visual handicaps and learning*. Belmont, Calif.: Wadsworth Publishing Co., 1976.

Barraga, N. C., & Morris, J. E. *Program to develop efficiency in visual functioning: Source book on low vision*. Louisville, Ky.: American Printing House for the Blind, 1980.

Basic optical concepts; Lenses, prisms and mirrors; Normal and abnormal vision; The human eye. Southbridge, Mass.: American Optical Corp., 1976.
Series of four programmed self-instruction courses.

Blindness, visual impairment, deaf-blindness: Semiannual listing of current literature. Nevil Interagency Referral Service, October 1976 to present.
Annotated bibliography of professional literature related to visual impairment.

Cholden, L. S. *A psychiatrist works with blindness*. New York: American Foundation for the Blind, 1958.

Faye, E. E. *Clinical low vision*. Boston: Little, Brown & Co., 1976.

Faye, E. E., & Hood, C. M. *Low vision*. Springfield, Ill.: Charles C Thomas, 1975.

Inde, K., & Bäckman, Ö. *Syntraining med optik* (Visual training with optical aids). Malmö, Sweden: Hermods, 1975.

Mehr, E. B., & Freid, A. N. *Low vision care*. Chicago: Professional Press, 1975.

Seagers, P. W. *Light, vision and learning*. New York: Better Light Better Sight Bureau, 1963.

Sloan, L. L. *Reading aids for the partially sighted*. Baltimore: Williams & Wilkins Co., 1977.

Statistical Briefs, *Journal of Visual Impairment & Blindness*. October 1976 to present.
Column prepared by the American Foundation for the Blind staff on social and demographic characteristics of the visually impaired and blind population in the United States and the characteristics of the U.S. service delivery systems.

DATA ON THE VISUALLY IMPAIRED POPULATION

Dickey, T. W., & Vieceli, L. A survey of the vocational placement of visually handicapped persons and their degree of vision. *New Outlook for the Blind*, 1972, **66** (2), 38-42.
Presents data on 1,733 visually impaired individuals placed by 77 vocational rehabilitation counselors; relates the degree of vision to type of job placement and states areas of concern voiced by employers.

Faes, F. F. A study of successful and unsuccessful low vision rehabilitation patients.

American Journal of Optometry & Physiological Optics, 1981, **58** (5), 404-407. Reports on a study of 84 visually impaired patients rehabilitated through a low vision clinic; data suggest factors that affect successful rehabilitation.

Goldish, L. H. The severely visually impaired population as a market for sensory aids and services: Part one. *New Outlook for the Blind*, 1972; **66** (6), 183-190. Presents statistics on age groups, services utilized, limitations of activity, percentage in the labor force, and financial sources of the visually impaired population.

Goldish, L. H. The severely visually impaired population as a market for sensory aids and services: Part two. *New Outlook for the Blind*, 1973; **67** (7), 289-296. Discusses the nature of partial sight, statistics on the primary objectives of low vision care patients and the types of aids prescribed, and the market for large-print books and closed-circuit televisions.

Hoover, R., & Kupfer, C. Low vision clinics: A report. *American Journal of Ophthalmology*, 1959, **48** (2), 177-187. Reports on 841 visually impaired cases seen at seven clinics in New York, Massachusetts, Maryland, North Carolina, and Ohio; data emphasize etiology and aids prescribed.

Kleen, S. R., & Levoy, R. J. Low vision care: correlation of patient age, visual goals, and aids prescribed. *American Journal of Optometry & Physiological Optics*, 1981, **58** (3), 200-205. Presents data on 185 visually impaired patients seen in a clinical setting, emphasizing the patients' goals and the aids prescribed.

Rosenbloom, A. A. Prognostic factors in low vision rehabilitation. *American Journal of Optometry, Archives of the American Academy of Optometry*, 1970, **47** (8), 600-605. Presents follow-up data on 276 visually impaired patients as to pathology, success in the use of low vision aids, and type of aid in relation to successful use.

Unruh, D., & Barraga, N. C. Data synthesis: Alternate approaches to research with low incidence populations. *Journal of Visual Impairment & Blindness*, 1981, 75(8), 317-320. Discusses the problems of obtaining extensive research information on a low-incidence population and describes four approaches to data synthesis as a means of integrating the limited information available.

Vision problems in the U.S.: Facts and figures. New York: Operational Research Department, National Society to Prevent Blindness, 1980.

PHYSIOLOGICAL AND FUNCTIONAL ASPECTS OF EYE DISEASES AND TREATMENT

Andriola, M. J. When visual disturbances are linked to neurological disorders. *Geriatrics*, 1976, **31** (3), 109-112. Discusses normal changes owing to aging seen in elderly patients and the abnormal changes associated with neurological problems; includes the symptoms, etiology, and treatment.

Ball, G. V. Anomalies of vision in low illumination. *American Journal of Optometry & Physiological Optics*, 1973, **50** (3), 200-205. Lists and briefly discusses the various causes of poor night vision, the most common being media irregularities (such as cortical cataracts), uncorrected refractive errors, and psychological considerations.

Basso, L. V. The condition known as diabetes mellitus. *Journal of Visual Impairment & Blindness*, 1978, **72** (9), 338-442.
Describes diabetes mellitus, its history, complications, current treatment, and research.

Beller, R., Hoyt, C. S., Marg, E., & Odom, J. V. Good visual function after neonatal surgery for congenital monocular cataracts. *American Journal of Ophthalmology*, 1981, **91** (5), 559-565.
Describes surgical treatment, the fitting of contact lenses, and amblyopia treatment in infants with congenital monocular cataracts; results indicate good visual acuities but no evidence of binocularity.

Ciuffreda, K. J. Retinitis pigmentosa and vision—An overall view and approach. *Optical Journal and Review of Optometry*, 1972, **109** (20), 38-46.
Describes retinitis pigmentosa, including its optical management, the history of nonoptical treatments, and suggestions for new optical aids.

Coughlin, W. R., & Patz, A. Diabetic retinopathy: Nature and extent. *Journal of Visual Impairment & Blindness*, 1978, **72** (9), 343-347.
Reports on the incidence and prevalence of juvenile- and adult-onset diabetes, retinal changes in background and proliferative diabetic retinopathy, current treatment, and theories about the causes of changes in the retinal tissue.

Faye, E. E. The role of eye pathology in low vision evaluation. *Journal of the American Optometric Association*, 1976, **47** (11), 1395-1401.
Classifies eye diseases according to patterns of field loss and discusses the functional implications of eye diseases in relation to the prescription and use of low vision aids.

Guth, S. K. Effect of age on visibility. *American Journal of Optometry, Archives of the American Academy of Optometry*, 1957, **32** (9), 463-477.
Reports on an investigation of visibility levels attained with various levels of illumination; data are broken into age groups to help determine the effect of age on illumination requirements.

Kalina, R. E. Treatment of retrolental fibroplasia. *Survey of Ophthalmology*, 1980, **24** (4), 229-236.
Describes the etiology of retrolental fibroplasia, reviews current treatments and results, and discusses surgical treatment for associated problems such as a detached retina.

Kleinstein, R. N. Intraocular lenses. *Optometric Monthly*, 1980, **71** (11), 616-617.
Lists the types of intraocular lenses and discusses the indications and contraindications for their use, complications, and the management of patients.

Marmor, M. F. Visual loss in retinitis pigmentosa. *American Journal of Ophthalmology*, 1980, **89** (5), 692-698.
Reports on a study of 93 patients diagnosed as having retinitis pigmentosa and presents data on visual acuity and changes in acuity with age.

Morin, J. D., & Bryars, J. H. Causes of loss of vision in congenital glaucoma. *Archives of Ophthalmology*, 1980, **98** (9), 1575-1576.
Reports on a study of 51 patients with congenital glaucoma and controlled intraocular pressure that showed the chief causes of vision loss to be damage to the optic nerve, medial opacities, and corneal irregularities.

Noble, K. G., & Carr, R. E. Stargardt's disease and fundus flavimaculatus. *Archives of Ophthalmology*, 1979, **97** (7), 1281-1285.
Reports on a study of 67 patients with Stargardt's disease or fundus flavimaculatus; describes the visual function and ophthalmoscopic appearance of both and concludes that there is no distinction between the two diseases.

Raab, E. Cataracts and glaucoma in the infant and preschool child: Detection, systemic aspects, and treatment. *Sight Saving Review*, 1980, **50** (1), 5-14.
States that the early detection and prompt treatment of congenital cataracts or glaucoma are essential and discusses the symptoms, diagnosis, and treatment.

Rosenberg, R., & Werner, D. L. Nystagmus and low vision. *Journal of the American Optometric Association*, 1969, **40** (8), 833-835.
States that the etiology and type of nystagmus may influence the success of low vision aids and that attempts should be made to increase visual function rather than to eliminate the nystagmus.

Schaffer, R. N., & Cohen, J. S. Visual reduction in aniridia. *Journal of Pediatric Ophthalmology*, 1975, **12** (4), 220-222.
Presents a basic discussion of the effect of aniridia on the retina, optic nerve, cornea, lens, and iris and changes in vision that occur with age.

Sloan, L. L. Congenital achromatopsia: A report of 19 cases. *Journal of the Optical Society of America*, 1954, **44** (2), 117-128.
Reports in detail about studies of the visual function of subjects with complete and incomplete achromatopsia; emphasizes the rate of dark adaptation in parafoveal and foveal regions.

Spitzberg, D. Ocular histoplasmosis. *Sight Saving Review*, 1980, **50** (1), 21-24.
Presents background information as well as the signs, symptoms, and treatment of ocular histoplasmosis.

Tanner, W. P. Adaption of vision following cataract removal. *New Outlook for the Blind*, 1971, **65** (9), 281-286.
Presents a personal account of adjustment to vision after the removal of cataracts; discusses color, the relationship of size and distance, the distortion of vertical surfaces, and peripheral vision.

Whinston, M., & Applebury, M. L. The unsolved mysteries of retinitis pigmentosa and retinal degeneration. *Nursing Care*, 1978, **11** (1), 28-35.
Briefly describes the retinal changes in retinitis pigmentosa with some theories about the cause of these changes.

Zimmerman, D. R. Birth defects and visual impairment. *Journal of Visual Impairment & Blindness*, 1977, **71** (1), 2-12.
Surveys the epidemiological studies on birth defects and visual impairment; discusses ophthalmic genetics, including research studies.

VISUAL FUNCTIONING

Barraga, N. C. Effects of experimental teaching on the visual behavior of children with low vision. *American Journal of Optometry, Archives of the American Academy of Optometry*, 1965, **42** (9), 557-561.
Reports on a study to determine the effect of an eight-week vision stimulation program for severely visually impaired children (6/200 or less).

Barraga, N. C. Learning efficiency in low vision. *Journal of the American Optometric Association*, 1969, **40** (8), 807-810.

Emphasizes the importance of visual functioning as opposed to acuity; discusses vision as a sequentially learned skill, including the stages of visual perceptual development, vision training, and efficiency; presents charts on the stages of visual discrimination and the sequence of activities.

Barraga, N. C. Utilization of low vision in adults who are severely visually handicapped. *New Outlook for the Blind,* 1976, **70** (5), 177-181.
Discusses the importance of emphasizing and increasing the use of residual vision by adults with severe visual loss and states that the increasing use of residual vision should be through perceptual reorganization for adventitious impairment and visual perceptual development for congenital impairment.

Barraga, N. C., & Collins, M. E. Development of efficiency in visual functioning: Rationale for a comprehensive program. *Journal of Visual Impairment & Blindness,* 1979, **73** (4), 121-126.
Outline of visual functions with corresponding age levels at which the functions occur in normal development and tasks that illustrate the presence of the functions; represents the theoretical base for the Program to Develop Efficiency in Visual Functioning.

Barraga, N. C., Collins, M., & Hollis, J. Development of efficiency in visual functioning: A literature analysis. *Journal of Visual Impairment & Blindness,* 1977, **71** (9), 387-391.
Describes the development of vision in unimpaired infants and children and relates it to the progression of visual function in visually impaired individuals. Discusses the recent literature; represents the literature base of the Program to Develop Efficiency in Visual Functioning.

Collins, M. E., & Barraga, N. C. Development of efficiency in visual functioning: An evaluation process. *Journal of Visual Impairment & Blindness,* 1980, **74** (3), 93-96.
Discusses the Diagnostic Assessment Procedure, including basic assumptions, the rationale for development, terminology, administration, interpretation, and use. Represents the practical base for the Program to Develop Efficiency in Visual Functioning.

Low, F. N. Some characteristics of peripheral visual performance. *American Journal of Physiology,* 1946, **146** (4), 573-584.
Reports on studies done to develop a standardized measure of peripheral visual acuity and to determine the practicality of training peripheral function; discussion of the nature of the peripheral visual process.

Valvo, A. Behavior patterns and visual rehabilitation after early and long-lasting blindness. *American Journal of Ophthalmology,* 1968, **65** (1), 19-24.
Describes a specialized surgical procedure that enabled a patient with long-lasting blindness to recover vision; the neurophysiological and psychological difficulties encountered are discussed.

PSYCHOLOGICAL AND SOCIOLOGICAL CONSIDERATIONS

Adams, G. L., Pearlman, J. T., & Sloan, S. H. Guidelines for the psychiatric referral of visually handicapped patients. *Annals of Ophthalmology,* 1971, **3** (1), 72-81.
Describes patients' reactions of acceptance, denial, and depression to visual loss, suggests when referral to a psychiatric consultant is appropriate, and includes specific case studies.

Cross, H. E. Genetic counseling and blinding disorders. *Blindness* (American Association of Workers for the Blind annual), 1974–75, 29-41.
Briefly describes the basic genetic principles; discusses the information to be sought by a genetic counselor, counseling for major forms of genetic diseases, how to determine the risk of recurrence; and suggests how to present and interpret data.

Cutsforth, T. D. Personality crippling through physical disability. In P. A. Zahl (Ed.), *Blindness*. Princeton, N.J.: Princeton University Press, 1950.
Describes and discusses the personality factors that are induced by blindness as the individual attempts to live in a world unaccustomed to blindness.

Emerson, D. L. Facing loss of vision: The response of adults to visual impairment. *Journal of Visual Impairment & Blindness*, 1981, **75** (2), 41-45.
Group therapy was used to treat psychosocial problems of adult clients. Most members went through phases of shock and reactive depression; all but a few were in a period of readjustment after six months.

Freedman, S. The assessment of older visually impaired adults by a psychologist. *New Outlook for the Blind*, 1975, **69** (8), 361-364.
Stresses the importance of psychological testing in the rehabilitation process, points out the need to inform the patient and the staff of information gathered, and suggests testing material.

Freeman, P. B. Evaluating the needs of the low vision teenager. *Optical Journal & Review of Optometry*, 1980, **117** (6), 49-50.
Presents a case history of a 17-year-old boy that illustrates the problems of cosmesis.

Lee, D., & Jose, R. T. Low vision care—Not everyone wants it. *Optical Weekly*, 1976, **67** (50), 1365-1369.
Presents a case report of a 25-year-old woman who ultimately rejected low vision aids; presents some ideas on possible reasons for the rejection.

Mehr, H. M., Mehr, E. B., & Ault, C. Psychological aspects of low vision rehabilitation. *American Journal of Optometry, Archives of the American Academy of Optometry*, 1970, **47** (8), 605-612.
Describes a discussion group for partially sighted individuals and discusses the implications for various age groups.

Perle, T. A matter of adjustment: A personal reaction to visual loss. *Journal of Visual Impairment & Blindness*, 1978, **72** (7), 255-258.
Describes personal experiences of a teacher of visually handicapped children, including his own visual loss, the problems encountered, and his solutions.

Schein, A. Counseling issues in retinitis pigmentosa. *A.A.R.T.*, Spring 1976, 9-14.
Presents a brief overview of the diagnosis and etiology of retinitis pigmentosa, lists the problems associated with it that may cause difficulties in rehabilitation, and discusses counseling issues, which are illustrated with some case histories.

Soll, D. M. Vision care for the partially sighted child. *New England Journal of Optometry*, 1973, **24** (7), 202-205.
Discusses the psychological aspects of examining and prescribing for partially sighted children; emphasizes the need to address problems early for better adjustment to aids.

The patient's view: Usher's syndrome. *Canadian Journal of Ophthalmology*, 1980, **15** (1), 51-53.
Presents personal reactions to visual loss from Usher's syndrome and gives ad-

vice to ophthalmologists about telling patients of such a diagnosis.

Welsh, R. L. The use of group strategies with the visually impaired: A review. *Journal of Visual Impairment & Blindness*, 1978, **72** (4), 131-138.
Reviews the literature on group therapy for visually impaired individuals, including therapeutic, assessment, and experimental groups; discusses the nature and strategies of these groups and some suggestions for further research.

OPTOMETRIC LOW VISION EXAMINATION

Bailey, I. L. Visual acuity measurement in low vision. *Optometric Monthly*, 1978, **69** (7), 418-424.
Compares several charts for measuring distance acuity and gives tips for taking more reliable measurements.

Bailey, I. L. Refracting low vision patients. *Optometric Monthly*, 1978, **69** (8), 519-523.
Describes specialized refracting techniques and stresses the need to take time with low vision patients.

Bailey, I. L. Visual field measurement in low vision. *Optometric Monthly*, 1978, **69** (10), 697-701.
Discusses the methods of testing the central visual field in low vision patients and describes some of the difficulties that may be encountered.

Bailey, I. L. Specification of near point performance. *Optometric Monthly*, 1978, **69** (12), 895-898.
Describes the systems in wide use for measuring near-point acuity and compares their relative merits; recommends using the M system or point system and gives conversion methods for these two systems.

Bailey, I. L. Combining accommodation with spectacle additions. *Optometric Monthly*, 1980, **71** (6), 397-399.
Explains how to estimate the accommodation of a young low vision patient who is using a high add by utilizing the formula given or measuring the working distance.

Faye, E. E. A new visual acuity test for partially-sighted non readers. *Journal of Pediatric Ophthalmology*, 1968, **5**, 210-212.
Describes the development, format, and testing procedure of the Lighthouse symbol acuity text card.

Flom, M. C. New concepts on visual acuity. *Optometry Weekly*, 1966, **57** (28), 63-68.
Discusses the reserve of resolving power, contour interaction, and psychometric analysis and how these concepts affect visual acuity measurements, particularly for low vision patients.

Genensky, S. M. Acuity measurements—Do they indicate how well a partially sighted person functions or could function? *American Journal of Optometry & Physiological Optics*, 1976, **53** (12), 809-812.
Discusses the fallacy of equating visual acuity with visual functioning; suggests the level of illumination and test charts to be used when examining a partially sighted individual.

Goodlaw, E. I. Assessing field defects of the low vision patient. *American Journal of Optometry & Physiological Optics*, 1981, **58** (6), 486-490.
Discusses the importance of assessing the fields of low vision patients; describes

a technique for assessing fields that can be used when fatigue or debility prohibits the use of standard tests.

Griffin, J. R. Historical summary of visual fields methods. *Journal of the American Optometric Association*, 1980, **51** (9), 833-835.
Sketches the methods and equipment used to determine visual fields from Hippocrates through the 1970s; briefly discusses the advantages and disadvantages of the hemispherical perimeter.

Kaiser, P. K. Colour vision in the legally blind. *Canadian Journal of Ophthalmology*, 1972, **7** (3), 302–308.
Reports on a study of the color vision of six legally blind individuals; discusses the use of the color-naming method as a clinical tool.

Kleinstein, R. N. Contrast sensitivity. *Optometric Monthly*, 1981, **72** (4), 38-40.
Defines contrast sensitivity and spatial frequency and briefly describes their clinical measurement. The clinical applications for their diagnostic uses have not yet been determined.

Larkin, M. Visual fields interpretation. *Journal of the American Optometric Association*, 1980, **51** (9), 837-842.
Describes many common visual field defects and their etiology and stresses the need to include visual field testing in ocular health examinations.

Levin, M. I., & Hirsh, M. J. A low vision patient's expectations: A partial case report. *American Journal of Optometry, Archives of the American Academy of Optometry*, 1973, **50** (10), 809-811.
Presents a case report of a 20-year-old female college student, lists 43 activities she wanted to be able to do, which provides insight into some of the basic needs of the low vision patient.

Lie, I. Relation of visual acuity to illumination, contrast, and distance in the partially sighted. *American Journal of Optometry & Physiological Optics*, 1977, **54** (8), 528-536.
Reports on a study to determine the differences among partially sighted people as to the dependence of their acuity on illumination, contrast, and distance; presents data and discusses the relationship of diagnosis to acuity and the practical implications of the study.

Mehr, E. B., & Freid, A. N. The measurement and recording of vision are near test distances. *American Journal of Optometry & Physiological Optics*, 1976, **53** (6), 314-317.
Discusses the various systems for recording near visual acuities and gives suggestions for standardizing measurements.

Myers, W. A. Color discriminability for partially seeing children. *Exceptional Children*, 1971, **38** (3), 223-228.
Reports on a study of the effect of various color combinations on the Snellen E when testing low vision myopic children.

OPTICAL AIDS

Berson, E. L., Rabin, A. R., & Mehaffey, L. Advances in night vision technology: A pocketscope for patients with retinitis pigmentosa. *Archives of Ophthalmology*, 1973, **90** (12), 427-431.

Describes the Generation II night-vision pocketscope and the results of an investigation of its use by 18 patients.

Drasdo, N. Visual field expanders. *American Journal of Optometry & Physiological Optics*, 1976, **53** (9), 464-467.
Discusses the magnification, acuity, and field diameter of reverse telescopes (field expanders), various designs of these systems, and suggestions for bioptic systems.

Hoffer, D. C. The handwriting low vision aid. *Optical Journal & Review of Optometry*, 1979, **116** (9), 63-65.
Discusses four visual levels that describe the ability to use visual feedback for writing tasks and the procedures for determining the correct power and type of aid for a patient.

Holm, O. C. A simple method for widening restricted visual fields. *Archives of Ophthalmology*, 1970, **84** (5), 611-612.
Describes the reversed Galilean telescope as a visual field widener and suggests that it be tested with all patients who have severely restricted fields.

Kelleher, D. K. A pilot study to determine the effect of the bioptic telescope on young low vision patients' attitudes and achievement. *American Journal of Optometry and Physiological Optics*, 1974, **51** (3), 198-205.
Discusses the effect of the successful use of a bioptic telescope on the attitudes and achievement of five selected low vision students and the training sequence with the bioptic. The study determined that there was a change in attitude, but no significant change in achievement.

Kelleher, D. K. Orientation to low vision aids. *Journal of Visual Impairment & Blindness*, 1979, **73** (5), 161-166.
Presents an overview of optical and nonoptical aids, including the categories, characteristics, instruction in use, and factors affecting success.

Kennedy, W. L., Rosten, J. G., Young, L. M, Ciufredda, K. J., & Levin, M. I. A field expander for patients with retinitis pigmentosa: A clinical study. *American Journal of Optometry & Physiological Optics*, 1977, **54** (11), 744-755.
Reports on a study on the use of field expanders by 10 patients with retinitis pigmentosa; describes the device, the methods used for taking acuities and fields, the results of the study, and short case reports of the 10 people.

Krefman, R. A. Working distance comparison of plus lenses and reading telescopes. *American Journal of Optometry & Physiological Optics*, 1980, **57** (11), 835-838.
States that the increase in working distance obtained with a reading telescope as compared to a plus lens should be significant enough to merit the decreased field view; suggests a critical difference in working distance.

Ludlam, W. M. Clinical experience with the contact lens telescope. *American Journal of Optometry, Archives of the American Academy of Optometry*, 1960, **37** (7), 363-372.
States that a contact lens telescopic system affords a wider field of view than a conventional telescope of the same power and that only lower powers of magnification can be achieved; four case studies are discussed.

Quillman, R. D., Frost, A. B., Shaw, H.K., & Goodrich, G. L. Low vision monocular field study. *Optometric Weekly*, 1976, **67** (44), 1202-1205.
Compares the static and dynamic fields and minimum focal distance of eight

monocular telescopes as measured by the authors and the measured fields with the fields indicated in the manufacturer's literature.

Ricker, K. S. Visual field wideners: A personal report. *Journal of Visual Impairment & Blindness*, 1978, **72** (1), 28-29.

Describes the use of a reverse telescopic system by the author, who has retinitis pigmentosa, and discusses the advantages and limitations of the system.

Rosenberg, R. A survey of magnification aids to low vision. *Journal of the American Optometric Association*, 1973, **44** (6), 628-635.

Describes the methods of magnification and how they are achieved through optical aids; the advantages and disadvantages of aids as to field, working distance, available powers, and illumination.

Sloan, L. L., & Habel, A. Reading aids for the partially blind: New methods of rating and prescribing optical aids. *American Journal of Ophthalmology*, 1956, **42** (6), 863-872.

Presents an outline of procedures for selecting the best optical aid determined by the power of the aid, visual acuity, and the near point of accommodation.

NONOPTICAL AIDS

Courtwright, G., Mihok, T., & Jose, R. Reading stands: A nonoptical aid. *Optometric Weekly*, 1975, **66** (16), 449-451.

Describes the advantages of a specially designed reading stand for low vision patients, comparing it to other stands available.

Duncan, J, Gish, C., Mulholland, M.E., & Townsend, A. Environmental modifications for the visually impaired: A Handbook. *Journal of Visual Impairment & Blindness*, 1977, **71** (10), 441-455.

Suggests environmental modifications and provides information about the Committee on Architectural and Environmental Concerns, references, and resource organizations.

Genensky, S. M. Some comments on a closed circuit TV system for the visually handicapped. *American Journal of Optometry, Archives of the American Academy of Optometry*, 1969, **46** (7), 519-524.

Presents a history of the development of a closed-ciruit television system; describes the system and future developments proposed at the time of writing.

Goodlaw, E. I., & Genensky, S. M. Headborne illuminator for the partially sighted. *American Journal of Optometry and Physiological Optics*, 1978, **55** (12), 840-848.

Describes in detail a headborne device that illuminates reading material even when the material is 1–2 centimeters from the eye, compares this device to other illuminated reading systems, and suggests the types of patients who may find it useful.

Hellinger, G. O., & Berger, A. W. The Optiscope Enlarger: A report of initial field trials. *New Outlook for the Blind*, 1972, **66** (9), 320-322.

Describes the Optiscope Enlarger, an opaque projection device; the results of an evaluation of 30 low vision patients' performance on a standard near-point chart and selected materials unaided, with customary low vision aids, and with the Optiscope.

Lehon, L. H. Development of lighting standards for the visually impaired. *Journal of Visual Impairment & Blindness*, 1980, **74** (7), 249-252.

Includes a history of the development of lighting standards for visually impaired students in the classroom and presents research on visibility, visual acuity, and illumination and general recommendations for a flexible lighting system in the classroom.

McGillivray, R. (Ed.). *Aids and Appliances Review*. No. 2. Newton, Mass.: Carroll Center for the Blind, July 1979.
Includes a definition of large print; an exploration of printing terms and measures; a discussion of the qualities of the best print; resources for large-print books, periodicals, and typewriters; a detailed list of the services and products offered.

McGillivray, R. (Ed.). *Aids and Appliances Review*. No. 3. Newton, Mass.: Carroll Center for the Blind, July 1980.
Includes a review of handwriting guides (letters, signature, full-page, envelope, and check guides), prices, ordering information, the advantages and disadvantages of commercial aids, and suggestions for homemade guides.

Mehr, E. B. The typoscope by Charles F. Prentice. *American Journal of Optometry, Archives of the American Academy of Optometry*, 1969, **46** (11), 885-887.
Is a reprint of an 1897 article by C. F. Prentice, the originator of the typoscope; discusses the physiological principles of the nonoptical aid.

Nilsson, E. U. L., Hall, P., & Nilsson, S. E. Reading table for low vision patients with severe motility handicaps. *Journal of Visual Impairment & Blindness*, 1978, **72** (1), 27-28.
Describes a special reading table designed for a low vision patient with severely restricted arm and hand movements.

Potts, A. M., Volk, D., & West, S. S. A television reader as a subnormal vision aid. *American Journal of Ophthalmology*, 1959, **47** (4), 580-581.
Describes an early closed-circuit television reading system.

Sicurella, V. G. Color contrast as an aid for visually impaired persons. *Journal of Visual Impairment & Blindness*, 1977, **71** (6), 252-257.
Discusses the use of color contrast in the home to increase the functioning of visually impaired people and presents specific suggestions for each area of the home.

Sloan, L. L., & Habel, A. High illumination as an auxiliary reading aid in diseases of the macula. *American Journal of Ophthalmology*, 1973, **76** (5), 745-757.
Reports on a thorough investigation providing (1) extensive data on the acuity-luminance functions of patients with active and inactive atrophic macular lesions and (2) describes a simple clinical test to determine if high illumination significantly improves reading ability.

Sloan, L. L., & Habel, A. Reading speeds with textbooks in large and in standard print. *Sight Saving Review*, 1973, **43** (2), 107-111.
Partially reports on a study of the advantages and disadvantages of using large-print texts in the classroom; presents data on reading speeds with large and regular print.

Taylor, C. D. The relative legibility of black and white print. *Journal of Educational Psychology*, 1934, **25** (8), 561-578.
Reports on an investigation to determine (1) which print, light on dark or dark on light, is more legible and (2) why there should be a difference in legibility; in-

dicates that, primarily because of irradiation effects, light print on a dark background is most beneficial when the print is larger and is sans serif.

Turner, P. J. The place of CCTV in the rehabilitation of the low vision patient. *New Outlook for the Blind*, 1976, **70** (5), 206-214.
Presents a brief history of the development of the closed-circuit television (CCTV); the properties, advantages and disadvantages of the CCTV; and guidelines for prescribing it.

Verma, S. B. Non-optical aids. *American Journal of Optometry & Physiological Optics*, 1974, **51** (10), 758-764.
Describes in detail aperture devices (pin-holes, typoscope, stenopaic slit, visors, filters) and illumination; briefly refers to other nonoptical aids.

TRAINING

Allen, D. Orientation and mobility for persons with low vision. *Journal of Visual Impairment & Blindness*, 1977, **71** (1), 13-15.
Discusses the need for orientation and mobility instruction based on the patient's use of remaining vision, teaching environmental patterns and assumptions, and the idea that seeing is a learned process.

Carter, K. The sonic guide and distance vision training. *Optometric Weekly*, 1975, **66** (33), 907-911.
Differentiates the problems in orientation and mobility training for the congenitally and the adventitiously visually impaired child, describes the Sonicguide system, and compares it to reverse telescopes and prisms.

Feinbloom, W. A study of visual rehabilitation after 30 years of braille. *American Journal of Optometry, Archives of the American Academy of Optometry*, 1936, **13** (8), 455-463.
Discusses the assessment of visual function, designing of an optical aid, and training the patient to read print for the first time.

Ferrante, O. Teaching abbreviated handwriting to visually handicapped children. *Journal of Visual Impairment & Blindness*, 1978, **72** (1), 27.
Briefly describes an abbreviated note-taking system the author found helpful for several students.

Finn, W. A., Gadbaw, P. D., Kevorkian, G. A., & De l'Aune, W. R. Increased field accessibility through prismatically displaced images. *New Outlook for the Blind*, 1975, **69** (10), 465-467.
Outlines the placement of Fresnel prisms and the training and adjustments involved for the patient with severely restricted visual fields.

Gadbaw, P. D., Finn, W. A., Dolan, M. T., & De l'Aune, W. R. Parameters of success in the use of Fresnel prisms. *Optical Journal & Review of Optometry*, 1976, **113** (12), 41-43.
Presents an interim report of a study of the parameters of the successful application of a prism with 39 patients, including specific training techniques.

Goodrich, G. L., & Quillman, R. D. Training eccentric viewing. *Journal of Visual Impairment & Blindness*, 1977, **71** (9), 377-381.
Discusses functional problems associated with central scotomas and describes four specific techniques for training eccentric viewing.

Goodrich, G. L., Mehr, E. B., & Darling, N. C. Parameters in the use of CCTVs and optical aids. *American Journal of Optometry & Physiological Optics*, 1980, **57** (12), 881-892.

Reports comprehensive data from a study of 96 veterans who used a CCTV over a two-year period (50 percent of the veterans also read with other optical aids), compares CCTVs with other optical aids, and presents suggestions for efficient reading with CCTVs.

Hennessey, J. J. A pragmatic approach to the orientation and mobility needs of a low vision client. *Blindness* (American Association of Workers for the Blind annual), 1974–75, 80-87.

Describes a method for assessing orientation and mobility skills of individuals with low vision and lists the essential mobility skills and the sample routes and evaluation forms used.

Holcomb, J. G., & Goodrich, G. L. Eccentric viewing training. *Journal of the American Optometric Association*, 1976, **47** (11), 1438-1443.

Reports on a study of the effectiveness of two eccentric viewing techniques using three subjects and two controls for each technique; the techniques are inexpensive and do not require extensive training.

Inde, K. Low vision training in Sweden. *Journal of Visual Impairment & Blindness*, 1978, **72**, 307-310.

Describes low vision clinics in Sweden in which training is the key to all services and discusses four functional categories of visual impairment.

Jose, R. T., & Smith A. J. Increasing peripheral field awareness with Fresnel prisms. *Optical Journal & Review of Optometry*, 1976, **113** (12), 33-37.

Discusses the use of prisms to increase efficiency in scanning of patients with restricted peripheral fields; prism placement and power, patient selection, and specific training techniques.

Jose, R. T., & Watson, G. Increasing reading efficiency with an optical aid/training program. *Optical Journal & Review of Optometry*, 1978, **115** (2), 41-48.

Describes an optical aid training program for six students; training includes instruction in the use of the aid and training visual skills adapted from Barraga. Includes a detailed subject evaluation and outline of the sequence of lessons.

Jose, R. T., & Watson G. Maximum use of residual vision: Optical aids orientation program, part 1. *Optometric Weekly*, 1975, **66** (46), 1239-1242.

Describes an optical aids training program carried out jointly by a college of optometry and a rehabilitation facility; includes three case histories.

Jose, R. T., & Watson G. Maximum use of residual vision: Optical aids orientation program, part 2. *Optometric Weekly*, 1975, **67** (4), 80-84.

Presents three case histories and five case sketches that emphasize the benefits of a structured training program and follow-up services.

Kelleher, D. K. Teaching the low vision patient—A new optometric area of responsibility. *Optometric Weekly*, 1975, **66** (24), 655-657.

Describes the benefits of having a teacher/counselor as the instructor in the use of low vision aids and the role and responsibilities of the instructor.

Kelleher, D. K. Training low vision patients. *Journal of the American Optometric Association*, 1976, **47** (11), 1425-1427.

Discusses the importance of training when optical aids are prescribed and presents general guidelines for training.

Kurpis, J. S. People with low vision can distinguish paper currency. *Journal of Vi-*

sual Impairment & Blindness, 1977, **71** (2), 75-77.
Presents a technique for using residual vision to differentiate paper currency that involves learning to recognize the unique patterns of lights and darks on the backs of the bills.

Quillman, R. D. *Low vision training manual.* Kalamazoo, Mich.: Western Michigan University, College of Health and Human Services, Department of Blind Rehabilitation, 1980.
Presents training procedures for near and distance aids and a series of low vision reading exercises in print sizes ranging from 1M to 3M.

Rosenberg, R. Training in low vision practice. *Journal of the American Optometric Association*, 1968, **39** (1), 57-60.
Discusses the visual-motor problems encountered when reading with optical aids and presents general ideas for training.

Watson, G., & Jose, R. T. A training sequence for low vision patients. *Journal of the American Optometric Associaiton*, 1976, **47** (11), 1407-1415.
Describes a training program at a rehabilitation facility; presents a sequence of training, examples of materials for training in the use of optical aids for reading, and several case sketches.

Workshop on low vision mobility: Final report of a workshop at Western Michigan University, November 3–5, 1975. Washington, D.C.: Veterans Administration, Department of Medicine and Surgery, 1976.
Presents conference papers on the evaluation of visual functioning, visual training without aids, visual training with optical aids, evaluation of distance vision with optical aids, and the psychological aspects of low vision; summary of conference recommendations.

DRIVING WITH BIOPTIC TELESCOPES

Allen, M. J. Tips for the older driver. *Optometric Weekly*, 1967, **58** (23), 31-32.
Discusses driving techniques related to normal visual changes caused by the aging process.

Burg, A. Vision and driving: A report on research. *Human Factors*, 1971, **13** (1), 79-87.
Compares the driving records of a population of drivers over a three- and six-year period with the drivers' performance on vision tests and driving habits. Dynamic visual acuity was found to be the most closely related factor; static visual acuity, mileage, age, and sex are also considered.

Feinbloom, W. Driving with bioptic telescopic spectacles. *American Journal of Optometry & Physiological Optics*, 1977, **54** (1), 35-42.
Reports on 300 low vision patients who used bioptic telescopes for driving, discusses the visual processes and skills that are important in driving, rebuts the major criticisms of driving with bioptics, and recommends regulations for driving with bioptics.

Jose, R. T., & Butler, J. H. Driver's training for partially sighted persons: An interdisciplinary approach. *New Outlook for the Blind*, 1975, **69** (7), 305-311.
Describes a multidisciplinary three-part program involving an eye care specialist, a special education driving instructor, and a specially trained road performance test officer to evaluation qualifications and training in the use of bioptic telescopes for driving.

Kelleher, D. K. Driving with low vision. *Journal of Visual Impairment & Blindness*, 1979, **73** (9), 345-350.

Discusses driving with low vision, with and without a bioptic telescope, including the problems encountered, the training involved, and licensing.

Korb, D. R. Preparing the visually handicapped person for motor vehicle operation. *American Journal of Optometry, Archives of the American Academy of Optometry*, 1970, **47** (8), 619-628.
Presents the rationale and technique for fitting bioptic telescopic systems for driving, the problems encountered with use, adaptation, and recommended criteria for licensing.

National conference on telescopic devices and driving. Morton Grove, Ill.: Health & Safety Associates, 1976.
Includes conference presentations by Gerald Fonda, William Feinbloom, Dennis Kelleher, and Arthur Keeney, major arguments for and against the use of bioptic telescopes for driving, and recommendations of the workshop sessions.

GERIATRICS

Arnold, C. Visually impaired persons in nursing homes. *New Outlook for the Blind*, 1972, **66** (7), 227-229.
Discusses variables for selecting an appropriate nursing home for elderly visually impaired adults.

Bailey, I. L. The aged blind. *Australian Journal of Optometry*, 1975, **58** (1), 31-39.
Discusses the strong association between blindness and aging and the need for practitioners to be aware of services available to the aged blind; outlines the use of specific aids.

Carroll, T. J. A look at aging. *New Outlook for the Blind*, 1972, **66** (4), 97-103.
Discusses the changing status of the aging in our society, age-related functional changes, and the need for a careful basic visual examination to maximize usable vision.

Corwin, B. C. Vision screening in nursing and retirement homes. *American Journal of Optometry, Archives of the American Academy of Optometry*, 1972, **49** (12), 1008-1011.
Reports on a vision-screening project for the aged in a nursing home in South Dakota; includes data on 4,383 individuals.

Crouch, C. L. Lighting needs for older eyes. *Sight Saving Review*, 1965, **35** (4), 213-215.
Discusses general changes in illumination needs related to aging.

Donahue, W., & MacFarland, D. C. Aging and blindness. *Blindness* (American Association of Workers for the Blind annual), 1964, 85-98.
Discusses the social aspects of aging and problems specific to the visually impaired older population and presents comprehensive recommendations for rehabilitation.

Faye, E. E. Visual function in geriatric eye disease. *New Outlook for the Blind*, 1971, **65** (7), 204-208.
Describes the four major eye diseases affecting the elderly (cataracts, macular degeneration, glaucoma, and diabetic retinopathy), how they affect vision, and the types of aids that may be of value for each disease.

Galler, E. H. A long-term support group for elderly people with low vision. *Journal of Visual Impairment & Blindness*, 1981, **75** (4), 173-176.
States that the benefits of a long-term support group include social interaction

and information as well as support and presents an outline for establishing a group and topics for discussion.

Gilbert, J. G. Aging among sighted and blind persons. *New Outlook for the Blind*, 1964, **58** (7), 197-201.
States that people who lose their vision late in life have to deal with more than the normal aging changes experienced and compares the physical, emotional, social, and economic aspects of growing old for non-visually impaired and visually impaired older adults.

Hellinger, G. Vision rehabilitation for aged blind persons. *New Outlook for the Blind*, 1969, **63** (6), 175-177.
States that because most legally blind persons have some residual vision, rehabilitation and low vision services can help elderly patients to maintain their independence.

Hiatt, L. G. Is poor light dimming the sight of nursing home patients? *Nursing Homes*, 1980, **29** (5), 32-41.
Describes the specific problems of nursing home patients and the lack of adequate screening and treatment programs and presents guidelines for utilizing information about patients once it has been collected.

Hiatt, L. G. The color and use of color in environments for older people. *Nursing Homes*, 1981, **30** (3), 18-22.
Discusses the factors to be considered in selecting and using color in environments for older people.

Pastalan, L. A. The simulation of age-related sensory losses: A new approach to the study of environmental barriers. *New Outlook for the Blind,* 1974, **68**(8), 356-362.
Reports on a study in which devices were used to simulate normal age-related visual losses (not pathology-related losses) and includes suggestions for organizing space that can be applied to environmental design; reinforces the need for further investigation in this area.

Werner, D. L. Perceptual training for the geriatric patient. *Journal of the American Optometric Association,* 1967, **38**(12), 1034-1036.
Compares visual perceptual problems of some low vision geriatric patients with the perceptual problems of children and suggests the use of programs to develop the perceptual skills of these patients.

EDUCATIONAL CONSIDERATIONS

Arensman, D. The role of the teacher for the visually handicapped in vision assessment. *Education of the Visually Handicapped,* 1975,7(1), 5-8.
Suggests procedures and materials for the visual assessment of students referred to special education visually impaired programs.

Bateman, B. Mild visual defects and learning problems in partially seeing children. *Sight Saving Review,* 1963, **33**(1), 30-33.
Reports on a study of the reading ability of 131 partially sighted students and discusses the determination of reading disabilities that are not directly related to visual impairment.

Bruce, R. E. Using the overhead projector with visually impaired students. *Education of the Visually Handicapped,* 1973, **5**(2), 43-46.

Presents specific ideas for using an overhead projector by teachers and visually impaired students, including room arrangements, illumination, and materials.

Bullard, B. M., & Barraga, N. C. Subtests of evaluative instruments applicable for use with preschool visually handicapped children. *Education of the Visually Handicapped,* 1971, **3**(4), 116-122.
Lists subtests of common evaluative instruments that are applicable to visually impaired preschool children, including a separate section for blind children and children with residual vision.

Carpenter, P. Low vision aids: The implications of education. *Blindness* (American Association of Workers for the Blind annual), 1974–75, 54-58.
Presents the training and social considerations for the successful prescription of an optical low vision aid in a classroom setting and two case histories.

Corn, A. L. Optical aids in the classroom. *Education of the Visually Handicapped,* 1981, **12**(4), 114–121.
Presents a rationale for using optical aids in the classroom, emphasizes the need for educators to understand optics and aids and to provide training in the use of the aids in the classroom, and outlines four knowledge areas with which educators should be familiar.

Daugherty, K. M. Monterey Learning Systems: Improving academic achievement of visually impaired learners. *Journal of Visual Impairment & Blindness,* 1977, **71**(7), 298–301.
Reports on a project in which the Monterey Learning Systems Reading and Mathematics Programs were used with 29 visually impaired print readers. The goal was to increase reading and mathematics skills, and the results showed an average gain of about one year in these skills.

Fridal, G., Jansen, L., & Klindt, M. Courses in reading development for partially sighted students. *Journal of Visual Impairment and Blindness,* 1981, **75**(1), 4-7.
Describes a short-term reading development course aimed at increasing reading speeds for students with acuities of 20/50 to 20/200; the results indicate an increase in reading speed for the six students who participated.

Friedman, G. R. The teacher/doctor coordinating form—An instrument in rehabilitation of the partially sighted child. *Journal of the American Optometric Association,* 1976, **47**(11), 1418–1422.
Presents and explains a model of a form used in several low vision clinics; the form is designed to elicit the most pertinent information from the teacher and the doctor.

Heron, E., & Zytkoskee, A. Visual acuity and test performance. *American Journal of Optometry & Physiological Optics*, 1981, **58** (2), 176-178.
Reports on a study comparing ACT scores and visual acuities and briefly reviews studies demonstrating a positive correlation between myopia and giftedness.

Hull, W. A., & McCarthy D. G. Supplementary program for preschool visually handicapped children: Utilization of vision-increased readiness. *Education for the Visually Handicapped*, 1973, **5** (4), 97-104.
Describes a preschool program for visually handicapped children that emphasized the use of residual vision; includes an outline of the curriculum content and the evaluation process.

Jones, J. K. Colour as an aid to visual perception in early reading. *British Journal of Educational Psychology*, 1965, **35** (1), 21-27.
Reports the results of a study of 110 nursery school children with normal vision that investigated the value of color as an aid to the visual discrimination of words and letters. The study showed that the children preferred colored test items and scored higher when using them.

Kastenbaum, S. M. Effects of reduced visual acuity on performance on the Wechsler Adult Intelligence Scale. *Journal of Visual Impairment & Blindness*, 1981, **75** (1), 25-27.
Reports on a study that found that with visual acuity reduced to 20/200, the experimental group performed significantly lower than the control group on parts of the Wechsler Adult Intelligence Scale; the decreased performance of the visually handicapped patients may have been due to reduced vision rather than reduced ability.

Kephart, N. C. Visual changes in children associated with school experience. *American Journal of Optometry, Archives of the American Academy of Optometry*, 1950, **27** (4), 195-199.
Reports on a study of myopic and hyperopic trends in school-age children at various grade levels over a school year and the summer months.

Livingstone, J. S. Evaluation of enlarged test forms used with the partially seeing. *Sight Saving Review*, 1958, **28** (1), 37-39.
Reports on a study to determine if using the enlarged print form of the Stanford-Binet Intelligence Scale improved scores for partially sighted children and presents brief comparison of scores for partially sighted and non-visually impaired children.

Murphy, A. T. Attitudes of educators toward the visually handicapped. *Sight Saving Review*, 1960, **30** (3), 157-161.
Reports on a study to measure through a rating scale the attitudes of 309 educators, grouped according to educational role, toward exceptional children; indicates that visually impaired children were least accepted possibly because of the educators' lack of knowledge.

Nolan, C. Y. A 1966 reappraisal of the relationship between visual acuity and mode of reading for blind children. *New Outlook for the Blind*, 1967, **61** (8), 255-261.
Reports data on 18,652 visually impaired children enrolled in various school programs in 1966; compares visual acuity with reading mode, visual acuity and reading mode in various educational settings, and 1966 data with 1963 data.

Prince, J. H. Relationship of reading types to uncorrectable lowered visual acuity. *American Journal of Optometry, Archives of the American Academy of Optometry*, 1957, **34** (11), 581-595.
Describes a project that studied the effectiveness of various type styles and interletter spacing used by individuals with lowered visual acuities; discusses legibility thresholds, the legibility of letters in groups, and the probable influence of age on reading speed.

Sabatino, D. A., Abbott, J. C., & Becker, J. T. What does the Frosting DTVP measure? *Exceptional Children*, 1974, **40** (6), 453-454.
Reports on a study using 129 children to determine test-retest reliability and distinct visual motor perceptual behaviors measured by the DTVP.

Sloan, L. L., & Habel, A. Problems in prescribing reading aids for partially-sighted children. *American Journal of Ophthalmology*, 1973, **75** (6), 1023-1035.
States that in prescribing reading aids for children, one must consider the print

size the children are working with and the amplitude of accommodation present. Gives examination procedures, monocular and binocular aids, and some typical results.

Swallow, R. M. Fifty assessment instruments commonly used with blind and partially seeing individuals. *Journal of Visual Impairment & Blindness*, 1981, **75** (2), 65-72.
Discusses the major concerns, modifications of testing procedures, and evaluation of test results when assessing blind and visually impaired children; 50 commonly used assessment instruments by age-grade level, and the time required to complete them.

Sykes, K. C. Print reading for visually handicapped children. *Education of the Visually Handicapped*, 1972, **4** (3), 71-75.
Discusses print size, illumination, quality of print, posture, reading distance, use of near aids, visual training, and various approaches to teaching reading to visually impaired children; substantial references to research literature.

Weber, G. V. Visual disabilities—Their identification and relationship with academic achievement. *Journal of Learning Disabilities*, 1980, **13** (6), 301-305.
Discusses two vision tests to assess the existence of visual functional problems when acuities are tested as normal; reports on a study to determine if there is a correlation between these vision tests and academic achievement.

MULTIPLY IMPAIRED PEOPLE

Bernstein, G. B. Integration of vision stimulation in the classroom: Part I—Individual programming. *Education of the Visually Handicapped*, 1979, **11** (1), 14-18.
Describes selected multiply handicapped visually impaired children and the vision-stimulation activities designed for them.

Bernstein, G. B. Integration of vision stimulation in the classroom: Part II—Group programming. *Education of the Visually Handicapped*, 1979, **11** (2), 39-48.
Describes classroom activities and materials for vision stimulation that can be used with groups; includes objectives and area of development for each activity.

Bernstein, G. B. Integration of vision stimulation in the classroom: Part III—A total approach. *Education of the Visually Handicapped*, 1979, **11** (3), 80-84.
Describes a vision-stimulation program at the Upsal Day School in Philadelphia, including specific techniques and activities..

Cech, D., & Pitello, A. Combining specialties to serve low functioning visually and physically impaired children. *Journal of Visual Impairment and Blindness*, 1977, **71** (10), 439-440.
Describes a preschool program for visually and physically impaired children involving a teacher for visually impaired children and a physical therapist and the specific programs designed for two of the children.

Deckard, D. K. Adapted visual efficiency scale: A comparison of performance obtained by multihandicapped children. *Education of the Visually Handicapped*, 1979, **11** (3), 75-80.
Reports on a study to determine the value of an adapted visual efficiency scale for multihandicapped children; includes descriptions of the adapted scale items.

Ficociello, C. Vision stimulation for low functioning deaf-blind rubella children. *Teaching Exceptional Children*, 1976, **8** (3), 128-130.
States that because of the nature of sensory loss in deaf-blind rubella children,

the functional visual assessment and vision stimulation programs must be modified to suit the individual; specific activities are suggested.

Jose, R. T., Smith, A. J., & Shane, K. G. Evaluating and stimulating vision in the multiply impaired. *Journal of Visual Impairment and Blindness*, 1980, **74** (1), 2-8. Describes a functional visual evaluation for multiply impaired low vision children adapted from Langley and Dubose and a vision stimulation sequence that includes 17 visual skills and recommends procedures for clinically establishing acuity, refraction, binocularity, and fields.

Kephart, N. C. Visual behavior of the retarded child. *American Journal of Optometry, Archives of the American Academy of Optometry*, 1958, **35** (3), 125-133. Describes theories of form perception and the developing belief that it is a learned rather than an innate process, relates learning difficulties of retarded children to inadequate form and figure-ground perception, and discusses reading problems associated with form-perception problems.

Langley, B., & Dubose, R. F. Functional vision screening for severely handicapped children. *New Outlook for the Blind*, 1976, **70** (8), 346-350. Presents extensive references to the literature on vision screening of multiply handicapped children and a detailed description of a procedure for screening functional vision, including management of the child, materials, what to observe, and a recording checklist.

Leach, F. Multiply handicapped visually impaired children: Instructional materials needs. *Exceptional Children*, 1971, **38** (2), 153-156. Reports on a survey by the American Printing House for the Blind of 159 organizations describing 3,443 multiply handicapped visually impaired children; presents data on the most helpful materials, characteristics of needed materials, and specific materials needed in seven basic instructional areas.

Smith, A. J., & Shane Cote, K. *Look at me: A resource manual for the development of residual vision in multiply impaired children*. Philadelphia: Pennsylvania College of Optometry Press, 1982. Describes the assessment activities utilized with a group of multiply handicapped children at the Upsal Day Care Center in Philadelphia and suggests a sequence for evaluating these children.

SERVICE DELIVERY MODELS

Brinkley, S. B. Optometry and the vocational rehabilitation program. *Blindness* (American Association of Workers for the Blind annual), 1970, 101–110. Presents guidelines by the Rehabilitation Services Administration for utilizing optometry in the general schema of vocational rehabilitation.

Carter, K. D., & Carter, C. A. Itinerant low vision services. *New Outlook for the Blind*, 1975, **69** (6), 255-260. Describes an itinerant low vision service in New Hampshire; discusses screening, referral and visit to the clinic, the prescription of aids, training, and follow-up.

Colenbrander, A. Dimensions of visual performance. *Transactions of the American Academy of Ophthalmology & Otolaryngology*, 1977, **83** (2), 332-337. Defines the terms "visual disorder," "visual impairment," "visual disability," and "visual handicap" in relation to the area affected, functional aspects, treatment, the role of ophthalmology, and psychosocial considerations.

Davis, L. Community resources—Why should we use them? *Journal of the Ameri-*

can Optometric Association, 1976, **47** (11), 1445-1448.
Discusses the assistance that can be provided by rehabilitation, education, and mobility personnel in training and counseling low vision patients.

Deur, G. Meeting the social needs of the visually impaired patient. *Optical Journal & Review of Optometry*, 1979, **116** (9), 83-88.
Describes the roles of members of the multidisciplinary low vision team in relation to the social needs of the low vision individual.

DiStefano, A. F. Rationalizing the delivery of eye care: Parts I, II, and III. *Journal of the American Optometric Association*, 1976, **47** (2), 216-221; 1976, **47** (4), 489-494; 1976, **47** (5), 627-632, respectively.
Discusses eye care delivery systems and the problems of various systems; describes a model for regionalized health services; and defines the primary, secondary, and tertiary levels of care.

Faye, E. E., & Hood, C. M. Low vision services in an agency: Structure and philosophy. *New Outlook for the Blind*, 1975, **69** (5), 241-248.
Provides a comprehensive description of the New York Lighthouse Low Vision Service, including its history, philosophy, and structure of service.

Friedman, G. R. Functional vision—A multidisciplinary approach as utilized by a low vision clinic model. *Journal of Optometry & Visual Therapy,* 1973, **4** (1) 10-18.
Discusses areas of concern in the rehabilitation of a low vision patient and describes the multidisciplinary services at the Low Vision Clinic of Boston University Medical Center.

Jose, R. T. What is low vision service? *Blindness* (American Association of Workers for the Blind annual), 1974–75, 49-53.
The multidisciplinary approach to low vision and the phases of the examination and treatment.

Jose, R. T., & Springer, D. Optical aids: An interdisciplinary prescription. *New Outlook for the Blind,* 1975, **67** (1), 12-18.
Interprets raw data from a follow-up study on 50 low vision patients seen at the University of Alabama College of Optometry; emphasizes the need for input from family, friends, teachers, counselors, and other health professionals as well as from the examining doctor before a prescripton is made; and discusses the need for training and follow-up.

Jose, R. T., Cummings, J., & McAdams, L. The model low vision clinical service: An interdisciplinary vision rehabilitation program. *New Outlook for the Blind,* 1975, **69** (6), 249-254.
Describes a low vision service in a rehabilitation agency; suggests that such a service should complement the rehabilitation program, maximize the client's vocational goals, and be provided by an interdisciplinary team; and discusses the roles of the team and ways to coordinate efforts.

Landwehr, R., & Hutcheson, K. Use of a mobile unit for delivering services to older blind persons. *Journal of Visual Impairment & Blindness,* 1979, **73** (3), 106-109.
Describes a mobile training unit used for delivering rehabilitation services to older visually impaired individuals and discusses the advantages and disadvantages of such a unit.

Olshansky, S. Some comments on the delivery of service. *Rehabilitation Literature,* 1973, **34** (7), 203-206.

Discusses the bureaucratic pitfalls associated with large organizational service systems (specifically vocational rehabilitation), and emphasizes how the running of such a system too often overshadows meeting the needs of people, which is the intended function of such organizations.

Rosenbloom, A. A. Research needs in low vision. *American Journal of Optometry & Physiological Optics,* 1978, **55** (11), 776-779.
Identifies six areas in which research on low vision is needed, including (1) reading and learning development in visually impaired children, (2) the development of new aids, (3) environmental modifications.

Smith, B. L. & Smith, T. E. C. Tips for itinerant service providers. *Journal of Visual Impairment & Blindness,* 1981, **75** (1), 34-35.
Presents basic ideas for maximizing the amount and quality of direct contacts with clients by itinerant service providers.

Sprague, W. D. Low vision: Its impact on an agency. *Journal of Visual Impairment and Blindness,* 1977, **71** (5) 197-202.
Describes a multidisciplinary low vision service in an agency for visually handicapped persons; discusses the concepts, philosophy, organization, and objectives of the low vision service at the New York Association for the Blind, as well as cost estimates, space, equipment, and manpower requirements.

Worden, H. W. Aging and blindness. *New Outlook for the Blind,* 1976, **70** (10), 433-437.
Describes a cooperative effort by various agencies in Rhode Island to provide comprehensive services to a geriatric visually impaired population.

About the Authors

R. Victoria Berg is a self-employed orientation and mobility instructor, and consultant on O&M, low vision, and blindness. She has a masters in education from Boston College, and has written on various topics in low vision and blindness.

Constance C. Carter is a self-employed orientation and mobility specialist and low vision consultant. She has published articles on low vision and electronic mobility aids, and has served on numerous regional and national interest group committees. She is a graduate of the dual program in visually handicapped education and orientation and mobility at the University of Northern Colorado.

Kent D. Carter is a doctoral candidate at the University of Massachusetts, College of Business Administration, with previous experience as an itinerant teacher, orientation and mobility specialist, and low vision services consultant. He has written extensively on low vision services and electronic mobility aids, and has served on numerous regional and national visually handicapped committees. He is a graduate of the dual program in visually handicapped education and orientation and mobility at the University of Northern Colorado.

John Ferraro is director of the Low Vision Clinic, University of Houston College of Optometry. He served on the faculty of the University of Northern Colorado and holds a masters degree in special education from San Francisco State University.

Sandra Ferraro is a low vision educational specialist at the University of Houston low vision clinic. She has a masters in orientation and mobility from San Francisco State University, and has previous experience as a visually handicapped classroom teacher at the University of Northern Colorado.

Kathleen Fraser holds an O.D. from Pennsylvania College of Optometry, and is assistant professor of optometry at the University of Houston, College of Optometry. She specializes in multiply handicapped low vision children. Dr. Fraser has co-authored several articles on low vision.

Terese Hritcko is doctoral candidate in school psychology at Pennsylvania State University. Previous experience includes working as an itinerant teacher and consultant and providing an in-service training component to cross train itinerant teachers, and industrial arts and vocational education instructors. She is a graduate from Illinois State University with a degree in education of blind and visually handicapped persons.

Frank (Skip) Johns is a vision specialist at the Cooperative Education Service Agency No. 14 in Fennimore, Wisconsin. Previous experience includes teaching in Idaho and New Hampshire. He is a graduate of the education of the visually handicapped program at the University of Northern Colorado.

Randall T. Jose is coordinator of the rehabilitative optometry tract, and an associate professor at the University of Houston College of Optometry. Dr. Jose is editor of the Journal of Rehabilitative Optometry, and has published numerous papers on low vision, and contributed to three texts on low vision. He graduated from the University of California in 1968 and is presently a diplomat in low vision, American Academy of Optometry and chairman elect of the low vision section, American Optometric Association. He is past chairman of the American Association of Workers for the Blind.

John L. Morse is a psychologist in private practice serving the handicapped. He is president-elect of the New Hampshire Society of Psychologists, is on the board of the AEVH, Northeast Region, and is a recipient of the Thomas Caulfield Award, New England Chapter of AAWB. He has conducted numerous workshops nationwide for the American Foundation for the Blind and has published over thirty articles. He is a graduate of and holds a doctorate from the counseling psychology program at Boston University, School of Education.

Sam Negrin is associate director for development, American Foundation for the Blind. He previously directed AFB's field services department and community services division, and served as a department director for the National Association of Social Workers. He served as assistant director for the Jewish Welfare Federation of Dallas, Texas and branch director for the Jewish Community Centers Association of St. Louis. Mr. Negrin received his masters degree in social work from Columbia University in 1955.

Karen Shane Cote is a vision consultant at Elwyn Institutes. She has conducted numerous workshops across the country on vision stimulation and has co-authored articles on vision stimulation for multiply impaired children. She is co-author of *Look at Me: A Resource Manual for the Development of Residual Vision in Multiply Impaired Children*. She has experience as a physical education teacher, mobility instructor, and coordinator of a low vision clinic. She received her masters from Boston College in 1975.

Audrey J. Smith is the director of educational programs in vision rehabilitation at the Pennsylvania College of Optometry. She has worked as a mobility instructor, low vision consultant, and has lectured extensively throughout the United States on low vision and vision stimulation. She is co-author of *Look at Me: A Resource Manual for the Development of Residual Vision in Multiply Impaired Children*. Ms. Smith received her masters from the University of Pittsburgh in 1971.

Gale Watson is a special education program coordinator at the office of academic development, Pennsylvania College of Optometry, where she is developing a network of low vision workshops for special educators, and is a low vision specialist at William Feinbloom Vision Rehabilitation Center, PA College of Optometry. Previous experience includes work as an education specialist, teacher and low vision coordinator. She has authored numerous articles on low vision and education.

Index

AAWB (*see* American Association of Workers for the Blind)

Abnormalities, refractive and ocular, 5-7 (*See also* specific references: Astigmatism; Myopia; Nystagmus; Scotomas; etc.)

Absorptive lenses, 328, 330-331

Abstract symbols, identifying, 426-427

Accommodation, 5, 7, 24, 27, 36, 44, 80 93, 95, 97, 193-194, 199-200, 201, 202, 203, 206-207, 220, 224, 225, 228, 229, 324-325, 337 (*See also* Optics, Refraction)

Acetate filters, colored, 328

Achromatism, 236

Achromatopsia, 8, 32

Acuity, central, 9, 11, 13-16, 18, 19, 22, 26, 29, 30, 36, 62, 69, 242, 382 (*See also* Blurred vision; Cataracts; Field loss)

Acuity measurements:
distance, 88-92, 146, 256-257
"finger count," 149
near, 92-97, 146-151, 158, 257, 320
(*See also* Assessment; Magnification, levels of)

Acuity, visibility, 88-89, 245

Adaptation, light/dark, 80, 121, 131, 235, 298, 405-406

Adaptive behavior, 380, 387-388

Adaptive chairs, 392

Adjustment
difficulties, 47-50
and intervention, 51-52
success in, 50-51

Adventitious vs. congenital low vision, 43

AEVH (*see* Association for Education of the Visually Handicapped)

Aging, aged, problems of, 55-56
and color vision, 405
and visual handicaps, 56-58
services for, 58-59

Aids, low vision (*see* Nonoptical; Optical)

"Aids and Appliances for the Blind and Visually Impaired," 263

Aids and Appliances Review, 331

Aids and services, listed by companies, 497-513

Albinism, 8, 31-32, 45, 120, 236

Alignment, telescope, 288

All-or-nothing concept, 278-279

Alliance for Education and Rehabilitation of the Visually Impaired, Inc., 444

Aluminum foil, 389

Amblyopia, 7, 23, 157

American Academy of Optometry, 495

American Association of Workers for the Blind (AAWB), 444, 445

American Foundation for the Blind (AFB), on low vision services, 257-258, 444, 454

American Optometric Association, 263, 495

Amniocentesis, 34

Amsler Grid, 99, 102, 119, 151, 152, 153, 257, 289, 363-364

Anatomy of the eye (*see* Eye)

Ancillary lighting systems (*see* Illumination)

Angular magnification, 208-210, 213, 326

Aniridia, 8, 14, 20, 21-22, 120, 381, 391

Ann Arbor Tracking Program, 260

Anterior chamber, 3

Antibacterial agents, 35

Antiviral agents, 35-36

Anxiety, 46-47

Apert's syndrome, 20

Apertures, 235, 243, 322, 335, 394

Aphakia, 23, 234, 417

Aqueous, aqueous humor, 3-4, 5, 13, 19, 21 (*See also* Glaucoma)

Arc perimeter, (*see* perimeter)

Arthritis, 314

Assessment of lighting, 403-414
color vision, 403-405
dark/light adaptation, 405-406
environmental, 406-413
macular degeneration, needs in, 410
minimal task lighting, 408-409
outdoor, 412-413
surface reflectance percentages, 407
(*See also* Illumination)

Assessment of low vision, 73-137, 266
comprehensive preliminary, 85-104
general considerations, 73-74
illumination levels, 83, 92-93, 103, 104
minimum sequence, 75-83
(*See also* Children; Clinical measure-

ments; Environmental measurements; Evaluation, O&M)
Assessment of the multiply handicapped, 379-402
  evaluation of specific conditions, 381-386
    recording forms, 384, 386
  observing child's behavior, 379-381
  vision stimulation sequence, 386-401
    generalization of activities, 399
    light stimulus, 390-399
    observation, 387-388
    stimulus, general, 388-390
    tracking and exploration, 400-401
Association for the Education of the Visually Handicapped (AEVH), 445
Asthenopia, 6-7
Astigmatism, 6-7, 31, 156, 203-204, 285, 286, 429
  congenital, 7
"Attachment" and vision, 44
Auditory information (see Hearing)
Auditory response, 383
Autosomal traits, 6, 21
  dominant, 6, 22, 25,33, 35
  recessive, 6, 20, 28, 31
Awareness, kinesthetic (see Kinesthetic)

Ball, colored, 265
Balloons, colored, 399, 400
Balls, 399, 401
Beeper balls, 283, 431
Bender Visual Gestalt Test, 124
Bifocal lenses, 24, 102, 225, 226-227
  microscope, 225, 346, 347
Bilateral integration, 395
Binocularity, binocular vision, 81, 97, 226, 326, 379
  with CCTV, 350
  examining and evaluating, 142, 156-157, 158, 168
  and reading telescopes, 222
Binoculars, 208, 219-220, 287
  techniques, 233-234
Bi-ocularity, 157, 158, 168
  and reading telescopes, 222, 223
Biomicroscope, slit-lamp, 14, 16, 20, 22, 23, 24, 145, 147, 158
Bioptic spectacles, and reverse telescopes, 374
Bioptic telescopes, 217-218, 221, 222-223, 225, 243, 245, 296-297, 342, 345, 346-347, 348, 431
  and driving, 243-244, 265
    references, 528-529
Black lights, 396
"Blind" and "sighted," 43-44, 47

Blind spot, normal, 98-99
Blind spots (see Scotomas)
Blindfolding, 438-439
Blindness agency or center clinics, 447-448
Blindness, and corneal ulceration, 19
Blindness and diabetes, 27
Blindness, legal, 63, 68, 254
Blinking, blink reflex, 116, 382, 395
  and glare, 413
Blinking lights, 389, 394
Blocking light source, 397-398, 399
Blocks, 399
Blue-violet hues, perception of, 405
Blurred vision, 9, 10, 19, 21, 22, 23, 25, 26, 35, 36, 241, 320
  blur interpretation, 421, 423, 427
  prism blur, 369, 372
Body adjustments, compensatory, 388, 419
Bold-line paper, 263, 328, 330, 346, 347, 351
Bolsters, 390-391, 399
"Bouncing," and use of telescope, 285, 326
Braille, 328, 352, 435
Brightness (see Luminance)
Brushfield spots, 12
Bubbles, soap, colored, 394
Building and house numbers, reading, 312, 433-434, 435
Bulbs, lamp, types of, 327, 398, 410-411
Bumping into things, 388
Buphthalmos, 12
Burns, chemical, 19
Bus numbers and destinations, reading with telescope, 312-313, 434
Business and typing courses, 128

Camper's flashlight, 375
Candle power (see Footcandles)
Canes, 82, 420, 438
  folding, and night travel, 374, 375
  and prisms, 241, 366
Cap, sunglass, 298
Carbonic anhydrase inhibitors, 36
Card playing, 263, 344, 347-348
Cards, reading, 118, 130-131, 260, 330, 345
Cardboard with punch holes, 394
Cardiac problems, 11, 12, 14, 16, 34, 35
Carpet remnants, 398
Carter, Kent, and driving with bioptics, 244n
Case histories, 86-88, 142-145, 158, 256, 266, 274, 417-418, 420-421, 426-427, 429, 435
  sheets, 159-166

Cataract(s), 8-10, 11, 12, 16, 22-25, 28, 36, 37, 58, 69, 236, 417
    and color vision, 404
    congential, 23-24, 34
        causes, 24
    cortical, 23-24
    posterior subcapsular, 23, 24-25, 28
        causes, 24-25
    secondary, 23
    surgery for, 22-23, 24, 28, 34, 157, 234
CCTV (*see* Television, closed circuit)
Central acuity (*see* Acuity)
Cerebral palsy, 287
Chairs, adaptive, 392
Chalkboards, 265, 299-303, 308-309, 405, 426
Chang mobility kit, 423-424
Charts, testing (*see* Testing)
Check-writing guide and training, 259, 329, 330, 331, 347, 351
Chemical burns, 19
Children, low vision assessment of, 105-137
    and classroom teachers, 111, 113, 114, 117
    educational media, 124-128
    evaluating visual function, 114-124
    low vision aids, 126-127
    observation, 111-114
    preschool child, 111, 117
    reading ability, 125-126
    roles and responsibilities, 106-111
    special classes, 127-128
    survey and recommendations, 128-137
    vision stimulation sequence, 386-401
    writing ability, 126
Chloralabe, 403
Choroid, 4
Christmas lights, 395, 398
Ciliary body, 4
Ciliary muscle, 4, 5
Circulatory problems, 314
Classroom management, 133-134
Clinical examination (*see* Examination)
Clinical measurements, data and assessment, 63, 69-70, 76, 85, 88, 102, 106
    (*See also* Children)
Clinical services, 64-70, 139-248, 441
    (*See also* Delivery systems; Examination; Optics; Treatment options)
Clinical specialist, low vision, 495
Clinics, 446-450
    blindness agency or center, 447-448
    medical center and hospital, 448
    mobile service unit, 449
    private practice, 449-450
    university-affiliated, 446-447

Clip-on occluders, 259
Clip-on telescope, 216-217, 218, 287, 290, 293
Clocks, large-number, 263, 329
Clocks, ticking, 283, 431
Closed circuit television (*see* Television)
"Closer Look at Low Vision Aids, A" (Dean), 263
Closure, visual, 123, 423
Collagen, 4
Coloboma, 10, 25, 32-33
Color blindness (*see* Achromatopsia)
Color clues while traveling, 419
Color contrast, 255
Color distortions, 18, 23
Color matching, 404
Color vision, and assessment of lighting, 403-405, 419
Color vision, impairment of, 27, 29, 30, 35, 36, 89, 97, 404-405
Color vision, testing, 119-120, 127, 142, 154, 158, 168, 257, 419, 447
Comfort cables, spectacle, 287
Comfort, physical, 235, 236
Comfort and proficiency, 279, 329
Communication and low vision services, 168, 248
Companies and organizations for low vision services, 497-513
Composite picture, 365
Concreteness and counseling, 51, 52
Cones, 5, 8
    and color vision, 403-404, 405
    and dark/light adaptation, 405
    dysfunction, 413
Conferences, 445
Confrontation and counseling, 51, 52, 53
Confrontation field assessments and tests, 99-100, 119, 290
Confusion of images, with prisms, 372
Congenital vs. adventitious low vision, 43
Congential visual impairment, and clear focus, 293, 297
Congested areas and telescopes, 313
Conjunctiva, 4, 35
    hemorrhage of, 36
Conjunctivitis, 35
Connecticut State Board of Education and Services for the Blind, 263
Constriction of visual field, 21, 22, 34
    (*See also* Field, measurement)
Consultant, medical, to low vision program, 496
Contact lenses, 20, 24, 26, 31, 33, 154, 155, 234-235, 252
    pin-hole, 22, 31

telescopes, 219-220, 234-235
tinted, 236
Contrast, problems, 235, 236, 327, 333, 397, 398, 404, 406
outdoor lighting, 412
(*See also* Nonoptical aids)
Contrast, control of, 127, 323, 328, 336, 338, 339, 343, 397, 404
CCTV, 332, 351
painting, 411
Convergence, 5, 44, 81, 116, 193, 196, 197-203, 229
(*See also* Optics)
Converging lens, 188
(*See also* Lenses, convex)
Coordination, visual-motor, 81
Coordinator-Instructor, low vision program, 496-497
Coping responses and skills, 45, 47, 52
Cornea, 3, 4, 5, 6, 14, 19, 22
and astigmatism, 6, 203-204
diseases of, 19-20
distorted, 155, 195-197, 200, 234, 235
examination of, 145, 147, 158
and glaucoma, 20-21
Corneal dystrophies, 20
Corneal lesions, ruptures, ulcerations, 19
Corneal transplants, 14, 20
Correcting lens, telescope, 285
Cortical cataracts, 23-24
Cortical and retinal activity, in evaluations, 245
Costs of low vison services, 450-452
Counseling, counselors, 51-52
Counterpart professionals, 444
Cratty "Body Image of the Blind Child," 123
Crawling, 399
Crocheting aids, 347
Crossed eyes, 81
Crying, 395
Cryosurgery, 15, 29
Crystalline lens (*see* Lens)
Cutouts, 342, 343
Cycloplegics, 36
Cylindrical correction, 320
Cylindrical lenses for astigmatism, 7

D-15 color test, 119, 257, 404
Dark/light adaptation, 80, 121, 131, 235, 298, 405-406
Day-glo tape, 396
Deafness and distance training, 316
Dean, Marybeth, 263
Decongestants, 36
Degenerative myopia, 5-6, 11, 15
Degree program, proposed, 457-460
De-icers, telescopes, 287

Delivery systems, 441-456
bibiography, references, 456, 534-536
costs and finances, 446, 450-454
budget, establishing, 450-452
funds, obtaining, 452-454
government agencies, 453-454
private agencies, 454
documentation, 455
model, developing, 446-450
blindness agency or center, 447-448
medical center & hospital, 448
mobile service unit, 449, 450
private practice, 449-450
university affiliated, 446-447
procedures, 454
steps and stages, 442-446
authorities and professionals, finding, 444
cooperation, professional, 443
timetable and plan, 443
training, obtaining, 444-446
"Deluxe Phosphor Mixture" bulbs, 412
Department of Health, Education, and Welfare, 441-442
Dependence and independence, 47
Depression, 46, 58, 59
Depth of focus, microscope, 226
telescopes, 285
Depth/space perception, 81, 89, 256, 326, 347
Designs for Vision, 260
minification devices, 243
Determination of movement, 418
Developmental Learning Materials, 310
Developmental Test of Visual Motor Integration, 124
Diabetes Mellitus, 10-11, 15, 18, 27-28, 29, 314
and blindness, 27
and motor control, 287
Diagnostic Assessment Procedure, 123
Diagnostic Reading Scales, 124
Dimmer switches on lamps, 327, 328, 396
Diopters; dioptic power, 188-203, 206-207, 220, 224, 225-226, 230, 324-326
(*See also* Magnification; Optics)
Diplopia, 10, 25, 27, 35, 37, 81, 241, 339, 350, 379
and prisms, 372-373
Directionality, 335-336
Directory of Agencies for the Visually Handicapped in the U.S. (AFB), 257-258, 444
Directory of Local Radio Reading Services (AFB), 258, 264

Diseases and treatments, references, 516-518
Displacement, prism, 369-371
Distance prescription glasses and telescopes, 293
Distance tasks, 82, 124-125, 416-417, 418
Distance training techniques, 256, 257, 264-265, 272-276, 277-316
  basics, 277-297
  and clinical examination, 279-280
  and deafness, 316
  de-icers, 287
  directing, 288
  and distance perception, 313-314
  elderly people, 314-315
  and eyeglasses, 286, 293, 298
  fixation, 292-295, 299
    exercises, 294-295
    focusing, 292-294
  games and activities, 436
  instruction in different settings, 280-282
  instruction room, 282
  integrating skills, 310-313
    bus numbers and destinations, 312-313, 434
    congested areas, 313
    house and building numbers, 312, 433-434, 435
    store signs, 311-312, 435-436
    street signs, 310, 435-436
    traffic lights, 310-311, 434
    unfamiliar areas, 313
  localization, 286-292, 297
    exercises, 291-292
    and instructor, 288-291
    and special problems, 287, 313-316
    and mental retardation, 316
    patches, patching technique, 289, 291
    physically handicapped people, 314-315
    psychosocial problems, 314
  scanning, 307-309, 310-313
  securing the aid, 286-287
  sequence, 282
  skills, development and practice of, 282-283
  spotting, 296-299, 310-313, 358, 360, 431-434
    exercises, 297-299
  tracing, 299-304, 305, 380n, 310-313
    exercises, 301-304
    and nystagmus, 300-301
  tracking, 299, 304-307, 310-313
    exercises, 305, 307
  (*See also* Role model; Training and instructional services)

Distance vision measurements, 88-92 104, 116-118, 125-126
  functional vision, 102-103
Divergence, 5, 191-195, 197-201
  (*See also* Optics)
Diverging lens, 189
  (*See also* Lenses, concave)
DLM Spatial Relations Cards, 123
Dogs, 82
Dolch word lists, 260
Dominant autosomal traits, 6, 22, 25,33, 35
Dominoes, large, 263
Double vision (*see* Diplopia)
Down's syndrome, 9, 12, 14, 20, 24, 34
Driving, bioptics and, 243-244, 265, references, 528-529
Drug-Induced Ocular Side Effects and Drug Interactions (Fraunfelder), 35
Drugs and eye troubles, 19, 25, 35-37
Dry-eye syndrome, 19, 37
Dynamic field, 366, 367

Eccentric fixation, 392
Eccentric gazing and viewing, 290, 304, 319, 321, 333, 334-335, 338, 339, 340, 343, 418, 422, 428,
  and glare, 413
Edema, macular, 6
Edna Lite stand-mounted magnifiers, 228
Educational considerations, references, 530-533
Educational materials, 132-133, 135
Educational media, and children with low vision, 124-128
Educational intern program, low vision curriculum, 461-491
Efficiency, visual, 112, 123
  without aids, 334
Elastic Velcro straps, 265, 287, 331
Electrodiagnostic testing, 15, 28
Electronic magnifiction, 231-233, 240, 332-333
Embroidery aids, 347
Emmetropic eye, 5
Empathy and counseling, 51, 52, 53
Engleman Unit, 234
Entoptic images, 18
  (*See also* Floaters; Spots)
Environmental aids against veering, 419 424
Environmental feedback, (*see* Adjustment)
Environmental illumination assessment, 406-413
  outdoor, 412, 413
Environmental (functional) measurements, 63, 68, 69, 70

comprehensive, 85-104
  case history, 86-88
  distance vision, 88-92, 104, 124-125
  functional vision, 102-103
  near-point vision, 92-97, 104, 125-126
  preliminary assessments, advantages of, 103-104
  visual field, 97-102, 104
  (*See also* Children)
Erythrolabe, 403
Evaluation, O&M, 416-421
  (*See also* Assessment)
Examination, clinical, 141-185, 266, 274, 279-280
  acuities, 142, 146-151, 158
    (*See also* Acuity measurements)
  binocular vision, 142, 156-157, 158, 168
  case history, 142-145, 158
    sheets, 159-166
  color vision,142, 154, 158, 168
  components, 142
  discussions with patient, 158-159
  fields, 142, 151-154, 158
    (*See also* Field)
  goals of, 141
  magnification, 142, 157-158
  observing, 256-257
  ocular health, 142, 145-146, 158
  reference outline, 158
  refraction, 142, 154-156, 158
  reporting, 168
    letter formats, 169-185
  stages and techniques, 141-142, 158-159
Expertise, areas of, 71
Eye, abnormalities of (*see* Abnormalities)
Eye, anatomy of, 3-5
  (*See also* Specific references: Cornea; Lens; Pupil; etc.)
Eye, diseases and disorders, 7-35
  (*See also* specific references: Aniridia; Cataracts; Glaucoma; Nystagmus; etc.)
Eye-hand coordination, 81, 122, 123,124, 256, 314, 325, 336-337, 373, 400, 401
Eye movements, and tracking, 394-396
Eye poking, 388
Eye preference, 16, 382
Eyeglasses (*see* Spectacles)

Family, problems, 48-49, 83, 108, 114, 167, 322, 417-418
Farnsworth D-15 color test, 119, 257, 404
Farsightedness (*see* Hyperopia)
Feedback, environmental (*see* Adjustment)
Feedback, kinesthetic (sensory), 224, 225, 279, 308, 370

Feinbloom Center (*see* William)
Feinbloom bioptic telescope, 221, 225
  and driving, 244, 265
Feinbloom Distance Test Chart, 116, 130
Feinbloom Subnormal Vision Reading Card, 260, 345
Feinbloom, William, and minification devices, 243
Felt washers, 265
Felt-tip pens, 204, 236, 297, 328, 346, 351
Field-enhancement devices (*see* Field-utilization aids)
Field loss, defects, 6, 9, 10, 12, 13, 14, 15, 16, 17, 16, 18, 19, 20, 21, 27, 30, 33, 37, 44-45, 62, 69, 81, 82, 97, 118, 151, 237, 240, 290, 304, 321, 335, 364-365, 393, 413
  central, 45
  degrees of restriction, 364-365
  and microscopes, 225
  (*See also* Field, visual, measurement of; Fields, restricted)
Field preference, 383
Field-utilization aids, 237, 240-243
  minification systems, 242-243
  magnification, 240-241
  training, 240
  (*See also* Fields, restricted, training for)
Field, visual, measurements of, 97-102, 104, 116, 119, 151-154, 158, 256, 289-290, 320, 363-364
  and light, 392-394
  normal, 98-99
  and prism, use of, 242
  response, checking, 382-383
  restriction, degrees of, 364-365
Fields, restricted, training for, 364-376
  definitions, 364-367
  and magnification, 240-241
  (*See also* Field-utilization aids; Night-vision aids; Prisms; Telescopes, reverse)
Figure-ground perception, 81, 89, 116, 123, 245, 278, 306, 323, 328, 404
  CCTV, 332, 351
Filters, 255-256, 263, 345, 394
  colored, 322, 328, 331, 339, 342, 373, 381, 391, 392, 395
    yellow, 236, 328, 392
Financing a delivery system, 446, 450-454
Fine motor tasks, 315
Fixation, near task:
  CCTV, 352
  with aids, 337, 343
  without aids, 319, 334-335
  Fixation skills, 80, 418, 422
Fixation skills and telescopes, 292-295, 299

exercises, 294-295
focusing, 292-294
Fixed pupil, 381, 391
Flash cards (*see* Cards)
Flashing lights, 6, 25, 27, 29
Flashlight(s), 391, 392
   camper's, 375
Flickering lights, 265, 381, 391, 392
Flicking, 380, 382, 388
Flip-down loupe(s), 293
Floaters, 6, 11, 18
Fluctuating vision, 18, 45, 80, 320
Fluorescent lights and lamps, 327, 404, 412
Focal distance, 188-189, 190, 255, 264,
   286, 319, 324, 325, 326
   and near training, 337, 338, 340
Focal point, optical, 188-190, 191, 294
   (*See also* Focusing)
Food as reinforcer, 398
Foot-hand coordination, 401
Foot lamberts, 406, 407-409, 411
Footcandles, 406-411, 412
Forms, recording, for training, 268-272,
   274-276
   for reports and evaluation, 168-185,
   384, 386
Foundation Center (*Foundation News;
   Foundation Grants Index: Subjects*),
   454
Fovea, foveal vision, 5, 289, 334, 406, 428
Fresnel page magnifiers, 228
Fresnel prisms (*see* Prisms)
"Frozen eyeball syndrome," 366
Frustration and training, 315
Functional field, 366
Functional losses, ocular, 7, 18-19
Functional measurements (*see* Environ-
   mental)
Functional O&M evaluation, 418-421
Functional vision, 102-103
   (*See also* Assessment)
"Functional Vision Inventory" (Langley),
   401,
Fundus, 10, 11
   peripheral, 6

Games and activities, nearpoint and
   distance, 436
Genetic counseling, 22, 24, 28-29, 32,
   34, 35
Genetics, genetic conditions (*see*
   Autosomal; Coloboma; Hereditary;
   Retinitis pigmentosa; sex-linked; etc.)
Genuineness and counseling, 51 52, 53
Geriatrics, 19
   references, 529-530
   (*See also* Cataracts; Elderly people)

Gestalt concepts, 240
   (*See also* Whole-part)
Glare problems, 23, 24, 31, 33, 83, 87,
   89, 111, 120-121, 133, 135, 136,
   229-230, 235, 298-299, 313, 327, 328,
   406, 412-413
Glaucoma, 8, 10, 11, 12-13, 16, 20-21, 22,
   25, 26, 27, 28, 33, 34, 36, 45, 58, 363
   congenital, 34
Goal locaters, 431
Goals, determining, 279, 315, 322
Goggles, night-vision, 365
Goggles, red lenses, for light-dark adapta-
   tion, 405-406
Good Start (film), 135
Groping, 388
Gross motor tasks, 315
Guides, sighted, 82

Half-eyes, 256, 325-326, 345
Hammocks, 393
Hand-eye coordination, 81, 122, 123,
   124, 256, 314, 325, 336-337, 373, 400,
   401
Hand-foot coordination, 401
Handicap(s), 62, 68, 69, 71, 107
   (*See also* Assessment)
Handicapped, multiply, assessment of
   (*see* Assessment)
Head-movement tracking, 394
Head-and-eye-movement tracking, 394
Head scanning, 366
Head-and-eye scanning, 366-367
Head tilt, 380, 387-388, 419
Hearing and environmental feedback, 47,
   51, 296, 306, 315
   (*See also* Radios)
Hemianopsia(s), 18, 237, 242, 335, 367
Hemorrhages, retinal, macular, 6, 26, 27,
   28
Hereditary conditions (*see* Congenital)
Herr, Selma, 135
Heterochromia iridis, 35
High-intensity lamps, 412
Hill Concept Inventory, 123
Hippus, 381, 391
Histoplasmosis, 13, 30-31
Home economics classes, 127-128
Hospital clinics, 448
House and building numbers, reading,
   312, 433-434, 435
Huntscope, 435
Hyaluronic acid, 4
Hyperopia (presbyopia), 4, 5, 6, 156, 198-
   200, 202, 203, 225-226, 229, 320, 325
Hypotonia, 12

Identifying objects and symbols, 423-427, 436
Illuminating Engineering Society (IES):
  on contrast, 406
  recommended reflective percentages, 407-411
Illumination levels and needs, 83, 92-93, 103, 104, 111, 112, 120-121, 127, 157, 168, 228, 229-230, 231, 235-236, 295, 322-323, 327-328, 345, 425-426
  ancillary systems, 365
  control aids, 327-328
  in distance training room, 264-265
  in near training room, 258, 321-322, 336
  (See also Assessment of lighting; Foot-candles)
Immediacy and counseling, 51, 52, 53
Impairment, visual, 62, 63
  (See also Assessment)
Implementing low vision service (see Delivery systems)
Incandescent lights and lamps, 327, 404, 411-412
Independence and dependence, 47
Independent travel (see Orientation and mobility; Training and Instructional services)
Industrial arts classes, 127
Infinity, optical, 188, 194, 264
Inflammations, 19
Information-processing systems, improving, 365
  (See also Night-vision aids; Prisms; Telescopes, reverse)
Injury, traumatic, 24, 25, 29
Instruction, instructional services (see Training)
Insulin, 27
Integration, bilateral, 395
Integration of skills, 310-313, 422
Intentional functioning, 52
Interaction with objects, 400-401
Interdisciplinary low vision service, 61-71
  instruction and training, 70-71
Intermediate tasks, 82
Intermediate training, 258, 262, 266
  (See also Near)
Intraocular pressure, 20, 21, 36
Iris, 4, 8, 33
  conditions of, 21-22
  (See also Aniridia)
Ishirhara Plates, 119
Islands of vision, 372
Itinerant teachers, 105, 107, 136, 258, 415-416
  (See also Role model)

Job descriptions, 492-494

Kaleidoscopes, 265
Keitzer checkwriting guide, 331
Keratoconus, 12, 14, 19-20
Keratometer, keratometry, 14, 20, 154, 155-156, 158
Keratoplasty (corneal transplant), 14, 20
Kinesthetic (sensory) feedack and awareness, 224, 225, 279, 308, 370
Knitting aids, 347
Kratz, L. E., 133

Labelers, 329
Lamberts (see Foot)
Lamps, flex-arm, 235, 236, 237, 259, 263, 265, 295, 322, 327, 332, 356
  dimmer switches, 327, 328, 396
Lamps and lights, incandescent and fluorescent, 327, 404, 411-412
Landmarks and orientation, 419
Large print, large-print editions and devices, 204-205, 236, 259, 262, 264, 314, 315, 323, 328-329, 330, 331, 345, 352
Laser beam surgery, 10, 15, 27-28, 29
Laurence-Moon-Biedel's syndrome, 15, 28, 420
Leber's syndrome, 15, 28
Legal blindness, definitions of, 63, 68, 254
Lens, 3, 4, 9-11, 195, 201
  disorders of, 22-25
  displaced, 8, 14, 22, 25, 35
  examination of, 145, 147, 158
  removal of, and color vision, 404-405
  and wavelengths of light, 404
Lenses:
  bifocal, 24, 202, 225, 226-227, 346, 347
  contact, 20, 24, 26, 31, 33, 154, 155, 234-235, 252
    pin-hole, 22, 31
    telescope, 219-220
    tinted, 236
  concave, 189-190, 194-195
  convex, 188-189, 194, 324, 325
  corrective, telescope, 285
  microscopic, 206
  NoIR, 236, 328, 330, 372, 406
  Olo, 236, 328, 331
  Polaroid, 236
  spectacle, 24, 197-204, 285,
    colored, 235, 322, 328
  sunfilters, 235, 236, 409
  sunlenses, slip-on, 328
  tinted, 235, 236, 322, 328, 330, 409, 412
  (See also Optics, Treatment options)

Letter of request, low vision services, 444
Leukocoria, 26, 381
Light boxes, 396, 399
Light, and color vision, 403-405
Light/dark adaptation, 80, 121, 131, 235, 298, 405-406
Light gazing, 380, 382, 388
Light meter, 259, 264, 327, 331, 406-408, 410, 412, 413
Light, nondiffuse, 396-398
Light reflectance (*see* Reflectance)
Light source, blocking, 397-398, 399
Light stimulus, 390-399
    with other stimulus, 390-391
Light and visual fields, 392-394
Lighthouse Flashcard/Symbol Cards, 116-117
Lighthouse Low Vision Service, 260
Lighthouse Near Acuity Card, 118, 130
Lighting (*see* Illumination)
Lighting, assessment of (*see* Assessment)
Lighting conditions,maximum use of, 421 425-426, 435
Lights, flickering, 265, 381, 391, 392
Lights, light reflectors, 389
Lights, reaching or moving toward, 385
Lights, in testing stimulus, 389-399
Limbus, 4
Line markers (*see* Typoscopes)
Loaner aids, 272-273
Local and state resources, 257-258, 444
Local workshops, 445-446
Localization, near tasks:
    with aids, 337, 338, 342
    without aids, 319, 334, 335-336
Localization, telescopic aids, 286-292, 297
    exercises, 291-292
Long cane (*see* Canes)
Loupe(s):
    clip-on, 226-227
    flip-down, 293
    Low vision aids (*see* Optical)
    Low vision aids kit, portable, 442
Low vision care, 61-62, 63, 249
    (*See also* Treatment options; Training and instructional services)
Low vision Clinical Society, 492
Low vision clinical specialist, 492
Low vision conferences, 445
Low vision educational intern program, curriculum, 461-491
Low vision instructors, 68, 69, 70, 86, 249
    degree program, 457-460
    itinerant, 105, 107, 136, 258, 415-416
    (*See also* Delivery systems; Role models; Training and instructional services)

Low Vision Referral Form, 76-80
    guidelines for, 80-83
Low vision screening, 420
    (*See also* Assessment)
Low vision services, 61-71
    costs, 450-452
    (*See also* Assessment; Delivery systems; Role model; Training and instructional services)
Low vision specialist(s), 61, 62, 63, 70
    job descriptions for, 492-494
Low vision student(s), 249n, 266
    (*See also* Training and instructional services)
Low Vision Training (Bäckman & Inde), 260
Low Vision Training Manual (Quillman), 260
Lumen(s), 406, 410
    (*See also* Footcandles)
Luminaires (*see* Lamps)
Luminance, 406-413
    measurements of, 406-411

Macbeth easel lamp, 404
Macula, macular area, 5, 6, 7, 8, 11, 13, 15, 17, 18, 26, 27, 28, 29, 30, 31, 33, 93, 195, 234, 364
Macular degeneration, 31-32, 86-87, 97, 320
    and luminance needs, 410
Macular edema, 6
Magnification (*see* Optics)
Magnification levels, 212-213
Magnification needs, measuring, 69, 92, 96-97, 142, 151-158, 225, 240-241, 278, 320, 321, 349
    (*See also* CCTV; Lenses; Optics; Treatment options)
Magnifiers, 227-233, 346, 347
    hand-held, 228, 229, 230, 255-256, 323, 324-325, 337, 345, 364, 436-437
    projection and electronic, 231-233
    spectacle, 437
    stand-mounted, 228-230, 255-256, 323, 324, 325, 337, 345, 354-355
    taking care of, 326-327, 354
    typical uses, 227
Marbles, in tube, with oil, 400
Marfan's syndrome, 9, 14-15, 20, 24, 25, 35
Maxfield Buchholz format, 109
Measuring aids, 329
Medical center clinics, 448
Medical consultant to low vision program, 496
Medications, side effects of, 320
    (*See also* Drugs)

Memory, visual, 81-82, 123, 240, 242, 245, 364, 365, 423, 425
Mental retardation, 10, 16, 28, 33, 34, 117
and distance training, 316
(*See also* Assessment of the multiply handicapped)
Metamorphopsia, 6, 11, 18, 19
Metronomes, 296
Microphthalmia, microphthalmus, 10, 16, 26, 33, 34
Micropsia, 15, 29
Microscope(s), 26, 157, 193, 224-227, 228 230, 232-233, 240, 255, 256, 262, 321, 324, 325-326, 377, 345, 346, 347, 356-357
advantages, 224
bifocal lenses, 225, 346, 347
depth of focus, 226
design of, 226-227
disadvantages, 225, 233
multilens, 225
optics of, 225-226
taking care of, 356
telemicroscopes, 157, 220-224
working distance, 225, 226
Microscopic spectacle, 323
Mild visual field restriction, 364-365
Minification systems, 242-243
Miotics, 36
Misalignment, telescope, 288
Mobile service units, 449
Mobility specialist(s), 71
Mobility evaluation and instruction, 240-242, 248, 421-427
(*See also* Role model)
Model for rehabilitation, 61-71, 441
clinical 69-70
postclinical, 70-71
preclinical, 63-69
(*See also* Delivery systems; Role model)
Moderate visual field restriction, 364-365
Mongolism (*see* Down's syndrome)
Monocular telescope, clip-on, 287
Monocular vision, monocular corrections, 156-157, 216, 220, 222, 223, 226, 278-279, 337
and distance judgment, 313-314
Mother, role of, 48
Motivation, factors, 87, 417
multiply impaired children, 387
Motor Free Visual Perception Test, 124, 131
Motor skills, coordination and control, 123, 124, 300, 385, 396
Motor tasks, gross and fine, 315
Movement awareness and identification, 424

Movement, determination of, 418
Movement and learning, 387
Movement patterns, 380
Movement Without Sight (Kratz), 133, 134
Multiple sclerosis, 287
Multiply handicapped, assessment of (*see* Assessment)
Mulitply handicapped children, 107
(*See also* Assessment of the multiply handicapped)
Multiply impaired people, references, 533-534
Munson's sign, 20
Muscle imbalance, 115, 381
Music classes, lessons, 128, 132
Music stands, 330
Musical instruments, 390, 391, 394-395
Mydriatics, 36
Myopia, 5-6, 11, 12, 14, 15, 16, 19, 26, 34, 35, 36, 93, 156, 196-204, 206-207, 224, 226, 226, 229, 320, 325, 429
degenerative, 5-6, 11, 15

Nanometer(s), 406
Nanometer levels, and aging, 405
National Accreditation Council for Agencies Serving the Blind and Visually Handicapped, 454
National Center for Health Statistics, 455
National Library Service for the Blind and Physically Handicapped, 257-258, 264
National Retinitis Pigmentosa Foundation, 375
National workshops, 445
Near-point vision measurements, 92-97, 104, 118-119, 125-126
field test, 101-102
functional vision, 102
Near tasks, 82, 125-126, 317, 420
and aids, 318
and color, 405
and illumination, 412
(*See also* Near training techniques)
Near training techniques, 252, 258-264, 266-272, 317-362
efficient use of visual skills:
with aids, 319, 337-344
without aids, 319, 333-337
fixation:
CCTV, 352
with aids, 337, 343
without aids, 319, 334-335
games and activities, 436
general guidelines, 317-318, 323
handouts, 263-264
home practice, 352-362

and identifying abstract symbols, 426-427
initial encounter, 318, 322-323
localization:
  with aids, 337, 338, 342
  without aids, 319, 334, 335-336
nonoptical aids, 327-332
  sources of equipment, 329-332
optical aids, 323-327
  sources of equipment, 329-332
performing specific tasks, 344-353
  CCTV training, 348-352
preparations for training, 319-322
problems and solutions, 338-341
scanning:
  CCTV, 350-351, 352, 358
  with aids, 319, 337, 339, 342-343, 436-437
  without aids, 319, 334, 336, 436
sequence, 266, 267-268, 318-319
tips for success, 343-344
tracking:
  with aids, 337, 343, 358, 360, 436-437
  without aids, 319, 334-335, 336-337, 436
(*See also* Role model; Training and instructional services)

Near Vision Symbol Test, 118
Nearpoint lighting, 410-411
Nearsightedness (see Myopia)
Needle-threading devices, 259, 263, 347
Needles, self-threading, 263
  large-eye, 330
Needlework, training in, 347
New York Lighthouse for the Blind, 444, 445
Night blindness, 15, 18, 28, 37, 83
Night vision, 23, 420
Night-vision aids, 365, 374-375
  cane, 374
  goggles, 365
  night-vision scope, 375
  wide angle mobility light, 374
  camper's flashlight, 375
NoIR lenses, 236, 328, 330, 372, 406
Nonoptical and accessory aids, 235-237, 255-256, 323-324, 345, 346
  contrast, 328
  near, 263, 327-332
    sources, 329-332
  references, 524-526
  (*See also* Large print; Reading stands)
Normal fields, 98-99
Not Without Sight (film), 135
Null point of fixation, 300, 306, 428

Nystagmus, 7, 8, 9, 10, 12, 14, 22, 23, 31, 33, 34, 35, 37, 92, 95, 101, 116, 133, 156, 235, 300-301, 379, 395, 418
  null point, 300, 306, 428
  and testing, 91, 145

Object/form recognition, 231, 424-425
Obstacle course, 401
Occluders, clip-on, 259, 265
  paddle type, 265
  (*See also* Patches)
Ocular abnormalities (*see* Abnormalities)
Ocular health, testing, 145-146, 158
Ocular, telescope, 284, 293, 294, 312
Oculocutaneous albinism, 31-32
Office of Management and the Budget, Washington, D.C., 452-453
Old age (*see* Aging; Geriatrics)
Olfactory response, 383, 422)
Olo lenses, 236, 328, 331
Opacification (*see* Cataract)
Ophthalmia neonatorum, 35
Ophthalmoscopy, 10, 12, 13, 14, 15, 16, 17, 20, 21, 22, 23, 26, 28, 29, 30, 145-146, 158, 448
Optic nerve, 5, 21, 33, 204
  atrophy of, 33, 363
  disorders of, 45
Optical aids, 80, 187, 211, 256, 266, 323-324,
  children, in school, 126-127
  problems with, 340
  and realistic expectations, 280
  references, 522-524
  taking care of, 326-327
  (*See also* Magnifiers; Microscopes; Prisms; Telescopes; Training and instructional services; Treatment options)
Optical axis, 189, 190, 191
  axis ray, 188, 189, 191, 204
Optical infinity, 188, 194, 264
Optics, 187-210
  basics, 187-195
  magnification, 204-210, 240-241, 255, 324
    angular, 208-210, 213, 326
    four ways, 204
    levels, 212-213
    projection, 210
    (*See also* Projection magnifiers)
    relative-distance, 205-208, 224
    relative-size, 204-205, 208
  refraction, 195-203
  (*See also* Diopters, Treatment options; Vergence)
Options, treatment (*see* Treatment)
Optistick, 381

Optometric low vision examination, references, 521-522

Organizations and companies for low vision services, 497-513

Orientation, clues and landmarks, 419

Orientation and mobility (O&M) programs, 304-305, 312, 315, 364, 365, 413
   functional evaluation, 416-421
   (*See also* Role model)

Oscillation, visual, 300-301
   (*See also* Nystagmus)

Oscillopsia, 18, 37

Osmotic agents, topical, 36

Oxygen, and premature babies, 25-26

Paddle-type occluders, 265

Padlocks, magnetic, 263

Painting and light reflectance, 411

Panoscopic tilt, 338, 340

Paper:
   bold-line, 263, 328, 330, 346, 347
   raised-line, 330, 346

Parallel light rays, 5   (*See also* Vergence)

Parkinson's disease, 314

Part/whole relationships and concepts, 123, 240, 242, 245, 364, 365

Patches, patching techniques:
   microscopes, 321
   pinhole, 322, 335
   telescopes, 289, 291, 305, 306, 330, 334, 337, 350, 353, 382

Pathologies, eye, 7-35
   (*See also* specific references: Albinism; Keratoconus; Retinitis pigmentosa; Toxoplasmosis; etc.)

Pathway disorders, 45

Pd measurements, 234

Peep holes, 243

Penlights, 259, 265, 338, 375, 381, 391

Pennsylvania College of Optometry, 445

Pens, lighted, 263, 375
   felt-tip, 204, 236, 297, 328, 346, 351

Percept (composite picture), 365

Perception, 244-245

Perceptual Communication Skills (Herr), 131, 135

Perimeter, 99

Perimetry, 151, 158, 242, 363, 448
   (*See also* Prisms)

Peripheral fundus, 6

Peripheral vision & fields, 21, 23, 45, 99-101, 116, 119, 151, 226, 237, 240, 241, 242, 289-290, 304, 363, 364, 365-367, 382-383, 447
   (*See also* Field measurement; Fields, restricted)

Phoropter, 156

Photocoagulation, 29

Photophobia, 8, 9, 10, 12, 13, 15, 18, 19, 21, 22, 28, 31, 35, 36, 37, 258, 320, 328, 412

Phthisis bulbi, 21

Physical comfort, 235, 236

Physical difficulties and problems, 340-341

Physical education classes, 128

Physically handicapped people and distance training, 314-315

Physicians Desk Reference for Non-prescription Drugs, 35, 36, 320

Physiological and functional aspects of eye diseases and treatments, references, 516-518

Picture, composite, 365

Picture puzzles, and object solving, 425

Pinhole apertures, 235, 322, 335

Playing cards, low vision, 263, 347-348

Plexiglass, 399

Polaroid lenses, 236

Polydactyly, 10, 33

Portable aids kits, 442

Positioning and sensory integration, 387, 392, 400

Positive regard and counseling, 51, 42

Postclinical services, 70-71, 441
   (*See also* Delivery systems)

Posters, 426

Postural behavior and response, 82, 380, 387-388, 419

Preclinical services, 63-69, 441
   (*See also* Delivery systems)

Preferential seating, classroom, 133

Presbyopia, 4
   (*See also* Hyperopia)

"Print-A-Log" (Services for the Blind), 263

Print, size and style, 328-329, 345
   (*See also* Large print)

Prism(s), 15, 28, 226, 241-242, 254, 326, 364, 365-373
   blur, 369, 372
   and canes, 241, 366
   and confusion, 372
   difficulties with, 372-373
   displacement, 369-371
   and double vision, 372-373
   exercises, 369-372
   functional use of, 371-372
   measurements for positioning, 367-368

Private practice clinics, 449-450

"Products for People with Vision Problems" (AFB), 263

Professionals, cooperation among, 442-443

Professionals, counterpart, 444
Project LUV (Virginia), 455, 495-496
Projection magnifiers, 157, 210,
  231-233, 240
  electronic, 231
  (*See also* CCTV)
Projection and telescopes, 292
Psychoeducational and psychological
  evaluations, 132, 416
Psychological and social considerations,
  references, 519-521
Psychosocial problems, 43-54, 321
  adjustment, 47-51
  and the aged, 55-59, 314
    services for, 58-59
  intervention, 47, 51-53
  implications of visual deficiencies,
    44-46
  and restricted fields, 363
  self-concept, 46-47
  stereotypes, 43-44
  and use of telescopes, 314
Psychosocial set, 340-341, 416
Ptosis, 36, 37
Punch-holes in cardboard, 394
Pupil, 4, 32-33, 36
  dislocated, mutiple, 14, 35
  hippus and fixed pupil, 381, 391
Pupillary response, 115, 381

Radio information (reading) services,
  258, 264
Radios, 283, 293, 296, 431
Raised-line paper, 330, 346
Reading caps, telescopic, 220-221, 222,
  255, 256, 285, 326
Reading cards, 118, 130-131, 260, 330,
  345
Reading skills, 82, 125-126, 259-262,
  339-340
  training in, 345-346, 436-438
    CCTV, 352
Reading stands, 127, 236-237, 238-239,
  256, 259, 263, 314, 315, 323, 324,
  325, 329, 330, 332, 337, 338, 342, 345
Reading telescopes (*see* Telemicroscopes)
Recessive autosomal traits, 6, 20, 28, 31
Recessive trait, sex-linked, 31
References, selected, 515-536
  data on the visually impaired popula-
    tion, 515-516
  driving with bioptic telescopes,
    528-529
  educational considerations, 530-533
  general, 515
  geriatrics, 529-530
  multiply impaired people, 533-534

  nonoptical aids, 524-526
  optical aids, 522-524
  optometric low vision examination,
    521-522
  physiological and functional aspects of
    eye disease and treatment, 516-518
  psychologial and social considerations,
    519-521
  service delivery models, 534-536
  training, 526-528
  visual functioning, 518-519
Reflectance, light, 406, 407-411
  and painting, 411
Refraction, 187-188
  (*See also* Convergence; Divergence;
    Optics; Retina)
Refraction, testing for, 154-156
Refractive error, 8, 10, 27, 37, 92, 97,
  155, 204, 215, 222, 229, 320
  astigmatic, 7, 156
  measuring, 69, 154-156
  (*See also* Astigmatism; Hyperopia;
    Myopia; Optics)
Refractive power; refractive index, 3, 5,
  6, 20   (*See also* Optics)
Rehabilitation service(s), 61-71
  evaluation, 416
  instruction and training, 70-71
  state, 257
  (*See also* Assessment; Delivery systems;
    Role model; Training and instruc-
    tional services)
Reports, examination (*see* Examination)
Resources: companies, aids and services,
  497-513
Resources, local and state, 257-258
Respect and counseling, 51, 52
Restricted fields (*see* Fields)
Retardation, mental (*see* Mental)
Retina, 3, 4-5, 6, 8, 9, 10-11, 16, 17, 195
  244-245, 289
  and astigmatism, 203-204
  disorders of, 26-33
    achromatopsia, 8, 32
    albinism, 8, 31-32, 45, 120, 236
    coloboma, 10, 25, 32-33
    detachment, 6, 9, 10-11, 14, 15, 16,
      21, 23, 25, 26, 27, 29, 35
    diabetic retinopathy, 10-11, 15, 18,
      27-28
    histoplasmosis, 13, 30-31
    macular degeneration, 31, 86-87, 97,
      320, 410
    occlusion, central, artery and vein, 26
    retinitis pigmentosa, 14, 15, 20, 25,
      28-29, 34, 97, 151, 234, 236, 241-
      242, 320, 363, 375

toxoplasmosis, 17, 29-30
examining, 145, 155, 156, 158
and magnification, 204-210
and refraction, 195-203
underdevelopment of, 22
(*See also* Cones; Macula; Rods)
Retinoscope, retinoscopy, 155, 156, 158, 448
Retrolental fibroplasia, 16, 25-26, 231, 435
Reverse(d) telescopes (*see* Telescopes)
RLF (*see* Retrolental fibroplasia)
Robert Wood Johnson Foundation, 454
Rods, 5, 28
and dark/light adaptation, 405-406
rod-cone dysfunction, 413
rod flare, 406
Role modeling, 51
Role model for instruction and teaching, 415-439
evaluation, 416-421
case history, 417-418, 420-421, 426-427, 429, 435
distance, 416-417, 418
fundamental evaluation, 418-421
indoor and outdoor, 419-420
night, 420
mobility training, 421-427
identifying objects and symbols, 423-427
visual awareness, 422-423
near point and distance games and activities, 436
near point activities, 436-438
questions about training, 438-439
telescopes, 427-436
basics, 427-430, 432
focusing, 429, 432
hints for effective viewing, 435-436
holding, 428-429
indoor training, 430-432
outdoor training, 432-434
practicing, 428-429
Rolling, 399
Rope, distance training, 265, 303-304
Rubella, rubella syndrome, 9, 16, 24
congenital, 33-34
Rulers, 259, 329, 381
Rural service, costs of, 451-452

Saccadic eye movements, and tracking, 394-395
Scanning, 81, 116, 122, 234, 240, 241, 242, 243, 259, 260, 290, 304, 365-366, 385, 401, 418, 421, 439
environmental system, 424-425
exercises, 261

near training, 319, 334, 336, 337, 339, 342-343, 436-437,
with CCTV, 350-351, 352, 358
with a telescope, 307-309, 358, 360, 433
reversed, 374
types of, 365-367
(*See also* Reading)
Sclera, 4, 14, 35
Scooting, 399
Scotoma(s), 13, 18, 30, 31, 97, 99, 118, 152, 288-289, 292, 321, 334, 335, 363-364
central, 153, 231-232, 260, 288-289, 320, 334, 335
migraine, 25
ring, 151-152
Script boards, 346
Seating, preferential, classroom, 133
Self-concept, self-image, 49-50, 69
development of, 46-47, 417
Self-pity, 48
Selsi telescopic aid, 265-266, 284, 417-418
Senile macular degeneration, 31-32
Sensitivity and counseling, 51, 52
Sensory behavior, functioning, 388
Sensory clues, 422, 438-439
Sensory (kinesthetic) feedback, 224, 225, 279, 308, 370
Sensory integration, 422, 439
Sensory responses, 380
Sequence, training (*see* Distance; Near)
Sequence, vision stimulation, 386-401
Service delivery models, references, 534-536
Services and aids, list by companies, 497-513
Severe visual field restriction, 364-365
scanning, 365-366
Sewing aids, 330, 347
(*See also* Needles)
Sex-linked recessive trait, 31
Shading problems, outdoor lighting, 412-413
"Shamming," 48
Shapes, spotting, 297
Shields, spectacle, 328
Shifting of visual attention, 385
Shoe gazing, 366
Shorelines, shorelining skills, 431-432
(*See also* Tracking)
Shrinkage, eye, 21
"Sighted" and "blind," 43-44, 47
Sighted guides, 82
Sighted peers, acceptance by, 49-50
Signature guide, 259

"Significant others," 45, 47, 51, 103, 322, 417

Signs, assorted, 265, 310

Signs, reading, 310, 435-436

Simple-to-complex concept, 278

Simulation of vision; simulation kits and uses, 37-41

Slide projectors, 231, 265, 293

Slingerland Prereading Screening Procedure, 124

Slit-lamp biomicroscope, 14, 16, 20, 22, 23, 24, 145, 147, 158

Sloan Continuous Text Reading Cards for Low Vision Patients, 118, 130-131, 260, 330, 345

Smooth eye movements, and tracking, 395-396

Sniffing, 388

Soap bubbles, colored, 394

Social worker, evaluation and information from, 416

Sonicguide™ 427, 439

Spatial awareness, 123

Specific Skill Series, 134

Spectacle-mounted telescopes, 215, 290, 360-361

Spectacle lenses, 24, 197-204
    colored, 235, 322, 328

Spectacles:
    comfort cables, 287
    microscopic, 323
    and prisms, (*see* Prisms)
    taking care of, 327

Spectrum, color, 403-405

Speed smear, 285
    (*See also* Bouncing)

Spots before the eyes, 6, 12, 18

Spotting, near tasks, 324, 358, 437

Spotting and telescopes, 296-299, 310-313, 358, 360, 431-434
    exercises, 297-299

Squint (*see* Strabismus)

"Standards for Providing Eyeglasses and Visual Services" (HEW), 444

State and local resources, 257-258, 444

State Library for the Blind and Physically Handicapped, 257, 264

Static field, 366

Static to dynamic concept, 278

Stencils, for writing, 329, 330, 346

Stereotypes, 43-44, 68

Steroid therapy, 30

Steroids and cataracts, 25

Stimulation, stimulus (*see* Vision)

Stopwatches, 259, 331, 335

Store signs, reading, 311-312, 435-436

Strabismus (squint), 9, 10, 12, 14, 17, 23, 30, 33, 34, 35, 36, 380

Straps, Velcro, 265, 287, 331

Street signs, reading, 310, 435-436

Stroboscopic effects, 412

Stroke, 287, 314

Study skills, 134-135

Sunfilters, 235, 236, 372

Sunglass cap, 298

Sunglasses, 22, 24, 33, 80, 121, 136, 298, 406, 412, 413
    transmission percentages, 409

Sunlenses, slip-in, 328

Support systems, 83, 287

Surgical telescopes (*see* Telemicroscopes)

"Swimming" effect and telescopes, 306

Symbols and objects, identifying, 423-427, 436

Tactile defensiveness, 389

Tactile reinforcement and clues, 315, 341

Tangent Screen tests, 99, 101, 150, 151, 152, 158, 289, 363,

Tape, day-glo, 396

Targets and telescope training, 430-434

Tasks, near, intermediate, and distance, 82-83

Tasting, 389

"Teacher's Guide to Low Vision Aids, A," 263-264

Teachers, itinerant (*see* Itinerant)

Tearing, excessive, 12, 35

Tears, 19

Telemicroscopes, 157, 220-224, 321, 324, 326, 333, 337, 345, 346, 347
    bioptic, 342, 345, 346-347, 348
    taking care of, 326-327
    working distance, 221

Telephone dials and attachments, 263, 330

Telescope(s), telescopic aids, 26, 86, 92, 135, 157, 158, 195, 211, 213-224, 240, 256, 265-266, 278-279, 364, 417-418, 421
    afocal, 294
    alignment, 288
    and angular magnification, 208-210, 213
    binoculars, 208, 219-220, 287
        techniques, 233-234
    bioptic, 217-218, 221, 222-223, 225, 243, 245, 296-297, 342, 345, 346-347, 348, 431
        (*See also* Driving)
    "bouncing," 285, 326
    categories, 216
    characteristics, 283-285
    clip-on, 216-217, 218, 287, 290, 293
    contact lens, 219-220, 234-235

exit pupils, 215, 222, 278, 284-285, 287
familiarization with, 285-286
field of view, 300
focusing, 285, 291, 292-295, 297, 358, 360, 429, 431, 432
full field, 218-219, 290
Galilean, 215, 284
hand-held, 215, 216, 218, 222, 283, 315, 358-359
Keplerian, 215
maintenance, 286, 359, 360-361, 428
negative working distance, 245
optics of, 213-215
parameters of, 215
prescription options, 222-224
problems in use of, 213
reading caps, 220-221, 222, 255, 256, 285, 326
and refractive examinations, 156
reversed, 242-243, 365-366, 373-374
spectacle-mounted, 215 , 290, 360-361
"swimming," 306
terrestrial, 284, 288
on tripods, 283, 315
in unfamiliar areas, 313
(*See also* Distance training techniques; Patches; Role model; Scanning; Spotting; Telemicroscopes; Tracing; Tracking)
Television, closed circuit (CCTV), 157, 210, 231-233, 240, 255-256, 259, 263, 332-333
attachments for, 351-352
near training with, 348-352, 358
"Test of Visual Analysis Skills," 260
Testing charts and cards, 91, 93, 116-120, 122-124, 147, 149-151, 256-257, 260
and focusing telescopes, 294-295
Textbooks, 125-126, 131
Theatrical gels, 331
Timers, large-dial, 329
Tinted lenses, spectacle, 235, 322, 328
Tonometry, 12, 16, 21, 145
Topical osmotic agents, 36
Toxoplasmosis, 17, 29-30
Toys, 381, 382, 390, 400
Tracing, and telescopes, 299-304, 305, 308n, 310-313
exercises, 301-304
and nystagmus, 300-301
Trachoma, 19
Tracking skills, 80, 116, 245, 383-385, 400-401, 421
moving objects, 434
saccadic eye movements, 394-395
smooth eye movements, 395-396
(*See also* Distance; Near)

Tracking, and telescopes, 299, 304-307, 310-313, 358, 360,
exercises, 305, 307, 431-434
Traffic lights, reading, 310-311, 434
Training and instructional services, 249-368
distance, 264-265
equipment and materials, 265-266
sequence, 273, 282
training room, 264-265
training sessions, 272-276
local and state resources, 257-258
low vision aids, 255-256
near, 258-264, 266-272
equipment, 259
materials, 259-264, 266
sequence, 266, 267-269
training room, 258-259
training sessions, 266-272
observation of examinations, 256-257
professional preparation, 251-258
professional reading, 251-255
program, establishing, 251-276
references, 526-528
training sessions, 266-276
distance, 272-276
near, 266-272
Trauma (*see* Injury)
Travel, independent (*see* Orientation and mobility; Training and instructional services)
Treatment options, 211-248
bioptics and driving, 243-244
magnification levels, 212-213, 240-241
optical aids, 211
perception, 244-245
stimulation of vision, 244
suggested aids, list of, 246-247
(*See also* Binocularity; Binoculars; Field-utilization; Lenses, Magnifiers; Microscopes; Nonoptical aids; Prisms; Projection and electronic magnifiers; Telemicroscopes; Telescopes)
Trial frame and lenses, 156
Tubes, paper and cardboard, 265, 292, 305
Tunnel vision, 21, 22, 34
Typewriters, large-print, 329
Typoscopes, 236, 255, 259, 262, 263, 328, 330, 338, 339, 342, 343, 345, 346, 356, 437
CCTV, 332

Ultraviolet light, 404-405
Unfamiliar areas and telescopic aids, 313
University-affiliated clinics, 446-447
University of Alabama at Birmingham

Low Vision Clinic, 263-264
University of Houston College of Optometry, 444, 445
outline of intern program, 461-491
University programs in low vision, 445
suggested outline, 457-460
Usher's syndrome, 15, 28
Uveal tract, 4, 21
Uveitis, 10, 16, 21, 26

Veering, 419, 424
Velcro straps, elastic, 265, 287, 331
Vergence, 187-188, 190-193, 195, 197-200, 202, 220, 221, 228, 229
(*See also* Convergence; Divergence; Refraction)
Vertex distance, telescope, 285
Veterans Administration medical centers, 447-448
Vibrator, therapy, 389
Viewing angle and focusing telescopes, 295
Viewing patterns, 419
Viewscan, 231, 233
Vineland Social Maturity Scale, 109
Virginia Commission for the Visually Handicapped, program of, 455, 495-496
Visibility acuity, 88-89, 245
Vision, fluctuating, 18, 45, 80, 320
Vision rehabilitation, 61-62
(*See also* Rehabilitation)
Vision, simulation of (*see* Simulation)
Vision stimulation, 244
Vision stimulation sequence, children, 386-401
Vision-up, 109
Visors, 24, 121, 136, 235, 298, 322, 328, 330
Visual attention, shifting, 385
Visual awareness, training in, 422-423
Visual closure, 123, 423
Visual clues, importance of, 47
Visual comfort, 329
Visual cortex, 5
Visual deficiency, psychological implications of, 44-46
Visual efficiency, 112
without aids, 334
Visual Efficiency Scale, 123, 131
Visual field (*see* Field)
Visual functioning, references, 518-519
Visual handicap (*see* Handicap)
Visual impairment (*see* Impairment)
Visual memory, 81-82, 123, 240, 242, 245, 364, 365, 423, 425

Visual-motor coordination and skills, 81, 122, 123, 124, 380, 386, 394
(*See also* Vision stimulation sequence)
Visual override, 439
Visual-perception skills, measuring, 121-124, 260, 380, 386
(*See also* Vision stimulation sequence)
Visual/postural behavior, 82, 380, 387-388, 419
Visual sensations, sensory responses, 380
Visual skills, with optical aids (*see* Fixation; Localization; Scanning; Spotting; Tracking)
Visually impaired population, data, references on, 515-516
Vitreous, 4, 5, 6, 16, 21, 23, 27, 196
problems with, 25-26

Walk–Don't Walk signs (*see* Traffic lights)
Wall Distance Acuity Charts, 116
Walters telescopic aid, 265-266
WAML (*see* Wide Angle Mobility Light)
Warmth and counseling, 51, 52
Washers, felt, 265
Watches, large-number, 263, 329
Wavelength, light and color, 403-404, 405
"When You Have a Visually Handicapped Child in Your Classroom: Suggestions for Teachers" (AFB), 264
Whole/part relationships and concepts, 123, 240, 242, 245, 364, 365
Wide Angle Mobility Light (WAML), 374
William Feinbloom Vision Rehabilitation Center, 444, 445
Word lists, Dolch, 260
Working distance:
microscopes, 225, 226
telemicroscopes, 221
Writing guides, 329, 330
Writing skills, 126
training in, 346-347
CCTV, 351

Xylophones, 394-395

Yellow filters, 236, 328, 392

Zero vergence (*see* Vergence)